AN ENCYCLOPEDIA

OF

THE VIOLIN

PLATE I—*Frontispiece*

EUGÈNE YSAŸE.

AN ENCYCLOPEDIA
OF THE VIOLIN

WRITTEN BY
ALBERTO BACHMANN

WITH AN INTRODUCTION BY
EUGENE YSAŸE

TRANSLATED BY
FREDERICK H. MARTENS

EDITED BY
ALBERT E. WIER

Preface to the Da Capo Edition by
Stuart Canin

A DA CAPO PAPERBACK

Library of Congress Cataloging in Publication Data

Bachman, Alberto Abraham, 1875-
 An encyclopedia of the violin.

 Reprint of the 1966 ed. published by Da Capo Press,
New York, in series: Da Capo Press music titles.
  1. Violin. 2. Violinists, violoncellists, etc.—Biogra-
phy. 3. Violin makers. I. Title.
[ML800.B13 1975]   787'.1   74-20867
ISBN 0-306-80004-7

First Paperback Printing – March, 1975
Second Paperback Printing – July, 1976
Third Paperback Printing – July, 1978
Fourth Paperback Printing – November, 1980

ISBN: 0-306-80004-7

This Da Capo Press Paperback edition of *An Encyclopedia of the Violin*
is a unabridged republication of the first edition
published in 1925 in New York and London.
It includes a new preface by Stuart Canin,
prepared especially for this edition.

Published by Da Capo Press, Inc.
A subsidiary of Plenum Publishing Corporation
227 West 17th Street
New York, N.Y. 10011

Manufactured in the United States of America

PREFACE TO
THE DA CAPO EDITION

Mr. Bachmann's romance with the violin and things violinistic is marvelous to behold. In this day of the cynic, with much loose talk of the music business, and the business of music, it is refreshing to find a professional who has written about the violin with his heart on his sleeve.

Alberto Bachmann, born in 1875 in Geneva, Switzerland, and a student of Ysaÿe and César Thomson, was a touring concert violinist, whose love and respect for the instrument impelled him to compose for it and to write about it. His compositions include three concerti, a violin sonata, and many arrangements; he is the author of *Le Violon* (1906), *Les Grands Violinistes du Passé* (1913), and *Gymnastiques à l'Usage des Violinistes* (1914).

Mr. Bachmann's love shows, and though some of the material is dated and the product of an earlier age, this writer found the *Encyclopedia of the Violin* to be charming and informative, covering in depth every aspect of the violin from its origins as a musical instrument, through its development, to its present position as the backbone of practically all instrumental music. Mr. Bachmann not only touches upon the violin, but the *Encyclopedia* also contains descriptions of hundreds of individual artists and ensembles, who themselves were touched by the violin and who built their lives around it.

Along the way, the reader will be fascinated, as I was, by a chapter which includes marvelous photographs of many famous and not so famous string quartets of the past, including capsule descriptions of their virtues and weaknesses. Another chapter, "How to Practise," has a full-page illustration giving a note photograph of the famous broken-octave entrance of the solo violin in Beethoven's Violin Concerto. The illustration contains exact interpretations, according to Mr. Bachmann's musical memory, of performances by Joachim, Wilhelmj, de Sarasate, Ysaÿe, Thomson, Kreisler, and Kubelik! It is amazing to see, rhythmically illustrated, the unique qualities with which these masters of the past endowed this most famous passage. On the other hand, if one is interested in practical matters such as essentials of violin and bow construction, precise and specific information is contained in the *Encyclopedia*. Mr. Bachmann takes one, step by step, through the entire process, from wood selection to the application of various varnishes. At any point one chooses, the professional or amateur can peruse the *Encyclopedia of the Violin* and be caught up in a wonderful web of information, practical and romantic. One example of the latter is to be found in the chapter entitled "Analysis of Master Violin Works." Referring to the *Andante* movement of Lalo's *Symphonie Espagnole,* Mr. Bachmann mentions that this "sublime slow movement seems to evoke that Berber Africa where the Moors of Spain took refuge after having been driven from their terrestrial paradise in Granada." For those aficionados of the violin, no explanation is necessary, and for others, in this space age, no explanation is possible.

As a performer and teacher who is involved daily with matters of the violin, I can say without fear of reproach that, of the many books written during the past few decades dealing with the violin and its practitioners, Bachmann's *Encyclopedia of the Violin* must be on the violinist's bookshelf with other outstanding works as van der Straeten's *History of the Violin,* Hodgson's *Motion Study and Violin Bowing,* Galamian's *Principles of Violin Playing and Teaching,* and Szigeti's *A Violinist's Notebook.*

Stuart Canin
Oberlin, Ohio

INTRODUCTION

Alberto Bachmann's first contribution to the literature of music was a work biographical and æsthetic in character: in it the lives of virtuosos, ancient and modern, were portrayed and their works analyzed. This volume, interesting from every point of view, clearly established the varying degrees of talent or genius of all the virtuoso composers from the 16th century to the present day. It was the more valuable since the author was an excellent artist himself, and consequently thoroughly at home in the subjects he discussed.

Having completed this work, in which the conclusions are well reached, and in which the critical comment is both intelligent and respectful, Mr. Bachmann did not feel, however, that he had exhausted his subject, for in this new book, whose sponsor I consider it an honor to be, the author has undertaken one of the most arduous tasks imaginable, that of presenting the violin and the art of violin playing from every possible angle, in a thoroughly exhaustive manner.

In the archives of literature relating to the violin, there would seem to be a gap which this new work will fill. Artists and amateurs alike will find it a kind of universal encyclopedia of the art of the violin, and the scope of the volume itself makes clear how vast this art-field really is, with its diverse elements and its abundance of forms and formulas. I feel that I do not prophesy too freely in predicting that it will meet with a cordial reception.

To write of the violin in a general way is an easy enough matter; to analyze, point by point, detail by detail, all the elements which constitute the virtuoso's art, is a far greater task. Only an author who knows the instrument perfectly can successfully undertake it.

The violin has its secrets: it has at one and the same time a soul and a mind. It is a poet whose enigmatic nature may only be divined by the elect. It is an instrument whose voice, since first it came into being, has stirred the heart-strings of the human race; and the lofty raptures which it has called forth have done their part, with other branches of the art of music, to raise the soul of man to the highest summits of the ideal.

This volume, in reality, needs no recommendation to the violinist who has once opened its covers, for its value will immediately become apparent, awakening interest which will increase with the turning of every page.

I heartily felicitate the author and remain his admirer.

AUTHOR'S PREFACE

While literature relating to the violin has been far from meager, there has never been projected, within the knowledge of the author, an encyclopedia covering adequately the matters of historical, mechanical, technical, critical and biographical importance which have profound interest for teachers, students and lovers of the "King of Instruments."

In endeavoring to produce such a comprehensive work in my *Encyclopedia of the Violin,* I have based my labors on personal experience, and upon that of the numerous famous violinists with whom I have lived on a footing of friendship and intimacy; while in transcribing my thoughts I have been careful to bear in mind that clearness and exactness are essential, in view of the marked difference between "feeling" and "expression" in the elucidation of æsthetic matters.

Were a work of this character to attempt to cover at length all the numerous subjects of vital interest, it would of necessity become a publication of many volumes. I have deemed it wiser to treat each topic with clarity and brevity, rather than exhaustively from the scholastic point of view, thus rendering it possible to produce the work in a single volume.

A certain degree of systematic procedure has been adopted in the construction of the work, beginning with important matters such as the origin of the violin, its mechanical construction and famous makers. An at least elementary knowledge of these subjects is essential in the intelligent study of the instrument, thereby laying a foundation for clearer understanding of essays upon technical and æsthetic matters which follow.

It would consume many pages of the book were I to attempt to enumerate by name all those broad-minded and kindly disposed virtuosos, pedagogues and scientific authorities on the violin who have encouraged me in the preparation of the manuscript and have aided with wise counsel and experience. I thank them one and all, and in particular my former teacher and life-long friend, Eugène Ysaÿe, who so whole-heartedly sponsors the work. May it be known to all those who derive instruction and pleasurable reading from this book that it was the constant encouragement and enthusiastic faith of this great artist which enabled me to labor unceasingly for many years toward its completion.

Alberto Bachmann

EDITOR'S PREFACE

The preparation of M. Bachmann's *Encyclopedia of the Violin* from the practical and commercial standpoint has been a source of great pleasure to the editor, due to the fact that not only has the author covered the entire field thoroughly, but the translator, Mr. Frederick H. Martens, has aided greatly by his lucid translation of the work.

Acknowledgment is also gratefully made to Mr. Jay C. Freeman and Mr. Franz Kneisel for the valuable advice and assistance rendered in the preparation of the volume; to Mr. Felix Kahn and Mr. Maurice Sternberger for the use of reference books and pictures; to Mr. Howard Semple for assistance in the art work and to J. H. Armour and Company, August Gemunder and Sons and The Rudolph Wurlitzer Company for information and photographs utilized in articles devoted to manufacturing or mechanical processes.

The plan of the work is to include in a single volume concise and accurate information on every subject connected with the violin. Its fulfillment will be a source of great satisfaction to the publishers.

ALBERT E. WIER.

CONTENTS

ILLUSTRATIONS

AN ENCYCLOPEDIA
OF
THE VIOLIN

AN ENCYCLOPEDIA
OF THE VIOLIN

CHAPTER I

THE ORIGIN OF THE VIOLIN

The origin of all stringed instruments is lost in the mists of time, and despite the most patient and laborious research on the part of famous savants, no positive information has as yet been furnished regarding this point. Knowledge of the subject is more or less conjectural, and all that has been definitely established is the existence of the predecessors of the violin—the English crewth, the rebec, the viol da Gamba, the Arabian rebab, the vielle played with the bow, the organistrum, and the vielle or chyphonie (Plates 2 and 3). Nor have I been able to discover, in spite of all my investigations, an exact definition of these two last-mentioned instruments. In his admirable work on stringed instruments, Antoine Vidal expresses himself as follows with regard to the origin of the violin and its development to the present form:

"I shall say nothing anent the vielle (Plate 3), played with a bow, of the Middle Ages, nor of the viols of the Renaissance, a family whose numerous and diversified members almost exclusively supplied the instrumental music heard up to the middle of the seventeenth century; special works have been devoted to these purely historical subjects, to which the more restricted scope of my own book compels me to refer the reader.

"Nevertheless, there is one instrument played with the bow which is no longer known in our day, and which is often designated as the three-stringed violin. I feel that I should give some account of this instrument, in order to establish its nature and restore its true character. It is the rebec, shaped like an elongated pear, often met with in old medieval sculpture, and in the miniatures which embellish the manuscripts of the Middle Ages.

"The rebec (Plate 3) is an instrument which has in common with the violin no more than its bow and its three strings tuned in fifths: G, D and A. In other respects, such as form and character, the two are altogether different, the rebec having no ribs, a convex back, and an absolutely flat sound board. Its origin is very ancient, and it probably came from the Orient. The *rebab* (Plate 2) introduced by the Moors of Spain after the conquest, toward the beginning of the eighth century, is nothing more than a rebec. The word rebec

1

is not met with in France until about the thirteenth century, when it is alluded to in Aymeric de Peyrat's lines:

> Quidam rebecam arcuabant
> Muliebrem vocem confrigentes

It is probable that the instrument was in use long before that period, however, though I can advance no historical proof to that effect."

Up to the fifteenth century it was described, in particular, by the words *rebelle, rubèbe,* and it is only beginning with this epoch that the name rebec [1] was definitely adopted to the exclusion of all others.   In 1483, we find the instrument thus designated in the accounts of King Charles VIII of France.[2] In connection with a voyage made by the king in September of that year, there was given, following his order, "35 *sols* to a poor witless man who played the rebec."

In the year 1490, we find in the accounts of King Charles VIII the following entry: "Paid to Raymond Monnet, a rebec-player"; and, listed from 1523 to 1535, the name "Lancelot Levasseur, rebec-player in ordinary to the King"; and, in the year 1559, that of "Jehan Cavalier, rebec-player to the King."   In England the rebec was one of the instruments of the royal band, "the state band of Henry VIII (1526) consisting of fifteen trumpets, three lutes, three rebecs, three taborets, a harp, two viols, four drums, a fife and ten sackbuts."

The rebec was an instrument with a hard, nasal tone, and was used to play for dancing.   Bride and groom proceeded to church to the sound of rebec and tambourin.

It was so well known that it even supplied a malicious popular allusion, "Dry as a rebec."   In "Florinde," a comedy which was very successful in its day—it may be found in the Adrien de Montluc's *Comédie des proverbes*—there is a description of the swashbuckling Captain Fierrabras, whom Florinde's father has chosen to be her husband, against her wish.   She says, "As to his face, it is but so-so; and above all he is as delicate and blond as a twice-washed prune; and as to his purse, it is none too well garnished; in that respect he is as dry as a rebec."

On March 27, 1628, an ordinance was issued by the Civil Lieutenant of Paris forbidding all musicians to play in taverns (*cabarets*) and places of ill repute, all high, low or other kinds of violins, but only the rebec.

---

[1] Juan Ruiz, Archpriest of Hita, mentions among the instruments used by the Spaniards during the Middle Ages, "the screeching *rabé* with its high notes," and somewhat later, "the *rabé* of the Moors."   The "screeching *rabé*" is evidently nothing else than our own rebec, "hard and dry."   As to the Moorish *rabé*, there can be no doubt as to its being the Arabian *rabeb*.   This word *rabé* has held its own in Spain through the centuries, for even to this day, in certain villages of Catalonia, the violin is called the *rabaquet* by the people.   *See* Mariano-Fuertes, *Historia de la Musica Española*, Madrid, 1855.

[2] *See* "*Les Comptes de l'argenterie du roy Charles VIII*," Arch. Nat.

PLATE 2

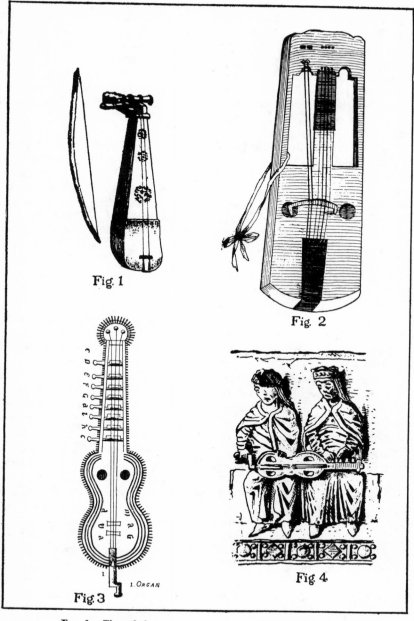

Fig. 1

Fig. 2

Fig 3

1. ORGAN

Fig 4

FIG. 1.—The rebab.
FIG. 3.—The organistrum.

FIG. 2.—The crewth.
FIG. 4.—The chyphonie.

It is only just to remark, however, that the unfortunate rebec was not always treated with such contempt. For a long time, in fact, it figured among the instruments whose use was permitted at the royal court. Its importance began to decline with the first years of the seventeenth century. This decline was an irrevocable one, since, a century later, in 1742, when Guignon was named "King of the Violins," after a sufficiently long interregnum had left this office—which he was the last to fill—vacant, one of his first acts of authority was to issue the following order:

"Since it would be at once impossible and opposed to the projects of the community, as well as to that perfection in the arts for which it is striving, to include among those making the effort a certain number of persons lacking capacity, whose talents are restricted to the amusement of the people in the streets and the public-houses, these last are to be allowed to play only a kind of instrument with three strings, which goes under the name of the rebec; but they are not to make use, under any pretext whatever, of the violin with four strings."

Thus the rebec went out of existence, although, as has been shown, it was still in use in France during the seventeenth century. Since then it has disappeared so completely that I have been unable to find a single specimen of the instrument either in public or private collections. The instrumental Museum of the Paris Conservatoire, however, possesses an exact copy made by J. B. Vuillaume, an example of great interest for students of the history of instrumental art.

According to Vidal, there is very little information to be had with regard to the manufacture of the instruments in use in the old days, and yet, in the third book of the *Bibliotheque de l'École des Chartes* he has discovered the name of a certain Henry, called "Henry of the Vielles," since he was one of the best-known vielle makers of his epoch.

Caspar S. Duiffopruggar (Plate 4), named Tieffenbrucker, a Bavarian who became a nationalized Frenchman, was long reputed to be the first maker of violins, but Vidal declares that all the so-called Duiffopruggar violins are spurious, having been made by Vuillaume, who, in 1827, conceived the idea of making violins after the pattern of a *viola d'amour* built by the former. That Duiffopruggar came to France with King Francis I, who, after the battle of Marignano, had proceeded to Bologna to confer with Pope Leon X, and brought back the viol maker with him, is proved by an engraving made by Woeriot, in Lyon in 1562. Vidal estimates that Duiffopruggar worked in Paris from approximately 1515 to 1530, but, in spite of their contentions that Duiffopruggar was a wonderful artist at inlay work, there is absolutely no proof existing, as Vidal asserts, of the authenticity of the violins he is said to have made.

PLATE 3

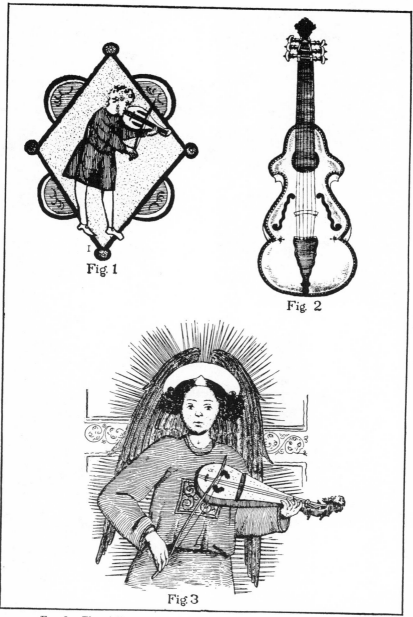

Fig. 1

Fig. 2

Fig. 3

Fig. 1.—The vielle.   Fig. 2.—The viola da gamba.
Fig. 3.—The rebec.

The labels of this master are conceived in the following terms:

> Gaspar Duiffopruggar à la
> costé St. André à Lyon
> (Gaspar Duiffopruggar at the
> side of St. Andrews' in Lyon)

and have the form of a reverse triangle. Count Louis de Waziers and the violin maker Chardon-Chanot, of Paris, possess bass viols by Duiffopruggar whose authenticity is beyond question.

The following Latin label, in which an allusion is made to the wood of which the viols were constructed, is also attributed to Duiffopruggar:

> Viva fuy in Sylvis; sum
> dura occisa securi;
> Dum vixi, tacui, mortua
> dulce cano
> (I was living in the forest;
> the cruel ax did slay me.
> Living, I was mute,
> Dead, I sweetly sing.)

The viols were the immediate predecessors of the violin, and the viols, in so far as form is concerned, were, as Vidal tells us, subject in construction to all the liberties which the builder might choose to take with them.

The creation of the violin of to-day in its actual shape is veiled in mystery, which the most ardent discussions on the part of specialists have not been able to solve. The opaque curtain of uncertainty which hides the truth from us has made it possible to ascribe the glory of having called forth the wonderful instrument to which this book is devoted to Testator the Older, Amati, Gasparo da Salo and Maggini respectively. A *luthier* (a viol and lute maker) named Kerlino, who lived in Brescia about the year 1450, is also credited with the discovery of the violin in the form known to us; and Kolitzer, a famous Parisian builder of the same epoch, is said to have effected the transformation from viol to violin by changing the neck of a *viola da braccio.* All in all, while it is possible that the paternity of the violin may be conceded to Gasparo da Salo, it seems most probable that Maggini of Brescia may be considered the first to give the violin its present form; and, at all events, the instruments made by this famous builder are authentic in all their parts.

It is evident that the actual form of the instrument is the fruit of a thousand and one successive changes, and that the present form has been in use for several hundreds of years. Innumerable experiments have been made with the object of varying the form, and of increasing the sonority of the violin as we know it; but none of those who would improve the violin has produced instruments which can equal in nobility of tone the instruments made by Stradivarius, Amati and other great Italian masters.

PLATE 4

GASPAR DUIFFOPRUGCAR
Luthier

1515

We may set the date of the actual creation of the violin somewhere between the years 1500 and 1550. It played a part in a fête offered by the city of Rouen to the King Henry III of France and to the Queen Mother Catherine de Médici "on their triumphant and joyous entry into the said town, which took place on Wednesday and Thursday, the first and second days of October, 1550." A feature of the entry was an artificial rock, with Orpheus and the Muses, "and in the middle of said rock, Orpheus was seated upon a block of polished marble . . . to his right stood the nine Muses, garbed in white satin, who together rendered madrigals and follias with their violins in excellent voice." In the year 1571, there were seven violins included in the royal band of Queen Elizabeth of England, which North mentions in his memoirs, published in London, in 1846: Item, "to the vyolons, being seven of them, every one of them at 20d. per diem for their wages, and £. 16, 2s, 6d., for their lyveries, in all per annum £. 325, 15. s."

The fabulous prices paid in these days for the great Stradivarius instruments—I know of many which have become altogether extinct—represent a later development, for the cost of violins was modest enough at first, as is shown by amounts quoted in the fragment of an account of King Charles IX of France where, in many cases, the prices are no more than those paid for ordinary, cheap commercial instruments at the present time.

CHAPTER II

VIOLIN MAKERS IN EUROPE

It is unfortunate, but nevertheless a fact, that almost nothing of consequence is known about most of the European violin makers; the labels, in many cases, being the only source of information. Even these are often not to be relied upon, because so many "genuine" counterfeit labels bearing the names of great makers have been placed in violins by imitators that it usually requires an expert to determine their authenticity.

This scarcity of information applies almost as well to the great masters of the art of violin making as to the lesser lights. At the time when violin making flourished, those who engaged in it were looked upon as artisans—not to be compared with the artists who performed upon their instruments. Therefore, while we have copious information regarding the great players of the violin, the only authentic facts regarding the makers are those which have been acquired by painstaking research on the part of antiquarians.

The list which follows presents the names of all violin makers of reputation in alphabetical order, irrespective of nationality, thus enabling one interested in the subject to find the name he seeks without difficulty. Wherever the maker's name has no special interest attached to it, beyond the fact that he was engaged in the business of violin making, the information is of the briefest character. In the case of those makers whose fame for the beauty and tone of their instruments has carried through the centuries, sufficient concise information is given to thoroughly place the maker's position in his particular field.

This chapter is illustrated by reproductions of the labels and the instruments of many of the most famous violin makers, and wherever such labels and instruments have been reproduced, reference has been made to same in the article under the maker's name.

ABBATI, GIAMBATTISTA, Modena, 1775 to 1795.

ABSAM, THOMAS, Wakefield (Yorkshire), 1810 to 1849.

ACEVO, ——, Tannenholz.

ACHNER, PHILIPP, Mittenwald, 1772 to 1798.

ADANI, PANCRAZIO, Modena, 1775 to 1827.

ADDISON, WILLIAM, London, 1665 to 1670.

AIRETON, EDMUND, London, b. about 1727, d. 1807.

ALBANESI, SEBASTIANO, Cremona, 1720 to 1744.

ALBANI, PAOLO, Palermo, Rome, Cremona.

ALBANUS (or ALBANI), MATTHIAS, Bozen, b. in Kaltern 1621, d. Bozen, 1712. One of the best-known makers in the Tyrol. His first violins were made in 1645, and he was still producing in 1712, at the age of ninety. His instruments are distinctive in that the backs are always made of acorn wood, finished in a light reddish-brown color. Like Stradivarius, he attained the height of his art at middle age. Albanus also was known as an ex-

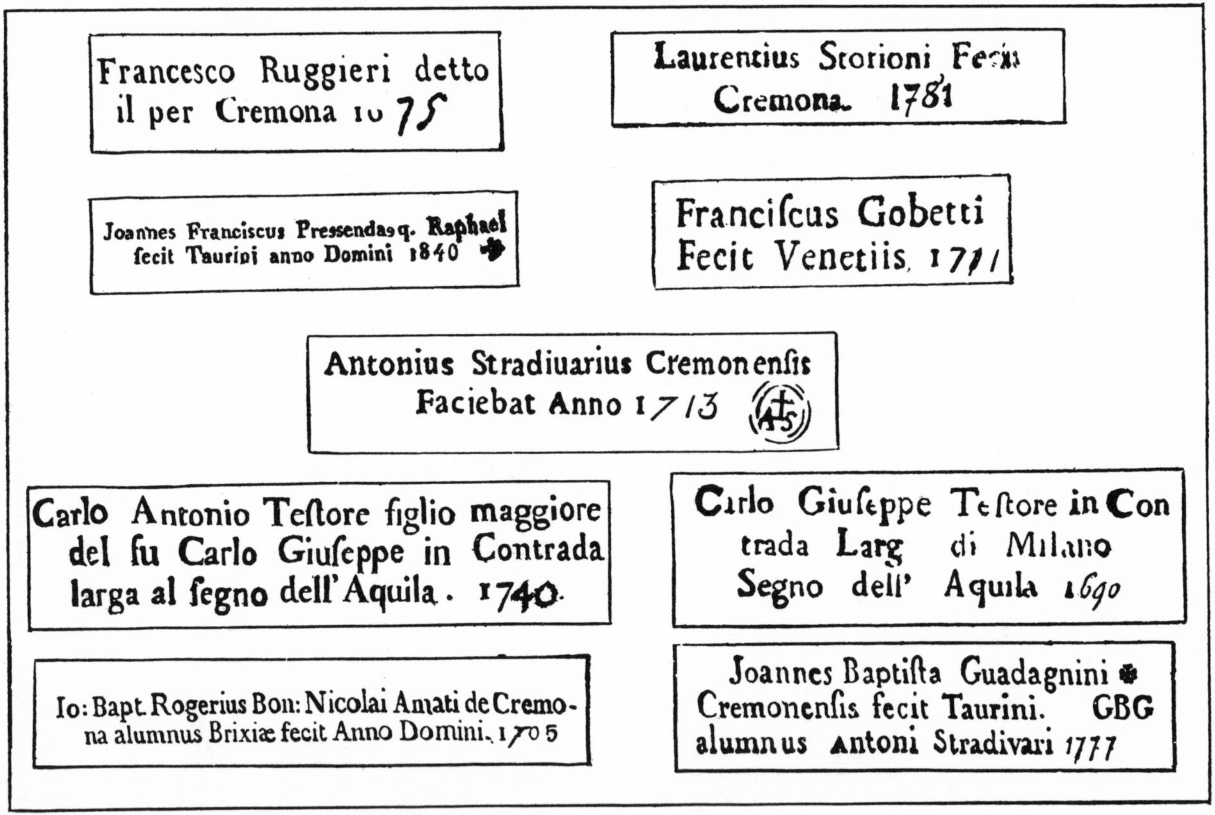

PLATE 5

Laurentius Storioni Fecit
Cremona. 1781

Francifcus Gobetti
Fecit Venetiis. 1711

Carlo Giufeppe Teftore in Con
trada Larg di Milano 1690
Segno dell' Aquila

Antonius Stradiuarius Cremonenfis
Faciebat Anno 1713

Francesco Ruggieri detto
il per Cremona 1075

Joannes Franciscus Pressendaeq. Raphel
fecit Tauripi anno Domini 1840

Carlo Antonio Teftore figlio maggiore
del fu Carlo Giufeppe in Contrada
larga al fegno dell'Aquila. 1740.

Io: Bapt Rogerius Bon: Nicolai Anati de Cremona alumnus Brixiæ fecit Anno Domini. 1705

Joannes Baptifta Guadagnini
Cremonenfis fecit Taurini.   GBG
alumnus Antoni Stradivari 1777

LABELS USED BY ITALIAN VIOLIN MAKERS.

cellent bow maker. His sons, Michael and Joseph, were also notable violin makers. The label used by Albanus is reproduced on Plate 17, and one of his instruments on Plate 18.

ALBERTI, FERDINANDO, Milan, 1737 to 1760.

ALBERTO, PIETRO, Rome 1578, still living•in 1598.

ALDRED, ——, London, 1600.

ALDRICH, JEAN FRANCOIS, Paris, b. Mirecourt 1765, d. 1843.

ALLARD, FRANCOIS, Paris, 1776 to 1789.

ALLETSEE, PAUL, Munich, 1698 to 1738.

ALVANI, PAOLO, Cremona, 1750 to 1755.

AMATI, ANDREA, Cremona, b. about 1535, d. after 1611. The founder of a famous violin-making family, but unfortunately very few of his excellent instruments are still preserved. His violins were of a small pattern, fashioned from the best of woods, and varnished either a reddish black or a dark yellow. The name "Amati" has been sadly misused, being applied to any instrument resembling an Italian maker's model. Twenty-four violins made by him for Charles IX of France were destroyed in the French Revolution.

AMATI, ANTONIO, Cremona, b. between 1555 and 1560, d. after 1640.

AMATI, HIERONYMUS (GIROLAMO) I, Cremona, b. about 1556, d. 1630. Antonio was eldest son of Andrea Amati, and worked jointly with his brother Hieronymus, their beautiful instruments resembling the work of their father. The best instruments known are credited to the brother Hieronymus. The varnish of their earlier violins was dark cherry brown, later they made it orange in color. After the death of his brother, Hieronymus labeled his violins only with his own name, and they became famous not only in his own country but also in France and other European countries. The label used by Antonio and Hieronymus Amati is reproduced on Plate 11, and one of their instruments on Plate 14.

AMATI, HIERONYMUS (GIROLAMO) II, Cremona, b. 1649, d. 1740. The label used by Hieronymus is reproduced on Plate 11 and one of his instruments on Plate 6.

AMATI, NICOLA, Cremona, b. 1596, d. 1684. Son and pupil of the talented Hieronymus Amati, and· the greatest artisan of his family up to 1625. He followed his father's model exactly for years, but upon reaching the apex of his art, he designed his own model, which he named the "Grand Amati Model," and forthwith became the greatest violin maker of his time. The woods he used were carefully selected, and the varnish a golden red. All masters of the first part of the eighteenth century were his pupils. A collection of his violins, including one made in 1673, may be found in Vienna. The label used by Amati is reproduced on Plate 11, and one of his instruments on Plate 10.

AMBROSI (AMBROGI), PIETRO, Brescia, Rome, 1712 to 1748.

AMELOT, ——, Lorient (Frankreich), 1821 to 1842.

ANSELMO (ANSELMI), PIETRO, Florence, Venice, 1700 to 1750.

ANTEGNATI, GIOV. FRANCESCO, Brescia, 1535.

ANTONIAZZI, GAETANO, Cremona, b. 1823, d. Milan, 1897.

ANTONY, H., 1750 to 1780.

ASKEY, SAMUEL, London, b. 1785, d. about 1840.

ASSALONE, GASPARO (GASPERO) D', Pesaro and Rome.

AUBRY, JACQUES, Paris, 1840.

AUDINOT, NICOLAS I, Mirecourt, 1742.

AUGIERE, ——, Paris, 1830.

BACHELIER, JEAN GASPARD, Paris, 1777 to 1789.

BACHMANN, KARL LUDWIG, Berlin, b. 1748, d. 1809.

BACHMANN, OTTO, Halberstadt, 1830 to 1835.

BAGATELLA, ANTONIO, Padua, b. 1755, d. 1829.

BAGATELLA, PIETRO, Padua, 1712, still living in 1760.

BAGNINI, ORAZIO, Florence, 1661 to 1667.

BAINES, ——, London, 1780.

BAKER, JOHN, Oxford, 1688 to 1720.

BALESTRIERI, TOMMASO, Mantua, 1720 to 1788. The opinions regarding Balestrieri differ greatly, some claiming he was a pupil of Pietro Guanerius while others claim he was a pupil of Stradivarius. This seems to be more correct, as Balestrieri took part in the last works of the great artist. His model is large, with a reddish-yellow or orange-yellow varnish, suggesting the Guadagnini instruments, and have improved, probably through age, greatly in beauty of tone. The label

PLATE 6

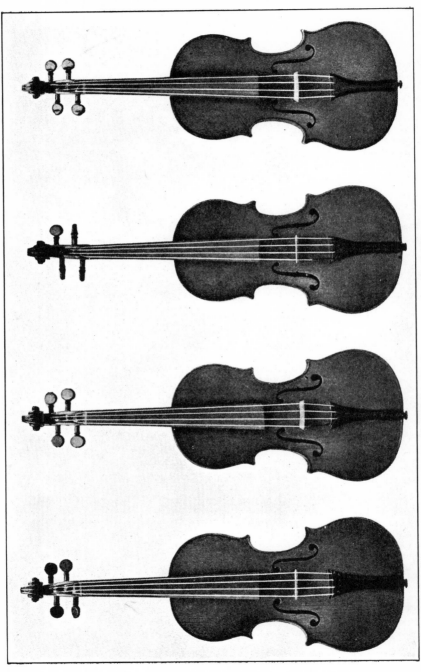

Hieronymus Amati.   Peter Guanerius.   Lorenzo Storioni.   Francesco Gobetti.

used by Balestrieri is reproduced on Plate 11, and one of his instruments on Plate 7.

BALLANTINE, ROBERT, Edinburgh, then Glasgow, 1850 to 1856.

BANKS, BENJAMIN I, Salisbury, b. 1727, d. 1795. One of the best English masters, and probably the first one who abandoned the highly regarded Stainer model to work over the Amati and Cremonese patterns. The color of his violins is a transparent, reddish black. He worked exclusively for the publishing firm of Longman and Broderip. The label used by Banks is reproduced on Plate 20, and one of his instruments on Plate 21.

BANKS, BENJAMIN II, Salisbury, later London, then Liverpool, b. 1754, d. 1820.

BANKS, JAMES, Salisbury, later Liverpool, b. Salisbury, 1756, d. Liverpool, 1831.

BARBANTI, SILVA FRANCESCO, Correggio, 1847 to 1850.

BARBIERI, FRANCESCO, Mantua, 1695 to 1750.

BARNES, ROBERT, London, 1765 to 1794.

BARNIA, FEDELE, Venice, 1760 to 1780.

BARRETT, JOHN, London (Piccadilly), 1714 to 1740.

BARTON, GEORGE, London, 1772, d. about 1810.

BASSIANO, ——, Rome, 1666.

BASSOT, JOSEPH, Mirecourt, Paris, b. in Mirecourt 1740, d. after 1805.

BASTOGI, GAETANO, Livorno, 18th century.

BAUSCH, LUDWIG CHRIST. AUG., Dresden, Dessau, Leipzig and Wiesbaden, b. Naumburg, 1705, d. Leipzig, 1771.

BAUSCH, LUDWIG D. J., Leipzig, b. Dessau, 1829, d. Pabstorf, 1871.

BAUSCH, OTTO B., Leipzig, b. Leipzig, 1841, d. 1875.

BECKMAN, SVEND, Stockholm, d. about 1761.

BELLOSIO, ANSELMO, Venice, b. after 1715, d. 1789. A son of Giovanni Bellosio and a pupil of Serafino Santo. Although not an equal to his master, he was one of the best violin makers of his time. His violins have an excellent tone, although his wood and varnish are not of the highest grade.

BELVIGLIERI (BILVEGLIERI), GREGORIO, Bologna, 1742 to 1772.

BENEDICT, JOSE, Cadix, 1667 to 1744.

BENTI, MATTEO, Brescia, b. 1580, d. after 1637.

BERATI, ——, Imola (Prov. Bologna), 18th century.

BERETTA, FELICE, Como, 1760 to 1789.

BERGE, ——, Toulouse, 1760 to 1771.

BERGONZI, BENEDETTO, Cremona, d. Cremona, 1840.

BERGONZI, CARLO I, Cremona b. 1686, d. 1747. One of the best, if not the best pupil of Stradivarius. After the death of Stradivarius' sons, Bergonzi took over the house and workshops of his master. The color of his instruments is reddish brown or amber, but is sometimes applied a little too thickly, and therefore shows a tendency to dissolve or melt. His instruments of late years have gained greatly in value, the last ones bearing the year mark of 1700. A violinist in Munich has one labeled 1696, but the *chef d'oeuvre* by Bergonzi is now in the possession of Baron Liebig at Vienna. The label used by Bergonzi is reproduced on Plate 11, and one of his instruments on Plate 9.

BERGONZI, CARLO II, Cremona 1780, d. about 1820.

BERGONZI, MICHEL ANGIOLO, Cremona, b. about 1715, d. about 1765. Bergonzi succeeded his father in 1747, working on several different models, but giving the broad Stradivarius pattern the preference. He did good work, but never equaled that of his father. His varnish is dull, and the tone often muffled. Only a few instruments of his make are in existence, as in early life he devoted himself to making mandolins.

BERGONZI, NICOLA, Cremona, 1740 to 1782.

BERGONZI, ZOSIMO, Cremona, 1750 to 1777.

BERNARDEL, AUGUSTE-SEBASTIEN-PHILIPPE, Paris, b. Mirecourt, 1802, d. Bougival, 1870. Bernardel came to Paris in 1820 and learned the trade with Nicolo Lupot. He founded his own business in 1826, and worked alone until 1859, when he took his two sons as partners into the business. He was one of the most skillful French violin makers of the nineteenth century, and was also considered one of the greatest connoisseurs of wood. In 1851 he exhibited some of his work at an exposition in London and received a prize. The label used by Bernardel is reproduced on Plate 15.

BERTASIO, LUIGI, Piadena, 19th century.

BERTI, ANTONIO, Cortona, 1721.

BERTOLOTTI, GASPARO, (Gasparo da Salo), b. Salo, 1540, d. 1609. Bertolotti was a pupil of his grandfather, and later a scholar of Girolamo di Viriki. In talent

PLATE 7

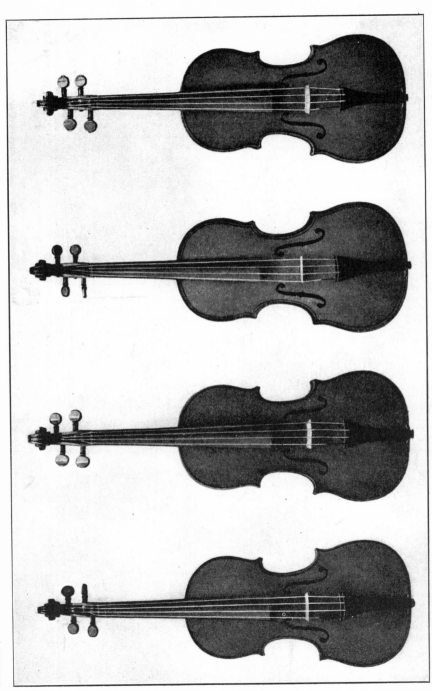

Antonio Stradivarius.   Giovanni Rogeri.   Paolo Maggini.   Tommaso Balestrieri.

he surpassed all his predecessors and soon became head of the Brescian school. His instruments were first of a beautiful amber color, but in time have taken on a much darker tone. Only a very few of his instruments are in existence at the present time. The label used by di Salo is reproduced on Plate 8.

BERTRAND, NICOLAS, Paris, 1687 to 1735.

BESSARD, LOUIS, Paris, 1753.

BETTS, EDWARD, London, b. Stamford (?), d. about 1815 or 1820.

BETTS, JOHN EDWARD (OLD JOHN BETTS), London, b. 1755, d. 1823. Betts was born in Stamford, Lincolnshire, and was a scholar of Richard Duke. He was better known as a dealer and connoisseur than a violin maker. The instruments which bear his name were mostly made by his sons and nephews who were working for him. His successor in the business was his brother Arthur. One of his instruments is at present owned by T. W. Japhouse. Betts is also famous for having first purchased a Stradivarius for twenty shillings ($5) which was recently sold for $60,000.

BIANCHI, NICOLO, Aix, Paris, Genoa, Nizza, b. Genoa, 1796, d. Nizza, 1881.

BINDERNAGEL, JOHANN WILHELM, Gotha, b. Remstadt bei Gotha about 1770, d. Gotha, 1845.

BLAISE, ——, Mirecourt, 1822.

BLANCHARD, PAUL FRANÇOIS, Lyon, b. Mirecourt, 1851.

BODIO, GIAMBATTISTA, Venice, 1790 to 1832.

BOIVIN, CLAUDE, Paris, 1730 to 1754.

BOLLER, MICHAEL, Mittenwald, about 1770.

BOLLES, ——, London, 1600 to 1620.

BOMBERGHI, LORENZO, Florence, 17th century.

BONORIS, CESARE, Mantua, 1568.

BOOTH, WILLIAM I, Leeds, b. about 1779, d. 1858.

BOOTH, WILLIAM II, Leeds, b. 1816, d. 1856.

BOQUAY, JACQUES, Paris, b. in Lyon, d. Paris, after 1736. A famous early French maker who copied Amati violins with great success.

BORBON (BOURBON), GASPAR, Brussels, 1673 to 1702.

BORELLI, ANDREA, Parma, 1720 to 1746.

BORLON (BURLON, PORLON), AERT (ARTUS OR ARNOLD), Antwerp, 1579.

BORLON (PORLON), FRANCIS, Antwerp, 1645.

BORLON (PORLON), JAN, Antwerp, 1670 to 1680.

BORLON (PORLON), PEETER, Antwerp, 1636 to 1647.

BORTOLOTTI, LUIGI, Milan, 1815.

BOSI (BASI), FLORIANUS, Bologna, 1756 to 1782.

BOUCHER, ——, London, 1764.

BOULLANGIER, C., London, 1889 to 1900.

BOUMEESTER (BOUWMEESTER), JAN, Amsterdam, 1637 to 1689.

BOURDET, JACQUES, Paris, 1750 to 1752.

BOURDOT (BOURDET), JEAN SEBASTIEN, Mirecourt, b. beginning of 18th century, still living in 1766.

BOURGARD, JEAN, Nancy, 1775 to 1786.

BOURLIER, LAURENT I, Mirecourt, b. about 1737, d. 1780.

BOUSSU, BENOIT JOSEPH, Eterbeek, Brussels, 1750 to 1780.

BRAGLIA, ANTONIO, Modena, 1790, d. about 1820.

BRANDIGLIONI, FILIPPO, Brescia, 1790 to 1800.

BRANZO, FRANCESCO BARBARO, Padua, 1620 to 1660.

BRENSIO, ANTONIO, Bologna, 1592.

BRENSIO, (GIROLAMO) HIERONYMUS, Bologna, 16th century.

BRESSANO, BAPTISTA, 16th to 17th century.

BRETON, FRANÇOIS, Mirecourt, b. about 1750, d. 1830. Breton's work was not as artistic as it was clean-cut. He preferred a large model and always used a light yellow varnish. He employed many workmen, and his instruments are not rare, but, as his business was taken over by a Mirecourt house, it is well to distinguish between the older and the newer instruments, as this firm places the old Breton label in new violins.

BRETON, JOSEPH FRANÇOIS, Paris, Mirecourt, 1740 to 1815.

BROSCHI (BROCCHI), CARLO, Parma, 1730 to 1744.

BROWN, JAMES (sen.), London, b. 1759, d. 1834.

BROWN, JAMES (jun.), London, b. 1786, d. 1860.

BROWNE (BROWN), JOHN, London (Cornhill), 1680 to 1743.

BRUGERE, FRANÇOIS, Mirecourt, b. 1822, d. Mirecourt, 1874.

BUCHSTETTER, GABRIEL DAVID, Stadtamhof bei Regensburg, 1752 to 1771.

BUONFIGLIUOLI, PIER FRANCESCO, Florence, 17th century.

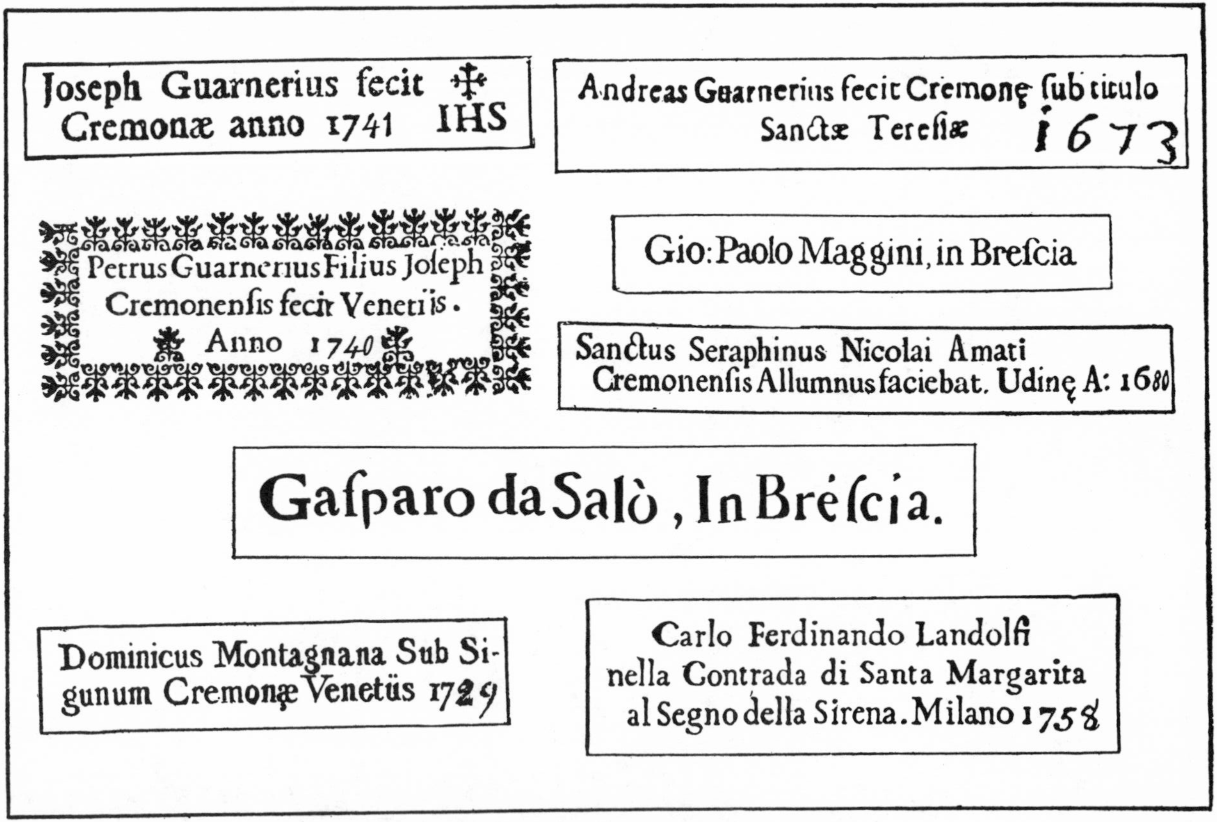

PLATE 8

Joseph Guarnerius fecit ✠ IHS
Cremonæ anno 1741

Andreas Guarnerius fecit Cremonæ sub titulo
Sanctæ Teresiæ 1673

Gio:Paolo Maggini, in Brescia

Sanctus Seraphinus Nicolai Amati
Cremonensis Allumnusfaciebat. Udinę A: 1680

Petrus Guarnerius Filius Joseph
Cremonensis fecit Venetiis .
Anno 1740

Gasparo da Salò, In Brescia.

Carlo Ferdinando Landolfi
nella Contrada di Santa Margarita
al Segno della Sirena. Milano 1758

Dominicus Montagnana Sub Si-
gunum Cremonę Venetiis 1729

LABELS USED BY ITALIAN VIOLIN MAKERS.

BUSAN, DOMENICO, Vicenza, Venice, 1740 to 1780.

BUSSETTO, GIOVANNI MARIA DEL, Cremona, Brescia, 1640 to 1681.

BUSSOLERO, LUIGI, Riva, Nazzaro, 1817.

CABROLI, LORENZO, Milan, 1716.

CAESTE, GAETANO, Cremona, 1660 to 1680.

CAHUSAC, ——, London (Strand), 1785 to 1788.

CALCAGNI (CALCANIUS), BERNARDO, Genoa, 1710 to 1750.

CALONARDI, MARCO, Cremona, 17th century.

CALOT (CALLOT), Paris, b. Mirecourt, 1810.

CALVAROLA, BARTOLOMMEO, Torre Baldone (Bergamo) and Bologna, 1750 to 1767.

CAMILLI, CAMILLO, Mantua, 1714 to 1760. It is generally claimed that Camilli was a pupil of Stradivarius, but his violins resemble more those of Peter Guanerius, so it is more than probable that he was a pupil of the latter. His instruments have a fine tone, excellent wood and light red or brownish red varnish of the first quality. One of his violins, marked 1734, is in the possession of a member of the Brussels String Quartet.

CAPO, ——, Milan, 1717 to 1718.

CAPPA, GOFFREDO, Saluzzo, b. Saluzzo, 1644, d. 1717. Son of Andrea Cappa. He was probably a pupil of Nicolo Amati, and is classed as one of the best of the Amati School. His violins have a noble tone and can easily be compared with those of G. B. Rogeri.

CAPPA, GIOACCHINO AND GIUSEPPE, Saluzzio, Turin, 1661 to 1725.

CARCANIUS, ——, Cremona, 1500.

CARCASSI, LORENZO, Florence, 1737 to 1757. He was a partner in the firm of Lorenzo and Tomasso Carcassi, although he worked independently. His violins have a high arch and a yellow varnish. Later the Brothers Carcassi manufactured only guitars. One of his violins is in the museum at Cologne.

CARCASSI, TOMASSO, Florence, 1747 to 1786. Probably a partner in the firm of Lorenzo and Tomasso Carcassi. His work is of the same high quality as his brother Lorenzo's.

CARLOMORDI (CARLOMORTI), Marco, 1654 to 1660.

CARON, ——, Versailles, 1775 to 1790.

CARRE, ANTOINE, Arras, 1750 to 1790.

CARTER, JOHN, London, 1780 to 1790.

CASPAN (CASPANI), GIOVANI PIETRO, Venice, 1658 to 1670.

CASSANELLI (CASANELLI), GIOVANNI, Ciano (Modena), 1770 to 1777.

CASSINI (CASINI), ANTONIO, Modena, b. about 1630, d. about 1698.

CASTAGNERI, ANDREA, Paris, 1730 to 1750.

CASTAGNERI, GIAN PAOLO, Paris, 1638 to 1665.

CASTELLANI, LUIGI, Florence, b. 1809, d. 1884.

CASTELLANI, PIETRO, Florence, 1780, d. 1820.

CASTELLO, PAOLO, Genoa, 1750 to 1780.

CASTRO, ——, Venice, 1680 to 1720.

CATENARI, ENRICO, Turin, 1671, still living in 1746.

CATENARI, GIUSEPPE FRANCESCO, Turin, 1703 to 1720.

CATI, PIERANTONIO, Florence, 1738 to 1760.

CAVALORIO (CAVALERIO).

CELONIATO, GIAN FRANCESCO, Turin, 1730 to 1737.

CERIN, MARCO ANTONIO, Venice, 1780 to 1824.

CERUTTI, ENRICO, Cremona, b. 1808, d. 1883.

CERUTTI, GIOV. BATTISTA, Cremona, b. about 1755, d. after 1817. A pupil of Lorenzo Storiomi, and later his successor. On account of ill health the business was afterwards transferred to his son. He worked on the Guanerius model, and made in all about five hundred violins. The varnish varies in color, sometimes light yellow, then again deep red. At times he used different woods for back and belly. The tone of his violin is loud and clear, and has quite naturally gained by age.

CERUTTI, GIUSEPPE, Cremona, b. about 1787, d. Mantua, 1860.

CHALLONER, THOMAS, London, 18th century.

CHAMPION DE ST. JULIEN, RENE, Paris, 1730 to 1770.

CHANOT, FRANCIS, Paris, b. Mirecourt, 1787 or 1788, d. Brest (Rochefort), 1823. François Chanot was not a professional but rather an amateur violin maker. He started a shop with the organ builder, Lebé, and tried to build an original model in which he only partially succeeded. The tone of his violins is too muffled and the varnish lacks luster.

CHANOT, FREDERIC W., London, 1890 to 1900.

CHANOT, GEORGES, Mirecourt, 1710 to 1714.

CHANOT, GEORGES, Paris, b. Mirecourt, 1801, d. Courcelles, 1883. The son and pupil of Joseph Chanot, he came to Paris in 1819 and worked in the shops of Lebé where he constructed violins for his brother. After

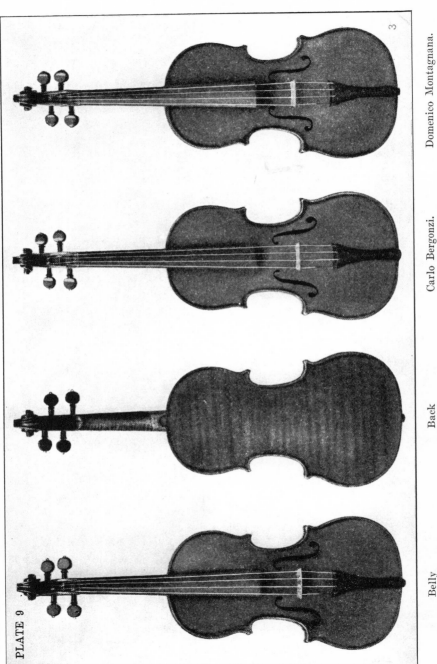

PLATE 9

Belly
"Sancy" Strad.

Back
"Sancy" Strad.

Carlo Bergonzi.

Domenico Montagnana.

this he went to Clement as assistant, and in 1823 started an independent shop. He worked mostly after the Stradivarius and Guarnerius models, and his wood and varnish are faultless. He was also a dealer in violins and undertook long journeys through Italy, Spain, Germany and Russia in search of instruments made by the masters. Chanot's son is also famed for his wonderful copies of Joseph Guanerius de Gesu's instruments. The label used by Chanot is reproduced on Plate 15.

CHAPPUY, NICOLAS-AUGUSTIN, Paris, Mirecourt, b. about 1740, d. 1784.

CHARDON, JOSEPH-MARIA, Paris, b. Paris, 1843.

CHAROTTE, ——, Rouen, b. Mirecourt, d. 1836.

CHERPITEL, NICOLAS-EMILE, Paris, b. Mirecourt, 1841, d. Paris, 1893.

CHEVRIER, ANDRÉ-AUGUSTIN, Paris, Brussels, 1830 to 1840; b. Mirecourt.

CHIARELLI, ANDREA, Messina, b. Messina, about 1675, d. 1699.

CHIAVELLATI, DOMENICO, Lonigo, 1780 to 1796.

CHIOCCHI, GAETANO, Padua, b. 1814, d. after 1880.

CHRETIEN, HIPPOLYTE, gen. Silvestre, Lyon, Paris, b. Sommerviller, 1845.

CHRISTA, JOSEPH PAUL, Munich, 1730 to 1776.

CIRCAPA, TOMASO, Naples, 1730 to 1735.

CLAUDOT, AUGUSTIN, Mirecourt, 1840 to 1850.

CLAUDOT, CHARLES II, Mirecourt, b. Mirecourt, 1794, d. 1876.

CLEMENT, JEAN-LAURENT, Paris, 1783 to 1847.

CLIQUOT, LOUIS-ALEXANDRE, Paris, 1756.

COLE, JAMES, Manchester, 1850 to 1910.

COLE, THOMAS, London (Holborn), 1672 to 1690.

COLLICHON, MICHEL, Paris, 1670 to 1693.

COLLIER, SAMUEL, London, 1775.

COLLIN-MEZIN, CHARLES-JEAN-BAPTISTE, Paris, b. Mirecourt, 1841.

COLLINGWOOD, JOSEPH, London, 1760.

CONTRERAS, JOSÉ, Madrid, b. about 1710, d. about 1780.

CONTRERAS, ——, Madrid, b. about 1751, d. 1827.

CONWAY, WILLIAM, London, 1745 to 1750.

CORDANO, GIACOMO FILIPPO, Genoa, 1770 to 1776.

CORNELLI, CARLO, Cremona, 1702.

CORSBY, ——, Northampton, 1770 to 1780.

CORSBY, GEORGE, London, 1789 to 1830.

COUSINEAU, GEORGES (OR PIERRE JOSEPH), Paris, 1769 to 1788.

CRAMOND, CHARLES, Aberdeen, 1800 to 1834.

CRASKE (CRASK), GEORGE, Bath, Leeds, Sheffield, Birmingham, Manchester, Stockport, b. Bury St. Edmunds, 1797, d. Stockport, 1888.

CRISTOFORI (CRISTOFALI), BARTOLOMMEO, Florence, b. about 1667, d. after 1720.

CROSS, NATHANIEL, London (Aldermanbury), 1700 to 1751.

CROWTHER, JOHN, London, 1755, d. about 1810.

CUNAULT, GEORGES, Paris, b. Paris, 1856.

CUNY, ——, Paris, 1777 to 1778.

CUPPIN, GIOVANNI.

CUYPERS, JAN, Hague, b. 1719, d. after 1806.

DALLA CORNA (DELLA CORNA), GIOVAN GIACOMO, Brescia, b. about 1484, d. after 1548.

DALLA COSTA, PIETRO ANTONIO, Treviso, 1700 to 1768. Dalla Costa modeled his violins after those of the brothers Amati and Stradivarius; his workmanship is particularly clean-cut. He used a brownish red or a yellow varnish, and worked in both Mantua and Venice from about 1720 to 1757. His name and label have been misused by inferior makers, but there are several genuine specimens of his art in the possession of European collectors and dealers.

D'AMBROSIO, ANTONIO, Naples, 1820.

DANIEL, EDMOND, Marseilles, 1800 to 1850.

DARDELLI, FRA PIETRO, Mantua, 1497 to 1500.

DAVIDSON, HAY, Huntley, 1870.

DAVIS (DAVIES), RICHARD, London, b. Bussage bei Stroud, about 1790, d. 1836.

DEARLOVE, MARK, Leeds, 1812 to 1820.

DE COMBLE, AMBROISE, Tournay, 1740 to 1785. A pupil of Stradivarius at Cremona. His violins are of great merit. The label used by De Comble is reproduced on Plate 15.

DECONETTI, MICHELE, Venice, Padua, 1752 to 1795.

DEFRESNE, PIERRE, Rouen, 1731 to 1745.

DE LANNOY, H. J., Lille, 1740 to 1775.

DELANY, JOHN, Dublin, 1808.

DELAUNAY, ——, Paris, 1775.

DELEPLANQUE, GERARD J., Lille, 1760 to 1790.

PLATE 10

4

Nicola Amati.   Alessandro Gagliano.   Joseph Guarnerius del Gesu.   Gianfrancesco Pressenda.

DENNIS, JESSE, London, b. 1795, d. after 1855.

DERAZEY, JEAN JOSEPH HONORE, Mirecourt, b. Darney, 1794, d. 1883.

DEROUX, SEBASTIEN AUGUST, Paris, b. Mirecourt, 1848.

DES ROUSSEAUX, NICOLAS, Verdun, 1755.

DEVEREUX, JOHN, London, Melbourne, 1840 to 1880.

D'HESPONT (DESPONT), ANTOINE, Paris, 1634 to 1636.

DICKINSON (DICKENSON), EDWARD, London, 1750 to 1790.

DICKSON (DICKESON), JOHN, London and Cambridge, b. Stirling (Scotland), about 1720, d. after 1780.

DIEHL (DIEL), FRIEDRICH, Darmstadt, b. 1814, d. 1888.

DIEHL, JAKOB, Bremen, Hamburg, b. Mainz, 1806, d. Hamburg, 1874.

DIEHL, JOHANN, Mainz, 1808 to 1843.

DIEHL, MARTIN, Mainz, 1770 to 1792.

DIEHL, NIKOLAUS, Mainz, Darmstadt, b. 1779, d. 1851.

DIEHL, NIKOLAUS LOUIS, Hamburg, 1860, d. 1876.

DIEULAFAIT, ——, Paris, 1720.

DINI, GIOVANNI BATTISTA, Lucignano, 1700 to 1707.

DITTON, ——, London, 1700 to 1720.

DODD, THOMAS (SON), London, beginning of 19th century.

DODD, THOMAS (FATHER), London, 1786 to 1820. Thomas Dodd, third son of Edward Dodd, the famous bow maker, was first a brewer, from 1786-1789 a bow maker, and from 1798 a violin maker and dealer, and finally a harp and piano builder. He was a great connoisseur of Italian instruments, and his violins and violoncellos bring a very high price, being in great demand. Dodd claimed to be the only man having a formula for the genuine Cremona varnish as used by the master makers. The label used by Dodd is reproduced on Plate 20.

DOMINICELLI, ——, Ferrara, 1695 to 1715.

DONATO, SERAFINO, Venice, 1411.

DONI, ROCCO, Florence, 1600 to 1660.

DOPFER, NIKOLAUS, Mainz, 1715 to 1768.

DORANT, WILLIAM, London, 1814.

DRINDA, GIACOMO, Pienza, 18th century.

DROULOT (DROULEAU), ——, Paris, 1788 to 1800.

DUCHERON, MATTHIEU (MATHURIN), Paris, 1700 to 1730.

DUIFOPRUGGAR, GASPAR (see Tieffenbrucker, Gaspar).

DUKE, RICHARD (FATHER), London, 1750 to 1780. A reproduction of one of Duke's instruments will be found on Plate 21.

DUKE, RICHARD (SON), London, beginning of 19th century.

DU MESNIL, JACQUES, Paris, 1655 to 1662.

DUNCAN, GEORGE, Glasgow, b. 1855 in Kingston-on-Spey.

EBERLE (EBERLL), JOHANNES UDALRICUS, Prague, b. Vils, 1699, d. 1768. A maker of highly arched violins, beautifully varnished. The label used by Eberle is reproduced on Plate 17 and one of his instruments on Plate 19.

EDLINGER, JOSEF JOACHIM, Prague, b. Prague, 1693, d. 1748.

EDLINGER, THOMAS I, Augsburg, b. 1656, d. 1690.

EGLINGTON, ——, London, 1800 to 1802.

ELSLER (ELSTER), JOHANN JOSEPH, Mainz, 1717 to 1750.

EMILIANI, FRANCESCO DE, Rome, 1704 to 1736.

ERNST, FRANZ ANTON, Gotha, b. 1745, d. 1805.

EVANS, RICHARD, London, 1742.

EVE, JACQUES CHARLES, Paris, 1758 to 1788.

FABRIS (FABBRIS), LUIGI, Venice, d. after 1873.

FACINI, FRA AGOSTINO, Bologna, 1732 to 1742.

FALAISE (FALAIRE), ——, Paris.

FALCO, PAOLO, Cremona, 1750 to 1752.

FARINATO, PAOLO, Venice, 1695 to 1725.

FARON, ACHILLES, 1701.

FENDT, BERNHARD SIMON (SIMMON), London, b. London, 1800, d. 1852. Eldest son and pupil of Bernhard Fendt. After working for John Betts and his successors for a long time, he formed the firm of Fendt and Purdy. He was a skillful but not a careful worker, and was especially clever at imitating the large Amati model. In the last year of his life (1851) he received the first prize at the London Exposition for one of these instruments. His wood was well selected, the varnish a light red. One of his violins of 1820 was exhibited by Hill and Sons in 1904 at the London Music Loan Exhibition.

FENDT, FRANCIS, London, Liverpool, 1850 to 1857.

FENDT, JAKOB, London, b. 1815, d. 1849. Third son of Bernhard Fendt and a pupil

PLATE II

Antonius, & Hieronymus Fr. Amati
Cremonen. Andreæ fil. F. 1630

Nicolaus Amatus Cremone &
Hieronymi filii fecit. An 1651

Hieronimus Amati Cremonensis
Fecit Anno Salutis 1640

Thomas Balestrieri Cremonensis
Fecit Mantuæ. Anno. 17 75

Magno dieffopruchar a venetia.

Lavrentius Guadagnini Pater;
& alumnus Antonij Straduarj
fecit Placentie Anno 1745

Gia. Bapt. Grancino in Contrada
Largha di Milano anno 1699

Anno 1741 Carlo Bergonzi
fece in Cremona

LABELS USED BY ITALIAN VIOLIN MAKERS.

of Bernhard, his eldest brother. Jacob
was a highly talented violin maker, who
copied the instruments by Stradivarius
and Lupot with great success. He generally worked for dealers, and had always
the ambition to make his instruments
appear a great deal older than they really
were.

FENDT, MARTIN, London, b. 1812, d. 1845.

FENDT, WILLIAM, London, b. 1833, d. 1852.
Youngest son of Bernhard Simon Bendt,
and an apprentice of his father. As he
died very young he only made a few instruments, but those he produced were of
the highest grade.

FENT, FRANÇOIS, Paris, 1765 to 1791. One
of the ablest Parisian violin makers of
his time. He worked upon the Stradivarius model, using only the best wood.
His varnish was a reddish brown which
now of course appears much darker and
seems nearly black. Vidal calls attention
to the fact that nearly all the Fent instruments are infested by worms. The
label used by Fent is reproduced on
Plate 15.

FERATI, PIETRO, Siena, 1754 to 1764.

FERET, ——, Paris, 1708.

FERRARI, AGOSTINO, Budrio, 18th century.

FERRARI, ALFONSO, Carpi (Modena), 1738.

FERRARI, CARLO, Siena, 1740.

FEURY (FERRY), FRANÇOIS, Paris, 1715 to
1762.

FEVROT, Lyon, 1779 to 1813.

FEYZEAU, ——, Bordeaux, 1740 to 1770.

FICHTL, MARTIN MATTHIAS II, Vienna, b.
about 1682, d. 1768.

FICHTOLD, HANS D. A., Fussen, 1616 to
1666.

FICKER, JOHANN CHRISTIAN I, (Mark-) Neukirchen, b. about 1735, d. 1780. Second
son and pupil of Johann Kaspar Ficker.
He made his masterpiece in 1755. One of
his instruments is now in Wurzburg,
made of fine wood with a high arch and
brown varnish.

FICKER, JOHANN CHRISTIAN II, (Mark-)
Neukirchen, b. 1758, d. 1822.

FICKER, JOHANN GOTTLOB I, (Mark-) Neukirchen, b. 1744, d. 1832.

FILANO, DONATO, Naples, 1763 to 1783.

FIORILLO, GIOVANNI, Ferrara, 1780.

FIRTH, ——, Manningham, 1877.

FISCER (FITTER), BRUDER, Milan, 1760 to
1764.

FISCHER, JOSEPH, Regensburg, b. 1769, d.
1834.

FISCHER, ZACHARIAS, Wurzburg, b. 1730, d.
1812.

FLETTE, BENOIST, Paris, 1745 to 1763.

FLEURY, BENOIT, Paris, 1751 to 1791.

FLORENO, FIORENZO, Bologna, 18th century.

FLORENO, GIOVANNI GUIDANTE, Bologna,
1685 to 1730.

FLORENO, GUIDANTE, Bologna, 1710 to 1740.

FONTANELLI, GIOVANNI GIUSEPPE, Bologna,
1733 to 1773.

FORSTER (FOSTER, OR FORRESTER), JOHN,
Brampton (Cumberland), b. Kirkandrews,
about 1688, d. Brampton, 1781.

FORSTER, SIMON ANDREW, London, b. 1781,
d. 1870. A violin maker and author of a
*History of the Violin and Other Bowed
Instruments.*

FORSTER, WILLIAM I, Brampton, b. about
1713, d. 1801.

FORSTER, WILLIAM II (OLD FORSTER), London, b. Brampton, 1739, d. London, 1808.
An English maker of Stainer and Amati
copies.

FORSTER, WILLIAM III (YOUNG FORSTER),
London, b. 1764, d. 1824.

FRANCK, ——, Ghent, 1800 to 1830.

FRANKLAND, ——, London, 1785.

FREY (FREI), HANS, Nurnberg, 1450, d.
1523.

FURBER, HENRY JOHN, London, 1830, still
living in 1865.

FURBER, JOHN, London, 1810, still living in
1841 in Cow Cross, Smithfield.

GABRIELLI, ANTONIO, Florence, 1760.

GABRIELLI, BARTOLOMMEO, Florence, 1730.

GABRIELLI, CRISTOFORO, Florence, 1730.

GABRIELLI (GABBRIELLI), GIOVANNI BAT-
TISTA, Florence, 1739 to 1770.

GAFFINO, GIUSEPPE, Paris, 1734, d. 1789.

GAGLIANO, ALESSANDRO, Naples, b. Naples,
about 1660, d. 1725. Credited with having been an assistant to Stradivarius for
thirty years, which seems doubtful, as his
oldest instruments are dated from 1695
and are noted for the fine quality of wood
and workmanship. The varnish is a
marvelous deep red or orange, and is easy
to distinguish from the Cremonese instruments. In model his violins remind one
of the best works of Carlo Bergonzi, for
which they are often sold. The label used
by Gagliano is reproduced on Plate 11,
and one of his instruments on Plate 10.

GAGLIANO, ANTONIO I, Naples, b. about 1728,
d. about 1795. Third son of Nicolo and
youngest brother of Ferdinando. He
worked exclusively with Giuseppe, using

PLATE 12

Giovanni Grancino.   Carlo Landolfi.   Lorenzo Guadagnini.   Carlo Antonio Testore.

good wood and a red varnish. Only a
few genuine violins of his make are in
existence.

GAGLIANO, FERDINANDO, Naples, b. Naples,
1724, d. 1781. Eldest son of Nicolo, with
whom he cannot compare, although he
was a good workman, his instruments resembling those of Alessandro. He imitated the last model of Stradivarius and
used a reddish brown or yellow varnish
of a warm color. In the selection of his
woods he was particularly careful.

GAGLIANO, GENNARO, Naples, b. about 1700,
d. after 1770. Second son and pupil of
his father Alessandro, whose influence in
his work cannot be mistaken. He imitated the Stradivarius models and his best
work was done between 1730 and 1750.
His violins are noted for their fine wood,
orange or red varnish and beautiful tone.
One of his violins, made in 1758, was sold
to Charles Mahillon for 10,000 francs.
Gennaro is considered the peer of his
brother Nicola.

GAGLIANO, GIOVANNI I, Naples, b. about
1740, d. 1806.

GAGLIANO, GIOVANNI II, Naples, b. 1800,
d. after 1867. A son of Giovanni I, and
classed as one of the better violin makers
of his time, although no one of his instruments is deserving of special mention.

GAGLIANO, GIUSEPPE, Naples, 1725, d. 1793.
Second son of Nicolo Gagliano and brother of Ferdinando, Antonio and Giovanni.
He worked scrupulously after his father's
model, and was able to give his instruments a beautifully clear tone. In later
years, he worked with his brother Antonio.

GAGLIANO, NICOLA I, Naples, b. about 1665
or 1670, d. about 1740. Eldest son of
Alessandro, but dissimilar in talent. He
usually imitated the Stradivarius models,
mostly the older periods of the master,
using a bright yellow varnish. One of his
instruments of the year 1750 was owned
by Prof. Jacob Grün of Vienna. Many of
Nicola's violins are decorated with
purfling of a highly ornamental nature.

GAGLIANO, RAFFAELE, Naples, b. about 1790,
d. 1857. A son of Giovanni who worked
most of the time in partnership with his
brother Antonio. The color of his violins
was brown, and the workmanship of an
ordinary character.

GAGLIANO, VINCENZO, Naples, 1870, d. about
1886.

GAILLARD-LAJOUE, JULES, Mirecourt, b.
about 1820, d. about 1870.

GALBANI, PIETRO, Florence, 1640.

GALBUSERA, CARLO ANTONIO, Milan, 1813 to
1833.

GALLAND, JEAN, Paris 1744, d. 1761.

GALRAM (GALRAN, GALRAO), JOACHIM JO-
SEPH, Lissabon, 1769 to 1825.

GALTANI, ROCCO, Florence, 17th century.

GAND, CHARLES-ADOLPHE, Paris, b. Paris,
1812, d. 1866.

GAND, CHARLES-FRANÇOIS, Paris, b. Versailles, 1787, d. Paris, 1845. Son of
Michael Gand and from 1807 to 1810 a
worthy pupil of Nicolas Lupot. After
Lupot's death in 1824, Charles took over
his business and his workshops. He was
unquestionably the most able French violin maker of his time. His instruments
compare favorably with those of the old
Italian makers, and bring high prices.
There are several splendid specimens in
the museum of the Paris Conservatory.
The label used by Gand is reproduced on
Plate 15.

GAND, CHARLES-MICHEL, Versailles, b. Mirecourt, about 1748, d. Versailles, 1820.

GAND, CHARLES-NICOLAS-EUGENE, Paris,
b. Paris, 1825, d. 1892.

GAND, GUILLAUME-CHARLES-LOUIS, Versailles, b. Paris, 1792, d. Versailles, 1858.

GARANI, MICHELE ANGELO, Bologna, 1685 to
1720.

GARANI, NICOLA, Naples, about 1700.

GAVINIES, FRANÇOIS, Bordeaux, Paris, b.
about 1700, d. after 1770.

GEDLER (GIDL), JOHANN ANTON, Fussen,
1752 to 1800.

GEDLER, JOSEPH BENEDICT, Fussen, b. about
1759, d. 1830.

GEDLER, NORBERT, Wurzburg, 1715 to 1723.

GEISSENHOF, FRANZ, Vienna, b. Vils, 1754,
d. Vienna, 1821.

GEMUNDER, GEORG, Astoria, Boston, New
York, b. Ingelfingen, 1816, d. 1899.

GERLE (GERLA, GERLEIN), CONRAD, Nurnberg 1460, d. 1521.

GERLE, GEORG, Innsbruck 1569, d. about
1589.

GERMAIN, EMILE, Paris, b. Paris, 1853,
d. 1906.

GERMAIN, JOSEPH-LOUIS, Paris, b. Mirecourt, 1822, d. 1870.

GERONI (GERANI), DOMENICO, Ostia, 1800 to
1820.

GHERARDI, GIACOMO, Bologna, 1677.

GIANOLI, DOMENICO, Milan, 1731.

PLATE 13

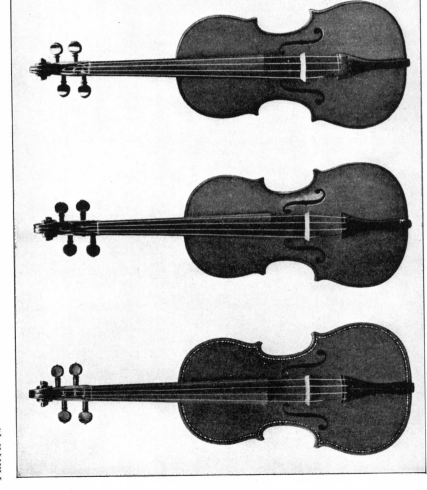

The "Hellier" Stradivarius.   Carlo Giuseppe Testore.   Francesco Ruggeri.   Andreas Guarnerius.

GIBBS, JAMES, London 1800, d. about 1845.

GIBERTINI, ANTONIO, Parma, Genoa, 1797 to 1850.

GIGLI, GIULIO CESARE, Rome, 1721 to 1762.

GILBERT, NICOLAS-LOUIS, Metz, 1701 to 1706.

GILCHRIST, JAMES, Glasgow, b. 1832, d. 1894.

GILKES, SAMUEL, London, b. Morton Pinkney (Northamptonshire), 1787, d. London, 1827. A pupil of Charles Harris, Sr., who worked with William Forster, and in 1810 opened his own shop. He copied the Harris model, and also tried the Amati model several times without success. He did good clean work, using the best wood and a good varnish. He was much sought after by dealers, and his violins are at the present time in great demand.

GILKES, WILLIAM, London, b. Tothill Field, Grey Coat Str. (Westminster), 1811, d. London, 1875.

GIORDANO, ALBERTO, Cremona, 1725 to 1740.

GIORGI, NICOLA, Turin, 1717 to 1760.

GIULIANI (GIULIANI), ——, Cremona, Saluzzo, 1660.

GOBETTI, FRANCESCO, Venice, 1690 to 1732. Judging by his work he must have been a pupil of Stradivarius. He is, next to Montagnana and Serafino, the most important Venetian violin maker. It is claimed that he did all his work in the years 1690 to 1725, but there always has been great doubt about these dates. In the monastery of St. Florian in Austria can be found a violin with his trademark of 1761, but it is most likely that the figure "6" can also be taken for an "0." His model may be called the happy medium between the Stradivarius and Amati model. The varnish is of a clear light red color. One especially fine instrument of his make can be found in a collection at Antwerp. The label used by Gobetti is reproduced on Plate 5, and one of his instruments on Plate 6.

GOFRILLER, FRANCESCO, Venice, Udine, 1690 to 1740.

GOFRILLER (GOFFRILER OR GAFRILLER), Matteo, Venice, 1690, d. 1742. His work suggests the old Italian school and he appears to have been a pupil of Carlo Bergonzi. His work is exemplary in the selection of the wood, the beautiful red varnish, and the excellence of tone. One of his instruments, dated 1742, is in a Museum at Cologne. Gofriller frequently omitted the label from his violins.

GOSSELIN, JEAN, Paris, 1814 to 1830.

GOUGH, WALTER, London, 1810, d. about 1830.

GRABENSEE, T. K., (OR T. G. OR J. A.), Dusseldorf, 1818 to 1861.

GRAGNANI, ANTONIO, Livorno, 1741, still living in 1800. Although not one of the master makers, Gragnani's violins have an excellent tone and pleasing appearance. One of his instruments is reproduced on Plate 14.

GRAGNANI, GENNARO, Livorno, 1730.

GRANCINO, FRANCESCO, Milan, 1690, d. 1746.

GRANCINO, GIOVANNI I, Milan, 1645 to 1682.

GRANCINO, GIOVANNI II, Milan, b. about 1675, d. after 1737. Second son and pupil of Paolo Grancino. As a violin maker, he is one of the best, and fully the equal of his brother Paolo. The arch of his violins is not as high but broader than that of Paolo, although the latter used better wood. He had a predilection for the smaller models. One of his instruments (1737) is in the Lobkowitsch collection; another of the year 1702 is owned by Alfred Keil in Lisbon.

GRANCINO, GIOVANNI BATTISTA I, Milan, Ferrara, 1690 to 1710. The label used by Grancino is reproduced on Plate 11, and one of his instruments on Plate 12.

GRANCINO, PAOLO, Milan, 1665 to 1692. A distinguished maker said to have been a pupil of Amati.

GRAND-GERARD, JEAN-BAPTISTE, Mirecourt, 1771 to 1820.

GRANDJON, J., Mirecourt, 1862 to 1868.

GREGORI, LUIGI, Bologna, 1793 to 1808.

GREIFF, HANS (JOHANN), Fussen, 1606 to 1622.

GRIESSER, MATHIAS, Innsbruck, b. Fussen, after 1700, d. 1784.

GRIMM, KARL, Berlin, b. 1794, d. Berlin, 1855.

GRISERI, FILIPPO, Florence, 1650.

GROSSET, PAUL FRANÇOIS, Paris, 1744 to 1765.

GROSSI, GIUSEPPE, Bologna, 1803 to 1804.

GRULLI, PIETRO, Cremona, 1870, d. 1898.

GUADAGNINI, ANTONIO, Turin, b. 1831, d. 1881.

GUADAGNINI, CARLO, Turin, 1780 to 1839.

GUADAGNINI, GAETANO I, Turin, 1775 to 1831.

GUADAGNINI, GIAMBATTISTA, Piacenza, Turin, b. Cremona, 1711, d. Turin, 1786. Son of Lorenzo, and a scholar of Stradivarius, as was his father. He built his

PLATE 14

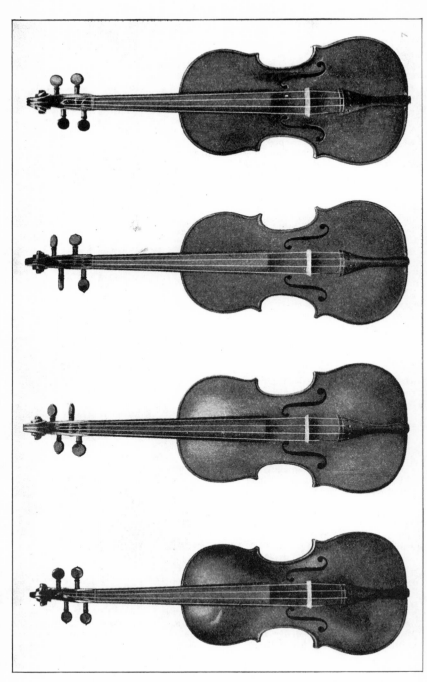

David Teechler.   Antonio and Hieronymus Amati.   Antonio Gragnani.   Giambattista Guadagnini.

instruments on the Stradivarius model, but always used the flat pattern, with a golden yellow transparent varnish. Still, with all the beauty of his finish, it cannot compare with Lorenzo, for it lacks the same purity. Nor in tone do his violins equal Lorenzo, although he did his best work in the latter part of his life. His instruments are highly esteemed and bring very high prices. The label used by Guadagnini is reproduced on Plate 5, and one of his instruments on Plate 14.

GUADAGNINI, GIUSEPPE, Brescia, 1697.

GUADAGNINI, LORENZO I, Cremona, Piacenza, b. about 1695, d. 1760. A pupil of Stradivarius who worked for his old master a very long time. In 1730 he started in business for himself, using a pattern of medium size and only the best wood. His reddish gold varnish is wonderful and is not surpassed by any of the Guadagnini's. The prices for his violins increase continually with the demand. The label used by Guadagnini is reproduced on Plate 11, and one of his instruments on Plate 12.

GUADAGNINI, LORENZO II, Turin, 1790.

GUARNERIUS, ANDREAS, Cremona, b. about 1626, d. 1698. Son of Bartolommeo, Andrea was the head of the entire violin-making family of that name. His violins are larger than those of his teachers. Besides making full-sized violins, he also made "half-size" instruments, one of which is still preserved in Berlin. The label used by Guarnerius is reproduced on Plate 8, and one of his instruments on Plate 13.

GUARNERIUS, ANTONIO, Cremona.

GUARNERIUS, GIUSEPPE (JOSEPH DEL GESU), Cremona, b. 1687, d. after 1742. The greatest master of the family of Guarneri and the son of Giambattista, but it cannot be proved that he was a pupil of Stradivarius. He often changed his models, but always used exclusively acorn wood. His work is faultless, the varnish transparent and the tone beautiful. In the latter part of his life, Giuseppe worked too fast, and instruments of that period have not the value of the former. At the present time (1924) his violins bring prices comparable with those of Stradivarius. The term "del Gesu" originates from his label, on which he always used the characters J. H. S. (Jesu Hominum Salvator) and a Roman cross. The label used by Guarnerius is reproduced

on Plate 8, and one of his instruments on Plate 10.

GUARNERIUS, GIUSEPPE GIAN BATTISTA (JOSEPH GUARNERIUS), Cremona, b. 1666, d. after 1738.

GUARNERIUS, PIETRO I GIOVANNI, Cremona, Mantua, b. Cremona, 1655, d. after 1728. First son of Andreas Guarnerius. Came to Mantua in 1680 and returned to Cremona in 1698. He was a pupil of the Amati, but his father was his principal teacher. He was a gifted violin maker. In form his violins differ greatly from those of his father and brothers. He made several attempts to create some new models, but failed in every instance. Generally speaking, his model is a composite of Amati and Stradivarius, and the tone often lacks volume. The wood is of good quality and the varnish is light red or brownish yellow.

GUARNERIUS, PIETRO II, Venice, b. Cremona, 1695, d. Venice, after 1760. The label used by Guarnerius is reproduced on Plate 8, and one of his instruments on Plate 6.

GUDI, HIERONIMO, Cremona, 1726 to 1727.

GUERRA, GIACOMO, Modena, 1810.

GUERSAN, LOUIS, Paris, b. about 1713, d. about 1781.

GUGLIELMI, GIO. BATTISTA, Cremona, 1747.

GUSETTO, NICOLA, Cremona, 1785 to 1828.

HAMBERGER, JOSEPH I, Pressburg, b. Vienna, 1808, d. 1864.

HAMM, JOHANN GOTTFRIED, (Mark-) Neukirchen, b. 1744, d. 1817.

HARBOUR (HARBUR), W., London, 1785 to 1786.

HARDIE, MATTHEW, Edinburgh, b. Edinburgh, 1755, d. 1826.

HARDIE, THOMAS, Edinburgh, b. 1804, d. 1856.

HARE, JOHN, London, beginning of 18th century.

HARE, JOSEPH, London (Cornhill), 1720 to 1726.

HARRIS (HARRYS), CHARLES I, Oxford, London, 1780 to 1800.

HARRIS, CHARLES II, Oxford, London, 1818 to 1830.

HART, GEORGE I, London, b. 1839, d. 1891. He was an excellent violinist and the successor to his father's business. Although he did not make any instruments himself, he was one of the best connoisseurs of his time and was also the author of two valuable books, *The Violin, Its Famous Mak-*

PLATE 15

Jean Baptiste Vuillaume à Paris
Rue Croix des Petits Champs

BERNARDEL *Luthier-Eleve de Lupot*
Rue Croix des Petits Champs, N° 23
A PARIS 1835

Georges Chanot à Paris
Quai Malaquais. Année 1856

Nouveau procédé approuvé par l'Institut.
THIBOUT, Luthier, rue Rameau,
N°. 8, à Paris, 1835

Pierre Silvestre
à Lyon 1848

Nicolas Lupot Luthier rue de
Grammont ; a Paris l'an 1798

GAND Luthier du Conservatoire de Musique
Rue Croix des Petits Champs N° 20. PARIS 18 18

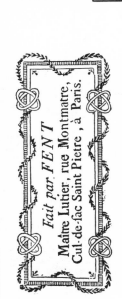

Fait par FENT
Maître Luthier, rue Montmatre,
Cul-de-fac Saint Pierre , à Paris.

Fait a Tournay par
Ambroise De Comble 1755

LABELS USED BY FRENCH VIOLIN MAKERS.

ers and Their Imitators (London 1875 and 1887) and *The Violin and Its Music* (London 1881).

HART, GEORGE II, London, b. London, Warwick, 1860. Son of George I. After finishing his education as a violin maker in Paris, he entered his father's business, and the firm name became Hart and Son, a highly respected house still in existence. His specialty is making exact reproductions of fine Italian instruments. A reproduction of the Hart & Son label will be found on Plate 20.

HART, JOHN THOMAS, London, b. 1805, d. 1874. In 1820 he associated himself with Samuel Gilkes as an apprentice, and soon developed into a first class master. He did not build many violins himself, but those he made are considered first class Amati copies. He was a great judge of Italian violins and an excellent repairer.

HARTUNG (HARTON), MICHAEL, Padua, 1602 to 1624.

HASSERT (HASERT), J. C., Eisenach, 1728.

HASSERT (HASERT), JOHANN CHRISTIAN, Rudolstadt, b. 1759, d. 1823.

HEESOM, EDWARD, London, 1748 to 1750.

HEL, PIERRE JOSEPH, Lille, b. Mazirot, 1842, d. Lille, 1902.

HELLMER, KARL JOSEPH, Prague, b. 1739, d. 1811. Successor to his father Johann Georg Hellmer and pupil of Joh. Eberle. After finishing his apprenticeship in Germany, he returned to Prague in 1763. His violins resemble those of his father, except that they are flatter in places and have a brown varnish. He was not only an accomplished musician, but also a publisher of musical literature. One of his violins (1796) is in the Museum at Salzburg and two more (1771 and 1791) are in the Monastery of St. Margaret in Prague.

HEMSCH, JEAN-HENRY, Paris, 1747 to 1763.

HENOCQ (HENOC), JEAN, Paris, 1763 to 1789.

HENRY, CHARLES, Paris, b. 1803, d. Paris, 1859.

HENRY, EUGENE, Paris, b. 1843, d. 1892.

HENRY, JEAN BAPTISTE, Paris, b. 1757, d. Paris, 1831.

HENRY, JEAN BAPTISTE FELIX, Paris, b. 1793, d. 1858.

HENRY, OCTAVE, Grenoble, b. Marseille, 1826.

HETEL, G., Rome, 1763.

HILL, JOSEPH I, London, 1660.

HILL, JOSEPH II, London, b. 1715, d. 1784. First a pupil of Banks and then of Wamsley. His workmanship is good and clean-cut. All his four sons were educated as violin makers, and became his apprentices. One of his violins of the year 1770 is owned by J. T. Chapman. A label used by Jos. Hill is reproduced on Plate 20.

HILL, LOCKEY, London, b. 1756, d. 1810.

HILL, WILLIAM, London, b. 1745, d. 1790.

HILL, WILLIAM EBSWORTH, London, b. 1817, d. 1895.

HILL AND SONS, London, 140 New Bond St. W. One of the largest and highest class violin-making institutions in the world. The present members of the firm are William Hill, Arthur Fred Hill, William Henry Hill and Walter E. Hill. They employ a large number of artisans at their shops in Hanwell, near London. The label used by Hill and Sons is reproduced on Plate 20, and one of their instruments on Plate 21.

HILLDEBRAND (HILDEBRANDT), MICHEL CHRISTOPHER, Hamburg, 1768, still living in 1807.

HILTZ, PAUL, Nurnberg, 1656.

HOFFMANN, JOHANN CHRISTIAN, Leipzig, b. 1683, d. 1750.

HOFFMANN, MARTIN, Leipzig, b. 1653, d. 1719.

HOFMANS, MATTHYS, Antwerp, 1689 to 1740.

HOLLOWAY, JOHN, London, 1794.

HORIL, JAKOB, Vienna, Rome, 1720 to 1759.

HORNSTEINER, ——, Mittenwald. A family of skillful violin makers, who have not only produced instruments of merit, but have also earned recognition as dealers and publishers. The Hornsteiners were the first to associate themselves with the Klotz family. A reproduction of the label used by one of the family, Jos. Hornsteiner, is reproduced on Plate 17.

HORNSTEINER, FRANZ, 1782 to 1820. Franz Hornsteiner imitated the Klotz model closely, and used a yellow or a golden brown varnish. The tone is of an even mellow character, and the instruments resemble those of Andreas Jais, another well-known Mittenwald maker.

HORNSTEINER, JOSEPH IV, b. Mittenwald, 1853.

HORNSTEINER, MATHIAS II, 1760 until after 1803.

HOSBORN, THOMAS ALFRED, London, 1629.

HULINZKY, THOMAS ANDREAS, Prague, b. 1731, d. 1788.

PLATE 16

Belly
Nicolas Lupot.

Back
Nicolas Lupot.

Belly
J. B. Vuillaume.

Back
J. B. Vuillaume.

HÜLLER (HULLER), AUGUSTIN, Schöneck, 1735 to 1775.

HUME, RICHARD, Edinburg, 1535.

HUMEL, CLAUDE, Mirecourt, 1820.

HUNGER, CHRISTOPH FRIEDRICH, Leipzig, b. Borstendorf, 1718, d. Leipzig, 1787.

INDELAMI, MATTEO, Rome(?).

JACQUOT, PIERRE CHARLES, Nancy, b. 1828, d. 1900.

JAIS, ANDREAS, Tölz (Mittenwald), b. 1685, d. after 1749.

JAIS, JOHANN, Bozen, b. Mittenwald, 1752, d. after 1780.

JAUCH (JAUCK), JOHANNES, Dresden, 1735 to 1750.

JAY (JAIE), HENRY I, London (Southwarke), 1611, d. about 1676.

JAY, HENRY II, London (Long Acre), 1744 to 1777.

JAY, THOMAS, London, 1690 to 1700.

JEANDEL, PIERRE NAPOLEON, Rouen, b. Meurthe, about 1812, d. Rouen, 1879.

JOHNSON, JOHN, London, 1750 to 1760.

JULIANO, FRANCESCO, Rome, 1690 to 1725.

KAISER, MARTINO, Venice, 1609 to 1632.

KAMBL, JOHANN ANDREAS, Munich, b. 1699, d..1781.

KARG (KARP, CARP), GREGORIUS, Konigsberg, 1694 to 1696.

KEMPTER, ANDREAS, Dillingen, b. Lechbruck, about 1700, d. Denklingen, 1786.

KENNEDY, ALEXANDER, London, b. Schottland, about 1695, d. London, 1785.

KENNEDY, JOHN, London, b. about 1730, d. London, 1816.

KENNEDY, THOMAS, London, b. 1784, d. 1870.

KIRCHSCHLAG, LOUIS, 1790 to 1796.

KLEIN, ALOYS, Rouen, 1884.

KLOTZ, AEGIDIUS I, Mittenwald, 1675 to 1711. There are in existence a large number of old violins under the name of Aegidius Klotz. His work is similar to the work of Aegidius II of the eighteenth century, but his violins are much better and worth about three times as much as those of his namesake. He must have been a pupil of Stainer. One of his violins may be found in a collection at Berlin.

KLOTZ, AEGIDIUS SEBASTIAN, Mittenwald, b. 1733, d. 1805.

KLOTZ, GEORGE I, Mittenwald, b. 1687, d. 1737.

KLOTZ, GEORGE II, Mittenwald, b. 1723, d. 1797.

KLOTZ, JOHANN CARL, Mittenwald, b. 1709, still living in 1790.

KLOTZ, JOSEPH I (THOMAS), Mittenwald, b. 1743, d. after 1809.

KLOTZ, MATHIAS I, Mittenwald, b. 1656, d. 1743. The real founder of the violin industry in Mittenwald. He was the eldest son of Urban Klotz and received his first lessons from Stainer, although his real education was accomplished in Italy where he worked for six years under Giovanni Railich in Padua. His work is of the highest grade and very praiseworthy. The tone is wonderful although he did not always use the best wood. There are a good many violins of his make in existence. In 1890 a bronze statue was erected to his memory in Mittenwald. A reproduction of the label used by Klotz will be found on Plate 17.

KLOTZ, SEBASTIAN I, Mittenwald, b. 1696, d. after 1767. A son of Mathias Klotz. Violins of his make with a later date than 1750 are not in existence. His instruments are built after the Stainer model. The varnish is thicker and better than that of his father and of different colors, mostly red or dark brown, resembling that of Albanus. His violins bring a high price in both Great Britain and the United States. The label used by Klotz is reproduced on Plate 17, and one of his instruments on Plate 19.

KNITL (KNITTEL, KNITTL), JOSEF, Mittenwald, 1756 to 1790.

KOLDITZ, JAKOB, Rumburg, b. about 1718, d. 1796.

KOLDITZ (KOLDIZ), MATTHIAS JOHANN, Munich, 1733 to 1760.

KOLIKER, JEAN GABRIEL, Paris, 1783 to 1820.

KRAMER, HEINRICH, Vienna, 1680 to 1718.

KRINER, JOSEPH, Landshut, b. 1836.

LAGETTO, LOUIS, Paris, 1745 to 1753.

LAMBERT, JEAN-NICOLAS, Paris, 1731, d. 1761.

LAMBLIN (LAMBIN), ——, Gent, 1795 to 1830.

LANDI, PIETRO, Siena, 1774.

LANDOLFI, CARLO FERDINANDO, Milan, 1734 to 1787. Most of Landolfi's violins were made on the model of Joseph Guarnerius, therefore, it is probable that he was a pupil of this great master. Many are made with the greatest care, while others were crudely executed of poor material, even in respect to the varnish which is sometimes very carelessly applied. The String Quartet of Brussels has one of his instruments dated 1742. The label used by Landolfi is reproduced on Plate 8, and one of his instruments on Plate 12.

LANDOLFI, PIETRO ANTONIO, Milan, 1750 to 1800. Son, pupil and successor of Carlo Ferdinando Landolfi, whose skill he was never able to equal. He was less painstaking and his work could never be classed with that of a master.

LANZA (LANSA), ANTONIO MARIA, Brescia, 1675 to 1715.

LAPAIX, J. A., Lille, 1840 to 1858.

LA PREVOTTE, ETIENNE, Marseille, Paris, b. Mirecourt, about 1795, d. Paris, 1856.

LARUE, PIERRE MATHIEU, Paris, 1767.

LASKE, JOSEF ANTON, Prague, b. Rumburg, 1738, d. Prague, 1805.

LAVAZZA, ANTONIO MARIA, Milan, 1703 to 1708.

LAVAZZA, SANTINO, Milan, 1718 to 1780.

LECLERC, JOSEPH NICOLAS, Paris, 1760 to 1777.

LECOMTE, ANTOINE, Paris, 1775 to 1800.

LE DUC, PIERRE, Paris, 1640 to 1649.

LEFEBVRE, J. B., Amsterdam, 1720 to 1786.

LEFEBVRE, NICOLAS, Rouen, 1630 to 1636.

LEFEVRE (LEFEBVRE), TOUSSAINT-NICOLAS-GERMAIN, Paris, 1762 to 1789.

LE JEUNE, FRANÇOIS, Paris, 1755 to 1789.

LELIEVRE (LE LIEVRE), J. C. PIERRE, Paris, 1731 to 1765.

LENTZ (LENZ), JOHANN NIKOLAUS, London, 1803 to 1813.

LEONI, CARLO, Treviglio, Treviso, 1851 to 1861.

LEONI, FERDINANDO, Parma, 1870.

LE PILEUR, PIERRE, Paris, 1703 to 1757.

LESCLOP, FRANÇOIS-HENRY, Paris, 1746.

LEWIS, EDWARD, London, 1687 to 1730.

LIGHT, EDWARD, London, 1798 to 1800.

LIGNOLI, ANDREA, Florence, 1681.

LINAROLO, VENTURA, Venice, 1577 to 1591.

LOLIJ (LOLLIJ), JACOPO, Naples, 1727.

LONGMAN & BRODERIP, LONGMAN LUCKEY AND CO., 1760.

LORENZINI, GASPARE, Piacenza, 1750.

LOTT, GEORGE FREDERIK, London, b. 1800, d. 1868.

LOTT, JOHN FREDERICK (SEN.), London, b. Germany, 1775, d. London, 1853. A celebrated maker of Cremonese imitations.

LOTT, JOHN FREDERICK (JUN.), London, b. 1804, d. 1871.

LOUIS, JOSEPH, Genf, Basel, Mulhausen, Besançon, 1813 to 1841.

LOUVET, JEAN II, Paris, 1750 to 1789.

LOUVET, PIERRE, Paris, 1739 to 1783.

LUDICI, HIERONYMO PIETRO DI, Conegliano, 1698 to 1709.

LUGLIONI (LUGLONI), GIUSEPPE, Venice, 1777.

LUPOT, FRANÇOIS I, Stuttgart, Orleans, b. Plombières, 1725, d. Paris, 1804.

LUPOT, FRANÇOIS II, Paris, b. Orleans, 1774, d. Paris, 1837.

LUPOT, FRANÇOIS-LAURENT, Mirecourt, Plombières, Luneville, Orleans, b. 1696, d. after 1762.

LUPOT, JEAN, Mirecourt, b. about 1652, d. after 1696.

LUPOT, NICOLAS, Orleans, Paris, b. Stuttgart, 1758, d. 1824. Son and pupil of François Lupot, with whom he came to Orleans at the age of eleven. His earliest instruments are dated from Orleans. In 1794 he came to Paris and was employed by Rique, but it is doubtful whether he gained much by this. In the year 1798 he opened his own shop, and became without question the greatest master of the French school, quite correctly being called the "French Stradivarius." His only fault was applying his varnish a little too thick, which very often caused it to crack, but nevertheless he was a great master and his violins were given as prizes to the pupils at the Paris Conservatory. One of the violins built in 1818 is in possession of the Brussels String Quartet. The label used by Lupot is reproduced on Plate 15, and one of his instruments on Plate 16.

MAC-INTOSH, JAMES, Blairgowrie, b. 1801, d. 1873.

MAFEOTTO, GIUSEPPE, Rovere, 1637.

MAGGINI, GIOVANNI PAOLO, Brescia, b. 1580, d. about 1632. A son of Giovanni Maggini. At the age of seven he was a pupil of Gasparo da Salo, where he remained until he attained his majority. In his first year, he worked strictly after the model of his teacher, and was often inexact and not sufficiently particular in the selection of his wood. He made frequent attempts to create a broader-toned violin, but failed in every attempt. His varnish was thinner than da Salo's, but more fiery and of different colors, mostly light brown. More than fifty of his instruments are in existence. Two are in the possession of Prince Chimay who paid 8000 francs for each. Professor Keller in Stuttgart has another, and one is owned by Theodor Hammerle in Vienna. The

PLATE 17

MATTHIAS ALBANUS fecit
Bulsani in Tyroli 1690.

Mathias Kloz, Lautenmacher
in Mittenwaldt, Anno 17)

443

§ Joannes Udalricus Eberle, §
§ fecit Pragæ, 17 §

JOACHIM TIELKE
in Hamburg/ An. 1676

Jacobus Stainer in Absam
prope Œnipontum 1659

Sebastian Kloz, in
Mittenwald, An. 17

Joseph Horenstainer Musicant
in Mittenwald an der Iser. 1735

Michael Boller, Geigenmacher in
Mittenwald an der Iser. 1796

LABELS USED BY GERMAN VIOLIN MAKERS.

label used by Maggini is reproduced on Plate 8, and one of his instruments on Plate 7.

MAGGINI, (PIETRO) SANTO, Brescia, 1630 to 1680.

MALER (MALLER, MAHLER), LAUX (LUCAS), Bologna, 1500 to 1528.

MALER (MALLER), SIGISMONDO, Bologna and Venice, 1460 to 1526.

MANN, JOHN ALEXANDER, Glasgow, b. 1810, d. 1889.

MANTEGAZZA, PIETRO GIOVANNI, Milan, 1750 to 1790.

MANTOVANI, ——, Parma, 18th century.

MARATTI, GIAMBATTISTA, Verona, 1690 to 1700.

MARCELLI (MARCELLO), GIOVANNI ANTONIO, Cremona, 1696 to 1697.

MARCHI, GIAN ANTONIO, Bologna, 1660 to 1726.

MARCO-ANTONIO, ——, Venice, 1700.

MARCONCINI, GIUSEPPE, Ferrara, b. about 1774, d. 1841.

MARCONCINI, LUIGI (ALOISIO), Bologna, Ferrara, 1760 to 1791.

MARIA, GIUSEPPE DA, Naples, 1770 to 1779.

MARINO, BERNARDO (BERNARDINO), Rome, 1770 to 1805.

MARSHALL, JOHN, London, 1750 to 1759.

MARTIN, ——, London, 1790 to 1800.

MAST, JEAN-LAURENT, Mirecourt, 1750 to 1789.

MAST, JOSEPH-LAURENT, Toulouse, 1802 to 1830.

MAUCOTEL, CHARLES, London, b. Mirecourt, 1807, d. after 1860.

MAUCOTEL, CHARLES-ADOLPHE, Paris, b. Mirecourt, 1820, d. 1858.

MAUSSIELL, LEONHARD, Nurnberg, b. 1685, d. after 1760.

MAYR, ANDREAS FERDINAND, Salzburg, 1721 to 1750.

MEARES, RICHARD, London, 1667 to 1680.

MEDARD, ANTOINE, Nancy, 1621, still living in 1666.

MEDARD, FRANÇOIS III, Paris, 1690 to 1710.

MEDARD, NICOLAS II, Nancy, Paris, 1620 to 1641.

MEIBERI, FRANCESCO, Livorno, 1745 to 1750.

MELLINI, GIOVANNI, Guastalla, 1768.

MELONI, ANTONIO, Milan, 1690 to 1694.

MENNEGAND, CHARLES, Amsterdam, Paris, b. Nancy, 1822, d. Villers-Cotteret, 1885.

MENNESSON, JEAN EMILE, Reims, b. Reims, 1842.

MERIGHI, PIETRO, Parma, 1770.

MERIOTTE, CHARLES, Lyon, b. about 1703, 1770.

MERLIN, JOSEPH, London, 1778 to 1780.

MEZZADRI, ALESSANDRO, Ferrara, 1690 to 1732.

MEZZADRI, FRANCESCO, Milan, 1700 to 1750.

MICHAUD, ——, Paris, 1788 to 1789.

MICHELIS, PEREGRINO (PELEGRINO) DI ZANETTO, Brescia, b. about 1520, still living in 1603.

MICHELOT, JACQUES-PIERRE, Paris, 1760 to 1800.

MIER, J., London, 1780 to 1786.

MILLER, GEORGE, London, 1669.

MIRAUCOURT, JOSEPH, Verdun, 1736 to 1749.

MIREMONT, CLAUDE-AUGUSTIN, New York, Paris, b. Mirecourt, 1827, d. Pontorson Ende, 1887. A French maker who received several medals for his fine instruments.

MOERS, JEAN HENRI, Paris, 1771.

MOHR, PHILIPP, Hamburg, 1650.

MOITESSIER, LOUIS, Mirecourt, 1781 to 1824.

MOLINARI, ANTONIO, Venice, 1672 to 1703.

MOLINARI, JOSÉ E., Buenos Aires, 1890 to 1895.

MONTADA, GREGORIO, Cremona, 1690 to 1735.

MONTAGNANA, DOMENICO, Venice, b. about 1690, d. about 1750. Although a master of first rank, there is little known about his life. Judging by his work he must have been a pupil of Nicolas Amati, others think he was a disciple of Stradivarius, as his violins undoubtedly show the influence of the latter master. He always preferred a large model, selecting the wood carefully. The workmanship is faultless, and the varnish of golden red color. His violins bring prices comparable with those obtained for the Cremonese masters. The label used by Montagnana is reproduced on Plate 8, and one of his instruments on Plate 9.

MONTICHIARO, ZANETTO (GIANETTO), Brescia, 1530.

MONTRON, ——, Paris, 1783 to 1789.

MORELLA, MORGLATO, Mantua, Venice, 1545 to 1602.

MORONA, ANTONIO, Isola bei Capo d'Istria, 1731.

MORRISON, JOHN, London, b. about 1760, d. about 1833.

MOUGENOT, ——, Rouen, 1763 to 1770.

NADERMAN (NADERMANN), JEAN-HENRI, Paris, 1772, d. about 1800

NADOTTI, GIUSEPPE, Piacenza, 1757 to 1789.

NAMY, JEAN-THEODORE, Paris, 1772, d. 1808.

PLATE 18

Belly
Jacob Stainer.

Back
Jacob Stainer.

Belly
Matthias Albanus.

Back
Matthias Albanus.

NAYLOR, ISAAC, Headingly, b. Leeds; 1778 to 1792.

NELLA, RAFFAELE, Brescia, 1659 to 1672.

NEUNER, MATHIAS II, Mittenwald, 1795 to 1830. A skillful violin maker who was the founder of the still established firm of Neuner and Hornsteiner. The violins which carry his name are not all genuine, because, after working at the business for a time, he engaged a large force of men, and the violins made by them are not so good in tone and workmanship as those made by himself, even though they bear the Neuner label.

NEZOT, ——, Paris, 1730 to 1760.

NICOLAS, DIDIER L'AINE, Mirecourt, b. Mirecourt, 1757, d. 1833. Son and pupil Antoine Nicolas. He made good cheap violins, but they cannot be judged as works of art, although they have all the same good characteristics. His model ·is flat and suggestive of Stradivarius. With his attempts to change the regular form of the violin, he had, like many others, very little success. His varnish is reddish brown inclining toward yellow. He conducted the manufacture of violins on a large scale, and at times employed as many as six hundred men.

NICOLAS, FRANÇOIS-FOURRIER, Paris, b. Mirecourt, 1758, d. 1816.

NICOLAS, JOSEPH, Mirecourt, b. 1796, d. Mirecourt, 1864.

NIGGELL, SYMPERT, Fussen, b. Schwangau, 1710, d. 1785.

NORBORN (NORDBORN), JOHN, London, 1723.

NORMAN, BARAK, London, b. about 1678, d. 1740.

NORRIS, JOHN, London, b. about 1739, d. 1818.

NOVELLO, MARCO ANTONIO, Venice, 1780 to 1795.

NOVELLO, PIETRO VALENTINO, Venice, 1790 to 1800.

NOVERCI (NOVERSI), COSIMO, Florence, 1662.

OBBO, MARCO I, Naples, 1712 to 1727.

OBICI (OPICI, OBIZI), BARTOLOMEO I, Verona, 1665 to 1685.

.ODANI, GIUSEPPE MORELLO, Naples, 1738.

ODOARDI, GIUSEPPE, Ascoli, 1786.

OHBERG, JOHAN I, Stockholm, b. about 1723, d. 1779.

ORTEGA, ASENSIO, Madrid, 1799 to 1840.

ORTEGA, SILVERIO, Madrid, 1785 to 1798.

OSTLER, ANDREAS, Breslau, 1730 to 1770.

OTT, JOHANNES, Fussen, 1727.

OTTO, CARL CHRISTIAN, Halle, b. Weimar, 1792, d. 1853.

OTTO, CARL GUSTAV, Markneukirchen, b. 1857.

OTTO, C. W. F., Stockholm, b. Jena, 1808, d. 1884.

OTTO, HEINRICH WILHELM, Amsterdam, Berlin, b. 1796, d. 1858.

OTTO, HERMANN, St. Petersburg, b. Holn, 1859, d. St. Petersburg, 1884.

OTTO, JAKOB AUGUST, Weimar, Jena, b. Gotha, 1760, d. 1829. A famous German maker who published a manual of violin building.

OTTO, LOUIS, Dusseldorf, b. Ludwigslut, 1844, d. 1920.

OTTO, LUDWIG, Erfurt, Koln, St. Petersburg, b. Jena, 1821, d. St. Petersburg, 1887.

PACHERELE, MICHEL, Mirecourt, 1779 to 1780.

PACHERELE (PACHEREL), PIERRE, Paris, Nizza, Genoa and Turin, b. Mirecourt, 1803, d. Nizza, 1871.

PACQUET, ——, Marseille, 1785.

PAGANI, GIAN BATTISTA, Cremona, 1735 to 1747.

PAGANONI, ANTONIO, Venice, 1750.

PALATE, ——, Luttich, 1710 to 1750.

PAMPHILON, EDWARD, London, 1660 to 1685.

PANDOLFI, ANTONIO, Venice, 1710 to 1740.

PANORMO, GEORGES LOUIS, London, b. about 1774, d. after 1842.

PANORMO, JOSEPH, London, b. London about 1773, d. after 1825.

PANORMO, VINCENZO TRUSIANO, Paris, London, b. Monreale bei Palermo, 1734, d. London, 1813.

PANZANI (PANSANI), ANTONIO, Rome, 1735 to 1785.

PAQUOTTE, HENRI-FELIX, b. Paris, 1857.

PAQUOTTE, PLACIDE, Paris, b. 1864, d. 1900.

PARDI, ——, Paris, 1785 to 1788.

PARDINI, BASTIANO, Florence, 17th century.

PARKER, DANIEL, London, b. about 1700, d. 1775.

PASTA, ANTONIO, Brescia, 1710 to 1730.

PASTA, DOMENICO, Brescia, 1710 to 1730.

PASTA, GAETANO, Brescia, 1710 to 1760. The most important member of his family and a pupil of Hieronymus Amati. His violins are on a flat model, and a brilliant tone, somewhat resembling those of G. B. Rogeri.

PAZZINI, GIOVANNI GAETANO, Florence, 1630 to 1666.

PEARCE, JAMES, London, 1780 to 1800.

PECCENINI, ALESSANDRO, Bologna, 1581 to 1595.

PEDRAZZI, FRA PIETRO, Bologna, 1784.

PEDRINELLI, ANTONIO, Crespano, 1781 to 1854.

PEMBERTON, EDWARD, London, 1660.

PERRY, THOMAS, Dublin, 1767 to 1830. A very industrious violin maker who was for a while connected with William Wilkinson. His violins are of good wood and have a fine tone. A reproduction of one of his instruments will be found on Plate 21.

PERTON, ——, Paris, 1757.

PFRETZSCHNER, CARL FRIEDRICH I, b. 1743, d. 1798.

PFRETZSCHNER, CARL GOTTLOB, b. 1807, d. 1863.

PIERRAY, CLAUDE, Paris, 1698 to 1726. One of the best representatives of the Paris school. His violins are made in small and large patterns, and are generally varnished light red or yellow which time has turned very dark. The tone is brilliant and very powerful. Authorities are agreed that Claude Pierray's violins compare favorably with Cremonese instruments. There are a great many of his violins still to be obtained.

PIETE, NOËL, Paris, b. about 1760, still living in 1810.

PILLEMENT (PILLEMENTI), FRANÇOIS, Mirecourt, 1774 to 1830.

PILOSIO (PELOSIO), FRANCESCO, Gorz, b. 1754, d. after 1778.

PIQUE, FRANÇOIS-LOUIS, Paris, b. Roret, 1758, d. Charenton Saint-Maurice, 1822.

PIROT, CLAUDE, Paris, 1795 to 1833.

PITET, ——, Paris, second half of 17th century.

PIZZURNO, DAVIDE, Genoa, 1760 to 1763.

PLACHT, FRANZ I, 1760 to 1788.

PLANI, AGOSTINO DE, Genoa, 1750 to 1778.

PLATNER, MICHAEL, Rome, 1735 to 1750.

PLUMEREL, JEAN, Mirecourt, 1727 to 1751.

POLIS, LUCA DE, Cremona, 1751.

PONS, CESAR, Grenoble, 1750 to 1808.

PONS, ——, Paris, 1788 to 1800.

POWELL, THOMAS I, London, 1780 to 1808.

PRESSENDA, GIANFRANCESCO, Alba, Carmagnola, later Turin, b. Sequio Berra or Turin, 1777, d. 1854. Son of Raffaelo Pressenda, a traveling musician who gave lessons in violin playing. Gianfrancesco was a pupil of Lorenzo Storioni. In 1814 he came to Alba and there settled down as a violin maker. He is one of the few violin makers of the nineteenth century whose work is much imitated at the present time. One of his violins, made in the year 1814, was in the possession of Waldemar Meyer. The label used by Pressenda is reproduced on Plate 5, and one of his instruments on Plate 10.

PRESTON, JOHN, York, 1789.

PREVOT (PREVOST), P. CHARLES, Paris, 1775 to 1788.

QUINOT, JACQUES, Paris, 1670 to 1680.

RAILICH, GIOVANNI (ZUANE), Padua, 1672 to 1678.

RAMBAUX, CLAUDE-VICTOR, Paris, b. Darney, 1806, d. Mirecourt, 1871.

RANTA, PIETRO, Brescia, 1733.

RASURA, VINCENZO, Lugo, 1785.

RAUCH, SEBASTIAN, Breslau, 1730 to 1779.

RAUT, JEAN, Rennes, b. 1719, d. 1791.

RAWLINS, HENRY, London, 1775 to 1781.

RAYMANN (RAYMAN), JAKOB, London, 1620 to 1657. A maker who copied the Stainer model, and is looked upon as the father of English violin making. The label used by Raymann is reproduced on Plate 20.

RECHARDINI, ZUANE, Venice, 1605 to 1609.

REICHEL (REICHELT), JOHANN CONRAD I, b. about 1715, d. 1762.

REICHEL, JOHANN GOTTFRIED II, b. 1759, d. 1819.

REMY, JEAN-MATHURIN, Paris, b. in Paris 1770, d. 1854.

REMY, JULES, Paris, b. 1813, d. 1876.

REMY, MATHURIN-FRANÇOIS, Paris, 1760 to 1800.

REMMY (REMY), ——, London, 1840.

RENAUDIN, LEOPOLD, Gent, Paris, b. Mirecourt, 1756, d. 1795.

RENAULT (REGNAULT, REGNAUT), JACQUES, Paris, 1666 to 1684.

RENAULT ET CHATELAIN, Paris, 1772 to 1811.

RENAULT, NICOLAS, Nancy, Paris, end of 16th and beginning of 17th century.

REYNAUD, ANDRE, Tarascon, 1755 to 1766.

RICHARD, ROBERT, Paris, 1756.

RICHARDS, EDWIN, London, b. 1859, d. 1894.

RICOLAZI, LUDOVICO, Cremona, 1729.

RIECHERS, AUGUST, Hannover, Berlin, b. Hannover, 1836, d. Berlin, 1893.

RIESS, ANDREAS, Bamberg, b. about 1720, d. 1777.

RINALDI, GIOFFREDO BENEDETTO, Turin, 1850, d. 1888.

ROCCA, GIUSEPPE ANTONIO, Turin, Genoa, b. Alba, about 1810, d. after 1868.

RODIANI (RUDIANI), GIOVITA, Brescia, Bologna, b. about 1545, d. after 1624.

ROGERI, GIOVANNI BATTISTA, Brescia, b. about 1650, d. 1730. A pupil of Stradivarius, who, when starting in business for himself, used the Stradivarius model exclusively. His work was in every respect perfect, and the varnish a golden or light red. Not many of his instruments are in existence at the present time. The label used by Rogeri is reproduced on Plate 5, and one of his instruments on Plate 7.

ROGERI, PIETRO GIACOMO, Brescia, b. about 1680, d. after 1730.

ROISMANN, JOHANNES, Breslau, 1630 to 1680.

ROL, ——, Paris, 1753.

ROMANO, PIETRO, Pavia, 18th century.

ROMARIUS, ANTÓNIUS, Cremona, 1703.

ROMBOUTS, PIETER, Amsterdam, b. 1674, d. after 1735.

ROOK, JOSEPH, London (Carlysse), 1777 to 1830.

ROPIQUET, ——, Paris, 1815.

ROSIERO, ROCCO, Cremona, 1730.

ROSS (ROSE, ROSA), JOHN, London (Bridewell), 1562 to 1599.

ROTA, GIOVANNI, Cremona, 1795 to 1810.

ROTH, CHRISTIAN, Nurnberg, 1675.

ROVETTA (ROVELTA), ANTONIO, Bergamo, 1840 to 1884.

ROZE, ——, Orleans, 1701 to 1760.

ROZET, ——, Paris, about 1691.

RUELLE, PIERRE, Paris, 1754.

RUGGERI (RUGIERI), FRANCESCO, Cremona, 1645 to 1700. The eldest and best violin maker of this family. His varnish is bright and transparent and of a deep red color. He always managed to give his violins a clear and broad tone. One of his instruments of the year 1665 was bought by Ole Bull for $2000. Another is in the possession of Theodore Hammerle of Vienna. The label used by Ruggeri is reproduced on Plate 5, and one of his instruments on Plate 13.

RUGGERI (RUGIERI), GIACINTO GIO. BATTISTA, Cremona, 1666 to 1696.

RUGGERI (RUGIERI), VINCENZO, Cremona, 1690 to 1735. A son of Francesco, but less important than his father. A fine instrument of his is in the Imperial Collection of Musical Instruments in Berlin. Beethoven had one labeled 1690, which was given to him by Prince Lichnowsky.

RUPPERT, FRANZ, Erfurt, 1800 to 1809.

SACCHINI, SABBATTINO (SEBASTIANO), Pesaro, 1670 to 1686.

SACQUIN, ——; Paris, b. about 1811, d. 1860.

SAINPRAE (SAINPRA), JAKOB, Berlin, 17th century.

SAINT-PAUL, ANTOINE, Paris, 1768 to 1789.

SAINT-PAUL, PIERRE, Paris, 1740 to 1743.

SAJOT, ——, Paris, 1720 to 1734.

SALLE, LE PÈRE, Paris, 1825 to 1850.

SALO, GASPARO DA, see Bertolotti.

SALOMON, JEAN-BAPTIST-DESHAYES, Paris, 1740, d. about 1772.

SANONI, GIOVANNI BATTISTA, Verona, 1680 to 1740.

SANTAGIULIANA, GIACINTO, Vicenza, Venice, 1770 to 1830.

SANTE, ——, Pesaro, 1670.

SANTE (SANTO), GIUSEPPE, Rome, 1778.

SANTO (SANTI), GIOVANNI, Naples, 1700 to 1740.

SANTO (SANZO, SANZIO), SANTINO, Milan, 1684 to 1700.

SAPINO (SERPINO, SARPINO), ——, 16th century.

SARACINI (SARACENI), DOMENICO, Florence, 1655.

SARDI, ——, Venice, 1649.

SAUNIER, ——, Mirecourt, 1740.

SAUNIER, EDMOND, Bordeaux, Paris, b. about 1730, d. after 1783.

SAVANI (SCAVANI), GIUSEPPE, Carpi, 1809.

SAVART, FELIX, Paris, b. Mezieres, 1791, d. Paris, 1841.

SAVICKI (SAWITZKI), CARL NIKOLAUS, Vienna, b. Lemberg, 1792, d. Vienna, 1850.

SCHEINLEIN, JOHANN MICHAEL, b. 1751, d. after 1794.

SCHEINLEIN, MATTHAUS FRIEDRICH, b. 1710, d. 1771.

SCHELLE (SCHELL), SEBASTIAN, Nurnberg, 1700 to 1745.

SCHMIDT, C., Butzow, 1841.

SCHÖNFELDER, JOHANN (HANS) ADAM, b. 1707, d. 1763.

SCHONGER, FRANZ, Erfurt, 1750 to 1776.

SCHONGER, GEORG, Erfurt, b. about 1666, d. about 1740.

SCHORN, JOHANN JOSEPH, Salzburg, 1716 to 1726.

SCHORN, JOHANN PAUL, Innsbruck, Salzburg, 1680 to 1716.

SCHOTT, MARTIN, Prague, 1680 to 1682.

SCHWARTZ (SCHWARZ), BERNHARD, Strassburg, b. Konigsberg, about 1744, d. 1822.

ANTONIO STRADIVARIUS—1698

NICHOLAS LUPOT—1814

SCHWARTZ, GEORG FRIEDRICH, Strassburg, b. 1785, d. 1849.

SCHWARTZ, THEOPHIL WILHELM I, Strassburg, b. 1797, d. 1861.

SCHWEITZER, JOHANN BAPTIST, Budapest, b. Vienna, about 1790.

SELLAS, MATTEO, Venice, 1600 to 1639.

SENI, FRANCESCO, Florence, 1634.

SENTA, FELICIO (or FABRIZIO), Turin, beginning of 18th century.

SERAPHINO, SANTO, Udine, Venice, 1678 to 1737. According to his own statement, Seraphino was a pupil of Nicolas Amati. In 1710 he was in Venice and became indisputably one of the best Venetian violin makers. In painstaking care as to detail, his work is only surpassed by that of Stradivarius. His varnish is red or yellowish brown, and only wood of the finest quality used. The tone is wonderfully clear and even, and it is not surprising that his violins bring a high price. A beautiful instrument of his is with Theodore Hammerle of Vienna. The label used by Seraphino is reproduced on Plate 8.

SHAW, JOHN, London, 1655 to 1698.

SICILIANO (CICILIANO), ANTONIO, Venice, 1630 to 1660.

SICILIANO, GIOACCHINO, Venice, 1670 to 1680.

SILVESTRE, HIPP C., vide Chretien.

SILVESTRE, HIPPOLYTE, Lyon, b. 1808, d. 1879.

SILVESTRE, PIERRE, Lyon, b. 1801, d. 1859. A pupil of Blaise in Mirecourt. As apprentice he worked with Lupot and Grand (père) and finished his artistic education with them. In 1829 he opened his own shop and conducted the business in partnership with his brother Hippolyte, who stayed with him until 1848. He was a trained master and worked with the Stradivarius model. After his death the business was conducted by his brother Hippolyte. The label used by Silvestre is reproduced on Plate 15.

SIMON, CLAUDE, Paris, 1783 to 1800.

SIMONIN, CHARLES, Genf, Toulouse, b. about 1815 in Mirecourt, still living in 1875.

SIMPSON, JOHN, London, 1785 to 1794.

SMITH, HENRY, London, 1629 to 1633.

SMITH, THOMAS, London, 1750 to 1799.

SMITH, WILLIAM, London, Hedon (Yorkshire), 1770 to 1786.

SNEIDER, JOSEPH, Pavia, 1701 to 1718.

SNOECK (SCHNOECK), EGIDIUS, Brussels, 1700 to 1730.

SOCCHI, VINCENZO, Bologna, 1661.

SOCQUET, LOUIS, Paris, 1750, 1800.

SOLIANI, ANGELO, Modena, b. 1752, still living in 1810.

SOMER, NICOLAS, Paris, 1725, d. 1776.

SORSANA, SPIRITO, Coni, 1714 to 1736.

STADLMANN, DANIEL ACHATIUS, Vienna, b. about 1680, d. 1744. One of the ablest violin makers in Vienna, and the best imitator of Stainer. His wood is of excellent quality and the varnish yellow. As he was a hard worker and very industrious, his violins can be found in many collections.

STADLMANN, JOHANN JOSEPH, Vienna, b. 1720, d. 1781.

STAINER, ANDREAS, Absam, 1660 to 1690.

STAINER, JACOB, Absam (Tirol), b. Absam, 1621, d. 1683. Son of Martin Stainer and the greatest master of the German school of violin makers who had as his only equals Amati and Stradivarius. It was never known whose pupil he was, but it is certain that he first went to work for the great organ builder Herz. It was Stainer who discovered the secret of the Italian varnish and made excellent use of his knowledge. Besides being a great violin maker, he was also a celebrated performer. His violins were first offered for sale in 1639. In 1645 he went to Venice and from there to Kirchdorf in Austria, where he stayed until 1648. There was hardly an instrument used in his time that was not of his make. The best Stainers are now to be found in England, and nearly all other violins claimed as his are not genuine. Some of the places where genuine Stainer specimens can be found are The Society of Music Lovers in Vienna, the museum of the Paris Conservatory of Music, the Imperial Collection of Musical Instruments in Berlin, and the Lobkowitch Collection in the castle Roudnic in Bohemia. Three of Stainer's finest violins are in the possession of Theodore Hammerle in Vienna. In 1898 a beautiful monument was erected to his memory in his birthplace at Absam in the Tyrol. The label used by Stainer is reproduced on Plate 17, and one of his instruments on Plate 18.

STAINER, MARCUS, Absam, Kufstein, Laufen, b. about 1619, d. after 1680. Marcus

Stainer was the younger brother of Jacob, and was probably a pupil of the same master as Jacob. The violins recognized by authorities as his are on a large model, and, although he was no equal in the art to his brother, he imitated his work in a fair manner.

STAUDINGER (STAUTINGER), MATHAEUS WENZESLAUS, Wurzburg, 1745 to 1775.

STEFFANINI (STEPHANINI), CARLO, Mantua, 1764 to 1790.

STEGER (STEGHER), MAGNUS, Venice, 17th century.

STEININGER, FRANZ XAVER (FRANÇOIS), Darmstadt, Frankfurt, Paris, St. Petersburg, b. Mainz, 1778, d. about 1850.

STEININGER, JAKOB, Passau, Mainz, Frankfurt, Aschaffenburg, 1775 to 1818.

STORIONI, LORENZO, Cremona, Turin, b. 1751, d. after 1801. Storioni may be singled out as the last of the great Cremona makers, although the passing of this great school is plainly evident. In later years, he neglected his work to such an extent that the instruments of this period are of small value. He always preferred a large model, similar to the Guarnerius, and obtained a fairly good tone. Vieuxtemps used one of his instruments for years. The label used by Storioni is reproduced on Plate 5, and one of his instruments on Plate 6.

STOSS, FRANZ ANTONI, Fussen, b. 1737, d. 1814.

STOSS, MARTIN (JOHANN MARTIN), Vienna, b. Fussen, 1778, d. 1838.

STRADIVARIUS, ANTONIO, Cremona, b. between 1640 and 1650, d. 1737. The past master of the art of violin making, and a pupil of Nicolas Amati. As a young man he inherited great riches, and was therefore independent, it being a proverb in his time "rich as Stradivarius." It is unfortunate that not a single likeness has been preserved for later generations. After serving his time as apprentice with Amati, it became evident by his work that he was going to be a great artist. He stayed with Amati from 1667 to 1670 and about this time started to work independently. The oldest violins which bear his name are dated from the year 1670. As he himself was a great violinist, he knew what was lacking in the Amati instrument, and he started to experiment in order to find its faults, continuing his labors for thirty years

until his efforts were crowned with success. No one can ever estimate the amount of money it required to accomplish his purpose. Only a few of the violins made in this experimental period are in existence, as he probably destroyed most of them, because in his critical eyes they were imperfect. His labors can be divided into three periods: the first between 1668 and 1686 (it took all this time to select what he thought to be the best wood); the second period from 1686 to 1694 during which time he made his violins considerably larger and the arch much flatter; the third and last period starts with 1695 and reaches its highest point in 1714. This was the period during which he reached the pinnacle of success, for at the age of fifty he had perfected the Stradivarius model, and no living man, although thousands of attempts have been made, has been able to produce an instrument so faultless as a Stradivarius of this period. There have been made admirable copies, perfect up to the smallest detail, but the soul is always missing. His ground varnish was golden yellow covered with a light red, which later turned to brown. It is soft and elastic and has up to this very day the peculiarity that, if the hand rests upon it only for a moment, one can plainly see the imprint. Stradivarius was a very industrious workman; on an average, he finished one violin a week. As he labored sixty years of his life, at this rate he must have completed about three thousand violins, and it is calculated there are about this number now in existence; yet if you would assemble the really absolutely genuine Stradivarius violins to-day, you would only find about one hundred. Sixty years after his death the price of his violins had tripled. The violin belonging to Prof. Waldemar Meyer from the year 1716, one of the finest specimens in existence and nominally made for King George I, was bought in the year 1889 for $5000 and shortly after sold for nearly $10,000. One of his violins, dated 1714, was owned by Alexander Batta, who in 1836 paid $1500 for it, and in 1893 sold it for $16,000. The famous "Betts" Stradivarius (pictured in this work) is now the property of an American who

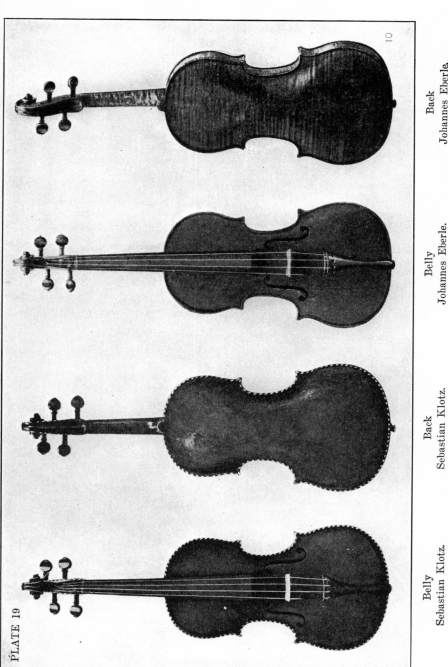

PLATE 19

Belly
Sebastian Klotz.

Back
Sebastian Klotz.

Belly
Johannes Eberle.

Back
Johannes Eberle.

is said to have paid the enormous sum of $60,000 for it. The label used by Stradivarius is reproduced on Plate 5, and some of his instruments on Plates 7, 9 and 13.

STRADIVARIUS, FRANCESCO, Cremona, b. 1671, d. 1743.

STRADIVARÍUS, OMOBONO, Cremona, b. 1679, d. 1742.

STRAUB, JOHANNES, Rothenbach, b. about 1760, d. 1847.

STRAUBE, JOHANN AUGUSTIN, Berlin, b. 1725, d. 1802.

STRAUSS, JOSEPH, Neuṣtadt, 1750 to 1775.

STRNAD, CASPAR, Prague, b. 1752, d. 1823.

STRONG, JOHN, Somerset, about 1640.

SULOT, NICOLAS, Dijon, 1829 to 1839.

TACHINARDI, ——, Cremona, 1690.

TANEGIA, CARLO ANTONIO, Milan, 1725 to 1731.

TANINGARD, GIO. GIORGIO, Rome, 1735 to 1750.

TASSINI, BARTOLOMMEO, Venice, 1740 to 1756.

TAYLOR, WILLIAM, London, b. 1750, still living in 1820.

TECCHLER (TEKLER), DAVID, Salzburg, Venice, Rome, b. 1666, d. after 1743. His name appears to have been written in various spellings of which the above are most frequently found. His violins are made after the Stainer model. In 1705 he went to Rome and there performed his greatest achievements. He is the most important violin maker of Rome, well-known for his clean-cut work and the fullness of tone imparted to his instrument. Tecchler always selected a large model, used wonderful wood and rich varnish of a yellow red color. A reproduction of one of his instruments will be found on Plate 14.

TEODITI, GIOVANNI, Rome, 17th century.

TERMANINI, PIETRO, Modena, 1755 to 1773.

TESTORE, CARLO ANTONIO, Milan, b. about 1688, still living in 1764. Son and scholar of Carlo G. Testore. He worked on the models of Amati, Guerneri and Stradivarius, used good wood and a gold-yellow varnish, making only large violins. In his last years he worked together with his son Giovanni. The label used by Testore is reproduced on Plate 5, and one of his instruments on Plate 12.

TESTORE, CARLO GIUSEPPE, Milan, b. in Novara about 1660, d. 1710. A pupil of Giovanni Grancino, and probably

Cappas. He was the most important artisan of his family, but only a few of his violins are in existence, either because he did not make many, or they are buried under the labels of Grancino or Cappas. The label used by Testore is reproduced on Plate 5, and one of his instruments on Plate 13.

TESTORE, PAOLO ANTONIO, Milan, b. about 1690, d. after 1760.

THERESS (THERESE), CHARLES, London, 1840 to 1850.

THIBOUT, GABRIEL-ADOLPHE, Paris, b. 1804, d. 1858.

THIBOUT, JACQUES-PIERRE, Paris, b. 1779, d. 1856.

THIERRIOT, PRUDENT, Paris, 1772 to 1775.

THIR (THIER), JOHANN GEORG, Vienna, 1738, d. after 1781.

THOMASSIN, LOUIS, Paris, b. Mirecourt, 1855.

THOMPSON, PETER, London, 1794.

THOROWGOOD, HENRY, London, 18th century.

TIEFFENBRUCKER, GASPAR, Lyon, b. 1514, d. 1570 or 1571. A lute maker who made instruments of great beauty. Vuillaume made wonderful imitations of these instruments.

TIEFFENBRUCKER, LEONHARD I, Padua, 16th century.

TIEFFENBRUCKER, MAGNUS, Venice, 1557 to 1621.

TIEFENBRUCKER, ULRICH (ULDRICH), Venice, Bologna, 1521.

TIELKE, JOACHIM, Hamburg, b. 1641, d. Hamburg, 1719. The label used by Tielke is reproduced on Plate 17.

TIELKE, JOHANN, Hamburg, 1635.

TILLEY, THOMAS, London, 1774.

TIPHANON (THIPANON), JEAN-FRANÇOIS, Paris, 1775 to 1800.

TIRLER, CARLO, Bologna, 17th century.

TOBIN, ——, London, 1844.

TOBIN, RICHARD, London, 1790, d. Shoreditch, about 1836.

TODINI, MICHELE, Rome, b. Saluzzo, 1625, d. 1676.

TOLBECQUE, AUGUSTE, Paris, Niort, b. Paris, 1830.

TONONI, CARLO, Bologna, 1689 to 1717.

TONONI, CARLO (ANTONIO), Venice, 1721 to 1768.

TONONI, FELICE, Bologna, 1670 to 1710.

TONONI, GIOVANNI, Bologna, 1689 to 1740.

TONONI, GUIDO, Bologna and Rome, 1690 to 1760.

PLATE 20

Jacob Raymann, at ye Bell
Yard, in Southwark
London, 1650

Made & Sold by Jos.ᴴ Hill
at yᵉ Violin in Angel Court
17 Westminster. 51

T. DODD,
VIOLIN, VIOLONCELLO
& BOW MAKER,
New Street,
Covent Garden.

Benjamin Banks
Musical Instrument Maker
In Catherine Street, Salisbury 1779

William E. Hill & Sons
Makers, Wardour Street,
London. 1882.

HART & SON.
MAKERS.
28, Wardour Street,
18. LONDON. 97.

LABELS USED BY ENGLISH VIOLIN MAKERS.

TOPPANI (TAPPANI), (MICHEL) ANGELO (DE), Rome, 1735 to 1750.

TORELLI, ——, Verona, 1625.

TOULY, JEAN (BAPT.), Nancy, 1730 to 1747.

TRAPANI, RAFFAELE, Naples, 1800 to 1826.

TREVILLOT, CLAUDE I, Mirecourt, 1697 to 1698.

TREYER, JEAN-BAPTISTE, 1750 to 1770.

TRINELLI, GIOVANNI, Scandiano, b. Villalunga, Reggio Em., d. about 1815.

TURNER, WILLIAM, London, 1650.

TYWERSUS, Nancy (Lothringen), 16th century.

UGAR, CRESCENZIO, Rome, 1788 to 1790.

UNGARINI (UNGHERINI), ANTONIO, Fabriano, 1762.

URQUHART (URQUEHART), THOMAS, London, b. 1625, d. 1666.

VAILLANT, FRANÇOIS, Paris, 1736 to 1783.

VALLENTINE, WILLIAM, London, 1870, d. about 1877.

VANDELLI, GIOVANNI, Fiorano (Modena), b. 1796, d. 1839.

VANDERLIST, ——, Paris, 1788 to 1801.

VAN DER SLAGHMEULEN, JOH. BAPT., Antwerp, 1660 to 1679.

VANGELISTI (EVANGELISTI), PIER LORENZO, Florence, 1700 to 1745.

VAROTTI, GIOVANNI, Bologna, 1786 to 1815.

VENZI, ANDREA, Florence, 1636.

VERLE, FRANZ, Padua, about 1590 to 1600.

VERMESCH (VERMERSCH), PATER, Beaumont vide Oise, 1781 to 1812.

VERON (VERRON), PIERRE-ANDRÉ, Paris, 1711 to 1750.

VETRINI (VETTRINI), BATTISTA, Brescia, 1629 to 1630.

VIARD, NICOLAS, Versailles, 1760 to 1790.

VIBRECHT (WIEBRECHT), GYSBERT, Amsterdam, 1700 to 1710.

VILLAUME ET GIRON, Troyes, 1791.

VIMERCATI, GASPARE, Milan, 1790.

VIMERCATI, PAOLO, Venice, 1660 to 1710.

VINACCIA, ANTONIO I, Naples, 1734 to 1781.

VINACCIA, GAETANO, Naples, 1779 to 1800.

VINACCIA, GENNARO, Naples, 1755 to 1778.

VINACCIA, PASQUALE, Naples, b. 1806, d. between 1881 and 1885.

VINCENZI, LUIGI, Carpi, b. 1775, d. after 1818.

VIVOLI, GIOVANNI, Florence, 1642.

VOBOAM, JEAN, Paris, 1676 to 1699.

VOGEL, WOLF (WOLFGANG), Nurnberg, d. 1650.

VOGLER, JOHANN GEORG, Wurzburg, b. 1692, d. after 1750.

VUILLAUME, CLAUDE I, Mirecourt, 1625.

VUILLAUME, CLAUDE-FRANÇOIS I, Mirecourt, b. about 1730, still living in 1760.

VUILLAUME, JEAN III, Mirecourt, 1702, d. 1752.

VUILLAUME, JEAN-BAPTIST, Paris, b. Mirecourt, 1798, d. Paris, 1875. Son and pupil of Claude Vuillaume V. He was scarcely nineteen years of age when he was called to the workshops of Lébé in Paris. After this he worked two years for Chanot but returned again to Lébé. The association with this highly educated man accomplished wonders in the perfecting of this young artist. In 1825 Lébé took him as partner into his business, but they parted in 1828 and Vuillaume started to work independently. He was very successful in imitating Stradivarius, and at the present day there are many of his violins sold as genuine Stradivarii. He used to haunt antique shops, and, finding an old piece of furniture of rare wood, purchased and used it for making violins. These are the ones which became famous for having a most beautiful tone. He paid great attention to the varnish he used, and is really the only violin maker of the nineteenth century who was able to equal the varnish of the old Italians. The label used by Vuillaume is reproduced on Plate 15, and one of his instruments on Plate 16.

VUILLAUME, NICOLAS IV, Mirecourt, b. 1800, d. about 1871.

VUILLAUME, NICOLAS-FRANÇOIS, Brussels, b. Mirecourt, 1802, d. 1876.

VUILLAUME, SEBASTIEN, Paris, b. about 1835, d. 1875.

WAGNER, BENEDICT, Durrwangen, Ellwangen, 1720 to 1796.

WAGNER, JOSEPH, Konstanz, b. 1729, d. about 1781.

WAMSLEY (WALMSLEY, WAEMSLEY), PETER, London (Piccadilly), 1715, 1751. Wamsley worked on the Stainer model, but was never able to be compared with his master. He used good wood, his varnish was red-brown, but only a few of his violins can be considered of any great value.

WEICKERT, ——, Halle, about 1800.

WEIGERT (WEIGERTH), JOHANN BLASIUS, Linz, 1717 to 1755.

WEISS, JAKOB, Salzburg, 1714 to 1740.

PLATE 21

Benjamin Banks.　　　Richard Duke.　　　Thomas Perry.　　　Hill and Sons.

WENGER, GREGORI FERDINAND, Augsburg, b. 1680, d. after 1757.

WETTENGEL, GUSTAV ADOLF, (Mark-) Neukirchen, 1820 to 1830.

WIDHALM, LEOPOLD, Nurnberg, b. 1722, d. 1776.

WILKINSON, ——, Dublin, 1820.

WILLEMS, JOORIS (GEORG), Gent, 1634 to 1642.

WISE, CHRISTOPHER, London, 1650 to 1661.

WITHERS, EDWARD I, London, 1808 to 1875.

WOLTERS, JEAN-MATHIAS, Paris, 1740 to 1777.

WRIGHT, DANIEL, London, 1743 to 1745.

YOUNG, JOHN, London, 1724.

ZANFI, GIACOMO, Modena, b. 1756, d. 1822.

ZANOLI (ZANIOL), GIACOMO, Venice, Padua, Verona, 1740 to 1757.

ZANOTTI (ZANNOTTI), CHRISTOFANO, Modena, 1685.

ZANOTTI, GIUSEPPE, Piacenza, about 1700.

ZANTI, ALESSANDRO, Mantua, 1765 to 1819.

ZANURA (ZANURE), PIETRO, Brescia, 1509.

ZENATTO, PIETRO, Treviso, 1680 to 1694.

ZWERGER, ANTON, Passau, Salzburg, 1788 to 1823.

CHAPTER III

VIOLIN MAKERS IN AMERICA

The remarks prefatory to the list of European violin makers apply equally well to the following list of American makers.

Information of an encyclopedic nature regarding those who have devoted themselves to this line of work in the United States has been available in only a few instances, and for this reason the list which follows does not lay claim to being complete. In endeavoring to get information regarding their life work from a number of contemporary American violin makers, the editor has had brought home to him forcibly the saying that "art is modest"—it is almost difficult to believe that several refused information regarding their work even for encyclopedic purposes.

The list of American makers is illustrated by reproductions of the labels and instruments of a number of representative makers. Wherever this has been the case, the plate numbers are referred to in the articles.

ADKINS, W. H., Minneapolis, Minn.

ALBERT, CHARLES F., Philadelphia, Pa.

ALBERT, JOHN, Philadelphia, Pa. Born at Freiburg, Germany. Came to the United States in 1854. Maker of the violin well-known as the "John Albert" and one of America's best-known artisans.

ALDRED, JOHN, Buffalo, N. Y.

ASCHOW, J. N., Oakland, Cal.

BADGETT, MAYS, Atlanta, Ga.

BALDWIN, WM. M., Racine, Wis.

BEEBE, BYRON E., Muskegon, Mich.

BENJAMIN, S. B., Bloomington, I'l.

BENTIN, HENRY, New Orleans, La. Was Born at Nakel in Posen, Germany, and learned the art of violin making from his father who came to the United States and settled first in Iowa and later in New Orleans. In 1921, Jan Kubelik became greatly interested in Bentin's re-productions of famous old violins and since that time other great artists have found much to commend in them. The varnish used on his instruments re-sembles greatly that employed by the Cremonese makers. The label used in Bentin's instruments is reproduced on Plate 22 and one of his violins on Plate 25.

BLASIER, H. E., Williamsburg, Ia.

BOHMANN, JOSEPH, Chicago, Ill.

BREDALL, J. B., Chicago, Ill.

BRETCH, BRAYTON S., Oswego, N. Y.

BRONSON, WILLIAM S., Grand Rapids, Mich.

CARLISLE, JOSEPH R., Cincinnati, Ohio. Was born in Ashland, Kentucky, April 8, 1886, and, having shown in early life a great interest in the art of violin mak-ing, received considerable encourage-ment and knowledge from a violin-making amateur who resided in Ashland. He spent the years 1909 to 1914 in scientific research, as well as experiments in var-nishes and colors, supplementing this work with practical experience in the employ of a violin maker in Charleston, W. Va. He later became associated with the house of Wurlitzer in Cincinnati and has been highly successful in his imita-tions of the old masters' instruments, and is now working upon a model entirely his own. The label used in his violins is reproduced on Plate 22 and one of his instruments on Plate 23.

CLARK, OSCAR L., Northampton, Mass.

COLLINGWOOD, JOSEPH, Ottumwa, Iowa. Was born April 17, 1853, and became interested in the art of violin making through learning to play on the instru-

49

PLATE 22

J. R. Carlisle.
CINCINNATI. OHIO
NO.
ANNO

PUEHLAND & FUCHS
MADE
BROOKLYN, N.Y. U.S.A.
1923

Joseph N. Copland,
fecit Chicago, Ill. anno 1923
L. III.

H. Bentin
New Orleans, F. A. 192

John Friedrich fecit
New York Anno 192

"GEMÜNDER ART VIOLIN
AUGUST GEMÜNDER & SONS NEW YORK 1920

Henry Richard Knopf,
New York, Anno 1923

MADE BY
WILLIAM LEWIS & SON,
CHICAGO, ILL. ANNO
TUNER

John A. Gould
Boston, Mass.

Made by
TREFLE GERVAIS,
Violin Maker.
BOSTON
NO.
18

FECIT.
OTTUMWA, IOWA.
ANNO 19
no.

LABELS USED BY AMERICAN VIOLIN MAKERS.

ment and desiring to create one for his personal use. The first instrument he produced proved to have exceptional tone qualities and he therefore adopted violin making as a profession and is still making instruments (1924) at the age of 72. Collingwood's instruments number nearly six hundred, and it would appear that he comes rightly by his talent, as he is a descendant of an English maker, Joseph Collingwood, who is credited with having made violins about 1750. The label in his violins is reproduced on Plate 22 and one of his instruments is reproduced on Plate 25.

COPLAND, JOSEPH N., Chicago, Ill. Became interested in the art of violin making at an early age, founding his own shop in 1905. Since that time he has made about fifty violins, all of which are of artistic appearance and a satisfying quality of tone. The label used in his instruments is reproduced on Plate 22.

COX, WILLIAM, Detroit, Mich.

DAVIS, J. WESLEY, St. Louis, Mo.

EINSELE, GEORGE N., see Lewis and Son, Chicago, Ill.

ELLETT, RAY, North English, Ia.

FARLEY, CHARLES E., Everett, Mass.

FERRON, FASSAUER, Chicago, Ill.

FIDIAM, JAMES, Scranton, Pa.

FISCHER, LORENZ J., Milwaukee, Wis.

FRASER, O. L., Saginaw, Mich.

FREEMAN, JAY C., New York City. Was born in Chicago, Ill., and apprenticed in 1887 to August Heck, violin maker, under whom he worked until March 1889, making his first violin in 1888. In addition to being a practical violin maker, Freeman has distinguished himself as an expert in the selection of authentic old instruments, having been employed in this capacity by Lyon and Healy, of Chicago, from 1889 to 1920 and since that time by The Rudolph Wurlitzer Company. He has made many trips to Europe in search of rare instruments, his purchases including the famous Hawley Collection (Hartford, Conn.) in 1901 and the Waddell Collection (Glasgow, Scotland) in 1923, the latter including the "Betts" Stradivarius. In the thirty-five years of his experience as a violin expert, it is safe to say that thousands of authentic masterpieces of the violin-making art have passed through his hands.

FRIEDRICH, JOHN, New York City. Established himself as a violin maker in New York in 1883, after having practiced his art with several of the great makers abroad, including Schonger of Cassel and Mockel of Berlin. His instruments are modeled after Stradivarius, Joseph Guarnerius and Nicola Amati, and have been used by a number of famous players. Friedrich has made over 250 instruments and has been awarded medals at several national expositions. The label used in his instruments is illustrated on Plate 22 and a reproduction of his copy of the famous "Le Messie" Stradivarius on Plate 24.

FUNK, CHARLES FRANCIS, Allentown, Pa.

GEIGER, JOSEPH, St. Joseph, Mo.

GEMUNDER, AUGUST MARTIN LUDWIG, New York City. Was born in Ingelfingin, Wurtemberg, Germany, March 22, 1814. He came to the United States in 1846. His copies of Stradivarius and Guarnerius instruments were regarded as creations of the highest quality, Sarasate having stated that his copy of an Amati violin was as good as the original. He died in New York, September 2nd, 1895.

GEMUNDER, AUGUST MARTIN, New York City. Is the son of August Gemunder and received his instruction in the art of violin making from his father. In 1905, Gemunder created a scientific model of his own design which was taken to Europe by him in 1906 and adjudged favorably by experts. Since that time, Gemunder has continued to make instruments which are highly endorsed by musicians of reputation. The label used in his instruments is reproduced on Plate 22 and a reproduction of the first 1905 model violin on Plate 23.

GERVAIS, TREFFLÉ R., Boston, Mass. Was born November 2, 1863, in Canada, of French parents and came to Boston in 1877. He made his first violin in 1882 and for a period of years gained experience in the employ of various Boston violin makers. For more than 26 years he has conducted his own shop, making a series of instruments which have earned the highest commendation. The label used in his instruments is reproduced on Plate 22 and one of his violins on Plate 25.

GILMORE, VIRGIL E., Coffeyville, Kansas.

GLAESEL, A. HERMAN, New York.

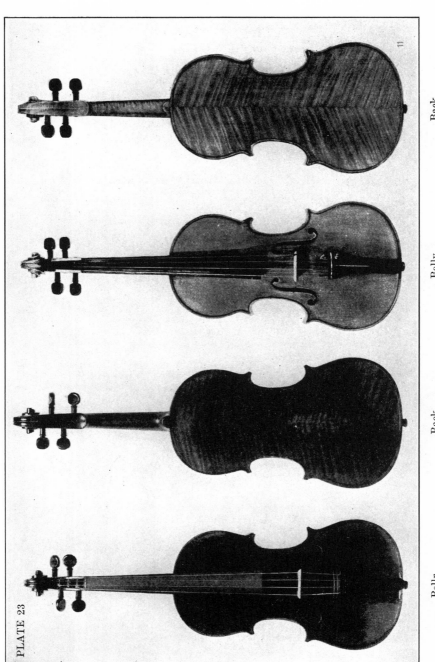

PLATE 23

Belly
August Gemunder.

Back
August Gemunder.

Belly
Joseph Carlisle.

Back
Joseph Carlisle.

PLATE 24

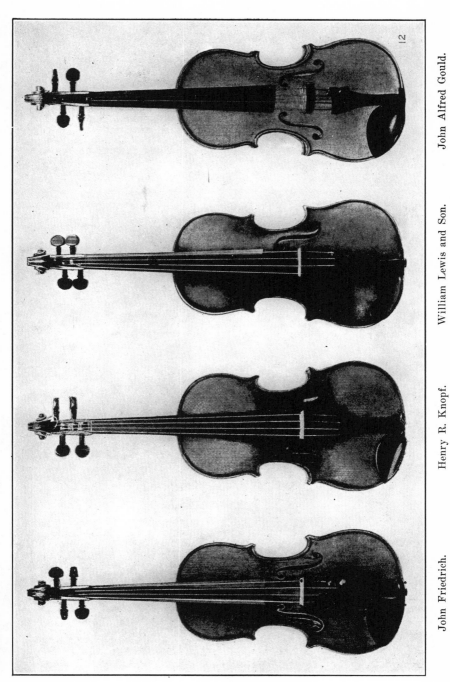

12

John Friedrich. Henry R. Knopf. William Lewis and Son. John Alfred Gould.

Goss, Walter Solon, Boston, Mass.

Gould, John Alfred, Boston, Mass. Was born March 11, 1860, in England and in 1883 migrated to Canada. In 1885 he came to Boston in the employ of Orin Weeman, and in 1889 established his own business, conducting it at the present time (1924) with the assistance of five sons, three of whom are practical violin makers. Gould's instruments are well spoken of by those qualified to judge them and his label is reproduced on Plate 22 as well as one of his instruments on Plate 24. His sons, Orin A. Gould and Ronald A. Gould are both in his employ as violin makers and repairers.

Hamburg, George, New York.

Harman, Lauren E., Cedar Rapids, Ia.

Heiges, Luther D., Baltimore, Md.

Heinl, George, Ottawa, Canada.

Holzapfel, Carl C., Baltimore, Md.

Horvath, Julius D., New York City.

Howe, Elias Co., Boston, Mass. Makers and collectors of old violins.

Hull, John Justus, Scranton, Pa.

Kaplan, Ladislav, New York.

Knopf, Henry R., New York. Was born in Markneukirchen, Germany, December 15, 1860, and was the son of a famous bow maker, Heinrich Knopf. He studied violin making with Otto Bausch in Leipzig and Christian Adam in Berlin, coming to America in 1879. In 1880, he established his own business in New York and has made a number of instruments of the highest quality and especially famous for the beauty of the varnish as well as responsiveness of the tone. His two sons, Eugene and Richard, are now in the firm of H. R. Knopf and Sons. His label is reproduced on Plate 22 and one of his violins on Plate 24.

Kretschmar, H. H., Chicago, Ill.

Krug, J. Adolph, Detroit, Mich.

Latterell, G. H., Paynesville, Minn.

Leonard, John F., Elizabeth, N. J.

Lewis and Son, Wm., Chicago, Ill. This well-known Chicago house employs violin makers, among them George N. Einsele, who produce instruments of exceptional quality, marketed under the name of Wm. Lewis and Son. The label used in their instruments is reproduced on Plate 22 and one of the violins on Plate 24.

Lindsey, George C., Los Angeles, Cal.

Lundh, Jacob O., Minneapolis, Minn.

Lutz, Ignaz A., San Francisco, Cal.

Martin, A. Will, Kansas City, Mo.

Mathewson, C. H., Providence. R. I.

Maxham, O. H., Erie, Pa.

Merrill, Albert H., Portland, Ore.

Moglie, Albert F., Washington, D. C.

Nebel & Brother, M., New York City.

Nute, L. M., Portland, Me.

Paulsen, Carl A., Detroit, Mich.

Paulsen, Peter Christian, Chicago, Ill.

Poehland, Bernhard, Brooklyn, N. Y. Was born in Klingenthal, Saxony, and spent most of his early life among violin makers. He came to America in 1886, opening a music store but devoting his personal efforts since 1903 to violin making, specializing in copies of Stradivarius and Gagliano. Most of his instruments are in the hands of professional musicians who speak highly of their appearance and tonal qualities. A reproduction of his label is to be found on Plate 22 and one of his violins on Plate 25.

Rider, G. C., Portland, Ore.

Roberts, Allen N., Southern Pines, N. C.

Robinson, Robert, Portland, Ore.

Rockwell, Edgar G., Akron, O.

Rodet, Paul, Buffalo, N. Y.

Roescher, William, Scranton, Pa.

Rowe, Frederick, Minneapolis, Minn.

Schetelig, Henry, Brooklyn, N. Y.

Schultz, Henry F., Boston, Mass.

Seymour, Abijah H., Lincoln, Nebr.

Snyder, J. H., Milwaukee, Wis.

Squier, J. B., Boston, Mass.

Struble, D. G., Washington, D. C.

Swett, Joel B., Rochester, N. Y.

Tauscher, Arno, Chicago, Ill.

Taylor, Nathan S., Lewiston, Me.

Thoma, Jacob, Boston, Mass.

Thomas, G. J., Oakland, Cal.

Tietgen, Hans, New York City.

Titus, Joseph A., Worcester, Mass.

Van Dorston, A. W., Chicago, Ill.

Weeman, Orin, Boston, Mass.

Whitcomb, W. B., Milwaukee, Wis.

Wickes, Milton O., Holyoke, Mass.

Wurlitzer, Rembert, Cincinnati, O. It is both interesting and illuminating to learn that even in these practical days, there are still those who desire to learn the art of violin making, among them being Rembert Wurlitzer, son of Rudolph Wurlitzer of the music house of this name. Although only a youth in the accepted sense of the word, he has produced three excellent instruments and at this time (1924) he is in Europe studying violin making and old instruments.

Zeigler, Dr. W. S., Clinton, Ia.

PLATE 25

Henry Bentin.   Bernhard Poehland.   Trefflé Gervais.   Joseph Collingwood.

CHAPTER IV

THE CONSTRUCTION OF THE VIOLIN

The Normal Type Violin and Its Variants

The violin which we are about to describe is the instrument of normal type, the large-form or full-sized violin, which is the best known and most widely used model.[1]

Violins are also constructed for children, and for the use of those with small hands, in reduced sizes, called three-quarter, half and quarter violins, whose proportions are based in every particular on those established for the full-sized instrument. These instruments, with but few exceptions, are constructed with less care than the large-form normal violin.

The following is a table of the correct dimensions of the violin as established by Vidal. These dimensions vary, of course, according to the individual instrument and its maker, but Vidal's figures may be accepted as the standard of measurement generally adopted, representing the exact principal dimensions of a very fine genuine Stradivarius which has been preserved in perfect condition since the latter part of the 17th century (the "Vuillaume" or "La Messie" Stradivarius, Plate 26).

	Figure	Millimeters	Inches
Total exterior length of body	1 B-E	355	14.0
Breadth across upper bouts	1 F-G	165	6.9
Breadth across lower bouts	1 O-P	206	8.2
Breadth across inner bouts	1 K-L	109	4.3
Length of inner bouts	1 H-M	076	3.0
Length from base of button to notch of F-holes	1 B-D	193	7.6
Height of sides, upper bouts	2 F-G	030	1.2
Height of sides, inner bouts	2 K-L	030	1.2
Height of sides lower bouts	2 O-P	031	1.25
Length of the neck	2 A-B	130	5.15
Length of finger board	2 A-C	260	10.25

The figures and letters in above table refer to the illustration presented herewith of the "Vuillaume" Stradivarius (Plate 26). The millimeter measurements have been figured out as accurately as possible into inches.

---

[1] The detailed historic and practical information presented here by Mr. Bachmann has been compiled after exhaustive research in old treatises, most of which had to be consulted in the reference departments of great libraries throughout the world. The subject matter carries great weight as the expression not of his individual ideas or theories, but of the authoritative knowledge of master violin designers. (The Editor)

PLATE 26

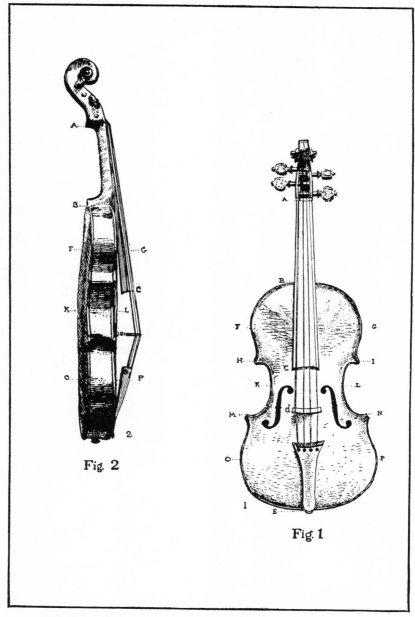

Fig. 2

Fig. 1

THE "LA MESSIE" STRADIVARIUS AS A MODEL FOR SCALE
MEASUREMENTS.

Although the violin is the best known and most generally used stringed instrument to be found in the world of music, very few laymen have any idea of how many individual parts it is composed. The writer has even been asked whether the arched form of the top and back was not secured by submitting these pieces first to a steam bath and then to strong pressure.

The violin (Plate 27), when belly and back each represent an individual piece, is composed of sixty-eight separate parts, and when the back and belly are each formed of two pieces, of seventy parts.

The instrument comprises

Part	Number of Pieces	
Belly	2	(sometimes 1)
Back	2	(sometimes 1)
Ribs	6	
Inside blocks	6	
Inside linings	12	
Inside bass-bar	1	
Purfling	24	
Finger board	1	
Neck and scroll	1	
Nut	1	
Lower nut	1	
Tailpiece	1	
Loop	1	
Tailpiece button	1	
Pegs	4	
Strings	4	
Bridge	1	
Sound post	1	
	70	

Several varieties of wood are used in the construction of a violin; maple or plane wood, fir or spruce, and ebony or rosewood.

Maple or plane wood is used for the back, neck, ribs and bridge. Spruce is used for the belly, the bar of the corners, the molds, linings and sound post. Ebony or rosewood is used for the finger board, nuts, pegs, tailpiece and the tailpiece button which supports it.

Back and belly are given the shape peculiar to them by means of various cutting tools, such as chisels, small planes and knives.

The neck is carved.

The ribs and linings are chiseled, and afterward smoothed by means of water and a hot iron.

The other string instruments are constructed in the same manner as the violin, the only difference being in their proportions, which are constantly increasing until the double bass is reached.

The viola, which is tuned five tones lower than the violin, is approximately one-seventh larger in dimension than the latter instrument.

PLATE 27

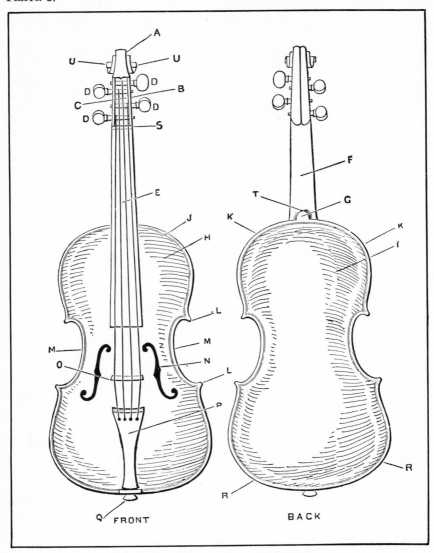

THE COMPONENT PARTS OF A VIOLIN.

A Scroll.	H Belly.	O Bridge
B Sides of Scroll.	I Back.	P Tailpiece.
C Peg Box.	J Purfling.	Q Tail Pin.
D Pegs.	K Edges over Ribs.	R Lower Edges.
E Finger-board.	L Corners.	S Nut.
F Neck.	M Center Bouts.	T Shoulder.
G Button.	N F-holes.	U Eyes of Scroll.

The violoncello, which is tuned an octave below the viola, doubles the violin in its dimensions.

The double bass is approximately twice the size of the violoncello.

It seems worth while adding to these general proportions assigned the string instruments, some information given by August Otto, a distinguished and skillful violin maker, of Halle, Saxony, published in a pamphlet issued in 1817, under the title of "An Essay on the Construction and Preservation of String Instruments."

"It is certain that the perfection of the violins built by famous makers is due to the fact that these genuine artist-craftsmen built their instruments according to plain and simple rules, established on a mathematical foundation, and without varying the proportions of their sound boards and backs. These proportions were fixed as follows:

The thickest part of the belly was that found beneath the bridge, between the two F-holes. In moving away, toward the sides, its thickness continued to decrease, in such wise that it was no more than half that of the belly in the places where the latter rests on the ribs and the moulds.

In the length of the instrument the thickness of the belly was preserved throughout the entire lengthwise extension of the bass-bar, finally coming to an end toward the upper molds and the lower molds in a thickness which was exactly half the thickness of the belly.

In their breadth it would appear that the cheeks of these instruments were only one-fourth as thick as their bellies.

These proportions are the sole ones which are capable of giving a violin the strength, brilliancy and sweetness of tone desired for the instrument. The backs of these violins had the same proportions at all points, save that most of them had backs which were somewhat thicker than the bellies."

Hieronymus Amati, the oldest of the Cremona makers, secured the greatest beauty in the plane-wood instruments he built, and, so far as we know, the greater number of his backs were constructed of a single piece of wood. These plane-wood backs were lowered a little from left to right.

His violins were large in shape, and were very agreeable to the eye. Their corners were very short, and their edges extended but very slightly beyond the ribs, which gave the instrument a most handsome appearance. The sides were very thick and perfectly rounded, as is the case with all the Italian instruments, and the purfling, very well made, was large in size.

The arch of Amati's instruments was somewhat more elevated than that of the Stradivarius violins; it rose from the groove in which the purfling is located in such an imperceptible manner that one would never believe it rose to the height of an inch (twenty-eight millimeters) above the horizontal line of the side, in view of the fact that it appears quite flat to the eye. The purfling was further removed from the sides than in other violins, and the lines of the ribs were not perpendicular in relation to the back and the sound board, since they had a slope of about a hundred degrees.

The back was made of a variety of spruce, whose large veins were equally spaced throughout the entire length of the instrument; the arch of the belly corresponded in every respect to that of the back. The F-holes were very clean-cut and their curved upper perforations were separated one from the other by the exact measurement of length of the width of the bridge. They were not very long, and approached each other quite closely at the head.

The neck was made of very fine plane wood, and the walls of the peg box were extremely thick; the scroll, perfectly rounded, was very large from one to the other button, and this scroll is decidedly one of the greatest beauties of the Cremona violins.

Finally, a yellow amber varnish was used, which gave them a brownish cherry color, although some of them were a mahogany color. In the case of most of these instruments, the varnish shows splits, since these violins are among the oldest Cremonas known, dating from 1614 to 1620.

The next in order are the violins of Antonius Amati, in all probability the son of Hieronymus. We have seen only a few of his instruments, some of which are still in Italy, while others may be found in England. There are but slight differences as regards construction between the violins of Antonius and those of Hieronymus Amati; their tone is perfect when they have not been spoiled by ignorant violin repairers.

Third in order are the violins of Nicolas Amati, and those of Stradivarius, which were built at practically the same period.

Those of Nicholas Amati are noticeable for their individual pattern, which is smaller than that of the preceding builders; and for their special arching, which, beginning at the purfling, remains somewhat flat at first, only to rise to the height of a full inch above the horizontal line of the sides.

The rise of this arch may be more easily traced in Nicolas' violins than in the violins of Hieronymus and Antonius Amati. As for the rest, these violins by Nicolas are fashioned with great care; though the purfling is not as well executed as that of the others, and the corners are somewhat more pointed. The sides are most admirably rounded and the F-holes, sufficiently approximated to each other, are perfectly cut. When these violins have not passed through incompetent hands, their tone in no wise yields to that of the violins built by Stradivarius.

The back is made of spruce wood smaller in grain than that used for the violins already described; yet the wood used in it is very handsome and very well smoothed.

The varnish used is an oil varnish, reddish yellow in color, though we have seen some instruments which were brown in color.

Stradivarius violins are the flattest among all the Cremonese instruments,

PLATE 28

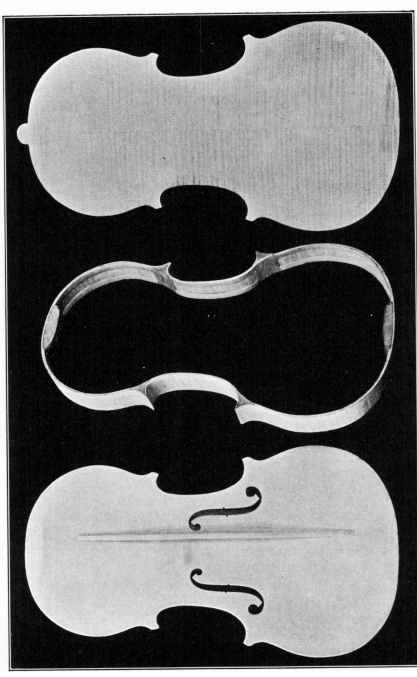

THE RIBS, BELLY AND BACK OF A VIOLIN BEFORE ASSEMBLY.

(Courtesy of the Rudolph Wurlitzer Co.)

their arch being raised no more than a half to three-quarters of an inch (fourteen millimeters). Those among them which have not been spoiled, possess a tone which is deep and brilliant. They are much sought after by virtuosos, who expend considerable sums of money in order to become the possessors of these famous instruments.

Their reputation is probably due to the construction of the belly, which, being flat, produces an easier and more vigorous vibration than an arched instrument. Unfortunately, many of these violins have been ruined, usually through the efforts of ignorant repairers to improve them.

These violins being all of them strong and well made, were provided, when coming from their maker's hands, with very weak and greatly curved bass-bars; hence all of them gave way at the belly on the bass-bar side, owing to the strain of the strings, and when violin makers who did not understand the nature of the defect were instructed to remedy it, they generally ruined the instrument.

In addition to this, the average amateur delights in having his instrument tampered with, and to have a large strong bass-bar placed in it—the very thing most calculated to kill the vibrations.

The Stradivarius model is a very beautiful one; the purflings of these violins are larger than those of the other Cremonese instruments, and they are farther removed from the sides. Their F-holes are perfectly cut and the wood is very handsome.

The varnish used is an oil varnish, and is dark brown in color; some of the Stradivarius violins, however, have a brownish yellow hue. Others again, arched nearly like those of Nicolas Amati, are mahogany colored.

The violins made by Joseph Guarnerius show a great resemblance to those of Nicolas Amati, and have a golden yellow varnish. The Rutheri and the Alvany violins are very similar to the Guarnerius instruments.

The violins of Jacob Stainer, of Absam in the Tyrol, in no wise yield in beauty or in excellence to the Cremonese instruments. They are far more arched than are the latter, and their interior construction is altogether different.

The distinction which may be made between the sound of the Stainer violins and that of the Cremonese instruments is that the former have more of the flute quality in their tone, and the latter more of the quality of the clarinet.

The backs of Stainer violins are more curved than are the bellies. The summit of this arch is exactly as wide in dimension as the bridge, and extends from the bridge to the middle of the back in the direction of both the upper and the lower sides, and then little by little descends to the spot where the purfling is located.

The sides are very well rounded, and the purfling lies nearer to them than in the case of the Cremonas, and is less thick. The F-holes are exceedingly well cut, and are individual inasmuch as the curves at their upper and lower end are almost triangular in form.

Finally, some of these Stainer violins, which are all slightly shorter than are the Cremonese instruments, have a neck terminating in a very well carved lion's head in place of the scroll.

The wood of which they are made is very handsome, and an oil varnish, reddish yellow in color, is characteristic of all of them. Some of the instruments have a dark brown body and a yellow back.

Labels are but rarely found in the Stainer violins; and when they do appear, they are not printed, but written by hand.

Many Tyrolean violin builders have endeavored to imitate the Cremona masters and Stainer; yet it is easy to recognize their work by examining the spruce used for the backs, which is very close grained, and by noting the ribs, which are narrower and not as well rounded. Their purflings, too, are much narrower and do not everywhere display a well-rounded form.

These Tyrolean violins have F-holes which are excellent imitations of those of the Cremonese and Stainer instruments, but their arches are altogether wrong. The maple used in their construction is of mediocre quality, and the scroll terminating the neck is at least a third smaller. Finally, the varnish used is an alcohol varnish and very weak. Their color, which strives to imitate that of old wood, is in nearly every case a pale yellow.

Among the Tyroleans there are but two makers who have produced good instruments: Egitia Klotz and his son Joseph.

TOOLS USED IN VIOLIN MAKING
(Figures refer to numbers on Plate 29)

1. Drawing knife
2. Spoke shaver
3. Large curved planes
4. Medium curved planes
5. Small curved planes
6. Small knife
7. Large knife
8. Peg-hole reamer
9. Steel scraper
10. Large round gouge
11. Small round gouge
12. Bradall
13. Peg-hole borer
14, 15. Peg-hole reamers
16. Broad scraper
17-20. Curved scrapers
21. Graduated calipers
22. Straight steel scraper
23. Hammer
24. Purfling tool
25. Bending iron
26. Round guage
27. Block plane

28, 29. Bass-bar clamp
30, 31a. Top clamps
32. Joint clamp
33. Hand clamp
34. Jointing clamp
35, 36. Steel scrapers
40. Inside form
44-49. Clamp blocks
50, 51. Neck gauges
52. Spacers
53, 54. Zinc outline patterns
55. Sound hole pattern
56. Finger board gauge
57. Peg shaver
58. Lining clamp
62. Flat wood rasp
63. Round wood rasp
64. Flat varnish brush
65. Round varnish brush
66. Oil stone
68. Sound post setter
A-M Assorted files

PLATE 29

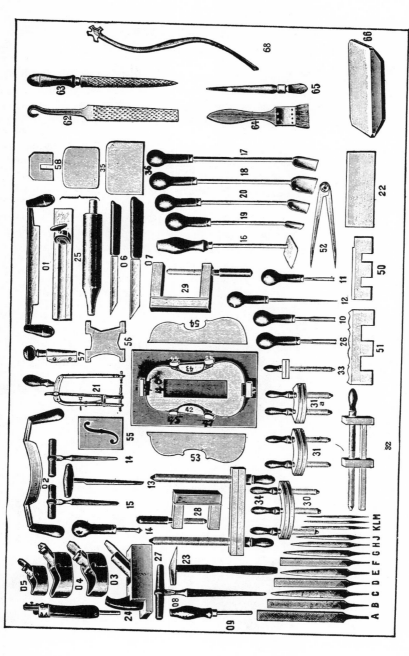

THE TOOLS USED IN VIOLIN MAKING.

(Courtesy of John Friedrich & Bro.)

One of the most essential factors toward success in violin making is the acquisition of a set of tools adequate for the purpose in both quality and variety. Many of the tools used are to be found in the shop of any carpenter or cabinet maker, but there are also many special tools which are absolutely necessary in the production of fine instruments.

Among the ordinary tools may be mentioned saws of various sizes and types, large and small planes, carving chisels, gouges, rules, T-squares, straight edges, iron cramps, bench and hand vises, oil stones, files and small hammers.

The special tools include toothed planes, scrapers of various styles, special knives, bending irons, lining chisels, oval planes, compasses, punches, calipers, violin screws, sound-bar clips and cramps, purfling gouges and chisels, as well as several other special tools expressly designed for delicate operations in violin making.

In this connection, Plate 29 illustrates the tool needs of violin makers very clearly and by referring from the numbers on this plate to the complete list of violin-making tools given on page 64, the reader will obtain a very clear idea of the instruments which are needed on the work bench.

How the Models of the Various Violin Parts Are Made

The models used by the violin makers in building their violins consist of small pieces of plane wood, planed down until they are no more than 2/25 of an inch thick, and which, representing with perfect accuracy the profiles and outlines of the various parts of the instrument, serve for tracing them in order that later on they may be given their proper form. These models should be traced and cut out with scrupulous care, since it is the perfection of the models which absolutely determines the beauty and value of the violins produced from them:

Figure 1, Plate 30, represents the model of the belly and of the back.

Figure 2, Plate 30, represents the curves of the belly and of the back in their respective lengths.

Figure 3, Plate 30, represents the arch across the instrument, at its greatest breadth.

Figure 4, Plate 30, shows the arch running across from the middle of the instrument to the F-holes.

Figure 5, Plate 30, represents the arch running across the violin at its point of greatest breadth, in the part which is next to the neck.

Figure 6, Plate 30, represents the cut and position of the F-holes.

Figure 7, Plate 30, finally represents the arch or curve of the neck of the instrument.

The surest way of tracing a fine violin model is to obtain an original or "creator's" violin. A "creator's" violin is one which was built, some two

PLATE 30

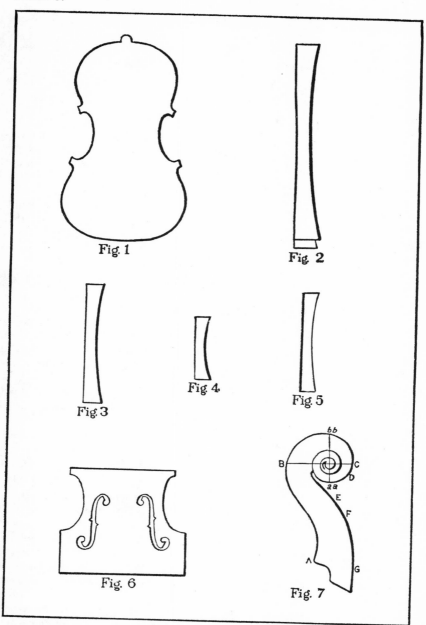

Fig. 1

Fig. 2

Fig. 3

Fig. 4

Fig. 5

Fig. 6

Fig. 7

MODELS USED IN VIOLIN MAKING.

hundred years ago or more, by the Stradivarii, the Amati, the Stainers and the Guarneri.

One begins by planing down a small piece of maple or some other hard wood to a line thickness of about 2/25 of an inch, taking care to give this piece of wood somewhat greater dimensions, as regards length and breadth, than those of the violin to be copied. The violin which serves as a model must then be "unboarded."

Unboarding a violin consists in separating the belly from the body of the instrument, to which it is attached by the ribs. In order to carry out this operation successfully, the greatest care must be taken so that neither the belly nor its sides be broken, since both are fragile. A knife especially meant for the purpose should be used. This knife, which ought not to be too flexible, should nevertheless be rather narrow at the sides and at its extremity, which is rounded, so that it can easily be inserted between the ribs and the sound-board. Little by little, while holding the thumb of the left hand on that portion of the soundboard which is being separated from the ribs, this opera-tion—which is a trifling matter for the experienced violin builder—can be brought to a successful conclusion. The knife to be used might most ap-propriately be compared to a paper knife, with a blade no more than about 2 3/4 inches in length.

When the belly is finally separated from the body of the violin, the piece of "model" wood is placed flat upon the workbench, and the belly upon the piece of "model" wood, on the side from which it has been removed; then, taking a tracer, which is nothing more or less than a well-tempered and pointed bodkin of steel, the exact outline of the belly is traced around it upon the wooden model (Fig. 1, Plate 30).

This tracing completed, there must first be removed, with the very finest kind of a saw, all the wood which lies outside the line of the tracing; while the greatest care must be exercised not to approach the traced line too closely. This operation is completed by giving the model its exact shape and form with the aid of a well-sharpened penknife and scrapers.

In order to trace the model of Figure 2, Plate 30, the curve of the instrument along its greatest length, one must take a piece of the "model" wood, one and a half inches broad by fourteen inches long, and place it on the middle of the sound board, on the varnish side. Then the sound board is rested against the workbench, a compass is opened about four inches, one of its points is placed flat on the sound board, and the other upon the "model" piece of wood which should be firmly held in the left hand; the compass, in the position indicated, is then moved from one end of the sound board to the other, care being taken that it bear constantly on the "model" piece, which in this way receives the imprint of the arch which it is desired that it obtain. The wood lying outside the tracing is then removed with a pen-knife, the "model" is once more placed on the sound board, and the points of the compass are approached in such wise that there is a distance of no more than a sixth of an inch, or a little over, between them. The same operation is then repeated and, as before, the unnecessary wood is removed; in this way the exact lengthwise arch or curve of the violin is obtained.

This curve model, as well as the models of the arches running across the breadth of the instrument, also answer for the making of the back as well as the belly.

The models, Figures 3, 4 and 5, Plate 30, are obtained in the manner already described.

The arch (Fig. 3, Plate 30) of the instrument, at the point of its greatest breadth, should be taken where the tailpiece is situated.

The arch for Figure 4, Plate 30, should be taken at the point which is situated between the two notches of the F-holes.

Finally, the arch, Figure 5, Plate 30, should be taken at the point of greatest breadth (or that part of the instrument) in which the base of the neck is set.

The model, Figure 6, Plate 30, is that of the F-holes. In order to make an exact tracing of it, it is necessary to take a piece of strong parchment, more than large enough to cover that part of the sound board occupied by the F-holes.

One should then take a piece of sheeting, or other similar material of any kind, fold it over some eight or ten times, then place it on the work-table or bench. The parchment is now laid upon the cloth, and turning over the belly of the violin, it is laid with its outer side upon the parchment in such wise that the latter entirely closes all the openings of the F-holes of the sound board, while with a pencil sharpened to a fine point, the interior lines of the F-holes are traced with exactness, and, following this, the exterior outline of the sides of the violin, as may be seen in Figure 6, Plate 30.

This done, the parchment is pasted on a small piece of maple wood which has been planed down to a mean thickness of about a twenty-fourth of an inch, and this is put under pressure, care being taken that the parchment is stretched in a manner which will prevent its forming creases and there is allowed to dry. Then, taking a well-sharpened penknife, the lines of the F-holes are cut out, together with the exterior outlines representing the sides of the violin. Thus the model of Figure 6, Plate 30, is obtained.

Then the parchment may be loosened and separated from the piece of "model" wood, by using a moistened sponge; the parchment once released from the wood, the latter should be replaced under pressure in order that it may not warp.

The model of the neck, Figure 7, Plate 30, is the most difficult to obtain. The neck which is to be copied is laid down flatly on a piece of parchment superimposed on a cloth. The exterior lines of the peg box and the scroll are then traced as exactly as possible with a pencil, the pencil moving from point

A to point *G,* passing from one to the other by points *B, C, D, E* and *F.* The neck is then raised from the parchment, and the tracing is corrected as far as possible where it is not in conformity with the original.

The compass is then returned to the parchment, at the places corresponding to those of the neck, the situation of the nut at the upper end of the neck is marked, and then the distance along the neck from the middle of the nut to the point *C,* and this, too, is marked on the parchment. The measurements necessary to establish the distance from the nut in question to the point *AA* and then to the point *BB,* are made in the same way. At point *bb,* one takes the measurements of every angle, figuring the degrees of distance from the spiral to the nut by straight lines which are set down on the parchment.

When by means of these points the distance between the spiral and the nut at the upper end of the neck has been marked, the pencil should be used to trace the spiral, from point to point, and the model thus obtained. The parchment should finally be pasted on a piece of "model" wood and pierced with little holes.

How to Prepare the Glue

In violin making, glue, known as Cologne glue, is employed, taking its name from the city in question, where it is manufactured in the form of tablets of a very pale yellow color. This glue has the advantage of not forming a thickness between the pieces or parts which it unites.

Since the various parts of which the string instruments are composed, are held together by this sole means, the first and indispensable necessity to this end is the obtaining of the best possible glue, and the taking of every precaution needful to prepare it properly.

After having reduced the tablet of glue to fragments by means of a hammer, it is well to allow it to soak in water for the space of three or four hours; it should then be boiled in hot water. If one were to use an ordinary pot to boil it in, the glue, within a short space of time, would deteriorate; it becomes necessary, therefore, to secure from the proper source the special type of glue pot which is used by cabinet makers and joiners for hot-water boiling.

In melting the glue, one must be careful to add water to it only little by little, and to add no more water than is absolutely required, so that, when it is completely melted, and one allows it to drop from the brush, it will appear to have the fluidity of a somewhat heavy oil. The glue should never be used save when it is really warm. The advantage which the hot-water gluepot offers is that of keeping the glue at the highest temperature possible without allowing it to burn.

In his gluepot the violin maker always has a brush proportionate in size to the nature of the work he is doing, as well as a very narrow wooden spattle.

It is by means of these two instruments that he places or introduces the glue where it may be needed.

In summer, two or three hours are sufficient to dry the glue, but in winter ten hours are none too long. When it is noticeably cold, it is well to heat slightly the pieces or parts to be glued before applying the glue.

When a part of any kind has been glued, the leavings of the glue should be washed off by means of a brush dipped into the hot water of the gluepot. This little operation, which is no trouble, and which if attended to at once, does away with the necessity of a longer one, that of removing the dried glue from all those places in which it should not remain, should not be forgotten.

Making the Molds and Their Accessories

The mold is a piece of wood so prepared and cut as to make it possible to fix in it, in such wise that they form a single unit, the brackets, the corners, the ribs and the linings of the instruments.

Figure 8, Plate 31, represents a mold as it should appear ready to receive the various parts which have been enumerated.

In order to make this mold, one must begin to fashion a model resembling Figure 1, Plate 30, in every point. A tracer should then be taken, should be opened to the extent of approximately 3/24 of an inch and a firmly marked line should be drawn entirely around the model which is to be made. All wood which may remain outside this line is then removed by means of a fine saw and a penknife. This done, we obtain what is known as the counter mold, as shown in Figure 9, Plate 31.

A piece of hard wood should then be taken (walnut is to be preferred, because it is a wood which may be easily cut or carved in any manner) and this piece of wood, well planed, should have a thickness of 9/12 of an inch along its entire breadth, and should be somewhat larger in its dimensions than the model Figure 1, Plate 30. The piece of wood which is to be made into the mold is now placed upon the workbench, and the "outside" or counter mold upon it. With a fine point the exact outline of all the contours of the counter mold should be traced on the piece of wood. Then, with a rule, measure off the notchings at top and bottom, *AA,* and the fourth of the two sides, *B,* as shown in Figure 8, Plate 31. All the unnecessary wood, that is to say the wood left without the line, should then be removed with a fine screw saw, and the work should be completed with knife and polishing stick.

A condition indispensable to this work is that the trimming be carried out all around the mold in such a manner that in all the rounded parts, the sides as well as the mortises, the edges are on an absolute level with the surface of the mold.

This explanation will be better grasped once the manner in which the new tool is used has been watched, for, properly speaking, the mold is nothing more or less than a tool.

PLATE 31

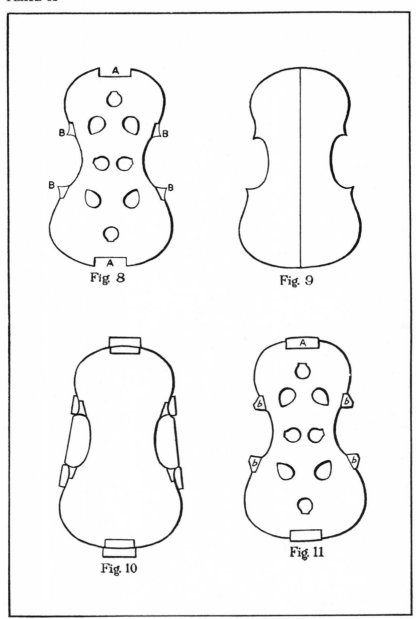

Fig. 8

Fig. 9

Fig. 10

Fig. 11

MOLDS USED IN VIOLIN MAKING.

Finally, the eight screw holes seen in Figure 8, Plate 31 (the two at the top and bottom, some 35 millimeters, 1 1/3 inches distant from the inside of the mortise A; the four others 28 millimeters, 1 1/10 inches distant from the inside of the mortise B; and the two center screw holes, one inch distant from the most indented part of the sides) should be made. The mold is then completed.

We now come to the eight counterparts or sections with which the mold should be provided in order to perform the service expected of it.

Casting our eyes on Figure 10, Plate 31, we notice that the eight counter sections surround the mold. These counter sections are made of the same wood of which the mold itself is composed; they are exactly as high as the ribs, and like the mold itself have been traced by means of the counter mold, in order that they will fit exactly in each of those portions of the mold corresponding to them.

We will return to the counter sections shortly after we have shown the manner in which the blocks and corners of the mold should be set up.

Figure 11, Plate 31, represents the mold fitted out or mounted with its blocks and its corners.

The pieces of spruce which may be seen glued in the mortises A and B are intended to establish the form and to furnish the blocks and corners of the violin. Nothing could be simpler than the preparation of these six pieces which represent the foundation of the entire instrument. By means of the jointer one faces a piece of spruce whose fibers are perfectly straight and gives it the dimensions necessary to fill exactly the notches or mortises. This piece of wood is cut to the height of 35 millimeters (1 1/3"), and, letting no more than one drop of glue fall into the notches, some glue is spread on each of the two pieces in the notches, taking care that they project out on the same side of the mold, and nearly touch the other side of the mold; that is to say, make sure that they jut out about an inch.

The same thing is done with the corners, and the glue is then allowed to dry.

When the glue has dried, the blocks will be found fixed in the mold as well as the corners. Then, using the knife and, after it, the file, these six pieces are made level with the surface of the mold on the side which is meant to receive the sound board. A rule will suffice to make clear whether the pieces have been set up parallel with the mold. It must not be forgotten that the spruce fibers of which the blocks and the corners have been made, should be placed crosswise to the notched rims of the mold, since, without this precaution, the violin would lose all its solidity. Incidentally, the spruce wood of these very pieces may be found in the body of the instrument.

When the above things have been done, the counter mold is taken and placed upon the mold, which last itself is put upon the workbench. Great care should be taken that the rounded portions of the mold and the counter mold are absolutely on a level, which should not be hard, seeing that both these molds have been fashioned one upon the other. Then, with the point, the outline of the counter mold only is traced on the blocks and corners.

Now, taking a suitable gouge or chisel, all the superfluous wood should be removed from these six pieces, finishing the work off with knife and file. When this has been done, Figure 11, Plate 31, will have assumed in every particular the form of Figure 8, Plate 31.

In order that the detail of the work last described leave nothing to be desired, it should be carried out slowly, the wood being removed little by little, and heed being paid at every moment that the correct level is maintained, as well as making sure that the corners and blocks, in every part, form a perfect right angle with the surface of the mold.

The Sides or Ribs

The ribs or sides are those parts of the wood which, in the violin, unite the sound board to the back, and give the instrument its outward shape. The pieces of spruce which serve to double the sides or ribs are known as linings, and are attached to the latter by means of glue.

To begin with, a piece of plane wood 835 millimeters (32 3/4") long by 105 millimeters (4 1/8") broad should be cut down to a thickness of 1/12 of an inch by means of the saw. Care must be taken that the fiber of the wood lies on the surface of the piece which is to be used.

This sheet of wood, once it has been reduced to the proportions already given, is placed on the edge of the workbench, to which it is fixed by means of a clamp whose end lies to the rear of the workbench. The reason this is done is that the sheet, being extremely narrow, and destined to become even more so, cannot be rested against the griper (the square bolt or iron pin which is fixed to the bench) in order to plane it, since it would not offer the needed resistance to the plane.

The sheet of plane wood having been clamped on the workbench as described, the end which is not attached is first planed with the joiner, since the part held in the clamp cannot be reached. This portion once well planed, the clamp is opened, and the sheet is turned in such wise that the part held in the clamp changes place with the part already planed. The clamp is once more tightened, care being taken to place a block of wood some 56 millimeters (2 1/5") broad and as long as the sheet itself between the clamp and the sheet. This serves to preserve the portion of the sound board already planed from becoming marked with the impress which the clamp would be sure to give it.

This precaution having been taken, this end of the sheet is planed in turn.

In the same way, and observing the same process, the other side of the sheet is planed, and reduced to a thickness of one millimeter (1/25").

It might be observed here that maple or plane wood is very hard to plane, probably because of its fibre, and care must be taken not to attack it too heavily with the steel of the plane, and to remove the wood only in thin shavings, since otherwise, if the planer is handled too vigorously, splits may result, which would mean beginning the work all over again, seeing that in such case the wood might as well be thrown into the fire.

At times the wood is so difficult to plane (and, as a rule, this applies to the best veined wood) that hardly any use can be made of the ordinary plane. In such case the toothing plane should be used.

We have already mentioned that the sheet of wood in course of preparation should be reduced to a thickness of 1/25 of an inch although the ribs or sides are not exactly of this size. The sides, in addition, should be scraped in order to give them the necessary smoothness, and to do away with the small inequalities which the plane, especially the toothing plane, may have left.

The sheet having thus been scraped with greatest care, in particular as regards the side which will be on the exterior of the instrument, the beam compasses should be taken, and, setting the points about 35 millimeters (1 1/3″) apart, a line should be drawn the entire length of the sheet. By means of the knife this piece is then separated from the sheet of wood, and the operation is continued until the sheet of wood has been divided into three distinct pieces.

Then, taking a strip of paper, one should measure on the mold which is already provided with its blocks and corners, the outline of the circle which, in the narrow part of the violin rises at the central line of the mold and terminates between the two points of the two corners. With a second strip of paper the interior outline comprised between the points of the two corners. This part is the C bout or inner bout.

With a third strip of paper the outline of the point of the interior corner of the instrument as far as the central line of the mold is measured and this will yield the proportion of length for each part of the ribs.

After having placed each of these strips of paper on the three planed pieces of wood, prepared as has already been described, one must cut by the rule two pieces of a length corresponding to that of each of the strips of paper, and the ribs or sides are completed. All that is left to do is to pound them.

It is well to cut these pieces of plane wood somewhat longer than the paper models, to avoid the possibility of getting them too short; since, once they are too short, the defect cannot be remedied; while, even if they are a little longer, no harm is done, as they may be shortened.

One should not forget to cut the ends of the ribs which are to meet at the point of the four corners neatly and exactly on the line.

We have omitted mentioning that after having separated into three pieces the sheet of wood of which the sides of the ribs are formed, and which has been described, the sides of the three pieces in question should be smoothed by the plane. In order to do so the tool should be used from above, holding its lower extremity between the knees and resting its end against the workbench. Then, presenting the surface of the piece of rib wood to the blade of the plane, its two sides should be planed in such wise as to give the piece an exact breadth of 1 1/4 inches (32 mm.).

The ribs or sides should then be bent in order to give them the form of the outlines of the mold. In order to do so, the bending iron should be heated, not to a degree which will cause it to blacken the wood, but merely enough to soften it and allow of its manipulation. While this tool is in the fire, the ribs side pieces are plunged once or twice into water. Then the bending iron should be clamped upon the bench, and sitting opposite it one should begin to bend the *C's* or inner bouts, which have to meet at the extremity of the corners of the mold. Whenever a bend has been made—gentle pressure should always be applied—the rib must be adjusted to that part of the mold where it is to be fixed, and, if necessary, the curve which the bending iron has given the rib in question must be rectified by once more working it against the iron.

This operation, simple enough in itself, should nevertheless be carried out with the greatest care. The wood must be bent little by little, for any attempt to hasten the work may result in splitting the sides. When the wood becomes too dry it is plunged into the water again.

Care should also be taken that the sides are not warped during the bending process, and that once fitted and glued to the mold they are perfectly adjusted. A little practice soon develops great skill in this procedure. When the ribs or sides have been given the exact shape of the rim of the mold, they must then be fixed on the blocks and corners.

The time has now arrived for us to make use of the counterparts, the linings, which, as has already been explained in speaking of the mold, are nothing more or less than pieces of wood of the same breadth and thickness as the ribs or sides, that is to say, 32 millimeters (1 1/4″) broad.

These pieces of wood represent the exact counterpart of the mold, provided with its blocks and trimmed corners, as may be seen in Figure 22. These linings or counterparts serve to press the ribs against the blocks and corners, and to fix them there definitely by means of glue.

Begin by rubbing all the edges of the mold with a piece of soap, taking the greatest care at the same time not to touch either the corners or the blocks with the soap. Then one of the inner faces of one of the *C* bouts should be covered with glue. (The *C* bouts are the two ribs which have the shape of the letter in question.) The rib is then taken, and the lining corresponding to it is pressed against it; then, while passing the end of the clamping iron into the hole adjacent to the *C* bout, the pivot of the clamping iron is rested on the flat side of the lining while, tightening the vise, pressure is applied until the lining touches the whole interior of the *C* bout formed by the mold and the corners with its entire surface. The same operation is then carried out for the other lining belonging to the opposite *C* bout.

Next in order come the lower or the upper ribs of the instrument, it being quite immaterial which are taken first, though we will begin with the upper ones.

The face of the corner turned toward the neck should be covered with glue, and the ends of the ribs corresponding should be fastened to them by means of the lining; and, using the clamping iron, the same thing is done on the opposite side. Then, covering the upper blocks with glue, and pressing the two ribs strongly against the mold, their ends are forced upon the blocks, where they must be fastened by means of the linings and using the clamping iron. Finally, the two lower ribs are treated in the same manner, and the mold has been "mounted."

The ribs or sides, and this applies as well to the blocks and corners, should be on a level with the mold on the one side, and project beyond it on the other.

An interval of about 8 millimeters (1/3″) may be left between the two ends of the ribs which terminate on the upper blocks, but this does not apply to the lower ribs, which must align perfectly. In order to make them do so, after the two ribs in question have been fastened and glued, they must be approached one to the other by pressing on the outline of the mold, and on the block; then, tracing a line at the spot where the one rib is directly opposite the other, the central line of the mold, the operation should be repeated for the other rib. The block of the latter is covered, and bringing together the two ends of the lower ribs, they are pressed like the upper ribs by means of the lining and the clamping iron.

When the glue has dried, the clamping irons and the linings may be removed, and whatever excess of height the blocks and corners show above the sides should be removed with the saw.

The height of the sides should be 32 millimeters (1 1/3″) at the lower blocks, and 3 centimeters (1 1/5″) at the blocks of the neck. One should now make the two sides or ribs in question take on an insensible slope of two millimeters (about 1/12″) along the whole body of the instrument. The knife and the scraper will suffice to ensure this.

Having reached this point, it will be found that the ribs, as well as the blocks and corners, are on a level with one side of the mold; while on the other they rise above it 10 to 11 millimeters (1/3″ to 5/12″). It is to this portion which rises above the mold that the linings must now be joined.

These linings are obtained in the same manner as were the ribs, with the sole difference that they are made of spruce. They are 2 millimeters (1/12″) thick, and 7 millimeters (1/3″) wide. They are bent in the same manner as the ribs. In order to glue them to the ribs small wooden clips, Figure 12, Plate 32, are used, and by means of a little notch cut into the corners and the blocks, their ends are introduced into these pieces in order to fasten them more firmly. The small clips straddle both the linings and the ribs themselves, and hold them together.

The linings having been glued and, the glue having dried, the clips are all removed, and the edge of the linings, near the mold, are removed with the knife, after which they are rubbed with glass paper. Finally, gouges are employed to round off the corners and the blocks level with the mold.

Before going any farther we would advise all those who make use of this treatise, as amateurs in violin building, always to have a group of the tools used before their eyes (Plate 29). The processes of work here described will then appear far less difficult to understand than would otherwise be the case.

How to Build the Back of the Violin

It is not hard to understand that the back of the violin must necessarily be that part of it which forms the under side when the instrument is being played.

The back and the sound board are made in the same way; the presence of the F-holes in the latter being the only difference between the two pieces, and the back should have absolutely the same arching, the same appearance as the sound board.

As has already been seen, there exists, in the middle of the pieces of maple or plane wood (Fig. 13, Plate 32) of which backs made of a single piece are to be formed, an elevation destined to form the arch of the instrument. In backs made of two pieces, the two heaviest sides of the slabs of wood (Fig. 14, Plate 32) are joined by means of glue, which gives the back the same character as one formed of a single piece of wood.

Hence, if the back is to be formed of two pieces, one must begin by splitting the piece of plane wood in the middle, following the marked line (Fig. 14, Plate 32).

This done, the two thickest and broadest sides of the split wood are smoothed by means of the plane, and when, fitting one to the other, it is evident that they form a perfect jointure all along the line, they are glued together. Once the glue has dried, the two pieces, which now form but one, are absolutely similar to a back made of a single piece, and from this moment on they are handled in the same way.

The flat slab of the back is placed on the workbench, and with the griper raised enough to provide a point of support for it, both sides should be planed down in such a way that both sides are equally thick at their opposite edges. Care must always be taken not to dig in the iron of the plane too deeply for fear of tearing out chips.

The two nether sides of the back having been carefully scraped and leveled, the piece of wood is turned around on the workbench in order that its flat surface may be scraped, and it is scraped until the application of a rule proves

PLATE 32

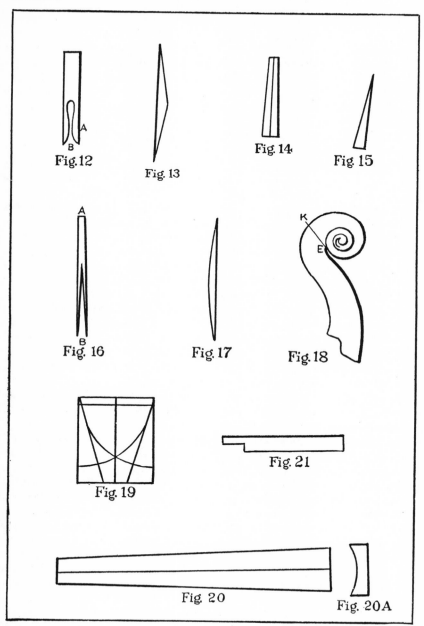

MODELS AND TOOLS USED IN VIOLIN MAKING.

that the surface is absolutely level. These procedures, as one may see, are not difficult.

If the back is to be made in one piece, a line should be drawn across the whole breadth of the back, with the point, on the level side, taking care that the line in question is absolutely parallel with the point of support above the wood, something easy enough to do if the tracing is done with a folding rule or square. This line, starting from the level of the back, ends in the most conical part below.

In the back made of two pieces, the jointure existing in the middle makes this traced line unnecessary.

The model, Figure 1, Plate 30, is now taken and laid on the slab of the back, attention being paid that the center of the model is fixed exactly on the line which has just been drawn; and then the entire outline of the model is traced with the point, the greatest care being used. The back which has been traced is then placed in the vise, and is cut out with the turning saw, heed being always paid not to approach the latter too near the line, since after the saw has been used, knife and scraper are employed to make the model exact. By frequent use of the rule the assurance may be gained that the edges form a right angle with the flat side of the form.

The outline completed, one should take the tracer and open it to the extent of 5 millimeters (1/5"). The back is then placed on the knees, and, resting the larger arm of the tracer against the wood, a line which serves to indicate the thickness which the edges should have is drawn completely around them.

The back should then be placed flat on the workbench and held there by means of clamps, while one begins to line out the arching, using the largest of the gouges. Here the craftsman should be doubly attentive, and move slowly and surely in order to attain his ends, since a single splinter of wood carried away may spoil his work.

One should begin removing, along the length of the back, all the wood necessary to obtain the arch shown in the model, Figure 2, Plate 30, frequently looking at the model while so doing, and not allowing the gouge to bite too deeply into the wood, lest too much of it be removed. When the lengthwise arch has been obtained one must, if necessary, place the back in a new position on the workbench, and get to such work as reproducing the arch shown in Figure 4, Plate 30, which is the central arch, crosswise. In order to find the exact joint, the model of the F-holes should be taken and placed upon the back, and the two interior curves of the F-holes marked. The model should then be removed, and a line drawn between these two curves; the center of this line will be the point on which the model, Figure 4, Plate 30, should be placed in order to carve this arch.

The placing of the models for the upper and lower transverse archings of the violin does not call for explanation, since it is at the broadest point of the upper and of the lower part of the instrument that this arch should be placed.

If the arches have been hollowed with all possible care, and if attention has been paid to removing only a little wood at a time, the marks of the gouges do not stand out prominently, and it is easy to remove them with the tooth plane. In addition the tooth plane serves to give an arched form to the throat of the back. The throat is the name given the small groove running all around the back, at 3 millimeters (1/8″) from the edges, in which the purfling is encrusted.

Having thus equalized the various parts of the exterior of the back, to as great a degree as the tooth plane will permit, small scrapers should be employed to do away with all asperities which may still exist, and one may end with smoothing down the exterior with glass paper.

All these operations having been completed, attention should be paid to hollowing out the back on the plane side, and to giving it the thickness demanded if the instrument is to have the proper tone when it is entirely completed.

A piece of rounded wood is placed in one of the holes of the work bench, and wedged firmly into place. This peg of wood serves as a point of support for the side of the back, which is held against it in the left hand, while the right hollows the wood by means of a gouge, working transversely.

In order to carry out this work, a layer of wood should be placed on the workbench, against which the finished side of the back may rest, in order to prevent its being scraped or trod upon. Certain precautions should be adopted in hollowing out the back: (1) all those portions of the outline against which the blocks, the corners, the ribs and the linings are to rest should be left perfectly intact; (2) the wood should be removed only with great caution, for fear of taking away too much, an evil for which there is no remedy, and care should be taken to leave a thickness of 1 millimeter (1/25″) in excess of that required all over the back and its parts. A caliper should be used as a guide in this work, and it should be completed with the tooth plane, scrapers and glass paper.

The back completed, it is laid on that side of the mold which has the ribs, linings, corners and blocks ready to receive it. The edges of the back should be examined in order to see whether they stand out equally above the entire outline of the ribs, for they should rise above them to the extent of 2 millimeters (1/12″). Then, attaching the back to the ribs by means of four fiddle screws or clamps holding together the two parts where they are largest, the wimble is used to make a number of small holes which, traversing the back, end in the blocks, opposite the point of junction of the upper and lower ribs. In order that these holes may not be visible later on, they are made in the very spot where the purfling is to be placed. When these holes have been made, two small pegs of plane wood are inserted in them.

This procedure serves to fix at once the place which the back is to occupy on the ribs when the glue comes to be applied; for if the attempt were made to find the resting place of the back after the glue had already been applied, it would be found impossible to do so, since the glue, which should never be used unless very hot, congeals very quickly.

When sure that the back is ready to be glued on the ribs, the small pegs already mentioned are withdrawn, and spreading the glue on blocks and corners and under the outline of the ribs, the back is at once laid down, the pegs are inserted in both, and driven in with the hammer; and finally the instrument is clamped down on every side with as many clamps and screws as may be needed.

These clamps or screws should be used in the following manner, in order to prevent the back from opening out if the glue should chance to grow cold in certain places. Two clamps are placed on the upper blocks, two on the lower blocks, one at each end of the upper and lower ribs, toward the corners; and finally in the *C* bouts, and anywhere else where they may be placed with profit.

A brush should then be dipped in the hot water of the gluepot, and any glue which may have found its way outside the ribs should be removed, and the whole then allowed to dry.

How to Construct the Sound Board and Pierce the F-Holes

As we know, the sound board is the upper part of the violin body, and as has already been remarked, the sound board of the instrument is made in exactly same manner as is the back. Even greater care should be taken in shaping the sound board of the instrument than the back, in view of the fact that spruce is far more fragile than plane wood and the fiber of this soft wood is often very irregular, which frequently forces a change of direction on the part of the tools being used in order to cut it properly.

When the sound board is in one piece, the procedure is the same as for the back.

When the sound board is made of two pieces of wood, care should be taken:

1. To line up the two surfaces which are to be joined with the plane in such a manner that, following the grain of the wood, the grain in both pieces runs parallel.

2. To see to it that the heart of the wood, that is to say that part of the wood where the grain is closest, is in the center of the sound board.

3. When setting up the model, not to trace the little half-circle which is found at the top of the sound board, and which goes under the name of the heel end, where the neck joins the body, as this prolongation is needed by the sound board.

All in all the F-holes represent the only difference between the back and

PLATE 33

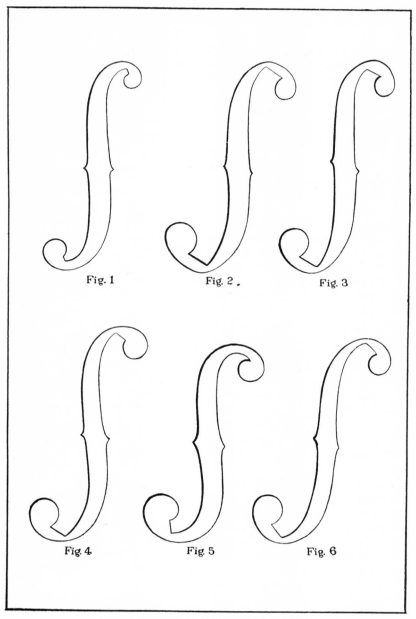

Fig. 1   Fig. 2 .   Fig. 3

Fig. 4   Fig. 5   Fig. 6

F-HOLES DESIGNED BY FAMOUS MAKERS.

1. Gasparo da Salo.	3. Guarnerius.	5. Stainer.
2. Bergonzi.	4. Amati.	6. Stradivarius.

the sound board. They are not pierced until the sound board has been entirely completed, and its degrees of thickness established.

In order to do so, take the model of the F-holes, Figure 6, Plate 30, and lay it on the sound board which has just been completed in such a way that the corners of the model as well as the C bouts are absolutely perpendicular with the corresponding parts, and then with a well sharpened pencil clearly trace the interior lines of the model.

Three perforations smaller than the curves of the F-holes should be made, cutting from above, and into the three perforations the knife blade should be introduced and, little by little, all the wood found within the pencil lines should be removed, until the F-holes have been entirely cut out.

Then the sound board is placed on the mold, on the side with which the ribs have been made level, and two holes are pierced, which, like those of the back, are plugged with two small pegs. This precaution is a necessary one, for as one will see later, when separated from the mold the ribs may at times warp, a disadvantage which is prevented by the pegs which we have just mentioned, since they compel the ribs to maintain the position given them when they were fixed in the mold.

At this point the mold should be removed from the inside of the ribs. This separation is carried out by means of a chisel whose cutting edge is between the blocks, the corners and the notches of the mold. When the chisel is thus in position, its handle should be given a short, quick tap, and the corners as well as the blocks will separate from the mold, to which they were fixed by means of a single drop of glue, as already has been explained.

It is now necessary as in the case of the back, to add the linings, which, as well as the ribs themselves, should be joined to the sound board. The blocks should then be rounded by means of knife and scraper, and the corners treated in the same manner, after any glue which may have run over from the ribs of the back has been removed with the chisel. Then the entire inner part of the blocks, the corners, the ribs and the linings should be smoothed with glass paper. The operation is completed by gluing the bass-bar to the sound board, and then gluing the sound board to the violin.

THICKNESS OF THE BACK AND SOUND BOARD; POSITION OF THE BASS-BAR

This work, that of giving back and sound board of the violin the requisite degree of thickness, is one of the most detailed tasks found in all violin making.

By drawing a straight line between the two interior curves of the F-holes, and taking the exact center of this line, we obtain a point which serves as the fundamental base of all the processes used to give the back and the sound board of the instrument the thicknesses necessary to ensure the vibration of the various parts of the two pieces. It is on this operation that the greater or lesser beauty of tone of a violin mainly depends.

Care having been taken, then, to establish with exactitude the point lying in the exact center of the two F-holes, on the inner side of the sound board, take the compasses and opening them at exactly 21 millimeters (4/5″), set one of the points exactly on the place selected, and the other on the line which moves directly toward one of the F-holes. This spot is marked on the line, and turning around the point of the compasses, another spot is marked on the opposite side of the same line. Consequently these two spots which have been marked have an interval of exactly 42 millimeters (1 2/3″) between them. Then take a rule, and from each of these spots draw a line which extends parallel to the joint along the length of the sound board, 83 millimeters (3 1/4″) from the line moving toward the top of the violin, and 56 millimeters (2 1/5″) from the line moving toward the bottom of the instrument. We will then have a square 139 millimeters (5 1/2″) long by 42 millimeters (1 2/3″) broad. All the wood of the sound board comprised within this square should have a mean thickness of 3 millimeters (1/8″).

Radiating out from all the exterior lines of this square, the proportion just given of 3 millimeters (1/8″) diminishes insensibly, to fade away toward the edges of the sound board, where the latter rests on the ribs, the blocks and the corners, until it ends in a thickness of 1½ millimeters (1/16″).

Thus, in order to make this perfectly plain, one might say that the thickness of the violin sound board, along the entire extension of its outlines, starting from the point where it no longer rests on the ribs, the blocks and the corners, is 1½ millimeters (1/16″). In moving up from the edges of the sound board toward its center, which is the length of the square already mentioned, this thickness insensibly augments until the square is reached, where it is 3 millimeters (1/8″) thick, which proportion should obtain with the most perfect exactitude throughout the interior of the square.

The degrees of thickness of the back are in every way comparable to those of the sound board, with the only difference that in all of its proportions the thickness of the former is greater by 1 millimeter (1/25″) than that of the latter.

In order to give the sound board the degrees of thickness which have just been described, the following process should be observed. A block of hard wood 56 to 83 millimeters long (2″ to 3″), should be set up in the form of a corner, as shown in Figure 15, Plate 32.

Three lines should be drawn at right angles on one of the sides of this block; the first at that part of the block which is no more than 3 millimeters (1/8″) thick; the second at the place where the block is exactly 2 millimeters (1/12″) thick; the third, finally, at the place where it is exactly 1½ millimeters (1/16″) thick.

It will be noticed that the first line indicates the thickness of the lengthwise; the second the thickness of the various parts of the sound board which are found between the square and the edges; the third, finally, the thickness where it rests on the blocks, corners and ribs. The block is introduced between its two buttons, as far as the line which has a thickness of 3 millimeters (1/8″); the compasses are then closed and it is thus given an opening of 3 millimeters (1/8″) which represents the thickness of the square.

With a scraper the superfluous wood of the sound board is then removed, and care should be taken that the sound board be often measured during the process, so that too much wood is not removed. Thus, little by little, the square is given the exact thickness which it should have.

This done, the block is once more placed between the dividers of the proportional compasses, and narrowing it down to the second line, they are opened to the extent of 2 millimeters (1/12″).

One should then commence to take away the wood all about the square, moving from each face of the square towards the edges. This is done in order that the thickness of those portions of the sound board found between the square in question as well as the edges, will have exactly the thickness given at that moment by the compasses. Finally, the block is introduced in the compasses for the last time, it is set on the third line, and the thickness at the edges of the sound board, 1½ millimeters (1/16″) is established.

As, in the process of establishing the various thicknesses, one cannot help but remove the lead-pencil lines with the scraper, it will be necessary to redraw them whenever it may be needed.

All the thicknesses indicated must be made somewhat broader than the indications demand, since the scraper and glass paper will still have to be used to smooth the surfaces, and these two small operations will, naturally remove a little of the wood.

Finally, it will be wise to prepare a second block for measuring the thicknesses of the back which, as has already been said, should correspond in all its proportions to those of the sound board but 1 millimeter (1/25″) thicker.

The construction of the interior of the violin is completed by the insertion of the bass-bar. This is a small piece of spruce, at the left side of the sound board, which serves, on one hand, to help the instrument support the weight and the tension of the strings, and on the other, gives the two heavy strings the depth of sound which, without it, they would not have.

The bass-bar is 278 millimeters (about 10 2/3″) long, 5 average millimeters (1/5″) thick, and 9 millimeters (1/3″) high in the middle. It is terminated at its two ends by bevels which stretch out on the sound board to which it is glued.

The bass-bar is made in the following manner: a piece of spruce about 18 or 19 millimeters (approximately 2/3″) in breadth is taken, and trimmed to 5 millimeters (1/6″) of thickness by means of the plane, care being taken that the grain of the wood is on the same side as this breadth, and runs parallel with that of the sound board itself, when the bar is glued to it.

This piece of spruce having been trimmed as indicated, the compasses are opened 21 millimeters (3/4″) and, placing one of the points on the central point of the bass-bar, the other point of the compasses is used to make a point which will be, consequently, 21 millimeters (3/4″) distant from the joint of the sound board. This is absolutely the same process described in order to find the square of the sound board itself. A line is then drawn at the point marked, parallel with the emplacement joint of the bass-bar.

In order to give the bar the curve necessary if it is to adapt itself naturally, and as though of its own accord to the sound board, one must proceed in the following manner:

The prepared bass-bar, as was the case when obtaining the models of the archings, is laid edgewise on the line which has been drawn on the interior or inner side of the sound board, and, opening the compasses as far as necessary, one of the points is laid down flat on the sound board, while the other is laid flat on the bass-bar. The compasses are moved from one end to the other of the bar, and thus the curve of the arch of the sound board is obtained.

The knife is then used to remove all unnecessary wood; the bar is brought to the place at the sound board where it is to be glued fast, and, little by little, all the wood which might prevent its entire adjustment to the sound board is removed. Then it is set up squarely and is ready to be glued fast. That part of the violin on which this bar rests should be cut slightly on a bias, since, being glued, it forms a right angle with the sound board.

In order to glue the bass-bar to the sound board, wooden tools, known as sound-bar cramps are employed, as shown in Figure 16, Plate 32.

The foot of the bass-bar is covered with glue and is then attached to the line already drawn on the sound board, in such a manner that the two ends are each equally removed from the top and the bottom of the sound board. The sound board is taken up by the four fingers of the left hand and held in place while the bass-bar is pressed and held in place by the thumb of the same hand. Thus the right hand is free to act, and is used to pass a bar clamp below the sound board on the one side, and one above the bass-bar on the other. Then, by pressing a little, the clamp is forced forward until the bar is adequately fixed in position, when five or six more of these bar clamps are introduced, at equal distances one from another, until the whole bass-bar has been attached to the sound board. Then, with a brush and some hot water, the glue which may have run over along the joint of the bar is removed, and it is allowed to dry.

The glue used in affixing the bass-bar having dried, the clamps are removed, and taking the sound board on the knees, the larger segments of superfluous wood are removed with the tooth plane or scraper. Compasses are then taken, opened to 10 millimeters (a fraction over 1/3″), one of the points is placed flat on the sound board, and, with the other in the center of the bar, the height it should have at the place in question is marked. A tooth-plane scraper is then taken, and the bar is planed in such wise that it assumes the form shown in Figure 17, Plate 32; the traces of the tooth plane are then removed by the scraper, and in conclusion the bass-bar is rubbed smooth with glass paper.

The next thing to do is to fit the sound board to the violin. This process does not offer any difficulties, for after having covered the ribs, the linings, the blocks and the corners of the violin with glue, as has already been shown, all that is left to do is to affix the sound board, first by means of the two small pegs of which we have already spoken, and then by means of clamps, employing the same process followed in gluing the back. After this has been done, it should be allowed to dry, and, as before, the glue which may have escaped and found its way outside the ribs should be washed off.

When this point has been reached and the violin has been disengaged from its clamps, the edges should be carefully examined, those of the back as well as those of the sound board, to see that they do not outpass the ribs in some places to a greater extent than in others, and if they do, the defect should be remedied by cutting away with the knife, and always cleanly and neatly, as much of the edging as may stand out above the ribs.

This accomplished, the back and the sound board should be purfled; that is, in small grooves or incisions made in them along the entire border of the instrument, there are introduced and fixed in place with glue, small filaments or tongues of wood whose only purpose is to embellish the instrument. There are usually three of these tongues or purflings, known as "sandwiches," two of wood stained ebony and one, between them, which remains white.

It is possible to purchase these purflings ready-made, especially from violin makers. They are all the better for having been cut by the bench saw, and may be had in any desired thickness. It is well, however, that the violin builder make whatever is to be made in connection with the instrument with his own hands, and for this reason we will describe how these purflings should be fashioned. First of all, the two intended to be black should be stained ebony color, for which purpose the recipe for making a black stain in the section treating of varnishes may be consulted.

The wood most easily obtainable for use in this connection is white hawthorn. One should begin by cutting a piece of this wood 35 millimeters (1 1/3″) thick by 167 millimeters (6″) long. Its length should be at least that which the purfling itself will have when it is put in place. It goes without saying that this piece of wood should have neither knots nor cracks. It is placed in the workbench vise, with its narrowest side presented to the steel of the plane; the plane is passed over it, and a single shaving of wood removed. When this first shaving has been removed, it is necessary to see whether the thickness desired has been obtained. If the side is still too narrow, the plane is used again, with more or less pressure as the case may require.

Two-thirds of each of these shavings or purflings are tinted black; three of the purflings are then glued together, the white one placed in the middle, while care must be taken to use glue which is fluid, weakened with water, in order that when these purflings come to be glued in their grooves, they will be flexible enough to adapt themselves to the outlines of the grooves in question.

When the purflings have been glued and dried, it is necessary to cut the groove which is to receive them. The operation, which is one requiring great care, is carried out as follows:

Taking the purfling gauge or marker, the vise is used to open it to the desired extent necessary to set away more or less of the edge of the purfling, a matter which depends altogether on the taste of the individual, unless when he is copying another violin faithfully, he would rather imitate it in every detail.

The violin is held on the knees, and, controlling it with the left hand, the cutter of the marker rests upon the back of the sound board, for it makes but little difference whether one begin with the one or the other. The marker being held as described, care must be taken to keep it in an upright position, while passing it all about the border of the instrument and raising it again at each of the four corners. This operation will result in a small line drawn upon the back of the sound board. Then, after having convinced one's self that the marker has drawn the line clearly wherever it has passed, it is used again wherever it may have failed to make a proper impression. This first operation accomplished, it is only necessary to cut the two lines destined to form the groove which is nearest the edge. The second groove line must now be drawn, bearing in mind the thickness of the three purflings taken together, and opening the purfling gauge or marker in conformity, and if necessary, forcing the purfling gauge a trifle with the hammer.

A tool composed of two blades carefully sharpened and closely set together, the purfling compasses, which makes it possible to cut two grooves at once, is also used.

The second groove of the purfling being similar to the first, a small space is left beneath the small half-circle at the heel of the neck where it joins the body.

In order to do away with this break in the tracing of the groove, one should take a small piece of very narrow wood, like the wood of the models which have already been described, and use the knife to give it the curve required by the groove in this place; after which, that portion which the marker has been unable to reach is traced with the point.

The entire purfling having thus been traced along the two sides of the violin, with the point of a knife, the lines which the marker has left are gone over with the knife in order to deepen the grooves sufficiently to permit of the purflings being introduced in them; while guarding against pressing the knife too powerfully into the wood, especially in the case of spruce wood, lest it cut through the sound board.

This work finished, the wood lying between the two grooves forming the purfling should be removed. This is easily done by means of a small purfling chisel or "picker," together with a fine awl. The awl is used in the places where its breadth is less than is the breadth of the groove. A chisel is given a sloping cutting edge on the grindstone resembling that of a marker chisel. It then becomes an actual purfling chisel, so-called, with which one may remove the wood that is to yield place to the purflings.

In order to place the purflings in the grooves, one should begin adjusting them by cutting them lengthwise, with nibs, care being taken to cut them with the knife where they are to join the corners of the violin. This done, the next thing is to take two purflings at a time in order to introduce them at one and the same moment into the corners, after first having placed the glue necessary in the grooves. Once adjusted in the corners, the purflings are filled into the grooves adjacent to the corners, and driven home with short blows of the chisel. Below the small half-circle where the heel of the neck joins the body, and at the bottom of the large ribs, since the purflings must necessarily be joined to one another, and present the appearance of forming one sole piece, they must be cut on the bias, and very cleanly so that their point of junction is not remarked.

One thing which it is very necessary to observe is that these purflings, before being used in the manner described, should be cut in such a way that they do not outpass the groove but very slightly.

In order to cut them down to a height of 8½ millimeters (a trifle over 1/3″) a scraper should be made of a triangular file, with one tooth resembling the tooth of a saw, and this tooth must rise 1 millimeter (1/25″) above the plane.

The purflings are placed on the flat surface of the plane, the tooth is then placed on the purfling and the flat surface of the scraper on the planer, the toothed scraper is drawn from one end to the other of the shaving, as though one were using the tracer or the compasses. The same thing is then done on the other side, and the wood is cut. All that is now necessary is to separate the piece of purfling intended to enter the groove from the other with the finger.

When the glue of the purflings has dried, whatever portion of them stands out too noticeably against the back or the sound board must be carefully removed. In order to do so, the larger portions are removed with the knife, guarding against chipping, while the scraper does the rest.

The body of the violin has now been completed, with the exception of the edges of back and belly, which are still square instead of being round. One might believe at first glance that the work of rounding off these edges is not hard, but, nevertheless, meticulous care is needed if the operation is to be successful.

By means of a small, well-sharpened knife the brim formed by the edges is removed on the side of the ribs, great care being taken not to cut away more wood in one place than in another, and to preserve, above all about the corners, the exact form of the model which has served to outline the back and the sound board; and also remembering not to touch the wood which forms the lateral part of the strings. Care should also be taken to change the direction of the knife whenever it is evident that it is cutting against the grain of the wood. The same process is observed on the side of the edge opposite to the ribs; and it is rounded by means of a sharp-grained file until all the squareness along the edges of the instrument has disappeared. The final smoothing is given by means of glass paper.

It is preferable to round off the edges on the side of the ribs before glueing back and sound board together, in order not to risk cutting into the ribs during the operation. This precaution is not necessary in the case of the edges opposite the ribs.

Again we feel it necessary to advise all those who think of taking up violin making as a labor of love, always to have a good violin in sight while they are working, to serve as a guide.

How to Construct the Neck

First of all, we must realize exactly what is meant by the neck of the instrument.

In order to construct this part, a piece of plane wood 278 millimeters (about 10 2/3″) long should be taken; it should be trimmed square on all four of its faces, two of which should be 45 millimeters (1 3/4″) in breadth, while the two remaining ones, which are to form the sides of the neck, should be 65 millimeters (2 1/2″) broad.

Once this piece of wood has been smoothed and squared, the model of the neck is placed on one of the sides, and its outlines are traced on the wood with a pencil, as shown in Figure 7, Plate 30.

A transverse line is then drawn with the T-square across the four faces, beginning at the point marked G, which is the place where the peg box is to begin, and from this line which has been drawn one should measure off, at point G, moving toward the opposite end of the neck, a distance of 148 millimeters (5 3/4″) and this length, which is the neck, beginning with the peg box up to the end which is to be fitted into the body of the instrument, should be marked off. Once more using the rule, a transverse line is drawn at the point just marked, and this line is repeated on each of the faces of the wood.

The compasses are then taken, opened to about 28 millimeters (about 1″)

and on the two straight lines of wood and along its entire length a dividing line is drawn which separates each into two equal parts.

Now the compasses are opened 13 millimeters (13/24″) and one of the points is placed on the line which is to be drawn, on the very spot where it is crossed at right angles by the line which has been drawn transversely at point G, in order to indicate the beginning of the peg box. To the left and to the right of the transverse line two points are marked off at a distance of about 25 millimeters (about 1″) from each other. This measurement gives the proportion of the neck at the beginning of its handle, and the proportion of the nut found in the same place, the upper end of the neck.

The compasses are then opened 17 good millimeters (3/4″) and, placing one of the points on the point where the lower transverse line is crossed by the one which divides the neck lengthwise into two parts, there should be marked, to the left and the right of the said line, two points which will be 35 millimeters (1 1/3″) apart. This is the proportion of the breadth of the neck at its extremity, which, later on, will be fitted into the body of the violin.

This tracing having been attended to, the neck is now set in the vise so that all that portion, of which the scroll and the peg box are to be formed by means of the turning saw, rises above the bench. Then all the superfluous wood about the lines, from letter A to letter G, Figure 7, Plate 30, is removed. The shape which it is ultimately to assume is now given to this part, and there is nothing left to do to it, save to use knife and file, or whatever other tools may best answer the purpose. The neck is then coupled in its length to the transverse lower line.

With compasses which have been opened 23 millimeters (7/8″) the central line is retraced along that part of the neck which is about to be sawed, from A to E.

Two straight lines are then drawn with the rule, running from the two points marked at the transverse line which separates the peg box from the neck, to the other two points which have also been marked at the bottom of the neck. The piece is then gripped in the vise in such a way as to leave on each side of the neck whatever lies outside of the last two lines which have been drawn, and the two saw lines are extended as far as the dotted line K——E, Figure 18, Plate 32.

Now all that remains to be done is to turn our attention to the scroll or volute, which we do by beginning with the button with which the scroll starts. Take a gouge or rounded chisel, whose cutting edge is exactly proportioned to the edge of the scroll—after the neck has been set on the workbench and laid down on its side—hold the tool perpendicularly, and thrust it into the wood, following with exactness the line traced on the scroll. By inclining the gouge, the rounded grooves are then formed, leaving as few inequalities as possible in the grooves in question, and finishing them off with scrapers and glass paper. The gouge should be changed conformably as the curve of the scroll grows broader as it leaves the button.

This done, there remains to work out the species of slide or groove on both sides of the neck, which, starting behind the neck, proceeds in turns to the top of the peg box, where it ends, and in which, eventually, the mortise is made. The construction of the neck is anything but easy; yet, given patience and practice, one will soon be able to build a fine neck.

We will indicate how the neck is to be completed up to the moment when it is joined to the body of the instrument.

Since the grip, which should have a thickness of 16 millimeters (2/3″) from top to bottom, offers no special difficulties, we will say no more about it, and turn our attention to the foot of the neck, which is the portion inset in the upper block of the violin on the one side, and on the other resting on the nut of the sound board where the neck joins the body.

Opening the compasses 35 millimeters (1 1/3″) and setting the two points on the lower end of the neck, exactly opposite the two points which were previously marked which indicate the breadth of this part, a circle is traced with one of the compass points while the other point remains on the spot in which it was set down. This first circle drawn, another is drawn inversely, and the point of meeting of the two circles serves as the point of departure for a line drawn from the center line of the neck, which is an extension of this line, dividing the end of the neck into two equal parts.

The breadth of the nut at the junction of neck and sound board is now measured, and equally divided by the compasses. It is marked on the foot of the neck by placing one point of the compasses on the line which has just been drawn, and marking a point to the right and to the left of this line, in the place which is to rest on the nut. As it is not possible to judge by the eye where this place should be, it is found in the manner described.

Since the neck should extend beyond the sound board of the violin 5 millimeters (1/6″), one should commence by drawing a line of this thickness with the compasses at the end of the neck, resting the tool on the flat surface which is to receive the finger board. An ordinary foot rule should then be used to measure the height of the ribs and of the sound board, beginning from the flat surface of the nut, below the line traced by the compasses. It is there that the breadth of the nut should be established by the two points already mentioned.

Beginning with the two lines at the right and the left of the neck respectively, at the spot where they stop at the end of the neck, two lines should be drawn which will come to rest on the two points just mentioned. The superfluous wood is then removed from either side of the neck, as well as any wood extending beyond the two points indicating the breadth of the nut, and now the neck is ready to be mortised into the instrument. Figure 19, Plate 32, shows a sketch of the base of the neck.

How to Make the Finger Board

The finger board is that portion of the instrument on which the left-hand fingers of the violinist fall when playing. Of all the parts of which the string instruments are composed, this is unquestionably the easiest to make. There are, however, several measures which must be taken to ensure its doing its full duty when joined to the other parts of the instrument which is being built.

Begin by making a model which will give the exact length and breadth of the finger board. This model should not offer the slightest difficulty since it is neither more nor less than a slab of wood, 27 centimeters (9 3/4") long and 44 millimeters (1 3/4") broad at one end 25 millimeters (1") at the other (Figure 20, Plate 32).

A piece of ebony 29 centimeters (10") long should be trimmed down to a thickness of 9 millimeters (1/3") and this model should then be laid upon the ebony which has been trimmed, and the finger board traced, and cut out.

When the finger board has been cut out, one of its sides should be smoothed with the plane. This side is the one which, later on, is to be glued to the neck; the other side should present a rounded surface as shown in Figure 20 A, Plate 32.

Since it would be impossible to round off the finger board while letting it lie flat on the workbench, a piece of beech wood 9 millimeters (1/3") broader than the finger board, and 56 millimeters (2 1/4") longer than it, should be taken. The model of the finger board should be placed in the middle of this piece of wood, which should have a height of 56 millimeters (2 1/4"); and two lines should be drawn, one to the right and one to the left, each about 5 millimeters (1/6") from the edge of the piece of beech wood. Two cuts are then made with the saw, to a depth of 3 millimeters (1/8"), along the two lines. Finally, the wood lying between the two saw cuts is removed to the same depth. It is within this slide or groove that the finger board is placed to round it off, first with a small plane, then with a large plane, using a small model in arch form as a guide.

In order that the piece in question may be held to the workbench, its broader end is half sawed through, as shown in Figure 21, Plate 32, and with the end placed directly against the workbench vise, the piece is tightened by means of the incision which has been made, and is held firmly in place with the clamps.

Fitting the Neck

Having left the neck of the violin ready to be fitted and joined to the body of the instrument, a description of this operation itself would now be in order.

It might be well to observe, before taking up the details of this fitting, that when the sound board of the violin is formed of a single piece, one should, before going any further, draw a pencil line along the sound board which, passing through the central point situated between the two F-holes, will divide the sound board in question into two equal halves.

This line, as will be seen, serves as a guide when fitting the neck, so that it may be placed exactly straight to the axis of the instrument, and to prevent bending it either to the left or to the right.

The neck, the foot of which is rested on the ribs at the place it is intended to occupy, should now be taken in the hand, paying attention that the central line which divides its grip into two equal parts is directly opposite the line which has just been drawn on the sound board. Take the tracing point in the right hand, and with the foot of the neck in your left, in the position already indicated, draw two lines with the tracer which, starting from the nut at the back, end at the sound board, thus marking the opening in which the foot of the neck is to be inserted. The neck is placed on the workbench, and together with it that part of the sound board comprised between them. The incision is cut to a depth of 7 millimeters (1/3″), care being taken to remove only the wood necessary to this end, so that when the foot of the neck is fitted to the incision, it cannot enter without a little forcing. Without this indispensable precaution the work will have no firmness.

When the foot of the neck has been adjusted in the hollow which has been cut for it, and when it rises exactly 5 millimeters (1/6″) above the sound board, care should be taken to incline it 1 millimeter (1/25″) toward the side of the E string.

This done, attention should be paid to giving the neck its backward slant. This slant of the neck serves to facilitate playing the instrument in passages where the violin neck enters in.

In order to make certain that the neck has the proper slant backwards, the following procedure should be observed.

The finger board having been prepared in the manner already indicated, and having a thickness of 5 millimeters (1/6″) on each of its sides and of 7 millimeters (1/4″) in the middle, it is laid on the neck, which should already have been adjusted on the workbench, as though it were to be glued.

Holding the neck and the finger board in the left hand, one should take a true rule and place it on the center of the finger board. While continuing to hold neck and finger board in position, the rule should be taken in the right hand, and stood upright on the sound board at the exact place where the point is to be found, making sure that the rule rises somewhat over 28 millimeters (a trifle over 1″) above the sound board.

This elevation gives the exact measure of the backward slant, which cannot fail to be exact if one does not forget to give the foot of the neck the

1/6 of an inch of elevation above the sound board which has already been recommended.

If, when verifying the back slant, the rule rises higher than 28 millimeters (1 1/6″) one should take the knife and remove a little of the wood in the hollow from the blocks at the side of the sound board, and once more test with the rule until the exact height desired has been secured. If the rule does not quite rise to the height indicated, a little wood should be cut away from the hollow on the side on which the nut of the sound board is placed. It might be remarked that this operation is a very delicate one, and that if it is not carried out well, it will exert a sensible influence on the tone quality of the instrument.

Before glueing the neck into its hollow, one must make certain that it is perfectly straight. In order to do this take a walnut rule no more than about 3 millimeters (1/8″) thick, so that it is capable of being bent. This rule should be placed on the pencil line which has been drawn on the sound board, and on the center line of the neck, in order to ascertain whether it inclines to one side or the other. If such be the case, the slant is remedied by cutting away a little of the wood in the hollow at the side which it is necessary to deepen, in order to ensure straightness. After that, all that remains to be done is to glue it.

To do so, take a clamp, open it to the desired extent, then lay it on the workbench, ready to hand, for later use. Then cut a wedge of cork, 12 millimeters (1/2″) thick by 56 millimeters (2 1/8″) long and 28 millimeters (little over 1″) broad. This wedge of cork is intended to be placed crosswise under the nut and the blocks of the sound board, to receive the screw button of the clamp, and prevent its causing strain or wrenching when the vise is tightened.

These preparations at an end, the brush is used to cover the entire interior of the hollow with glue before attempting to fit in the neck, and the piece of cork is put in place. Under the nut and the block the screw button of the clamp is rested against the cork, and the screw handle on the flat surface of the neck at its extremity, while the neck is tightly pressed, supporting it with the left hand in order to prevent its turning aside from the hollow. The remnants of glue are then washed away with hot water and a brush, and the violin is put in a place where it can dry.

It might be mentioned that when the sound board of the instrument has been constructed of two pieces of wood, it is unnecessary to trace the pencil line which has already been mentioned down its center, since the jointure of the two pieces itself supplies the line.

During wet weather it is well to heat the neck a little, and this is done by holding it to the fire before introducing it in the hollow. This is the best way to ensure quick drying of the glue.

It is also well to make a number of small holes with the point of the tracer or a knife point in the flat surface of the foot of the neck and in that portion of it which is to rest on the nut. This will allow the glue to act more effectively.

PLACING THE FINGER BOARD ON THE NECK; THE NUT AT THE UPPER END OF THE NECK AND THE NUT AT THE TAILPIECE

The glueing of the foot of the neck having been completed and the glue having dried, the next thing to do is to glue the finger board to the neck.

The finger board, being perfectly trimmed and having the thickness and the proportions already indicated, is now glued fast to the neck, care being taken to leave an interval of 5 millimeters (1/6″) between the top of the finger board and the bottom of the peg box and its right-hand end. This space is intended to receive the nut at the upper end of the neck.

To glue the finger board it is only necessary to cover the flat of the neck with glue and then set the finger board on this glue, pressing it tightly into place, and taking care that it does not shift over to either side, which may easily be prevented, since the two lines drawn on the neck at the right and left indicate its position.

A piece of ebony of the right size to supply a nut should now be taken and planed down to a height of about 8 millimeters (about 1/3″) and a breadth of 6 millimeters (1/8″) and then should be glued in its place. This piece will naturally project slightly beyond the two sides of the violin neck.

The nut at the tailpiece is a piece of ebony placed above the end pin of the instrument, that is to say, at the opposite extremity of the violin. It is intended to support the piece of gut string which attaches the tailpiece to the tailpin. This nut is usually 28 millimeters (little over 1″) long by 7 millimeters (7/25″) high.

In order to make it more solid, it is forced to enter into the sound board about 7 millimeters (7/25″) and as far into the ribs.

This part is so simple that the least practiced eye need only to see one in order to make a duplicate at once. The only precaution which should be taken when making it is to bring it high enough above the sound board to prevent the tailpiece from touching the latter, and then to round it off at the angle which is to hold the loop of the tailpiece, in such a way that the latter will not cut it.

When the glue of the nuts and of the finger board has dried, the larger portions of the superfluous wood about the two nuts are removed with the knife, and a file is used to give the desired shape to these two pieces. Then the nut over which the strings pass is arranged in such wise that it is only 1 millimeter (1/25″) higher than they are.

In conclusion the knife is used to shape up the grip or haft of the neck, which should just touch the finger board at its sides; the knife marks are filed away and the whole smoothed with glass paper.

A rat-tail file is then used to cut the four notches in the nut at the upper end of the neck intended to receive the strings, care being taken to make them as shallow as possible and to smooth them with glass paper. Then the hole intended to receive the button is pierced in the middle of the ribs and at the point of their junction.

How to Place the Sound Post, the Pegs, the Bridge and Other Accessories

When the violin has been varnished, attention should be paid to polishing the finger board and the nuts. In order to do so, five or six bunches of shave grass whose knots have been removed should be allowed to steep for a few minutes, and the ebony should be rubbed with them, moistening them continually, until it has taken on a fine polish. A linen rag impregnated with oil mixed with Tripoli, as well as sieved and powdered charcoal, should be used to rub with, until the pieces have acquired a varnishlike luster.

This done, with a borer of smaller size than the pin of the pegs, the holes which are to receive the latter are pierced and are enlarged with the peg-hole finished in such wise that the pegs will fit into them. This adjustment of the pegs, which does not seem very hard, calls for much care, nevertheless.

The most disagreeable thing which can happen to any string instrument player is to have to use pegs which jump, or which move only by jerks, or which come out. To do away with this inconvenience, the violin maker should be careful, in adjusting the pegs, to use only a file which is neither too fine nor too coarse. He must also be careful to fit the pegs equally in the holes of the peg box, to prevent their first twisting and then breaking; the holes, furthermore should be made very round, which is easy enough to do if the peg-hole finisher is ground in such fashion as to cut cleanly and without any effort on the part of the hand using it.

There is a little trick which is not generally known to make the pegs turn evenly and prevent their coming out. We will explain it.

Take two parts of Spanish white, reduced to a very fine powder, and add to it one part of colophonium, also reduced to powder. Mix these two substances well, and when the pegs have been adjusted, take a piece of very dry soap, and rub the pins of the pegs lightly with it, then covering them with the mixture of Spanish white and colophonium. If this is done they will function admirably.

Before proceeding it might be well to remark that the pegs and the buttons being made by means of the turner, the violin maker can procure them from the carpenter shop ready-made. In Mirecourt, bridges and tailpieces may be bought so cheaply that there are hardly any violin builders who make these parts themselves. Those who prefer to fabricate these parts themselves, however, will succeed in making their tailpieces without much difficulty, but, as to bridges, it takes a good while before one as shapely and graceful as those made in Mirecourt can be turned out. In this manufacturing town the workmen who make bridges do nothing else, hence they are able to turn out perfect specimens of the best workmanship.

The bridge should be sufficiently solid to be able to resist the tension of the strings; at the same time it is preferable that the under portion, upon which the strings rest, be as narrow as possible, since this greatly augments the brilliance and the purity of tone of the instrument.

The pegs once adjusted, the borer is used on each of them to pierce the little hole which is necessary to hold the end of the strings.

The true bridge is then taken and prepared to receive the four strings which are to be mounted on the instrument, a dummy or guide, in the shape of an old bridge being used to prop up the strings while the real bridge is being fitted.

Begin by fitting the feet of the bridge to the sound board, adjusting them absolutely to the arching of the belly in such wise that not the least space is left between the two parts, for the tone of the instrument grows hoarse and rough if the feet of the bridge are not perfectly adjusted along their whole length of the sound board.

The lower part of the bridge should be rounded, in such a way that when the bow is used, the player does not touch several strings at once against his wish. At the same time it should not be too much rounded, since this would result in difficulties for the player, who would be obliged to make too many movements when bringing the bow from the E string to the fourth string. In short, it should be given approximately the same arching indicated for the finger board. Incidentally, the four small notches which serve to hold the strings in place on the bridge should be made as shallow as possible.

Finally, the height of the bridge should be approximately such that the fourth string, the G string, will rise about 6 millimeters (1/4″) above the finger board, the D string and A string somewhat less, and the E string about 5 millimeters (1/6″). The distance separating the G string from the E string should be about 37 millimeters (about 1 1/3″).

We have still to make a sound post and to fit it into the instrument.

This part, a small one in itself, has a great deal of influence on the tone of the instrument. We will give all the details necessary for making it and for its subsequent adjustment.

Take a piece of soft pine, well dried and without knots, and trim it square with the plane. Each face of this rod of wood is diminished until, when presented at the opening of the right-hand F-hole it can enter the same. Then the four corners of the square are cut away with the knife, and the rod is rounded in cylinder shape by the file. The height which the sound post should have is then tested, and it is cut down and smoothed with glass paper.

In order to ascertain the height of the sound post, one should take a piece of steel wire or a knitting needle, let us say, and passing it through the upper curve of the F-hole, lower its end until it rests on the inside of the back of the violin. The steel is then nicked or marked at the surface of the sound board, it is drawn out and the proper length which the sound post should have has been established.

The grain of the pine or spruce of which the sound post is made should run in the direction contrary to the grain of the spruce of which the sound board is made. This important detail should not be forgotten, in order that the remainder of our explanation may be entirely understood.

The back and the sound board of the violin not being perfectly flat, but well arched, it is necessary, in order that the head and the foot of the sound post join the two parts in question absolutely and perfectly, to cut them slightly on a bias. A perfectly sharpened knife is used to give this slight bias to the sound post, and the bias should be cut *with* and not *against* the grain of the pine or spruce of which the sound post is made.

A sound post setter is then taken, its point is thrust into the sound post, at about 10 to 11 millimeters (1/4″ to 1/3″) below its head, and in the tender part of the wood. Then the sound post is passed through the curve of the right hand F-hole of the violin, and its foot is rested against the back, its head inclining toward the lower end of the violin. Once the foot has been placed approximately in the position it is to occupy definitely, the sound post is raised and allowed to slide beneath the sound board, until it has assumed a vertical position. The point of the sound post setter is then withdrawn from the sound post, and, laying this tool aside, the work of giving the sound post its proper position is completed by means of hooks.

The place it should occupy is 2 millimeters (1/12″) to the rear of the bridge, and exactly 21 millimeters (3/4″) distant from the central point of the sound board; that is to say, if we imagine a line drawn parallel to the joint of the sound board of the instrument, the exterior part of the foot of the bridge and the exterior part of the outer portion of the head of the sound post will both be on this line, whose distance from the joint is about 21 millimeters (3/4″).

The sound post having now been put in position, it is necessary to place the button, which should be introduced somewhat forcefully into the block, in order to fix it there solidly.

The mounting of the strings is now all that remains in order to complete the violin, and they should be most carefully strung, care being taken that they do not become entangled in the peg box. This operation is so simple a one that it seems superfluous to detail it.

CHAPTER V

COLORS AND VARNISHES

The old makers whose works serve as models for the violin builders of to-day mingled color with their varnish. Whether it be that their processes have not been handed down to us, or that the preparation which these varieties of varnish demanded has discouraged violin makers of the present time from employing them, the fact remains that but very few craftsmen use the color varnishes. They are, nevertheless, much to be preferred to those which are applied to the instruments, after the latter have been colored by painting.

Since it is our wish to make this manual as comprehensively informative as possible, we will describe the two processes by giving receipts for the colors which are applied to the instruments before they have been varnished.

Colors Used by the Violin Makers

Black.—Black is used to color the nuts when, owing to reasons of economy, the maker does not care to employ ebony. Violin makers who manufacture cheap violins also use black to tint the tailpiece, the frets, the pegs, and, in short, all those parts which in choicer instruments are usually made of ebony.

To obtain this black, one should boil 5 1/3 ounces of horse-chestnut wood in 1 5/8 quarts of water for three quarters of an hour. The vessel should then be removed from the fire, the color gently poured into a pan, and 14/15 of an ounce of ground copperas should be added to it while it is still warm.

This color is applied by means of a brush to the parts which are to be blackened; they are then allowed to dry, and the operation is repeated until the black seems to have acquired the proper degree of consistency desired.

It might be mentioned that the longer the coloring matter is allowed to boil, the finer is the black resulting from the operation.

When the manipulation just described has been completed, the brush is also used to apply to the parts which have been tinted two layers of a composite which is prepared in the following manner, and which serves as a fixative for the color used.

An earthenware pot is half filled with strong vinegar of the very best quality obtainable, and into this vinegar are thrown pieces of rusty iron, the rustier the better.

The vinegar in the pot should rise about .117 inches above the fire, and the composition should be stirred frequently while boiling, and should be allowed to macerate for two or three weeks, the supply of vinegar being renewed whenever the process of evaporation makes this necessary.

Red.—This is a very solid color, and one which costs almost nothing to prepare. All that is necessary is to boil 5 1/3 ounces of Pernambuco wood, chopped very fine, together with 1 1/15 ounces of alum, in 1 5/8 quarts of water. These ingredients should be allowed to remain on the fire for a full half-hour, and then set aside to settle. The coloring matter may then be withdrawn, and applied by means of a brush. The longer the mixture is allowed to boil, the darker it will be in color.

Brown.—To obtain a brown one must boil 10 2/3 ounces of campeachy wood (logwood) chopped fine, together with 1 1/15 ounces of alum, in 1 5/8 quarts of water for a full half-hour. The resulting mixture is applied as already indicated after it has been allowed to settle.

The Tyrolian violin makers employ the following process in order to give the instruments which come from their workshops an air of antiquity:

After having applied a brown color to all portions of the instrument, they dip their brushes into hot water and remove the color in those spots which are known to suffer from abrasion when the violin is constantly used, such as the half of the neck, the ring and that portion of the sound board against which the chin of the musician is pressed, as well as all other outstanding parts.

Yellow.—A very fine yellow color may be obtained by boiling 2 3/5 ounces of curcuma (tumeric) with 1 13/15 ounces of alum in 1 5/8 quarts of water. While these ingredients are boiling, one may ascertain whether the color has gained the lighter or darker shade which may be desired, by dipping a brush into it, and applying it to a piece of wood. When the color has gained the desired shade, the vessel is withdrawn from the fire, and the fluid color is taken from it and preserved for future use.

Orange Yellow.—This color is one used almost exclusively by the violin makers of Mirecourt, and is very beautiful.

In 7/8 of a quart of water boil 2 3/5 ounces of arnotto, with 1 3/10 ounces of potash. After the mixture has boiled up three or four times it should be withdrawn from the fire and allowed to stand for twenty-four hours; then the portion which is clear should be poured into a scrupulously clean bottle, and it is ready for use.

Since arnotto spoils very quickly, only a small quantity of it should be prepared at a time, and, in general, arnotto should be prepared only when needed and in the quantity required.

In making this color, as well as when decanting it into a bottle after it has been boiled, the greatest care should be taken that no foreign substance be mingled with it, since in that case the mixture would at once change and lose all its qualities.

Before boiling the arnotto it should be well ground in a small quantity of water intended for its decoction, so that it may be entirely dissolved.

Brownish Red.—This color, which is the color generally found in the old German violins, is obtained by boiling 1 3/10 ounces of arnotto with 1 3/10 ounces of Cassel yellow and 1 3/10 ounces of potassium in 7/8 of a quart of water.

As in the case of the preceding color it is necessary to grind the arnotto and the Cassel yellow before exposing them to the action of the heat.

The composition should be allowed to boil for a somewhat longer time than the one preceding, since it takes longer for the Cassel yellow to dissolve than it does for the arnotto.

After having let it stand for twenty-four hours, the liquid is decanted and poured into a bottle which should be hermetically sealed.

Mahogany Color.—This color is obtained by boiling 21 1/3 ounces of madder root together with 5 1/3 ounces of fustic or yellow wood in 1 5/8 quarts of water. By so doing a light mahogany-hued coloring fluid is obtained.

If a darker shade of mahogany is desired, 5 1/3 ounces of campeachy or sandalwood should be used in place of the yellow wood.

These colors—the light and the darker mahogany—having been applied to the wood, 1/3 of an ounce of potash should be dissolved in 7/8 of a quart of water, and a layer of this should be placed on the wood after the first coats have dried thoroughly.

How to Obtain All These Colors in Their Greatest Perfection

In preparing these colors, one must endeavor, as far as possible, to make use of river water or rain water, and to employ in the preparation of each color an earthenware pot glazed on the inside, in order that the same pot may be invariably used for the same color. While the color is boiling it should be stirred with a piece of maplewood.

An equalized fire should be maintained beneath the pots, and each pot should be withdrawn from the fire when the mixture contained in it boils up, and replaced once the ebullition has gone down.

It is well to allow coloring matter to thicken somewhat in order that the color may be a little darker than is desired, for the simple reason that it is always easy to make a color lighter later on, by adding a little water; while, on the contrary, when the color is too light, it will not answer, and it cannot be put back on the fire to boil without changing. Finally, a coal fire is preferable to a wood fire, since it is possible to regulate the heating of the pot as may be desired, by throwing a few cinders on the coal fire when the latter becomes too hot.

Colors Meant to be Mixed with Alcohol Varnishes

Black.—The only means known to us by which fine black may be obtained are the following:

A glazed earthenware dish should be filled with good ink and exposed, if it be summer, to the direct heat of the sun, if it be winter placed upon the stove, and in either case left until the liquid portion of the ink has been entirely absorbed by evaporation, leaving nothing in the dish but a kind of black deposit. With a rounded knife or a piece of wood, this black deposit is detached from the bottom of the dish, and is ground by means of a glass pestal together with a little spirits of wine; it is then mixed with the varnish in whatever quantity may be necessary to furnish a solid black color.

The Germans grind lamp black with the varnish and then apply it, a process which is much more rapid, but which yields a black offensive to the eye, since it shades over into gray.

Red.—To obtain a red color the process already explained is followed, the red being drawn after settling, as already indicated for the colors applied before varnishing. If a dark red is desired, however, one must proceed in the following manner:

In a new, glazed earthenware vessel about 2 3/5 ounces of flat lacquer, the darkest colored obtainable, should be boiled together with 1/6 of an ounce of green copperas. It is taken from the fire when approximately four hours have passed, is drawn after settling, and dried as in the case of the black. Then it is ground together with spirits of wine to be mixed with the varnish.

Brown.—In order to obtain a brown employ the same process as for black, using the color indicated in place of the ink in the preceding case for the colors applied before the varnish.

For a red-brown or brownish red, the process is exactly the same as for a black, as has already been explained on p. 101.

Yellow.—In order to obtain a yellow, all that is needed is to steep tumeric or curcuma, or else saffron in spirits of wine for about twenty-four hours, and then mix it with the varnish.

Tumeric, which also goes by the name of *terra merita,* and saffron both yield a yellow color, but there is a difference, nevertheless, between the two color principles.

There is a third drug which, dissolved in alcohol, also produces a handsome yellow: gamboge. This, however, must be dissolved in a hot-water bath. It will be shown, later on, under the head of varnishes, how the hot-water dissolved bath is employed.

Mahogany Color.—There should be steeped in 8 ounces of spirits of wine 14/15 of an ounce of tumeric and 14/15 of an ounce of dragon's blood. These ingredients should be allowed to dissolve in the spirits of wine for some four or five days, care being taken to stir the bottle containing them often, since, when the gums have thoroughly dissolved, this color is mixed with the varnish.

The quantity of tumeric or of dragon's blood to be dissolved may be somewhat in excess or somewhat less than the amounts indicated, according as the color desired is to approach more or less closely to yellow, or is to assume more of a reddish tint.

When time is an object, there is a way of making the ingredients in question dissolve more quickly, by placing the bottle containing them, loosely corked, on a warm stove, taking care to insert between bottle and stove a fourfold thickness of paper, in order to prevent the bottle from bursting in consequence of too great a development of heat.

Orange Yellow.—Place 7/8 of a quart of spirits of wine, 2 ounces of arnotto and 1/3 of an ounce of potash in a bottle, and let them steep for three days, stirring the mixture at frequent intervals. After having allowed it to stand for three days more, that portion of the liquid which has clarified should be poured, with the greatest precaution, into another bottle, in order to be mixed with the varnish later.

ORDINARY SOLID VARNISH

This varnish, like all the varnishes of the same kind which we are about to describe, might almost be said to make itself, since all that is necessary is to leave its component materials in a well-corked bottle. However, since it is well to know how any piece of work may be done quickly and well, we will indicate the process of fusion by means of a water bath which may be used for all the alcohol varnishes.

This process consists in enclosing in a bottle all the ingredients required to make a varnish.

1. The bottle in question should be at least a third larger than necessary to hold the matter contained in it.

2. The bottle should be corked with a paper cover, and one must not forget to perforate this paper cover with a needle or pin, in order to supply a vent for the air in the interior of the bottle, which, if the vent did not exist, might burst.

Once these precautions have been observed, one takes a vessel of any kind, a casserole, for instance, either made of earthenware or of tin, and places a strip of wood or some straw or sawdust at the bottom. The bottle is then placed in the casserole, or whichever one of the substances mentioned that may have been selected, in order that its bottom will not touch the bottom of the casserole itself, a contact which might result in the bursting of the glass. This done, water is poured into the casserole, care being taken that the water remains .117 inches below the liquid enclosed in the bottle. The casserole may then be placed on a coal fire which should be regulated in such manner that the bottle does not boil up too strongly. From time to time the bottle may be taken out of the water in order to see whether the ingredients it contains have entirely dissolved. When no undiscovered particles are to be seen, and the contents of the bottle have become completely merged, the casserole may be withdrawn from the fire, which then may be banked.

The bottle should then be uncorked, and the varnish strained through a linen cloth, one which is neither too fine nor too coarse. It is then poured into a second bottle, which must be absolutely clean and dry.

The varnish of which we have spoken before should be made up of the ingredients which follow in the proportions given:

Gum lac .... 5 3/5 ounces
Powdered gum sandaric .... 14/15 of an ounce
Mastic in tears .... 14/15 of an ounce
Spirits of wine .... 7/8 of a quart

Before placing these three varieties of gum in the bottle together with the spirits of wine, they should be coarsely pounded; if they are pounded too fine they will not dissolve as easily, since in that case they are inclined to cling together in mass.

The quality of the spirits of wine employed may be tested in the following manner:

One should take 3 4/5 ounces of this varnish, mix it with 16 ounces[1] of spirits of wine and add 2 ounces of prepared turpentine. All these ingredients should be enclosed in the bottle, which is exposed to the sun, or placed on a moderately heated stove. In this way a very fine varnish, one which dries in a very short time, is obtained.

GOLDEN ORANGE

Steep 1 ounce of tumeric and 23/100 ounces of oriental saffron for twenty-four hours in 26 2/3 ounces of spirits of wine. This infusion is filtered, then pounded out on a well-mixed powder composed of 1 ounce of gum gutta (gamboge Gum), 2 3/5 ounces of gum sandrach, the same amount of gum elemi, 1 13/15 ounces of dragon's blood in reeds, an equal amount of seed lac; and the whole is then dissolved in a water bath.

RED INDIA VARNISH

This varnish is prepared by dissolving in a water bath the ingredients which follow, placed in 7/8 of a quart of spirits of wine, pulverizing them before the operation:

Cochineal .... 14/15 of an ounce
Dragon's blood .... 1 13/15 ounces
Gum lac .... 1 13/15 ounces

After they have been entirely dissolved, the resulting mixture is withdrawn from the water bath and filtered before preserving for use.

---

[1] The various weights and measures here given have been translated from the metric system and every endeavor has been made to approximate them as closely as possible to our domestic equivalent. Where weight instead of measure is applied to liquids, the translation is made from the metric *gram*. "The *gram*, unit of *weight*, is a cubic centimeter of pure water at greatest density."

DRYING OIL OR OIL VARNISH

All the famous Italian and German violin makers, such as the Amati, the Stradivarii, the Stainers, and others, have made use of drying oils or oil varnishes, which are far more beautiful and also far more durable than the spirit varnishes. They have another great advantage over the latter, that of not requiring so much polishing. In addition, two layers applied to an instrument cover the wood as thoroughly as seven or eight layers of varnish prepared with spirits of wine.

The ingredients composing this varnish are: (1) resin of amber, (2) linseed oil, (3) essence of terebinth.

Before occupying one's self with the varnish, the oil must be prepared in order to render it siccative, for if it were to be employed in its original state, the varnish would take an incalculable time to dry. This oil may be rendered siccative in two different ways, the first of which is known to every house painter. The process is the following one:

Take 21 1/3 ounces of linseed oil, 14/15 of an ounce of litharge, the same amount of sulphate of lead, umbra and plaster; boil the whole in a glazed pot on a slow and even fire, taking care to skim the mixture while boiling. As soon as the scum begins to grow red and scanty, the fire is banked and the oil is allowed to settle, in order to be decanted later on in its clarified form.

It seems worth while remarking that this operation should be carried out in a yard or somewhere in the open, if possible, in order to avoid accidents and the disagreeable odor which is given off during the boiling process.

The second process does not offer these inconveniences, but is a much longer one.

Add to 1 5/8 quarts of linseed oil, 8 7/15 ounces of muriatic acid (spirit of sal ammoniac) and allow the mixture to stand until the acid has separated from the oil, which becomes clear and limpid.

A bottle is then filled one-quarter full with carefully cleansed and dried sand, and into the bottle thus prepared one part of oil and two parts of boiling water are poured, care being taken to stir the mixture several times a day. When the oil has been deposited upon the sand, it should be carefully withdrawn, the water being poured off, and the oil then replaced on its sand bed, while fresh water is poured into the bottle. The operation is repeated until the water is no longer clouded. It is then allowed to stand for several days, when the oil is placed in a clean, dry bottle.

Once the oil has thus been prepared, the preparation of the varnish itself may be undertaken.

Take 5 1/8 ounces of amber varnish, from which any extraneous matter which may have become mixed with it has been carefully removed, break this amber into fragments of the size of small peas, and place them in an iron pot which has not been used before. On these pieces of amber a ladleful of essence of terebinth is poured, and it is then placed on a coal fire where it should be allowed to boil for about a quarter of an hour, and the mixture stirred from time to time with a piece of spruce wood, care being taken to replace the cover after each stirring. When the amber varnish has entirely dissolved, the pot is withdrawn from the fire, and the mixture stirred with the stirrer until it is no longer at its highest degree of temperature. Then 2 3/5 ounces of the oil which has been prepared in the manner indicated are very carefully poured into the mixture, and the two are thoroughly amalgamated. Finally 5 1/8 ounces of essence of terebinth, colored by whichever gums may have been employed are added.

In order to color the essence of terebinth, various gums, such as dragon's blood, gamboge gum and others are taken and crushed fine, and then allowed to dissolve in the essence, in the same way that they are dissolved in spirits of wine.

Varnishes for the Bow

We will bring our consideration regarding this subject to an end by indicating how the varnish used in the manufacture of bows, to lend luster to the stick, should be prepared.

Gum lac .... 5 1/8 ounces
Dragon's blood .... 1 3/10 ounces
Copal .... 1 3/10 ounces
Spirits of wine ....21 1/3 ounces

We might here observe that this varnish is used for bow sticks of red wood, such as Brazil wood and Pernambuco wood, while in the case of bow sticks made of brown woods, such as iron wood and campeachy or logwood, the dragon's blood is omitted.

Begin by pounding the copal into a fine powder, and when this has been done, mix with it 3 4/5 ounces of very dry chalk, also ground dust-fine. These two substances should then be placed in a very narrow white glass bottle together with 10 2/3 ounces of spirits of wine, and the mouth of the bottle should be properly corked, with a double paper stopper, well tied up. By means of a pin a hole should be made in the paper stopper to prevent a possible explosion of the glass. The bottle should then be placed on a warm stove and left there for several hours. Care must be taken to place a fourfold thickness of paper between the bottle and the top of the stove. A new paper stopper should be placed in the bottle mouth every morning before replacing the bottle on the stove, and after having removed the residue which has been precipitated to the bottom of the bottle, the operation should be continued every day until the spirits of wine have assumed the color of old Xeres (Spanish wine). When, after pouring out a drop into a glass of water, the water turns white as milk, it is a sign that the copal has dissolved. It should then once more be left to settle so that the residue is sure to be well separated from the liquid, and following this should be poured carefully into another bottle. The lac and the dragon's blood, well crushed, are then added, together with the remaining half of the spirits of wine (10 2/3 ounces) which has been reserved. The substance used being essentially inflammable, the dissolving process by application of heat should be made by means of a water bath.

The varnish thus obtained is applied by means of a pad on the sticks of the arches. The process of applying by pad is carried out by laying the varnish on the piece of wood to be polished, using a rag or pad of cloth soaked in oil.

The process is as follows: a piece of white linen cloth is taken and folded back tightly on itself several times. This pad is covered with a piece of old linen on which a drop of drying oil has been placed. The surface of the cloth is then dipped in the varnish, a little being taken up at a time and the pad is then passed lightly along the stick, from one end to the other, thus warming the varnish.

As soon as it is evident that the pad sticks to the wood, it is once more dipped into the varnish, as before, and, changing the linen coverpiece, another drop of oil is placed upon it and the frictional process is resumed and continued, the varnish being distributed in the most equalized manner possible.

PRELIMINARY OPERATIONS

Before concluding the subject of color and varnishes, a word should be said anent the condition of the instrument which is to receive the coat of varnish.

Before the varnish is applied a well-edged scraper should be taken, and all exterior surfaces of the wood lightly scraped, to remove any small rough places or inequalities which may remain, as well as any particles of glue or other substances which handling may have left. This operation completed, all the exterior parts of the instrument should be polished with sandpaper.

A very clean sponge should then be taken, moistened in water, and the violin should be lightly wiped with it and allowed to dry.

Finally, these various operations should be repeated until the wood, perfectly smoothed, presents a dully varnished appearance.

When this is the case, some very clear glue should be prepared, and the instrument should be given a coat of it, and, when this coat of glue is perfectly dry, the wood should once more be polished with emery paper. The instrument is then ready to be varnished.

APPLICATION OF THE VARNISH

A special brush should be provided for each variety of color. The brushes used for varnishing should be made of very fine pig's bristles.

There should be placed in the orifice of the tailpiece of the violin a bit of wood long enough to make it possible for the violin to be held in an isolated position, when it is grasped in the left hand; it is while holding it in this position that it is varnished.

When the violin has been covered with varnish, it should be suspended by the scroll from a piece of brass wire in some well ventilated place where, however, no dust is liable to settle on it, and allowed to dry.

If the first coat of varnish does not appear to be sufficient or is not deep enough in color, a second coat may be applied, only, however, after the first has dried thoroughly. After each coat of varnish has been applied, the violin should be wiped with a piece of linen which is old and worn, but clean.

In order to apply the varnish one should begin by pouring into a clean dish the quantity considered needful for the purpose. Not much should be taken at a time.

A flat hair brush should be dipped in the varnish, and before applying the latter, it should be tried on the edge of the dish; for the varnish must be spread out as finely as possible, whatever part of the instrument is being varnished receiving but two strokes of the brush, one forward and one back.

One must wait until the first coat of varnish is perfectly dry before applying a second coat to the violin.

Finally, for the alcohol varnishes, seven or eight coats should be given, while only two are called for in the case of the oil varnishes.

The alcohol varnishes should be polished with a rag steeped in tripoli, care being taken that the hand describes small circles while rubbing.

The same place should not be rubbed too long a time, lest all the varnish itself be removed, and the rag should be dipped into oil again as soon as it seems to stick to the varnish.

The instrument then should be wiped with a piece of clean, soft linen. In order to obtain a really fine varnish, one must polish after each layer has been applied.

It is unnecessary to polish the oil varnishes. Nevertheless, if one chooses to do so, the gloss, though less pronounced, is none the less agreeable to the eye. In order to polish them one should use water, as we have indicated, and very finely powdered pumice stone which has been strained through a silk sieve.

It will be of great assistance in preparing violin varnishes for the reader to acquaint himself with the nature, character and origin of the ingredients used by carefully reading the information given in the list appended herewith:

Alum. Alum occurs in commerce as a rule in three forms: ammonium, potassium and sodium, which are used as mordants in dyeing. In the manufacture of colors, ammonia alum answers quite as well as potash alum, hence both salts are sold under the common name of alum.

Amber (amber lac). A fossil gum or resin principally found along the shores of a large part of the Baltic and North Seas, especially off the promontory of Samland. It is cast up by the sea, and collected at ebb tide with nets; and is also brought up by divers and dredging. It is partly soluble in alcohol and entirely so in chloroform. It decomposes when heated rather below 300° C., yielding "oil of amber," and a black residue called "amber pitch." This last, when dissolved in oil of turpentine or linseed oil, forms "amber varnish" or "amber lac."

Animé. See copal.

Arnotto. A small South American tree of the Indian plum family producing the yellowish-red dye also known as annatto.

Asphalt. The bituminous pitch coming principally from Trinidad, sparingly soluble in alcohol, but more so in naphtha, turpentine or ether.

Benzoin (gum benzoic). (1) A balsamic resin obtained from the *Styrax benzoni*, a tree native to Java and Sumatra, and from other varieties of the *Styrax*; (2) the *Lithocarpus benzoni*, a tree found in Siam. The Siamese benzoin occurs in the form of small "tears." This Siamese benzoin is reddish yellow to white in color, consisting of 10 to 14 per cent of benzoic acid, and the rest resin. The Sumatra benzoin occurs only in masses of dull red resin enclosing white tears.

Brazil wood. The red wood of the Brazilian *Cœsalpina* used as a dye. The dark, yellowish-red heart-wood of the *Cœsalpina echinata*, or Pernambuco wood (*bois de Fernambouc* is largely used for the making of violin bows.

Campeachy wood. See logwood.

Cassel yellow. A patent yellow pigment.

Chagual gum. See gum Arabic.

Cinnabar (vermilion). An ore of mercury, cochineal-red to lead-gray mercury sulphite, found in crystals and powder, and used as a pigment.

Cochineal. A dyestuff consisting of female cochineal insects, killed and dried by heat, which gives a brilliant scarlet dye and the pigment carmine.

Copaiba. Copaiba or Copaiva is an oleoresin from trees of the *copaifera* species found in the West Indies and the valley of the Amazon. From its golden colored, viscous liquid, there is disengaged a volatile oil.

Copal. Copal, from the Mexican copalli, incense, is a hard, lustrous resin, and the term is generally and vaguely used for resins which, though similar in physical properties, are altogether distinct as to their sources.

Mexican copal, generally considered the best, is obtained from a species of *Hymenœa*. It is tasteless, odorless, almost colorless, transparent, and lemon-yellow or yellowish brown in color. It forms one of the most valuable of varnishes when it has been dissolved in alcohol, spirits of turpentine, oil of turpentine which has been exposed to the air, or any other suitable medium. The addition of

oil of spike or rosemary promotes its solubility in alcohol. As a gum it ranks next to amber in hardness. Copal is also obtained from Sierra Leone, and, in a fossil state, from the west coast of Africa, as well as from Brazil and other South American countries, from trees of the *Guibourtia, Trachylobium and Hymenœa* families.

Anim is the hard copal resin obtained from the *Hymenœa courbaril*, a South American tree; while gum animé is the name also given to the resin known in commerce as Zanzibar or East African copal. The raw copal yielded by the Zanzibar *Trachylobium hornemannianum* is inferior, and used only in India and China for making a coarse varnish. The fossil East African copal is dug from the ground over a wide belt of the mainland coast of Zanzibar. A gum obtained from the *Vateria indica* is also known as gum animé, and is often confused with true copal in commerce.

Curcuma. See tumeric.

Dragon's blood. The best gum dragon or dragon's blood is obtained from the *Calamus draco*, a rotang or mattan palm of the eastern Archipelago and India. It is a dark red-brown in color, brittle, nearly opaque, and when ground supplies a fine red powder soluble in ether, alcohol and fixed and volatile oils. Much of the dragon's blood of commerce is obtained from the *Pterocarpus draco*, of South America.

Elemi (gum elemi). This is a fragrant resin obtained from the Egyptian *Amyris elemifera* and the Mexican *Elaphirium elemiferum*, and is greenish yellow and semitransparent. The oleoresin known as Manilla elemi is obtained in the Philippines, probably from the *Canarium commune*, and is pale yellow in color, soluble in alcohol. In the 17th and 18th centuries the term elemi usually denoted a Brazilian elemi obtained from trees of the *icœiu* species.

Gamboge (gum gutta). Externally a dirty orange in color, gamboge, which occurs in commerce as pipe or roll gamboge, which is purer, and cake gamboge, inferior in quality, is a gum resin coming from Cambodia and Siam. It is tasteless, hard and brittle, affords a brilliant yellow powder, and is often adulterated with rice-powder or pulverized bark.

Garance (Fleur-de-garance or madder-bloom). This "flowers of madder" is a refined dyestuff obtained by macerating commercial madder.

Gum arabic. Gum arabic is of the type of the gums which are entirely soluble in water. It is obtained from a variety of sources as it exists in the juices of almost all plants. It is largely obtained from the *Acacia arabica* of Nort.. Africa and eastern Asia, and varies in color from straw yellow to deep red. Varieties are: gum senegal produced by the *Acacia verek*, occurring in rounded pieces, reddish or yellow, and supplying a very clear, tough mucilage. Shagual gum, from Santiago, Chili, resembles gum senegal.

Lac or gum lac. This is a resinous incrustation formed of the twigs of various trees by an infesting insect, the *Coccus lacca*, allied to the cochineal insect, in the East Indies and southeastern Asia. To obtain the largest amount of both resin and red dyestuff, which is segregated in the ovaries of the females, the twigs with their living inhabitants are gathered in June and November. "Stick lac" is the lac encrusting the twigs when gathered; the resin crushed small and washed in hot water to free it from coloring matter is known as "seed lac," and this, melted and strained is the "shellac" of commerce. Lac forms the basis of some of the most valuable of varnishes.

Litharge. Lead monoxid, straw yellow in color and used as a pigment.

Logwood. The Mexican and Central American *Hæmatoxylon campechianum* supplies the dark red heart wood, whose color pigments readily dissolve in boiling water. It is also known as campeachy wood.

Madder. The Dutch *Rubia tinctorum* is the plant whose peeled roots supply madder, a pigment whose coloring principle is alizarin. The madders are brown, madder carmine and madder orange in color.

Mastic (gum mastic). A resinous exudation from the lentisk, *Pistacia leatiscus,* an evergreen shrub found along the Mediterranean coast, Portugal, Morocco and the Canaries. Mastic occurs in commerce in the form of roundish tears as large as peas, transparent, with a pale yellow or greenish tinge. It is soluble in alcohol and oil of turpentine.

Muriatic acid. Hydrochloric acid; a corrosive gaseous compound, very soluble in water, generally sold under the name of muriatic acid.

Oil of lavender. The product of the distillation of flowers of lavender with water. The variety most often used for varnishes is oil of spike, obtained from the *Lavandula latifolia.*

Orpiment. An arsenic-sulphur combination yielding a brilliant yellow color known as king's yellow.

Pernambuco wood. See Brazil wood.

Saffron. The dried, deep orange-colored stigmas of the saffron plant, *Crocus sativus,* which yield a much-used pigment for coloring varnishes.

Sal ammoniac. A soluble ammonium chlorid, white in color, and vitreous.

Sandalwood. This wood, much used as a dye, is not the *Santalum yasi,* but the *Pterocarpus santalunis,* and grows in India and Ceylon. The close grained heart wood is a dark red in color.

Sandarach. This is a yellowish transparent resin obtained from the *Callitris quadrivalvis,* a conifer of northwest Africa; analogous resins coming from the *Callitris sineusis* of China and the *C. reessii* of South Australia, which last product is known as pine gum. Sandarach reaches commerce in the form of small round balls or elongated tears, is yellow in color, and somewhat harder than mastic for which it is sometimes substituted. *True* Sandarach is obtained from the common juniper, and is another name for juniper gum.

Sulphate of lead. A mixture of lead carbonate and hydrated oxid, used as a pigment.

Terebinth. The liquid oleoresinous exudation of the *Pistacia terebinthus,* a small tree common in southern Europe and the Mediterranean area, known as Chian, Scio or Cyprian turpentine.

Tragacanth (gum tragacanth). This gum, a product of the *Astragalus tragacantha,* comes from Smyrna and Constantinople, occurs in opaque whitish flakes, and is an excellent thickener of colors. It may be considered one of the varieties of gum arabic.

Tumeric. Tumeric, *terra merita* or curcuma (*safran d'Inde:* Indian saffron), is made of the old roots of the *Curcuma longa,* a plant of the ginger family; and curcumin is the yellow compound contained in this root.

Turpentine. The oleoresins which exude from certain trees, especially of the conifer family. These resins are separated by distillation into rosin or colophony, and oil or spirit of turpentine. Venetian or Venice turpentine, collected principally in the Tyrol, from the larch tree, is the most esteemed variety. The result of its distillation with water is a colorless volatile oil (essential oil or spirits of turpentine) soluble in alcohol, ether and other oils, and a ready solvent of nearly all resins. Cyprian turpentine is inferior in quality to the Venice turpentine.

Umber. A hydrated ferric oxid, chestnut brown to liver brown in color, used as a pigment. As found in nature, the oxid is called raw umber, and when heated, so as to produce a reddish brown, is known as burnt umber.

Vermilion. See cinnabar.

Lesser used gums include: frankincense, the pinkish, fragrant exudation of the silver fir; *Aloes hepatica,* a brown resin from Socotra (Bombay aloes); and myrrh, the resin of the Arabian and Baesynnian *Balsamodendron myrrha,* exuded in thick yellow drops, and found in commerce in the shape of tears and lumps, varying from yellow to reddish brown.

CHAPTER VI

THE VIOLIN BOW

EUROPEAN BOW MAKERS

The following is as complete a list of the most famous bow makers as is possible, in view of the meager sources of information:

ADAM, JEAN DOMINIQUE, 1795 to 1864. Pupil and successor to his father Jean Adam. Only the best of his work was labeled with his trade-mark. His bows with an eight-cornered stick were very much in demand.

BAROUX, ——. Very little is known about Baroux beyond the fact that he was an extremely skillful maker.

BURR, ——, Paris.

CASADESUS, ——, Paris.

DODD, JOHN, 1752 to 1839. This distinguished bow maker is esteemed as much in England as Tourte is in France. His bows are fully equal to those of his French rival, even if they do not attain the same degree of elegance. His sticks have the one fault of not being long enough. Although he was always working, and was often given financial aid by rich people, he died in a workhouse at the age of eighty-seven. He never had a pupil, as he did not want the secret of his pattern known to any one. Many times, although in dire need of funds, he refused offers of 1000 pounds sterling for a copy of his pattern. At the present time his bows are in great demand at high prices.

FONCLAUZE, HEHRY, Mirecourt, about 1812.

FONCLAUZE, JOSEPH, 1800 to 1864. One of the best French bow makers. He was trained by Dominique Pecate in Mirecourt and in 1820 went to Paris, working first for Lupot, then for Tourte, and, finally, for ten years for J. B. Vuillaume. In 1840 he started to work independently. Most of his bows carry his name as trade-mark.

LAFLEUR, JACQUES, 1760 to 1832. Lafleur's bows are better known than his violins. He was an apprentice under François Tourte. His bows are noted for their elasticity and lightness.

LAFLEUR, JOSEPH RENÉ. Son, pupil and successor to Jacques Lafleur. He was originally a violinist and only later turned to bow making. Several fine specimens of his work are in the museum of the Paris Conservatory; also a bow with a flat stick.

LAMY, ALFRED JOSEPH, 1850. One of the best French bow makers of all time. In 1862 he started as an apprentice with Ch. A. Husson and left him in 1868 to work with Goutrot in Château-Thierry. From 1877 to 1885 he was with Voirin, after whose death he worked independently, always considering Voirin his real teacher. In 1889, he received the silver and gold medals at the Paris Exposition.

LUPOT, FRANÇOIS, 1774 to 1837. One of the sons of François I, and a brother of Nicolas. He was principally a bow maker, although he claims to be a pupil of Stradivarius, but this has always been questioned. His bows are considered among the best in France.

MARIE, NICOLAS, Mirecourt.

NURNBERGER BROTHERS.

Franz Albert I, son of Karl Gottlieb Nurnberger, was a widely known bow maker, and founder of a bow-making school in Markneukirchen where he was the instructor for twenty-five years.

Franz Albert II established himself as a maker in 1880, and used Vuillaume, Tubbs and Tourte bows as models. He is now one of the most prominent bow makers in the world.

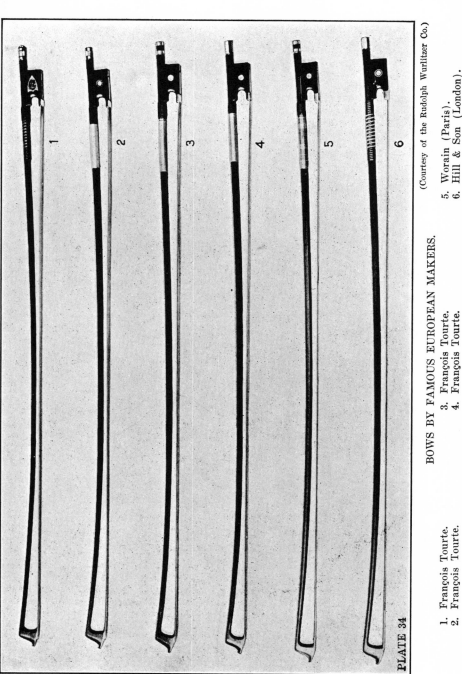

PLATE 34

BOWS BY FAMOUS EUROPEAN MAKERS.

1. François Tourte.
2. François Tourte.
3. François Tourte.
4. François Tourte.
5. Worain (Paris).
6. Hill & Son (London).

Johann Christoph, a highly skilled bow maker who worked more than five years with Vuillaume.

Karl Albert, another greatly esteemed bow maker.

Philipp Paul, son of Franz Albert II, who established himself as a bow maker in 1897, and has acquired an enviable reputation.

PANORMO, GEORGES LOUIS, 1774 to 1842. Son of Vincenzo Panormo, and also a violin and guitar maker, although his bows have made his reputation. Panormo was the successor of John Dodd, the famous English maker.

PECATE, DOMINIQUE, 1810 to 1874. An apprentice to J. B. Vuillaume from 1826 to 1837, after which he established himself as a bow maker. His sticks equal, and in some ways surpass, those of Tourte. Unfortunately he seldom used a distinguishing trade-mark, making recognition of his work possible only to experts.

PERSODT.

PFRETZCHNER, HERMAN RICHARD, 1857. An excellent bow maker, first a pupil of his father, and later of J. B. Vuillaume in Paris. In 1880 he established his own business, working on the Tourte and Voirin models. He created the Wilhelmji bow which is used by the greatest artists. His sticks are not varnished and bear the name H. R. Pfretzchner.

SARTORY, ——, Paris. An excellent bow maker and pupil of his father. He went to Paris in 1890 to Charles Peccatte (not "Peccate"), then to Alfred Lamy and in 1893 established his own business. His bows are marked "Sartory."

SCHWARTZ, GEORGE FREDERIC, 1785 to 1849. Son and pupil of Bernhard Schwartz. He assumed charge of his father's business in 1821, making exclusively bows, trade-marked "Schwartz Strassbourg." They were formerly in great demand, although they appear a little too heavy for use at the present time.

SIRJEAN, ——, Paris. A bow maker of great distinction who established himself in Paris. Little is known of his antecedents or career.

TOURTE, FRANÇOIS, 1747 to 1835. The "Stradivarius" of the art of bow making. He was originally a watchmaker, and after working at this trade for eight years joined his father and brother in making bows. The painstaking accuracy learned at watchmaking was of such great benefit to him at his new trade, that in a short time he attained great results and rose to be one of the best masters. At first he used the staves of old sugar barrels for his bows, which he sold for from twenty to thirty sous. He soon found out however that the principal part of a good bow was the wood, and after experimenting with different kinds, he selected Pernambuco (Brazil wood). This was in 1775 to 1780, and after that time he worked ceaselessly to improve his bows and at last gave them their present form, receiving—instead of twenty sous—fifteen Louis d'Or for each one. Every bow not entirely faultless was destroyed. He never varnished his bows but only rubbed them with pumice powder and oil. At the age of seventy-seven he was still making bows, and familiarly known as "Tourte le jeune" (Tourte the young).

TUBBS, London. A family of prominent bow makers for four generations. The name of the present firm is James Tubbs and Son, Wardour Street 94, London. All the bows made by members of this famous family are of the highest grade, and greatly sought after by collectors and artists.

ULLMAN, GEORGES, Milan.

VOIRIN, FRANÇOIS NICOLAS, 1833 to 1885. Brother of Joseph Voirin. After learning the art of violin making, he came to Vuillaume in 1855 and stayed with him for fifteen years, after which time he established himself as a bow maker. In France he was given the title "the modern Tourte." English dealers and violin makers made tempting offers to him to work for them, but he refused them all, saying that his work belonged to his country. His bows carry the trade-mark "F. N. Voirin." Among his pupils may be mentioned the famous maker Alfred Lamy.

PLATE 35

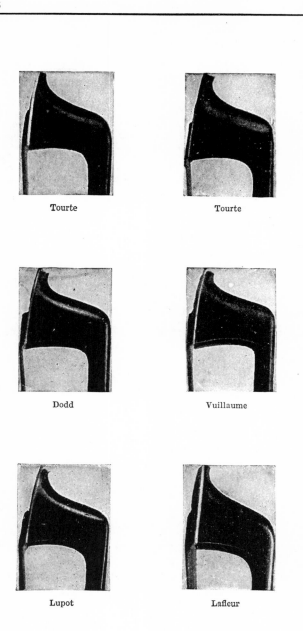

Tourte   Tourte

Dodd   Vuillaume

Lupot   Lafleur

(Courtesy of August Gemunder & Sons)

BOW HEADS DESIGNED BY FAMOUS MAKERS.

American Bow Makers

A number of bow makers, some of foreign birth and several American born, reside in the United States, and produce bows of real excellence. The following list will prove of interest:

ALDRED, JOHN, Buffalo, N. Y.	MANY, JOHN A., Washington, D. C.
BENDER, E. W., Newman, Ill.	MATHEWSON, C. H., Providence, R. I.
COPLAND, J. N., Chicago, Ill.	REINDAHL, KNUTE, Madison, Wisc.
CUSHMAN, JOHN, Collins, O.	ROBINSON, ROBERT, Portland, Ore.
GUETTER, JULIUS, Philadelphia, Pa.	ROY, BEN J., Seattle, Wash.
KARR, ALBERT H., Kansas City, Mo.	TUBBS, EDWARD, New York City.
KNOPF, HENRY R., New York City.	VALIANCE, FRED G., Detroit, Mich.
LYEKI, LOUIS, St. Louis, Mo.	ZIMMERMAN, JAMES S., Asheville, N. C.

Construction of the Bow

It is absolutely essential that the violinist have some knowledge of the construction of this mysterious wand which, externally of incomparable lightness and elegance in appearance, is nevertheless subjected to the hardest usage. The building of the violin bow has attained its present day perfection largely owing to the genius of the French craftsmen of the Tourte family, the greatest of whom was François Tourte, who died in Paris in 1835.

Vuillaume has the following to say anent the Tourte bow:

"Tourte established the length of the violin bow, from one end to the other, as being between 29.13 inches and 29.52 inches.

"The bow is composed of a cylindrical or prismoid portion whose dimensions are fixed, and whose length is 110 millimeters (4 3/10″). When this portion of the bow is cylindrical it is about one-third of an inch in diameter.

"From this cylindrical or prismoid portion on, the diameter of the bow decreases until its head has been reached, where it is deduced that the stick has ten points where its diameter is necessarily reduced 3/10 mm. (2/27″), beginning at the cylindrical portion.

"I discovered, by examining a large number of Tourte bows, that these ten points are always found at lessening distances from each other; and this not alone in the case of one and the same stick, but that on various other bows which I have compared as well, the distances between the points were practically the same."

Vuillaume carried on investigations for the purpose of discovering whether it would not be possible to verify the positions of these ten points graphically, so that they could be exactly determined in every case. If this could be done, it would be possible to construct bows whose excellence would always be fixed in advance. Vuillaume achieved his purpose in the following manner:

"At the end of the straight line AB (Plate 37), having a length of 0 m, 700 (27 5/10″), that is to say, the length of the bow, a perpendicular

PLATE 36

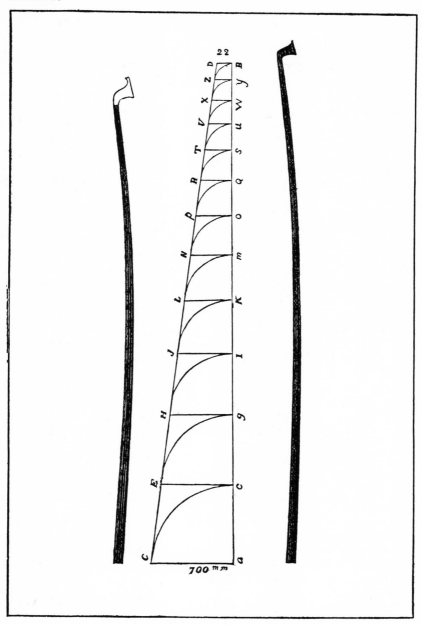

CHART FOR CALCULATING BOW MEASUREMENTS.

line, *AC*, is drawn, representing the length of the cylindrical portion, that is, 0 m, 110 (4 3/10″). At the extremity, *B*, of the same line, another perpendicular one is drawn, *BD*, whose length is 0 m, 022 (17/20″); and a straight line, *CD*, is used to unite the upper extremities of these two perpendicular lines or uprights in such wise that between them the two lines *AB* and *CD* form an angle.

"Setting down the length, 0 m, 110 (4 3/10″) of the upright *AC*, by means of the compasses, this length is carried back upon *AB*, and at its extremity another upright, *EF*, is ruled until the line *CD* is met, the new upright *EF*, consequently, being shorter than the upright *AC*. It is between these two uprights *AC* and *CF*, that the cylindrical portion of the violin bow is located, its diameter being, as has already been established, 0 m, 008 6/10 (1/3″).

"Now, having established the length of the upright *EF*, it is brought back to the line *AB*, starting from the point *F*, and a point *G* results, on which a third upright, *GH*, is ruled, whose length is also established in order to bring it back from point *G* on the *AB* line, and to fix a new point, *I*, on which the fourth upright, *IJ*, is ruled, whose length similarly brought back to line *AB*, establishes the point at which the fifth upright, *KL*, is ruled. This, under the same conditions, established the sixth *MN*, and the procedure is continued in this manner until the upright before the last is reached.

"The points *G, I, K, M, O, Q, R, S, V, W* and *Y*, thus obtained after starting from point *E*, are those at which the diameter of the bow is successively reduced 3/10 of a millimeter (about 2/27″).

"Now these points have been determined by the successively decreasing lengths of the uprights ruled on the said points, and their respective distances from one another are decreased progressively, from point *E* to point *B*.

"If these results are submitted to mathematical consideration, it will be found that the profile of the bow is represented by a logarithmic whose uprights increase in arithmetical progression; while the long lines increase in geometric progression, so that in the end the curvature of the bow profile may be expressed in the following equation:

$$\text{gr} - 3, 11 \quad 2, 5 \, \log. \, X$$

and by varying the *X* from 175 to 765 tenths of a millimeter, the values corresponding will be those of the rays.

"Thus the exact theoretic schema of the violin bow may be formulated. By an analogous process of line drawing, it is easy to establish the proportions of the viola bow and of the violoncello bow."

Another important point, which calls for elucidation is that of the bow with fixed nut, and we give the following explanation of the invention in Vuillaume's own words:

"The bows of stringed instruments, as they have hitherto been constructed, present two serious disadvantages, admitted by all artists: the first lies in the difficulty experienced in arranging the hairs in such wise that they form a perfectly flat ribbon along their entire length; in fact, it is decidedly rare to find bows whose hair is properly arranged. The second disadvantage is that the nut, to which one of the ends of the length of hairs is affixed, is constantly changing position, and that hence the length of the hairs necessarily varies. In consequence the artist, whose thumb should always remain near the nut, places it at various distances from the head of the bow itself, which varies the length and, as a result, the weight of this part of the bow stick, which is sufficient to disturb the extreme tactile sensitiveness which is transmitted from the artist's hand to the head of the bow.

"To remedy these two disadvantages it would be necessary, on the one hand, to find a less crude method of fastening the hairs, and on the other, to see to it that the nut be made immovable. I believe that I have succeeded in accomplishing this double task.

"The nut ordinarily is made of ebony, is hollow inside, and always fixed to the stick; the hairs are attached to a kind of inner nut, made of copper, which is set in movement, as in the case of the ordinary violin, by means of a nut screw fixed in the stick.

"As may be seen, the inner nut is able to move forward or backward as much as may be necessary, without the hairs comprised between the head and the exterior nut of the bow being in any way affected. The ribbon of hair used for the violin bow is formed of hairs carefully arranged parallel to one another, side by side, and are uniformly strung and solidly fixed at each of their extremities in a species of cylindrical wedge.

"The inner nut and the head of the bow are pierced on each side to receive these small wedges, in such a way that the artist himself may place the ribbon of his bow hair with the greatest ease, and hence may renew it whenever he desires."

In addition to François Tourte, John Dodd, known as "the English Tourte" in his native land, should not be forgotten. He was the only contemporary of the great Tourte himself to acquire a European reputation. His bows are remarkably well made,· but, unfortunately, somewhat too short.

In his splendid work, *La Lutherie et les Luthiers,* Antoine Vidal says, anent Dodd:

"I am indebted to Dr. Selle, of Richmond, who knew John Dodd for forty odd years, for some biographical notes regarding this master, which I take pleasure in communicating:

"I first met John Dodd in Kew, when I was no more than twelve years of age. At that time he made me a violin bow remarkable for its length and elegant shape. A distinguished teacher in Kew, Mr. Richard Platt, was his patron, and later this gentleman and myself did much to support him, not alone by buying his bows, but also by coming to his assistance at times when he lacked the common necessities of life.

"We visited him at the Richmond workhouse, where he died on October 4, 1839, of bronchitis, at the age of eighty-seven. He was buried in Kew, and not, as Forster declares, in Richmond.

"He was very small of figure and tripped rather than walked along. He was negligent in his dress, wore a wretched coat, old and frayed, short breeches and a broad-brimmed hat. He was most regular in his irregular habits, even to visiting the bars and public houses four times a day. His favorite beverage was a mixture of gin and beer called 'purl.'

"He would never consent to take an apprentice, insisting that he did not wish to initiate any one into his manner of building bows, and it has been said on good authority that he refused £1,000 which was offered him for his secret.

"On his deathbed, when asked whether he were a Catholic or a Protestant, he replied: 'A little of both.'"

Louis Panormo, the son of the violin maker Louis Panormo, succeeded Dodd in the mastery of bow manufacture, and his bows are much esteemed by violinists and command a high price.

THE BOW

For each one of the string instruments which have been considered in the first part of this work, there exists a particular variety of bow. The bow of the violin has a length of 73 centimeters (29 1/2").

The viola bow differs from the violin bow in only one respect: its stick is somewhat heavier, since the viola bow is obliged to cause strings to vibrate which are larger than the violin strings.

The bow of the bass or violoncello is 67 centimeters (25") long.

Double-bass bows are infinitely varied in form and dimension, and nothing very definite can be said regarding them. Incidentally, they are so easy to make, that the first chance craftsman at home in cabinet work could make a double-bass bow once he has seen one.

The same does not hold good of the other bows; making a violin bow, for instance, calls for a great deal of skill, and an experienced hand, and workmen who can make good violin bows are very rare.

The bows of the violin, the viola and the violoncello are haired with white horsehair. Black hair is always taken for those of the double bass; the stronger the better. The idea that red horsehair is preferable to white—it is sometimes recommended on the theory that it "bites" better, consequent on the action of the dye—is a mere fallacy, an increased coarseness of tone being the only noticeable results of its use.

PLATE 37

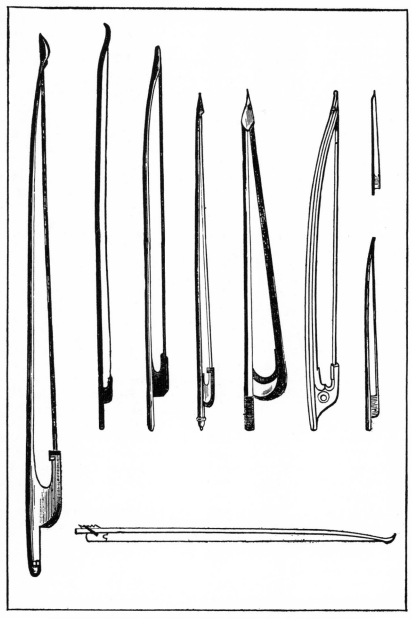

ANCIENT FORMS OF BOWS FOR STRINGED INSTRUMENTS.

Bows that are at all expensive are made of the wood used in cabinet work, such as campeachy wood, iron wood, Brazil wood, Pernambuco wood and others. The nut is made of ebony and, sometimes, ivory.

The best among the woods just mentioned is Pernambuco wood. Hence any really fine violin bow seen these days is made of this wood, the hardness and flexibility of which cause it to be preferred to all other woods in the manufacture of bow sticks.

Iron wood, too, is not without its good qualities, and is especially well adapted for the making of violoncello bows. Aside from the fact that it is somewhat heavy, however, it also has a great tendency to warp, and the bows made of it are rarely altogether straight.

Bows are also made of local woods of various kinds, but the best of them are not worth much.

Tools Used in Bow Making

The bow maker does not need nearly as many tools as does the violin maker. The tools he uses are the following:

A work bench similar to that employed by the violin maker, clamps, two steel planes, drills, chisels, knives, saws, files, a bench vise, and a hand vise.

The Steel Planes.—The first of these steel planes resemble an ordinary plane (Fig. 1). The only difference is one of dimension, the bow maker's plane being smaller. This plane is 14 centimeters long by 3 centimeters broad (5 1/2″ by 1 1/5″) at its base.

Figure 1, Plate 38, represents the small steel plane: *A,* the plane ready mounted; *B,* the base. It is made like the steel planes used by the violin makers.

The Drill.—Figure 2, Plate 38, represents this tool, which is familiar, since there is not a locksmith who does not possess one, although it has probably been replaced in modern bow-making shops by a more modern type.

In order to set this in movement a so-called bow drill is required. This bow drill is a dagger or sword blade recurved at its point so as to form a hook to which a strip of leather or a violoncello *D* string is fixed. Two or three turns are given the drill, and the strip or string is then fixed to the handle of the bow drill, while by alternate pushing and pulling back a rotary movement is communicated to the drill.

The vise *B* serves to hold down the platform of the drill, and prevents it from jumping while it turns. In the inner part of the end *C,* a square has been made into which the end of the drill fits. This square is about 2 centimeters (about 4/5 of an inch) deep, and the drill is fixed in this square by means of the small vise, *D.*

The bow maker should be provided with drills of various dimensions, and all these drills should, naturally, be made so that they are in proportion to the respective holes they are intended to bore. Thus, two are needed for the violin bow.

PLATE 38

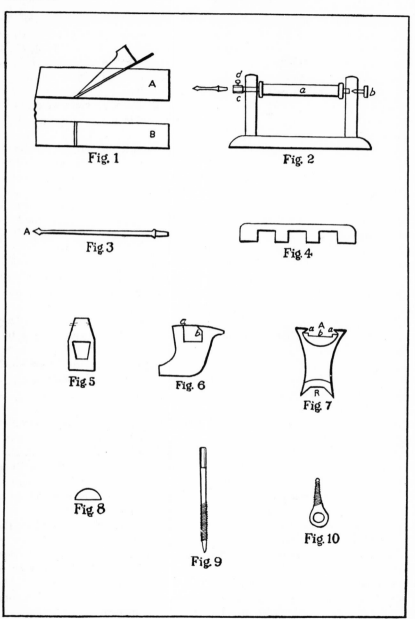

TOOLS AND MODELS FOR BOW MAKING.

One of these drills is intended to bore the hole in the lower end of the stick which is to hold the screw that makes the nut advance and recede, as well as to drill the holes meant to open the wedge box in which the clamp which holds one side of the nut, and whose screw turns in the said wedge box, is to be placed.   Finally, the same drill may also be used to bore the hole which is to receive the plate which carries the screw in the nut.

Another drill, larger but shorter, will serve to drill the holes in the head of the stick and at the nut which are intended to hold the hair, as will be explained later.

The drill (Fig. 3, Plate 38), is made of steel highly tempered at the point. This double-faced point should be beveled so as to form narrow cutting edges, and one edge should be on each face of the drill, so cut that one and the same rotary movement allows them to bite into the wood simultaneously.

The points of the drill alone should be tempered, since, were the entire drill to be tempered, it would break too easily.   These are, practically, all the tools used for drilling the holes.

In general it is well to have all the steel tools and iron tools made by a tool maker, or by some workman who is accustomed to tempering metals, since he will invariably make a better job of it than a stranger unacquainted with this sort of work, who will only make one good drill in a hundred.   One must have a special drill for each kind of bow.

The Chisels.—The bow makers' chisels are very short, and rightly so.   They are fitted into wooden handles in mushroom form, and they look exactly like an engraving chisel.

Two inches of blade and as many of handle is the correct proportion which this tool should have.   If it were larger it would be cumbersome, and, in addition, the person using it would be liable to cut himself.

The tools should not be very long, so that the hand which is using them has all the more strength to force them to bite into the wood of the bow, which is always very hard.

These chisels are adapted to the various species of chiseling for which they are intended.   Thus, the chisel used to cut out the wedge box in the head and in the nut should be larger than the one used to cut out the lower mortise in the stick.   By merely looking at a well-made chisel, one can at once recognize the proportions which the various bow making tools should have.

The Knives.—Since these are in all respects similar to those used by the violin maker, we refer the reader to the first part of this work.

The Saws.—Two saws are all that are needed in bow making.   One saw, 16 centimeters long by 4 centimeters broad (6 3/10″ by 1 3/5″), mounted in the German style, serves to divide the wood which furnishes the stick.   The blade of this saw must be very highly tempered, since otherwise it will not long resist the extreme hardness of the wood which it is used to saw.

The other saw, a spring saw, very fine-toothed, clamped (a hack-saw) is used to saw iron, brass, ivory, mother-of-pearl and, in general, all hard substances used in bow making. It is a tool which may be purchased in any hardware shop.

The Files.—Files of various sizes and forms are necessary to the bow maker.

For the stick, flat files and half-round files, as we will explain later, are used; while round files are required for the nut.

These files, in general, should be fine rather than coarse, but not too fine. Practice and experience will soon teach the user which files are best adapted for various purposes.

The Drawing Plate and Its Gauges.—This is another tool which may be purchased ready-made at a tool shop, and all that need be done when choosing it is to select one whose guide screws are in conformity with the article which is to be made. To this end one should calculate the size of the smallest hole of the drawing plane on a violin bow screw, and the largest size of the largest on the bow screw of a double bass.

The Vises.—Finally, the bow-maker must have two vises: one with a jaw or clamp width of 7 centimeters (2 3/4″), and a screw and plate at one end by means of which it may be fixed to the end of a board, which in turn is attached to the workbench by means of a jack. In addition a small hand vise which serves to clamp the small pieces which cannot be held in the hand, such as the screw of the nut, the screw of the bow, etc., is necessary. Both these tools may be purchased in a hardware shop.

Scrapers are also tools which the bow maker uses. Having described them in the first part of this work, it is needless to revert to them here.

The Actual Making of a Bow

Like the violin maker, the bow maker also has different models, which are made on planks or boards of hard wood, about 2 or 3 millimeters (about 1/8″) thick.

The most important among these models is that of the stick. In order to obtain it, the first thing to do is to secure a bow which leaves nothing to be desired as regards beauty and shapeliness.

Then a small piece of flat wood should be taken, and three small notches, like those shown in Figure 4, Plate 39, should be cut in it.

This small piece of wood will serve as a guide to establish the various thicknesses which the bow should show along its length.

The largest notch should have the exact thickness of the end of the stick, where it joins the button of the screw. The second notch should show the exact thickness at the middle of the stick. The third notch, finally, should give the exact thickness of the stick at the head of the bow.

PLATE 39

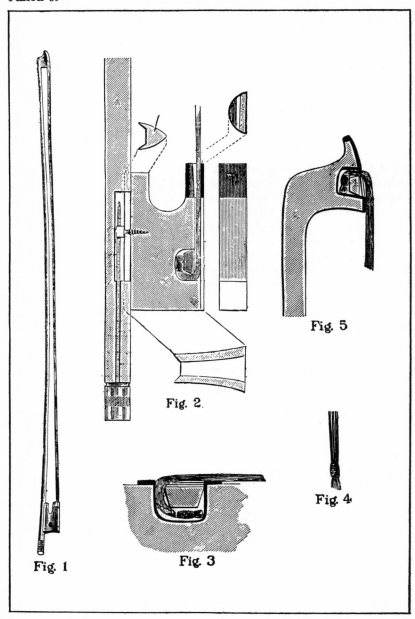

Fig. 5

Fig. 2

Fig. 4

Fig. 1

Fig. 3

THE VIOLIN BOW AND ITS PARTS BEFORE ASSEMBLY.

1. A complete bow.   2. Working parts of frog.
3. Method of wedging hair in frog.   4. Method of tying hair.
5. Method of wedging hair in head.

How the Stick is Made

One of the greatest essentials in making a good violin bow is the proper choice of the wood of which it is to be made. One should guard against using a piece of wood which a glance shows to be full of knots, cracks or other defects, for any labor spent on it would be a total loss. Any bow which has these defects in the wood of which it was originally made will not remain straight, nor will it possess the elasticity which should be its first recommendation.

When a good, healthy piece of wood has been chosen, one whose grain instead of being twisted is very straight, one should begin planing and trimming one of the faces of the piece of wood in question. The face to be trimmed should be selected in such a way as to get as much out of the wood as possible, for the woods used in cabinet making, Pernambuco wood, for example, are very dear.[1]

Taking for granted then, that the piece of wood of which the bow is to be made has been cut lengthwise, say to a length of 73 centimeters (29″) and that one of its faces offers a breadth sufficient to make two bows of it, one upon another; while the other face is only large enough to supply a bow and a half bow, the wood should be resplit in such a manner that the back of the stick will be on the side or face of which it is impossible to make two bows from the same surface of wood.

The model is first placed on the trimmed face of which mention has been made, and the outlines of the model are traced with a piece of chalk, placing the model in such a way that the grain of the wood conforms to the grain of the model as closely as possible. This done, the compasses are used to trace the thickness of the stick on the side which forms a right angle with that of which the model of the stick has just been traced.

It is necessary to remark in connection with this operation, that the stick of the bow should be split in such a manner that it measures at least 2 millimeters (about 1/10″) over and above all its actual future dimensions, in order that later on these exact dimensions may be definitely established by means of the necessary tools.

The piece of wood is then clamped in the workbench vise, and the stick-to-be is cut out by means of a circular saw.

---

[1] At the time when Tourte made his famous bows, from about 1775 to 1780, the wars carried on at sea between France and England, with their consequent interruptions of commerce, presented a serious obstacle to the importation of Pernambuc or Pernambuco wood on the continent, and the price of the precious dye wood rose to five shillings a pound. The rarity of the wood at the time Tourte made his bows explains the enormous prices the maker asked and received for them. He sold a bow with tortoise-shell nut, inlay mother-of-pearl head, and gold-mounted nut and button for nearly £12. His best silver-mounted bows with ebony nuts sold for about £3, 3s, and his ordinary unmounted bows fetched some 30 shillings.

The wood is then once more dressed with the plane, and the operation repeated until the work is finished.

When the sticks have thus been cut out into rough forms, they should be trimmed down, following the outlines of the model.

A large steel plane should be taken, and that side of the stick which shows the marks of the circular saw should first be planed smooth.

Then one should begin to plane the sticks toward one end, holding them by the head with the left hand, and resting the body of the stick on the workbench in order that the plane may be guided in the desired direction.

In this manner the two sides are first planed, great care being taken to look at them frequently, and to note whether, beginning at the end of the stick, its back is in straight alignment with the top of the head. When the two slides have been properly trimmed, and their thickness properly diminished in proportion as the head is approached, the back and belly of the stick should be trimmed, taking care to make the four faces form a perfect square, whose back or under side, once properly aligned with the head of the stick, will serve as a foundation for the work which remains to be done.

This accomplished, one must endeavor to place the end of the stick in the gauge (Fig. 4, Plate 38), in order to know exactly whether or not it has the right degree of thickness, and then plane down the four faces until this degree of thickness has been obtained.

The same gauge should be used for the middle and for the end which is near the head of the stick, in order to supply the necessary thickness. The bow must in this instance be taken in the left hand at its lower extremity, and should be planed, pushing the plane somewhat obliquely toward the head of the bow, thus giving it the three dimensions of thickness indicated by the gauge, while at the same time seeing to it that the square form of the stick is preserved.

The knife is then taken in hand, and any excess of thickness is carefully removed on each side of the head of the stick, without however, cutting away more wood on one side than on the other.

The next thing to do is to prepare the piece of ivory which embellishes the tip of the head, and which is known as the plate (Figure 5, Plate 38).

In order to give the ivory plate the form it should have the following process should be observed:

After cutting out a piece of ivory about 3 millimeters (about 1/8″) thick with the circular saw, its other dimensions being in conformity, a piece of wood is clamped in the vise upon which the plate is rested, and it is filed until it has assumed the curved form necessary for the upper face of the head, leaving a small elevation which rises above the front of the head. Then the plate should be fitted to the head, and should be filed until it adjusts itself perfectly. It is then glued fast to the bow head, is tightened by means of a band, and left to dry.

It would be advisable for those who wish to experiment with bow making always to have a well-constructed bow in sight, to serve as a model, since even the most detailed explanations are not always sufficient.

We have left the bow in a square form. The time has now come to give it an octagonal or round shape. If one desires that the bow be entirely octagonal from one end to the other, the four edges which form the four faces of the stick must be planed down equally with a small plane, care being taken never to remove more wood in one place than in another, so that the octagons may be perfectly regular. In order to plane down these four edges, the bow is taken in the left hand by the head end and placed on the workbench, with the end of the stick turned toward the body.

There is one portion of the stick which the planes cannot reach, that portion of the belly which lies near the head, and here the file must take the place of the plane.

If the stick is to be round, it is first blocked out in octagons as already described, and then, always using the small plane, the edges of each of these eight octagons are planed away. This is the only manner by which a stick can be given proper roundness.

Before attempting to give the stick either an octagonal or a round shape, the wedge box which is intended to hold the ribbon of the hair, should be dug in its head.

One should take a drill whose size is in proportion to the size which one wishes to give the wedge box, and at the proper place in the head of the bow a hole 7 millimeters (1/4″) deep should be made; then, holding the head of the bow firmly in place on the workbench with the left hand, take a chisel whose dimensions are suited to the purpose in the right hand, and give the hole the square form which has already been traced on the plate, as shown in Figure 6, Plate 38.

Side A of this wedge box drops perpendicularly into the head of the bow, while side B, as it enters the bow head, grows larger than its exterior orifice. This slope serves to hold solidly in place the small piece of wood cut with an edge which keeps the hairs in position and which is known as the wedge.

The next thing to do is to cut the elongated mortise in which the screw of the nut slides back and forth. Ordinarily this mortise is 2 centimeters (about 4/5″) long by approximately 6 millimeters (1/5″) broad, which is easily hollowed out, since all that is necessary is to drill three or four holes in its center, and afterwards, by means of knives and chisels, give it its actual dimensions, dimensions which, as to their length, are determined by the space taken up by the button of the screw of the nut.

This mortise properly finished, the hole is drilled which is to receive the screw which governs the forward and backward movement of the nut. This hole, perhaps, represents the most difficult piece of work on the whole bow, for it must be placed well in the center of the stick, along its entire length, so that the button which forms the head of the screw may be able to turn around smoothly on the head of the stick, supporting itself with the utmost regularity on all parts of the lower end of the stick; and so that the screw of the nut, in its forward and backward movement, may also follow the perpendicular line of the bow along its entire length. The drill intended for the purpose should be taken, and, while working, care should be taken that the drill be held horizontal to the stick of the bow.

Whenever the drill-lathe is to be used, it should be fastened to the end of the bench by means of a vise.

At the end of the stick, on the side which is to receive the button of its screw, a small circle is made in the wood of the stick itself, to prevent the button from shifting, and to keep it constantly on a level with the stick. It is unnecessary to give any explanation of this little process; by merely looking at a stick, it is easy to see that with a circular saw a line may be drawn entirely around the stick, in order that with the aid of the knife and file the small circle in question may be made.

The Nut.—The nut is unquestionably the most difficult part of the bow to make. No matter what pains one may have taken, no matter how hard one may have labored on the stick, if the nut is not set in the right way, the bow will always be a poor one. The essential thing is to fit the nut in such a manner that it allows the wedge box which receives the hairs to be placed in the correct alignment with the head of the bow.

A piece of ebony from 22 to 27 centimeters (8 1/2″ to 10 1/2″) long, is trimmed with the plane and given the same thickness as the bottom of the bow, and the same breadth as that of the nut when the latter has been mounted on the bow.

A model of the nut should then be made, taking that of the bow which is being copied, and using the process which we have already described in making other models. The model is placed on one of the flat sides of the piece of ebony and, as usual, the outlines of as many nuts as the piece of wood can furnish are traced.

This done, the saw is used to separate each of the pieces which is to be made into a nut; then, the superfluous wood should be removed with the saw, the small crosspiece which is found on the front of the nut should be formed, and a knife should be used to give this little piece the graceful shape which it ought to have, while avoiding hollowing out the two sides or cheeks of the nut.

The hole which is to form the wedge box to hold the hairs is then drilled, the procedure being the same as that used for the wedge box at the head of the bow.

If it seems desirable that the heel end of the nut be rounded, the angle found at this place should be sawed and rounded off afterward with the file.

The heel end of the nut is that part of it which, beginning behind the hairs, rejoins the stick.

All this should be done in such a manner that the upper and lower surfaces of the nut remain perfectly level and flat.

On that part of the nut which is to hold the hairs, there is then traced the sliding plate which is to enclose the hairs, and which is covered with a layer of mother-of-pearl closed by the band. This is the name given the half-oval piece of silver which is fitted on the front end of the nut.

The nut is then rested against the workbench, and held in the left hand, unless it be found preferable to clamp it in the jaws of the vise, in which case it should be guarded against pressure, by two pieces of soft wood intercalated between it and each jaw of the vise. A chisel should then be taken, one that seems best adapted to the purpose, and, little by little, following the two lines of the sliding plate, enough wood is dug out to form the groove or hollow which the hairs are to occupy, as shown in Figure 7, Plate 15, letters A to B. The two small angles AA of the same Figure are then made along the whole length of the sliding plate, and the silver leaf which ornaments the plate of the nut should be put in place, beginning by tracing the outline of the place it is to occupy, and then removing from the nut as much wood as the thickness of the silver calls for. Once the silver plate is in position and perfectly adjusted, it is held in place by two small silver nails made of a piece of silver wire, whose heads are driven in with blows of a hammer.

The two small angles AA, of Figure 7, Plate 38, A, are meant to receive a plate.

This plate is a small piece of ebony on which a sheathing of mother-of-pearl has been glued. These two pieces which form one unit, slide into place into two angles AA, and hide the hairs wherever they rest upon the nut.

This plate is affixed to the end of the nut, which looks in the direction of the bow head through a silver ring whose form is shown in Figure 8, Plate 38, B. Below the end of the nut a notch is made which, being proportionate to the thickness of the bow, makes it possible for the latter to remain level with the ebony.

When all this has been done, attention must be given to the slide, which should be mounted on the base of the stick, thus hiding the wedge box, and adapt itself to the three panels of the belly of the stick with such exactness that the nut cannot possibly become loosened.

To attain this end, the nut, as before, must be clamped in the vise, and, using small chisels, the slide must be given the form shown in Figure 7, Plate 38 and X. In order to carry out this task successfully, it should be done little by little, and the slide must be frequently tested along the stick of the bow in order that a perfect fit may be developed. One must also be very careful not to touch the two angles which form the cheeks of the nut with the slide, for if this be done, the nut, no longer having the required height, the hairs would not fail to rest against the stick itself; that is to say, it would be impossible to use the bow.

The work having thus far been carried out as described, it is now necessary to make the screw which fixes the nut on the stick, and at the same time causes it to move.

In order to do so, begin by filing a piece of steel round, until it has the dimension which will allow it to occupy the hole which has been drilled into the end of the stick. It is necessary that this piece enter the hole without difficulty, and it should be gauged with whichever one of the turning-plate gauges is best adapted to the purpose, until it has assumed the form shown in Figure 9, Plate 38.

A piece of brass is then taken and flattened at one end in such wise that after having been given the form shown in Figure 10, Plate 39, it is able to enter the mortise at the lower end of the bow stick without overmuch difficulty. In the middle of the brass a hole is drilled, and taking the gauge which corresponds to that used for the hole of the turning plate which made the guide screw of the piece of steel which was mentioned above, the brass is gauged and set in the hand vise. As is well-known, in order to gauge a guide screw it is necessary to grease either the turning plate or the gauge itself with a drop of oil.

After the vise has been carefully gauged, it also becomes necessary to gauge the end of the piece of brass which is to enter the nut. A hole must be bored in the nut so that the guide screw may enter with a little effort, though not so much as to split the nut. The brass is then fixed in this last part, causing it to slide forward and back through the action of its screw, in such a way that the hole of the screw is exactly opposite the line which is formed by the hole drilled in the stick, and the steel guide screw when entering will make the nut rest on the bow, without any shifting.

The piece with screw which is set square upon the posterior part of the button is the next to be placed.

We might remark here that the bow maker, like the violin maker, needs a turning lathe in order to make this button; and he also is obliged to call on the goldsmith for the band at the heel end of the nut, and the two ferrules which ornament the two extremities of the button.

It is true that the violin builder and bow maker can provide himself with a lathe and the necessary goldsmith tools in order to make the button and the ornamental ferrules; yet it is beyond question that it would be a pity to spend so much money for things which in themselves amount to so little that they are hardly worth mentioning.

The button is made in the following manner. The turner is given the two ferrules which the goldsmith has made according to instructions, and he is requested to make the button somewhat larger in diameter than the thickness of the end of the stick. The turner mounts these two ferrules on the button, taking care that the hole which is to receive the screw on the bow is situated in the center. Then the bow maker causes the square end of the screw to enter the hole of the button by main force, guarding against the screw's sliding to one side in the process.

This done, he mounts the nut upon the bow, and, using the vise, compels the screw of the nut to rise to the edge of the wedge box. Thus the button is placed in position against the end of the stick, and with a file the eight panels which exist on the stick are formed on the button.

On the head of the button the turner has left a small circle to which a bit of mother-of-pearl is to be affixed. It is quite easy to take off the piece of mother-of-pearl while filing, hence the glue should be used a little more liberally than usual, and after the glue has dried it should be filed once more, and then put in flowers of vitriol.

Finishing, Polishing and Varnishing of the Bow

When all the processes we have described have been completed, the nut of the bow is mounted and the stick is bent in order to make it slant backward to a somewhat greater degree than the various manipulations to which it has already been exposed have accomplished.

First, one should study out, holding the end of the stick at which the button is placed close to the eye, whether the bow is perfectly straight. If it leans to either one side or the other, this must be rectified by exposing it to the heat of a fire.

To carry out this operation, which is a delicate one—if it is clumsily done the stick may easily be broken—coal should be lit in a furnace, and when it begins to glow, the stick should be heated at the place where it is evident that it is not straight. It is then bent, holding it in both hands until it has become perfectly straight.

The secret of successfully carrying out this operation lies in heating the stick only little by little, until, having become perfectly hot, it yields freely to manipulation. Care must be taken that the stick does not begin to smoke, for in such case the wood has been burned.

When a careful visual examination shows that the stick is perfectly straight, the time has come to mount the nut, and to see whether, when looking through the nut, and at the same time glancing at the lower plate of the head of the bow, the belly is sufficiently curved to allow it to appear on the optical line which runs from the nut to the head. If this is not the case, the belly of the bow should be curved somewhat more. Finally, the head of the stick should be taken in the left hand and the other end in the right, and forcing the belly of the bow to rise on the side of the stick, one should make sure that there are no places left which are insufficiently curved. If there are, the bow may be reheated.

At this point all that remains to be done is to polish every part of the stick with scrapers and glass paper and, finally, to varnish it with the varnish best suited to it.

As to the nut, the problem of polishing such of its parts as cannot be reached by hand is solved in the following manner: the nut is fixed on the stick by means of the screw and, placing the upper end of the bow on the shoulder and the button on one end of the workbench, the little hollows which are found beneath the ring of the nut are polished by drawing over them with both hands a small bit of rag, steeped in oil and powdered pumice stone.

How to Hair the Bow

When the bow has reached this point of completion, it should be haired, and the first thing to be done is to make the two small wedges which have already been mentioned, and which have the exact shape of the wedge boxes of the plate.

The wedge is a small piece of wood whose edges have been cut slantwise so that, entering the wedge box with a little effort, it will press against the hairs and prevent them from escaping.

These wedges are made of a piece of plane or beech wood, in the following manner. Taking a knife, the piece of wood is so cut that it perfectly closes the largest side of the opening of the wedge-box. The piece of wood is then pressed against the opposite side of said wedge box with the result that a little mark is left which indicates the length of the wedge, which is cut square on this side.

Before proceeding, we will mention which hairs should be preferred in making a choice.

The finest and rounded hairs are the best. Those which are flat, coarse or uneven are worthless. The hairs, before being used, should be washed with soap and water in which a little common table salt has been dissolved, and should then be rinsed in fresh water, to carry off the soap, which would detract from the effect of the rosin.

A satisfactory quantity of hairs are united in a ribbon, and are strongly tied together at that end which was nearest the horse's tail, with waxed silk. Then dipping this end into powdered rosin for a few moments, it is held to a candle flame or spirit lamp in order that the rosin may melt, and thus cause the hairs to harden and cling together. This end is then thrust into the head of the bow, the wedge is set against it, turning back the coil of hair in the wedge box in the direction of the head of the bow, and then forcing the wedge in by pressing against the workbench.

The hairs are then passed through tepid water, and the coil or ribbon is pinched in the vise at about 16 centimeters (about 6 1/4″) distant from the head, with the wedge box of the head in the air, first wrapping a rag about the coil so that it will not be crushed in the vise in which it is placed. Then take a comb used only for this purpose, and comb and equalize the hairs. The nut is then set on the wedge box, and in the position nearest the head of the bow, the proper length which the hair should have is measured off, and it is then tied about 5 millimeters (about 1/6″) higher up than the wedge box of the nut, and is heated as was done for the other end. The hair is then passed into the wedge box and is fixed in the nut by means of the wedge, the screws being tightened somewhat to stretch the hair; the mother-of-pearl slide is slid into its groove, the band over the slide, and the operation is completed.

Tf, while holding the hair, the band slips a little to one side, the nut should be urscrewed and heated as already described to rectify it.

The last thing done is to lap the silk around the handle.

When the hairs are dry, care should be taken to powder some rosin with a wooden pallet, on a clean corner of the workbench, and to lightly rub the rosin on the hairs, pressing against them with the pallet

CHAPTER VII

VIOLIN BRIDGE, STRING AND ROSIN MAKING

The crude character of ancient pictures portraying the earlier stringed instruments, lacking quite naturally the detailed accuracy of modern photographic reproductions, leaves us with very little definite knowledge as to the exact forms of ancient bridges for such instruments, although it is quite evident that they were in actual use.

It is fortunate, therefore, that we do not have to concern ourselves to any extent either with their form or its results in a tonal sense, because the violin bridge, as universally used to-day, dates back only as far as Stradivarius, whose master mind created the design.

Many of the bridges fashioned by the Cremonese makers are of highly ornamental design, and the question as to whether this ornamental cutting plays any part in strengthening or adding to the beauty of the tone quality of their instruments is a much mooted one. Experiments, however, by scientists have proved that alterations in the form of these bridges does seriously alter or impair the tonal qualities of violins, due to the fact that vibrations of the strings through the bridge and into the belly of the violin or the bass bar are affected by the various forms of bridge design.

Another important point regarding the making of bridges is the fact that the height of the bridge from where its feet rest upon the belly of the violin to the top of the bridge should always be the same, any necessary alterations being made in the finger board rather than in the bridge in order to place the strings at the correct height from the finger board.

The best bridges are made of "spotted" maple, carefully selected so that the grain is horizontal and the wood of a medium degree of hardness. Bridges which bring the best results from a tonal standpoint are half as thick at the top where the strings are placed as at the feet. The fitting of the feet is also of the utmost importance, as they must be curved in exact accordance with the curve of the belly of the violin. Any open spaces between the feet and the belly causes a hollow tone lacking sonority or power.

Plate 40 shows a historically interesting array of bridges made in both ancient and modern times, although the former predominate. There is no doubt that any one who has sufficient craftsmanship to produce an artistic violin with his own hands is perfectly capable, by working consistently and carefully from a good model, to produce a satisfactory bridge of his own handicraft but, in the opinion of the writer it would seem far more advisable

PLATE 40

ANCIENT AND MODERN BRIDGES FOR STRINGED INSTRUMENTS OF
THE VIOLIN FAMILY.

and economical to use bridges already prepared in the rough by modern French or Italian specialists in bridge manufacture. The real art in bridge making consists in the skill with which each individual bridge is fitted to the particular instrument on which it is to be used, and the violin maker can well dispense with the time and labor necessary to prepare semifinished bridges.

VIOLIN STRING MAKING

After the great violin maker has perpetuated one of his marvelous instruments, and the equally skilled bow maker has provided a stick which will satisfy the most exacting artist, there yet remains the vitally important accessory of strings, which must be of the right character and thickness in order to bring forth the glorious tone of the instrument.

The following articles describe the manufacture of gut, silk and covered strings, first as made in Europe by time-old processes, and then as made in the United States at the present time by one of the largest packing houses. The average player knows so little of the methods by which strings are made that these articles will undoubtedly have the greatest interest. The illustrations of the article on the manufacture of strings in the United States are from photographs made while the workmen were engaged in the actual preparation of gut strings.

EUROPEAN PROCESS

The strings of the violin are made of the guts or small intestines of the sheep. The animals which supply the strings of the best quality are those raised on dry pastures and in hilly countries. The small-sized sheep found in the district of Berri and in several parts of Germany, also supply gut of an excellent quality.

As is generally known, the small intestines comprise the duodenum, the jejunum and the ilion. These subdivisions, however, are in reality one, whose size is not uniform at either end, and which is largest at the duodenum and smallest at the ilion.

Each of these three intestines or, better said, each of these parts of the entire intestines is made up of three distinct membranes, that is:

1. The external or peritoneal membrane.
2. The internal or mucous membrane.
3. The muscular or fibrous membrane, enclosed between the two others.

Of these three membranes the first two are removed as useless, and it is the third, the middle one, of which the violin strings are manufactured. It is, incidentally, the only one of the three made of fibers which are sufficiently strong and tough for the purpose in view.

The string makers buy these intestines from the butcher, but prefer to extract them from the bodies of the sheep while still warm, or to have this done by workmen experienced in so doing. Without taking this precaution

PLATE 41

THE INITIAL PROCESS OF STRING MAKING—CLEANSING THE MATERIALS.

they would risk receiving them in a state of alteration which would make them unfit for their purpose.

Removing the Intestines

The removing of the intestines is the first operation which they undergo. In order to remove them, the string maker's helpers go to the slaughterhouse, disembowel the sheep which have just been killed, and detach the intestines; then, at once placing them on an inclined plane or board, they scrape them with a knife blade, in order to cleanse them of any fecal matter and blood, as well as of bile and grease. This cleansing process must be carried out very quickly and while the intestines are still quite warm. If it were deferred until they had cooled, the fecal matter and other substances would not have failed to color indelibly any portion of the membranes with which they might have come in contact, and would also give rise to chemical changes which would either diminish or entirely destroy the tenacity of the membranous fibers.

Once emptied, the intestines are tied up in bundles, and are placed in vessels in order to be brought to the factory.

The First Steeping

As soon as they have been brought to the factory, the intestines are divided into bundles of ten, and are placed for tempering purposes in cold water, where they are left for twelve to fifteen hours.

This soaking should take place, when possible, in a running stream, or in a vat filled with spring or well water; only, care should be taken in the latter case, since such water is apt to be somewhat hard. to correct its hardness by the addition of about two grams of carbonate of soda to a quart of water.

After they have been removed from the water, the intestines are again immersed for some four or five hours in tepid running water, maintained at a temperature of approximately 25 degrees, after which the operation of scraping the intestines may be proceeded with.

Scraping the Intestines

The action of the water in the soakings which have just been described, will have given rise to a slight fermentation, which helps separate the membranes from each other.

The scraping of the membranes, with the object of separating the external mucous and peritoneal membranes from the fibrous membrane, is usually done by workmen divided into two groups.

The workmen in the first group stretch out the intestines on a wooden slab or board, slightly inclined; then, grasping them in their left hands, they scrape them from one end to the other, along the side of the external membranes with a split, beveled cane, which they hold in their right hands.[1] The workmen in the second group go through the same process in the same manner with the intestines, scraping along the side of the internal membrane.

The fragments detached by the canes are run off into buckets or a trough. Those of the internal membrane can only be used for fertilizer.

The fragments of the external membrane are later on subjected to appropriate treatment, which permits of their employ in the manufacture of racquets, whips and other rougher articles made of grit. The process used to make them adaptable is very simple: they are placed in a sulphuring room, where they are bleached and partly dried, after which they are drawn and rubbed with dog's grass brushes.

Second Soaking

After they have been scraped, the intestines have lost 19/20 of their original volume, for they are now reduced to the fibrous or muscular membrane, and it is on this that the entire attention of the manufacturer is now concentrated.

The fibrous membranes are separated into bundles of about ten, and are set in stone jars in order to soak for three or four hours in a solution of two quarts of potassa lye, even, preferably, an ammoniacal solution marking two on the salt gauge.[2]

After soaking for three or four hours, the membranes are passed one by one between the first finger of the left hand, protected by a ring and a rubber glove, and the thumb of the same hand, armed with a copper thimble. They are then subjected to a species of very careful and gentle rubbing or scraping, by whose means any small fragments either of the external or the internal membranes which may have escaped the initial scraping are removed. In carrying out this operation, which is usually repeated three times, at intervals of two hours during the same day, the workman has at his left the stone jar in which the intestines are kept, and while he is working he places them in a similar jar standing at his right which, like the first jar, contains a solution of permanganate of potassa. The fourth repetition of the process is a "dry" one, since the intestines this time are not dipped into a jar containing the potassa solution. After this fourth rubbing the membranes are dipped into water containing a weak solution of sulphuric acid. On the day following and for several days to come, the operations of wet and dry rubbing and scraping are repeated, morning and evening, care being taken that with each succeed-

---

[1] In France the cane used for this purpose is the *Arunda Donax*, vulgarly known as Provence cane, a large briar.

[2] The salt gauge is constructed on the same principle as the aerometer, with the difference that each of the degrees of the latter has ten subdivisions. As to the alkaline solution, it is usually prepared by mixing good quality potassa and graveled cinders in two equal parts.

ing passage through the water, the strength of the alkaline solution is increased. This is continued until the liquid registers 16 on the salt-gauge, which corresponds to a little less than one and a half degrees of the aerometer degrees. The guts are now sufficiently cleansed to be ready to be made into strings, but, before anything else, they must first be sorted and, if necessary, split.

Sorting the Membranes

The sorting of the membranes calls for great skill. Hence, as a rule, it is only entrusted to workmen who are thoroughly experienced and know what is needed to make a good string. The guts, in fact, have to be classified according to their whiteness, their length, and their stretching or tension power, so that each will be used to make the kind of string for which it is best adapted. At least two lots of strings are made, one of them consisting of the thin guts which seem fit to be transformed into *E* strings (*chanterelles*) with three threads, while the other includes those only suited to making coarse strings. In both lots those guts which are approximately the same size, and those which are more or less colored, are laid aside.

Splitting the Guts

Since the guts, as we have already remarked, are not uniform in size, and since this circumstance adds to the trouble of preparing strings of a regular cylindrical form, this difficulty is avoided by splitting—that is to say, dividing—such guts lengthwise into long threads, using for the purpose a special knife with several blades, known as a soutil or subtle, from the Italian word *sottile,* meaning narrow, thin, slender. As the threads are obtained by the splitting process, they are placed in a jar, care being taken that their ends lie inversely, that is to say, the thick ends at one side and the thin ends at the other.

There is a very simple way of telling whether a string has been made of a whole gut or of a split gut. All that is necessary is to dip an end of the string in question into a solution of tartaric or sulphuric acid. After a short immersion, the component parts of the string will separate. If the string has been made of a whole gut, the detached fragments will take the shape of small cylinders, which will not be the case if the string is made of a split gut.

Twisting the Strings

The twisting of the guts into violin strings is carried out by the aid of looms or frames which will carry about three lengths of violin string. The three strings are twisted at the same time, as a rule, a wheel with two hooks being necessary. These wheels are simple frames, about 66 centimeters (about 26″) broad by 1 meter (3 1/12′) long, one of whose ends is provided with several fixed pegs, while the opposite end is pierced to receive other wooden pegs, which, however, are moveable.

The twisting process is repeated several times, each repetition being separated from the other by various manipulations, carried out in different ways.

A start is made by selecting two, three or even a greater number of guts which are quite humid, according to the string which is to be made, and assembling them in such a way that the thick end of the one lies beside the thin end of another. Thus prepared, the guts are attached, at one extremity, to a little peg which is placed on one of the hooks on the wheel, and it is then twisted around one of the fixed pegs of the frame. After this the guts are cut to a suitable length, and their free end is fixed on a small peg, resembling the preceding one, which is set on the second wheel. The wheel is then set in motion, and while the guts are being transformed into fiddle strings, the fingers are passed along them their entire length in order to prevent the formation of inequalities!

As a rule the wheel is only allowed to make a small number of turns, since, thanks to the way in which its mechanism is arranged, this is enough to give the guts a torsion of several hundred turns.

The twisting of the strings having been completed, the small pegs of the wheels are removed; they are introduced into the two holes opposite the fixed pegs of the frame, and the operation just described is repeated in the same way with a new bundle of guts, until the frame is completely filled.

The Sulphur Bath

The sulphuring of the strings follows after this first twisting process, with the object of whitening the strings. The frames are placed in a special room, the sulphuring room, usually in the evening. After having been put in the middle of the room the frames, with the strings which have been wound on them during the day, are left there, and flowers of sulphur are ignited in a vessel, while all the cracks and openings of the door are hermetically sealed with putty. While burning, the sulphur releases sulphuric acid gas which, as is well known, has a bleaching effect on animal and vegetable matter.

It must not be forgotten that the *quantity* of sulphur, large or small, which is used, has no influence whatever on the success of the operation. Since the sulphur can only burn in proportion to the amount of air contained in the sulphuring room, the result is that, if too much be employed, whatever portion is in excess liquefies instead of producing sulphuric acid gas, which is an actual loss. Experience has shown that 25 grams of sulphur, as a rule, will be enough for a room of 2.616 cubic yards.

The frames are left overnight in the sulphuring room. They are withdrawn the following morning, and are then placed on benches or on a species of inclined chest or box, called the freshening box, where they are exposed to the open air, but not to the rain, until the strings have partly dried. The latter are then moistened with sponges, and after once more having been placed in the frame, they are twisted a second time, given a torsion sufficiently strong, and returned to the sulphur room.

The sulphuring process as a rule, lasts two days in the case of the fine strings and as long as eight days for the coarse ones.

Thinning the Strings

The work or operation next in order after the strings have been sulphured, is that of thinning them. This is done for the purpose of cleaning and removing all grease from the strings by means of an energetic polishing which, at the same time, removes all inequalities and asperities, as well as the isolated threads and filaments whose agglutination is imperfect.

To carry out this operation, the strings, still stretched on the frames, should be enveloped by several turns of horsehair cord, grouped in sheaves or masses of some ten to fifteen each. These preliminaries over, the workman takes one of these hair cushions in each hand, and, after having moistened them with a sponge dipped in potassa water, he rubs hard, passing the hair cushions from one end to the other of the strings as many as fifty times, taking care to stop from time to time to moisten his cushions with the alkaline water. This rubbing by hand being very taxing, it is nowadays, in all establishments of any size, carried out by means of a special apparatus, consisting of a carriage which holds the frame, and two inner jaws provided with hair cushions. When the machine is in action, the jaws, which are placed, one above the strings, the other below them, are held together by screws, and polish the strings in a forward and backward movement imparted by the motor of the factory.

After the thinning, the gut strings are disengaged from the hair, and then wiped with a fresh sponge to clean away the dirt which the rubbing may have left. They are then moistened with fresh water, and once more returned to the sulphur bath, where they are kept for at least one night. On the following day they are given one more twisting and then dried.

Polishing the Strings

After the strings have been dried they are polished, though in the case of the *E* strings this process is usually omitted.

The frames are first laid flat on trestles or on the freshener, and the strings, one by one, are placed in little gutta-percha cushions, or between folds of cloth, with a little olive oil, fine ground glass, or powdered pumice stone, and they are rubbed from one end to the other by hand until they are perfectly polished. In this case, also, in the larger factories, the hand polishing process is rejected in favor of a polishing machine similar to that used in the thinning already described.

PLATE 42

(Courtesy of the Armour Co.)

THE SECOND PROCESS OF STRING MAKING—SPINNING THE RAW GUT.

Finishing the Strings

After having been polished, the strings are well wiped, and are then lightly covered with olive oil of the best quality. Some manufacturers regard this last operation as harmful, owing to the ease with which oil turns rancid. This disadvantage, however, may be rectified by adding 1/10 its weight of laurel oil to the olive oil.

When the strings have been passed through the oil, they are carried to the drying stove, so that they may be dried perfectly. They may be considered thoroughly dry when, after having been taken from one of the pegs, they do not snap back upon themselves.

Once dried, the strings are cut close to the pegs. There only remains, after this, to roll them in circles by means of a cylinder roll mold, to attach them one to another, and, finally, to collect them in bundles of thirty, in the case of fine strings, or half-bundles of fifteen, for those which are coarse.

This section should not close without a word having been said with regard to the number of guts which are used in the manufacture of the various sorts of strings. The number not only varies according to the strings themselves, but also according to the individual manufacturer. We might quote as a generally adopted standard the number used by the maker, Henry Savarnesse.

The E string or *chanterelle* is composed of four, five or six threads, according to the size of the gut itself, and each thread is formed of half a gut, longitudinally divided. The A string, like the E, has four threads (or three) but stronger ones than those of the E, which are very fine. The D string has from 6 to seven threads.

For guitar strings threads finer than those used for the violin are employed.

Violoncello strings have as many as ten full threads, and those of the harp as many as twenty-two, also full.

Violoncello strings have six threads for the *chanterelle,* and ten for the D string.

Finally, the strings of the double bass have forty threads for the E string, and as many as eighty-five for the D string.

External Indications of Good Strings

How is one to tell at first sight whether a violin string is good or not? "The E string," declares Savarnesse, "should be transparent, perfectly rounded and quite regular in size. It should not be too white, since this is a sign that it has been made of the gut of too young a lamb, and when a bundle of E strings are pressed together in the hand, the strings should have an elastic feel, and should spring back just as a thin steel rod would. It is possible to make strings stiff by using aluminum salts in their manufacture, yet such strings are apt to snap when the bundle is pressed, for they are not flexible, and do not easily resume their former cylindrical position. They are also liable to change color when compressed. Hence, it is always a sign of good quality when strings do not change color, and when they at once resume their cylindrical form.

"The coarser strings, the second and third, on the contrary, should be transparent and very white. If rolled they should be flexible when pressed together; yet they should not change color, and should promptly return to their cylindrical form. If they are too stiff, it is a sign that they have been made with guts of too resistant a character, and in that case they will have a poor tone quality."

It must be remembered that the making of good strings depends largely on the care exercised by the workmen, and the routine they have in their work. Experience is the greatest master in this connection, and is the true secret of good string making. A lack of attention in any of the various processes and operations, too alkaline a water bath, poor twisting, etc., may and will proportion very defective products. The sulphuring process, too, has a great deal of influence on the quality of the strings. The process is an indispensable one if good strings are desired; yet at the same time, there is a point in the process which must be rightly seized, or else poor results are inevitable. If, in fact, this point be passed, the strings will have less tension, and if it be not attained, they will lack resisting power. It is evident, therefore, that the art of manufacturing violin strings depends practically altogether on experience, which, as Bacon has said, is the demonstrator among demonstrators.

Colored Strings, Silk Strings and Spun Strings

Colored Strings.—As is known, certain ones among the harp strings are colored red, and others blue. This artificial color is given them before they are split, and those guts which are most spotted are reserved for making the blue strings.

The red color used is prepared by boiling cochineal in a solution of potassa to one degree of the aërometer. The liquid is strained, the guts are then placed in it, and care is taken to stir them from time to time. One precaution which should not be forgotten is that of seeing to it that the larger the size of the strings, the lighter the coloring matter should be. The red strings are passed through the sulphur bath in the same manner as the white ones. In fact, it is worth noting that the action of the sulphuric acid contributes largely to give them a livelier and more brilliant gloss.

The blue color is obtained, as a rule, by macerating Dutch orchal or tournesol in flags in the same solution of potassa used for the red. The liquid is strained and the guts are then placed in it, care being taken to stir them from time to time. As has already been remarked in connection with dyeing the red strings, the liquid used should be thinner in proportion as the strings are thicker. The blue strings, however, must not be put through the sulphur bath, since, as chemistry teaches, all acids have the property of turning Dutch orchal and, in general, all vegetable blues, red. This will also explain why blue strings usually end up by turning red, especially if they are always in the neighborhood of sulphurated strings. When the blue strings, however, have taken on a red color, it is easy enough to make them return to their original tint by exposing them to an ammonia vapor bath.

Silk Strings.—Besides the gut strings, the violin makers use others made of silk. These came from China originally, but are now made in America as well as in Europe. The Chinese silk strings were twisted or plaited strings (Chinese watercord) enveloped in a layer of gelatin. They have been reproached with a tendency to stretch when mounted, and with not holding their tone. In spite of this serious defect, open-air musicians, especially village fiddlers, used them largely at one time. Many were also sent to colonial possessions in warm countries, where the action of the humidity together with the heat softens gut strings so that they not only break very easily, but are also incapable of rendering service when needed.

American and European silk strings, especially those made in Paris, are far superior to the silk strings of furthest Asia, because, before putting them on the market, they are subjected to a very severe tension which at once allows them to rise to pitch and to hold the pitch for a considerable time. They are usually composed of some 140 filaments, each filament made of 12 silk-worm threads, which gives a total of 1,680 filaments. After the skein of threads has been softened in an acid vapor bath, it is twisted together by means of a special wheel, then, when the string has been completed, it is covered with a light layer of gum arabic, and polished with a piece of white wax until it exceeds in uniformity and transparency the best of gut strings.

Covered Strings.—It only remains for us to mention the strings covered with wire ribbon, which are generally known as covered strings, in order to distinguish them from ordinary strings. The fourth or G string is the only covered string used on the violin.

These covered strings are strings of gut or of silk covered with silvered copper or with silver wire, whose spirals are very close to one another. When the interior string is of gut, they are not subjected to a sulphur bath, nor are they oiled. In the smaller factories the metallic outer sheath is applied by means of a wheel similar to that employed by the lace trimmers. For this purpose the string is attached to the hook of the wheel, while the opposite end is fastened to a turning loper, which is suspended by a weight from a band which, passing over a pulley, is attached to the loper. A workman then winds the extremity of the metal wire about the string, quite close to the loper, while giving the wheel a uniform movement. The string then begins to turn and communicate the same movement to the loper, and, while the workman supports it with his left hand, with his right he directs the metal wire in such wise that it rolls itself upon the string with the most perfect regularity. In

PLATE 16

(Courtesy of the Armour Co.)

FINAL PROCESS OF STRING MAKING—CUTTING THE STRINGS IN FINISHING ROOM.

the larger factories this operation is carried out in these days by means of an ingenious machine which, run by steam, makes the string turn fourteen or fifteen times in the course of a single minute.

AMERICAN PROCESS

Violin strings are frequently referred to as "catgut," and to this day the general public, not familiar with the process, believes that they are made from the intestines of cats. The origin of the term "catgut" has never been definitely ascertained. The *Encyclopedia Britannica* gives a reasonable explanation, stating that the Italian term for violin is "kit." At first steel strings were used on the kit, hence the term "kit steel." Later when gut strings were used the term "kit gut" became common. This in time developed into "catgut." Another explanation of the terms states that when gut strings were first manufactured in Europe the best strings came from Catagniny, Germany, and they were so much superior to strings from other parts that violinists demanded Catigniny gut or "catgut."

Catgut is not made from any part of the cat, and the feline family has no connection whatever with gut strings. They are made from the small part of the sheep intestine. The best violin strings are made from the fresh intestines, which are, like all animal products, very perishable. The largest makers of musical strings are usually found near the slaughterhouses. These intestines cannot be shipped any distance without being salted or dried. Sheep intestines are usually about 60 feet long and most of it is used as sausage casings and only the narrow ends which average about 8 yards, are sufficiently tender to enter into the manufacture of violin strings. This part is not much larger in diameter than a pencil, and is sometimes used as the casings of small breakfast sausages. This narrow sheep intestine must be thoroughly cleaned and scraped (Plate 41), most of which is done by hand, although machinery takes care of a few operations. Usually the intestines are split in half and great care must be exercised in handling these small pieces, as they are very tender and break easily. Every bit of fat and grease must be removed so that only the firm texture of the intestine is made into strings. Strings made from intestines that are not cleaned thoroughly deteriorate rapidly, as the fats that are not removed decay. Some string makers do not split the intestines, but specialize on what they call "whole gut" strings.

After the intestines are thoroughly cleaned, the best lengths of uniform size are set aside to be used in making the finest strings. They are cut to uniform lengths, and while still moist are bunched together to be spun. The number of strands in these strings depend upon what is wanted; for instance, in making good violin E strings, at least six or seven ply is used, violin A strings require eight to ten ply, D strings eleven to thirteen, cello strings eighteen to thirty and some double-bass strings have as many as fifty strands. These figures are for split intestines, that is, there are fifty half or twenty-five whole intestines in a double-bass string. The material is then put on frames and the excess moisture is removed.

The spinning of strings (Plate 42) requires great skill. If not spun sufficiently the strings will be weak, and if spun too much they will be hard. This is also true of woolen yarn which can be broken easily, but when the yarn is spun into a hard thread, it is very hard to break. The strings are then transferred to a drying room, and before they are completely dried, they are examined and are spun again if additional spinning is required. A dried string could not be recognized as a violin string as it is very rough and hard and must be polished until smooth and perfectly cylindrical in shape. Every violinist is familiar with faulty strings which do not vibrate uniformly because of varying sizes and shapes from one end to the other. This polishing was always done by hand in the past, but machinery has been invented which revolves the rough strings so that the polishing surfaces take uniformly on all parts of the strings. All so-called "perfect fifth" strings are polished by machinery. Great care must be taken in polishing strings so that the finished strings are of a usable size.

It is impossible to make gut strings exactly the same size as raw materials vary in weight, and the amount of moisture in the air frequently affects their size. It has been proven that strings gauge as No. 2 on a dry day, and will gauge 2 1/2 or 2 3/4 on a rainy day as the gut absorbs moisture. If every violinist demanded exactly a gauge 2, strings would have to sell at far more than the present price, as the majority of them would have to be thrown away. It is a good thing therefore that different violinists require strings of different gauges.

The strings are allowed to season on the drying frames for a few days, then cut down into single lengths (Plate 43) or two or three length coils. The strings must again be sorted out for color and finish, after which they are gauged very carefully. A large percentage of strings made to sell at the highest prices must be thrown out because of gauge, and sold as a cheaper grade. The strings are then coiled, tied and packed up in envelopes and cartons to be sent out to the trade.

The color of strings has nothing to do with the strength or trueness of tone, and very frequently the darker strings last longer than the best looking.

How Rosin is Prepared

Colophony or rosin is probably the smallest in size of all the accessories used in violin making and violin playing; yet it is, nevertheless, one of the most essential to those who use string instruments.

There is not a violin player who does not know how valuable a really good piece of rosin is to him, and how injurious a poor quality of rosin may be to the best instrument and the playing of the greatest virtuoso. Good colophony should be transparent, and the color of citron. When applied to the bow hair it should whiten it and not give it a yellowish tinge.   When the bow rubs against the strings, the colophony should fall to the foot of the bridge in a white powder, and should not blacken the strings where the bow attacks them.   Finally, good colophony should not stick to the fingers when a small piece is broken off.

We have seen many musicians cook white resin or terebinth with vinegar. This is the worst thing possible to do, for the vinegar, mixing with the resins, produces a rosin whose use, in place of tone, yields only a detestable whistling.

The real secret of making good rosin makes clear that there is nothing complicated about its preparation in itself, and yet it is decidedly worth knowing.

White resin or galipot should be melted in an unused glazed pot over a moderate coal fire.   As the resin melts it should be poured into a second pot, being filtered through a clean cloth, rather coarse in texture.   This second pot, similar to the first, should be ready at hand, near the fire.   The colophony is then poured into small paper rolls, or into small boxes or cartons which will give it a tablet form.

The best and finest rosin can be made by distilling Venetian terebinth, and this variety of colophony is practically white in appearance.

CHAPTER VIII

VIOLIN TEACHING AND STUDY

The goals toward which most of those strive who undertake the study of the violin seriously are either the professions of soloist or teacher. In the majority of cases the latter is the one which is finally settled upon, due to the fact that solo playing as a profession is not sufficiently lucrative, except for the favored few who come to be known as virtuosos.

Where the serious student has one or the other of these aims, the selection of an able teacher is of the utmost importance. As a matter of fact, it is extremely difficult for a student or his parents to be sure that the choice they have made in a teacher is a wise one. The musical world is full of people who, with nothing more than a smattering knowledge of the art, undertake boldly to educate others and bring them to heights of musical knowledge which these so-called "teachers" have never attained.

Many of these teachers "graduate" pupils who exhibit, through natural talent, a superficial ability of a showy type in which real musicianship plays no part whatsoever. The editor himself has been in contact with apparently brilliant performers on the violin, who could fiddle their way through showy pieces of the salon type, and yet were unable to even name the keys that they were playing in, or to denominate them as major or minor, or to play the ordinary scales in different keys properly.

Any person desiring to study the violin in a serious way is entitled to receive from the teacher who proposes to instruct him real proof in some form that the instruction which he proposes to impart will be of a high character and capable of forming the student into a violinist rather than a fiddler. Every teacher who has had the proper fundamental training and is himself a musician, in the true sense of the word, can be readily judged by the course of training he lays out, by the type of instruction books which he uses and by the firm stand he will take with every pupil as regards his mastering the fundamental principles of music in general and the art of violin playing in particular. Teachers who make light of scale study, chord practice, the use of exercises and études, but who substitute a slovenly system of easy pieces or "recreations" are to be avoided because the student who wastes time with them only finds later that he must begin his work all over again if he desires to become a finished player or teacher.

The situation is, of course, exactly the same with the pupil, who, if he is so fortunate as to be under the tuition of an able, conscientious and painstaking teacher, must follow exactly the course laid out for him, practicing scales, chords, exercises, etc., with the greatest patience, and allowing himself no deviation from the course prescribed by the master.

In this connection it is impossible to recommend too strongly that the student affiliate himself wherever possible with an established conservatory or college of music where the courses of study are laid out by the directorate of the institution. This means that the student gets systematic training not only in the art of playing the violin itself, but also in harmony, composition, theory, musical history and other subjects in which it is necessary for the thorough musician to be grounded. The instruction in this type of institution is usually not only more thorough but also more systematic and more broadening. The student must take his lessons at regular hours, he is examined frequently by impartial persons as to his progress and he is also enabled to hear others play and to observe their progress at the concerts or recitals which are a feature at all such institutions.

Furthermore, in the first and middle stages of violin study, class instruction, where two or three pupils are given their lessons within the hour period, all being at about the same stage of advancement, benefits the individual through the instruction given his fellow students, and after a time a spirit of friendly rivalry is established which leads him to give more thought and care to the preparation of his lessons.

Last, but not least, conservatory courses of instruction are far less expensive in the long run. The individual violin teacher rarely undertakes to instruct in the theoretical branches, thus requiring the student to seek knowledge of these subjects from specialists through private lessons. The conservatory, which requires most of its students to take these courses in order to secure a diploma, is enabled to mass a number of pupils in theoretical classes at one time, which is naturally a more economical method for every one concerned.

The student usually reaches a fairly advanced stage of study before he makes up his mind that he is going to pursue music as a profession, and it is at that time, that a decision must be made as to what branch of the profession—solo playing or teaching—is to be followed, as quite naturally the courses of study from this period on will be entirely different. If the student wishes to become a teacher it will be well for him to turn his attention to the more solid elements of violin playing and to instruction in normal courses which will teach him how to impart the knowledge which he has gained himself to others. If the ability shown by the student, and his success as a budding soloist on recital programs, etc., is sufficient for him to come to the conclusion that a virtuoso career may be safely sought, his course of study must be directed along lines of advanced technique and interpretation. In connection with the question of study for a virtuoso career there arises a question of the necessity of finishing one's education in the musical circles of Europe, and it is a question to which there are indeed many sides. Up to the time of the Great

War, there seems to be hardly any question that it was necessary for those who wished to be regarded as virtuosos and who proposed to undertake concert tours of this country, to finish their musical education under violin masters abroad, and to round off the edges of their musical education by plunging into the artistic atmosphere of old Europe.

There is a question in the editor's mind, however, as to whether this is nearly as necessary to-day as it was ten or more years ago. We have among us in the United States, permanently settled and a part of our musical life, many great teachers of the violin, represented by Auer, Flesch, Thomson and many others who find the New World a more lucrative and perhaps a more pleasant place in which to pursue their artistic and pedagogic activities. In addition to these newly acquired masters we have many eminent artists and teachers who have been with us for a score or more of years, among whom Franz Kneisel is preëminent and representative.

There is no doubt in the editor's mind that, so far as actually training in the art of violin playing is concerned, everything that ever could be done abroad in matters of instruction is now possible in this country, not only in the matter of individual instruction but also in the particular of concerts, recitals, operatic performances, lectures, musical club events and all other functions which tend to broaden the artistic instinct. There is one thing that perhaps it will be many years before the American born and American educated musician will find it difficult to overcome, and that is the lure which a name of foreign sound seems to exercise upon patrons of the box office in a concert hall. For some reason the music-loving layman who patronizes concerts appears to anticipate greater enjoyment of the playing of an artist whose name sounds foreign than some name which is the same as that of his next-door neighbor. Perhaps that is the reason why American singers, pianists and violinists are so successful in Europe—perhaps it is human nature to look down upon that which is a part of everyday life and to find greater pleasure in something which has in it the element of novelty or foreign association. Nevertheless, the time is coming—is almost upon us—when American born and American educated musicians will be as highly regarded in America as they are elsewhere—and this will be all the measure of success which an artist can desire.

CHAPTER IX

THE EVOLUTION OF THE ART OF VIOLIN PLAYING

There is but one art, or school of violin playing, and that is the Italian school founded by Arcangelo Corelli, and from which all other schools are derived.

The number of violinists who have made an actual, historical impress on the development of the art of violin playing is very small. They will be found in the following list:

Arcangelo Corelli	1653—1713
Giuseppe Tartini	1692—1770
Gaetano Pugnani	1727—1803
Pietro Nardini	1722—1793
Pietro Locatelli	1693—1764
Nicolò Paganini	1784—1840
Pierre Rode	1774—1830
Jean-Baptiste Viotti	1753—1824
Ludwig Spohr	1784—1859
Rodolphe Kreutzer	1766—1861
Charles de Bériot	1802—1870
Henri Vieuxtemps	1820—1881
Henri Wieniawski	1835—1880
Heinrich Wilhelm Ernst	1814—1865
Pablo de Sarasate	1844—1908
August Wilhelmj	1845—1908

Would it be possible to find a more difficult question for consideration than that of determining exactly who the actual founders or creators of the art of violin playing were? At first glance it seems simple enough, but in reality it is very complex.

Yet, as regards actual "creators" of schools in violin playing, there are but two names to be mentioned: those of Corelli and Tartini, and their standing as founders of "schools" of violin playing was, so to speak, established by Gaetano Pugnani, who was the pupil of both. Pugnani in turn, was the teacher of Viotti.

And now let us see which masters of the instrument may be traced back to Viotti, as wonderful a teacher as he was a violinist. The list is a distinguished one. It includes de Bériot, who was the teacher of Vieuxtemps; Kreutzer, who taught Lafont and also Bazzini the violin; Rode, who instructed Mayseder and Böhm, as well as many other great artists who, carrying on the teachings and traditions handed down to them, justify my opinion that the one true head of all the "schools" in existence at the present time was Jean-Baptiste Viotti.

The preceding table gives a clear exposition of the founders of the art of violin playing. Arcangelo Corelli, so to speak, was the father of our admirable school, and it was destiny's desire that this artist, a great master in every sense of the word, should be destined to transmit to future generations the essence of his message.

The great heads of the schools of violin playing are the following:

```
Arcangelo Corelli ........................................1653—1713
Gaetano Pugnani .........................................1727—1803
Giuseppe Tartini ........................................1692—1770
Jean-Baptiste Viotti ....................................1753—1824
Pierre Rode .............................................1774—1830
Rodolphe Kreutzer .......................................1766—1831
Louis Massart ...........................................1811—1892
Joseph Böhm ............................................1795—1867
Pierre Baillot ..........................................1741—1842
Nicolò Paganini .........................................1784—1848
François Habeneck .......................................1781—1849
Charles Dancla ..........................................1818—1907
Delphin Alard ...........................................1815—1888
Charles de Bériot .......................................1802—1870
Joseph Joachim ..........................................1831—1907
Henri Léonard ...........................................1819—1890
Ludwig Spohr ............................................1784—1859
Henri Wieniawski ........................................1835—1880
Ferdinand David .........................................1810—1873
Henri Vieuxtemps ........................................1820—1881
```

In these twenty masters there is concentrated the whole art of violin playing, and it is worth while giving an idea of the source of the development of the various schools.

After Tartini, the true founder of the whole art of violin playing, comes Viotti. It is not too much to say that whenever we may have occasion to admire some violinist at the present time, we can go back to Viotti in order to discover the origin of his art. Let us take, for example, the violinistic predecessors of Ysaye:

Viotti
>   Kreutzer
>   Massart
>   Wieniawski
>   Ysaye

The violinistic antecedents of Kreisler may be presented as follows:

Viotti
>   Kreutzer
>   Massart
>   Kreisler

Joachim's line of violinistic descent runs as follows:

Viotti

Rode

Bohm

Joachim

By head of a school, using the expression in connection with the violin, we mean those masters who have trained pupils who have become famous, and whose principles have been handed down to the present day. Art, in the final analysis, knows but one truth—the endeavor to attain a high ideal, one which is void of all low artifice. All the great artists have much in common, all are guided by the same lofty principles: it is their personality alone which differentiates them.

Nicolò Paganini may be regarded as the most radiant star in the great galaxy of violinists. He transformed the violin, the wonderful instrument which has been the delight of millions, and his greatest merit lies in his having very considerably extended the boundaries of violin virtuosity. Before his day, audiences were enraptured when a violinist could play as high as the fourth position. The genial Italian not only made the use of the entire range of the violin an ordinary matter, but also enriched the mechanism of fingers and bow to an almost miraculous degree. Long before his day Locatelli had registered a notable advance on the mechanism preceding his own epoch with his "Twenty-four Caprices," drawn from his twelve concertos, each containing two caprices. The best known among these caprices is the one called "The Harmonic Labyrinth."

It is interesting, to-day, to review with all honesty the so-called evolution of the art of violin playing. Progress since Paganini died has been nil, and this is proved by the fact that no violinist who has since arisen has been his equal; for he was not alone a formidable mechanician, but a great artist who knew how to charm and touch his auditors as well.

At the same time it is only just to pay a tribute of deep respect to Joachim and Ysaye, for their service and influence in the art of violin playing has been of the highest character. Ysaye is assuredly to be reckoned among those who have created a violinistic ideal. I regard Ysaye as the most perfect incarnation of the violin. In his playing the appeal to the heartstrings, the fervor of exultation, is always present. He awakens enthusiasm, and produces a genuine impression of wonderful mastery. He dominates the violin and, especially, those who hear him play it.

Vieuxtemps and Wieniawski are among the composers who have written most effectively for the violin, for to a noble technical development they added imagination in their treatment of the classic style, and deprived it of its frequent monotony and aridity.

CHAPTER X

HOW TO PRACTICE

The ability to practice without loss of valuable time is an art in itself. The teacher should indicate the course to be pursued, and should insist on being implicitly obeyed with regard to all that touches on the proper care taken of the pupil's instrument.

Patience is the secret of all real progress. One should learn how to practice very slowly, and reach the greatest difficulties by a process of natural progression.

The following examples give an analysis of certain difficulties; how they are to be studied and how overcome by means of a species of musical homeopathy:

In the Mendelssohn Concerto, for example, the original passage is written as indicated but may be practiced to advantage in all of the four ways indicated:

In the Beethoven Concerto, the opening passage is written as indicated, but as well may be practiced in all of the four ways indicated:

By these different means it is possible to become practically sure of the attack of the octaves. One very efficacious manner of playing this difficult beginning with exactness is to take the octaves, placing the fingers on them alternately instead of simultaneously. This beginning of the Concerto is unusually complicated and ungrateful, and most violinists are actually afraid of it, since, although they have little respect for the exact notation and can avail themselves of the pretext of a personal interpretation, the fact remains that it is preferable to use the composer's notation integrally as it stands. Beethoven indicated the sixteenth note followed by a quarter note with evident intention. The following illustration gives a note photograph of the interpretations of Joachim, Wilhelmj, Sarasate, Ysaye, Thomson, Kreisler and Kubelik.

The table just adduced is in exact conformity with the interpretations of the violinists mentioned as my musical memory records them.

I consider Joachim's interpretation as ideal, and I fail to see why Wilhelmj should be adjudged correct in interpreting this phrase in the manner he has chosen.

The work should not be made heavy and clumsy under the pretext of interpreting it. Beethoven is perfectly clear and concise in his indication of his wishes; it might be said of his works that not a note in them need be changed, and whoever transgresses the supreme logic of this immortal composer takes far too much upon himself.

Kubelik sometimes makes inoffensive "readjustments" in his playing of Paganini; but he does so in very dangerous places, where it is almost impossible to make certain of success, as in the wizard violinist's "Witches' Dance."

And now we come to one of the most delicate questions to be considered in this chapter, that of the progress made in the teaching of modern violin technique.

There has come into being a whole legion of specialists in violin technique, who are ready to turn out "Paganinis" in double quick time. All these destroyers of art in its purity should be shunned, for they are manufacturers of mechanical musicians, the most skilful among whom earn but little glory, and are the cause of disquiet to genuine artists. The pupils of such teachers may reach a certain point of development but in nearly every case they remain standing on the threshold of the temple of art, which they are musically unfit to enter.

One should wage unrelenting war against these mere technicians of the violin. Paganini was the possessor of a phenomenal mechanism, but he was a great artist as well; Mendelssohn declared that the famous Genoese sang the simplest things on his violin with the most affecting sentiment. My aversion for the mechanician violinist has always been intense, and has been measurably increased during the last few years. The number of violinistic acrobats has developed at a prodigious rate, and the public, easily impressed, reacting to all that is brilliant and, especially, all that "sounds," is frequently unduly pleased over what is nothing but unmusical "fireworks."

The public is sometimes sadly lacking in good judgment in selecting its musical idols, for few laymen are competent to judge the real musicianship of a performer. Clever advertising and the way in which the artist is presented establish his success rather than ability. I remember—it was when a certain technically skilful but musically deficient virtuoso played for the first time in the Théâtre du Vaudeville in Paris—the remark of a gentleman sitting beside me. The performer was playing Vieuxtemps' First Concerto, and after the first few measures my neighbor exclaimed "He is playing on hangman's rope!" that is, "He has the devil's own luck!" (In France a bit of the rope which has been used to hang a man is supposed to bring good fortune to its possessor.) Incidentally, the amusing incidents which take place in the concert hall supply valuable documents with regard to the mental state of audiences, and later I hope to mention some which will introduce a measure of humor into a work which is otherwise serious and purposeful.

As has already been remarked, the charlatans of violin technique must be opposed in an energetic manner, and the violinist should content himself with using the technique placed at his disposal by Gaviniés, Rode, Kreutzer, Baillot and their illustrious predecessor, Paganini.

In this connection it may be well to give some exercises calculated to develop the strength of the fingers, of the hand and of the lower arm:

1. Open and close the hand slowly, keeping time to a metronome beat of 100.

2. Clench the fist, using considerable power, then turn it very slowly to the right and to the left.

3. Lay the hand flat on a table and then slowly raise the fingers, to let them fall back again forcefully.

These three exercises are better calculated to develop the strength of the hand than any exercise a technician might be able to invent.

The time has come to take serious measures for relegating technical acrobats to an inferior rather than a superior place. True musicians should receive recognition rather than gymnasts of the E string!

It is all a matter of endowment. If you are really gifted, you will reach art's Parnassus with three hours of hard work a day; if you have missed your vocation you may practice ten hours a day, and the only advance you will register will be along the line of mechanical development. It is only just to remark, however, that example counts for a great deal in the development of talent, and that for this reason every student should endeavor to entrust himself to the guidance of a good teacher.

The popular fallacy that the violin virtuoso rarely makes a good teacher is of course not founded on fact or the real experience of talented students. There is, after all, nothing comparable to a virtuoso who is willing to take the trouble to teach; from such an instructor the intelligent pupil can derive an immense advantage and much serious profit.

In art there is but one truth and one logic: that each individual must himself discover the road which leads to the sublime and the beautiful.

CHAPTER XI

TONE AND ITS DEVELOPMENT

In my opinion every violinist who reaches a certain age should learn how to breathe properly, something which would be of great advantage to him, not only in aiding the proper exposition of his violin phrasing, but also in view of what I am about to explain.

It is very difficult to play the violin when the player's breathing is labored; and when heart and lungs are deprived of their freedom of circulation, it is impossible to obtain the maximum results which the exercise of a given talent permits. Experiments which I myself have made in breath control have been perfectly successful. For instance, ascending six flights of stairs, I have taken several deep inhalations before ascending each flight, with the surprising result that I walked the sixth flight without fatigue, and without finding myself out of breath.

I was moved to apply my experiences in this direction to the violin, and here, too, I obtained unexpected results. Being extremely nervous by nature, and finding that the quality of my playing was often at the mercy of the insensate terror inspired by an approaching performance in public, I made it a practice to inhale deeply at the moment when I commenced to play a composition on the platform, and soon found that my performance gained noticeably in calmness and equality.

The emission of the singing voice is identical with the emission of the violin tone, the voice of the violin, and by exercising great care it is quite possible to play in a manner which will make it impossible for any listener to notice the falling of the bow upon the strings. Amplitude of tone and the manner in which it should be secured from the viewpoint of breadth and power is also most important, and calls for consideration.

The manner in which a violinist is able to control the volume of his violin tone at once reveals whether he is an artist of the robust or of the effeminate type. Effeminacy in artistic matters should be regarded as in extremely bad taste, for the effeminate, affected artist has no place among the masters of his art. There are only two classes of violinists: artists, and those players who might be called "scrapers." The true artist always has a smaller tone than a mediocre one, for he pays greater attention to the *quality* of his tone, while the inferior player is so eager to obtain a big tone—a great volume of sound— that he neglects entirely the proper attention to the quality and purity of the sounds he produces.

The French and Italians, in general, have an attractive quality of tone; the Belgians and Dutch, in addition to the qualities of the French and Italians, show grandeur and virility in their mode of playing.

It might be said that the violinist of every race presents in his playing something of the character, the defects and the qualities of the people of which he is a member. It is, however, strange to see the Spaniards, when they happen to be musicians, the children of a land of ardent sun, of pulsing life, where the air is balmy with captivating perfumes, where the women are entrancing, the home of the most chivalric spirit in the world—quiescent with a calmness which almost wakes despair.

The cellist, Pablo Casals, is the most ardent among the artists Spain has produced; all others whom I have known and heard play were great musical pacifists, and never inclined to take the bit in their teeth and bolt. Sarasate was very witty and clever, but also very calm; Arbos was chilling, and many others were altogether frozen. The further north one goes, the more temperament the violinists seem to have, the Russians in particular, and the Slav in general, offering the most noticeable proof of this contention. The Hungarians, too, have supplied the world with a number of great artists. Hungary has been a veritable nursery for violinistic talent, and has produced Joachim, Auer, Hubay and others. I mention Hubay in particular, since he is much younger than the other masters cited, although he holds an enviable position among violinists. Without any other, incidentally, Joachim, that high priest of the violin, suffices to glorify a whole country.

The Germans cultivate a style of playing far more severe and studied than do the Slav peoples; yet as a rule they are less gifted.

By tone we understand the quantity of sound which may be drawn from an instrument, and it is not too much to say, under this head, that the violin, in so far as tone is concerned, may be transformed into a trumpet or trombone.

On the other hand, the *quality* of the tone plays a very great part in the endowment of the solo player, and is a point of capital importance in the consecration of an artistic talent. The fact that a solar artist must play to an accompaniment of six stands of first violins, eight stands of second violins, eight cellists, ten violas, and eight double basses, makes it necessary for him to possess a very powerful instrument in these days, and for this reason, Guarnerius' and the Maggini violins, which exceed all other master instruments in power and brilliance of tone, are extremely popular with concert performers.

Many instruments having a big tone are to be found, but those in which the tone is absolutely equalized on all four strings are decidedly rare. The strength of each individual player is unequal, that is to say, the strength of the individual violinist is a mystery. One may see violinists who are small and slight in stature draw an enormous tone from their instruments, while large men only produce one which is small and disagreeable.

I am convinced that the violin tone increases and becomes more and more sonorous while playing, and that when the player is sufficiently carried away he can obtain a superb tone—provided that he plays a high-grade violin.

Orchestra playing is excellent for broadening the violin tone, the symphonic orchestra above all, provided, of course, that the conductor is a musician of high culture.

THE STACCATO

The *staccato* is a succession of notes played in a single bowing; it is produced by either down-bow or up-bow, though the up-bow is generally used. Charming effects may be obtained by the use of the *staccato,* and nature has been prodigal of her benefits in this connection to some violinists, while refusing them to others. I am acquainted with many remarkable violinists who find it impossible to produce a brilliant *staccato;* it is only with the greatest difficulty that they manage to play from eight to sixteen notes of *staccato* to a measure. A curious point in this connection is that the violinists who have a natural *staccato* hardly ever can play it in time, they hurry it noticeably. It seems that Wieniawski had the most marvelous *staccato* imaginable, and Vieuxtemps also possessed a superb one, while in our own day Ysaÿe seems to have inherited their qualities. Marteau has a good but somewhat heavy *staccato,* while Kreisler produces one which is brilliant but without much power. Sarasate did not have a grandiose *staccato,* but his playing of it was graceful and correct. A few suggestions for the improvement of the *staccato* will not be out of place:

Play the following exercise with the whole bow, using first the down- and then the up-bow:

Play this same exercise first quickly and then slowly, always using the whole bow.

Then practice the same exercises, employing the section from the middle to the point of the bow. When satisfactory results have been obtained by the use of the preceding exercises, they should be practiced, using the second third of the bow length, at the point.

In order to concentrate the entire attention on this bow stroke, it would also be well to practice it on the open strings.

The essential thing in *staccato* is to accent the first note of every group, for on this accentuation the successful playing of the group depends, as may be seen in the following examples:

The *staccato* should not come from the wrist, but directly from the elbow, and in a passage of some length the arm has an involuntary tendency to stiffen.

Those players who produce their *staccato* from the wrist, have a *staccato* which is too weak, and is absolutely lacking in vigor.

THE SPICCATO

It is the dream of every violinist to have a perfected *spiccato;* yet this is one of the most delicate features of violin technique, and in order to gain a certain measure of perfection in this bowing it is necessary to work very hard and, in particular, to devote the utmost attention to studying the wrist.

One may secure a "leaping" *spiccato* only with the exercise of great patience and by commencing to study it with the following exercise, which should be played in the middle of the bow:

The same exercise should also be studied at the point of the bow.

It is generally understood that the *spiccato* should be produced at the middle of the bow; but violinists merely fix the middle of the bow as the point best suited to their physical requirements, or most advantageous for the handling of the bow itself. Sarasate has a marvelous *spiccato,* and he produced it at the point of the bow; other violinists play their *spiccato* exactly at the middle, and still others play it considerably below the middle of the bow. The majority of the best violin teachers declare that the *spiccato* should be played with the first third of the bow.

It is impossible to give exact indications here as to how the *spiccato* is to be played in each individual case. I merely give advice which is based on a large experience, and will leave every reader to select what best answers his own needs.

One should guard against hurrying when playing *spiccato* passages, although undue precipitation in movement when playing them, to tell the truth, is often caused by accompanists. These indispensable auxiliaries to performance are in many cases averse to keeping strict time, and must constantly be sermonized in order to compel them to observe the proper tempos. To choose a tempo and adhere to it strictly is, naturally, quite a complicated process; yet the violinist should be able to control his nerves sufficiently to do so without bolting or growing confused. The greatest aid in achieving this end is the metronome, which may always be referred to with confidence.

At certain points it is at times necessary to turn the *spiccato* into a *détaché*, for instance:

The same work:

There is also the important question of the balance of the bow, the maintenance of its equilibrium, a question generally ignored, and to which not enough attention is paid.

In order to obtain perfect equality on all the strings, a string should be tied to the wrist from which a piece of lead weighing somewhat less than a quarter of a pound should be suspended, and then, very slowly at first and then more rapidly, the following exercise should be played:

The *spiccato* becomes especially difficult when a rapid change of string takes place, and this is due to the lack of study material necessary to obviate this difficulty.

The player should obtain perfect equality by practicing the following examples:

In movements written in 6/8, 9/12 or 12/8 time, an accent is involuntarily given to the first six notes: this tendency should be avoided, since it is anti-musical. For instance:

This incorrect accentuation rarely occurs in movements written in 4/4 time, as for instance:

At every moment the question of the logic of certain bowings arises. As regards the following example, for instance, violinists are very much divided as to which bowing should be used. Many play with the bow on the string, others use a *spiccato:*

In my own opinion, the rather sprightly movement of this famous Rondo in itself indicates that a *spiccato* should be used at this point, since the phrase would be rendered heavy and clumsy if played with the bow on the string. Paganini's celebrated "Moto Perpetuo," the most famous of all perpetual movements owing to its superb verve and its lofty musicality, contains numerous passages, however, which are played with the bow on the string, especially at the close of sections.

The *spiccato* is an essentially violinistic effect, and is ravishing when it is properly played.

The bow should not jounce or bound too much on the strings, and the less leaping the bow does the more clear and limpid the resulting tones will be.

The Trill and Grace Notes

The birds, no doubt, were the first to call the attention of the musician to this charming ornament, and the violinist should endeavor to imitate the nightingale and other feathered songsters whose harmonious trills are model instances of what a trill should be.

A perfected trill has always been much coveted by artists, even the greatest, and it actually plays a great rôle in the virtuoso's technical equipment, in that of the singer as well as of the instrumentalist. Sarasate's trill could stand comparison with those of Patti, Melba and other famous *prima donnas,* and actually made the impression of being an uninterrupted succession of triplets, which I consider the highest point of perfection to be attained in trilling. The trill on two notes:

is not as perfect as the trill in triplets:

and hence this uninterrupted trill in triplets is the form to study in order to obtain a good trill. The fingers must be strong; if they are weak they must be strengthened. The following exercise is an excellent one if practiced slowly, cutting the second note very short:

Continue in this manner by tones and half-tones. This exercise will yield astonishing results, and it also has the advantage of notably strengthening the third finger.

In the following example various trill abbreviations are shown, together with the manner in which they should be played. According to its definition the trill is an ornamented note, in which the ornament lasts throughout the duration of the note value.

In accordance with the degree of mechanical perfection to which the violinist has attained, and on which all depends, the alternation of the trill notes should become more and more regular as the fingers gain the power and precision demanded. Joachim, to whom I wrote for advice on the question of trill endings, replied that he could not imagine a trill without an ending. The question was one we had discussed as friends in connection with the beginning of the Tenth Sonata by Beethoven, and on which we had been unable to agree. The point at issue was whether the trill at the beginning.

Sonata Nº 10 - Beethoven

called for an ending. According to Joachim, the trill *did* call for a termination; that is, it should be played thus:

Sonata Nº 10 - Beethoven

Now it is worth mentioning that though Beethoven often indicated terminations for his trills, on the other hand, he often omitted them. He was so exact in all that he wrote that a splendid example of the clearness of his exposition is to be found in the profound Sonata Op. 30, No. 2 (Sonata VII). In the example which follows:

the fragment might easily have been provided with indications for its playing in the following manner:

as, in fact, Joachim has provided in his edition (Peters). In the Allegro Vivace of Sonata Op. 30, No. 2, the end of the trill is written out:

Further on, however, no termination is indicated:

The most complicated trills to play are the short, broken or brief trills. An example in point which might be cited is the trill in the Twenty-second Concerto of Viotti, which always fills violinists with anxiety:

Several examples which shed much light on the manner in which the trill should be analyzed and understood in the music of the master of Bonn might be drawn from the Beethoven Violin Concerto.

In the Larghetto we find:

Here Joachim indicates a termination:

In the trill in the first movement the following termination is generally used:

Here, however, the termination has been indicated by Beethoven himself, and it is clear that it is better to follow the master in the development of his idea:

Trills may be found in works by Florillo, Wieniawski and Sarasate which are played as an accompaniment to a phrase, and which are difficult to make stand out. A passage of this kind may be found in Wieniawski's "Airs Russes":

This passage is complicated because of the great stretch made by the fingers of the left hand. A phrase found in Sarasate's "Le Rossignol" is equally difficult; yet, since it lies almost altogether in the third position, the real difficulty is to be found in the very limited amount of room left for the fingers to move in.

It is imprudent to attempt to force the swiftness with which the alternations of the trill notes are played, since this gives rise to a nervosity which totally does away with clearness and balance.

For the sake of completeness, some of the abbreviations employed by the older composers should be presented. The composers in question include: J. H. d'Anglebert, 1689; J. S. Bach, 1720; C. Ph. E. Bach, 1787; Dr. John Blow, 1700; Dr. Thomas Busby, 1786; F. Couperin, 1713; W. Calcott, 1817; E. Loulié, 1686; N. de St. Lambert, 1697; F. W. Marpurg, 1762; J. P. Milohmeyer, 1797; J. S. Petri, 1782; and J. G. Walther, 1732. Though these composers, with the exception of Bach, have written nothing for the violin, it is nevertheless decidedly useful to be acquainted with the abbreviations they employed.

ANCIENT MUSICAL ABBREVIATIONS

⁀	Vibrato	⁖ or ..	Play with double suavity
⁎ ✻ ⌗	Double sharp	//	Repeat words
:‖:	Repeat twice	:▌:	Repeat four times
,	Return	,,	Double return
C	Accent, portamento	Ↄ	Plucked or twanged
⌒	Double appogiatura	⌒	Suspension
\	A grace (obsolete)	/	Simple time
\ or /	Accent, portamento	>	Drop, portamento
|	Grace note	‖	Double grace-note

To return to the trill, the various schools differ so radically in their teachings concerning it, that I take pleasure in giving an absolutely convincing example of the fact by citing J. B. Viotti's views regarding the manner in which he thought the trill should be attacked; that is to say, beginning it with the note above, and not with the note itself.

The trill, however, must begin with its principal note:

Romance in F - Beethoven (1)

This should not be played as follows:

Romance in F - Beethoven (2)

Let us now take the following fragment of the Fifth Concerto by Viotti:

Fifth Concerto - Viotti (1)

Andantino

Viotti believed that it should be played in the following manner:

Fifth Concerto - Viotti (2)

With regard to double trills, their playing is regulated by the same principles covering those of the simple trills. Perfect independence of the fingers must be observed, and there should also be a sufficient degree of pressure on the two strings.

THE DÉTACHÉ

This bowing is the one most generally used, and is employed with much success in place of others which the player is incapable of using.

The *détaché* should be played in the exact middle of the bow.

The player should know how to choose his natural point of descent or attack, that is to say he should give the *détaché* a breadth in keeping with the strength and the length of his arm. If his arm be long enough, he must see to it that he secures sufficient breadth of bow; and if his arm be short, he himself must determine the amount of bow to be employed.

The player should not use a convulsive, irregular *détaché*. It is a direct result of a lack of judgment in the manner by which he tries to obtain the desired breadth in playing.

A combination which is quite difficult to bring about, is that of giving the same amount of breadth to the notes of a passage played with mixed bowings:

Concerto - Beethoven

It is evident that the breadth of the *détaché* varies, and the point is to play *piano, mezzo forte, forte* or *fortissimo*.

There are violinists who, so to speak, never use the *spiccato*, but use in its stead a very short *détaché* which makes the impression of being a *spiccato*.

Several famous artists play the Paganini "Moto Perpetuo" with a *détaché* from beginning to end of the composition.

For a professional violinist it seems decidedly strange to hear the famous "Moto,"

Moto Perpetuo - Paganini

played with the bowing as indicated over the notes instead of the proper bowing as shown under the notes.

It is anything but enchanting, to be perfectly frank, and it serves to make clear that the player's right arm is not as well developed as his left hand.

The Saltato, or Staccato with Springing Bow

In order to carry out successfully this difficult bowing, the wrist must be very flexible and, above all, exercise an indisputable mastery over the bow. The player must always have absolute control of his movements, and as everything is done on a very small scale, he must first of all possess great presence of mind.

There is an interesting difference of opinion with regard to the manner in which the Introduction to Saint-Saëns' "Rondo Capriccioso" should be played, Several virtuosos play the passage in the following way:

Rondo Capriccioso - Saint Saëns (1)

The majority of violinists, however, play it thus:

The two bowings are equally good, yet I would give the preference to that shown in the second example.

The *saltato* is used to quite an extent in rapid passages; but it should only be employed in these with circumspection, since the opportunities for its successful use are considerably limited.

It is customary to play the repetition of the variation in the Beethoven "Kreutzer Sonata" with a *saltato*:

The *saltato* is distinguished from the *staccato* by the indication of an elongated point or dot in place of a simple dot.

The "springing bow" is also used in places where the bow is "thrown" on the string, as follows:

In general the *saltato* is little used by composers; though, in order to lend additional interest to a subject, violinists like to embellish certain passages by employing it.

THE MARTELÉ

This bowing is essentially an energetic one, and may be used with success in passages where strength and decision are objects:

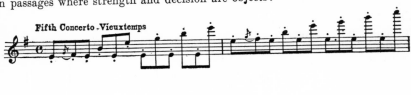

The *martelé*, if taken rightly, means that the notes are played very short and with great strength:

RHYTHM

What an austere and redoubtable word! The whole science of music is summed up in it.

It might be said at once that the perfect "rhythmician" is extremely rare, and the fact that orchestral conductors pass years conducting orchestras does not prevent them from being without any rhythmic sense. Is it possible to conceive a musician without rhythm? It is not. And yet, there are a great number of musicians, who have risen high, who lack the rhythmic sense.

Though there is every reason to believe that a sense of rhythm is, more or less, innate in the average human being, it is true, nevertheless, that where this is not the case it may be taught and developed.

As a rule not much attention is paid to the rhythmic development of the student; though, in truth, it should be the object of special care.

From the very beginning of the pupil's studies it is necessary to be absolutely inflexible as regards rhythm, and to prevent the student, by every possible means, from taking liberties with time and measure.

That faithful auxiliary, the metronome, plays a most important part in musical education, and at least makes it possible for the student to avoid precipitating himself upon a passage as misery does on a hospital. A few examples will suffice to convince the reader as to his ignorance regarding rhythm. Play the following example, for instance, once through without the metronome beat, and the second time with the assistance of Maelzel's invention, with the quarter note at 120 on the scale:

Romance in F - Beethoven

You will at once realize that you are exaggerating the movement, and that you have, in reality, all the time necessary to play the phrase calmly. Matthias Lussy's famous book *Rhythm* presents a number of intensely interesting considerations regarding its subject, and at the beginning of the volume may be found the following:

"Design corresponds to honesty and sincerity in painting" (Ingres). In the same author's *History of Musical Notation,* written together with Ernest David, he adds:

"Since rhythm bears the same relation to music that design does to painting, we in turn declare that rhythm is the honesty of music. . . ."

To this I might add that without rhythm music could not exist. Rhythm and balance are synonomous. A musician without rhythm is no more than an amateur, but an amateur without rhythm is a destroyer. Aristide Quintillian in his *De Musica* declares: "Time is the measure of movement and pausation," and again, "Rhythm is an aggregation of time arranged according to certain rules." Aristogenus, the disciple of Aristotle, regarded as the greatest musicologist of ancient Greece, said: "Rhythm is made recognizable to us, and perceptible to our senses by means of one or more measures. We do not constitute measure by means of indeterminate periods of time, but rather by periods fixed and determinable as regards their relative size and number, and the symmetry and order which reign among them. Nor do we constitute rhythm by means of indeterminate time-units, because all rhythms are formed by the assembling of determined measures. The essence of rhythm lies in the perception, by the listener, of a division, a dismemberment of the time or duration preferred, which the execution of a musical or poetic work may take." And Westphal, in his *Elements of Musical Rhythm,* defines rhythm as follows: "When we recognize a movement, we recognize it owing to the fact that its time or duration may be regularly divided into various small fragments or parts: we then say that it has a rhythm."

Again Gaevert, in his *Histoire de la Musique de l'Antiquité* states: "The laws of beauty demand that the time occupied by the performance of a musical work be divided in such a manner that the feeling of the auditor is able to discern, without effort, a regularity in the various groups of sounds and of words, as well as in the periodical return of pausation. Such an order is nothing less than rhythm, the manifestation of the principle of unity, of symmetry applied to the arts of movement." And, according to Charles Lévêque, "Rhythm is order in time or measure."

Lussy qualifies, in part, what has already been said by asserting: "It should not be thought, however, that it is enough to introduce large values of movement and pausation into a succession of sounds, in an irregular and fortuitous manner, in order to lend them meaning. It is necessary that these notes coincide with the physiological moments which impress upon our soul the sensation of repose, of an end; it is also necessary that the sounds be obedient to the laws of attraction, of appellation, which rule our tonal system." As Charles Gounod admirably put it, writing in "Le Ménestrel" of January 22, 1882: "Sounds in themselves alone no more make music than words alone constitute language. Words make a sentence, an intelligible phrase, only when they are interassociated by some historical tie responding to the laws of understanding. It is the same with regard to sounds, which must obey certain laws of attraction, of appellation, whose successive or simultaneous production is registered in order to make them a musical reality, a musical thought. Then they enter into the domain of art."

The word rhythm, like the word measure, says Lussy, has two meanings; a general and a specific one. One speaks of rhythm in general, and of one or another rhythm just as one does of measure and of one or several measures. "What is measure?" he continues. "What is the term of comparison by means of which it is possible to measure, to divide time? In other words, what is the origin of rhythm? It is evident that this origin can only be found in a phenomenon whose regular movements offer an alternation of strength and weakness, the periodical return, by twos or by threes, of a stress, a sound, a syllable, whose greater strength more especially impresses the sensibilities, and brings with it a sensation of rest, of pausation. Now, respiration alone possesses this peculiarity. Hence respiration, breathing, is the prototype of measure in music, and the generator of rhythm. It is in respiration that there dwells the faculty and power of measuring time, and of supplying our soul with the sensation of rest and pausation of time. In fact, respiration consists of two movements: inhalation and exhalation. Inhalation is equivalent to action; exhalation represents repose, the time of pausation. Exhalation is symbolized by the strong or down-beat of the bar, that is, the thesis or accented syllable. Inspiration corresponds to the weak or up-beat, that is, the arsis or mute, unaccented syllable, of the measure."

Dr. Hugo Riemann, the distinguished musicologist, seeking a means of comparison for duration of sound and the origin of rhythm in some physiological function, found it in the pulse beat. The comparison is a poor one, since pulsation is regular in strength, one pulse beat is no better than another for conveying the sensation of pause or rest.

Since we are discussing rhythm, a definition of the "ictus" should be given. The ictus, from the Latin icere, to strike, marks the down-beat, the first beat of the measure, its strong syllable; in a word, the strong sounds of the rhythms. The difference between the ictus and the thesis is that the word thesis is applied to all the strong beats contained in a measure, in a rhythm; while the word ictus is applied only to the first and last strong beats contained in the rhythm on which, so to speak, it rests.

Hence the very great importance of rhythm cannot be too strongly dwelt upon, and the violinist has at his disposal a rhythmic weapon which is not to be found in the pianist's armory, and which gives him a tremendous advantage—the bow. With the aid of the bow he is able to overcome a thousand musical and rhythmical problems which the pianist cannot even perceive.

Rhythm also is a help, a powerful help, on occasion, as a preventive against threatened "breakdowns" in public performance. If all factors were invariably favorable to the artist, public performances would be universally fine. Unfortunately, difficulties are apt to arise at the last moment, when they are least expected, and in the main these difficulties are due to the lack of musicianship on the part of those with whom the artist is obliged to play.

When playing with pseudo-musicians, the artist is often forced to stress the rhythm of the music he is playing to the detriment of the logical accentuation, which gives rise to disastrous interpretations.

Ysaÿe and Kreisler play in a superbly rhythmical manner. Kubelik's rhythm is less decisive; while that of other violinists of great reputation is practically non-existent. I must repeat that, if the violinist wishes to play in a truly rhythmical manner, he must choose his fellow player—in the case of sonatas or other ensemble works—or his accompanist, with the greatest care, and, if he himself be lacking in rhythmic sense, he must have recourse to their advice as regards playing in clean-cut rhythmic fashion, seeing that the rhythm he thinks he possesses may exist only in his imagination. In any event, he must learn to cultivate a genuine liking for the metronome, or the rhythmicon. The rhythmicon is a newer discovery, derived from the metronome, which beats out the most difficult rhythms with mathematical regularity. The more customary rhythmic figures are very perceptible, and are shown by means of cardboard perforations, each of which represents a different movement. For purposes of study and instruction, and as an aid to securing rhythmic accuracy in playing, this instrument is a very valuable mechanical accessory.

ACOUSTICS

Only a scientist can treat the subject of acoustics in all its aspects, and in presenting its essentials I will refer to those investigators who have made it the study of a lifetime. It should be remembered, of course, that acoustics are here considered exclusively from a violinistic point of view, and especially with regard to virtuoso violin playing.

Take the young artist who plays in public. The word acoustics has a very real meaning for him. He steps out upon the concert platform, makes his bow and begins to play. And from the moment his bow touches the strings he is unnerved and annoyed by the various echoes which come to him, echoes of sounds which he had thought ended, and which continue; by the duration of sounds accented by the kettledrums, for instance. In my opinion, the violinist should never be too near the orchestra when he plays, but should stand at a distance of at least five feet away from it, where he will be less at the mercy of the acoustic echoes. Playing with the piano is a different matter: here he must draw as near as possible to the piano, since the tonal quality of sound is altogether different in each instrument, and one supplements the other without interference.

Acoustics, from the Greek *acono*, "I listen," is that branch of physics whose object is to define the properties and relations of sounds, distinguish between tones and noises, and determine the laws according to which sound propagates itself.

Sound is generated by the movement given by percussion, or in any other way, to the molecules of some tone-producing body. The molecules of this body, whose equilibrium has been momentarily disturbed, return to their former position while executing rapid movements which constitute the vibrations already mentioned.

These vibrations, in turn, generate sound. Hence sound in itself is not a body, but is produced by the molecular movements of various bodies.

These vibrations may be easily determined. All that is necessary is to suspend a glass bevel from the extremity of a metal rod, of approximately .039 inches distant from its rim, in such wise that it can move. Then give the bell a light tap. Mingled with the resulting sound will be a noise produced by its striking the metal rod with its edges, which did not touch the rod before the production of the sound.

We must remember that the atom is the last final element in any body. The atoms in the most complex bodies are simple, and do not, as a consequence, give a complete idea of the body to which they belong.

The molecule is the combination or union of the system of atoms which compose the body. It is a complete sample of the body to which it belongs, and is the smallest one.

The particle is a combination or union of molecules, a small portion of a body, yet one more or less considerable.

Light, heat, magnetism and electricity are produced by atomic movement; sound is produced by molecular movement.

Hence one may say, with Tyndall, that the production of sound is analogous to that of light or heat rays, which also, in actuality, move in waves. Like the sound waves, the heat and light waves spread indefinitely in space, diminishing in intensity in consequence of the same laws, and, like sound waves, they lose but very little of their intensity when they are propagated in tubes whose interior surface is highly polished. Incidentally, all experiments in light refraction have had results analogous to those given by sound refraction.

It should be mentioned that a "vibration" as it is defined in America, England and Germany, comprises at one and the same time, a forward and backward movement. In France, the term "vibration" is applied to a single one of these movements, that is to say a French "vibration" is one half that of an English one. This complete vibration of the English and Germans is also known as an oscillation or undulation, a "wave"; while the French vibration is only half an oscillation or undulation, half a wave.

E. F. Chladni (1756-1827) hit upon the idea of making sound waves visible by pouring sand on the surface of a vibrating body, and attacking it with the bow. In this manner he obtained some surprisingly beautiful designs. It is astonishing to note, as soon as the vibrations are generated, not alone the rapidity with which the lines are formed, but their clearness as well. Metal or glass plates fixed by the center are generally used for these experiments.

CHAPTER XII

TONE AND THE VARIOUS BOWINGS

Like the human voice, the violin becomes a marvelous musical instrument when the player has learned to draw from it a tone at once mellow and powerful.

Quality of tone is the most important point in violin playing, and on his tone depends the talent of the artist.

Vieuxtemps, Joachim and, in our own day, Ysaÿe have marked a great advance on the older school of violin playing with regard to the tie, and to sustained notes.

The tie or syncopation of tones or sounds consists in expressing them without noticeable change of bow. In order to do so, the notes must be given a breadth of bow which extends them beyond their actual time value.

Sustained playing is a means by which a certain moving "roundness" of tone is secured in the interpretation of phrases expressive of emotion, by using a length of bow proportionate to the movement.

In the following examples I shall give an illustration of the curve described by the bow in passing across the strings:

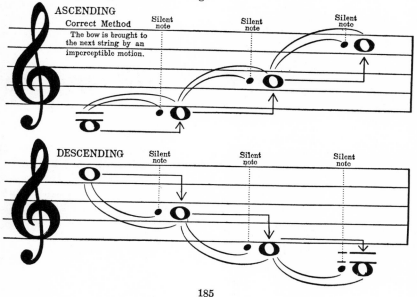

The method indicated by the slurs *above* the notes is the correct one; the method indicated by the arrows *underneath* the notes is the incorrect one.

Tone may be improved by study, but usually it is a natural gift (?) and excellent violinists sometimes have all the trouble in the world in securing a quality of tone which will be at the same time valid and charming.

I have made a profound analysis of the best manner of working to secure a good tone, or, rather, a sustained tone, and have come to the conclusion that in order to gain the desired result, the violinist should be able to sustain his tone for a full minute without using the tremolo or playing with harshness.

The tone should gradually gain perfect evenness and equality:

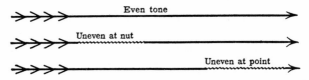

It may be perfected by practicing the production of an even, sustained tone without *crescendo* or *diminuendo,* using the lower or the upper third of the bow.

Furthermore, in securing a genuine sustained tone, the problem has to be solved which is offered by the passage of the bow without shock across the four strings.

The idea is by no means new, since the immortal Viotti—and, no doubt, other masters before him—have anticipated its application.

It has been claimed that the tone of Pietro Nardini was of unequaled beauty, and that his mode of playing was sustained to such a degree that his audiences never failed to react to its charm.

The following exercise makes an excellent study in this connection:

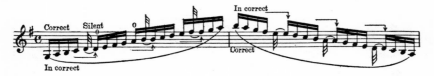

A certain amount of preparation on the part of the bow should precede the taking of the note to be played. Besides, where the execution is concerned, this preparation is absolutely essential and should be employed at all times.

This preparation is applicable as well to the sustained playing of the notes, to the sustained tone, as to technique pure and simple, and any student who cares to take the trouble to learn how to judge the great artists will soon realize that their playing is based on three essentials:

1. Prudence
2. Calmness
3. Preparation

One of the most complex details of violin playing is the art of introducing an initial *pianissimo* without any audible falling of the bow on the string, or a cutting short without attack. It is altogether a matter of flexibility, and the degree of virtuosity to which a violinist has attained may be very soon estimated by the manner in which he produces his *ton filé,* that even, sustained tone without *crescendo* or *decrescendo.*

CHAPTER XIII

THE EVOLUTION OF VIOLIN TECHNIQUE

When we consider the time which has elapsed from the creation of the violin, properly speaking, to the appearance of Paganini, it must be admitted that the evolution of progress was slow up to the moment when the tremendous genius of the great Italian illumined the firmament of art by the deploy of his magic powers.

In order to understand the evolution of violin technique it is necessary to understand Paganini's genius; the formidable results of what he created in the field must be studied. Liszt and Chopin, so to speak, are the creations of Paganini, and it might even be said that Liszt did for the piano what Paganini did for the violin. We are compelled to pay the most enthusiastic tributes to these geniuses who made violin and piano the kings of instruments, and it is not going too far when we bestow the title of emperor on the violin, and that of king on its keyboard rival.

The organ, naturally, holds a place apart: it is an orchestra played by a single individual, and equipped with nearly all the wealth of the orchestral tone palette.

The unforgettable Corelli, the father of violin technique, opened new horizons of violinistic achievement by extending the variety of bowings, for until his epoch the violin was a mere vulgar instrument of accompaniment.

Then came those "Airs with Variations" which were born of Tartini's inspiration, and whose flight came to an end only a few years ago, when they were replaced by the variations "without melodies" of modern music. Musical snobs may, if they choose, treat this primitive musical form with disdain; it has, for all that, been productive of savory virtuoso fruit.

There are even airs with variations (and under this head I classify all themes musically varied) which are magnificent. We may take, for example, the sixty variations which Tartini wrote on a Corelli gavotte: they are a genuine treasure, and, incidentally, wonderfully valuable for the study of the bow; they are even known as "the art of bowing." The violinist who to-day is able to play these variations perfectly may be regarded as a finished artist. It is a pity that this superb work has been mutilated by editors minus a conscience, who have been guilty of such monstrosities as putting forth the complete work in partial and abridged editions. It should be played only in the original edition and in its completed form, and those who take the liberty of cutting it in any way deserve the severest censure.

In his *Twenty-four Caprices,* Locatelli (1693-1764) has discovered various technical procedures of genuine interest. Several editions of this work have appeared in the course of the past few years; but the fact that these Caprices have been extracted from the Twelve Concertos of Locatelli, each of which contains two Caprices, is not generally known.

The following is a quotation from a publisher's notice of a forthcoming edition of the Locatelli Caprices:

"If we are to judge by the astonishment aroused by the appearance of the Paganini Caprices, and by other works written by composers of the present day, it would seem that the violin has only at this day and hour entered the period of virtuoso difficulty. Yet those who believe this to be the case can have but a superficial acquaintance with the older composers for the instrument. If we go back a hundred years, and examine the works of able violinists, we will find that they often combine a profound scientific knowledge of the instrument with the ripest musicianship. Among such artists must be included: Corelli, Porpora, Tartini, Nardini, J. S. Bach, Kenis, Leclair and others.

"Every period has its own style; yet as to schools, there is undoubtedly one first and original school which will endure through the centuries, and it is certain that the artist who most assiduously studies the ancient masters will find in them greater resources for the development of his own talent.

"Some ninety-one years ago the Locatelli Caprices were published for the first time, for they appeared in 1733, in Amsterdam, and since their appearance all capable of genuinely appreciating the best in violin study material have admired this master work. Gaviniés, the glory of the French school, who, at the age of twenty-three, composed and played his study work known as the 'Twenty-four Matinées,' a work which has sufficed to establish his reputation, made his début in 1740, at the 'Concerts Spirituels,' at the age of fourteen playing Concertos by Locatelli, and roused astonishment by the skill with which he performed the Caprices.

"In the twenty-third Caprice, known as 'The Labyrinth,' Locatelli went beyond the boundaries of the ordinary, and undoubtedly amused himself for a moment at the expense of his contemporaries, by giving them a problem to solve. How often, for this very reason, have not certain violinists, too indolent to take the trouble to study out the actual positions, declared that Locatelli had caused the ligatures connecting the fingers of his left hand to be cut, in order that he might play the composition. To-day it is evident that this theory will not hold water, and that the Caprices are very playable."

As to "The Labyrinth" which the composer has given us—though in abbreviated form and without any indications regarding the manner in which the arpeggios are to be played—it may be taken for granted that he wished to make it easy for those who performed it to vary the different kinds of arpeggios at will. M. Woldemar and J. B. Cartier, however, have edited the composition in accordance with the traditions handed down to them, and have developed the abbreviations in such a way that they may be played by the generality of musicians, and the latter has supplied a valuable note, which will be found on page 40 of the edition in question.

"As is generally known, these Caprices are in reality solo cadenzas of flourishes, which usually stop on a suspended chord; but the editor, with all due respect for the tradition established by the composer, has nevertheless thought proper, in order to rest the ear of the player, to add a single chord at the end of each Caprice.

"It is also a matter of common knowledge that in these older compositions the last sharp or the last flat was often dropped from the clef, hence one should not be surprised to find various ones among the Caprices engraved in this manner. Again, in many cases, to nullify one of the sharps given in the key signature, it was customary to place a flat before a note in the course of the composition, where a natural should actually be played; and in the same way a sharp was used to invalidate a flat when a flatted note was to be played as a natural.

"An analysis of these Caprices shows quite plainly that they were intended to be played with accompaniment.

"In general, one should not gain a false idea of the musical value of these Caprices. Their value is above all a documentary one. The numerous wonderful works written by Locatelli offer such eloquent testimony of a creative genius superior to these compositions, that they must be considered far inferior to his other works.

"An example of the monotony which becomes so evident in connection with Caprice No. 2 is here given:

Caprice N♀ 2 - Locatelli

"Later on we meet with abbreviations which are troublesome; in Caprice No. 5 a phrase of this kind is set down in the following manner:

Caprice N♀ 5 - Locatelli (1)

"This phrase should be played as follows:

Caprice N♀ 5 - Locatelli (2)

"I would recommend every violinist to study these Caprices with the greatest care, as he will gain greatly by their study."

Johann Sebastian Bach (1685-1750) followed the road taken by the ancient masters of the violin, and often made use of their figurations in the composition of his master works. He has, of course, employed them with the greatest latitude, and left their manner of performance to the artists who may play them. The latter, however, at times exceed the bounds of the artistically permissible, and entirely change the frame within which these works should be confined.

When Arcangelo Corelli (1653-1713) handed on his artistic legacy to Giuseppe Tartini (1692-1770), the latter in turn extended the horizons of violin achievement by important technical developments in the musical master-pieces he wrote; and numerous notable violinists were trained in the school he founded in Padua, in 1728. In Tartini's famous sonata "The Devil's Trill," the technical innovations he introduces in trilling are most important. Unfortunately, I have been unable to discover an edition of Tartini's own day, and owing to the great diversity of the signs which I had previously found in manuscript written by the Paduan master, I am inclined to believe that any number of supplementary ones have been added to those originally given. In the Allegro Moderato of "The Devil's Trill" Sonata, the trill marked by the sign *tr* should unquestionably be marked with the sign ⌁ or ⌁ ; and besides, the trill, like every other technical combination, is not practicably playable unless the tempo in which it is executed is left to the player. It is impossible to play a true trill on a sixteenth note with the tempo set at $108 = \flat$, M.M.

Le Trille du Diable-Tartini (1)

Again, further on, we find:

Le Trille du Diable-Tartini (2)

When playing at the expense of rhythm and measure, it is quite evidently possible to execute a rich, well-nourished trill on any note desired, and at any degree of speed; but the first thing to be done is to obey the laws of music and of rhythm, which inexorably reject all that is in poor taste, and all liberties detrimental to them.

In the allegro assai of "The Devil's Trill" Sonata (see complete analysis elsewhere in this work) we undoubtedly have one of the earliest examples of a trill used to illustrate a theme, a departure in which Tartini has been followed by other famous composer violinists, one of the most outstanding of whom,

Henri Wieniawski, employs the same device in the introduction to his brilliant "Airs Russes."

The abbreviations used by the older masters have given rise to numberless controversies in our own day, to which each individual edition of their works adds its own apple of discord, and a trifle more of confusion.

For instance, in the fugue in the Johann Sebastian Bach Sonata in G Minor, the following fragment is written as shown:

Fugue (Sonata in G Minor) Bach

Who can tell us exactly what Bach had in mind?   Could it have been that he meant it to be played as follows?

First Interpretation

Hellmsberger gives the following formula:

Second Interpretation

It would be more logical to play this, however, with the same idea in mind as shown in the following example:

Third Interpretation

It is well to note the fact that the violinists themselves have been the greatest obstacles toward progress and development in violin technique, a fact which is as strange as it is true.

And we have not changed. We are still the same at the present day, and take but little interest in new things unless they are placed on the market with a great outcry of advertisement.

Whenever some great virtuoso plays a new composition with success, all the young artists take it up.

When Brahms showed the manuscript of his violin Concerto to Wieniawski, the latter was terrified and refused to play it, and yet all who were acquainted with Wieniawski regarded him, not only as a genial violinist, but as a serious musician as well. He said that the Brahms' Concerto could not be played on the violin; and, to be candid, though it is a fine work, it is not a violinistic one.

Then we have the reception given the famous Sonata which Beethoven dedicated to Kreutzer. That violinist called the work an "insane" one, and never played it. This stigma will always remain with the memory of Kreutzer, who should have gone down on his knees before this work, which Vieuxtemps has declared imperishable.

Paganini is the father of modern violin technique. He was the first to make the violin sparkle with a radiance incomparable; he was the magician whose bow opened up illimitable horizons in the violin mechanism, and it was he who gave a hitherto unimagined richness to the most fantastic passages.

The "Twenty-four Caprices" written by the great Genoese constitute a work whose powerful musicality, originality and invention merit the admiration of the most exacting musician. Brahms considered these "Twenty-four Caprices" a finished masterpiece.

Paganini, by means of his compelling virtuosity, not only created number-less new possibilities for the violinist, but he also provided opportunities for the pianist and composer.

Vieuxtemps, who followed the path blazed by Paganini, made discoveries of his own. At the same time he was often responsible for exaggerations, and, for instance, used ascending sequences of triple chords which compel a pressure on the violin strings that is rather disagreeable:

Finale (Fourth Concerto) Vieuxtemps

Thomson changes the passage thus:

The above as played by Cesar Thomson

This is far more violinistic, and, at all events, the violinist would have to possess the muscles of Hercules in order to express properly the atrocity first instanced.

At the present time violin development has reached a halting point from which further progress will only be made when a new Paganini appears.

Wieniawski was another artist who relied on a technique which was aston-ishingly musical, and who displayed a flamboyant virtuosity.

At the present time the demands made on the violinist are very great, and the orchestra musician, to mention a case in point, is subject to tests which would have stupefied his ancestors.

Liszt, as is well known, was the direct predecessor of Wagner, and was the first to overstep the narrow limits imposed on the orchestral violins in his day. This great artist gave the violins wonderful opportunities in his orchestrations, and deserves gratitude for being the first to make it possible for good musicians living an obscure life to put into practice the results of their studies.

Gustav Saenger of New York, by the way, has edited five books of the most complex passages to be found in the most difficult orchestral scores. His splendid compilation is one that is of the greatest value to the orchestra violinist, for many orchestra conductors cannot understand the impossibility of playing certain passages without having studied them thoroughly.

The preceding examples prove beyond all doubt that modern orchestra music contains passages which are far more complex than any encountered in the Brahms' Violin Concerto, that of Bruch, or others. These composers indubitably consulted Joachim, and took his advice in order to make the passages they invented violinistic.

It took some twenty-five years at least before the violinists decided to include the Brahms' Concerto in their repertory. Not long ago Ysaÿe played the Concerto with his habitual talent, and the pleasure of listening to him was enhanced by the thought that the beauties of his playing were shown forth in a work worthy of them.

Zdislaw Birnbaum, one of the conductors of the Warsaw Philharmonic Orchestra, told me one day it was after he had played the Brahms' Concerto with Ysaÿe—that the Belgian master decided to add the work to his repertory. He scored an enormous success with it, and I may say with conviction, after having heard all the violinists at present before the public in it, that his interpretation is the one which made the greatest impression upon me.   It would be interesting, nevertheless, to know whether Brahms himself would have been content with the slight pause and the brief playing of the last notes of the first and second measures of the finale, as Ysaÿe presents them.   The original version is as follows:

Finale - Brahms Concerto

Ysaÿe plays it thus:

In the first movement, on the other hand, Ysaÿe has introduced an innovation which deserves to be appreciated, since it gives the chords in question a meaning and an importance which they lose absolutely when they are drawn out.

Concerto - Brahms

I do not claim that Ysaÿe is altogether within his rights in doing this, but I can bear witness to the satisfactory effect which results from this bowing.

It was Joachim who popularized the Beethoven "Kreutzer Sonata," a work of considerable extent, and impregnated with the atmosphere of genius from beginning to end.

The music publishers, as a rule, have recourse to the most famous violinists for the revision of the celebrated works of the violin repertory, yet, though this idea is logical enough, the revisions are not always carried out in a manner creditable to the authority making them.

J. Becker, for instance, the famous head of the Florentine Quartet, made an excellent revision of the Paganini *Caprices* for the Edition Peters; yet his ideas with regard to the Caprice No. 1 are decidedly open to question.   He indicates:

Caprice Nº 1 - Paganini (1)

which is quite illogical. It would be preferable not to strive for ease and convenience in so marked a manner, and use a more natural fingering instead:

Caprice N⁰ 1 - Paganini (2)

Further on we find:

Caprice N⁰ 1 - Paganini (3)

Why increase the difficulties encountered fivefold? One should try, on the contrary, to lessen them. It is so easy to use the following fingering:

Caprice N⁰ 1 - Paganini (4)

There are numerous other examples of this kind which prove that the violinist, instead of employing logic has made use of subterfuge. In Becker's edition of the Paganini Caprice No. 24, in the fourth variation, the fingering which is indicated can be used, it is true; but its application is quite impracticable, and I call attention to it because it is a fingering which might be termed, speaking as an electrician, a "poor conductor."

Caprice N⁰ 24 - Var. IV - Paganini (1)

Though it is always preferable to select a position which is to be held for as long a time as possible as quickly as may be, it is better to avoid all danger of playing out of tune. Hence I recommend the following fingering, the more so that Gaviniés indicates the same tendency toward progression by "periods," that is to say, by the employ of the same fingering for ascending passages, or for descending ones, of the same design. The fingering which follows will be found simple and practical:

Caprice N⁰ 24 - Var. IV - Paganini (2)

In an arrangement of the "Twenty-four Caprices" by Paganini which I have supplied with a second violin accompaniment, I have indicated the necessary alteration which should facilitate the playing of the Caprices for a violinist whose hand is small, and who, as a result, usually finds it impossible to play these Caprices as they were written by the Genoese master.

I will give some examples of the changes which I have indicated while respecting the original text:

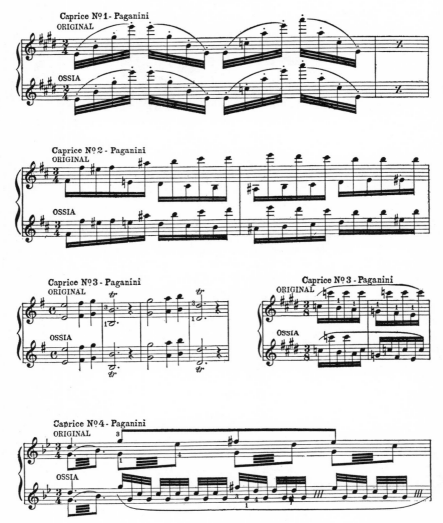

It is quite evident that passages will be met with in the Caprices written by various violinists which, at first sight, it seems impossible to play, but which, nevertheless, once they are taken up in the right way, may be mastered with rapidity. In one of my thirty "Caprices d'Artiste" the following passage occurs:

Caprice d'Artiste (Bachmann)
Allegro

It is in this case merely a question of shifting with the necessary dexterity. The moment a passage ceases to be violinistic, it should be altered. Saint-Saëns, for whom I entertain the greatest veneration, did not disdain to ask Sarasate's advice with regard to various passages in his violin compositions. It is certain that in the technical development used in the violin concertos written by this illustrious French master, the true inwardness of its mechanism is the most difficult thing to grasp, for it is a mechanism more akin to the piano than to the violin. A violinist can lay aside the Beethoven or the Mendelssohn Concertos, and not play them for three months, and can then take them up and play them in tempo. I defy him to do the same with the Concertos of Brahms and Saint-Saëns, which must be studied over again thoroughly every time they have been laid aside. The instrumental artist is less favored than the painter or the writer in this respect, since he must work with mathematical regularity if he wishes to preserve his ability. Painter and sculptor can lay aside their work for several months and take it up again without any decrease in their skill. Anton Rubinstein, whom I had the pleasure of knowing in Dresden, in 1891, once told me that when he let a day go by without practicing he noticed it, and that when he allowed two days to pass without working, the public noticed it.

CHAPTER XIV

THE USE OF THE BOW

The manner in which a violinist handles his bow at once betrays whether he is a musician or a mere amateur.

The intelligent violinist will always have recourse to logic in order to give balance to his bow strokes; he will ground his bowing on fundamental principles, and will observe a strict line of conduct with regard to handling the bow.

Among those who are most guilty, in so far as poor bowing is concerned, are the orchestral conductors, in nearly every case disrated pianists or violinists who, thanks to a fortunate combination of circumstances, have become distinguished orchestral leaders. Very often they are no more than petty musicians, placed at the head of large organizations. Hearing the blunders of which these persons are guilty, one can hardly believe one's ears.

In Europe this evil is not half so pronounced, for if it were to run its whole course, the orchestral musicians would break all the bones in the bodies of these time beaters. In America, what is accomplished in this direction is past belief, and enough to make one die of laughter.

The following are some of the bowings used by certain of the Symphony Orchestras:

It is in extreme bad taste to begin this Scherzo with a down-bow. Again we find:

The quality which lends this passage its strength and grandeur is inevitably transformed into a jig, for, the orchestral conductor indicating no rhythm, the instrumentalists who follow change the movement of the theme from 2/4 time to 6/8 time, as in the following example:

Thus this splendid theme is turned into a species of cradle song.

200

What is done in the G major Symphony of Mozart passes all bounds, and actually turns things upside down. The following example shows the bowings used at its beginning when played by Symphony Orchestras:

G Major Symphony - Mozart

On a number of occasions the violinists may be seen playing with inverse bowings, which is a decisive proof of incapacity.

And now I shall "outrage" the convictions of a number of my colleagues when I declare that I do not believe in a precise or exactly defined way of playing the *martelé,* at the point, or at a two-third bow length; or the *spiccato* with the middle of the bow or at the point.

Sarasate had a *sautillé* unique of its kind, and he played it nearly at the point, and at all events notably higher than the middle of the bow.

In the application of his bow stroke, every student should be guided by his individual physical conformity, or, better said, every teacher should study and realize the individual student's "type" before teaching him principles which may not be in accordance with his physical capacities.

In order to make a natural and normal application of the various styles of bowing, the student should first take a composition and make it the subject of exhaustive investigation. He can thus tell whether there is occasion to use the *sautillé,* the *détaché* or the *martelé* in this, that or the other passage. For example, in the Beethoven "Romance" in F, if the passage which follows be played *spiccato,* it becomes cheapened, and is in direct contradiction with the well-nigh austere character of the composition:

Romance in F - Beethoven (1)

The passage in question should be presented, using a short *détaché* and playing nearly at the point of the bow.

Further on, however, the bowing must be broad and full of marrow, and every note must be given that due majestic qualify which it calls for, as follows:

Romance in F - Beethoven (2)

Also the passage:

Romance in F - Beethoven (3)

which should be played with the whole length of the bow.

A defective bow technique is the point of departure for a poor application of the various strokes, and this, in turn, is due to the fact that a teacher capable of teaching the correct handling of the bow is very rarely to be found, for the very good reason that only too often the teacher does not know how to use the bow himself. And, to be quite candid, the violinist who is at home in every detail of bow technique is a very great artist indeed, and the really great artists are rare.

The bowing used often influences the character of the work interpreted. Sarasate, for instance, always began the Saint-Saëns' Violin Concerto in B Minor in the following manner:

B Minor Concerto - Saint - Saëns (1)

the first four notes falling like blows of the fist on a drum head.

Ysaÿe was the first to understand the beauty of the beginning of this magnificent Concerto, and stamped the two measures with the power of his interpretation by playing them in this manner:

B Minor Concerto - Saint - Saëns (2)

In the finale of the same Concerto, the interpretations of Sarasate and Ysaÿe were of equal value, for if Ysaÿe brought more of vigor to his exposition, Sarasate was superb in the lightness of imposing character of his playing:

Finale - B Minor Concerto - Saint - Saëns (3)

Ysaÿe's tempo is notably slower than that of Sarasate; yet to my mind it is preferable, wherever possible, because it stresses beauty at the cost of the trifling, and hence should be unhesitatingly approved. And, on the violin, beauty of tone is secured by the use of a broad and powerful bow stroke.

The powerful bowing may be employed quite as readily for music which is to be played lightly, as for music which calls for the exercise of strength, and it recalls Vieuxtemps' saying that the violinist should have an arm of steel and a wrist of velvet. The profound truth of this maxim uttered by the great master of the strings is well-nigh beyond sounding in all its phases, and it responds absolutely to the demands made by the technique of the bow.

CHAPTER XV

ACCENTUATION OR EMPHASIS

Accentuation lends life to musical execution, and if the musical phrase is to be intelligently expressed, it is necessary to follow its natural inflection, marked by accenting the first note of a tie. (We will consider the subject of accentuation in technique later on, since this is a variety of emphasis of a very special nature, and is employed only by a few artists.)

In order to make clear my views with regard to accentuation and its proper application, I have selected as examples phrases from the violin works of Beethoven and Mendelssohn.

The first note of the second and third measures at the beginning of the Mendelssohn Concerto should be accented without abruptness, for emphasis must not be confounded with brutal stress. There are strong accents and weak accents.

This is a decidedly important accent, since it at once establishes the affectionate happiness of mood of the commencement of this movement. This joyous beginning of the Concerto might, in fact, be described as a love story, whose heroine is an innocent young girl.

Turning to the following example fragment:

we find when played as indicated above the phrase is insipid; whereas, when the correct accentuation is given:

an admirable rhythmic symmetry results.

Again, if the following phrase, for instance, is played *détaché,* without accent, thus:

the result is monotony itself, while if the accent really demanded be given, as follows:

the phrase thus played will be full of life and decision.

We now come to a two-measure section in the Mendelssohn Concerto which the majority of artists accent incorrectly, in the following manner:

The accentuation really should be employed here in the manner as illustrated:

During the moving phrase which follows, certain most important accents should be applied:

and later on:

This last accent, on the *G*, is the expression of an ill-restrained impatience; and in view of the entirely lifeless manner in which this phrase is generally understood and interpreted, this accentuation may be advised as a most happy one.

In the technical two-measure example which follows, we find a celebrated passage which offers insoluble difficulties to many violinists. Its lack of accentuation is their worst enemy, and yet this same section, as may be seen in the following example, falls readily into line under the direct application of the proper accents.

A violinist who plays without accentuation or emphasis must be regarded as a mediocre player, a "whipped cream" violinist, and not, in the true sense, an artist.

In the andante from the Mendelssohn Concerto there are also characteristic passages which demand accentuation.

In the allegretto which precedes the vivace, the *E* must be accented wittily and with intelligence, for this introduction appears to be a bit of playful teasing:

So far as the finale is concerned, it must be taken measure by measure, so to speak, in order to prove the efficacy of its accentuations:

The accent on the *A,* for instance, is excellent; yet it should appear as an isolated stress, and the volume of tone should not be augmented either before or after the note in question is played.

And now we have reached a phrase which serves to prove either the student's artistic maturity or his ignorance; it is the two measure section following upon the *tutti:*

The illustration which follows shows what ought to be done:

In this vigorously martial two-measure phrase, the accent is *sforzando* rather than a mere stress; yet, though it must be forcefully played, this by no means implies that it should be attacked in a brutal manner.

In Beethoven's "Romance" in F Major, the phrase which follows must be accented, to avoid the risk of being monotonous, since monotony is the relentless enemy of all beauty in music. The passage in question should be accented as here shown:

Further on, in the same "Romance," we find a phrase whose correct accentuation has been the subject of considerable discussion.

This phrase is contained in a musical sentence of great dramatic intensity, and when the accentuation indicated is used—it is, incidentally, the one preferred by Joachim—a truly grandiose effect is secured.

Louis Spohr's Eighth Concerto, the so-called "Vocal Scena," offers a number of examples which may be used for similar applications of accent.

These two accents may be said to express a grief poorly disguised and illustrate the saying that "there is no rose without its thorn." Returning to Beethoven's admirable "Romance" in F Major, it is emphatically a composition devoid of all life and expression when played without accentuation. In the passage which follows, it is important that the notes which control the direct upward movement of the theme be well marked:

Marks of accentuation are written in various ways. I would suggest that the following signs be used:

> Strong Accent <
> Medium Strong Accent >
> Weak Accent ▷

In this way much confusion would be avoided, and the execution of the player would gain greatly in clearness.

The Technical Accentuation

And now we reach a species of accentuation which is of greatest importance, and which forms a pendant to the rhythmical or poetic accent we have been considering. This is technical or mechanical accentuation, by means of which phrases and passages acquire an intense vitality. Sarasáte, who had the most intensely "living" mechanism which could be imagined, was an adept at this species of accent, and it was the secret, I believe, of the pyramidal and perfected technique which he possessed. His technique showed mad ability, and at the same time, an intelligence which bordered on the miraculous.

Ernst's "Othello" Fantasy furnishes us with several examples of the technical æsthetics of the unforgettable Spanish master.

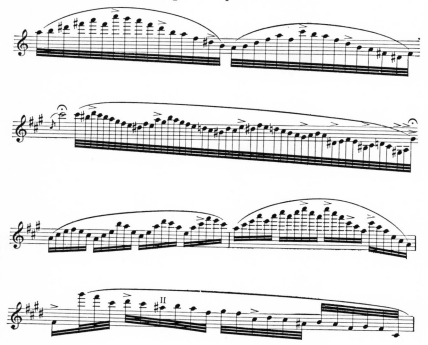

These examples prove that the student must practice change of position at a lightning rate of speed if he wishes to infuse his technique with vitality.

My aversion for the ordinary "mechanicians of the violin" is sincere, yet it must be admitted that an easy and flexible technique is required to overcome the difficulties scattered through the majority of violin compositions.

If, ordinarily, teachers of the violin do not cultivate in their pupils a sufficiently rational application of sane and exact technical and mechanical principles, it is because they themselves know but little regarding them. Incidentally, the system generally followed of giving instruction in violin mechanics is altogether lacking in foundation, and hardly any but the finished virtuoso could demonstrate it satisfactorily. Hence, the student should endeavor, as far as possible, to approach the genuine virtuoso and ask his advice.

CHAPTER XVI

THE GLISSANDO OR PORTAMENTO

This name is given to one of the most important violin effects and, in fact, purity of intonation in violin playing and seriousness of style are based on the *glissando*. A serious artist is at once recognized by the manner in which he conceives the bearing that one tone has on another. The various theories regarding this subject have never been thoroughly threshed out, and many violinists have not even taken the pains to apply principles of any kind to the practical development of this important branch of their art.

I myself am a believer in the principle of direct action, as shown herewith:

Glide with the *first* finger to a fourth below the principal note and not in the principle of indirect action, as illustrated by:

This procedure, which cannot be commended, consists in gliding with the *fourth* finger from the fourth succeeding to the first note.

Sarasate had one great quality amid a number of others; he practiced the *glissando* with circumspection.

Many violinists of undoubted talent absolutely spoil their playing as a consequence of the poor taste which they display in this respect, and which results in particular from a wrong use of the *portamento*. It would be easy to find excellent examples which might be submitted to the violinist desirous of cultivating artistic good habits, and with a higher outlook than that of captivating the common herd.

The Third Violin Concerto by Saint-Saëns, for instance, is a work from which we may glean an abundant harvest of excellent examples for study, for this Concerto is one of the most finished from the standpoint of virtuosity allied to genuine musicality.

At the very beginning, we have the following two measures:

This movement from *B* to *F* is all too often played with a *glissando* which is really pitiable if we consider the lofty and severe manner in which the beautiful theme should be presented. No *portamento* is called for between these two notes, and the violinist should concentrate on carrying out his change of position without effort, and without its being noticeable.

Further on we find another passage:

Here, too, there should be no *glissando* between the *B* and the *F*.

Every note should be given its exact value, and there should be no curtailment of even the shortest note as regards its duration; whether it be the case of an eighth-note triplet or of a whole note, each should be treated with the same regard for its rights of duration.

As a rule the ear is offended by the unseasonable *glissando* applied in the following fragment:

As a general thing a real voyage is made of the transit from the *G* to the *D*; whereas, were one to pass rapidly from the first to the third position, a *glissando* in very poor taste would be avoided.

In the admirable phrase which follows:

it is heartbreaking to have to listen to it played:

as this voyage from *B* to the *D* is so often carried out. It is the combination of actual worth and good taste which distinguishes the real artist.

The andantino of the Saint-Saëns' Concerto is prolific in useful examples. The following moving phrase:

is one which often suffers from the violinist's mania for using the *glissando* without excuse. Played with a *glissando*, a "sliding" effect is produced between the *G* sharp and the *G* natural which, rankly speaking, is horrible. Nevertheless, this terrible *glissando* delights the masses, and one can hear people listening to it say: "What sentiment! How soulful!"

It will be seen that the student must above all things, avoid what is anti-artistic, and the misapplied *glissando* is one of the most inartistic things which violin playing has to offer. Its excessive and inappropriate employment is a present-day tendency which should be opposed, in order to make way for ideals which stand for something higher than arousing the enthusiasm of the artistically perverted by so sorry a means.

CHAPTER XVII

ANALYSES OF MASTER VIOLIN WORKS

For the purpose of demonstrating the proper methods of advanced violin study, this section of the *Encyclopedia* presents analyses of several of the master works in the violin repertory, the observations being founded on the author's personal experience, and his many interesting discussions of technical and interpretative matters with great contemporary virtuosos.

As it would be manifestly impossible to analyze at length all the wonderful works which have been written for the violin by great composers, the following have been selected as representative of the entire group:

Chaconne (from the Fourth Sonata), by Johann Seb. Bach
Romance in G Major, Op. 40, by L. Van Beethoven
Romance in F Major, Op. 50, by L. Van Beethoven
Devil's Trill, Sonata by Giuseppe Tartini
Concerto in D Major, Op. 61, by L. Van Beethoven
Kreutzer Sonata, Op. 47, by L. Van Beethoven
Concerto in E Minor, Op. 64, by Felix Mendelssohn
Concerto in D Major, Op. 77, by Johannes Brahms
Concerto in A Minor, Op. 20, by Camille Saint-Saëns
Symphonie Espagnole, Op. 21, by Eduard Lalo
Concerto in G Minor, Op. 26, by Max Bruch
Concerto in B Minor, Op. 61, by Camille Saint-Saëns
Introduction and Rondo Capriccioso, Op. 28, by Camille Saint-Saëns

CHACONNE

By Johann Sebastian Bach

(1685-1750)

Bach's "Chaconne," notable for the seriousness of its style, is a work in which the Leipsic master has given the utmost freedom of expression to his genius. One might affirm that the melodic and harmonic beauties of Bach and the technical brilliancy of Paganini have united to enrich the violin with a composition of miraculous beauty.

The periods of the composition are each eight measures in length. The numbers which follow (1, 2, 3, 4, etc.) indicate the beginning of successive periods.

212

1

The very decisive beginning should be presented in the most sustained fashion, and the chords played with great breadth.

In order to obtain a big tone it is advisable to play the chords long drawn out, and with the up-bow. In this matter, incidentally, the author ventures to disagree with Joachim, who thought that the rhythm of the "Chaconne" was rendered too heavy by a strong third beat. The character of the Bach "Chaconne" is austere to the highest degree, and does not suggest in any way, shape or form a composition (in vogue during the seventeenth and eighteenth centuries) written for the dance.

2

Since the melody must be sustained, the chords should be broken in such wise as to give all the importance it may rightfully claim to the first theme, an interpretation preferred by all violinists who are genuine musicians. Nevertheless, any crassness or roughness in the enunciation of the chords should be avoided, and they should be given as much pith and tonal marrow as possible.

3

The final sixteenth note of the first measure, and the first beat of the second measure must be played without abruptness, and in order to follow the text of the original as closely as possible, the quarter note on the first beat of the eighth measure should be sustained.

4

We have here the beginning of an improvisation which does not conclude until the eighth period is reached. The tempo should be slightly slackened and the whole bow should be used. After the fifth measure of this period, the tone should be veiled.

5

This passage is often played in too rough a manner; the *détaché* notes of the first three measures should not be played abruptly; nor should they be enunciated like blows with a hammer; but they should be delivered in a broad and impressive manner.

6

This passage should be played with a touch of restless feeling; while taking care not to give free rein to a *rubato* which, on the contrary, should be carefully avoided.

7

Play the four first measures with tenderness and somewhat of abandon; the remaining measures anticipate the energetic period which follows.

8

Play the eighth notes as indicated,

with great vigor and marked rhythm.

9

Period of Twelve Measures

Play without hurrying, and with great clarity and contrast in shading.

10

This passage should be played with a flowing tone and with great calmness. From measure 5 to measure 8 play on the fingerboard.

11

Period of Four Measures

Play this period reverting to *tempo* little by little, bringing out the *martelé* or "hammered" notes with the fingers of the left hand.

12

Use the whole bow, and accent delicately, yet with precision.

13

There is a difference of opinion with regard to this passage, that is, as to the manner in which the chords should be varied. The question is one which should be submitted to the judgment of authorities, who, however, one should remember, are in no wise agreed on such questions.

14

Beginning with the fourth measure, and up to the end of the period, a strongly marked *crescendo* should be made, a *crescendo* which gradually attains to *fortissimo*.

15

The first note of each beat should be lengthened a little; at the second beat of the fifth measure the original text of the composition should be followed, since the chords, arranged in the following manner, would seem to be the chords as Bach himself conceived them:

16

Period of Four Measures

This period of four measures only is a transition period, reintroducing the principal theme. The first as well as the last note in the first three measures should be played in a very sustained manner, and the first thirty-second notes of each of these same measures should be stressed. The fourth measure should be played with full power.

17

This should be presented in the same spirit as the beginning, with genuine majesty, and with the last *D* played in a very sustained manner.

18

This marvelous phrase should be played with great calm and with an expression of sublime serenity; the first six measures without shading. In the fifth measure it is impossible to play the chord without abruptness. It is preferable to pass over the three strings, with a *piano* shading, thus avoiding all shock.

19

Play with the utmost rhythmical conciseness, dwelling upon the first and the last eighth notes of each measure.

20

Period of Four Measures

Play with much contrast in shading; the chords should be enunciated with a certain degree of roughness.

21

This should be played with a very light *spiccato,* yet not in a dry, short manner, dwelling upon the second sixteenth of the second and third measures.

22

Make a *crescendo* from the third to the fourth sixteenth note.
Make a *diminuendo* from the fifth to the seventh sixteenth note.

23

Carry out a voluminous *stretto* in the *crescendo,* leading up to a resounding *fortissimo;* the four *A*'s should be literally "hammered" out:

as well as the four *A*'s and the *D*'s of the fifth, sixth and seventh measures.

24

The first four measures should communicate a feeling of poignant grandeur; at the beginning of the fifth measure hasten the movement, and broaden out in the last two measures.

25-26

We have now reached the critical period of the "Chaconne"; for when he has reached this place the violinist is, so to speak, usually exhausted. The movement must be hastened somewhat, and a great deal of importance must be given the last eighth of measures one, two, three, four, five, six and seven, and in period 26, to measures one, two, three, five, six and seven.

27

Play lightly and sustain the basses.

28

Here the player has an opportunity to regain his strength to some degree. Great serenity is needed for the interpretation of this sublime phrase; the chords should be played with breadth and without abruptness.

29

Play with great expression stressing the ninth sixteenth note in measures one, two, three and four.

30

Period of Four Measures

Play in a very measured manner, and with a strongly pronounced *crescendo.*

31

These measures should be played with a decidedly diaphanous tone color. Sustain the note with the sign, that is to say, the third sixteenth of each measure. Play increasingly *piano.* The methodic order of the "Chaconne," so strongly marked, is varied by the seven measures of the present period.

32

These five measures are most characteristic. They are like a storm suddenly unloosed and ending in a whirlwind.

33

Period of Four Measures

The last eighth of these four measures should be played in a strongly sustained manner to secure the following effect:

The last measure is played in the following manner to obtain practically the effect of sustained chords:

34

Period of Thirteen Measures

Play with the whole bow, and with an expression of true grandeur; the fourth measure should be serene and well balanced. The conclusion should be very much retarded, and played with the greatest possible exertion of power.

THE ROMANCE IN G MAJOR

By L. van Beethoven Op. 40

(1770-1827)

The manuscript of these sublime pages, composed in 1803, is to be found in the library of the publishing house of Peters in Leipsic. In the manuscript, no tempo or expression marks are indicated. The Beethoven "Romance," a pearl of exceptional violinistic beauty, is "thought out" for the violin to such an extent that it is hardly possible to imagine it written for any other instrument. It is, however, a composition difficult to interpret, and the best violinists approach it with apprehension. It appears too infrequently on the recital program, and the compositions which are substituted for it by the fashion of the day take its place most unworthily. Its periods are each thirty measures in length, with the exception of the last, which is thirty-three measures long.

1

Measures 1 to 5: begin delicately, with a well sustained tone, and not too slowly, playing with a certain amount of decision. Give the last two beats of the second measure a slight *crescendo,* and observe a *decrescendo* in the first two beats of the third measure. Another slight *crescendo* should be made in the last two beats of the fourth measure. In measure 1 the fingering to be preferred from the point of view of sureness is the following one:

although the more musical fingering is that shown below:

In measure 11 observe a slight *crescendo.* In measure 21 the fingering given below is a musical abomination:

In measure 24 avoid dramatizing the fragment in question, yet, at the same time, do not play it in a cheap and commonplace fashion.

In measures 24 and 25 do not play the thirty-second notes shortly and abruptly, and see to it that they are well detached from the eighth notes.

In measure 26 give a slight accent to the *D*; and also accent the first *E* in measure 27 in the same manner.

2

Do not exaggerate the *crescendo* in measure 1. Measures 4 to 7 are to be played with a slight acceleration, with a return to *tempo primo* at measure 7. From measure 7 to measure 11 strive to give the violin tone the quality of the organ tone; play in a sustained manner, and with precision, and without any shading at all, on a *mezzo forte* dynamic plane.

The same observation holds good for the interval from measures 15 to 18.

The many different editions of the Beethoven "Romance" treat the composer's original text with scant respect. Alterations such as an editor may see fit to make are always permissible; but the original text, in such cases, should always be indicated on the margin.

At all events this is an energetic period, followed by one in imitation, in solid point-lace style of tonal embellishment, which, however, has nothing in common with the delicacies of *point d'Alençon* in its character.

3

We give below the bowing which we have found to be the best for playing measures 2 to 5 of this section:

It should be played with breadth, with an equal division of the bow into four parts, and in as extended a manner as possible.

In measure 7 accent the *D* sharp.

The three last sixteenth notes of measure 9 form a little poem in themselves, and should be played tenderly, without, however, exaggerating the *glissando* on the *A* string.

Measures 16 and 18 must be expressed simply, with an equal tone.

The sextolets of measure 18 should be produced without exaggeration. Violinists are apt to make them ungainly by dwelling too heavily on the individual notes. Be sure to observe the *crescendo,* and give its full value to measure 23, playing the two groups without a slackening of the movement.

In measure 28, the *D* sharp is of great importance, and should be slightly accented.

Measures 30 and 31 should be played with great calmness; and there may be a trifle more of expansion in measure 31.

Play the chords of measure 32 broadly, yet without roughness. It is always a shock to hear a beautiful composition such as this brought to a peculiar conclusion. These final chords might be termed the surprise of the "Romance in G," for in spite of its marvelous charm, the "Romance" seems to have a soporific effect on many of the older persons among the audiences that listen to it. These final chords rouse them for a moment, and the sight is an amusing one to witness.

THE ROMANCE IN F MAJOR

By L. van Beethoven Op. 50

(1770-1827)

The original manuscript of this "Romance in F Major," first published in 1803, was the property of Joseph Joachim. The *adagio cantabile* indicated at the beginning of the "Romance" as the proper tempo, should not be taken strictly as an *adagio,* but rather as an *adagio assai.*

The periods consist of 30 measures each, and the *tutti* are included in the periods.

1

In measure 1 the group or turn should be expressed as shown in the following example:

Play *mezzo forte,* with a slight *crescendo* up to the end of the measure 3. Accent the *D* flat of measure 5, as well as that of measure 6. Make a *crescendo* at the end on the last three eighth notes of measure 6, prolonging it into measure 7, and making a *decrescendo* in measure 8. The group in measure 7 should be played as shown below:

Play measures 20 to 23 in a calm and uniform manner as regards tone.

Measure 24 should be played *forte.* The *G* is hard to reach, hence it is well to use some means which will ensure its attainment, such as the following: while playing the *A,* at the same time prepare for the *G* by placing the fingers on a chord of the seventh in such a way that the *G* has the best possible chance of lying at hand when it is to be played.

The three small notes in the above illustration are, of course, silent.

In measure 26 play the group cleanly.

Play measure 28 *forte,* and in measure 29 produce the thirty-second notes without hurrying them, and with a large bow. In measure 30, nearly all editions indicate a *spiccato,* which is most objectionable. One should play here with the bow on the string.

2

In measure 1 sustain the three *G's,* and accent the three last eighths. Play measures 4 and 5 with restless sentiment and feeling.

Measures 7 and 8 should be played as shown in the following example:

with a generous breadth of bow.

In measure 9 observe a *rallentando* when playing the six final sixteenth notes.

With measure 28 begins a period of tragic grandeur. Attack the *F* with power, and sustain this forceful attack until measure 13 of the third period is reached. In measure 29 sustain and emphasize the sixteenth note.

3

In measure 1 the triplets should be played broadly and in a detached manner. In measure 2 emphasize the last *A*. In measure 3 emphasize the first B. Play the triplets broadly, with a slight retard on the six last notes of the measure.

Measures 4 to 9 disclose an admirable phrase, which is suddenly cut by the *tutti*. Why? That is a secret which Beethoven has carried with him to the grave. With all due respect and deference to the genius of the Titan of music, one might be allowed to suggest that a single phrase be made of measure 4, up to the first sixteenth note of measure 9, as shown in the following example:

In measure 9 play four notes *détaché* and four notes *martelé*.

Observe the same procedure in measures 10 and 12.

Play measures 14 and 15 *détaché,* emphasizing the fundamental notes, and with a big *crescendo*.

Play measure 16 with the whole bow and *forte*.

Play measures 17 and 18 without hurrying.

4

Measure 1 should be played broadly and with warmth.

In measure 2 accent the first note of each beat.

Play measure 3 with great breadth.

In measure 6 make the small notes very broad.

Measure 8 should be very calmly played.

Play measures 9 and 10 *mezzo forte,* without any *rallentando,* until the last two sixteenth notes of measure 10 are reached. End on the final notes, together with the orchestra, with the two final eighths well sustained.

THE DEVIL'S TRILL

By Giuseppe Tartini

(1692-1770)

"The Devil's Trill" Sonata is one of those works which leave the musician overcome with admiration. Musically it is a masterpiece of the first rank, and violinistically it is one of the greatest compositions which have been written for the instrument.

Tartini himself has told how his Sonata was conceived, as the result of a dream; and the mood of suffering and bitterness which dominates it suggests that the master was influenced by a spirit of fatalism when he gave this poem of sorrow and despair to the world.

1

Larghetto Affettuoso

Though in keeping with its character, this *larghetto* should be taken very slowly, it is an *adagio, ma non troppo* rather than a *larghetto*.

The plaintive melodic voice heard at the beginning:

should be expressed with great tenderness and in a very sustained manner, the last eighth note of the first measure being prolonged. A slight *crescendo* in measure 3 brings us to the sorrowful measure which succeeds it, and in this measure 4 a slight accent on the first *D* should be followed by a *diminuendo.* Play measures 5 and 6 *mezzo forte,* measure 7, *mezzo piano,* and measure 8 *piano.* The *forte* in measure 10 should be produced with the maximum of expression and with a broad bow, and this *forte* should be maintained until the last dotted half note of measure 12 is reached. Play measures 13 and 14 very sustained; and measures 15, 16 and 17 meditatively, while in measure 18 a pronounced *crescendo* should lead up to the chord. A slight agitation should mark the playing of measure 19, and the last eighth note of measure 20 should be much prolonged. Play the last three measures in a very sustained manner, and with an accent of the greatest sorrow.

2

Allegro

Play the beginning in a very energetic and vigorously accented manner. The difficulty in this movement lies in the proper use of a very strident trill, and it is preferable to regulate the trill by the small notes, since it is physically impossible to develop a well nourished trill on passing sixteenth notes, as:

Another difficulty to be overcome in this movement is the player's tendency to "bolt." The word "bolt" should be graven in the violinist's memory, for though it is easy enough to understand the anxiety of the soloist, he must control it, and must not budge from the initial tempo set.

3

The seven measures which follow should be conceived on a majestic plane and played correspondingly.

4

Allegro Assai

We have now reached the outstanding moment of the Sonata. The first four measures should be played rather sharply, especially the sixteenth notes, as follows:

In measure 5 avoid scratching, and never give way to an impulse to blurt or roar, even in the *fortissimos*. Even here the tone must be deployed in a broad and noble manner. In this famous "Devil's Trill," the trill itself must be continuous, uninterrupted, to the end of the period. It is possible to play this difficult period properly, with the exercise of a great deal of patience, but the student must not hurry too much, for he is face to face with one of the most arduous problems in all violin literature.

5

Grave

The same remarks made for section 3 apply here. What is left is a repetition of preceding periods, except the *cadenza* which should be played without haste, with a true understanding of the recapitulation of the different themes, and with perfect intonation.

THE CONCERTO IN D MAJOR

by L. van Beethoven Op. 61

(1770-1827)

Beethoven wrote this immortal work in 1806, and the original manuscript is preserved in the (former) Imperial and Royal Library of Vienna, now the National Library of the Austrian Republic. The manuscript bears the inscription: "Concerto Written for Clement, First Violin and Director of the Vienna Court Theater, by Ludwig van Beethoven, 1806." It was played for the first time in Vienna, by Clement, for whom it was written, on December 23, 1806, was very warmly received and scored extraordinary success.

Nevertheless, the critics of the day dwelt upon its length, and pointed out that its unity was "often broken." This is not surprising in view of the fact that, in our own age, too, there have been found those who take it upon themselves to criticize this work. After its initial performance, the Beethoven Concerto was not played for a long space of time, and the performances given by Luigi Tomasini in 1812 in Berlin; by Pierre Baillot in 1833 in Paris; by Henri Vieuxtemps in 1836 in Vienna, and by Ulrich in Leipsic, stand out during the long period of its neglect.

Joachim made it one of the principal works in his repertory, and attained a perfection of style in its playing which has never been equaled. The work was literally Beethoven himself as Joachim presented it to the public—a performance never to be forgotten.

Beethoven's Violin Concerto may be said to be a work which gives the accolade to the virtuoso artist, and if he can present it as it should be presented, he may be classed among the masters, for he has achieved the measure of greatness which lies in a valid reaction to the inspiration of the titanic composer of what is, in the opinion of many, the greatest concerto ever written for the violin.

There are not two violinists in the world who interpret this work in the same manner, and it may be said with entire frankness, that many are guilty of crimes against art in allowing themselves liberties in its interpretation which would have shocked Beethoven himself. The very first solo measures in this Concerto are played in distinctly different ways by great artists, as the author has demonstrated in one of the interpretative articles in this *Encyclopedia*. The various editions of this work also display a tendency to improve upon it which may truly be deplored, for, from the moment when editors allow themselves to "correct" Beethoven, one cannot take them seriously. Some years ago, while reading a book of collected criticisms by Paul Scudo, I was shocked to find the following passage: ". . . a talented young violinist named Henri Vieuxtemps came before the public with a Concerto by L. van Beethoven—a composition which I take the liberty of admiring not over-much." Shortly afterwards I asked M. Saint-Saëns what he thought of Scudo. His opinion was, and I give it word for word, "Scudo was an old fool who knew nothing at all about music." And yet Scudo in his day was accounted one of the most famous of music critics.

It has become a habit, when young artists discuss this master work, to dwell upon its beauty but to complain of its length. The length of a work is often more or less apparent in connection with the character and length of other works presented on the program together with it. Too many big works should not be crowded together on one and the same program, lest all of them suffer. Too long and sustained an attention on the part of the auditors is sometimes demanded. I remember attending one of the Concerts-Colonnes some years ago, and hearing a program devoted to the works of Camille Saint-Saëns. That master himself conducted one of his symphonies, Ysaÿe played the "Violin Concerto in B Minor," and Raoul Pugno the "Fifth Concerto" for piano, and some of the symphonic poems were also presented. This music was all admirable, but in its entirety the program was overpowering, and the auditor left a concert which he had attended for enjoyment's sake in a state of utter mental exhaustion. A concert should never last longer than two hours, and a program, if it is to be logical, should never have a symphony preceding a concerto.

In order to facilitate my comments on the Beethoven Concerto, I shall simply take each period of 32 measures in succession and discuss it, beginning with the solo after the first *tutti*.

1

The beginning should be played calmly and without any striving for exterior effect, as well as with a certain restraint, which may be brought out by a slight holding back on the first triplets,

with a very brief stop on the *F*. Too academic an execution of this beginning would give it a stiffness which is by no means in accordance with the composer's thought. At the end of the triplet figuration the measure should broaden out

in such manner that the succeeding fragment begins naturally with a sustained playing of its first note.

The various phrase fragments of the following period should be, so to speak, detached, while the player is attentive to maintain a balance of sonority, avoiding any *crescendo* before the end of the period has been reached:

In the following measures:

each note should be played with an increasingly broader bowing and the *D* should be well sustained. The first note of the first and third beats should be underlined, and too marked a dwelling on the second eighth results in an incorrect accent.

This first period, in accordance with my plan, ends at the *tutti,* and the second period begins with the solo.

2

Although the expression mark given be "dolce," this period must be conceived as one whose keynote is majesty, and it should be played with eloquence, and with a bowing generously broad. The last four notes of measures 2 and 4 should be stressed. The groups in measure 6 should be played exactly in time, as follows:

Measures 7 and 8 should be played with grandeur and without the player's allowing himself to be influenced by the change of rhythm which occurs in measure 8. In the following eight measures, every violinist uses a different bowing. One should remember to maintain the interpretation on a level of simple grandeur, and to avoid all buffoonery. In the following measure:

it is necessary to take the *E* on the open string, in such wise as to recall the first measure of the first *tutti;* make a slight *rallentando* and revert to tempo at the trill. The resumption of the phrase by the violin should be marked by a restful calm, and by a slight holding back in measure 26 of this period. When the appealing variation of the main theme in minor begins, the player must allow himself to be guided by his inspiration and stress the important notes.

3

At measure 10 a slight *crescendo* and *decrescendo* will add weight to the chromatic fragment:

Measures 17 and 18 should not be played stiffly as regards the rhythm, but rather with a light stressing of the first four notes of the measure.

Measures 19 and 20 are characterized by the importance which should be given the first notes of the fragment:

The period beginning with measure 24 should be played with repose and grandeur, and the expressional shade "dolce" applies only to the first four measures. It must not be forgotten that this period supplies a species of adjunct for the bass, hence the *crescendo* should begin with measure 32 of the period.

4

Play *sempre crescendo,* the four last notes in particular, until the triplets— which should be played with great breadth—have been reached. The chromatic scale which follows should begin *pianissimo* and end with a slight *crescendo.* Play measures 11, 12, 13 and 14 eloquently and with a broad bow, while making a big *crescendo,* terminating in *forte,* at the *E* of measure 15; then accent the first trill which follows and return to *piano.*

The trill should begin with a slight accent on the *B,* but the trill throughout its course should not be accented save that there is a slight *crescendo* at measure 27.

5

From measure 28 of period four to measure 2 of period five, play with great calmness, almost metronomically, so to speak. Measure 2 should be presented broadly and the last nine notes with an accent of eloquence.

6

We take up period six after the end of the *tutti.*

The first 14 measures are to be played in the same mood which characterizes the beginning of the Concerto. In measures 15 and 16 the *crescendo* should end at the *mezzo forte.* Measures 17, 18, 19 and 20 should be serene and reposeful in expression. In measure 21 give a light touch of importance to the first *F.* Beginning with measure 22, we have an illustration of the principal theme,

whose details should be properly stressed; as shown in measure 24:

The shading at this point should be uniform, and the performance marked with great calm, which will give the playing of the passage a quality of repose absolutely in keeping with the phrase.

The final measure of this period should be played with a *détaché* akin to a short *spiccato,* and the player must keep his accompaniment in mind.

7

Measure 7 of this period should be played without harshness. I have often asked myself why violinists scan the first note with such roughness and harshness, as follows:

Possibly it is with the idea in mind of recalling measure 1 of the Concerto; yet this has nothing to do with the exposition of the initial theme. Nor should the first sixteenth note be harshly struck out, since it results in a false adaptation of the rhythm.

Measures 10, 11, 12 and 13 should be played free in time, and eloquently, while measure 13 should be vehemently expressed. Play the end of the trill at measure 15 with abandon. The period under consideration is one of the most moving in this great work; accent plays a large and extremely important part in it, and the whole question is one of making a correct use of accentuation. In measure 18, for instance, accent as follows:

From measure 16 to measure 32, a supreme degree of serenity must be preserved; while at the same time endeavoring to extract from this sublime phrase the greatest possible degree of emotion contained in it.

8

Play as though expressing a mood of gentle reproach, with a suspicion of impatience. It is quite out of the question to employ the expression mark *piano* here indicated. Beginning with measure 1, a slight *crescendo* should be made which, little by little, climaxes in a *fortissimo.* Hence, from measure 1 to measure 9 make a slight *crescendo,* then from measure 9 to measure 17 develop a formidable one, ending at measure 1 of the following *tutti.*

9

We begin period nine after the *tutti.*

A distinction must be made between this period and the period of the first solo resembling it. In itself the tonality of *D* major lends a brilliance which is in striking contrast with that of *D* minor. The expression mark *piano* is out of the question, however. The violinist must play *mezzo forte,* with a slight *crescendo* at measure 6, and a *decrescendo* at measure 8.

Measures 9 and 10 should be played very evenly, and measures 11 to 14 without any shading and calmly. In measures 15 to 20 introduce a moderate *crescendo* and *decrescendo,* as in the following example:

At measure 22 a big *crescendo* terminating in a *forte* which is sustained to measure 29 should be made, followed by a *diminuendo* at measure 30, running to the trill.

10

Play measure 4 calmly; measures 5 and 6 without nervousness; and introduce a slight *crescendo* and *diminuendo* between measures 7 and 8. Otherwise the remainder of this period should be interpreted as was the first solo.

11

After measure 7 observe the most rigorous tranquillity in your playing and do not depart from it until measure 19 is reached. Measures 20 and 21 should be presented eloquently; and the first sixteenth notes of each beat in measures 22 and 23 must be strongly accented. The chromatics in measures 24 and 25 must be played evenly and *mezzo forte.* Make a *crescendo* at measure 26 and broaden out powerfully in measure 27. The trill must be played evenly, while slightly accenting each change of note.

The cadenza is of necessity left to the individual choice of the violinist, and it is with regret that I find myself obliged to declare that too many virtuosos are content to introduce the most pitiful makeshifts in the guise of cadenzas. From the moment when technical display becomes the keynote of a cadenza the spirit of Beethoven's work suffers inartistic profanation.

12

The sublime phrase which follows the cadenza should be played with simplicity, *piano,* and in the actual tempo of the beginning of the Concerto. A big *crescendo,* entering five measures before the close, should end with a formidable *fortissimo.* The *D* of the measure before the last should be sustained, the chord played without harshness, and the final *D* uttered broadly.

Larghetto

Beginning with the solo: play with great calmness. Measure 2 should be played as an echo, yet without exaggeration. A slight *crescendo* should be made at the end of measure 3.

1

The trill of measure 4 should be sufficiently prolonged and any *glissando* after the short cadenza should be avoided.

The accentuation of measure 7 is most important. See the following example:

It is understood, of course, that this accentuation should be employed with discretion. In the period of the larghetto which follows, the effect of an improvisation should be made, though the player, in endeavoring to achieve his purpose, must show good taste and restraint.

Make a short *rallentando* before the sublime phrase which veritably seems to have been set down "by the hand of God." To do justice to it the violinist should seek inspiration in the principle of *bel canto* song, and carry the note with distinction.

2

Avoid all shading while playing measures 3 to 27 of period two, and at measure 28 introduce a slight *crescendo,* followed by a *diminuendo* on the three last notes. A big *crescendo* marks measure 32 of this period.

3

The short cadenza of measure 3 in period three should be played *forte* and in declamatory style, and should be equally divided, while stressing the last seven notes.

The first two trills of measure 4 should be played without terminations, the third trill with termination.

Play the final measures of this admirable larghetto with calmness, while giving the conclusion a slight touch of impatience.

Rondo (*Allegro*)

1

Accentuation plays a large part in the proper exposition of this simple and noble hunting air which Beethoven has invented. Certain violinists use false accents when playing it, thus making themselves guilty of a serious attack on good style. The best way to make sure of the right accentuation is to give an exact illustration of the position of the accents of the principal theme, as follows:

The following measure should be presented as shown below:

Use the same accentuation when the theme is repeated in the higher position, and use the shading *mezzo forte* for the initial appearance of the theme, and the shading *mezzo piano* for its repetition.

2

Beginning this second period the first measure following the *tutti,* the *A* should be played without shock, yet with precision, and a big *crescendo* made at measure 13. Play measures 16, 17 and 18 *fortissimo* and with powerful accentuation. Measures 24 to 32 should be played broadly, taking care not to sustain the highest sixth in measure 25, in order to avoid giving rise to comparisons with those Italian tenors who have good voices but sing in wretched taste.

3

Play measure 5 *forte,* and measure 6 *piano.* A tradition exists which prescribes that measure 7 should be played an octave higher. Logically this may be attributed to absence of mind on Beethoven's part, since this traditional playing would be the natural melodic continuation of the period. Play measure 14 very broadly and with stress; and, beginning with measure 13, a powerful progression of the three *G's* of measure 14, which must be vigorously accented, should be prepared.

4

From measure 15 on allow the adorable period which is approaching to be forecast by a carefully graduated *diminuendo.* From measure 18 on the most exquisite pastorale imaginable develops until measure 25 is reached. Play this simply yet with feeling, making a slight *crescendo* at measure 25 and a *decrescendo* at measure 26. The variation which develops up to measure 1 of the fifth period should be presented without ostentation.

5

Many violinists give this variation altogether too brilliant a character. It must be held within its proper bounds and not forced, and the artist should remember that it ought to be played primarily from the standpoint of music, and not from that of the public.

At measure 2 the second fraction of the theme indicates a natural *crescendo,* which continues until the end of the measure following. There should be a *decrescendo* from measure 5 to the end of measure 6, and measures 7, 8 and 9 should be played with simplicity. The variation which follows offers a contrast to the variation of the first portion of the theme. Here the violinist must be more persuasive, more expressive in his playing. There is a big *crescendo* at measure 14 and a *decrescendo* at measure 17. Play increasingly *piano* from measure 18 to measure 26. Measures 28, 30 and 32 should be played with a *crescendo* increasing in vigor in order to attain a truly gigantic *forte.*

6

We begin period six after the *tutti.*

Play without any shading from measure 1 to 12, and without jolting the bow. If the interconnection of the notes is defective, a hardness is bound to be developed which is not at all in keeping with the elegance of the phrase. From measure 13 on to the *tutti* make a big *crescendo,* and from measure 18 to 20 "whip up" the *crescendo* with a powerful accent on the first and ·fourth beats of measure 19. Play *crescendo* at measure 25 and *diminuendo* at measure 26.

7

Rigorously observe all contrasts throughout period seven. The *crescendo* on the trill starts on measure 20.

8

Period eight begins after the cadenza. Allow the trill which begins *forte* gradually to die away into a *pianissimo* at measure 13. The repetition of the theme should also be *pianissimo,* and a subject for meditation on the part of the serious violinist. There is a great difficulty here which must be overcome;

it is that of maintaining a rigorous rhythm while accenting without jolting or pushing, as in the following example:

Play measures 18 to 23 *sempre pianissimo,* and make a rapid *crescendo* at measure 24, playing *mezzo forte* at measure 25 and *forte* at measure 26, while sustaining the *D.* The three eighths of measure 29 should be strongly accented and eloquently played, and a big *diminuendo* should occur on the trill, in order to achieve the *pianissimo* of measure 32 of this period and the first four measures of period nine.

9

Play measures 5 to 11 with imperturbable calmness and *piano.* From measure 12 to the *D* of measure 18 make an even and well balanced *crescendo* which should lead up to a *fortissimo* on the *D.* Since this period is one abounding in power and enthusiasm, it should be played broadly, emphasizing the basses, and with genuine authority of manner. The player should not strive to shine, yet his bowing should be broad and powerful. At measure 32 a little roughness may be employed as a radical contrast to measure 1.

10

What has already been said anent measure 14 of period eight applies to the last four measures of this period.

THE KREUTZER SONATA
by Ludwig van Beethoven Op. 47
(1770-1827)

This marvelous violinistic jewel, created by the Master of Bonn, confronts us with a problem whose solution is anything but easy. After having heard it played by the majority of the greatest violinists, the writer retains the impression that Joachim interpreted it in the manner which best revealed its profundity, hence it is upon his interpretation that the present analysis is based.

1

Adagio Sostenuto

The first chord should be played broadly, yet without harshness; though the *piano* which follows should be observed, the impression of a prelude on the organ is the one desired. The fingering of the first two measures has given rise to much discussion; they are very difficult and the one which is best and most reliable, and which in addition conforms to the exigencies of what is really musical, is the following one:

The *sforzando* on the *C* of measure 12 should be strongly accented. The sixteenth notes of the following measures should be played with an elongated bow; and a noticeable *ritardando* should be observed for the last five sixteenth notes in the measure before the last of this section.

2

Presto

The first two notes should come like a cry of despair. Do not take the tempo indicated at the very beginning, but work up to it gradually, commencing *quasi allegretto* in the first two measures and increasing the movement from measure 3 on. At the following *a tempo* continue with the tempo indicated.

The following periods should be played without any undue haste and very clearly:

The chords that follow:

should be played with breadth and without harshness. In the phrase which succeeds:

the group should be played as shown below:

In the succeeding phrase the first two notes of measures 6, 10, and 14 should be strongly accented:

The 20 measures preceding the first repeat should be played with strength and breadth. At the fragment following:

do not hasten, but rather hold the pianist down strongly to the proper tempo, and make him keep to it.

Here the movement should slow up very perceptibly, and should not revert to tempo again until the following:

is reached. This movement in general should convey an impression of power allied to tenderness. It is vital and energetic to a tremendous degree.

3

Andante con Variazioni

This delightful theme should be shaded and inflected without exaggeration. Its soulful quietude and calmness should be voiced, and to do so the following accentuation is to be observed: nine measures before the end of the theme mark a slight *rallentando,* but revert to tempo in the succeeding measure.

4

Variation I

Play very calmly; in measure 3, before the second repeat, *crescendo* and *diminuendo.*

5

Variation II

This famous variation, as a rule, is treated in too flippant a manner. The player should prove that he has an artistic conscience in a variation which usually only serves the purpose of showing off the brilliancy of the virtuoso's bowing. For the sake of variety, it is preferable to use this stroke of the bow at the first playing:

poco rall. tempo

and the following one at the repeat:

At the last measure, it is better to make the *F* a harmonic:

instead of playing it at the top of the fingerboard.

Variation III

This variation should be played with the greatest degree of poignant expression, especially the delivery of the opening phrase:

Nowhere in the pages of violin music is greater opportunity given to the musician than in this wonderful series of melodic phrases.

6

Variation IV

The player should have recourse to all his stylistic ability in order to bring out the marvelous Beethovian soul in this unique variation, and not suggest a mandolin in the *pizzicati*:

which should be rendered softly. Take measure 3 of the *tempo primo* succeeding the *molto adagio* very tranquilly.

Do not "elbow" the small notes out of the way, but rather turn them into large ones.

The measure before the last should be played with a decided *rallentando,* and the two last sixteenth notes:

should be very much prolonged.

7

Finale

Let the presto be a very moderate one, and play the opening measures:

in a somewhat mordant and sarcastic spirit, and the major theme that occurs later:

in a more genial and friendly spirit.

Immediately before the change to 2/4 time, make a short stop, for—though it is not usually indicated—the 21 measures in 2/4 time should be played twice as slowly as the 6/8 time preceding, with a *crescendo* and *decrescendo* in measures 7 and 8.

Revert to tempo primo after these 21 measures.

Play measures 3 and 4 of the tempo primo before the last adagio:

very *rallentando,* and be sure that you check all tendency to "bolt" in the final passages of this movement.

THE CONCERTO IN E MINOR

by Felix Mendelssohn-Bartholdy, Op. 64

(1809-1847)

When Mendelssohn first showed this Concerto to Ferdinand David, the latter unquestionably gave the young composer much valuable advice, for he

was a violinist of great talent, and as such was able to give the work a
violinistic form and cast. As a result this splendid Concerto is so well written
for the violin that, once it has been thoroughly learned, one may play it several
months after it has been studied, and it will still be at one's finger tips. His
fingers are the violinist's memory—in fact, it is possible to recall a piece which
has been forgotten by taking up the violin, for, no sooner is the instrument in
your hand, than the composition comes back to you with astonishing clearness.

This great Concerto, classic in all its lines, is also highly romantic. It is
magnificently proportioned, and those who would dismiss Mendelssohn as a
"talent" should have this Concerto placed before them as a challenge and as
proof positive that "genius" is the word which ought more properly to be
applied to its composer.

After all the years which have passed since it was written, the "Concerto in
E Minor" is still played with fervor, and audiences still acclaim it with joy.
It is, above all others, *the* most beautiful violin concerto.

This lovely music must not be played too quickly. Moderate tempos are
the ones which should preferably be used. Sarasate was accustomed to give a
bad example of this too rapid playing of the work by taking the finale at an
extreme tempo.

In considering the Mendelssohn Concerto it has been taken by its periods,
which have 30 measures each, and in which the *tuttis* are included.

The beginning of the Concerto has no element of the solemn in its concept,
and is expressive of tenderness rather than force. The *B* of measure 3 should
be lightly accented, as well as the *E* of measure 4. Give life and vitality to
this charming phrase with which the work begins, a beginning which is exquisite
beyond all measure. A suspicion of a *crescendo* from measures 7 to 10 might
very well serve to lead back to the shading of the beginning at the third quarter
note of measure 10.

At measure 17 a pronounced *crescendo* should move gradually to measure 24.
Measures 25 and 26 and the first two beats of measure 27 should be played with
the whole bow, while strongly accenting the first eighth of each triplet group.

Play measure 28 without harshness, as in the following example:

Avoid the objectionable, but commonly used, rendering which follows:

At measure 6 the shading must be abruptly broken, in order to begin with a
piano the forceful *crescendo* which ends at measure 10.

The octaves of measures 10 to 12 should be played broadly, but without accentuation.

If, as it is claimed, David had a hand in the shaping up of this Concerto, it seems strange that he omitted to add a lower *B* to the octave in measure 13, as shown in the following example:

The isolated upper *B* does not sound well. The octaves should not be played with precipitation, but calmness and balanced playing are emphatically in order as regards them.

In measures 14, 15 and 16 strongly accent the first notes of the triplets, yet not to the detriment of the other notes; all should be distinctly audible.

3

In the following measures, 16, 17 and 18—the solo resumes after the *tutti* at measure 16—

the *crescendo* should be made without exaggeration while, at the same time, it must necessarily be shaded on the same plane as the phrase itself. This, after all, is no more than the peroration of the four last measures of the preceding *tutti,* which commences the phrase to which the violin replies.

At measure 25 we enter upon a period of feverish movement, in which the difficulty lies in convincingly maintaining the feeling of agitation. The first *B* of measure 25 should be played with a strong accent, the remainder of the measure with a broad bow. The detached notes should be played as broadly as the tied notes, an arduous problem, yet one whose solution is logical.

4

Accent the second of the tied eighths in measures 3, 4, 5 and 6.

Maintain equality in the gradation of the *crescendo* from measure 7 to measure 10, that is to say the eighths should not sound jerky. In treating measure 10 some editions display lack of logic. The measure may be fingered as follows:

but not as shown in the next example:

Play measures 15 to 22 *mezzo forte,* if not *forte,* since otherwise the violin tone will be covered by that of the wind instruments. Measures 23 to 30 should be played broadly, laying a great deal of weight on the basses. The following fingering best suits the inner logic of the exposition:

5

Play measures 1 to 10 with a certain amount of expansion; somewhat softly and tenderly. In measures 4 to 7 there should be a slight *crescendo* and in measure 10 a pronounced *crescendo* ending on the G of measure 11.

The G sustained in the bass from measures 11 to 18, which supports the melody played by the wind instruments of the orchestra, must necessarily be played *forte.* Measures 19 to 30 offer a marvelous phrase, full of charm and depth, and which should be played with a smile, that is to say as though it were purity itself. This is a section in which the player may give free rein to his talent and show his artistry in one of its fairest aspects, that of sincerity.

It is all too easy for the violinist to yield to the dictates of poor taste, and the phrase under consideration is a species of stumbling block whose proper playing serves to measure the true worth of the artist. We have heard this fragment played times without number in the most insipid manner, the artist "letting himself out" in the most ridiculous way. Owing to the beauty of the admirable Stradivarius which he possessed, and also to the quality of the tone he produced, Sarasate was able to approach this phrase with a kind of aristocratic deference which was sincere enough, yet his interpretation as a whole was marked by the "bored" manner which this great violinist liked to affect.

6

Measures 1 and 2 should be played a trifle breathlessly, hurrying a little and retarding on the B of measure 3. In measure 4 there is a reversion to calmness subsequent to the preceding brief agitation, to which measure 4 offers a characteristic contrast.

Beginning with measure 12 and up to measure 18 we have a little poem of joy and gratitude, and the four A's of measure 15 seem to enclose a whole world of charm and delicacy of their own. The *glissando* from the upper A to the *A* in the third position is very tricky. The following example endeavors to describe it graphically:

Glide with the second finger.

Sustain the second *A*. Descend with a very slight *glissando* from the fourth *A* of measure 15 to the first *B* of measure 16, thus conveying a very marked feeling of tenderness. This is one of those exceptions to rule which explain themselves. It may not be correct from an *absolute* point of view, but absolutism is an essentially academic formula, and too rigorous academic principles are fatal to art.

At measure 18 revert to tempo. The triplets of measure 23 should be played without precipitation and *mezzo forte,* while those of measure 25 should be played forcefully. Play from measure 27 to measure 30 with clean-cut rhythm. In measure 29 take care to accent the *C* and the *C* sharp well, and in measure 30 the *D* should be heavily accented.

7

In the interval from measure 1 to measure 8 the violinist has an opportunity of displaying his musicianship. The impression of clarity which this period should make depends entirely upon true accentuation, which must be secured by means of a bowing all the more famous because it was the invention of a pianist. The section must be played strictly in time.

The following example will show my version of how the shading of the four measures 17 to 21 should be carried out:

Play measures 28 and 29 with great breadth.

8

Measures 1 to 13 should be presented eloquently, and measures 9 to 15 with a kind of sorrowful depression.

Hold back slightly in measure 15 and revert to tempo in measure 16. Accent the *G* sharp in measure 17.

Play both *D's* in measure 28 with great tranquillity.

9

Measures 29 and 30 of period eight as well as measures 1 and 14 of this period should be played chronometrically in time.

In measures 22 to 30 recall the beginning with an added tenderness and a kind of despondency.

10

In measures 7, 8 and 9 of this period we find an apparent contradiction between Joachim's own interpretation and the interpretation indicated in his edition of the work. Joachim, in fact, when playing this passage, tied the three G sharps, thus:

Henri Petri, one of Joachim's most distinguished pupils, acquainted me with this tradition.

Play measures 10 to 15 with great calmness.

Introduce a *rallentando* in measures 16 to 19, then revert to the previous movement at measure 20.

11

The Cadenza

Every violinist plays this cadenza in his own individual way. At the same time there are some valid points regarding its interpretation, which should be established. In the first *arpeggio* sustain the bass without accenting. The trills should be well nourished. After the final organ point "a tempo" is wrongly indicated. One should play in prelude style, sustaining the lower or bass notes until measure 30 has been reached. Then, little by little, the original movement is resumed at measures 1, 2 and 3 of the period.

12

The original tempo is resumed at measure 5.

At measures 18 and 19 another Joachim tradition calls for mention, the manner of playing shown in the following example:

13

Play measures 3 to 12 very calmly.

Play more broadly in measures 13 to 16, making a *ritenuto* at measure 16. Revert to tempo at measure 17.

14

For the remainder of period thirteen and for this period the remarks already made in connection with the first part hold good.

15

In measures 5 to 8 the octaves should not be hurried.

Play measures 10 to 22 with eloquent feeling and making a big *ritenuto* at measure 22. At the *più presto* play with passion, and augment in power until measure 12 of period sixteen has been reached.

16

This period comprises 32 measures.

At the *presto* play with uniform breadth, strongly accenting the double stops.

Andante

($\mathbf{\char`\d} = 96$)

The first period begins at the solo.

1

If the metronome indications given above are exceeded, the risk is run of making this charming phrase appear trivial. The violinist should play with calmness and avoid Sarasate's error—his performance made one feel that he was playing a slow waltz. The custom of exaggeration in whatever is played is, too, an unfortunate characteristic of our day, and this exaggeration is manifest in style as well as in tempo.

The beginning of this divine andante should be played with serenity, and with a broad and generous bow.

Present measures 7 and 8 with the shadings indicated.

Make a pronounced *crescendo* in measures 13 to 16.

Play measure 17 with sweetness, and accent the *D* in measure 18.

Measures 21 and 22 should be well sung and measure 22, in particular, played with great expression.

In measure 25 sustain and underline the first *E* and the second *C*.

Tranquillity should mark measure 26, and in measure 29 take the following fingering, which offers a relative certainty of sureness:

2

Measures 2 to 12 should be played with some agitation, without, nevertheless, exaggerating the tempo.

In measure 11 let the *D* stand out. In measure 17 pay attention to separating the last thirty-second notes of the measure, as follows:

The same applies to the last four thirty-second notes of measure 18.

In measures 20 and 21 accent the first and fourth eighths.

Eloquence should mark the playing of measure 22.

In measures 22 to 29 a tendency to bolt is noticeable in the case of nearly all violinists. A much nobler effect is secured by maintaining the initial movement and making a voluminous *crescendo* at measure 30, emphasizing the two *C's*.

3

Period three has 41 measures.

Both measures 5 and 6 should be played with great breadth, and the thirty-second note *A,* in measure 8, should be sustained.

Measures 9 and 10 should be played greatly *rallentando diminuendo.* The *pianissimo* here is an exaggeration; play *piano.*

There should be a big *crescendo* in the measure 20. In measure 21 bring out all the small notes clearly. There should be a *crescendo* in measure 22. Play measures 23 to 26 with a large, warm volume of tone. Press forward a little in measures 27 and 28. Hold back considerably in measures 29 and 30, above all on the three last eighths. Play measures 31 to 38 with great calmness, and introduce a slight *crescendo* in measures 37 and 38, with a pronounced *ritardando* in measure 39. Let measures 40 and 41 die away with a sigh.

Allegretto Non Troppo

(♪ = 100)

Periods of 30 measures each, in which the *tuttis* are comprised.

This genial scherzo should be played with grace, and the question of its interpretation is entirely one of accent.

1

Play measures 2, 4 and 5 *mezzo forte,* and make the second *A* very brief, as shown below:

In measures 6 and 7 develop a great *crescendo.*

The first *B* of measure 9 and the first *G* of measure 10 should be accented, but without being sustained.

According to the Joachim edition, measure 12 should be played *sempre pianissimo*. These *pianissimos* are out of place, however, when the solo instrument is playing against the orchestra, and especially so in this measure. A light accent on the first *A* is absolutely required.

Make a *crescendo* at the end of measure 16 and a big *crescendo* at measures 20 and 21.

2

In measures 19 to 22 sustain the basses, and sustain also the first *F* in measure 23.

3

The accentuation here should be as follows:

and not as in the next example:

A sudden *piano* should be marked in measure 6 on the last eighth.

Play measure 11 *forte*, with an accent on the second *D*.

Measure 12 should be played *forte piano* on the first *F*, then with a *crescendo* ending on a *sforzando* on the second *D* of measure 15.

Make a big *sforzando* in measure 16, on the *B*. Measures 16 to 20 should be well sung and sonorously declaimed.

Play measures 21 to 30 with a light *spiccato*, and introduce a *crescendo* in measure 29.

4

Play measures 1 to 5 *crescendo*, sustaining the *D* of measure 6.

Do not make the *C* of measure 7 short, but give it rich sonority.

Play measures 8 to 10 very evenly and without hurrying, something harder to do than might appear.

Measures 16 to 25 should be well sung, and the delightful design which the wind instruments of the orchestra embroider should be sustained.

Make a big *crescendo* in measures 24 to 26, terminating on the *E* of measure 26.

Sustain the first *E* in measure 28.

Sustain the first *D* in measure 29.

Sustain the first *E* in measure 30.

5

Measures 1 to 4 should be played with grace and with an even tone.

Measures 7 to 9 offer a stumbling block, in as much as it is very hard to play them evenly, without hurrying or holding back, but in strict time. The dynamic plane should be *mezzo forte,* for here again *piano* is out of place.

Measure 29 should be played as strictly in time as possible. It is a very difficult measure, and, as is usually the case, is all the more complicated because it is written in a simple scale.

The two measures of *tutti* should be played *fortissimo.*

6

Measure 30 of period five and measure 1 of period six are followed by two measures which form a direct response to them, and should be played with a *crescendo* at measure 2 and a heavy accent on the second *C.*

Play measures 5 to 15 with enthusiasm, and measure 16 calmly.

In measures 26, 27 and 28 sustain the basses, or lower notes.

7

The entire phrase included in measures 3 to 12, should be played *forte,* and with a well nourished trill.

Put eloquence into the playing of measure 13, and lend measures 14 to 17 an accent of warmth and grandeur.

Hold back greatly in playing measure 22, and revert to tempo in measure 23. In measures 24 to 30 guard against bolting.

Play measures 8, 9, 10 and 11 with great passion and with powerful accentuation.

Sustain the upper *E* in measure 23.

Coda

The coda proper should be played without precipitation, and the performer should not fall into the error made by some famous violinists, whose playing of it suggests a race against time rather than a dignified interpretation of this noble music, a work which gives its composer a secure place among the purest geniuses of the art.

THE CONCERTO IN D MAJOR
by Johannes Brahms, Op. 77
(1833-1897)

The Brahms "D Major Concerto" was played for the first time by Joseph Joachim, to whom it is dedicated, at a concert in the Leipsic Gewandhaus, on January 1, 1879, Brahms conducting the orchestra.

This magnificent work is more musical than it is violinistic, and contains numerous passages in which violence rather than strength must be employed to vanquish the difficulties which present themselves. When Brahms showed the manuscript of his Concerto to Wieniawski, the latter declared that it would be impossible to play it, and it is quite probable that Joachim made a number of alterations before producing it in public. The hand of Brahms is in evidence in Joachim's own Hungarian Concerto, just as Joachim's intervention in this Concerto of Brahms is clearly to be recognized. We know that Chausson's "Poème" was reconstructed by Ysaye; and we rather imagine that Sarasate influenced the Saint-Saëns "Concerto in B Minor."

The Brahms Violin Concerto should be regarded as a symphony with a solo violin, whose majesty lends surprising relief to the imperishable beauties of this powerful work. In order to play it well the violinist must rise above all trifling considerations, all personal interests, since it is an aristocratic work and one which must be played royally. In it the player must show that he is an accomplished musician, and all the little customary tricks of the virtuoso are out of place in a composition of such grandeur of conception and wide scope of musical interest.

I will begin my consideration of the Brahms Concerto with the first measure of the solo, and continue by periods of 30 measures.

Allegro Non Troppo

($\textbf{J} = 126$)

1

The first measure should be declaimed, without hurrying the tempo, and with a very broad *détaché*.

Sustain the first *F* of measure 4.

Play the chord in measure 5 without harshness.

The first *D* of measure 8 should be played in sustained fashion.

From measures 9 to 13 introduce a *crescendo, forte* to *fortissimo*.

The sextolets and the quintuplets in measures 13 to 22 should be played very calmly, and without conveying the impression that the player is anxious to finish with them.

Measures 23 to 26 should be played with a *spiccato* closely approaching a *détaché*.

Measures 27 to 30 should be played in the following manner:

observing the — over the *D*.

2

A *pianissimo* shading not being possible because of the character of the melodic line, measures 1 and 2 should be played *piano,* with a *crescendo* from measures 3 to 4, followed by a rapid *diminuendo* in the last-mentioned measure.

Stress the first six notes of measure 5, and play measures 6 to 9 with the greatest calmness. These measures vaguely recall the beginning of the Beethoven Violin Concerto, and it may be said positively that the first 45 measures of this Concerto form a genuine interlude following the first *tutti,* serving to introduce the initial theme.

Measures 11 to 13 should be played with a gradual *rallentando* up to the *ritardando,* which should not, however, drag.

The small notes preceding the trill in measures 15 and 16, should be played clearly and without undue haste. The theme itself should be presented in *mezzo forte,* and, especially from measures 17 to 22, should be kept on the same uniform *mezzo forte* level.

From measures 23 to 30 play freely and without accentuation, not even on the trill, which should not have any definite end.

In measures 28 and 30 make a fine *crescendo* leading up to the high *D,* which should be emphasized in the strongest fashion.

3

The trill and the accompanying small notes should be played as follows:

From the 13th to the 14th measure play very tenderly, and with considerable freedom, as well as without any rhythmic constraint.

Measures 15 to 20 should be presented without roughness and without any scraping; the chords should be struck out with one stroke and not in the usual way, that is to say, sustained:

because it is impossible to sustain the last chord as written by Beethoven.

Measure 29 should be played very freely and with a rapid *diminuendo.*

4

Beginning with measure 30 of the preceding period and moving to measure 18 of the succeeding one, we find ourselves confronted with a most delightful illustration of the melody orchestrally developed; the principal notes of the theme should, therefore, be sustained as in the following example:

The *crescendo* from measure 7 to measure 10 should be played without violence; it should be a gentle *crescendo* with, at measure 10, a rapid *diminuendo*.

The first *A* in measure 11 should be sustained, as well as the *A* in measure 12; and the same observation applies to measure 14.

From measure 11 to measure 18, everything should be held on a very lightly colored plane of expression.

Measures 21 and 22—counting in the two measures of the *tutti*—should be played calmly, and with a slight *crescendo* at the end of measure 22.

The ideally lovely phrase of measures 23 to 30 is marked "amabile," and should be played with great expression; while a heartfelt transport should mark measures 27 to 28.

5

Play measures 1 to 9 without forcing and with great breadth.

Measures 10 to 16 should be played flowingly, lightly and softly, and transparently, with a *crescendo* in measure 16; while in measure 17 the *C* should be brought out with decision. Measures 17, 18, 19, and 20 should be declaimed, and measures 21 and 22 should be played very expressively and with great freedom. Measures 23 to 30 should be played as shown in the following example:

6

Measures 3, 4, 5, and 6 belong to those fragments of an antiviolinistic type which are to be found in this great work, and in trying to make up for their deficiencies no recourse must be had to roughness or harshness. In measure 4 the second chord should be sustained. In measures 5 and 6 the sixteenth note should be prolonged, and played without harshness.

From measure 7 to measure 16 play brilliantly and broadly. In measure 23 prolong the first *E,* and in measure 24, prolong the *F.*

Play measures 25, 26 and 27 calmly and without hurrying.

We pass over the 31 measures of the *tutti.*

7

The superb phrase which runs from measures 1 to 8 should be played with fervor, and with a clear, somewhat *mezzo forte* dynamic coloring.

Measures 9 to 28 clearly expose the intellectual capacity of the violinist who undertakes to interpret the work; for the manner in which they are to be played is very adequately indicated in the Joachim edition. These measures should be played in the following manner:

with the first eighth sustained, as well as the two notes following, as indicated, with grace and above all without skipping.

In measures 29 and 30 strongly sustain the trill and see that an energetic accent is given to each note.

8

The sextolets in measures 4, 5 and 6 should be played with repose, holding back somewhat on the third beat of the measure 6. Measures 15 to 27 set the violinist the problem of how to avoid ridicule. The period is a grotesque one, and it seems clear that Brahms wished to depict a species of the hilarity appropriate to some bibulous person, whose silly mirth is followed by a brief and atrocious drama of some kind. The dramatic effect of measures 28, 29 and 30 of this period, and of the 17 measures of period 9, is tremendous.

9

The 16th and 17th measures of this last period seem to echo the triumph of a rage assuaged.

10

Period ten begins after the *tutti*. Measures 1 to 4 should be played with delicacy, yet with a prolonged bow stroke, and measures 5 to 9 with a feeling which evokes the graceful flight of a swarm of swallows.

Up to the *tutti* preceding the cadenza, we have a repetition of the first part; hence all that is necessary is to apply it to what has already been said.

11

Beginning period two after the cadenza, we may note that this period comprises the last 45 measures of the first part.

The first 21 measures should be played in contemplative fashion, with calmness and on a *mezzo forte* dynamic plane, since the *piano* indicated does not raise the violin sufficiently above the orchestra. The phrase is one of ideal beauty, and one in which His Majesty the Violin displays his tonal resources in the happiest manner.

Measures 22 to 31 should be played very evenly and strictly in time, except that, at measure 29, a *stringendo* should be carried out in the *crescendo*, which should end with a big *forte* on the chord of measure 32.

The tempo of the animato is approximately *MM—138*. One should start at once in the tempo of the animato, and not allow it to lapse until the end is reached.

Play the chords without harshness.

Adagio
(♩ = 72)

We begin after the *tutti*.

1

This beautiful movement should be played with simple sincerity, and the player should concentrate on the inner depth of the music. He should play with sentiment, yet not sentimentality.

It is all too easy to fall into errors of exaggeration, and certain virtuosos permit themselves liberties in the *portamento* which are absolutely ridiculous.

Nor should convenience be sought after at the expense of the truly musical, and it is with regret that I notice many a fingering indicated in the Joachim edition of the Brahms Violin Concerto, which would seem to be at variance with the ultra-academic principles professed by that master.

Measures 4 to 5 should be played upon the *E* string, as follows:

Measures 17 and 18 should be played freely and in a manner which shows that they are deeply felt.

Measures 21 and 22 should be played with impatience, emphasizing the three last notes of measure 22. Sustain the *C* sharp of measure 23, and give it its integral value.

Measures 25 to 28 should be played with power and breadth; emphasizing the *G* sharp of the measure 28.

Play measures 29 and 30 sadly and with resignation.

2

In measure 2 do not give the impression of playing a cadenza, but play

strictly in time. The organ point should be very short. The *C* should be accented, as well as the second *A* and the second *F* of the measure 3.

Measure 5 should be played in declamatory style.

Present measures 5 and 7 with a suspicion of impatience.

Measures 8 and 9 should be played with great calmness.

At measure 10 a voluminous *crescendo* should be made.

Measure 12 should be very broadly conceived, and measure 13 played without precipitation.

Measures 14, 15 and 16 must be played with sublimity of expression making a slight *ritardando*.

Revert to tempo at measure 17, and play the broken octaves flexibly.

A slight *ritardando* should be made to the end of measure 18.

Play measures 22 to 25 with great repose.

3

Measure 30 of period two and measure 1 of period three must be presented with a feeling of deep meditation and admiration.

Measures 2 to 9 are presented with fervor and nobility, playing broadly, and giving all its merited importance to this superb phrase.

At measure 9 a *crescendo* begins and is continued to measure 11, the *decrescendo* setting in at the second beat of the same measure. Emphasize the last two eighths.

In measures 14 and 15 accent the first notes tenderly.

Measures 16 to 25 should be played calmly and expressively, without exaggeration, but with a great feeling of amiability, charm and retrospection.

Allegro Giocoso, Ma Non Troppo Vivace

($\textstyle\int$ = 104)

The periods omit the *tuttis*.

Measures 1 to 8 should be played in a martial manner, and with great rhythmic squareness. (The *tutti* runs from measures 9 to 15.)

The descending scale in measure 16 must be played with precision, with a *sforzando* attack, and should conclude on a *mezzo forte* plane in measure 17. The *piano* indicated does not apply.

Measures 20 to 22 are in no wise violinistic. From measures 18 to 27 play almost *metronomically,* with a prolonged *spiccato,* and a very great *crescendo* from measures 25 to 27.

2

Brahms might have dispensed with the chords in measures 5 and 6, since their keynote is elegance, and chords are therefore out of place. At all events they should be played without harshness.

Measures 7 to 10 should be played with exquisite delicacy.

Measures 11 and 12 are summaries of measures 7 to 10.

In measures 7 to 14 use a fairly well nourished *spiccato.*

Keep the bow on the strings in measures 15 to 18, accenting the second sixteenth note of each one of these measures.

In measure 19 sustain the first *F.*

In measures 20, 21 and 22, sustain the first note of each measure in a noticeable manner.

Play measures 22 to 26 with great brilliancy, forecasting, so to speak, the powerful and energetic period which follows this one, in measures 27 to 30.

3

Strongly accent measures 1 to 12 of this third period.

It occurs at times, in this period, that the orchestra forgets that this is a violin concerto which is being played. The orchestral conductor must be given to understand that brass violins will never be the fashion!

Play measures 9 to 12 without constraint, and take your time while playing in order to avoid breaks.

4

The remarks made at the beginning apply to measures 1 to 17.

(As regards the *tuttis,* we refer the reader to measures 3 to 9.)

Play measures 18 to 21 in tranquil style, lightly sustaining the first note of each measure.

The expression mark *diminuendo,* at measure 24, does not apply. Incidentally, composers who write for the violin are continually making mistakes as regards expression marks, and it is a question whether any violinist observes the expression marks indicated to the letter, from measure 18 to measure 24 of this period of the Brahms Concerto. This phrase, without being played explosively, should nevertheless, be played with brilliance.

5

The ravishing episode which begins with measure 30 of period 4 and continues to measure 4 of period five is decidedly characteristic of Brahms' manner.

From measures 8 to 11 play fluently and transparently.

In measures 12 to 15, there should be a light, sustained accent given to the fourth sixteenth note of each beat. The signs for *crescendo* and *diminuendo* should not be regarded as applying here, since they cannot be carried out on a note as short as the sixteenth in question.

Play measures 16 to 19 very expressively, and connect the four sixteenth notes on the third beat of measure 17.

Measures 23 to 30 as measures 1 to 15 of this period.

6

The same observations apply to period six which were made in connection with period two and period three.

7

The same observations apply to period seven which were made in connection with period one.

8

In measures 12 to 20, take all the time needed and do not jostle the chords.

The phrase may be said to represent gladness after effort, and is a very lovely fresco, with outlines which combine grace and power.

Play measures 21 to 30 with almost metronomic exactitude, and, above all, with grace.

9

Beginning with measure 7, the approach of the coda or finale makes itself felt. Play measures 9 and 10 *mezzo forte*.

Measures 21 to 24 should be energetically played, and the chord well sustained.

Measure 26 (the first two sextuplets of the cadenza) should be enunciated with repose, and measure 27 (the remainder of the cadenza) without any precipitation.

10

Measures 1 to 19 are in the style of a hunting air. Be sure to accent the first quarter notes of measures 1 and 2 strongly.

Introduce a rapid *crescendo* in measures 6 and 7, and prolong the *C* of measure 8.

Play measures 10 to 19 gracefully, and with rhythmic accentuation.

Measures 23 to 30 should be played very broadly and a *diminuendo* made at measure 30.

11

Play measures 1 to 4 lightly, not *piano,* but rather *mezzo forte.*

Use a prolonged *spiccato* in measures 5 to 10, not playing harshly but giving the tone the mellowness of a horn.

In measures 16 to 25 use the bow as the shadings may require, and play measures 26 and 27 *fortissimo.*

12

Measure 30 of period eleven and measure 1 of period twelve should be played with enthusiasm.

Gradually allow the sonority of the violin tone to die away, from measures 10 on to measure 16.

Play measure 17 without any *rallentando.*

Measure 18 should be played in a broad and powerful manner, and sustained for the length of three ordinary measures.

THE CONCERTO IN A MAJOR

by Camille Saint-Saëns, Op. 20

(1835-1921)

This is a marvelously beautiful work, written in a single movement, with a short andante which serves as an interlude. Its ensemble is magnificently conceived, and its architecture is as elegant in lines as it is powerful in structure.

The chords at the beginning should set the tempos from the very start. They should be played as though on the piano, and with practice this result may be obtained. Incidentally, the tempo ($\downarrow = 144$) is not exaggerated. All grating effects should be avoided as being quite incompatible with the impression which is to be given.

Accent the third and sixth beats of measure 2 of the beginning strongly, as follows:

Nevertheless, these third and sixth beats should not be sustained, but should be played as shown in the next example:

At the beginning of the next period (letter *A* in the edition of the work published by Hamelle, in Paris) the measure should be divided into two bow strokes, as follows:

It is decidedly difficult to play here with an even tone, yet the passage is excellent for study purposes, and the wrist plays a large part in it.

The noble phrase which follows after the trill should be rendered in a spirit of concentrated grief. A remarkably expressive phrase, the player should be able to draw from it the tears and despair it so eloquently expresses. We are now confronted by one of those phrases which demand proper restraint in their expression, and the dilemma which at once arises is that of avoiding exaggeration in one or the other direction. Six measures after letter *C* a noticeably pronounced *ritardando* should precede the breathless fragment which follows. Play with a whole stroke of the bow to each note in the four measures preceding the letter *D*. Two measures before *D* take care to accentuate the principal design:

After the *tuttis* of the *C* major period we come to a phrase of such exquisite and ravishing charm that its playing raises the artist to the heights of emotional enjoyment.

It is not dots which should be placed above the following notes, but short stress lines:

At letter *E,* the skies grow overcast, hence at the end of the *crescendo* in the second measure, one should, so to speak, play the last two eighth notes with brutal roughness.

The delightful andante should be played in a spirit of quietude and of love rewarded. It is a species of thanksgiving, and its lovely theme should be played with a bowing of generous breadth and with nobility of feeling.

At seven measures after the letter *L,* the first note of each group of six eighths should be sustained, as follows:

Four measures before letter *M* play with great calmness and, as it were, with metronomic exactness.

At letter *M* the violinist has an opportunity of showing what he can do in the matter of sustained bowing, and how perfectly he is able to effectuate his changes of tone.

Measures 7, 8 and 9, after letter *M,* should be played most expressively.

The expressional phrase "con grazia sempre tranquillo," found eight measures before the letter *N,* is entirely devoid of good sense; the period is one of transition, which only forecasts an unmixed joy to come.

Two measures before letter *N*—and avoiding all melodramatic effect—one should play with deep feeling.

The letter *N* indicates the coda, and when I had the honor of playing this concerto with Saint-Saëns in Geneva, in 1896, he made a reservation with regard to my conception of the tempo of this period. The tempo should be slightly augmented and the eight measures should be divided by a well proportioned *crescendo.* At measure 9 the player must resist the tendency to bolt, and I know from my own experience that he will be almost obliged to force himself to restraint here.

Letter *O* : play here with great passion and a manifest sentiment of nobility.

These last measures are extremely difficult to render, they should be presented in a consecutively moving *diminuendo,*

ending, as it were, in the clouds, but followed by two abrupt *fortissimo* chords.

THE CONCERTO IN B MINOR

by Camille Saint-Saëns, Op. 61

(1835-1921)

The fact that Saint-Saëns should have added so noble a work as is this Concerto to the literature of the violin calls forth the reflection that there is not a single violinist who has composed a similar work of the first order for his instrument.

Vieuxtemps, it is true, wrote superb concertos, but they in no wise stand comparison with the concertos of Beethoven, Mendelssohn or Bruch. The concertos written for the violin by violinists are better adapted to the instrument than those written by the composers, but they are less musical in the real sense of the word. The Concerto under consideration is one of those which may be placed in the category of works which, though not very violinistic, are, nevertheless, admirably musical.

The first movement is authoritative and structurally worthy of Beethoven.

The andantino is a charmingly inflected barcarolle, which, however, seems out of keeping in a concerto as grandiosely conceived as is this one.

The finale is alive with verve and power, perfect as regards form and its creative values.

The beginning should be played broadly, with concentrated passion, and lyric fullness.

The letters referred to hereafter are to be found in the original French edition of this work.

Take care not to "bolt" in the following passage:

Further on we find the subject which is later taken up by the orchestra; the sustained playing of the basses or lower notes should be imitated as follows:

This effect may easily be obtained by playing the basses *fortissimo* and the upper notes *mezzo forte*.

At letter *A* sustain the *F*, as well as the first eighth note of measure 3.

The phrase which occurs eight measures after letter *A* should be broadly sung. Take care not to bolt in the two measures before the letter *B*.

Four measures before *E major* avoid the tendency to dramatize, and play simply and naturally.

The exquisite phrase in *E* is ideally conceived. It is as artless and lovely as could be imagined; hence, play it without ostentation, and with a soft quality of tone.

An intensive effect may be obtained at measure 11 of this *E* major section, although *"dolcissimo"* is the expression mark indicated. It is preferable to play first *piano* and then *pianissimo,* as follows:

Play the scale twelve measures before letter *C* with great serenity.

Do not bolt in the passage which follows the trill (at letter *C*). The tempo should be adhered to strictly. Throughout this period the violin must dominate the orchestra or else be drowned out by it, the more so since orchestral conductors, as a rule, fail to subdue the accompaniment.

At letter *F,* beginning with measure 4, play broadly, and at measure 10 accent each one of the first eighth notes in the groups, as follows:

Up to the end of the first movement, the violinist must play exactly in rhythm and must not depart from the tempo originally set.

Andantino Quasi Allegretto

Avoid falling into the error of playing this movement like a slow waltz. The movement is one ideally attractive and intensely poetic.

As regards the beginning there exists a controversy among violinists which deserves to be explained: the second note of measure 1 is often played as though it were a thirty-second note, as follows:

instead of being played in this wise:

The whole piece should be played on a plane of gentle calmness. Accentuation plays a preponderating part in it, and it affords the artist a unique opportunity to show what he is able to do by applying the principles of the art of song.

The subordinate theme in this movement is also one of poetic beauty:

and should be deeply studied in order to be interpreted in a musicianly way.

The harmonics at the close of this movement should be played without harshness, and somewhat broadly, as indicated:

Third Movement

The recitative at the beginning should be well enunciated and should not be unduly hastened by the player.

Allegro Non Troppo

Here the violinist has a chance to show his quality in every way, shape and form, and to display rhythmic precision in presenting the opening theme.

This beginning, full of nobility, should show clearly that the artist intends to adhere strictly to the indicated tempo, and there should be a slight *rubato* in the playing of the subordinate theme:

The phrase on the *G* string which occurs later should be clearly enunciated, but without undue force:

The greatest difficulty which the student will encounter in this movement is a tendency to "bolt" on passages of this type.

The whole movement is of such a superbly virile character, and so splendidly orchestrated that the player's enthusiasm is prone to speed up his tempos and thereby lessen the artistic effect of his performance.

THE SYMPHONIE ESPAGNOLE

by Edouard Lalo, Op. 21

(1823-1892)

The violinist who has a real understanding of the resources of his instrument, knows that Lalo's "Symphonie Espagnole" is a work extremely rich in effect, and the reason why it is such a favorite on the concert program will be found in the possibility it offers for virtuoso display which is at the same time thoroughly musical.

Are we to consider it a symphony in the accepted meaning of the word? Discounting agreement with the exact rules of form, in our opinion it deserves its title in the broader sense; since it is a work of serious beauty and lofty musical architecture, as well as full of charm and vigor.

1

Allegro Non Troppo

Declaim the theme with firmness and decision. The accent on the *C* sharp should not be too greatly prolonged. The first measure in tempo is decidedly characteristic and very complicated, since it presents the problem of playing groups of three and of two notes as equal units of time——

a figuration often found in Spanish music—with sufficient ease and lack of effort to produce a truly musical effect. Such groups are often played in the following manner:

This, of course, is a gross error. The following measure,

is a complicated one to play. In every important work of the violin repertory we find two or three redoubtable passages: in the "Symphonie Espagnole" the measure cited above is a nightmare to many a violinist.

It may be made less difficult by playing the whole measure with a single bow stroke, and by accenting each individual *G*.

Avoid drowning the individual notes while playing the following passage rapidly. Remember to play calmly and clearly:

In general, up to the end of the first period, play everything with marked emphasis and a strong accent.

Endeavor to bring out the profound sorrow and deep emotion concentrated in the following measures:

In the following very charming thought:

play with all the tenderness and feeling of which you are capable, and do not fall back on the vulgarity of the *glissando*. In the period which follows, emphasize the passages with strong accents, all of which have been clearly indicated by the composer. As a rule the violinist is too apt to see only the note itself, and not what may be placed above or below it.

At the following period:

slightly hasten the movement, but in a reasonable and well balanced manner.

The subsequent period,

should be played with a very concise *détaché,* or with an adequately heavy *spiccato,* that is to say, with the exception of the last measure.

Mark the rhythm firmly in the conclusion.

2

Scherzando

This exquisite movement is one of the loveliest jewels contained in this superb composition. Tenderness is the keynote of its mood throughout. Sarasate was accustomed to play a delightful *glissando* from the *D* to the *A*:

and somewhat further on we find a detail characteristic of Spanish music, one which should be underlined. In the following example:

if the rhythm is followed too closely, the figure becomes monotonous, and within the narrow limits of the measure the player must strive to secure the following effect:

In the passage which follows:

do not hurry the movement, but play with a bow that is flexible and drawn out. At the *poco più lento* mark the tempos with exactness. Sarasate always made a *ritardando* in the following two measures:

3

Intermezzo

As a rule this movement is not played, for the simple reason that the "Symphonie" when it is included becomes so very long. Yet this intermezzo is very characteristic. It is written in the style of a Habanera, and its rhythm must be thoroughly understood and clearly indicated.

Do not play this as follows:

This last manner of playing is grossly wrong. The velocity passages should be played clearly and without hurrying, with what Sarasate was accustomed to call "the rhythm of mechanism," which he controlled with incredible mastery. As regards the playing of the "Symphonie Espagnole," no other violinist has been able to play it with so prodigious an artistry as Sarasate, combining grace, clean-cut brilliancy and bewildering vitality in so remarkable a degree.

4

Andante

This sublime slow movement seems to evoke that Berber Africa where the Moors of Spain took refuge after having been driven from their terrestrial paradise in Grenada. It breathes a mystic poesy, a captivating charm, and an eloquence which is profoundly moving. It is a poem of love and suffering, where hope and illusion speak in turn. In order to interpret this wonderful andante worthily, the player must strive to exceed the limits of the commonly possible, the opening theme,

requiring more than ordinary musical understanding.

In the tempo following the *poco rit,* the rhythmic figure:

should be kept in mind, and the player should guard against letting the music take on a Hungarian character, one from which the spirit of the work is immeasurably removed. The difference is a very important one, and should be emphasized by playing the sixteenth notes without harshness, while the sixteenth notes in Hungarian music are played, so to say, as though they were thirty-second notes. The cadenza:

before the next tempo should be played tranquilly, and without attempting to make it brilliant. Play the first notes of the chromatic scale in the same tranquil manner, then hasten the tempo, little by little, after the trill, taking care not to hurry too much.

At the close see that the final *D* is played with a pure and ideal quality of tone, long and sustained.

5

Rondo Allegro

This rondo, full of vitality and spirit, brimming over with the joy of life, is anything but simple. The player should be able to present it with a rhythmic sureness which nothing can disturb. See to it that the *poco più lento* is presented with the greatest clarity, and also that the accents—which are very fully indicated—are all observed, since they are essential. Do not mistake the following measure:

for the subsequent one:

To do so simply reverses their rôle. It is an offense against musical ethics committed by many professional violinists.

Play the remainder of the movement with the assured elegance appropriate and in character with Spanish music, and see that the whole work is permeated with a feeling of vigor and strength. The combination of pizzicato and trills at the conclusion,

requires particular study in order to be performed without suspicion of "trick" playing. It is the ability of a player to render just such passages musically that stamps him as one of the elect.

The Concerto in G Minor

by Max Bruch, Op. 26

(1838-1920)

This magnificent inspiration must be ranked among the greatest violin concertos and is a work peculiarly impressive and noble in style—a work at once profound and beautiful, using the latter word, which is much abused, advisedly.

1

Allegro Moderato

See to it that the first *G* vibrates clearly, obtaining your effect by means of the following combination:

Produce the vibrato with the third finger, but do not play on the third (*D*) string.

The first recitation, as well as that which follows, should be played with great breadth and tranquillity; but always on the same level of tone, and the last note should be decidedly prolonged. As for the rest, up to the end of the period, play on the *G* string, with power and in an authoritative manner, enunciating the notes clearly and without any haste. Avoid all abruptness in playing the triad chords, and take enough time to make them stand out clearly.

In the charming phrase which follows, retard somewhat, and play in singing style, increasing the movement a little at the measure with the four trills. The succeeding *ritardando* should not be too pronounced.

The technical period which now follows should be played without hurrying, but in a somewhat lively tempo.

In the passage which follows:

sustain the notes in such a manner as to create the impression that double chords are being played, sounding as below:

Do not fail to use a large and generous bow. Take two thirds of the bow for the final trill. At the concluding fraction, the four-measure Allegro, each one of the first three measures should be introduced slowly, then each subsequent note should be played with greater speed.

2

Adagio

In order to execute this unique movement properly, it will be very helpful for the student to hear it interpreted by some great violinist such as Ysaÿe or Kreisler, who infuses into his performance the amount of depth and kindling ardor which it calls for in a musical sense. Some of the younger virtuosos do not play this movement with sufficient balance, nor with a sufficiently slow tempo. Even Sarasate, when he played this adagio, took it in far too rapid a tempo. It should not, of course, be played so slowly as to become tiresome; but, notwithstanding, the true character of the movement is one of breadth and poise.

A special effort should be made to play the following passage,

with as great a tranquil effect as can be achieved with the fingers and bow working in perfect synchronism.

Also in the last nine bars of this movement:

the various nuances, *crescendo* and *decrescendo,* must be fully carried out in order to bring the movement to a fitting artistic close.

3

Finale

This movement, with its distinct military stamp, is a mortal enemy to any lack of clean-cut rhythm.

When playing this allegro the violinist should bear in mind the device: "In union there is strength." Here he must know how to combine strength and beauty, and not permit a hard, brutal manner of playing to get the upper hand. Incidentally, one of the first conditions for playing this movement, and the whole concerto, for that matter, is the possession of a violin with a powerful tone. After the fine phrase on the *G* string:

the *grazioso* passage should be played with elegance and delicacy. The accentuation has everywhere been very adequately indicated by the composer, and should be used. Employ great breadth of bow for the whole of the finale, and remember that it is distinctly a finale of the heroic type. Avoid all tendency to "bolt" at the *presto con fuoco* movement.

The student must endeavor to realize that tempo markings are always relative, and that the composer always assumes that clarity will be the keynote of the performance of any movement, whether it be *adagio* or *prestissimo*.

INTRODUCTION AND RONDO CAPRICCIOSO
by Camille Saint-Saëns, Op. 28
(1835-1921)

The late illustrious master, Camille Saint-Saëns, was truly inspired when he composed this famous rondo, for it stands out in the entire literature of violin music as one of the most sparkling, most brilliantly varied and interesting of pieces, and one which is calculated to display in the highest degree the virtuosity and musical ability of the violinist.

It was one of Pablo de Sarasate's favorite program numbers, and he played it with a sprightliness and charm which made him its unique interpreter. It seems that Saint-Saëns originally wrote the Rondo as a final movement for the "Violin Concerto in A," Op. 20; but that later he changed his mind, and published it separately in the form in which it is known to us.

1
Introduction

The adorable *andante malinconico* at the beginning should be played strictly in character, as indicated. It is past understanding why nearly every violinist plays this beginning too fast. One should, in fact, even exaggerate the indicated phrasing a little when playing. The student should allow himself to be guided by the following example:

These *crescendos*, it goes almost without saying, should be played with great discretion, yet must be accented correctly—this is something the student must learn—in harmony with the laws of rhythm and the movement of the melody.

2
Animato

The player should begin slowly, and play more quickly in the proportion shown in the following example. Pay attention to the fingering:

Also make a *crescendo* at the commencement of the *animato,* beginning the *crescendo* with a *piano,* and rising to a *forte* when the *G* sharp eighth note is reached. The *tempo primo* is resumed at once at the *G* natural, at the brilliant passage 8 measures before the *allegro* begins. Do not hurry, and play clearly. This passage is so brilliant in itself that it is unnecessary for the violinist to try to introduce any pyrotechnical effects. Reserve your energies for the *allegro* movement. See to it that the trill occurring 2 measures before the *allegro* begins be full and well nourished.

3

Allegro, Ma Non Troppo

The first notes should be played as follows; this is the traditional and generally accepted opening:

Saint-Saëns' own expression marks are not detailed enough, and if those he has set down are followed to the letter, the glow and fire of this tonal gem will not be properly disclosed, and its music will produce a cold and glacial impression.

For instance, in the following:

a *crescendo* is necessary, and the final *F* should be accented.

The following trill:

should cover the whole part of the two first eighth notes of the measure, and not merely a small part of their time value.

After the organ point and the scale passages have been played, make a *rallentando* in the case of the first three notes, and do not return to the original tempo until the following measure has been reached. After the *tutti* play the energetic period which follows with emphasis, but do not hurry it. At the 2/4 time play somewhat *rubato,* and develop a *crescendo,* continuing it until measure 7 is reached. Then make an abrupt *diminuendo,* 7 measures before the 6/8 time signature, followed by a *crescendo* ending in a *fortissimo* 2 measures before the 6/8 time.

The rhythm, in the section in 6/8 time, should be well accented; yet without playing the first note of each group of six too forcefully. At the end of the chromatic passage played *sautillé* (with springing bow), pause for a moment on the *E,* play the scale brilliantly, and the three eighth notes with a *rallentando,* then at once resuming the original tempo.

When the following ravishing passage is reached:

play more slowly and with greater expression; hold to the idea, while you are playing, that you are voicing the love song of a young girl; remain on a *mezzo forte* level, and introduce a *diminuendo* 2 measures before the trill.

The arpeggios throughout should be held well in hand, and accented without ostentation, as they form a contrast and serve as an embellishment to the theme which is worked out at the same time in the orchestra.

The sequence of chords occurring before the *più allegro,*

should not be taken at too lively a tempo; all scratching and scraping should be avoided, and the chords themselves presented with a full sonorous tone.

4

Più Allegro

Here the tempo should be chosen with care, and the violinist should play without hurrying until the end of the movement has been reached. Do not play too quickly; you do so at the expense of clearness, and with the result that your interpretation misses fire.

This is particularly true of the series of scales and .arpeggios occurring just before the conclusion.

The "Rondo Capriccioso" is a violin number which has the most immediate effect on any and every audience. It is one of the most generally appreciated virtuoso violin pieces written, and though it makes great demands on the artist, he is sure of his reward after a good performance.

CHAPTER XVIII

VIOLIN COLLECTING IN EUROPE AND AMERICA [1]

Old violins, like paintings, porcelains and other works of art, have many devotees. Because of their exterior beauty as well as tone, fine violins give unbounded pleasure, and consequently violin collecting has become a recognized artistic hobby.

For similar reasons, violin collecting has been prevalent in nearly all European countries, commencing apparently as early as Nicola Amati's time (1596-1684). As in other things there is to be noted a very wide range of intelligence on the part of collectors, and an equally wide range in the quality of the instruments assembled.

Some seek only the finest specimens of the greatest old makers; others search for what may be termed "speculative" specimens, that is, genuine instruments in poor preservation that can be purchased for comparatively small sums. Still others. seeking quantity rather than quality, satiate their acquisitive propensities with cheap old commercial copies, usually of German make, picked up here and there, usually with more or less interesting histories attached, and delude themselves and others into the belief that they possess genuine works of art. Generally, such collectors are blissfully ignorant of real values, but more often their knowledge is influenced by monetary considerations. The latter group is not common alone in America but to all other countries where the violin is played. Furthermore it has existed everywhere for many years. It is by far the most numerous, and since such collections have no artistic and very little commercial value, we shall not consider them here but confine our attention to real works of the masters of the sixteenth to the nineteenth centuries.

While we have to do primarily in this article with private collections in the United States we shall digress, for the purpose of obtaining proper background, and briefly review famous European collections because the violin itself and violin collecting as a business or a hobby originated in Italy.

Violin playing and violin collecting may be said to have been coëxistent. About the year 1650 violin playing had developed far enough for the violin sonata and violin solo to have taken definite form. As early as 1604 a violin part appeared for the first time in an operatic score, that of Monteverde. As violin playing assumed the dignity of a profession and soloists began to be heard throughout the principal countries, popular appreciation of the pos-

---

[1] Contributed to the *Encyclopedia of the Violin* by Mr. Jay C. Freeman.

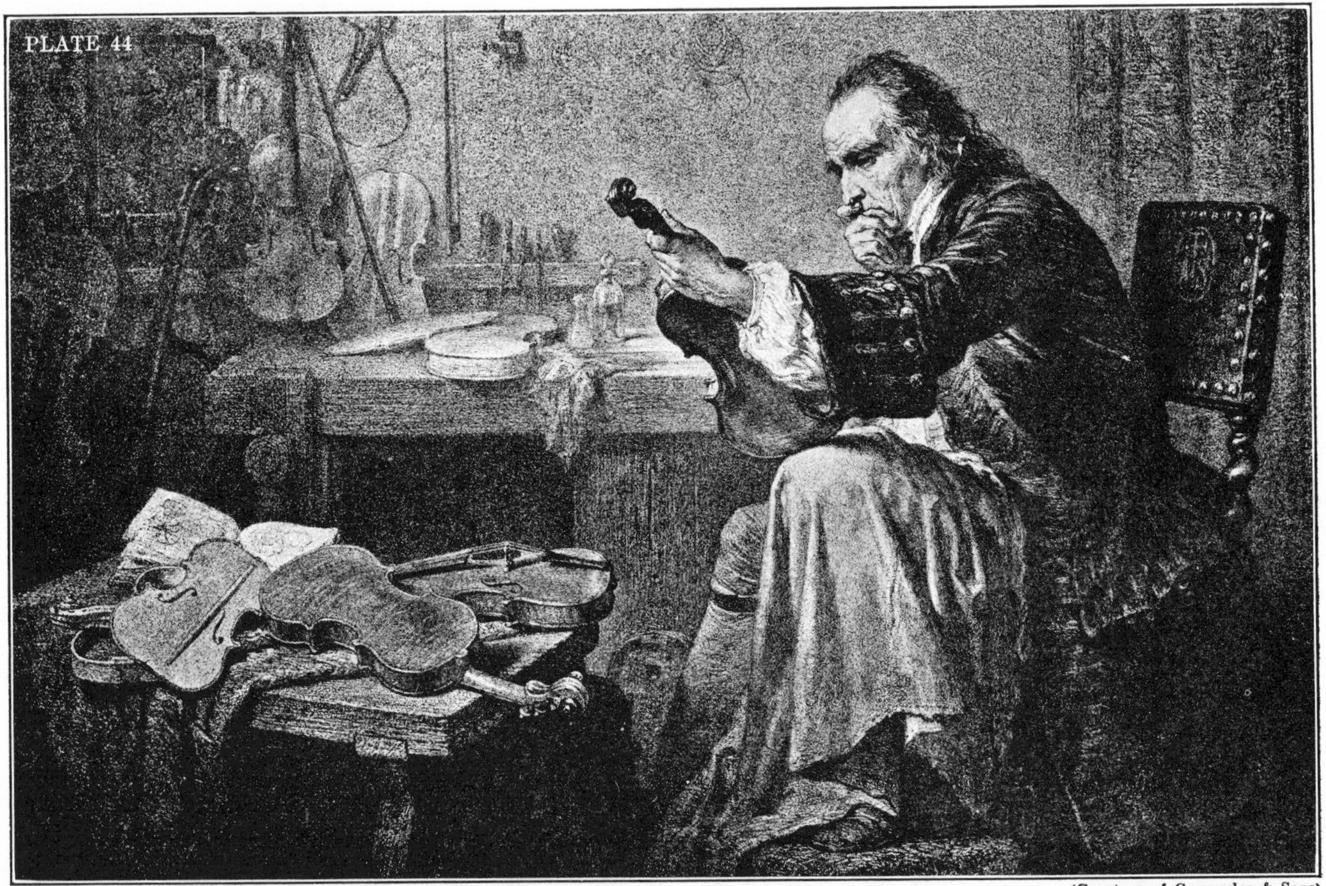

PLATE 44

STRADIVARIUS IN HIS WORKSHOP.

sibilities of the instrument rapidly spread. With the advent of Vitali, Corelli, Vivaldi, Locatelli and others of their time, love of the violin and its music became very general and princes of state and church began to form collections for their private use. Violin making likewise spread very rapidly over Italy, Germany, France and finally was introduced into England, and the makers of Cremona, Brescia and Venice probably owed not a little to the collaboration of the contemporary players already mentioned as well as of others who might be named.

The church also, appreciating the value of the violin and kindred instruments, assembled sets for use in their church services, and emperors, kings and princes collected the choicest violins and cellos for their private home.

Thus violin collecting began and private collectors who were usually amateur players also sought out their favorite instruments in the same manner as at the present time.

Violinists then, as to-day, were often collectors and some of them operated on a large scale. They had better opportunities than others, and those with business instinct assembled collections, generally of a few violins and sometimes of many, which they sold to their pupils and others. The public has always, in a certain sense, placed a premium on violins which have been in the possession of famous players—not always with good reason.

The most famous amateur collector of Italy undoubtedly was Count Cozio di Salabere, who, being an ardent admirer of Stradivarius, formed a large collection of both his instruments and his pupils; also the finest examples of Guarnerius and earlier makers. He was a patron of J. B. Guadagnini and possessed many of his violins which he appears to have bought as an investment.

This great collection contained many of the very choicest works of Stradivarius (including the famous "Messiah")—all that remained in the family having been purchased in 1775 from Paola Stradivarius, Antonio's son—the lot comprising ten instruments. Paganini owned a quartet of Stradivarii which were sold at his death. One of the violins of this quartet is now owned in New York.

Other Italian noblemen were intelligent collectors; their instruments, however, like that of Count Cozio di Salabere, were forced on the market by the financial depression which fell on Italy after the Napoleonic Wars. Count Cozio began to dispose of his large collection, containing perhaps a hundred or more instruments, in 1801, and at his death in 1840 he owned but one violin—a Nicola Amati.

By that time the preference in other European countries for the violins of Stainer, Klotz and other German makers had changed, and violinists and violin lovers were keen to acquire the treasures of Italy, and they then began to migrate rapidly to other countries.

PLATE 45

(Courtesy of the Rudolph Wurlitzer Co.)

A MODERN, TWO-STORY STEEL FIRE-PROOF SAFE FOR STORING
VALUABLE OLD VIOLINS.

In France and Belgium, collections of violins were formed and included many of the finest specimens by the master Italian makers of the sixteenth to the nineteenth centuries.

Several of the best known collectors restricted themselves entirely to the instruments of Stradivarius and Guarnerius. Among these, the most important were the Duc de Campo-Selice, who at his death in 1887, owned eight of the finest examples of Stradivarius.

Others were the Count de Choponay, Vicomte de Janze and M. de St. Senoch both of whom possessed a quartet of instruments made by Stradivarius.

M. Welmothe of Antwerp owned many fine instruments, and M. L'Evêque of La Rochelle formed a large and important collection.

In England, violin collecting was more general than in either France or Italy. Amateur quartets have been popular there for many years, and due to this fact, many sets of the finest Italian instruments were formed, in addition to several very important large collections.

Of the latter, that of Gillot, the pen manufacturer, was the largest, containing many splendid violins which were the work of Stradivarius.

The Goding collection contained a number of good violins, several of which are now in the United States. Other important collections were made by Plowden, Fontaine, Bennett and Waddell. The latter collection was purchased in Glasgow in August, 1923, by an American music house and brought to New York. It contained the famous "Betts" Strad of 1704 and the LeDuc Jos, Guarnerius del Jesus of 1743, besides a number of other very choice violins of different makes.

Other collections of note were made by Mr. Frederick Snitch of Manchester, Mr. Croall and Mr. Crawford of Edinburgh and David Laurie of Glasgow. Three magnificent quartets of Stradivarii are now or were owned in England by Mr. Charles Oldhand, Baron Knoop and Mr. R. E. Brandt.

The novelist, Charles Reade, was a keen violin lover, and owned many violins during his life. The names of Englishmen who possessed Stradivarii in the last two or three decades would form a long list.

Germany, after 1871, began to acquire some of the world's finest violins and cellos. Prior to that time, there were numerous Stradivarii and Guarnerii in the possession of her famous violinists, but it was after the Franco-Prussian war and during the ensuing prosperity, ending with the outbreak of war in 1914, that German amateurs entered the lists in Paris and London, and began carrying off to Germany some of the very choicest examples.

Joseph Joachim had a number of Strads during his career. At his death he possessed three fine ones of the year 1715. David, Spohr, Wilhelmj, Bott, Ernst and other famous German artists possessed numerous fine instruments. Baron Mendelssohn and his brother own a fine quartet of Stradivarii. It will now be in order to consider violin collecting in the United States, and to

PLATE 46

THE BETTS STRADIVARIUS (1704)—VIEW OF BELLY.

PLATE 47

(Courtesy of Mr. John T. Roberts.)

THE BETTS STRADIVARIUS (1704)—VIEW OF BACK AND SIDES.

trace as far as possible some of the interesting instruments which have found their way into the possession of Americans, many of which have at one time or another been in one or the other of the European collections mentioned above. I shall pass over collections of the ordinary kind, of which there are many, and confine the ʋpace at my disposal to a consideration of collections of Stradivarii, Guarnerii, Amati and other of the more famous Italian makers, which may be cited as representative specimens.

Good instruments were appreciated and purchased by the very few in pre-revolutionary days. Recently the writer had in his hands a fine 7/8 size Nicola Amati cello which was brought to Boston about 1760, and there is good evidence that few excellent old English and French violins were brought over in the early days of the last century.

There were many German and French commercial violins—copies of Stradivarius, Guarnerius and Amati—imported during those years, and not a few of these to-day masquerade as genuine works of art. In Louisiana and that part of the South, one meets with occasional Vuillaume, Chanot, Silvestre and Gand violins which were imported by wealthy planters, and others returning from France.

It was not until 1868, however, that a violin of the first class was purchased by an American, John P. Waters of Brooklyn. This was the "King" Joseph Guarnerius, 1737, and was secured through George Hart of London from the Plowden collection. Mr. Waters was an ardent lover and keen judge of Italian violins and owned several others besides the Joseph, among them being a few Nicola Amati and a Stradivarius, 1725.

In May of 1876 he sold the "King" to Mr. R. D. Hawley of Hartford, Connecticut, who then began the formation of the first collection of fine violins ever made in the United States. Mr. Hawley's collection attracted wide attention and aroused general interest in violins of the better kind, and, as a direct result, others emulated his example and many choice Cremonas began to find their way to America.

At his death, Mr. Hawley owned twelve violins; in addition to these he had owned as many more which he disposed of during his lifetime. The collection was sold by his executors to Ralph Granger of San Diego, California, and was purchased by the author of this article, on behalf of a large Western music house in 1901.

Mr. Albert H. Pitkin of Hartford also formed a modest collection of good violins, one of which was a Nicola Amati imported from London in 1872 by a Mr. Johnston of Chicago. This, as far as I know, was the first notable Cremona owned in that city.

Another collection of first importance was made by the late Dwight J. Partello of Washington, D. C. He was an enthusiast of enthusiasts. First as consul, then as special agent of the Treasury Department, he lived in

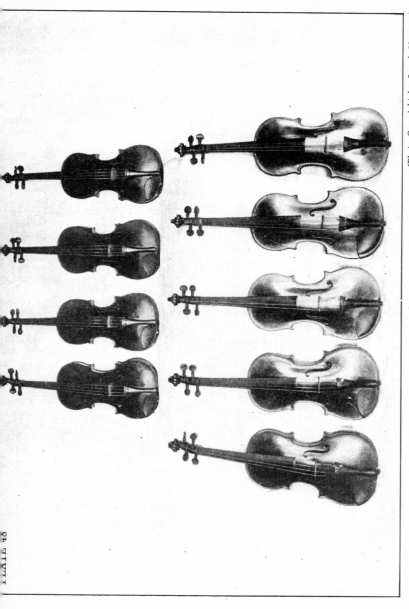

PLATE 46

(Photo Copyright by Joseph Muenzer.)

AN INTERESTING ARRAY OF STRADIVARII VALUED AT $150,000.

Top—Left to right—The Lord Nelson, the Spanish, the Duke of Edinburgh and the Ludwig Strads. Bottom—Left to right—The Paganini, the Huggins, the Rougemont, the Grün, and the Leonora Jackson Strads.

Germany many years, having the opportunity to gratify his love of music and passion for violins. His judgment was not always equal to his opportunities for the acquisition of the choicest specimens, but he nevertheless acquired a collection which comprised several very fine Gaglianos, Amati, Lupots, Rogerii, Guadagnini, etc., as well as two good examples of Stradivarii of 1722-1723 and one of 1690; an excellent Bergonzi and a fair Jos. Guarnerius del Jesu.

His collection of bows may be ranked as one of the finest ever assembled. It consisted of over a dozen choice Tourtes besides good examples of other great makers. After his death, Mr. Partello's collection was sold by his executors in 1922 and many of the most desirable violins it contained have now been disposed of to musicians and collectors.

Mr. John Coggeshall, of Providence, Rhode Island, owns probably the largest private collection existing in the United States to-day. He is an excellent amateur player and takes keen delight in old violins of the different schools. He possesses a very beautiful Stradivarius of 1716.

The increasing value of fine specimens of Cremonese and other Italian makers renders the collection of a large number prohibitive in cost except for the very wealthy. Where, in years gone by they were owned largely by a comparatively few individuals, they are now widely distributed over the country. In this connection it will be of interest to the fine violin lover to peruse the following list of celebrated instruments which are owned either by private persons residing in the United States, or by artists who make frequent visits to this country:

Antonius Stradivarius

1679	Mr. Max Adler
1683, ex Madame Bastard	Mr. David S. Carter
1683, ex Lord Aylesford	Rudolph Wurlitzer Collection
1685, ex Le Marquis Daria	Mr. Michael Gusikoff
1690	Partello Collection
1691	Prof. Leopold Auer
1692	Mrs. Senator Clark
1694	Mrs. Mathews Bryant
1697, ex Prince Uchtomsky	Mr. John T. Roberts
1698, ex Marie Schumann	Mr. Jacques Gordon
1698, "Martinelli"	Wurlitzer Collection
1698, ex Joachim (Long Model)	Mr. Hugo Kortchak
1699	Mr. Ben Roeder
1701	Mr. Mischa Dushkin
1701	Mr. Nahan Franko
1701	Mr. E. Fradkin
1703, ex De Rougemont	Rudolph Wurlitzer Collection
1704, "The Betts"	Mr. John T. Roberts
1708, "The Huggins"	Mr. Gustavo Herten
1708	Mr. Bernard Sinsheimer
1708, ex Soil	Rudolph Wurlitzer Collection
1709, ex Havemeyer	Mrs. Archibald Mitchell
1709	Mrs. Norton
1710, "The Roederer"	Mr. Geo. H. Andrews

PLATE 49

THE WILHELMJ STRADIVARIUS (1725).

Antonius Stradivarius (*continued*)

1710 .... Mr. Charles Martin Loeffler
1710 .... Mr. Joseph Fuchs
1711, "The Healy," ex Hawley collection........... Mr. Geo. Pettinos
1712 .... Ralph Granger
1712 .... Mr. Michael Press
1712 .... Mrs. Toscha Seidel
1713, "The Sancy"............................. Mr. Felix E. Kahn
1713, ex Pingrille............................. Dr. Evans O'Neill Kane
1714, ex Gruen................................ Mr. Franz Kneisel
1714, ex Smith................................ Mr. Albert H. Wallace
1714 .... Mrs. Leonora Jackson McKim
1714, ex Joachim............................. Mr. Albert E. Stephens
1715, ex Lipinski .... Mr. A. P. Malozemoff
1715 .... Mr. Roderick White
1715 .... Mrs. B. C. Ellery
1716 .... Mr. Horace Havemeyer
1716 .... Mrs. Olive Mead Green
1716 .... Mr. Efrem Zimbalist
1717, ex Piatti................................ Mr. John W. Coggeshall
1717 .... Mr. Sascha Jacobson
1717 .... Mr. Michael Banner
1718 .... Mr. John Frothingham
1720 .... Mr. and Mrs. Storn
1720, ex L'Eveque............................. Mr. F. C. Frost
1721 .... Mr. Carl C. Conway
1721 .... Mr. Francis C. Macmillan
1721 .... Mr. Morton Barker
1721, ex Jansa................................ Mr. Chas. Ringling
1721 .... Mrs. Mathews Bryant
1722, "The Earl".............................. Mr. W. T. Cousens
1722 .... Mr. Rudolph Polk
1722, "Imperator"............................. Mr. John S. Phipps
1722 .... Mr. Mischa Elman
1723, ex Bott, ex Spohr....................... Mr. M. Zamustin
1723, "The Spanish Strad"...................... Partello Collection
1724 .... Mr. William Wainright
1725, ex Wilhelmj............................. Mr. J. E. Greiner
1725, ex Duke of Edinburgh.................... Partello Collection
1727, ex Rode................................ Mr. H. S. Grimes
1727, "The Nestor" fatto di anni 83............... Mr. H. S. Grimes
1727, ex Kreutzer............................. Senator Wm. Clark
1731, ex Kiesewetter.......................... Mr. Horace Havemeyer
1733, ex Des Rosiers.......................... Mr. John H. Bennett
1733 .... Mr. Francis Underhill
1733 .... Mr. Socrates Barozzi
1735 .... Mr. Mischa Elman

Joseph Guarnerius del Gesu

1726 .... Mr. Horace Havemeyer
1732, ex Ferni................................ Miss Amy Neill
1732, ex Kreisler, ex Nachez .... Mr. R. C. Durant
1732, ex Ferni................................ Mr. Sascha Culbertson
1735 .... Mr. Albert Spaulding
1737, "King Joseph".......................... Mr. Horace Havemeyer
1737 .... Mr. Jascha Heifetz
1737, ex Hart, ex Kreisler..................... Mr. Howard W. McAteer
1738 .... Mr. Wm. Kroll

PLATE 50

CARLO BERGONZI (1740).

Joseph Guarnerius del Gesu (*continued*)
1739 .... Rudolph Wurlitzer Collection
1740, ex Ferdinand David........................ Mr. Jascha Heifetz
1741, "The Jarnowich"........................... Rudolph Wurlitzer Collection
1742, "The Wieniawski".......................... Mr. M. Zamustin
1742 .... Partello Collection
1743, "Le Duc".................................. Mr. John S. Phipps

There are of course many famous and excellent violins by other distinguished makers owned by American amateurs, collectors and performers, but I have deemed it best, bearing in mind the necessary limits of space, to deal only with the violins of Stradivarius and Guarnerius.

The greatly increased demand for authentic instruments, and the correspondingly decreased available supply has caused an upward trend of prices for such instruments in the open market, especially in the last twenty years. The schedule on page 286 of market values in 1900 and in 1924 will elucidate very clearly the distinct increase in values.

In view of the fact that authentic instruments, possessing a good tone and in a proper state of preservation, bring prices which involve a considerable outlay of money in the case of even the least expensive makes, it may be plainly seen that a knowledge of all that has to do with the violin, in every way, shape or form, is indispensable to the violinist. The manner in which the violin is made is interesting in the highest degree, and the most subtle of physical laws are put out of countenance by the logic and simplicity dictating the construction of His Majesty, the King of Instruments.

It is undoubtedly of the greatest importance that the violinist be acquainted with the various schools of violin building in order that he may not be at a loss when they become the subject of conversation. Yet, if you ask a violinist for information regarding violin making, you will find that, as a rule, his knowledge his limited. He will admit that the sellers of violins are not always scrupulous, but should you inquire *how* the violin maker shows his want of scruple, the violinist would be quite at loss for an answer. The truth is that there is no craft in the world in which so many questionable transactions are carried out as in that of violin making. Any number of inferior instruments have been provided with authentic labels of celebrated makers such as Stradivarius, Guarnerius, Amati, Ruggeri, Guadagnini, etc., through the clever falsifications of those who make a trade of such trickery.

I would recommend that every young violinist and future artist who is desirous of purchasing a fine master instrument act with the greatest circumspection, and take counsel with competent and disinterested advisers. It will always be possible to find some competent connoisseur willing to examine a violin under consideration, and in every case the prospective purchaser should proceed as follows: he should choose his violin, make a deposit on it, and obtain from the dealer a duly signed authorization to keep the violin

PLATE 51

JOSEPH GUARNERIUS DEL GESU (1743). USED BY NICOLO PAGANINI.

Name of Maker	Value in Dollars in 1900	Value in Dollars in 1924
Albani, Paolo	350—600	500—1000
Albani, Matteo	250—400	400—800
Aldric	100—150	250—600
Amati, Nicola	1000—5000	2000—8000
Balestrieri, Tommaso	500—1000	1500—4000
Banks, Benjamin	200—400	400—800
Bergonzi, Carlo	2000—4000	4000—12,000
Betts	150—300	300—750
Breton	50—100	125—200
Cappa, Gioffredo	300—1000	1000—3000
Carcassi, Lorenzo e Tommaso	200—500	500—1250
Ceruti, Giambattista	200—400	300—1000
Chanot, George	250—500	350—800
Clement	100—160	250—500
Decomble, Ambroise	150—250	250—500
Eberle, Johann Ulrich	125—350	200—500
Fent	175—400	400—800
Forster, William	200—500	300—600
Gagliano, Nicola	350—750	1000—2500
Gagliano, Gennaro	500—1500	1000—3500
Gagliano, Ferdinando	400—1000	1000—3000
Gasparo, da Salo	800—1550	1500—3000
Gobetti, Francesco	700—1500	1500—4000
Goffriller, Mateo	500—1500	1500—4500
Grancino, Paolo	300—500	1000—1800
Grancino, Giovanni	300—600	1000—2000
Guadagnini, Giov. Battista	600—2500	2000—8000
Guarnerius, Pietro	800—2500	2500—8000
Guarnerius, Joseph del Jesu	3000—12,000	7500—25,000
Helmer, Karl	125—300	200—400 and up
Klotz, Sebastian	200—400	350—700
Klotz, Egidius	200—350	350—700
Landolfi, Carlo	400—1000	1000—2500
Lupot, Nicolaus	750—1000	1500—4000
Maggini, Giovanni Paolo	800—1500	1500—4000
Montagnana, Dominico	750—2500	3000—8000
Nicolas, Didier	100—200	250—600
Panormo, Vincenzo	250—500	500—1500
Pierray, Claude	150—350	350—600
Pique, F. L.	400—500	800—1800
Pressenda, Giovanni Francesco	400—1000	1000—1500
Rauch, Jacob	75—100	200—300
Rugieri, Francesco	800—1500	1500—4000
Santo, Serafino	1000—3500	1500—4500
Stainer, Jacobus	600—1200	800—1500
Storioni, Lorenzo	400—1000	800—2500
Stradivarius, Antonio	4000—12,500	9000—30,000 and up
Stadelman, Daniel	150—350	350—600
Tecchler, David	300—1000	1000—2500
Tononi, Carlo	500—1200	1000—4000
Vuillaume, Jean Baptiste	400—850	750—1500
Widhalm, Leopold	150—250	250—500

JOSEPH GUARNERIUS DEL GESU—1741

DOMENICO MONTAGNANA—1730

in question for a reasonable length of time before deciding definitely on its acquisition. In this way the prospective purchaser will have plenty of time to study and examine in detail the instrument which he thinks of buying, and cannot fail to discover whatever faults or weaknesses it may possess. He can easily come to a decision with regard to the sonority of the instrument, either by playing it himself or having it played for him in his home by some good violinist. An instrument played at a violin dealer's place of business will frequently have a sonorous tone, due to the fact that the glass in the show windows and counter cases tends to act as a resonator. The chief protection for the person without experience who wishes to purchase a violin is to enter into a transaction only with a dealer of established reputation.

CHAPTER XIX

CHAMBER MUSIC

There is nothing more satisfying, more moving, than chamber music well played, the string quartet in particular. Nothing makes a greater impression on the musical sensibilities than hearing four genuine artists playing a Beethoven quartet. It is at a comparatively recent date that chamber music has taken its rightful place in the domain of the musically popular, and there are still to be found at the present day those who regard music of this type as wearisome.

The truth is that a certain degree of musical education is necessary in order to appreciate *any* music at its true value, and chamber music, in particular, appeals only to those of cultivated musical taste.

When we think of the marvelous treasure of ensemble music which constitute the legacy left the world by Joseph Haydn, in his 83 wonderful string quartets, one cannot help but enthuse over works which have been written with as much good taste as genius. But Haydn is not the only composer who has endowed the chamber music repertory with beautiful works, for ensemble literature has been highly developed by almost all the great composers, and the music contributed to it reaches the highest point of musical inspiration. The greatest of composers, Beethoven, Mozart, Schubert, Schumann, Mendelssohn, Brahms and others have given of their best in order to enrich the noble variety of ensemble which is known as "chamber music."

The origin of "chamber music" dates back to the year 1555, when it is mentioned in the *Antica Musica Ridotta alla Moderna* of Nicolas Vicentinos. In 1612, S. d'India is named as being the director of the chamber music at the Ducal Court of Turin; in 1635 we find Giovanni Giaccoma Arrignoni giving concerts of chamber music in Venice; and in 1637 Torquinio Merula published his *Canzoni overo Sonate concertante per Chiesà e Camera*. At this epoch all music not intended to be performed in the church or in the theater was classed under the head of chamber music, but to-day this expression applies only to sonatas, trios, quartets, quintets, sextets, septets and octets, written in the classic forms or such modern developments as have been added to the chamber music repertory by Schonberg, Stravinsky, Goosens, Poulenc, Milhaud, Bax and others during recent years.

The wonderful chamber music of the masters has been unquestionably the source of inspiration whence have sprung up in the last century so many splendid organizations which have devoted themselves to the interpretation of

PLATE 32

THE KNEISEL QUARTET AT THE TIME IT DISBANDED (1917).

these great works of art. It would require an entire volume to even mention only by name the thousands of amateur quartets which have been formed in Europe, most of whom have met for years at least once or even oftener each week to study religiously the pages of Haydn, Schubert, Beethoven *et als* written for four stringed instruments. We will therefore undertake to deal in these pages only with those organizations which have won international fame in the performance of chamber music, listing their names alphabetically, and presenting the essential facts regarding their artistic careers.

ARMINGAUD QUARTET. Was composed of Jules Armingaud, Leon Jacquard, Edouard Lalo and Mas. From 1820 to 1900 it won an enviable reputation for the technical perfection and musical beauty of its performance, and later, by adding wind instruments, it achieved an equally great reputation under the name "Societé Classique."

BOHEMIAN QUARTET. Was composed of Karel Hofmann, Joseph Suk, Oskar Nedbal and Hanus Wihan. Of all the quartets which have toured Europe, none has achieved the success of this organization. Its performances of the Beethoven and other classical quartets are the acme of perfection, while their renditions of modern quartets by Smetana, Dvorak and Brahms are full of fire and virility.

BOLOGNA QUARTET. Was composed of F. Sarti, A. Massarenti, A. Consolini and F. Serato. Chamber music in Italy did not flourish up to 1862 when A. Bosevi, the editor of a music magazine, founded this quartet which gained an enviable reputation for the interpretation of master chamber works.

BRODSKY QUARTET. Was composed of Adolf Brodsky, O. Novacek, Hans Sitt and L. Grutzmacher. It was at first a private undertaking but achieved such immediate and remarkable success as to be engaged for the Imperial Quartet. Brodsky was an exceptional leader, understanding how to bring out equally well the thoughts of Beethoven and the naïve humor of Haydn.

BRUSSELS QUARTET. Was composed of Franz Schorg, H. Daucher, P. Miry, and J. Gaillard. The playing of this quartet was highly regarded from both the standpoints of intonation and musical feeling.

BUDAPEST QUARTET. Was composed of Jeno Hubay, V. von Herzfeld, J. Waldbauer and David Popper. This ensemble was of such a character as to lead Johannes Brahms to say that it was the best string quartet he had ever heard.

CAPET QUARTET. Was composed of Lucien Capet, Tourret, Casadesus and Hasselmanns. A French quartet which has developed an ensemble calling forth enthusiastic encomium from both critics and the music loving public.

COLOGNE (GURZENICH) QUARTET. Composed of Willy Hess, Willy Seibert, Joseph Schwarz and Friedrich Grutzmacher. The leader of this quartet, Willy Hess, is a violinist and musician of the highest musical caliber and the performances of this quartet under his guidance have elicited the heartiest commendation from critics as well as the music loving public.

DANNREUTHER QUARTET. Was composed of Gustav Dannreuther, E. Schenk, O. Schill and J. Kovarik. This quartet is much older than the Kneisel quartet, its leader being a brother of the celebrated pianist, Edward Dannreuther, who for many years conducted regular chamber music soirées in London. For many years it was the means of advancing the appreciation of chamber music throughout the United States.

DRESDEN QUARTET. Was composed of J. Lauterbach, K. Hullweck, G. Goring and Fr. Grutzmacher. This quartet was in great favor with the King of Saxony, himself a musician of real attainments. It performed more than sixty times in his presence.

DUESBURG QUARTET. Was composed of August Duesburg, H. Matlocha, R. Pirschl and O. Krist. This quartet was one of the first to popularize chamber music concerts by making the price of admission very low and by giving con-

PLATE 53

ABOVE—THE JOACHIM QUARTET.   BELOW—THE BOHEMIAN QUARTET.

PLATE 54

ABOVE—THE FLONZALEY QUARTET.   BELOW—THE LETZ QUARTET.

certs on Sundays which every one might attend.

FITZNER QUARTET. Was composed of R. Fitzner, J. Czerny, O. Zert and F. Buchsbaum. One of the most popular of European quartets, not only on account of its technical excellence but also through its musicianship.

FLONZALEY QUARTET. Composed of Adolfo Betti, Alfred Pochon, Felicien d'Archambeau and Iwan d'Archambeau. This quartet was organized twenty-one years ago and has made eighteen hundred appearances in more than four hundred American cities and more than five hundred appearances in Europe. Its name, like that of the Kneisel quartet is inseparably linked with the growth of chamber music art in this country. Its performances of the classic works are irreproachable in both technical and musical respects. It has also presented in this country and abroad the greatest works of American as well as foreign composers. Another field which has developed for the enjoyment of music lovers has been the making of records for the phonograph, a partial list which is presented herewith:

Canzonetta (from String Quartet, Op. 12)   Mendelssohn
Drink to Me Only with Thine Eyes
                          Arr. by Alfred Pochon
Interludium in Modo Antico (from
  "Five Novellettes")   Glazounow
Molly on the Shore (Irish Reel)
                    Percy Aldridge Grainger
Music of the Spheres—Molto Lento
  ("Sphärenmusik")   Rubinstein
Nocturne   A. Borodin
Quartet in A Minor—Scherzo (Op.
  41, No. 1)   Schumann
Quartet in A Minor—Adagio (3rd
  Movement)   Schumann
Quartet in A Major—Assai agitato
  (Op. 41, No. 3)   Schumann
Quartet in A Major—Theme and
  Variations (Op 18, No. 5)   Beethoven
Quartet in C Major—Fugue (Op. 59,
  No. 3)   Beethoven
Quartet in C Minor—Allegretto (Op.
  51, No. 1)   Brahms
Quartet in C Minor—Scherzo (Op.
  18, No. 4)   Beethoven
Quartet in D Major—Allegro moderato (Op. 64, No. 5)   Haydn

Quartet in D Major—Adagio cantabile (2nd Movement)   Haydn
Quartet in D Major—Minuetto and
  Finale (Op. 64)   Haydn
Quartet in D Major—Andante   Mozart
Quartet in D Major—Menuet   Mozart
Quartet in D Major Presto   Beethoven
Quartet in D Major—Adagio (3rd
  Movement)   Mozart
Quartet in D Minor—Allegretto ma
  non troppo   Mozart
Quartet in E Minor—Scherzo (2nd
  Move., Op. 44, No. 2)   Mendelssohn
Quartet No. 3, in E Flat Minor—
  Scherzo (Op. 30)   Tschaikowsky
Where it is not possible for the members of amateur quartets actually to hear this remarkable organization, one can scarcely imagine a more inspiring method of securing a good idea of ensemble playing than by listening to these records.

FLORENTINE QUARTET. Composed of Jean Becker, Enrico Masi, L. Chiostri and Fr. Hilpert, the latter succeeded by L. Spitzer-Hegyesi. The classical performances of this quartet earned them a well-deserved reputation in musical centers all over Europe.

FRANKFORT QUARTET. Composed of Hugo Heerman, Bassermann, Naret-Koning and Hugo Becker. The association of these four artists resulted in performances of classical chamber music of the very highest character.

FRENCH-AMERICAN QUARTET. Composed of Gustave Tinlot, Reber Johnson, Saul Sharrow and Paul Kefer. This is an American quartet, composed of musicians residing in New York City, which has already achieved a splendid reputation with both press and public.

GELOSO QUARTET. Composed of Albert Geloso, Schnelzlud, Monteux and Tracol. Geloso was a Spanish violinist unusually well equipped in a musical sense for quartet playing. This quartet was accustomed to giving an annual concert devoted to Beethoven's last quartets, which were played with admirable science and sincerity.

GOMPERTZ QUARTET. Composed of Richard Gompertz, H. Inwards, Emil Krenz and Charles Auld. An organization which made a specialty of the finest classic chamber works, interpreting them with an unusual degree of musical insight.

PLATE 55

ABOVE—THE HELLMESBERGER QUARTET (2ND). BELOW—THE
WALDEMAR MEYER QUARTET.

HALIR QUARTET. Composed of Carl Halir, Gustav Exner, Adolph Muller and Hugo Dechert. Halir was the second violinist in the Joachim quartet from 1897 to 1907, and turned his experience to good account in forming his own quartet which enjoyed the highest degree of artistic success.

HAMBURG QUARTET. Composed of Florian Zajic, J. Schloming, M. Lowenberg and A. Gowa. One of Europe's finest ensemble organizations which presented not only the greatest of classic but also of modern quartet works with a more than satisfying degree of musical authority.

HANFLEIN QUARTET. Composed of George Hanflein, Hugo Piening, Edward Kirchner and Emil Blume. Another European organization which performed all the masterpieces of chamber music in a manner which won universal approbation.

HELLMESBERGER QUARTET. Composed of Joseph Hellmesberger, Sr., M. Durst, C. Heissler and C. Schlesinger. This quartet monopolized chamber music playing in Vienna for more than a quarter of a century. It was succeeded by another quartet of the same name, composed of Joseph Hellmesberger, Jr., Th. Schwendt, J. Egghard and Ferdinand Hellmesberger.

HOLLAENDER QUARTET. First composed of Gustav Hollaender, Bari, Schwartz and Grutzmacher. Later Hollaender formed a new quartet in Berlin with Willy Nirking, Heinrich Brandler and Leo Schrattenholz. Both organizations reached a high standard of excellence.

JOACHIM QUARTET. Composed of Joseph Joachim, Heinrich De Ahna, Emanuel Wirth and Robert Hausmann. This quartet remained intact for many years except for changes in the second violin, first to Johann Kruse and later to Carl Halir. The Joachim quartet is regarded as the greatest quartet organization of all time; it was equally admirable in respect to musical enthusiasm, ponderation of thought and correctness of execution. Joachim also had a quartet in London which he conducted yearly from January to March. It was composed of Joachim, Ries, Webb and Piatti. In Joachim's absence his place was taken by Lady Halle or Ysaÿe.

KNEISEL QUARTET. Founded by Franz Kneisel in 1885 with E. Fielder, L. Svecenski and F. Giese. Otto Roth suc- ceeded Mr. Fielder in 1887 and Anton Hekking Mr. Giese in 1889. In 1891 Alwin Schroeder succeeded Mr. Hekking; in 1899 Karl Ondricek succeeded Mr. Roth and J. Theodorowicz succeeded Mr. Ondricek in 1902. The final formation of the quartet was made up of Franz Kneisel, Hans Letz, L. Svecenski and Wilhelm Willeke. The quartet disbanded in 1917 after thirty-two years of chamber music concerts. It ranked with the finest organizations of its kind in existence, and as it appeared in practically every city of size in the United States, it spread appreciation of chamber music from the Atlantic to the Pacific Oceans.

LEIPZIG QUARTET. This quartet was for about forty years under the leadership of Ferdinand David, one of the world's greatest violinists. During that period it gave hundreds of concerts, performing the greatest chamber music masterpieces with precision and musical feeling, gaining continuous recognition as one of the greatest organizations of this kind in the world.

LENER QUARTET. Composed of Teno Lener, Joseph Smilovitz, Sandor Roth and Imre Hartmann. A Hungarian quartet which has toured Europe and Great Britain with great success. Its members are all comparatively young men and the quartet gives promise of being ranked among the best in Europe.

This quartet has also made a splendid contribution to the archives of music for future generations in its recordings for the phonograph, made in Europe and procurable in this country through The Columbia Phonograph Company. The following list will have interest for every lover of chamber music:

Adagio-Quartet Op. 74—Beethoven
Adagio-Quartet Op. 59, No. 1—Beethoven.
Allegro-Quartet in B♭—Mozart
Andante-Quartet Op. 51, No. 2—Brahms
Andante-Posthumous Quartet—Schubert
Andantino-Quartet Op. 10—Debussy
Scherzo-Quartet Op. 11—Tschaikowsky
Serenade-Quartet Op. 3, No. 5—Haydn
Their recordings also include complete renditions on several records of works such as:

Quartet in C♯ Minor, Op. 131— Beethoven (In 10 parts)

PLATE 56

ABOVE—THE LONDON QUARTET.   BELOW—THE LENOX QUARTET.

PLATE 57

ABOVE—THE PETRI QUARTET. BELOW—THE ARNOLD ROSE QUARTET.

Quartet Op. 76, No. 5—Haydn
(In 6 parts)

Quartet in C Major—Mozart
(In 8 parts)

LENOX QUARTET. Composed of Sandor Harmati, Wolfe Wolfinsohn, Nicholas Moldavan and Emmeran Stoeber. A New York organization which has toured the United States with great success and has attained a degree of musicianship in its ensemble performance which gives it great promise.

LETZ QUARTET. Composed of Hans Letz, Edwin Bachmann, William Schubert and Horace Britt. This is a New York quartet which is in a way an outgrowth of the Kneisel quartet as Hans Letz was a member of the latter organization during its concluding seasons. The Letz quartet is now regularly engaged in different cities of the United States for performances at institutions and before societies which formerly used the services of the Kneisel quartet.

LONDON STRING QUARTET. Composed of James Levey, Thomas Petre, H. Waldo Warner and C. Warwick-Evans. This organization was founded in 1908 and has given over one hundred and fifty concerts in London in addition to touring Europe, South America and the United States. Its repertoire includes modern as well as classic works and it is highly regarded from the standpoints of ensemble and interpretation.

This quartet has also made some remarkable recordings of chamber music for the Columbia Graphophone Co. in England, procurable through the same company in the United States. These include:

Andante Cantabile—Quartet Op. 11—
Tschaikowsky

Londonderry Air—Arr. by Frank
Bridge

Molly on the Shore—Grainger

Quartet No. 14—Mozart

Quartet in G, Op. 18—Beethoven

Andante & Agitato—Quartet Op. 67—
Brahms

Quartet in A—Schumann

Quartet No. 15—Mozart

Quartet Op. 18, No. 1—Beethoven

Hornpipe Quartet Op. 64, No. 5—
Haydn

MARTEAU-BECKER QUARTET. An organization presided over by Henri Marteau when he was professor of the violin at the Hochschule in Berlin. The cellist of the quartet was Hugo Becker, a musician of no less attainments and the performances of this organization placed it in the front rank of chamber music exponents.

MASON AND THOMAS QUINTET. Founded by William Mason in 1855, he himself playing the piano in conjunction with a string quartet composed of Theodore Thomas, Joseph Mosenthal, George Matzka and Carl Bergmann. The chamber music soirées given from 1855 to 1868 by this remarkable organization were the source of both musical education and unalloyed pleasure to New York music lovers, acquainting them with the chamber music works of Schumann and Brahms which had not been previously performed in this country.

MENDELSSOHN QUINTET CLUB. This organization was founded in Boston in 1849 and was the first chamber music ensemble to give concerts at regular periods and to tour the United States. Its members were August Fries, Francis Rzika, Edward Lehmann and Wulf Fries. The fifth member was Thomas Ryan. This organization held together for nearly fifty years, with occasional changes in the personnel.

MAURIN QUARTET. This quartet was founded by its first violin, J. P. Maurin, in 1822 and continued uninterruptedly until 1894. Its reputation in Paris, the city of its birth, as well as in the French provinces, was of the highest character.

MEININGER QUARTET. Composed of Bram Eldering, August Funk, Alfons Abbas and Carl Pienning. This quartet was founded in 1894 and developed an unusual degree of excellence, touring Europe, particularly Belgium, with great success.

MULLER BROTHERS QUARTET. Composed of Karl Friedrich, Theodor Heinrich, Franz Ferdinand and August Theodor Muller, all brothers, who were trained by their father, Christoph Muller, especially for quartet playing. They first performed exclusively at the court of the Duke of Brunswick, but in 1831 they appeared first in Hamburg and later in all the principal cities of Germany, France and Russia. They devoted themselves almost exclusively to the works of Haydn, Mozart and Beethoven. The leader of

PLATE 58

ABOVE—THE DANNREUTHER QUARTET.   BELOW—THE NEW YORK
QUARTET.

this quartet, Karl Friedrich Muller, also had four sons who were known as the younger Muller Brothers, who also formed a quartet which toured Europe. This organization, however, never attained the heights of artistic skill developed by the elder quartet.

NADAUD QUARTET. A chamber music organization founded in Paris by Edouard Nadaud, a well-known soloist and teacher at the Paris Conservatory.

NEW YORK STRING QUARTET. Composed of Ottokar Cadek, Jaroslav Siskovsky, Ludvik Schwab and Bedrich Vaska. It was founded by Mr. and Mrs. Ralph Pulitzer in 1919 with the object of creating a permanent organization for the advancement of chamber music. Three years of practice preceded the first really public appearance of this quartet in October, 1922. Since that time it has made a transcontinental tour winning approbation wherever it played for its vitality and its brilliant interpretations.

PETRI QUARTET. Composed of Petri, Bolland, Unkenstein and Alwin Schroeder, the latter afterwards becoming the cellist of the Kneisel Quartet. This quartet was founded while Henri Petri was professor of violin at the Dresden Conservatory and rivaled the Brodsky quartet in popularity.

PETROGRAD QUARTET. An organization founded by Charles Gregorovitch, a pupil of Basekirskji, Wieniawski and Joachim. Due to the disturbed state of affairs in Russia it is difficult to secure accurate information as to the present status and personnel of musical organizations.

PRILL QUARTET. Composed of Carl Prill, August Siebert, Anton Rusitzka and Joseph Sulzer. At the time this quartet was founded (1897) there were a number of brilliant ensemble organizations in Vienna, but nevertheless the thorough musicianship of the members of this quartet has brought it conspicuously before the music loving public.

RASOUMOWSKY QUARTET. Founded at Vienna in 1808 by Andreas Rasoumowsky, a Russian nobleman, with Schuppanzigh, Weiss and Lincke, he himself playing second violin. The organization for many years met in the evenings and played Beethoven's quartets with the master himself as instructor. Beethoven's three quartets Op. 59 were dedicated to Rasoumowsky.

ROMAN QUARTET. Composed of Tito Monachesi, Vincenzo Desamtis, Romolo Jacobavi and Gaetano Morelli. It was organized in 1893 by imperial decree under the supervision of the celebrated Italian composer Sgambati and has been the means of furthering the interests of chamber music in Italy.

ROSÉ QUARTET. Founded at Vienna in 1882 by Arnold Rosé with T. Fischer, Rusitska and Buxbaum. This quartet toured Europe several times and underwent several changes in its personnel. It is considered at the present time one of the finest organizations in Europe, due largely to the fact that Rosé himself is considered to be a born quartet leader.

ST. PETERSBURG QUARTET. This quartet is mentioned at some length in Leopold Auer's brilliant account of his musical career (My Long Life in Music). It was composed of Leopold Auer, Jean Pickel, Weickmann and Charles Davidoff. It had the distinction of playing the chamber music written by Tschaikowsky, Arensky, Borodin, Cui and Rubinstein from the original manuscript and was also known as the Imperial Russian Quartet.

SCHUPPANZIGH QUARTET. An organization in which Ignaz Schuppanzigh, one of Beethoven's closest friends, played the first violin, at the home of Prince Carl Licknowsky, who played second violin, Weiss the viola and Kraft the cello. This organization met every Friday during 1794-95, and developed a high degree of musicianship. Beethoven was present at many of its rehearsals and concerts.

SOLDAT-ROEGGER QUARTET. A famous ladies' quartet founded in 1887 by Marie Soldat-Roegger, with Frau Finger-Boilette, Frau Lochner-Bauer and Miss Campbell. This organization was very successful particularly in its interpretation of Brahms. Madame Soldat-Roegger also formed another quartet in Vienna which is still active.

STUTTGART QUARTET. Founded in 1861 by Edmund Singer with Barnbeck, Debuysere and Goltermann. During its career this quartet gave about six concerts annually and was greatly honored and patronized by the royal family.

TRIESTE QUARTET. This quartet enjoyed an active career in Trieste for more than forty years and was first composed of Julius Heller, Guido Echhardt, Menotti

PLATE 59

ABOVE—THE ST. PETERSBURG QUARTET. BELOW—THE BRUSSELS QUARTET.

PLATE 60

ABOVE—THE OLD MUELLER BROTHERS QUARTET. BELOW—THE SOLDAT-
ROEGGER QUARTET.

Remporat and Artura Cuccoli. Many changes have taken place in the personnel, the leader only remaining with it during its entire career.

WALDEMAR MEYER QUARTET. Composed of Waldemar Meyer, Max Heinicke, Dagobert Lowenthal and Albrecht Loeffler. One of the finest European chamber music organizations which toured Europe many times with the greatest possible degree of success.

WALTER QUARTET. Founded by Benno Walter, a violinist and musician of unusual ability who brought his organization to the highest point of musical as well as technical proficiency.

WARSAW QUARTET. Founded by Stanislaus Barcewicz, a Polish violinist of great reputation. He became professor of the violin at the Warsaw Conservatory in 1885, founding at the same time this quartet which immediately became one of the leading Polish organizations of this kind.

WINKLER QUARTET. Composed of Julius Winkler, Fritz Wahle, Alfred Finger and Alexander Timpel. This organization was one of the most popular of its kind in Vienna. Winkler was a great admirer of Haydn's quartets and his concerts invariably included some one of the lesser known works of the great master.

The above lists include most of the quartets whose labors in this field of music have tended to increase the love for and appreciation of the master chamber music works. It has been necessary of course to leave out the names of hundreds of lesser organizations in Europe but it will not be amiss to mention in connection with the United States such ensemble groups as the Boston String Quartet, the Chicago Quartet, the Chicago Scandinavian String Quartet, the Gordon String Quartet of Chicago, the Culp String Quartet at Cincinnati, the MacManus Quartet at Corvallis, Oregon, the Philharmonic and Zoellner Quartets of Los Angeles, the Spargur Quartet at Seattle, Washington, and the West Sisters Quartet at Omaha, Nebraska.

The playing of string quartets presents delicate problems in various ways. The chamber music player must be a thorough musician and an excellent instrumentalist from the technical standpoint. He must know how to handle his bow and his fingers perfectly, and must be fully conscious of the fact that in ensemble music it is absolutely necessary to sacrifice every kind of virtuosity. Mediocre virtuosos often make excellent quartet players, and this is due to the fact that these players have a better right arm than a left hand.

When beginning the study of a string quartet the player must resolve upon an act of self-abnegation. He must not say, "I am the first violin," or "I am the second violin," but must look on himself as merely forming an integral part of a combination, an *ensemble*. He must also know how to efface himself when it is the turn of another instrument to play the leading part. I have often heard chamber music played in the most lamentable fashion by very great artists who, each taken by himself, would have played marvelously well.

The listener should never allow himself to be unduly impressed by the magic of a great name, and those artists whose mission it is to reveal music in all its true beauty to the public are in error when they profane their art for mere display purposes.

PLATE 61

ABOVE—THE LEIPZIG QUARTET. BELOW—THE ORIGINAL KNEISEL
QUARTET.

In the Mozart String Quartet No. I, dedicated to Haydn, the first violin has the preponderating part because it carries the melody.

Accentuation plays a tremendous part in the proper playing of chamber music, as may be seen in the following passage from the work just cited:

In the Beethoven Quartet, Op. 18, No. 1, the initial theme should be played with spirit and intelligence, cutting the two final notes rather short:

The beginning of the Quartet, Op. 131, has always given rise to discussions regarding the correct tempo in which it is to be taken. The tempo indicated is adagio, *ma non troppo e molto expressivo:*

The string quartets of the Bonn master are the last word as regards perfection of musical form. In addition to this, there breathes in them so great an atmosphere of genius that we are astounded as we realize that the brain of one man has created these marvels which neither time nor progress have been able to effect.

When playing a chamber music work with a pianist, it is customary to keep the lid of the instrument closed, and to avoid all tonal effects which would tend to bring the piano part of the work being performed into more prominence than the string parts. A gentle reminder sometimes is necessary, when the services of a pianist of virtuoso type are utilized, to the effect that *ensemble* rather than solo playing is desired.

The correct tempos to be observed in the playing of chamber music have always been a matter of endless discussion. Every artist conceives them more or less in accordance with his own temperament; there are as many differences of artistic temperament as there are leaves on the trees; and scientists tell us that no two leaves of any tree are exactly alike. We give, therefore, on the following pages, a list of the principal Haydn and Beethoven string quartets, with the approximate *rational* tempo indicated for each of the movements in same:

THE HAYDN QUARTETS

1. Moderato ♩ = 96
   Menuetto ♩ = 120
   Adagio ♪ = 96
   Presto ♩ = 126

2. Moderato ♩ = 96
   Menuetto ♩ = 120
   Adagio ♩ = 76
   Allegro molto ♩ = 126

3. Andante ♪ = ï04
   Menuetto ♩ = 126
   Adagio ♪ = 88
   Allegro molto ♩ = 126

4. Moderato ♩ = 108
   Menuetto ♩ = 120
   Adagio ♪ = 88
   Allegro 𝅗𝅥 = 16

5. Moderato ♩ = 92
   Menuetto ♩ = 120
   Adagio ♪ = 80
   Presto ♩ = 126

6. Presto ♩. = 96
   Menuetto ♩ = 120
   Largo ♪ = 100
   Largo ♩ = 126

7. Moderato ♩ = 80
   Menuetto ♩ = 112
   Adagio ♪ = 84
   Presto ♩ = 132

8. Allegro moderato ♩ = 112
   Menuetto ♩ = 126
   Adagio ♪ = 84
   Allegro molto ♩ = 120

9. Allegro moderato ♩ = 104
   Menuetto ♩ = 116
   Largo ♪ = 66
   Presto ♩ = 126

10. Allegro ♩ = 138
    Adagio ♪ = 84
    Menuetto ♩ = 112
    Finale ♩ = 132

11. Vivace ♩ = 138
    Adagio ♪ = 80
    Menuetto ♩ = 120
    Vivace assái ♩ = 132

12. Allegro con brio ♪ = 132
    Andante più tosto allegretto ♩ = 72
    Menuetto ♩ = 132
    Presto ♩ = 132

13. Allegro moderato ♩ = 120
    Adagio ♪ = 104
    Menuetto ♩ = 152
    Presto ♩ = 144

14. Allegro moderato ♩ = 112
    Menuetto ♩ = 144
    Andante ♪ = 104
    Vivace ♩ = 138

15. Andante ♩ = 69
    Menuetto ♩ = 116
    Adagio ♪ = 108
    Presto ♩ = 132

16. Allegro moderato ♩ = 108
    Menuetto ♩ = 120
    Adagio ♩ = 66
    Presto ♩. = 96

17. Poco adagio ♩ = 54
    Menuetto ♩ = 120
    Largo ♪ = 88
    Presto ♩ = 132

18. Presto ♩. = 80
    Menuetto ♩ = 126
    Adagio ♩ = 69
    Allegro ♩ = 120

19. Allegro ♩ = 120
    Allegretto ♩. = 52
    Menuctto ♩ = 120
    Presto ♩ = 120

20. Vivace 𝅗𝅥 = 96
    Adagio ♪ = 84
    Menuetto ♩ = 126
    Adagio ♪ = 80
    Presto ♩ = 152

21. Allegro ♩ = 138
    Largo ♪ = 76
    Menuetto ♩ = 120
    Presto ♩ = 126

22. Allegro ♩ = 84
    Adagio ♪ = 76
    Menuetto ♩ = 120
    Vivace ♩. = 104

23. Andante più tosto allegretto ♩ = 66
    Allegro 𝅗𝅥 = 84
    Menuetto ♩ = 120
    Presto ♩. = 84

24. Vivace assái ♩ = 144
    Adagio ma non troppo ♪ = 80

	Menuetto	♩ = 120		Menuetto	♩ = 120
	Presto	♩. = 88		Presto	♩ = 120
25.	Allegro	♩ = 126	37.	Allegro	♩ = 116
	Andante	♪ = 96		Adagio	♪ = 88
	Menuetto	♩ = 120		Menuetto	♩ = 120
	Fuga	♩. = 66		Vivace	♩ = 120
26.	Allegro moderato	♩ = 112	38.	Adagio	♪ = 88
	Poco adagio	♪ = 100		Allegro	♩ = 116
	Menuetto	♩ = 120		Adagio	♪ = 80
	Vivace	♩. = 84		Menuetto	♩ = 126
27.	Allegro	♩ = 116		Allegretto	♩. = 92
	Poco adagio	♪ = 92	39.	Vivace	♩ = 132
	Menuetto	♩ = 120		Andante con moto	♪ = 100
	Allegro	♩ = 108		Menuetto	♩ = 120
28.	Allegro	♩ = 116		Vivace	♩. = 96
	Andantino	♪ = 96	40.	Allegretto con spirito	♩ = 132
	Menuetto	♩ = 120		Adagio	♪ = 80
	Vivace	♩ = 120		Menuetto	𝅗𝅥. = 96
29.	Allegro	♩ = 116		Allegro	𝅗𝅥 = 96
	Andante	♪ = 96	41.	Allegro	♩ = 112
	Menuetto	♩ ≐ 120		Andante	♪ = 108
	Presto	♩ = 112		Menuetto	♩ = 126
30.	Allegro	♩ = 132		Vivace	♩ = 138
	Largo assái	♪ = 96	42.	Allegro	♩ = 104
	Menuetto	♩ = 120		Adagio	♩ = 76
	Allegro	♩ = 116		Menuetto	♩ = 126
31.	Allegro moderato	♩ = 108		Presto	♩ = 144
	Menuetto	♩ = 120	43.	Allegro moderato	♩ = 104
	Allegretto	♩ = 84		Menuetto	♩ = 120
	Presto	♩. = 76		Affectuoso	♩ = 100
32.	Allegro	♩ = 112		Presto	♩ = 132
	Adagio non troppo	♩ = 96	44.	Moderato	♩ = 104
	Menuetto	♩ = 120		Adagio	♪ = 76
	Presto	♩ = 108		Menuetto	♩ = 120
33.	Vivace assái	♩ = 120		Allegro	♩. = 80
	Adagio	♪ = 84	45.	Allegro	♩ = 108
	Menuetto	♩ = 120		Menuetto	♩ = 120
	Allegro	♩ = 108		Poco adagio	♪ = 92
34.	Allegro	♩ = 108		Allegro molto	♩ = 120
	Menuetto	♩ = 120	46.	Allegro molto	♩ = 126
	Adagio	♪ = 76		Poco adagio	♩ = 60
	Presto	♩. = 96		Menuetto	♩ = 120
35.	Allegro moderato	𝅗𝅥 = 76		Presto	♩ = 132
	Adagio	♩ = 84	47.	Allegro moderato	♩ = 104
	Menuetto	♩ = 120		Menuetto	♩ = 120
	Vivace	♩ = 126		Adagio	♪ = 88
36.	Allegretto	♩ = 112		Fuga	𝅗𝅥 = 100
	Andante	♪ = 104	48.	Allegro molto	♩. = 66
				Adagio	♩ = 72

Menuetto	♩ = 120
Fuga	♩ = 100
49. Allegro	♩ = 116
Adagio	♪ = 84
Menuetto	♩ = 132
Finale	𝅗𝅥 = 80
50. Allegretto	♩. = 72
Allegro	♩. = 88
Largo	♩ = 72
Menuetto	♩ = 126
Finale	♩ = 132
51. Allegretto	♩ = 96
Fantasia	♪ = 88
Menuetto	𝅗𝅥. = 80
Finale	♩ = 126
52. Presto	♩. = 104
Menuetto	♩ = 120
Adagio	♪ = 88
Menuetto	♩ = 120
Presto	♩ = 132
53. Allegro molto	♪ = 138
Menuetto	♩ = 120
Adagio	♪ = 84
Menuetto	♩ = 120
Presto	♩ = 138
54. Adagio	♪ = 88
Menuetto	♩ = 120
Presto	♩ = 138
Menuetto	♩ = 120
Presto	♩. = 80
55. Presto	♪ = 152
Menuetto	♩ = 120
Adagio	♪ = 84
Menuetto	♩ = 116
Presto	♩ = 138
56. Allegro	♩ = 126
Andante	♩ = 72
Allegro molto	♩. = 80
57. Presto assái	♩. = 108
Menuetto	♩ = 120
Adagio	♪ = 100
Menuetto	♩ = 120
Presto	♩ = 138
58. Allegro	♩ = 120
Menuetto	♩ = 120
Poco adagio	♪ = 100
Menuetto	♩ = 116
Allegro molto	♩ = 132

59. Allegro	♩ = 120
Menuetto	♩ = 120
Adagio	♪ = 76
Menuetto	♩ = 120
Presto	♩ = 138
60. Allegro molto	♩ = 132
Menuetto	♩ = 120
Adagio	♪ = 76
Menuetto	♩ = 116
Allegro	♩ = 120
61. Presto	♩. = 84
Menuetto	♩ = 120
Adagio	♪ = 88
Menuetto	♩ = 120
Allegro	♩ = 120
62. Presto	♩. = 84
Menuetto	♩ = 120
Largo	♩ = 56
Menuetto	♩ = 116
Presto	♩ = 144
63. Adagio con variazioni	♩ = 100
Menuetto	♩ = 126
Presto	♩ = 138
Menuetto	♩ = 116
Presto	♩ = 144
64. Allegro molto	♩ = 132
Menuetto	♩ = 120
Andantino	♪ = 120
Presto	♩ = 138
65. Fantazia con variazioni	♩ = 66
Menuetto	♩ = 120
Presto	♩ = 144
66. Presto	♩. = 84
Largo	♪ = 76
Menuetto	♩ = 120
Presto	♩ = 144
67. Allegro molto	♩ = 116
Adagio	♪ = 80
Presto	♩ = 152
Adagio	♪ = 80
Presto	♩ = 152
68. Presto	♩. = 72
Andante	♩ = 96
Menuetto	♩ = 120
Scherzetto	♩ = 108
69. Presto	♩ = 152
Adagio	♪ = 80
Menuetto	♩ = 120
Scherzando	♩ = 104

70. Allegro molto ♩ = 116
    Menuetto ♩ = 126
    Andante ♩. = 52
    Presto ♩ = 144

71. Allegro molto ♩ = 112
    Menuetto ♩ = 120
    Largo ♪ = 72
    Presto ♩. = 92

72. Allegro molto ♩. = 116
    Scherzo ♩ = 120
    Adagio ♪ = 84
    Rondo ♩ = 144

73. Allegro molto ♩ = 112
    Scherzo ♩ = 120
    Largo ♪ = 76
    Presto ♪ = 132

74. Vivace assái ♩ = 126
    Largo ♪ = 96
    Scherzo ♩ = 120
    Finale allegretto ♩. = 69
    Presto ♩. = 96

75. Vivace assái ♩. = 88
    Andante ♩ = 60
    Scherzo ♩ = 120
    Allegretto ♩ = 88

76. Maestoso ♪ = 84
    Pater, dimitte illis, non enim sciunt, qui faciunt Largo ♪ = 72

77. Amen dico tibi; hodie mecum eris in paradisio Grave ♩ = 63

78. Mulier, ecce filius tuus, et tu ecce mater tuas Grave ♩ = 63

79. Eli, Eli lama sabacthani Largo ♪ = 72

80. Sitio Adagio ♪ = 80

81. Consumatum est Lento ♩ = 53

82. Pater in maus tuas commendo spiritum meum Largo ♩ = 53
    Il terremoto presto ♩. = 69

83. Andante ♩ = 76
    Menuetto ♩ = 126

THE BEETHOVEN QUARTETS

Quartet Op. 18, No. 1
    Allegro con brio ♩ = 126
    Adagio ♪ = 104
    Scherzo ♩. = 80
    Allegro ♩ = 116

Quartet Op. 18, No. 2
    Allegro ♩ = 84
    Adagio ♪ = 120
    Scherzo ♩ = 132
    Allegro molto ♩ = 152

Quartet Op. 18, No. 3
    Allegro 𝅗𝅥 = 96
    Andante con moto ♪ = 76
    Allegro 𝅗𝅥. = 69
    Presto ♩. = 138

Quartet Op. 18, No. 4
    Allegro ma non tanto ♩ = 104
    Scherzo ♪ = 125
    Minuet ♩ = 144
    Allegro 𝅗𝅥 = 120

Quartet Op. 18, No. 5
    Minuet ♩. = 84
    Minuet ♩ = 144
    Andante ♪ = 96
    Allegro 𝅗𝅥 = 100

Quartet Op. 18, No. 6
    Allegro con brio 𝅗𝅥 = 112

Adagio non troppo ♪ = 69
Scherzo ♩ = 132
La malinconica ♪ = 80
Allegretto quasi allegro ♪ = 152

Quartet Op. 59, No. 1
    Allegro ♩ = 160
    Allegretto vivaci ♪ = 176
    Molto adagio ♪ = 52
    Theme Russe ♩ = 104

Quartet Op. 59, No. 2
    Allegro ♩. = 76
    Molto adagio ♪ = 86
    Allegretto ♩ = 152
    Presto 𝅗𝅥 = 138

Quartet Op. 59, No. 3
    Allegro vivace ♩ = 132
    Andante con molto ♩. = 72
    Minuet ♩ = 132
    Allegro molto 𝅗𝅥 = 132

Quartet Op. 74
    Poco adagio ♩ = 60
    Allegro ♩ = 132
    Adagio ma non troppo ♪ = 54
    Presto 𝅗𝅥. = 88
    Più presto 𝅗𝅥. = 152
    Allegretto ♩ = 104

Un poco più vivace — ♩ = 112
Allegro — ♩ = 152

Quartet Op. 95
  Allegro con brio — ♩ = 144
  Allegretto — ♩ = 63
  Allegro assái vivace — ♩ = 176
  Larghetto espressivo — ♪ = 60
  Allegretto agitato — ♩. = 84

Quartet Op. 127
  Maestoso — ♪ = 92
  Allegro teneramente — ♩ = 152
  Adagio ma non troppo — ♪ = 120
  Andante con moto — ♪ = 112
  Adagio molto espressivo — ♪ = 108
  Scherzando vivace — ♩ = 108
  Allegro — ♩ = 144
  Presto — ♩. = 126
  Finale — 𝅗𝅥 = 126
  Allegro commodo — ♩. = 58

Quartet Op. 130
  Allegro ma non troppo — ♪ = 92
  Allegro — ♩ = 144
  Presto — 𝅗𝅥 = 138
  Andante con moto — ♩ = 63
  Allegro assái — ♩. = 76
  Cavatina — ♪ = 80
  Finale — ♩ = 138

Quartet Op. 131
  Adagio non troppo — ♩ = 80
  Allegro molto vivace — ♩. = 126
  Allegro moderato — ♩ = 120

Adagio — ♪ = 100
Andante non troppo — ♩ = 56
Più mosso — ♩ = 76
Andante moderato — ♩ = 84
Adagio — ♪ = 116
Allegretto — ♩ = 69
Adagio — ♩ = 108
Presto — 𝅗𝅥 = 160
Allegro finale — ♩ = 126

Quartet Op. 132
  Assái sostenuto — ♩ = 84
  Allegro — ♩ = 120
  Allegro non tanto — ♩ = 138
  Molto adagio — ♩ = 60
  Andante — ♪ = 88
  Molto adagio — ♩ = 60
  Andante — ♪ = 88
  Molto adagio — ♩ = 60
  Assái vivace — ♩ = 126
  Più allegro — ♩ = 138
  Presto — 𝅗𝅥 = 120
  Poco adagio — ♩ = 92
  Allegro appasionato — ♩ = 160

Quartet Op. 135
  Allegretto — ♩ = 76
  Vivace — ♩. = 108
  Lento assái — ♪ = 104
  Più lento — ♪ = 88
  Grave non troppo tratto — 𝅗𝅥 = 72
  Adagio — ♩ = 53
  Allegro — 𝅗𝅥 = 100

CHAPTER XX

THE PHONOGRAPH AND THE VIOLIN

There has always been an impression among musicians that mechanical reproductions, known in the vernacular as "canned music," could be of no material assistance in the development of a singer or a student of any instrument, and it is quite true that actual instruction is something which must be imparted orally in order to produce results.

There can however exist no doubt, except in the minds of those unduly prejudiced, that the higher grade of phonograph reproductions of music rendered by real artists has been a wide-spread and tremendously effective method not only of acquainting the general public with hundreds of classic and modern standard compositions which it would never have heard in any other way, but that they have also elevated the taste of musically uneducated people.

All the larger phonograph companies have reproduced violin music in a series of mechanically perfect records, and in doing this they have employed the services of almost every great virtuoso who has appeared in the United States in the last twenty years. Some of these reproductions have a historic as well as musical value which cannot be measured in money. The writer possesses a record, made by Joseph Joachim about a year before his death, of his own arrangement of the Brahms "Hungarian Dance, No. I," also a record made by Sarasate of his "Caprice Basque." Both of these records were made of course at a time when the phonograph was far from being as mechanically perfect in recording and reproducing as it is to-day, but both are still faithful reproductions of the marvelous artistic style of these two great virtuosos and can convey to any intelligent student, in no uncertain manner, just how the masters interpreted these numbers.

There is no question that, where a student can have instruction from only mediocre teachers, listening to records by great artists of standard pieces will be a source of genuine musical education, especially in regard to interpretation. This does not mean that records should be used with the idea of copying such interpretations exactly in a musical sense, but rather that listening to them tends to form a general impression upon the listener's mind as to the poetic thought or intent of the compositions themselves.

Many of the most important violin compositions are recorded for the different companies by several artists, and it becomes very interesting to make comparisons in interpretation. As a single instance, the "Meditation" from

Thaïs by Massenet may be mentioned, recorded by at least six great artists—every interpretation distinctly individual.

For those who will be interested in investigating the extent to which the phonograph has been used as a means of perpetuating the playing of great artists the following list will have interest. This list does not lay claim to being complete in any sense of the word, but it will serve to give an excellent idea of the work which has been done along these lines by the various phonograph companies.

The name of the record company is indicated by a single letter or letters following the name of the artist:

A	Aeolian (Vocalian)
B	Brunswick
C	Columbia
E	Edison
HMV	London Victor Co.
V	Victor

Albeniz, I.
  Tango in D — Elman (V)
Ambrosio, A. d'
  Canzonetta, Op. 6 — Elman (V) Heifetz (V)
  Seidel (C)
  Serenata, Op. 40 — Zimbalist (V)
Aurin, Tor
  Humoreske — Marie Hall (HMV) Zimbalist (V)

Bach, J. S.
  Air for the G String — Elman (V) Hubermann (B)
  Kubelik (V)
  Allegro (Sonata No. I) — Isolde Menges (HMV)
  Gavotte in E Major — Marie Hall (HMV) Kreisler (V)
  Prelude — Sarasate (HMV)
Bazzini, A.
  Ronde des Lutins — Heifetz (V) Hubermann (B)
Beethoven, L. van
  Minuet in G — Elman (V) MacMillen (C)
  Parlow (C) Powell (V)
  Spalding (E) Zimbalist (V)
  Turkish March — Elman (V) Heifetz (V)
Boccherini, L.
  Minuet in A — Kreisler (V)
Bizet, G.
  Adagietto (L'Arlésienne) — Kreisler (V)

Brahms, Joh.

Hungarian Dance No. 1	Heifetz (V)	Hubermann (B)
	Kochanski (A)	Kreisler (V)
	Seidel (C)	Spalding (E)
Hungarian Dance No. 2	Joachim (HMV)	
Hungarian Dance No. 5	Spalding (E)	Ysaÿe (C)
Hungarian Dance No. 7	Elman (V)	Spalding (E)
Hungarian Dance No. 17	Elman (V)	
Hungarian Dance No. 20	Zimbalist (V)	
Waltz in A From Op. 39	Menges (HMV)	Kreisler (V)

Bruch, Max

Kol Nidrei	Powell (V)

Chabrier, E.

Scherzo Valse	Spalding (E)	Ysaÿe (C)

Chaminade, C.

Sérénade Espagnole	Brown (C)	Kreisler (V)
	Spalding (E)	

Chopin, Fr.

Mazurka, Op. 67, No. 4	Kreisler (V)	
Nocturne, Op. 9, No. 2	Elman (V)	Heifetz (V)
	Hubermann (B)	Parlow (C)
	Spalding (E)	
Nocturne, Op. 27, No. 2	Elman (V)	Heifetz (V)
Nocturne, Op. 72	Brown (C)	Seidel (C)
Waltz, Op. 64, No. I	Powell (V)	Zimbalist (V)

Couperin, Fr.

Aubade Provençale	Kreisler (V)
Chanson et Pavane	Kreisler (V)

Cui, Cesar

Orientale, Op. 50, No. 9	Brown (C)	Elman (V)
	Seidel (C)	Spalding (E)
	Zimbalist (V)	

Deberiot, Ch.

Allegro (7th Concerto))	Powell (V)
Andante (2nd Concerto)	Spalding (E)

Debussy, C.

La Plus que Lente	Isolde Menges (HMV)

Delibes, L.

Passepied	Elman (V)

Dittersdorf, K. von

Deutscher Tanz	Elman (V)

Drdla, Fr.

Serenade	Brown (C)	Elman (V)
	Spalding (E)	Kubelik (V)
Souvenir	Elman (V)	Jacobsen (C)
	Kreisler (V)	MacMillen (C)
	Powell (V)	Zimbalist (V)

Drigo, R.

Serenade	Elman (V)	Jacobsen (C)
	Parlow (C)	Zimbalist (V)
Valse Bluette	Heifetz (V)	Jacobsen (C)
	Parlow (C)	Spalding (E)

Durand, A.

Chaconne	Brown (C)

Dvorak, A.

Humoreske, Op. 101, No. 7	Elman (V)	Marie Hall (HMV)
	Kreisler (V)	Parlow (C)
	Powell (V)	Seidel (C)
Indian Lament	Kreisler (V)	Parlow (C)
Slavonic Dance, No. 1	Heifetz (V)	Kreisler (V)
	Thibaud (HMV)	
Slavonic Dance No. 2	Kreisler (V)	

Elgar, Ed.

La Capricieuse	Heifetz (V)	Hubermann (B)
Concerto, Op. 61	Marie Hall (HMV)	
Salut d'Amour	Powell (V)	Zimbalist (V)

Gabriel-Marie

La Cinquantaine	Elman (V)

Glazounow, A.

Meditation, Op. 32	Heifetz (V)
Valse from "Raymonda"	Heifetz (V)
Grand Adagio (Raymonda)	Heifetz (V)

Gluck, C. W. von

Ballet Music "Orfeo"	Spalding (E)
Melody from "Orfeo"	Elman (V)

Godard, Benj.

Berceuse from "Jocelyn"	Jacobsen (C)	
Canzonetta (Concerto Romantique)	Morini (V)	Spalding (E)

Goldmark, C.

Andante (Concerto Op. 28)	Heifetz (V)

Gossec, F. J.
    Gavotte in D   Zimbalist (V)
    Tambourin   Elman (V)

Granados, E.
    Playera, Op. 5   Heifetz (V)   Kreisler (V)
                       Rosen (B)   Spalding (E)
                       Thibaud (HMV)

Grieg, Ed.
    Nocturne, Op. 54, No. 4   Elman (V)
    Solveig's Song   Brown (C)
    To Spring, Op. 43, No. 6   Kreisler (V)   Powell (V)

Handel, G. F.
    Largo   Kreisler (V)   Powell (V)
                       Spalding (E)
    Sonata, No. 6   Kubelik (HMV)

Haydn, Jos.
    Minuet in D   Elman (V)

Hubay, Jeno
    Hejre Kati, Op. 32, No. 4   Powell (V)   Seidel (C)

Juon, Paul
    Berceuse   Heifetz (V)

Kreisler, Fritz
    Caprice Viennoise, Op. 2   Kreisler (V)   Seidel (C)
                       Spalding (E)   Ysaÿe (C)
    Liebesfreud   Kreisler (V)   Parlow (C)
                       Seidel (C)
    Liebesleid   Jacobsen (C)   Kreisler (V)
    Schon Rosmarin   Kreisler (V)   Spaulding (E)
    Tambourin Chinois   Jacobsen (C)   Kreisler (V)
                       Parlow (C)

Lalo, Ed.
    Andante (Symphonie Espagnole)   Chemet (HMV)   Elman (V)
                                  Heifetz (V)
    First Movement "   "   Chemet (HMV)
    Scherzando   "   "   Chemet (HMV)
    Finale (Rondo) "   "   Chemet (HMV)
    Romance (Violin Concerto))   Chemet (HMV)
    Symphonie Espagnole (6 Parts)   Strockoff (C)

Mascagni, P.
    Intermezzo (Cavalleria Rusti-
        cana)   Parlow (C)

Massenet, J.
  Elegie, Op. 10 — Brown (C)
  Meditation (Thaïs) — Chemet (HMV) — Elman (V)
    Jacobsen (C) — Kreisler (V)
    Parlow (C) — Powell (V)
    Rosen (B) — Spalding (E)

Mendelssohn, F.
  Andante (Concerto) — Parlow (C)
  Finale (Concerto) — Heifetz (V) — Powell (V)
    Ysaÿe (C)
  Cradle Song, Op. 67, No. 6 — Elman (V)
  Spring Song — Jacobsen (C) — Zimbalist (V)

Moszkowski, M.
  Guitarre, Op. 45, No. 2 — Heifetz (V)
  Serenade, Op. 15, No. 1 — Powell (V) — Zimbalist (V)

Mozart, W. A.
  Landler — Elman (V)
  Minuet in D Major — Heifetz (V)
  Rondo in G Major — Heifetz (V)

Paderewski, Ig.
  Minuet à l'Antique — Brown (C) — Kreisler (V)
    Seidel (C)

Paganini, N.
  Caprice No. 13 — Heifetz (V)
  Caprice No. 20 — Heifetz (V)
  Moto Perpetuo — Hall (HMV) — Heifetz (V)

Pierne, G.
  Serenade — Chemet (HMV) — Jacobsen (C)
    Spalding (E) — Zimbalist (V)

Raff, J.
  Cavatina — Brown (C) — Elman (V)
    Powell (V) — Spalding (E)

Rameau, Ph.
  Tambourin — Kreisler (V) — Thibaud (V)

Ries, Franz
  Perpetuum Mobile, Op. 34, No. 5 — Kubelik (V)

Rimsky-Korsakow, N.
  Chanson Arab — Kreisler (V)
  Chanson Indoue — Kreisler (V)
  Hymn to the Sun — Brown (C) — Elman (V)
    Kreisler (V) — Menges (HMV)

Rode, Pierre
  Minuet Caprice — Thibaud (V)

Rubinstein, A.
  Melody in F   Spalding (E)
  Romance Op. 44, No. 1   Kubelik (V)

Saint-Saëns, C.
  Le Cygne (The Swan)   Hall (HMV)   Powell (V)
                                    Zimbalist (V)
  Prelude (Le Déluge)   Spalding (E)   Zimbalist (V)
  Rondo Capriccioso   Elman (V)   Spalding (E)
Sarasate, Pablo
  Caprice Basque   Brown (C)   Elman (V)
  Carmen Fantasy   Parlow (C)   Spalding (E)
  Habanera   Spalding (E)
  Jota Navarra   Vidas (C)
  Malaguena   Kochanski (A)
  Romanza Andaluza   Elman (V)   Kubelik (V)
                                    Morini (V)
  Spanish Dance, Op. 21, No. 1   Heifetz (V)
  Spanish Dance, Op. 23, No. 3   Elman (V)
  Tarantelle, Op. 43   Heifetz (V)   Sarasate (HMV)
  Waltz from "Faust" Fantasy   Morini (V)
  Zapateado, Op. 23, No. 6   Heifetz (V)   Kubelik (V)
  Zigeunerweisen, Op. 20, No. 1   Heifetz (V)   Powell (V)
                                    Seidel (C)   Spalding (E)
  Zigeunerweisen, Op. 20, No. 2   Heifetz (V)
Sauret, E.
  Farfalla   Powell (V)
Scarlatti, D.
  Capriccio   Elman (V)
  Pastorale   Elman (V)
Scharwenka, X.
  Polish Dance, Op. 3, No. 1   Seidel (C)
Schubert, François
  L'Abeille (The Bee)   Powell (V)
Schubert, Franz
  Ave Maria   Elman (V)   Flesch (E)
                                    Heifetz (V)   Powell (V)
                                    Ysaÿe (C)
  Ballet Music (Rosamune)   Kreisler (V)   Vidas (C)
  Moment Musical, Op. 94, No. 3   Kreisler (V)   Thibaud (V)
                                    Parlow (C)
  Serenade   Elman (V)   Seidel (C)
                                    Spalding (E)

Schumann, Robert
  At the Fountain   Morini (V)
  Traumerei   Elman (V)   Seidel (C)
                         Spalding (E)   VonVecsey (HMV)
  Widmumg (Dedication)   Heifetz (V)
Simonetti, A.
  Madrigal   Seidel (C)
Smetana, Fr.
  Bohemian Fantaisie   Kreisler (V)
Svendsen, J.
  Romance   Brown (C)   Morini (V)
                         Parlow (C)
Sibelius, J.
  Valse Triste   Powell (V)

Tartini, G.
  Fugue in A Minor   Menges (HMV)
  Sonata in G Minor
    Andante con moto   Chemet (V)
    Allegro commodo   Chemet (V)
  Variations on a Corelli Theme Gardner (E)   Kreisler (V)
Thomé, Fr.
  Simple Aveu   Elman (V)
Tschaikowsky, P.
  Andante Cantabile, Op. II   Kreisler (V)   Seidel (C)
  Canzonetta (Concerto)   Heifetz (V)   Seidel (C)
  Chant d'Automme   Zimbalist (V)
  Chant Sans Paroles   Kreisler (V)   Zimbalist (V)
                         Spalding (E)
  Melodie, Op. 42, No. 3   Elman (V)   Hubermann (B)
                         Parlow (E)
  Sérénade Mélancholique   Heifetz (V)   Spalding (E)
  Valse from Op. 48   Heifetz (V)

Vieuxtemps, H.
  Ballade and Polonaise   Hubermann (B)
  Rondino, Op. 32   Flesch (E)   { Hansen (V)
                                    { Ysaÿe (C)
  Serenite, Op. 45, No. 5   Thibaud (V)

Wagner, R.
  Album Leaf   Ysaÿe (C)
  Prize Song (Meistersinger)   Elman (V)   Spalding (E)
Weber, C. M. von
  Waltz   Chemet (V)

Wieniawski, H.

Carnival Russe	Kochanski (A)	
Concerto Op. 22		
Romance	Heifetz (V)	Morini (V)
	Powell (V)	Seidel (C)
Finale	Brown (C)	Kubelik (V)
Faust Fantaisie	Parlow (C)	
Garden Scene (Faust Fantaisie)	Elman (V)	
Kujawiak	Brown (C)	Powell (V)
Legende, Op. 17	Zimbalist (V)	
Menetrier (Mazurka)	Flesch (E)	Hubermann (B)
	Ysaÿe (C)	
Obertass (Mazurka)	Ysaÿe (C)	
Polonaise in A	Spalding (E)	
Polonaise in D	Menges (HMV)	
Saltarelle	Thibaud (V)	
Scherzo Tarantelle	Heifetz (V)	Spalding (E)
Souvenir de Moscou	Elman (V)	Spalding (E)
Valse Caprice	Morini (V)	Powell (V)

Zarzicki, A.

Mazurka, Op. 26	Morini (V)	Powell (V)

In recording music of any description on the phonograph a serious difficulty is experienced in that, as a record can only run for a very short period unless made in an unwieldy size, compositions must either be selected which are comparatively short, or double-sided records made, necessitating a break in the performance of the composition and a consequent interruption of the musical thought it conveys. In this respect the player piano possesses a decided advantage because the length of rolls is practically unlimited.

This is probably the reason why so few violin records have been made of movements from the great classic and modern concertos and sonatas which would bring so much pleasure to the music lover. Whether this difficulty will be overcome is a scientific problem which is undoubtedly being worked upon by laboratory experts—in the meantime it is interesting to note that the Bach "Concerto in D Minor" for two violins has been recorded by the Victor Company, interpreted by Kreisler and Zimbalist; also that the English branch of the Victor Company has recorded the Beethoven Concerto (played by Isolde Menges with orchestral accompaniment) using five double-sided twelve-inch records. It might be well to mention that all the records in the above list which are initialed "HVM" are procurable in the United States through any regular Victor dealer.

CHAPTER XXI

GLOSSARY OF MUSICAL TERMS

Abandon (Fr.). Giving away without restraint to natural emotion.

Abbreviation (Eng.). The contraction or shortening of a musical word or expression. A list of the abbreviations most used is given herewith.

Accel. Accelerando.

Accomp. Accompaniment.

Ad lib. Ad libitum.

Allo. Allegretto.

Al seg. Al segno.

Cantab. Cantabile.

Con exp. Con expressione.

Cres. or Cresc. Crescendo.

D.C. Da capo.

Decres. or Decresc. Decrescendo.

Dim. Diminuendo.

Div. Divisi.

Dol. Dolce.

D.S. Dal segno.

Esp. or Espress. Espressivo.

ff or fff. Fortissimo.

fz or forz. Forzando.

Intro. Introduction.

L.H. Left hand.

Leg. Legato.

m f. Mezzo forte.

M. Metronome.

M.M. Maelzel's metronome.

Mod. Moderato.

m p. Mezzo piano.

M.S. Manuscript.

8va. Ottavo alta (octave higher).

P. Piano (soft).

Perd or Perden. Perdendosi.

Pizz. Pizzicato.

PP. Pianissimo.

Recit. Recitative.

rf or r f z. Rinforzando.

R.H. Right hand.

Scherz. Scherzando.

2 do. Secondo.

Seg. Segne.

Semp. Sempre.

sfz or sf. Sforzando.

Sim. Simile.

Smorz. Smorzando.

Stacc. Staccato.

String. Stringendo.

Tempo Prim. or Tem. Io. Tempo primo

tr. Trill.

Trem. Tremolo.

Var. Variation.

Viv. Vivace.

Vni. Violini.

Abendgebet (Ger.). Evening prayer.

Abendlied (Ger.). Evening song.

Abeille (Fr.). Bee.

Abtheilung (Ger.). Division or part, as of a book or series of volumes.

Accelerando (It.). Increase the speed. Abbreviated *accel.*

Accent (Eng.). The stress or emphasis on certain notes.

Accidental (Eng.). A chromatic sign not found in the signature, set before a note in the midst of a composition.

Accompaniment (Eng.). The part played by the orchestra, piano or some combination of instruments during a solo to enhance and enrich the effect. Usually abbreviated *accomp.*

Acoustics (Eng.). The science of sound or vibrations.

Adagio (It.). Slow. The metronome indicates 100 to 126 beats per minute for *adagio.*

Adaptation (Eng.). An arrangement of a composition for some instrument other than the one for which it was originally written.

Ad libitum (Lat.). At pleasure. Abbreviated *ad lib.,* or *ad libit.*

Affabile (It.). Sweetly and gently.

Affetuoso (It.). With tender feeling.

Affretando (It.). Hurrying. Similar to *stringendo.*

Agilita (It.). Agility, rapidity.

Agitato (It.). Agitated, restless. Used chiefly with *allegro* and *presto.*

Air (Eng.) **or Aria** (It.). A melody without any definite form and usually after the nature of a song. It is often preceded

321

by an elaborate introduction and followed by one or more variations. Bach's Aria for the *G* string (as arranged by Wilhelmj) is one of the finest examples.

Al (It. and Fr.). Up to, as in *D.C. al fine* indicating a repeat as far as the measure with the word *fine* printed in it.

Alla (Fr.). In the manner of, as *alla militaire*, indicating that the composition is to be played in military style.

Allargando (It.). Becoming broader and slower, with increase of tone.

Alla stretta (It.). Increase the time.

Allegramente (It.). Gayly, quickly.

Allegretto (It.). Moderately fast.

Allegro (It.). Fast. Metronome marks are 152 to 184. Often modified by the use of other words such as *allegro marziale*, *allegro non troppo*.

Allein (Ger.). Alone, unaccompanied.

Allemande (Fr.). A German dance which often serves as a prelude to a longer composition. It is of moderate tempo and is in 4/4 time. Used in Bach's solo sonatas and other older compositions.

Alle saiten (Ger.). On all strings, same as *tutte corde.*

Allongé (Fr.). Prolonged; as *allonger l'archet*, which means to prolong the stroke of the bow.

Alto. The viola, tenor or bratsche. It is somewhat larger than the violin having the same general shape but is a fifth lower in pitch. The lowest string is *C.*

Alto Clef. The clef used in viola music, where middle *C* is written on the third line instead of on the first lower leger line.

Am (Ger.). At.

Amabile (It.). Amiable, gentle.

Amateur (Fr.). One having a taste for, and a knowledge about music, but not in a professional capacity.

Amoroso (It.). Lovingly, sweetly.

Amour (Fr.). Love.

Andacht (Ger.). Devotion.

Andante (It.). Slow, graceful, peaceful. *Più andante*—a little faster than *andante.*

Andantino (It.). Slightly faster than *andante* according to Italian lexicographers.

Anfang (Ger.). Beginning.

Anglaise (Fr.). An English country dance of lively character, closely resembling the *écossaise.*

Anima (It.). Spirit, animation.

Animato (It.). Lively. Same as *animando.*

Animé (Fr.). Animated, lively.

Anmerkung (Ger.). Notice.

Antico (It.). Ancient.

Anwachsen (Ger.). Increase.

Appassionato (It.). With feeling or passion.

Appoggiando (It.). Drawing out, lengthening.

Appoggiatura (It.). A grace note.

Après (Fr.). After, next to.

Arabeske (Ger.). A light, graceful form of composition.

Archet (Fr.). The bow.

Arco (It.). With the bow, used after a pizzicato passage to indicate a return to regular bowing.

Ardente (It.). Ardent, fiery, passionate.

Arioso or Ariosa (It.). In the style of an air.

Armonici or Arm (It.). Harmonics. Usually indicated by hollow round or diamond-shaped notes.

Arpa (It.). Harp.

Arpeggio (It.). In the style of a harp. The notes are played consecutively and not simultaneously as in a chord, indicated by a special wavy line in front of the notes of the chord.

Arrangement (Eng.). The adaptation of a composition to an instrument for which it was not originally written.

Arrêter l'Archet (Fr.). Stop the bow, indicated by two short lines at the point where the pause is to be made.

Assez (Fr.). Enough, sufficiently.

A Tempo (It.). In time. Used when the *tempo* has been changed to faster or slower, to indicate a return to the *tempo* previously used.

Attaca (It.). Commence at once without a pause, used when one movement of a composition immediately follows the preceding without pause.

Aubade (Fr.). A title for short instrumental pieces in lyric style.

Auffuhrung (Ger.). Performance.

Auffuhrungsrecht (Ger.). Right of performance.

Aufstrich (Ger.). Up-bow. Marked with a sign similar to the letter *V.*

Auftritt (Ger.). Scene.

Augmented Chord. A chord that is one-half tone greater than a major chord of the same kind.

Aus (Ger.). From, out of.

Ausdruck (Ger.). Expression.

Ausdrucksvoll (Ger.). Expressively.

Avec (Fr.). With.

Ave Maria (Lat.). "Hail Mary!" a favorite name for either a vocal or instrumental sacred composition.

Babillage (Fr.). Babble, chatter.

Badinage (Fr.). Sport, jest, fun.

Bagatelle (Fr.). A trifle, used frequently as the title of a graceful instrumental composition.

Ballade (Ger.). Strict meaning "a dancing song" often used as the title of a more pretentious violin composition.

Ballet (Ger. Ballett; Fr. ballet; It. ballo, balletto). A spectacular dance introduced in an opera or other stage productions.

Band (Ger.). A volume or book.

Bar (Eng.). The line crossing the stave separating the measures, is often used incorrectly instead of "measure."

Barcarolle (It.). Boat song, from the songs peculiar to the gondoliers of Venice. Frequently used as the title of a violin composition.

Bassgeige (Ger.). Familiar term for the cello.

Basso Continuo (It.). A kind of ancient musical shorthand where the bass part was written with numbers indicating the correct chords to be played.

Bayadere. East-Indian dancing girl, Rubinstein's "Dance of the Bayaderes" is a well-known composition.

Bearbeitet (Ger.). Adapted, arranged, revised.

Bearbeitung (Ger.). Adaptation.

Beat (Eng.). The motion of the hand or foot in marking time.

Beaucoup (Fr.). A great deal.

Begleitung (Ger.). Accompaniment.

Ben or Bene (It.). Well; as *ben marcato*, meaning well marked.

Berceuse (Fr.). A cradle song or slumber song having a soft and swinging melody. The German name is *schlummerlied*.

Bewegung (Ger.). Movement, agitation.

Bezeichnet (Ger.). Explained, defined.

Bibliothek (Ger.). Library.

Bien (Fr.). Well, good.

Bluette (Fr.). A light, graceful composition of no fixed form.

Bogen (Ger.). Violin bow.

Bogenfuhrung (Ger.). Management of the bow.

Bogenstrich (Ger.). Stroke of the bow.

Bogentechnik (Ger.). Technic of the bow.

Bois (Fr.). Wood.

Bolero (Sp.). A Spanish national dance, mostly in the time of a minuet, with a sharply marked and peculiar accent.

Bord (Fr.). Side, border, bank.

Bourée (Fr.). An old French dance of lively tempo found in many of the old sonatas.

Bowing (Eng.). The manner in which the bow is drawn across the strings upon which the quality of the tone is largely dependent.

Braccio (It.). The arm.

Bratsche (Ger.). Viola.

Bravura (It.). Dash, brilliancy.

Breve (Eng.). Ancient name for half note.

Brilliante or Brilliant (It. and Fr.). With brilliancy.

Brindisi (It.). A drinking song.

Brio (It.). Fire; as *con brio* meaning with fire.

Brioso (It.). In a fiery manner.

Brise, le (Fr.). Short detached strokes of the bow.

Bunte (Ger.). Bright or varied.

Cabaletta (It.). Strict meaning *little horse*. A simple, pleasing melody with a "trotting" accompaniment.

Cadence (Eng.). A concluding strain.

Cadenza (Eng.). A portion of a violin concerto, fantasia, etc., where the composer himself either writes a series of brilliant passages or variations, or indicates that the performer may extemporize at his pleasure.

Calando (It.). With decreasing volume of tone.

Campanella (It.). A little bell. Often used as the title of a pleasing bell-like composition.

Canon. The strictest form of contrapuntal composition, in which each voice imitates exactly the part sung or played by the preceding voice.

Cantabile (It.). In a singing style.

Cantando (It.). Similar in meaning to *cantabile*.

Cantilena (It.). Melody, air.

Canzonetta (It.). A light, airy, song-like piece of no great length.

Capo (It.). Head or beginning; as *da capo* or *D.C.* from the first.

Capriccietto (It.). A little capriccio.

Capriccioso (It.). Whimsical.

Caprice (Eng.) or **Capriccio** (It.). A species of free composition not subject to rule as to form or figure. The first caprices for violin were those by Locatelli, composed about 1750.

Causerie (Fr.). Chat, conversation.

Cavatina (It.). Smooth, melodious composition in song style. The "Raff Cavatina" is the best known composition for the violin with this title.

Cedez (Fr.). Decrease the tone.

Celere (It.). Quick, rapid.

Chaconne or **Ciaccona** (It.). An ancient Spanish dance, moderately slow in tempo. The best known chaconne is the one found in Bach's Fourth Solo Sonata. Vitali's "Ciaccona" is also well known.

Chamber Music. Vocal or instrumental music suitable for performance in a room or small hall; ordinarily applied to quartets and similar concerted pieces for solo instruments.

Chanson (Fr.). Chanson, or song. Some are written for the violin, such as the "Chanson-Polonaise," by Wieniawski.

Chant (Fr.). Song.

Chaque (Fr.). Each.

Characteristic piece (Eng.). A characteristic composition depicting a definite mood.

Chord. A combination of notes sounded simultaneously, and not consecutively (as in the arpeggio). It may be played on two, three or four strings, although the effect on the violin is somewhat like an arpeggio owing to the curve of the bridge.

Chromatic (Eng.). From the Greek, meaning *colored*, usually applied to passages or scales where the notes progress by half tones.

Ciaccona (It.). Same as *chaconne*.

Cinquantaine (Fr.). Fifty.

Classic. A composition which belongs to an acknowledged style in music written by an acknowledged master of that style.

Clavier or **Klavier** (Ger.). Piano.

Clef. The sign placed at the beginning of a musical staff indicating the line or space which represents the note from which the clef takes its name, such as "G Clef," "F Clef," etc.

Clochette (Fr.). A little bell.

Coda or **Finale.** The ending of a composition by an extra melodic phrase, for more completely establishing the final cadence.

Col, Coll', or **Colla** (It.). With, as *col arco*—with the bow.

Colla parte (It.). Accommodate the accompaniment to the solo.

Color (Eng.). The characteristic rhythms, harmonies and melodies of a composition. The word "timbre" is more frequently used to express the same meaning.

Come (It.). As, exactly, in manner indicated.

Common chord. A major or minor triad.

Common time. The most frequently occurring time—⁴/₄.

Comodo or **Commodo** (It.). Easily, at will, without haste.

Componirt (Ger.). Composed.

Composition (Eng.). A musical production for singing or playing.

Con (It.). With.

Concert. A public music performance.

Concertante (It.). In concerted style, each part playing alternately the solo and subordinate part with little or no difference in the difficulty of the respective parts.

Concerted Music. Music for several instruments at once.

Concertino. The concertino is similar to the concerto but much more concise, usually consisting of only one movement with change of time near the middle rather than of the typical three movements of the concerto.

Concerto (It.). A pretentious musical composition, usually in three movements, for a solo instrument with orchestra accompaniment, designed to show the technical and musical skill of the performer.

Concerto doppio (It.). A concerto for two or more solo instruments. The double concerto by J. S. Bach for two violins is a splendid illustration of this type of composition.

Concerto grande (Fr.). An orchestral concerto for two or more solo instruments accompanied by full or string orchestra.

Concert Pitch. A higher pitch with middle *C*, having 274 vibrations per second.

Concertstuck (Ger.). A concert piece.

Conservatory. A school of music.

Consonance (Eng.). A combination of two or more harmonious tones, requiring no further progression to make it satisfactory to the ear.

Conte (Fr.). Tale, story, used as the title of short pleasing violin pieces.

Corda (It.). A string.

Count. An accent, beat, or pulse of a measure.

Counterpoint (Eng.). A more elaborate form of musical harmony where one or more parts are added to another part.

Courante (Fr.). An old dance in triple

time, having rather a lively movement with notes of equal value, found in Bach's second and fourth solo sonatas and in many other of the old style compositions.

Couronne (Fr.). Crown, lengthens the note *ad lib.*

Cracovienne (Fr.). A Polish dance similar to the mazurka.

Crescendo (It.). Increase the volume of sound, abbreviated *cres.* or *cresc.*

Crotchet (Eng.). A quarter note.

Cygne (Fr.). Swan.

Czardas (Hung.). A Hungarian or Magyar dance.

Da Capo or **D. C.** (It.). Repeat from the beginning. The words *senza replica* are often added to show that in the D. C. no repeats are to be played.

Dal Segno (It.). Repeat from the sign placed at some previous measure in the composition.

Début (Fr.). A first appearance in concert or recital before the general public.

Deciso (It.). Decided, energetic.

Decrescendo (It.). Decrease the volume of tone. Abbreviated *decresc.*

Delicatemente (It.). Delicately.

Delicato (It.). Delicate.

Dernière (Fr.). Last.

Détaché (Fr.). Detached or staccato notes.

Deutch (Ger.). German.

Deux (Fr.). Two.

Deuxième (Fr.). Second.

Dextra (Lat.). Right, opposite to left.

Di (It.). With or of.

Diatonic. Through or embracing the tones of the standard major or minor scale.

Die (Ger.). The.

Diminished Chord. A chord which is one half tone less than the minor chord of the same kind.

Diminuendo (It.). Decreasing. Abbreviated *dim., dimin.*

Discord. A dissonance.

Dissonance. A chord of two or more tones requiring resolution.

Divertimento (It.). A short, light, cheerful composition.

Divisi (It.). Divided, indicating that one violin takes the upper line of notes and another violin takes the second line, etc. Found in orchestral music, and abbreviated *div.*

Doigt (Fr.). Finger.

Doigté (Fr.). Fingered.

Dolce (It.). Sweetly.

Dolcissimo (It.). As sweetly as possible.

Doloroso (It.). Sorrowful.

Dominant (Eng.). The fifth tone in the major or minor scale.

Doppelgriff (Ger.). Two notes played at once, forming a double stop.

Doppio (It.). Double; as *doppio movimento*—twice the speed.

Double-stop (Eng.). In violin playing, to stop two strings together, thus obtaining two-part harmony.

Double String (Eng.). Where the same note is to be played on two strings at once. In violin music it is very often used as nearly every note may be produced in a number of places with a surprising difference in the character of tone.

Douleur (Fr.). Sadness.

Doux (Fr.). Soft.

Down-bow (Eng.). In violin playing, the downward stroke of the bow from nut to point.

Dritte (Ger.). Third.

Droite (Fr.). Right, as applied to the hand.

Duet (Eng.). A composition for two instruments of the same or different character. In violin music, sometimes applied to a piece where the double stopping gives the effect of two players.

Duettino (It.). A short and easy duet.

Dumka (Bohemian). Lament. Compositions having this title are usually extremely emotional in character.

Durch (Ger.). Through.

Ecole (Fr.). School or method, applied to places for musical instruction, or to works of an educational character in music.

Ecossais (Fr.). Scotch. Many compositions with this title have been written for the violin.

Editeur (Fr.). Editor or publisher.

Effet (Fr.) Term used in violin music to indicate the sound produced when the note is to be played either in its natural or artificial harmonic form.

Egalement (It.). Evenly.

Eingerichtet (Ger.). Arranged or adapted.

Einmal (Ger.). Once.

Elan (Fr.). Impetuosity, vehemence.

Elégante (It.). Elegant, graceful.

Eleganza (It.). Elegance.

Elegy (Eng.). A composition depicting feelings of sadness, longing or ardent love. Usually of soft, plaintive character in slow tempo.

Embellishment. *See* grace note.

Empfindung (Ger.). Emotion.

Employez (Fr.). Use.

Encore (Fr.). A request for the repetition of the performance of an artist, evidenced by the clapping of hands. Also applied to the composition played in response to such a request.

Enegico (It.). With energy, forcibly.

Enharmonic. In modern music, enharmonic tones are those derived from different degrees, but practically identical in pitch. On the piano, *C* sharp and *D* flat are enharmonic, both being played on the same black key, but on the violin there is theoretically at least a difference in the pitch and position of the finger on the violin string.

Ensemble (Fr.). Together, combined, perfect harmony of parts in a musical composition.

Entr'acte (Fr.). The title given a musical composition played between the acts of an opera or play.

Erinnerung (Ger.). Remembrance.

Erklarung (Ger.). Explanation.

Erlauterung (Ger.). Explanation or illustration.

Erleichtern (Ger.). To simplify.

Erlichterung (Ger.). Simplification.

Eroica (It.). Heroic.

Erotic (Eng.). Amorous in character.

Erwachen (Ger.). Awakening.

Erzahlung (Ger.). Story, tale.

Espagnol (Fr.). Spanish.

Espoir (Fr.). Hope or faith.

Espressivo (It.). Expressive.

Esquisse (Fr.). Sketch.

Etude (Fr.). A study or exercise similar in style to the caprice. Many études have been written for the violin by Mazas, Fiorillo, Kreutzer, Rode, Gavinies and many of the modern composers and teachers.

Exercise (Eng.). A composition to develop technique or expression.

Expression (Eng.). The intelligent presentation of the emotional and intellectual meaning of a composition.

Extemporize. To improvise.

Extrait (Fr.). Extract.

Facilité (Fr.). Simplified.

Fackeltanz (Ger.). Torch dance. The music for a torch-light procession at royal marriages in Germany, usually in march time.

False (Eng.). Applied to an incorrect relation of two tones, or to a violin string which fails to tune correctly.

Fandango (Sp.). A Spanish dance in three-four time accompanied with castanets.

Fantasia (Eng.). A very old form of musical composition, having no set form, now used as the title of any composition of a free and somewhat rhapsodical character.

Ferne (Ger.). Distance.

Fertig (Ger.). Ready; completed, finished.

Fest (Ger.). Holiday.

Fête (Fr). Celebration.

Feu Follet (Fr.). Will o' the wisp.

Feuille (Fr.). A leaf.

Feuillet d'Album (Fr.). Album leaf.

Fiddle. A common name for the violin.

Figuration (Eng.). The variation of a theme by accompanying it with runs and passages.

Fileuse (Fr.). A spinner.

Finale (It.). Conclusion.

Fine (It.). End, close; indicates either the end of a repeated section (after the sign *D.S.* or *D.C.*) or the conclusion of a piece in several divisions.

Fingering (Eng.). The method of applying the fingers to the strings of a violin.

Fingersatz (Ger.). Position of the finger.

Flageolet (Fr.). Harmonics, the tones produced upon a violin by placing the fingers lightly upon the strings at certain points.

Fleur (Fr.). Flower.

Florid (Eng.). Embellished with figures, runs or passages.

Fois (Fr.). Times, used in connection with instructions for repetition.

Folge (Ger.). Succession, series, order.

Folia (Sp.). A slow Spanish dance in three-four time. Also used for an air with variations such as Corelli's "La Folia."

Forte (It.). Loud. Abbreviated *f*. The degree of loudness is indicated by the number of *f*'s used as *ff*, *fff* or *ffff*, etc.

Forza (It.). Emphasis.

Fugue (Eng.). The highest form of the contrapuntal style, introducing the theme in different places, often with three or more parts. The best examples for violin are found in Bach's Solo Sonatas which, however, are extremely difficult.

Fuhrer (Ger.). Guide.

Fucco (It.). Fire, passion.

Furiant. A rapid Bohemian dance varying in rhythm and accent.

Furioso (It.). Furious, vehement.

Gaiement (Fr.). Merrily, gayly.

Gamme (Fr.). Notation; the scale.

Ganz (Ger.). All, whole.

Ganzer Bogen or **G.B.** (Ger.). Whole bow. Play with the entire length of the bow.

Gauche (Fr.). Left, as applied to the hand.

Gavotte. A lively composition suitable for dancing.

Geboren (Ger.). Born.

Gedicht (Ger.). Poem.

Gefuhrt (Ger.). Directed.

Geige (Ger.). Violin.

Geiger (Ger.). A violin player.

Geordnete (Ger.). Arranged.

Gesang (Ger.). Song, melody, air.

Gesangscene (Ger.). A dramatic musical composition conceived in singing style. Spohr's Eighth Concerto has this title.

Gewidmet (Ger.). Dedicated.

Gezogen (Ger.). Indicated, pointed out.

Gigue (Fr.). The gigue or giga is a dance form much used in old sonatas of a joyful and lively character.

Giocoso (It.). Sportively.

Glissando (It.). A gliding or sliding.

Glissez (Fr.). Glide.

Glocke (Ger.). Bell.

Gnomes (Fr.). Goblins, fairies, misshapen imaginary spirits used as the title of a large number of compositions attempting to portray fanciful creatures of the night.

Gondoliera (It.). Venetian boat song. German "gondolied."

Grace Note. A small note whose time value is shortened, serving as an embellishment on the melody, also called the *appoggiatura*. There are two kinds of grace notes; the long, with plain stems, and the short, with a line through the stem.

Gracieuse (Fr.). Agreeable, graceful.

Grande (It.). Grand or great.

Grandioso (It.). In a lofty manner.

Grave (Lat., It., Fr. or Eng.). Slow or solemn.

Grazia (It.). With grace, elegance.

Grazioso (It.). Gracefully, elegantly.

Guitarre (Ger.). Guitar.

Habanera (Sp.). A popular Spanish dance in two-four time, with the rhythm in each measure equally divided between eighths and triplets.

Harfe (Ger.). Harp.

Harmonic Minor. A scale consisting of a tone, a half tone, two tones, a half tone, a tone and a half, a half tone, as *A, B, C, D, E, F, G* sharp, *A*.

Harmonics. Harmonics are overtones produced by the vibration of the string in segments such as halves, thirds, fourths, etc., while vibrating as a whole. The harmonics have a vibration rate that is an exact multiple of the rate of the fundamental tone upon which they are dependent. The second, third or fourth finger touches the string lightly, dividing it into segments, the non-vibrating point being where the finger touches the string. The fundamental may be the open string or any length as stopped by the first finger.

Harmony. In general, a combination of tones or chords producing music. The study of harmony consists in acquiring knowledge of the fundamental triads, chords and their combinations and interrelation.

Hebraischen (Ger.). Hebrew.

Heft (Ger.). Book.

Herunterstrich (Ger.). Down-bow.

Heure (Fr.). Hour.

Heureux (Fr.). Happy.

Hexantanz (Ger.). Witches' or goblin dance.

Hinaufstrich (Ger.). Up-bow.

Hinstrich (Ger.). Up-bow.

Hirtenlied (Ger.). Shepherd's song.

Hold (Eng.). The sign over or under a note or rest, indicating that it is to be prolonged at the performer's discretion.

Hommage (Fr.). Homage.

Hongrois (Fr.). Hungarian.

Humoresque or **Humoreske** (Fr.). A composition of humorous or fanciful style.

Idylle (Fr.). A composition in pastoral style.

Il (It.). The.

Imitando (It.). Imitate.

Imitation. The repetition of a motive or theme presented by one part (the antecedent) in another part (the consequent), with or without modification.

Immer (Ger.). Always.

Impromptu (Fr.). A composition of extemporaneous character.

Inhalt (Ger.). Table of contents.

Innig (Ger.). Heartfelt, fervent.

Instrumentation (Eng.). The theory and practice of arranging music for a body of instruments of different kinds.

Intermezzo (It.). Coming between, as between two acts or in the old suites between two other movements.

Intime (Fr.). Intimately.

Intonation. The production of sound on the violin; when properly produced in pitch it is said to be "pure" or "true"; when improperly produced to be "false."

Introduction (Eng.). A prelude.

Inversion. The transposition of the notes forming an interval or a fundamental triad.

Irlandais (Fr.). Irish.

Istesso Tempo (It.). The same tempo.

Jetez (Fr.). Throw.

Jig (Eng.). Probably derived from the French *gigue*, a country dance played in a rapid tempo, much favored in their suites by the older composers.

Jota (Sp.). A Spanish national dance in fast triple time.

Kadenz (Ger.). Cadence; *cadenza*.

Kammermusik (Ger.). Chamber music.

Key. The succession of tones forming any major or minor scale, named from the first tone of the particular scale.

Kinderlied (Ger.). Children's song.

Klang (Ger.). A sound.

Klavier (Ger.). Formerly the name of the older type of piano, now the name of any style of piano.

Kol Nidrei (Heb.). A Jewish song of worship.

Konzert (Ger.). Concerto.

Krakowiak (Pol.). *See* cracovienne.

Kronung (Ger.). Coronation.

Kunst (Ger.). Skill, art.

Kunstler (Ger.). Artist.

Kurz (Ger.). Short.

Kuyawiak (Pol.). A Polish dance similar to the mazurka.

Lage (Ger.). Position; as *erste lage*—first position.

Lagenwechsel (Ger.). Change of position.

Lamentoso (It.). Plaintive.

Landler (Ger.). A German country dance in two-four or three-eight time. The peculiar swing to the dance is brought about by the use of dotted eighth followed by sixteenth notes.

Langsamer (Ger.). Slower.

Largamente (It.). Broadly, in a grandiose manner.

Larghetto (It.). Not as slow as *largo*.

Largo (It.). Slow, broad.

Leader. The first violin in an orchestra who directs other musicians while playing at times himself.

Lebhaft (Ger.). Lively, quick.

Leçon (Fr.). Lesson, exercise.

Legato (It.). Bound, closely connected, not staccato.

Légende (Fr.). A slow, melancholy composition based upon a poem of sentimental character.

Léger (Fr.). Light.

Légèrement (Fr.). Lightly.

Leger Lines. The lines added to the staff either above or below.

Leggenda (It.). Legend.

Leggieramente (It.). Lightly, swiftly.

Leggierezza (It.). With lightness.

Leggiero (It.). Light, easy, swift.

Leggierissimo (It.). Very light, easy.

Legno (It.). Wood; *coll'legno*—with the back of the bow.

Lehrer (Ger.). Teacher.

Leise (Ger.). Low, soft, piano.

Lento (It.). Slow.

Levez (Fr.). Raise or elevate.

Libitum (Lat.). Pleasure, will.

Lied (Ger.). A song.

Linken (Ger.). Left hand.

L'istesso Tempo (It.). The same tempo.

L', La, Le (Fr.). The.

Loco (It.). Play in the proper place. Used after playing passages marked *8va*.

Longeur (Fr.). Length.

Loure (Fr.). An old dance in triple time with the accent well marked on the first beat. Used in many of the older violin sonatas and suites.

Lunga (It.). Long; as *lunga pausa*—long pause.

Lusingando (It.). Caressingly, coaxingly.

Lutins (Fr.). Elfs, goblins.

Madrigal (Eng.). The madrigal is a short composition of lyric character similar to the short poem of three stanzas by the same name, popular about the middle of the sixteenth century. Simonetti's "Madrigal" is the best known composition of this title.

Maestoso (It.). Majestic, dignified.

Maestro (It.). A master.

Maggiore (It.). Major.

Main (Fr.). Hand; as *main droite* or *m.d.*—right hand; *main gauche* or *m.g.*—left hand.

Major (Eng.). Applied to intervals, chords or scales and keys. A major chord is one that is greater by a semitone than a minor chord. Major keys are always used where the composition is of a bright or gay character.

Malaguena (Sp.). A Spanish dance.

Mandolin. A musical instrument descended

from the ancient lute family (pear-shaped) with four steel strings, tuned *E*, *A*, *D* and *G* like the violin, except that it has *two* strings tuned in unison for each note, a fretted fingerboard and is played with a plectrum or pick.

Marcato (It.). Marked or emphasized. Abbreviated *marc.*

March. A composition primarily designed for marching purposes in either slow or fast rhythm. For military purposes a quick march is usually used; for stage productions or solemn occasions, a slow march is most effective.

Martellato (Fr.). Hammered. Applied to a particular form of violin bowing.

Marziale (It.). Martial, warlike.

Massig (Ger.). Moderately.

Matinée (Fr.). A variety of étude for the violin, the chief examples of which were left by Gavinies, who wrote an important series of twenty-four exercises with this title.

Mazurka (Eng.). A lively Polish dance, usually in three-four time, the music of which has a peculiar and pleasing rhythm.

Measure. The group of beats or rhythm contained between two bars, establishing a metrical unit of fixed length and regular accentuation.

Mécanisme (Fr.). Technique.

Mediant (Eng.). The third degree of a scale.

Mehr (Ger.). More.

Melancholico (It.). Sad, sadly.

Melodic Minor. A scale containing a tone, a half tone, four tones, a half tone, as *A*, *B*, *C*, *D*, *E*, *F* sharp, *G* sharp, *A*.

Melodieux (Fr.). Melodious.

Melody. A pleasing succession of tones depicting some particular feeling. Used as the title of a composition in which a simple motive is prominent.

Même (Fr.). The same.

Menetrier (Fr.). Minstrel or rustic musician.

Meno (It.). Less, not so much, as *meno mosso* meaning "less fast." Abbr. men.

Mesure (Fr.). Measure, time.

Metronome. A mechanical contrivance for regulating the speed at which a musical composition is played, claimed by J. N. Maelzel to have been his invention in 1816. The principle is a double pendulum with a weight at one end and a sliding piece of brass at the other, which, when moved in either direction, causes the pendulum to oscillate at varying degrees of speed.

Metronome mark. A mark set at the head of a composition for exactly indicating its tempo in connection with a metronome.

Mezza or **mezzo** (It.). Half, medium or hushed, as *mezzo forte*, half loud, abbreviated *m f.*

Militaire (Fr.). Military.

Minim (Fr.). A half note.

Minor. Applied to scales or chords. The minor chord is a semitone less than the major chord. The minor mode is used to portray sorrow, sadness or kindred emotions.

Minuet. A graceful and stately dance of French origin. In the earliest form it consisted of two eight-bar phrases each repeated.

Misterioso (It.). Mysteriously.

Mit (Ger.). With.

MM. Metronome. Indicates the *tempo;* as *MM.* = 120, meaning that 120 quarter notes are to be played in one minute.

Moderato (It.). Moderate.

Modulate. To pass from one key or mode into another; to effect a change of key or tonality.

Moll (Ger.). Minor.

Molto (It.). Much or greatly.

Morceau (Fr.). A short piece of pleasing music.

Mordent (It.). A musical ornament resembling a portion of a trill, indicated by a short wavy line sometimes accompanied by an accidental.

Morendo (It.). Dying away.

Morris Dance. A kind of country dance still performed in England.

Mosso (It.). Rapid, moved.

Motive (Eng.). A short phrase or figure used in the development of a musical composition.

Moto (It.). Movement or motion.

Mouvement Perpetual (Fr.). Perpetual motion, a title sometimes given a composition where the notes throughout are of one value played at a considerable degree of speed. Paganini's "Perpetual Motion" is an excellent example in violin composition.

Mouvement (Fr.). A principal division or section of a composition, containing themes and their development.

Musette (Fr.). An ancient dance in triple time, formerly accompanied by bagpipes, a drone bass note being used to make the music resemble that of the bagpipe.

Nacht (Ger.). Night.

Nobile (It.). With noble spirit.

Nocturne. The nocturne is a night piece or serenade, the form of which originated with John Field.

Non (It.). Not; as *non troppo allegro*—not too fast.

Notation. The art of representing musical tones by means of written characters. Letters, numerals and signs of different kinds are used.

Novellette. A musical title first used by Schumann (Op. 21) for an instrumental composition of romantic character.

Obligato (It.). Usually applied to an independent melodic part for a violin or other instrument in conjunction with a song.

Obertass (Ger.). Literally "over the cup." Used by Wieniawski as a title for a mazurka.

Octava or **8vo** (It.). An octave higher, as far as the mark extends.

Octet. A composition for 8 instruments.

Oeuvre (Fr.). Work.

Ohne (Ger.). Without.

Ongarese (It.). Hungarian.

Opus or **Op.** (Lat.). A work, as *Opus 3*, which indicates that the work is the third in numerical order written by the composer.

Opus Posthumus (Lat.). A composition published after the death of its composer.

Orchestration (Eng.). The arrangement of music for orchestral rendition.

Ornament (Eng.). A grace note or embellishment.

Ornamental Notes. Any notes added to the melody to embellish the simple part.

Ossia (It.). Or. Usually indicates an easy substitute for a harder passage. The simplified version is written in a smaller staff above the original music.

Ou (Fr.). Or.

Overture. A musical prelude or introduction.

P, PP, PPP, PPPP (It.). Piano, pianissimo, etc. Indicating different degrees of softness.

Papillon (Fr.). Butterfly.

Paraphrase. A free transcription of a composition for some other instrument than the one for which it was originally written.

Paroles (Fr.). Words.

Partito (It.). Scored, divided into parts for various instruments in combinations.

Pas (Fr.). A step; also, a solo dance in a ballet.

Passage. A short portion or section of a piece.

Passepied (Fr.). An old French dance.

Pastoral (Eng.). An instrumental composition depicting rural scenes or events.

Patetica (It.). Pathetic, exciting pity, sympathy and sorrow, etc.

Pensées (Fr.). Thoughts.

Perpendosi (It.). Dying away in speed and sound.

Perpetuo (It.). Perpetual.

Perpetuum Mobile (It.). Perpetual Motion. A musical composition written in rapid tempo and intended to give an exhibition of technique.

Pesante (It.). Ponderous, heavy.

Petit (Fr.). Little, small.

Peu à peu (Fr.). Little by little, gradually.

Phantasiestuck (Ger.). A fantastic piece or fantasy.

Phrase. A short musical figure or passage complete in itself.

Phrasing. Grouping the notes of a musical figure to bring out the meaning.

Piacere (It.). Pleasure. Used to indicate freedom of interpretation in a musical phrase or melody.

Piacevole (It.). Pleasant.

Pianissimo (It.). As soft as possible—marked *pp. ppp. pppp.* to denote the degree.

Piano (It.). Soft, gentle—marked *p.*

Piece. A composition.

Pince (Fr.). *Pizzicato* (in violin playing).

Pitch. The height or depth of a musical tone.

Pitch, International. The Vienna Congress in 1885 assigned 435 vibrations to the *A* above middle *C*. This is used as the standard in tuning pianos and in manufacturing tuning forks and pitch pipes for all other instruments.

Pittoresque (Fr.). Picturesque.

Più (It.). More; as *più vivace*—more lively.

Pizzicato or **Pizz.** To pick with the finger on the violin strings. *Pizzicato* may be played with either hand.

Pochissimo (It.). As little as possible.

Poco (It.). A little; as *poco a poco*—little by little.

Pointe (Fr.). Point or head (of a bow).

Polacca (Pol.). The polacca (or polonaise) is a Polish national dance of slow movement in three-four time, always beginning and ending with a full measure.

Polichinelle (Fr.). A grotesque dance, also used as the title of a fanciful composition.

Polonaise (It.). *See* polacca.

Ponticello (It.). The bridge; as *sul ponticello*—near the bridge.

Portamento (It.). Gliding while bowing from one note to another; bringing out all the intermediate tones.

Position (Ger. Lage; Fr. position; It. posizione). The place of the left hand on the finger board of the violin.

Potpourri (Fr.). A medley or selection of airs from an opera.

Pour (Fr.). For.

Poussez or **Poussé** (Fr.). "Pushed." Used to indicate the up stroke of the violin bow.

Preghiera (It.). A prayer.

Preludio (It.). An introduction, serving the purpose of ushering in the main movement of an elaborate composition.

Premier (It.). First.

Presto (It.). Very fast.

Prière (Fr.). Prayer.

Prima (It.). First; as *prima volta*—first time; *prima corda*—first string.

Primo (It.). Principal, first.

Principale (It.). Chief; as *violino principale*—solo violin.

Principalstimme (Ger.). Solo part.

Program. A list of compositions to be performed at a concert.

Quartet. A group of four players whether string, brass or wood instruments, with or without the piano.

Quasi (It.). As if, or almost. *Andante quasi allegro*, means *andante* almost *allegro*.

Quatrième (Fr.). Fourth.

Quintuple. A species of time seldom used, having five parts to the measure.

Quintet. A group of five players.

Quitter (Fr.). To leave; *sans quitter la corde*, without leaving the string.

Rallentando (It.). Gradually slower.

Rapidement or **Rapido** (It.). With rapidity.

Rebec. The primitive violin of medieval Europe. See article on "Origin of the Violin."

Recital. A concert at which all the important pieces are executed by one performer, who, however, may be assisted to some degree by other performers.

Recitative. A series of musical phrases frequently used in violin music having no definite rhythmical arrangement, no decided or strictly constructed melody or any strict time and often written without time or tempo marks of any kind.

Reigen (Ger.). A circular dance.

Relation. The degree of connection between keys, chords and musical tones.

Relative Key. The minor key that is three half tones below any major is called the relative minor of that major. Conversely the major that is three half tones above any minor is called the relative major to that minor.

Religioso (It.). Religious, sacred.

Repeat Mark. The sign on the musical staff, usually in the form of two dots in the second and third spaces before the bar mark, indicating that all or a part of a composition is to be repeated.

Répertoire (Fr.). The compositions which an artist has prepared for immediate use in concert.

Répétez (Fr.). Repeat.

Replica (It.). Repeat.

Resolution. The progression of a dissonant interval or chord to a consonant interval or chord.

Resonance. The communication of vibrations from one body to another.

Rest. Silence. Rests have the same value as notes.

Restez (Fr.). Remain. *Restez à la position*—remain in the position.

Retardation (Eng.). A gradual slackening of speed.

Retour (Fr.). Return.

Rève (Fr.). Dream.

Réveil (Fr.). A military signal in the morning for rising.

Reverie. A dreamy composition.

Rêveuse (Fr.). *See* reverie.

Revidirt (Ger.). Revised.

Rhapsody. A brilliant composition, national in its character, embodying characteristic dance movements, slow and fast, with changes of key and time. Hauser and Hubay have written distinctive compositions of this kind.

Rhythm. Measured movement in time.

Rinforzo or **Rinforzando** (It.). Strengthened.

Risoluto (It.). With resolution.

Ritard (It.). Slower.

Ritardando (It.). Same as *ritard.*

Ritenuto (It.). Holding back the speed.

Ritornello (It.). An interlude, postlude.

Romance or **Romanza** (Eng., Fr., Sp. and It.). A short sentimental or romantic composition without definite form, usually written in slow tempo.

Romanesca (It.). Romance.

Romantique (Fr.). Romantic.

Rondeau (Fr.). *See* rondo.

Rondo. A very early form of musical composition which has a symmetrical or rounded form, owing to the return of the principal subject after new matter has been introduced.

Rubato (It.). Stolen; as *tempo rubato*— one note deprived of part of its time value so that another note may be made a little longer.

Ruhig (Ger.). Restful, tranquil.

Run (Eng.). A rapid scale passage.

Russe (Fr.). Russian.

Rythme (Fr.). In rhythm, measured.

Saite (Ger.). String.

Salon Music. Compositions intended for performance in a drawing-room as contrasted with more pretentious and lengthy works for concert hall use.

Saltarello (It.). An old Italian or Spanish dance, quick and springing in its nature, usually in six-eight time and very similar to the tarantella.

Saltato (It.). Leaping, a special kind of violin bowing.

Sammlung (Ger.). Collection.

Sans (Fr.). Without.

Saraband (Fr.). A stately Spanish dance in triple time, its regular place being in sonatas between the *courante* and the *gigue.*

Sattel (Ger.). The nut of the finger board.

Satz (Ger.). Movement of a concerto, sonata, etc.

Sautille (Fr.). Hopping, a special kind of violin bowing, marked with a dot over or under the notes so to be played.

Scale. A succession of tones taken in direct succession through the interval of an octave.

Scharf (Ger.). Sharp, acute.

Scharf Abgestossen (Ger.). Broad, staccato, a special violin bowing.

Scherzando (It.). Jestingly, gayly.

Scherzo (It.). A jest, sportive, playful. A sonata or symphonic movement.

Scherzoso (It.). Jestingly, in fun.

Schlag (Ger.). A beat, blow, stroke.

Schlummerlied (Ger.). Slumber song.

Schluss (Ger.). Conclusion, end.

Schmerz (Ger.). Pain, grief, sorrow.

Schmetterling (Ger.). Butterfly.

Schnell (Ger.). Quick.

Schule (Ger.). School, method.

Schwach (Ger.). Weak, soft.

Schwer (Ger.). Difficult.

Schwierigkeit (Ger.). Difficulty.

Scintillante (Fr. and It.). Brilliant, sparkling.

Score. All the orchestral parts of a composition written in parallel lines, the bars extending the full length of the page, thus showing what notes the various instruments have at the same time.

Sec (Fr.). A cold, sharp, dry quality of tone.

Secunda (It.). Second; as *secunda volta*— second time.

Segno (It.). A sign.

Segue (It.). Follows, comes after. Used to indicate that what follows is to be played in the same manner.

Seguidilla (Sp.). A Spanish dance in ³/₄ time.

Sehr (Ger.). Very.

Selon (Fr.). According to.

Semitone. The smallest interval employed in modern music.

Semper (Lat.). Always. Abbreviated *semp.*

Semplice (It.). Simply.

Sennerin (Ger.). Shepherd girl.

Senza (It.). Without; as *senza sordino*— remove the mute.

Septet. A combination of seven instruments.

Sérénade (Fr.). A soft, melodious piece expressing longing or love, intended to be played at night, usually played with mute.

Sequence (Eng.). The repetition, more than twice in succession, of a fragment of melody or harmony by regularly ascending or descending intervals.

Serenata (It.). *See* sérénade.

Serioso (It.). Serious.

Serrez (Fr.). Check; as *serrez un peu*— check the speed a little.

Seul (Fr.). Alone.

Sextet. A combination of six instruments.

Sforzando, Sf. or **Sfz.** (It.). Forced or unusually emphasized.

Shake. Same as *trill.*

Shift. A change in the position of the left hand, in playing the violin.

Siciliano. An ancient quiet dance in ⁶/₈ or ¹²/₈ time, pastoral in its nature.

Signature. The sharps or flats at the beginning of each line of a musical composition to indicate the key.

Signe (Fr.). Sign.

Simile or **Simili** (It.). Like.

Simplified. Free from difficult passages.

Sinfonia Concertante (Fr.). A concerto symphony.

Singend (Ger.). Singing, melodious.

Sinistra (Lat.). The left hand.

Smorzando (It.). Gradually fading away.

Soave (It.). Agreeably, sweetly.

Solo (It.). A composition (or a portion of one) for a single instrument with or without accompaniment.

Somma (It.). Utmost, highest.

Son (Fr.). Sound; tone. *Son harmonique,* a harmonic note on the violin.

Sonata. The most important and a.mired set form for classical and modern instrumental music.

Sonatina. A smaller form of sonata both in musical significance and length.

Song without Words. A poetical melody partaking of a lyric nature.

Sonore (Fr.). Sonorous, resonant.

Sons (Fr.). Tones. In violin music *sons harmoniques*—harmonic sounds.

Sorcières (Fr.) Witches.

Sordino (It.). A mute.

Sostenute (Fr.). Sustained.

Sostenuto (It.). Sustained. Abbreviated *sost.*

Sotto (It.). Below, under—*Sotto voce,* in an undertone, aside.

Sound. Vibrations between 16 and 40,000 times per second which are audible to the ear.

Sourdine (Fr.). A mute.

Souvenir. A composition written in remembrance.

Space. The interval between two leger lines in the musical staff.

Spiccato (It.). Distinct, detached, pointed, separated. Played with the point of the bow and with the wrist stroke.

Spiel (Ger.). Play, performance.

Spiritu (It.). With spirit.

Spitz (Ger.). The point of the bow.

Staccato (It.). Detached. Each note is brought out sharply as opposed to legato. Staccato may be played on the up- or down-bow.

Staff or **Stave.** The five parallel lines and four intervening spaces upon which the notes are written. Violin music adds two lines below and sometimes as high as eight lines above, although usually, where more than three or four lines are needed, the passage is written an octave lower with the mark *8va.*

Stark (Ger.). Vigorous.

Steg (Ger.). Bridge. *Am steg*—near the bridge. See *ponticello.*

Stem. The line drawn from the head of a note.

Stentando (It.). Delaying, retarding. Abbreviated *stent.*

Step. A progression to the next note or tone, equal to a major or minor second.

Stimme (Ger.). A part. *Solostimme*—solo part; *orchesterstimmen*—orchestral parts.

Strain. In general, a song, tune, air, melody; also, some well-defined passage in or part of a piece which has become popular.

Streich (Ger.). A stroke of the bow.

Streichen (Ger.). To draw the bow across the strings of a violin.

Strepito (It.). Noise.

Stretch. A wide interval on the finger board of the violin.

Stretta (It.). A closing passage, *coda* in faster time than the preceding movement.

Strich (Ger.). Stroke, manner of bowing.

String. The materials chiefly used for manufacturing musical strings are gut (intestines of lambs and sheep). There is a general erroneous impression that the entrails of the domestic cat are used through the expression "cat gut."

Stringendo (It.). Hastening the time.

String Quartet. A group of four stringed instruments—usually two violins, violin and violoncello.

Stuck (Ger.). A piece.

Study (Eng.). An exercise for developing technique or musical expression.

Suave (It., Sp. and Fr.). Sweet, mild, pleasant.

Subito (It.). Immediately, suddenly.

Subject. A theme or melody upon one or more of which a composition is built.

Suite. A series of five or six dance forms so arranged that the tempos and time signature change with the successive movements.

Suivant (Fr.). According to, in accordance with.

Suivez (Fr.). Follow, continue in the same style.

Sul (It.). On (or near) the bridge as *sul ponticello*, near the bridge.

Suono (It.). Sound.

Sur (Fr.). On, over or near. *Sur la touche* —over or near the finger board.

Suss (Ger.). Sweet(ly).

Sustain. Give full time value.

Symphony. A composition for full orchestra consisting of from three to six movements of great length and richly developed.

Syncopate. To change the accent on a naturally strong beat, by tying it over from the preceding weak beat.

System. Two or more staves braced together for writing out a score either for a solo instrument with piano or any combination of instruments.

Tacet (Lat.). Be silent.

Takt (Ger.). A beat.

Tambourine. An ancient dance form which was accompanied by tambourines.

Tanto (It.). So much.

Tanz (Ger.). Dance.

Tarantella. An ancient Italian dance in six-eight time constantly increasing in speed and alternating between the major and minor.

Tartini's Tones. In 1714 Tartini discovered the science of "resultant tones," often called Tartini's tones. The phenomenon is this: When any two notes are produced steadily and with great intensity, a third note is produced whose vibration number is the difference between the number of vibrations of the notes themselves.

Technic (Eng.). That part of music that can be taught—fingering, bowing, etc.

Tedesca (It.). German style.

Tempo (It.). Time in an exact sense.

Tempo mark. A word or words indicating the speed of a movement.

Tenuto (It.). Held. Indicates that a tone so marked is to be sustained for its full time value. Abbreviated *ten.*

Terzen (Ger.). Thirds.

Theme. The subject from which a composition is developed.

Thranen (Ger.). Tears.

Tie. A curved line joining two or more notes of the same pitch indicating that they are to be sounded as one note equal to their combined time value.

Timbre. Quality of tone.

Time. The duration of notes in their relation to one another.

Tirez (Fr.). Down-bow.

Toccatta (It.). An ancient form of composition consisting of runs and arpeggios. In modern music it has become a brilliant, showy composition.

Ton (Fr.). Tone; pitch.

Tonarten (Ger.). Scales.

Tone. Sound having musical quality. Also used to denote the amount of distance between notes of different pitch as *half tone* or *semitone.*

Tonic Minor. The minor scale beginning on the same note as the major.

Tonischen (Ger.). Scales.

Tonkunst (Ger.). Music.

Tonleiter (Ger.). Scales.

Touche (Fr.). The fingerboard of the violin.

Toujours (Fr.). Always.

Tout (Fr.). All. *Tout l'archet*—the whole bow.

Trainez (Fr.). Slurred, bound.

Tranquillo (It.). Tranquil.

Transcription. The adaptation of a musical composition for an instrument other than that for which it was originally composed.

Transition (Eng.). Modulation.

Transpose (Eng.). To change the pitch.

Transposing Instruments. Instruments which give higher or lower sounds than the notes indicated when playing from ordinary music. Thus the *B* flat clarinet sounds the scale of *B* flat when playing the notes of the *C* scale.

Traumerei (Ger.). Dream, fancy.

Traurig (Ger.). Sad, heavy.

Tremolo (It.). A trembling of the tone caused by a rapid movement of the wrist, holding the finger firmly on the string.

Très (Fr.). Very, most.

Triad. A chord of three tones.

Trill or Tr. A shake. One finger is held firmly on the string and the next finger is moved rapidly up and down thus affording alternate notes either a tone or a semitone apart. Double trills are also frequently used.

Trio. A group of three players; piano, violin and violoncello being the most common arrangement.

Triomphale (Fr.). Triumphal.

Triple Concerto. A concerto for three solo instruments.

Triplet. A group of three notes played in the same time as two of the same kind. Usually indicated by a small *3.*

Tristesse (Fr.). Sadness.

Trois (Fr.). Three.

Troisième (Fr.). Third.

Trovatore (It.). A minstrel.

Turn. An ornament at the end of a trill or other form of musical ornamentation.

Tutta Forza (It.). Full force.

Tutti (It.). All. When placed in an orchestral passage it indicates that everybody is to play.

Tziganes (Hung.). Gipsy.

Uebungen (Ger.). Exercises.

Umfange (Ger.). Compass or range of instruments or music.

Unbekannt (Ger.). Unknown.

Ungar or **Ungarisch** (Ger.). Hungarian.

Un Poco (It.). A little. *Un poco più*—a little more.

Up-Bow. When the bow is pushed in such a way that the frog constantly approaches the string. Up-bow, like down-bow, may be played with any part of the bow as it refers simply to direction.

Valaque (Sp.). Farewell.

Valse (Fr.). A dance form in three-four time.

Variantes (Fr.). Variations. Abbreviated *var.*

Variation. A modification or transformation of an original theme by means of different embellishments, melodic and harmonic changes.

Variazioni (It.). Variations.

Veloce (It.). Rapid, swift.

Velocité (Fr.). Swiftness.

Velutato (It.). Veiled.

Verlassen (Ger.). Abandon, leave; as *ohne die saite zu verlassen*—without leaving the strings.

Verzetzen (Ger.). To transpose.

Verve (Fr.). Spirit, animation.

VerzeicÌniss (Ger.). List, index.

Vibrante (It.). Full resonance of tone.

Vibrato,-a (It.). A wavering effect obtained by vibrating or "trembling" the finger on the violin string.

Viel (Ger.). Much.

Vielle (Fr.). Hurdy-gurdy, an old stringed instrument.

Vier (Ger.). Four.

Viert (e) (Ger.). Fourth.

Vif (Fr.). Lively.

Vigoroso (It.). Firmly.

Volkslied (Ger.). Folk song.

Villanelle (Fr.). An Italian dance.

Viol (Eng.). An ancient type of bowed instrument; the progenitor of the violin family.

Viola (It.). The tenor violin.

Violino Principale (It.). The solo violin.

Violino Secundo (It.). The second violin.

Violinschule (Ger.). Violin school or method.

Violinstimme (Ger.). A part for the violin.

Virtuoso (It.). A skillful performer.

Vite (Fr.). Quickly.

Vivace or **Viv.** (It.). Lively.

Vivacissimo (It.). Very lively.

Vivamente (It.). In a lively manner.

Vivo (It.). Lively.

Vollstandig (Ger.). Complete.

Volta (It.). Time. *Secunda volta*—second time.

Vorbehalten (Ger.). Reserved.

Vorher (Ger.). Before.

Vorige (Ger.). Preceding.

Vorschlag (Ger.). *Appoggiatura.*

Vorspiel (Ger.). Introduction or prelude to an opera or other pretentious musical composition.

Vortragsstucke (Ger.). Concert pieces.

Waltz. An old German dance said to have come originally from Bohemia, and is still in vogue. It is in three-four time and has a moderate tempo.

Weinend (Ger.). Weeping.

Weise (Ger.). Melody, air, song.

Weisen (Ger.). In the manner of.

Wenig (Ger.). Little.

Werk (Ger.). Work.

Wie (Ger.). As.

Wiegenlied (Ger.). Cradle Song.

Zapateado (Sp.). Meaning *cobbler*. A Spanish dance whose rhythm is emphasized by stamping the heel.

Zeit (Ger.). Time.

Zigeuner (Ger.). Gipsy music of a wild, passionate nature without regular form.

Zingara (It.). In the style of the gipsy music.

Zum (Ger.). To the.

Zuruckhalten (Ger.). To retard.

Zwei (Ger.) Two.

Zweite (Ger.). Second.

Zwischen (Ger.). Between.

CHAPTER XXII

BIOGRAPHICAL DICTIONARY OF VIOLINISTS

This dictionary is designed to present the essential facts regarding violinists of both past and present, following the same general procedure in each case—nationality, date and place of birth, musical training, artistic accomplishment, compositions, etc. In many instances, complete information has not been available, largely due to disturbed conditions in Europe since the Great War.

ÁBACO, EVARISTO FELICE DALL', Italian violinist and composer, b. Verona, July 12, 1675. Leader of orchestra for the Duke of Bavaria. Compositions include twelve violin sonatas. His works represent the highest type of Italian chamber music, and are considered superior in expressional power to those of Corelli. D. Munich, July 12, 1742.

ABEILLE, JOHANN, German violinist and composer, b. Bayreuth, Feb. 20, 1761. Concertmaster of the Duke of Wurtemburg's orchestra. Compositions include interesting chamber music. D. Stuttgart, March 2, 1838.

ABEL, LUDWIG, German violinist and composer, b. Eckartsberga, Thuringia, Jan. 14, 1834. Studied under Ferd. David. Concertmaster of the Munich Orchestra in 1867. Taught the violin at the Royal Music School, Munich. Compositions include a number of violin solos and a violin method. Held in high repute as a performer on the violin. D. Munich.

ACHSHARUMOW, DEMETRIUS, Russian violinist, b. Odessa, Sept. 20, 1864. Studied under Krassnoktutski, Auer and Dont. Made numerous successful tours from 1890 to 1898. Now teaching and conducting an orchestra in Pultawa, Russia.

ADAMOWSKI, TIMOTHÉE, Polish violinist and composer, b. Warsaw, March 24, 1858. Studied under Massart at the Paris Conservatory. Appeared as soloist with Colonne and London Philharmonic Orchestras. Toured the United States and became a member of the Boston Symphony Orchestra in 1884. Has taught the violin since 1907 at the New England Conservatory of Music. Compositions include a number of attractive violin pieces. Conducted the Boston Symphony Promenade Concerts for seven years, and organized both quartet and trio ensembles bearing his name.

ADELBURG, AUGUST RITTER VON, violinist and composer, b. Constantinople, Nov. 1, 1830. Studied under Mayseder, who made a remarkable performer of him. Compositions include a number of valuable studies, sonatas and concertos. As a performer on the violin, his tone was said to have been matchless in its sonority. D. (insane) Vienna, Oct. 20, 1873.

AFANASSIEV, NIKOLAI J., Russian violinist and composer, b. Tobolsk, 1821. Compositions include several effective violin pieces. D. Petrograd, June 3, 1898.

AGOSTINO, ALFONSO D', Italian violinist and composer, b. Naples, Sept. 5, 1883. Studied under Deworzak and De Nardis. Made numerous successful tours through South America. Now at the head of his own music school in Birmingham, Ala. Compositions include studies and solos for the violin.

AHNA, HEINRICH KARL D', Austrian violinist, b. Vienna, June 22, 1835. Studied under Maysder and Mildner. Made successful tours throughout Europe. Taught the violin at the Berlin Hochschule. Became second violin in the Joachim Quartet. D. Berlin, Nov. 1, 1892.

ALARD, DELPHIN, French violinist and composer, b. Bayonne, March 8, 1815. Studied under Baillot. Taught the violin at the Paris Conservatory 1843-1875, Sarasate being among his distinguished pupils. Compositions include a famous violin method and many solos, as well as modernized arrangements of classical works. As

336

PLATE 62

1. TOR AULIN. 2. RICHARD ARNOLD. 3. LEOPOLD AUER. 4. A. d'AM-BROSIO. 5. TIMOTHÉE ADAMOWSKI. 6. DELPHIN ALARD. 7. MAX BENDIX. 8. MICHAEL BANNER.

a performer on the violin he was highly regarded. D. Paris, Feb. 22, 1888.

ALBINONI, TOMMASO, Italian violinist and composer b. Venice, 1674. Compositions include sonatas and concertos for the violin, as well as symphonies and more than forty-five operas. D. Venice, 1745.

ALBRECHT, EUGÈNE MARIA, Russian violinist and musicologist, b. Petrograd, July 16, 1842. Studied under Ferdinand David. Appeared as soloist with Petrograd Orchestra with great success. Author of many valuable musical essays. In 1872 was made inspector of all Russia's Imperial Orchestras. D. Petrograd, Feb. 9, 1894.

ALDAY, PAUL, French violinist, b. Lyons, 1764. Studied under Viotti. Appeared frequently as soloist at the Concerts Spirituels. Came to England in 1791 and founded the Dublin Conservatory about 1812. Compositions include three violin concertos and a number of smaller pieces now forgotten. D. Dublin, 1835.

ALFVÉN, HUGO, Swedish violinist and composer, b. Stockholm, May 1, 1872. Studied at the Stockholm Conservatory. Member of the Court Orchestra. Compositions include symphonic poems and a romance for violin.

ALLEGRI, GREGORIO, Italian violinist and composer to whom is attributed the composition and performance of the first string quartet.

ALLEN, CHARLES N., English violinist, b. York, 1837. Studied under Saenger at Paris. Member of Paris Opera Orchestra. Came to Boston in 1871. Became a member of the Boston Symphony Orchestra and the Mendelssohn Quintet Club. Taught the violin for thirty years, Henry K. Hadley being one of his pupils. Compositions include some easy teaching pieces. D. Boston, April 7, 1903.

ALTÈS, ERNEST EUGÈNE, French violinist and conductor, b. Paris, March 28, 1830. Studied under Habeneck. Awarded a gold medal and various other prizes. Member of the Paris Conservatory Orchestra. Assistant conductor and later conductor of the Paris Opera. Compositions include a sonata for piano and violin as well as smaller works. D. Paris, 1899.

ALTHAUS, BASIL, English violinist and composer, b. 1865. Famous as a teacher as well as a writer of charming *genre* pieces, and editor of violin exercises. Mr. Althaus was a very prominent figure in London edu-

cational musical circles, and his early demise, Dec. 28, 1910, was keenly felt. He was also the author of an interesting book entitled *Advice to Violin Students and Teachers.*

ALTMANN, WILHELM, German violinist and musicologist, b. Adelnau, April 4, 1862. Studied under Otto Leistner. Transcribed Bach's violoncello suites for violin, and edited the first published edition of Haydn's violin sonatas.

AMBROSCH, LOUIS, Austrian violinist, b. near Vienna, May 15, 1879. Studied under Spiering, Sitt and Prill. Taught the violin for seventeen years in the United States.

AMBROSIO, ALFREDO D', Italian violinist and composer, b. Naples, June 13, 1871. Studied at Naples Conservatory. Made numerous successful tours of Italy, Germany and France. Compositions include a violin concerto, and many successful light pieces such as his "Canzonetta." Founded a string quartet at Nice which still bears his name.

ANCOT, JEAN, Belgian violinist and composer, b. Belgium, Oct. 22, 1799. Studied under Baillot and Kreutzer, afterwards becoming professor of the violin at the London Athenaeum. Compositions include several violin concertos. D. 1829.

ANET, BAPTISTE, French violinist, b. about 1680. Studied under Corelli and appeared as soloist in Paris with great success, but soon left to spend the balance of his life conducting the private orchestra of a Polish nobleman. There seems to be no doubt that he was a pioneer in introducing the advanced principles of Italian violin playing into France. D. 1755.

ARA, UGO, Italian violinist and violist, b. Venice, July 19, 1876. Was violist with the Flonzaley Quartet for a number of years.

ARBOS, FERNANDEZ-ENRIQUE, Spanish violinist, conductor and composer. B. Madrid, Dec. 25, 1863. Studied under Monasterio, Vieuxtemps and Joachim. Became concertmaster of the Berlin Philharmonic Orchestra, made numerous successful tours through Europe and taught the violin at the Hamburg and Madrid Conservatories. In 1890, became professor of the violin at the Royal College of Music, London, and of recent years tours Spain for three months each season as conductor of the Madrid Symphony Orchestra. As a performer he is in the first rank of artists, and his compositions include a large number of musicianly violin solos.

ARDITI, EMILIA, woman violinist, b. about 1830. Achieved remarkable success on the concert stage.

ARMINGAUD, JULES, French violinist, b. at Bayonne, May 3, 1820. Member of the Paris Opera Orchestra, and also founded a string quartet which, later reinforced by wind instruments, became known as the "Societé Classique." His quartet is said to be the first to introduce the Beethoven String Quartets to Parisian music lovers. Compositions include several interesting violin pieces. D. Paris, Feb. 27, 1900.

ARNOLD, RICHARD, German violinist, b. Eilenburg, Jan. 10, 1845. Came to the United States in 1853, but returned to Leipzig in 1864 to study under Ferdinand David. Came back to the United States in 1867, becoming a member of the Theodore Thomas orchestra, and from 1880 to 1909, he was concertmaster of the New York Philharmonic Society, under a series of distinguished conductors. Founded the Richard Arnold String Sextette in 1897, and spent the rest of his life teaching and playing in New York. D. New York, June 21, 1918.

ARTOT, ALEXANDER JOSEPH, Belgian violinist, b. Brussels, Jan. 25, 1815. Studied under Snel and Kreutzer, becoming member of several famous Parisian orchestras. Made numerous successful tours of Europe and came to the United States in 1843, where he contracted a lung disease which proved fatal. May be described as possessing a magnetic personality with a very delicate manner in performing on the violin. Compositions include a concerto, several fantasias and sets of variations. D. Paris, July 20, 1845.

ASCHENBRENNER, CHRISTIAN H., Austrian violinist, b. at Altstetten, Dec. 29, 1654. Studied under Schütz, Theile and Schmelzer. Appeared as soloist in 1690 before the Emperor of Austria and was conductor of several ducal orchestras. Compositions include six violin sonatas. Led what may be termed a struggling existence, dying almost in want at Jena, Dec. 13, 1872.

AUER, LEOPOLD, Hungarian violinist and teacher, b. Veszbrem, July 7, 1845. Studied under Kohne, Dont and Joachim. Appeared as soloist before the late Czar of Russia and became professor of violin at the Petrograd Conservatory as well as conducting the concerts of the Imperial Russian Musical Society. Founded a string quartet, with the cellist Davidoff, which played an important part in Russian musical life. Came to the United States in 1918, devoting himself to teaching. His pupils include Elman, Zimbalist, Parlow, Seidel, Heifetz, Rosen and many other distinguished artists of the younger generation. Has edited and revised many musical works, including the Tschaikowsky violin concerto which was originally written for and dedicated to him. Has also written a book expounding his theories on teaching and a remarkably interesting autobiography. As a performer on the violin, he possesses a nobility of style second only to Joachim.

AULIN, TOR, Swedish violinist, b. Stockholm, Sept. 10, 1866. Studied under Emil Sauret, became concertmaster of the Royal Opera at Stockholm. Founded the Aulin String Quartet in 1912, an organization which gave exceptionally fine renderings of Scandinavian music. The most remarkable violinist produced in Scandinavia since Ole Bull. Compositions include three violin concertos and many agreeable pieces. D. Stockholm, March 1, 1914.

AUSTIN, FLORENCE MURIEL, American violinist, b. Galesburg, Mich., March 11, 1883. Studied under Schradieck, Urso and Musin, awarded first prize at the Royal Conservatory of Music, Liége. Returned to the United States in 1901 and has toured successfully since that time, giving recitals in 1913 and 1914 at Aeolian Hall, New York.

BACHMANN, ALBERTO ABRAHAM, naturalized French violinist, b. at Geneva, Mar. 20, 1875, of Russian parents. Studied under Ysaÿe, Thomson, Brodsky, Hubay and Petri and was awarded first prize at the Lille Conservatory. Made numerous successful tours of Europe. Came to the United States in 1916 touring with great success, afterwards becoming a member of the New York Philharmonic Orchestra. Taught the violin privately. Compositions include three concertos, a sonata, two suites and many light violin pieces. Has also written important works dealing with the violin and violinists including this encyclopedia. As a performer on the violin is equipped with a splendid technique and a broad tone. Returned to Paris in 1922 where he has opened a studio for teaching and concertizing. (Editor.)

BACHRICH, SIGISMUND, Hungarian violinist, b. Zsambokreth, Jan. 23, 1841. Professor of violin at the Vienna Conservatory. D. at Vienna, July 13, 1913.

BAGATELLA, ANTONIO, Italian violinist and author, born at Padua, about 1750. Wrote a valuable treatise on the construction of the violin and other stringed instruments which was later translated into German.

BAILLOT, PIERRE MARIE FRANÇOIS DE SALES, French violinist and composer, b. at Passy, Oct. 1, 1771. Studied under Polidori, Saint-Marie and Pollani. In 1802 became solo violinist in the private band of Napoleon Bonaparte. Made numerous successful tours of France, the Netherlands and England. Taught the violin at the Paris Conservatory where he finally became the chief exponent of the new French school of violin playing. As a performer on the violin he possessed a splendid technique and sonorous tone. D. Paris, Sept. 15, 1842. Compositions include his well-known violin method, ten concertos and many other interesting works.

BALOKOVIC, ZLATKO, Jugo-Slav violinist, b. Zagreb, Croatia, March 21, 1895. Studied under Vaclav Huml, a pupil of Sevcik, and later at the Meisterschule in Vienna under Sevcik himself. Toured Russia, Austria, Germany, Switzerland, France and England. Came to the United States, and made his debut at the National Theater on Feb. 17, 1924, giving sixteen recitals in a period of four weeks. Has since toured the entire country.

BALTARAZINI, Italian violinist. Brought from Piedmont in 1577 by Marshall de Brissac as leader and soloist of Catherine de Medici's private band. He brought Italian dances into Paris and had much to do with the introduction of ballets and operas.

BALTZAR, THOMAS, German violinist, b. Lubeck, 1630, John Banister's predecessor as leader of Charles II's band of twenty-four violins. As a performer on the violin he was a prodigy at this early period, playing with a plentiful degree of technique and especially sweet tone. D. at London, 1663, and is buried in Westminster Abbey.

BANISTER, JOHN, English violinist and composer, b. about 1630. Succeeded Baltzar as leader of King Charles II's band of twenty-four violins but lost the position because he stated in the King's presence that English violinists were superior to the French. He was the first performer to publicly advertise the giving of concerts in England. His son, John Banister (1673-1735) was violinist at the Drury Lane Theater as well as composer of stage music. D. 1679. Compositions include several pieces for the violin.

BANNER, MICHAEL, American violinist, b. Sacramento, Cal., Oct. 20, 1868. Studied under Padovani, Jacobsohn and with Massart at the Paris Conservatory where he was awarded the first prize. Toured Europe and the United States with success, but of late years has interested himself in composition and teaching, ill-health having forced his retirement from the concert stage.

BARBELLA, EMMANUELE, Italian violinist and composer, b. Naples, 1704. As a performer on the violin his tone was said to be marvellously sweet and pleasing. D. at Naples, 1773. Compositions include sonatas and a lullaby which has been transcribed by Edward Deldevez.

BARCEWICZ, STANISLAUS, Polish violinist, b. Warsaw, April 16, 1858. Studied under Laub and Hrimaly. Made numerous successful tours through Europe and became director of the Warsaw Imperial Musical Institute in 1911.

BARGHEER, KARL, German violinist, b. Buckeburg, Dec. 31, 1831. Studied under Spohr, David and Joachim. Taught the violin at the Hamburg Conservatory until 1889 and then became concertmaster under Von Bulow. As a performer on the violin he was a virtuoso of the high rank. D. Hamburg, May 19, 1902.

BARNS, ETHEL, English violinist, b. London. Studied under Sainton and Sauret and was awarded several prizes. Appeared first as soloist at Crystal Palace Saturday Orchestral Concerts. Made numerous successful tours throughout Great Britain. Taught the violin at the Royal Academy. Compositions include a violin concerto, three sonatas and many charming light pieces.

BARSTOW, VERA, American violinist, b. Celina, O., June 3, 1893. Studied under Luigi von Kunits. Appeared as soloist with Vienna and Berlin Philharmonic Orchestras and made numerous successful tours of the United States. Was soloist with the Boston Symphony, New York Philharmonic and Philadelphia Symphony Orchestras. Gave first performance of Leo Ornstein's Violin and Piano Sonata at Mac-Dowell Club in 1916.

BARTH, RICHARD, German violinist, b. Grosswanzleben, June 5, 1850. Studied un-

PLATE 63

1. ADOLF BRODSKY. 2. OLE BULL. 3. CHARLES DE BERIOT. 4. WILLY
BURMESTER. 5. EDDY BROWN. 6. PIERRE DE BAILLOT. 7. CECIL
BURLEIGH. 8. ALBERTO BACHMANN.

der Beck and Joachim. Concertmaster and conductor of several German orchestras. As a performer on the violin he has the distinction of being a left-handed player, capable of performing everything ordinarily executed with the right hand, using an instrument especially altered for this purpose.

BARTHELEMON, FRANÇOIS-HIPPOLYTE, French violinist and composer, b. Bordeaux, 1741. Made numerous successful tours of Europe, and came to England in 1765 as leader of the Opera Orchestra. He once composed the music for a song while looking over David Garrick's shoulder as he was writing the lyric. Compositions include a concerto, several duets and quartets. D. London, 1808.

BASSANI, GIOVANNI BATTISTA, Italian violinist and composer, b. Padua about 1657, and generally accredited with having been the teacher of Corelli. His compositions include sonatas which demonstrate a knowledge of the finger-board and bow far in advance of his predecessors. D. Ferrara, 1716.

BAZZINI, ANTONIO, Italian violinist and composer, b. Brescia, Mar. 11, 1818. Studied under Camisoni and toured Europe with great success for many years. Became director of the Milan Conservatory in 1882. His compositions include many effective pieces for the violin, including the famous "Ronde des Lutins." D. Milan, Feb. 10, 1897.

BECK, FRANZ, German violinist and composer. B. Mannheim, 1731. Studied under Stamitz and fled to Paris to escape the consequences of a duel, finally settling in Bordeaux, spending the remainder of his life concertizing and teaching. Many of his pupils, among them, Blanchard and Bochsa, became eminent musicians. His compositions include several string quartets. D. Bordeaux, Dec. 31, 1809.

BECK, JOHANN HEINRICH, American violinist and composer, b. Cleveland, O., Sept. 12, 1856. Studied at the Leipzig Conservatory and has taught the violin in Cleveland for many years. His compositions are chiefly works in the larger forms, orchestral and operatic, highly praised by eminent authorities.

BECKER, DORA, American violinist, b. Galveston, Tex. Studied under Joachim, appearing as soloist with the Berlin Philharmonic Orchestra. Made numerous successful tours of the United States, includ-

ing soloist performances with the Theodore Thomas and Seidl Orchestras, introducing many important violin works to American audiences.

BECKER, JEAN, German violinist, b. Mannheim, May 11, 1833. Studied under Kettenus, Lachner and Alard. Appeared successfully in Paris and London, settling in Florence in 1866, where he founded the Florentine String Quartet, one of the finest organizations of this character in Europe. His violin playing displayed at once the seriousness of the German school and the brilliancy of the French. D. Mannheim, Oct. 10, 1884.

BEEL, SIGMUND, American violinist, b. in California, Mar. 13, 1863. Appeared as soloist at the Crystal Palace Saturday Concerts in London and made successful tours of both Europe and America. Now concertmaster of the Los Angeles Symphony Orchestra.

BENDA, FRANZ, Bohemian violinist and composer. B. Alt-Benatky, Nov. 25, 1709. Became leader of the orchestra for Frederick the Great of Prussia, an amateur flutist whom he accompanied during the course of forty years in the playing of thousands of concertos. His violin playing was notable for its lyric style and his compositions include concertos, solos and études for the violin. D. Potsdam, Mar. 7, 1786.

BENDIX, MAX, American violinist, b. Detroit, Mich., Mar. 28, 1866. Studied under Simon Jacobsohn and made numerous successful tours of the United States. Later became concertmaster of the Germania and the Theodore Thomas Orchestras, in addition to organizing a very successful string quartet in 1900. His compositions include a violin concerto and a number of smaller works.

BENNEWITZ, ANTON, Bohemian violinist, b. Privat, March 26, 1833. Concertized extensively and taught the violin for many years, becoming in 1882 Director of the Prague Conservatory.

BERBER, FELIX, German violinist, b. Jena, Mar. 11, 1871. Studied under Brodsky and became concertmaster of the Leipzig Gewandhaus Orchestra and Leader of the Gewandhaus Quartet. In 1910, toured the United States with great success and has taught the violin at the Royal Academy, London, and other famous institutions. He once played nine different concertos in three consecutive concerts at Berlin, and is noted for his broad tone and splendid intonation.

BERGH, ARTHUR, American violinist, b. St. Paul, Minn., March 24, 1882. Studied entirely under teachers in America and was a member of the New York Symphony Orchestra from 1903 to 1908, in addition to teaching the violin at the New York Institute of Music. Compositions include a number of interesting violin pieces.

BERIOT, CHARLES AUGUSTE DE, Belgian violinist. B. Louvain, Feb. 20, 1802. Studied under Viotti and Baillot, appearing with great success as soloist both in Paris and with the London Philharmonic Society. He made numerous successful tours of England, France and Italy, in company with his wife, Maria Malibran, the famous singer, whose death prostrated him with grief. Became Professor of the violin at the Brussels Conservatory, but retired when overtaken by blindness. As a performer on the violin he was esteemed in the highest degree for musicianly artistry. His compositions include seven concertos, eleven airs variés and many minor works. D. Brussels, April 8, 1870.

BERTHELIER, HENRI, French violinist. B. Limoges, Dec. 27, 1856. Concertized and taught successfully in Europe, becoming professor of violin at the Paris Conservatory, among his pupils being Raoul Vidas, the distinguished young French violinist.

BESEKIRSKY, VASSILY VASSILIEVITCH, Russian violinist and composer, b. at Moscow, Jan. 26, 1835. Studied under Leonard, appearing as soloist with the Leipzig Gewandhaus Orchestra in 1868. Made numerous successful tours of Europe, and became professor of the violin at the Philharmonic Society Conservatory of Moscow, instructing personally more than five hundred pupils, among them Charles Gregorowitsch. His musical activities extended over a period of more than sixty years and his compositions include a concerto, many violin pieces and cadenzas to the Brahms, Beethoven and Paganini concertos.

BESEKIRSKY, VASSILY, Russian violinist, b. Moscow, 1879. Studied under his father, Vassily Vassilievitch Besekirsky, and appeared as soloist with the Moscow Symphony Orchestra in 1891. Made numerous successful tours of Russia, Germany and Scandinavia coming to the United States in 1914, on a concert tour, throughout

which he was received with great enthusiasm.

BETTI, ADOLFO, Italian violinist, b. Tuscany, March 21, 1875. Studied under César Thomson, and was awarded a gold medal at the Liège Conservatory in 1896. Toured Austria, France and Italy for years and taught the violin at the Brussels Conservatory from 1900 to 1903. Since 1903, he has been first violin of the Flonzaley Quartet, one of the most important organizations of this character in the world.

BIEBER, HEINRICH JOHANN FRANZ, German violinist and composer, b. Wartenberg, Bohemia, Aug. 12, 1644. Became conductor of music at the Court of the Prince-Archbishop of Salzburg and was one of the founders of the school of German violin playing, which gradually removed itself from the influence of cheap Italian charlatans. His compositions include a number of sonatas, one of which is included in Ferdinand David's "Hoch-schule." D. Salzburg, May 3, 1704.

BIGNAMI, CARLOS, Italian violinist and composer, b. Cremona, Dec. 6, 1808. He had the distinction of being considered by Paganini the premier violinist of Italy. Compositions include a concerto, studies and various smaller pieces. D. Voghera, Aug. 2, 1848.

BILBIE, EDWARD NORMANTON, English violinist, b. Nottingham, May 19, 1865. Studied at the Stern Conservatory at Berlin, and privately with Emil Sauret. Has given numerous recitals and is now a member of the Pittsburg Symphony Orchestra and String Quartet. His compositions (in mss.) include several works for the violin.

BINI, PASQUALINO, Italian violinist and composer. B. Pesaro, in 1720. Studied under Tartini, whom he soon equaled as a performer, appearing in Rome as soloist under the protection of Cardinal Oliveri. He later pursued his studies further with Tartini who had, in the meantime, changed his style of playing and greatly developed the technique of the bow. Bini was highly regarded by Tartini, who spoke of him in highest terms in a letter to an English acquaintance, a Mr. Wiseman. His compositions include a concerto and a sonata for the violin. D. Stuttgart in 1754.

BLAGROVE, HENRY GAMBLE, English violinist, b. Nottingham, Oct. 20, 1811. Studied under Spagnoletti and at the Royal Academy of Music, where he was awarded a silver medal for proficiency. Appeared as soloist with Queen Adelaide's private orchestra and founded a string quartet which gave London some of its choicest ensemble concerts. Blagrove also studied with Spohr and later taught the violin in London, among his pupils being the Duke of Cambridge. For more than thirty years he held a high position as solo, ensemble and orchestral player. D. Dec. 15, 1872.

BLIGH, ELDINA, English violinist, b. Geneva, of English parents. Studied at the Brussels Conservatory, and at the Berlin Hochschule under Joachim. Appeared with great success at St. James Hall, London, and made many tours of Great Britain, appearing by royal command before Queen Victoria, in Dublin, during one of Her Majesty's visits to Ireland.

BLOCH, JOSEF, Hungarian violinist and composer, b. Budapest, Jan. 5, 1862. Studied under Hubay and Dancla and was a member of the Hubay-Popper Quartet for six years. Taught violin at the Hungarian National Conservatory and has composed a concerto, études and pieces for violin solo, as well as a violin method.

BÖHM, JOSEPH, Austrian violinist and teacher. B. Pesth, Mar. 4, 1795. Studied under Rode and appeared with great success as soloist in Vienna. Toured for years all through Europe and became professor of violin at the Vienna Conservatory, where for fifty years he numbered among his pupils such great artists as Ernst, Joachim, Singer, Hellmsberger, Rappoldi and Hauser. As a performer he was possessed of a splendid technique and a masterly style, while as a teacher he ranks among the greatest of all time. D. Vienna, Mar. 28, 1876.

BORGHI, LUIGI, Italian violinist and composer, b. about 1750. Studied under Pugnani and became renowned as a virtuoso. In 1784, he led the violins at the Handel Commemoration Services at Westminster Abbey. His composition include sonatas, concertos and duets for the violin.

BORISSOFF, JOSEPH, Russian violinist, pupil of Sarasate and Auer. Toured Russia both as soloist and as leader of a string quartet, making frequent appearances before the late Czar and the Royal Family. After the Great War, he toured Turkey, Arabia and Greece, afterwards coming to the United States, where he has been cordially received.

BORNSCHEIN, FRANZ CARL, American violinist, b. Baltimore, Md., Feb. 10, 1879. Studied at the Peabody Conservatory, where he was awarded a prize for the composition of his "String Quartet in D." In 1905 he became violin instructor at the Peabody Conservatory, and in addition has gained distinction as a music critic and writer on pedagogical subjects. His compositions include a violin concerto and numerous smaller pieces.

BOROWSKI, FELIX, English violinist and composer, b. Burton, England, Mar. 10, 1872, of Polish parents. Studied under Rosenthal and Pollitzer, also at the Cologne Conservatory with Japha. Came to the United States in 1897, teaching violin and musical composition at the Chicago Musical College of which he is now president. Compositions for the violin include many pieces of which one entitled "Adoration" is best known.

BOUCHER, ALEXANDRE JEAN, French violinist and composer, b. Paris, Apr. 11, 1770. At the age of 8, he appeared as soloist at the Concerts Spirituels. Later, he made successful tours all through Europe. As a performer on the violin, his technical proficiency was second only to that of Paganini, but he appears to have had little regard for the musical significance of his playing and to have advertised himself and his concerts in a manner more suited to a quack doctor. D. at Paris, on Dec. 29, 1861.

BRASSIN, GERHARD, French violinist, b. Aix-la-Chapelle, June 10, 1844. Made numerous successful tours of Switzerland, Sweden and Germany. Taught the violin at the Berne Conservatory and the Stern Conservatory, Berlin. Compositions include some valuable double-stop exercises and a number of musicianly solos. Brother of Louis Brassin, well-known pianist and composer-arranger.

BRIDGE, FRANK, English violinist and composer, b. at Brighton, Feb. 26, 1879. Studied at the Royal College of Music. Member of several string quartets and has been chosen assistant to the Joachim Quartet in the performance of works requiring additional performers. Compositions include several string quartets which have won great praise. Mr. Bridge is well-known also as a violin player of the highest rank.

BRIDGETOWER, GEORGE AUGUSTUS POL-

GREEN, mulatto violinist, b. Poland about 1780. Studied under Barthelemon and Giornovichi. Was a remarkable violinist at the age of ten. Appeared as soloist at the Concerts Spirituels and in London at Drury Lane. Became chamber musician to the Prince of Wales. As a performer on the violin his playing was marred for the truly musical by extravagant gestures. In 1803 he played the "Kreutzer" Sonata with Beethoven in Vienna at a concert. D. England about 1850.

BRISTOW, GEORGE FREDERIC, American violinist and composer, b. Brooklyn, Dec. 19, 1825. Member of the New York Philharmonic Society for over thirty years. Compositions include symphonies (all performed at Philharmonic Concerts) and string quartets. Mr. Bristow had a wide experience in American music and was highly regarded as a man as well as a musician. D. New York, Dec. 13, 1898.

BRODSKY, ADOLF, Russian violinist, b. Taganrog, Mar. 21, 1851. Studied under Hellmsberger and Laub. Appeared as soloist with the Leipzig Gewandhaus Orchestra and organized a quartet which won great favor. Made numerous successful tours of Europe. Came to the United States in 1890 as concertmaster of the Damrosch Symphony Society, but returned to Europe in 1894, becoming concertmaster of Sir Charles Halle's Orchestra in Manchester, England, also principal of the Royal College of Music and Organizer of another splendid string' quartet. As a performer on the violin he makes a strong appeal through the sound musical quality of his playing.

BRODSKY, FRANK J., American violinist, b. Pittsburgh, Feb. 3, 1883. Studied under Becker and Sevcik. Appeared as soloist at the German Music Festival in Prague. Member of the Prague, Leipzig and Pittsburgh Orchestras. Conducts a school of music at Pittsburgh. Published compositions include a set of exercises preparatory to the study of Kreutzer.

BROWN, EDDY, American violinist, b. Chicago, July 15, 1895. Studied under Hubay and Auer. Awarded artist's diploma at the Royal Conservatory in Budapest at twelve years of age. Appeared as soloist with all important European orchestras. Since 1916, has concertized all over the United States. Compositions include several original numbers and classic arrangements for the violin.

BROWN, JOYCE, Australian violinist, b. Hobart, Tasmania, Mar. 21, 1899. Studied under Ysaÿe and Thomson. Made her debut as soloist at Queen's Hall, London, playing the Wilhelmj version of the Paganini "D Major Concerto." Made numerous successful tours of the British Provinces.

BRUN, ALFRED, French violinist. Studied under Massart. Appeared as soloist with the Paris Opera Orchestra and became professor at the Paris Conservatory.

BRUNETTI, GAETANO, Italian violinist and composer, b. Pisa in 1753. Studied under Nardini. Compositions include several violin sonatas. Brunetti has been immortalized through the fact that it was for him that Mozart composed a complete sonata in the exact space of one hour. D. Madrid in 1808.

BUCKLEY, GEORGE PARKER, American violinist, b. Battle Creek, Mich., Feb. 7, 1885. Studied under Schradieck, Hartmann, Sevcik and Press. Member of the Prague Philharmonic Orchestra and other famous organizations. Taught the violin at Eichelberg Conservatory, Berlin. Now teaching privately in Spokane, Washington.

BULL, OLE, Norwegian violinist, b. Bergen, Feb. 5, 1810. Studied under Lundholm, a pupil of Baillot, but really gained most of his knowledge of violin playing through experience. Made numerous successful tours of Europe and Great Britain. Came to the United States first in 1843 touring with enormous success artistically and financially, making in all five visits, the last in 1879. Compositions include several pieces for violin of the program type. As a performer on the violin he had few equals in technical proficiency, and while not a musician in the highest sense, he played with a splendid warmth and verve. D. Bergen, August 17, 1880.

BURLEIGH, CECIL, American violinist and composer, b. Wyoming, N. Y., April 17, 1866. Studied under Witek, Grunberg, Sauret and Heerman. Made numerous successful tours of the United States and Canada. Taught the violin at the University of Montana and is now professor at the University of Wisconsin. Compositions include concertos, sonatas, and numerous charming and musicianly pieces in the smaller forms.

BURMESTER, WILLY, German violinist, b. Hamburg, Mar. 16, 1869. Studied under Joachim. Has appeared as soloist with all

PLATE 64

1. RICHARD CZERWONKY. 2. JOHN T. CARRODUS. 3. ARCANGELO CO-
RELLI. 4. RENÉ CHEMET. 5. SASHA CULBERTSON. 6. FERDINAND
DAVID. 7. RAFAEL DIAZ-ALBERTINI. 8. JOHN DUNN.

the great European Orchestras. Made numerous successful tours of Europe and came to the United States for the second time in 1923 touring with great success. Has transcribed numerous compositions by ancient masters with an unusual skill and delicacy. As a performer on the violin, he is a remarkable interpreter of Bach and Spohr, with a prodigious technique and a beautiful quality of tone.

CALCAGNO, CATARINA, Italian violinist, b. Genoa about 1797. Studied under Paganini. Had an extremely brilliant but short career, as she totally disappeared from the public concert platform in 1816.

CAMPAGNOLI, BARTOLOMEO, Italian violinist and composer, b. Cento, Sept. 10, 1751. Studied under pupils of Lolle and Tartini and afterwards with Nardini. Lead opera orchestras in Rome and Florence and made numerous successful tours conducting the Leipzig Gewandhaus Concerts in 1797. Compositions include a violin school as well as concertos, sonatas and many smaller pieces. As a performer on the violin he had a noble tone and adequate technique.

CAMPANARI, LEANDRO, Italian violinist and conductor, b. Rovigo, Oct. 20, 1857. Studied at the Milan Conservatory. Made numerous successful tours of Europe and came to the United States in 1881 to organize the Campanari String Quartet. Taught the violin at the New England Conservatory of Music and the Cincinnati Conservatory. Conducted opera in Milan and New York. In 1907 he settled in San Francisco as a teacher. Has written text books for the violin.

CAPET, LOUIS LUCIEN, French violinist, b. Paris, Jan. 8, 1873. Appeared as soloist with all the famous French orchestras and is leader of a well-known string quartet. M. Capet is a master performer on the violin with a wonderful technique and a warm, powerful tone.

CARPENTER, NETTIE, American violinist, b. New York, 1865. Studied at the Paris Conservatory and was awarded first prize for violin playing in 1884. Appeared as soloist in London at the Promenade Concerts. Made numerous successful tours through Europe and the United States. Was married for a short time to Leo Stern, the cellist.

CARPENTER, PAUL SIMONS, American violinist, b. Philadelphia, Jan. 18, 1892.

Studied under Schradieck and was a member of Henry Schradieck's String Quartet. In 1914 became director of violin department at the University of Oklahoma.

CARRODUS, JOHN TIPLADY, English violinist and composer, b. Keighley, Jan. 20, 1836. Studied under Molique. Became concertmaster of numerous famous English orchestras and appeared as soloist at the Crystal Palace. Taught the violin at Trinity College and the London National Training School. Compositions include several pleasing violin pieces, useful exercises, and he has also written several instructive books on violin playing for "The Strad" series. D. London, 1895.

CARSE, ADAM, English violinist and composer, b. Newcastle-on-Tyne, May 19, 1878. Studied at the Royal Academy of Music and was awarded the McFarren scholarship. Has taught the violin for many years and saw active service in the world war. Compositions include a Norwegian fantasy and a sonata, as well as many orchestral numbers.

CARTIER, JEAN BAPTISTE, French violinist and composer, b. Avignon, May 28, 1765. Studied under Viotti. Appeared as soloist with all great French orchestras and as accompanist to Marie Antoinette. Compositions include sonatas, variations, duos and exercises for the violin, and also published a valuable collection of ancient music entitled *L'art du Violin*. D. Paris, 1841.

CASLOVA, MARIE, American violinist, b. in the Ozark Mountains, Mo., Mar. 29, 1895. Studied under Sevcik, Flesch and Serato. Appeared as soloist with Bluthner Orchestra, Berlin. Made her United States debut in 1913 with the New York Symphony Orchestra and toured with Johanna Gadski, in addition to appearing with many of the larger symphonic organizations.

CASTRUCCI, PIETRO, Italian violinist and composer, b. about 1690. In 1715 entered the service of the Duke of Burlington, whose private orchestra concerts were directed by Handel. Compositions include sonatas rich in originality and musical feeling.

CATHIE, PHILIP, English violinist, b. Manchester, 1874. Studied under Sainton and Sauret at the Royal Academy of Music. In 1891 appeared as soloist at St. James Hall, London, introducing the Goldmark Concerto. Made numerous successful tours of Great Britain. Taught the violin at the Royal Academy of Music since 1897.

CATTERALL, ARTHUR, English violinist, b. Lancashire. Studied under Hess and Brodsky. Appeared at Hans Richter's invitation at Bayreuth, where he played at the home of Cosina Wagner. Became leader of the Queen's Hall Promenade Concerts in 1909 and taught the violin at the Royal Manchester College.

CELESTINO, ELIGIO, Italian violinist and composer, b. at Rome about 1739. Appeared in London in 1772 and became concertmaster to the Duke of Mechlenburg in 1780, retaining this position the rest of his life. Dr. Burney, the celebrated music historian, considered him the best Italian violinist of the period. D. Jan. 14, 1812.

CHAPEK, JOSEPH HORYMIR, Bohemian violinist and composer, b. Jestrebice, Mar. 12, 1860. Studied under Bennowitz and graduated from the Prague Conservatory. Made numerous successful tours throughout Europe in 1882. Since that time, he has been in the United States occupied in the highest fields of musical art, establishing the Chapek Music School at Chicago in 1910. Among his accomplishments may be mentioned the first American performance of Fredrich Smetana's "Am Mein Leben" Quartet at Milwaukee in 1914. Compositions include a number of attractive pieces for violin.

CHARTRES, VIVIEN, English violinist, b. Italy, daughter of an English lawyer, John Chartres, and Anna Vivanti, a well-known Italian poetess. Studied under Sauret and Sevcik. Appeared as soloist with the Prague Philharmonic Orchestra when only nine years old. Made numerous successful tours throughout Europe and Great Britain. Miss Chartres appeared as a child before King Edward VII who presented her with a brooch bearing his monogram.

CHEMET, RENÉE, French violinist, b. Boulogne-sur-Seine. Studied under French teachers developing a remarkable technique and a general musical style which has led to her being named the "female Kreisler." Has appeared as soloist with most of the famous European and British orchestras and has given many recitals in Germany, England and France. Has visited the United States twice, winning the highest approval, her interpretation of the Tartini "G Minor Sonata" being but a single instance of her thorough musicianship.

CHERNIAVSKY, LEO, Russian violinist, b. Odessa, Aug. 30, 1890. Studied under Wilhelmj. Member, with his brothers, Jan and Mischel, of the Cherniavsky Trio which has toured the world for a number of years.

CLAPISSON, ANTOINE LOUIS, Italian violinist and composer, b. Naples, Sept. 15, 1808. Excellent violinist who devoted himself later to the composition of twenty operas and more than 200 songs. He made a collection of ancient musical instruments, purchased by the French government in 1861 and placed in the museum of the Conservatory. D. Paris, 1866.

CLEGG, JOHN, Irish violinist, b. Dublin in 1714. Studied under Dubourg and Bononcini. Appeared as soloist in London at nine years of age, playing a Vivaldi concerto. He afterwards became a great performer, surpassing his contemporaries in execution and tone, but became insane and died at London about 1750.

CLEMENT, FRANZ, Austrian violinist, b. Vienna, Nov. 17, 1780. Studied under his father and a teacher named Kurzwiel. Appeared as soloist at the Imperial Opera House at the age of nine. Made numerous successful tours through Europe and England, where he was presented at the Haydn and Salomon Concerts. His performance on the violin was specially characterized by extraordinary technique and a beautiful tone. For a time he traveled as conductor for the famous singer Catalini. It was for Clement that Beethoven wrote his violin concerto, first performed by him, Dec. 23, 1806. D. Vienna, Nov. 3, 1842.

CLENCH, NORAH, Canadian violinist, b. St. Mary's. Appeared as soloist in that city in 1886, followed by numerous successful tours of Canada and Europe. Since her marriage, she appears to have relinquished entirely her public career.

COLONNE, JUDAS (called Edward), French violinist and conductor, b. Bordeaux, July 24, 1838. Studied at the Paris Conservatory, and awarded first prize for violin playing in 1863. Became member of the Opera Orchestra, leaving it to establish, after years of struggling against permanent institutions of similar character, the "Concerts du Chatelet," which have become world-famous.

COLYNS, JEAN-BAPTISTE, Belgian violinist, b. Brussels, Nov. 25, 1834. Studied at the Brussels Conservatory, where he was awarded a prize for violin playing. Made numerous successful tours of Europe and England. Taught the violin at Brussels and Antwerp Conservatories. Compositions include a number of solos for the violin.

CONRADI, ARTHUR, American violinist and teacher, b. Baltimore, Md., Jan. 5, 1884. Studied at Peabody Conservatory and under Issay Barmas in Berlin and Leopold Auer in Petrograd. Made many successful tours of Germany and the United States. Has taught the violin both in this country and abroad. Mr. Conradi has also contributed many articles to the music magazines of the United States.

CORBETT, WILLIAM, English violinist and composer, b. about 1675. Appeared as leader of the Haymarket Opera Orchestra in 1705. Compositions include sonatas for violins, flutes and oboes as well as orchestral concerts. Traveled abroad for years, making a collection of music and Italian violins, which upon his death were sold at auction, as the authorities of Gresham College refused to accept them as legatees under his will.

CORDIER, JACQUES, French violinist and rebec player who lived in the reign of Louis XIII, and who later came to England. He became a favorite of Charles I who heard him play many times.

CORELLI, ARCANGELO, Italian violinist, composer and teacher, b. Fusignano, Feb. 12, 1653. Studied under Bassani; outside of this fact little is known of his earlier career. Traveled in Germany, and also appeared in Paris, and finally settled in Rome under the protection of his friend, Cardinal Pietro Ottoboni, in whose palace he lived up to the time of his death, Jan. 10, 1713. Compositions include numerous sonatas, suites and concertos, all of which are characterized by technical perfection for the instrument, as well as by musicianly earnest feeling. As a performer on the violin he was a serious, dignified artist, and as a composer he accomplished more than any one of his predecessors in aiding the violin to assume gradually the position which it assuredly now occupies as the "King of instruments."

COURVOISIER, KARL, German violinist and composer, b. in Basel, Nov. 12, 1846. Studied under David, Rontgen and Joachim. Member of several famous European orchestras. Made numerous successful tours until 1876. Taught the violin and singing for a number of years in Liverpool, England. Has written a violin concerto, violin method, special exercises and a well-known essay "The Technic of Violin Playing," translated into English by Henry E. Krehbiel.

CRAMER, WILLIAM, German violinist and composer, b. at Mannheim in 1743. Studied under Stamitz and Cannabich. Member of the Mannheim Orchestra at the age of sixteen. Came to London in 1772 where he soon attained a high position as conductor, particularly at the Handel Festivals in 1784-87. Compositions include three concertos. As a performer on the violin he was said to have combined the skill of Lolli with the expressional power of Franz Benda. D. London, Oct. 5, 1799.

CULBERTSON, SASHA, American violinist, b. United States, Dec. 29, 1893. Studied under Suchorukov and Sevcik. Appeared as soloist in Vienna at the age of nine. Made numerous successful tours of Germany and England. As a performer on the violin he is accredited with a technique almost without rival.

CUTTER, BENJAMIN, American violinist and teacher, b. Woburn, Mass., Sept. 6, 1857. Studied under Eichberg and Singer. Upon his return to the United States he became a member of the Boston Symphony Orchestra. Taught the violin at the New England Conservatory of Music, although later he became exclusively professor of harmony and musical analysis. As a teacher of the violin he was intelligent and painstaking, and those who studied under him received a thorough grounding in the art. He also edited the *Kreutzer Exercises* in a masterly and highly illuminating manner. D. Boston, May 10, 1910.

CZERWONKY, RICHARD, German violinist and composer, b. Birnbaum, May 23, 1886. Studied under Florian Zajic at the Klindworth-Scharwenka Conservatory in Berlin, where he held a scholarship for three years, and at the Royal High School in Berlin under Joachim. Appeared as soloist with the Berlin Philharmonic Orchestra. Made numerous successful tours through Europe. Came to the United States in 1907 as assistant concertmaster of the Boston Symphony Orchestra, followed by an engagement as concertmaster with the Minneapolis Symphony Orchestra. Now teacher of the violin at the Bush Conservatory, Chicago, in connection with which he has organized an orchestra composed of students, which has grown to be a part of the city's musical life. As a performer on the violin he has a splendid technique and a warm, pure tone. His compositions include violin pieces and concerted works exhibiting remarkable talent.

DAMROSCH, LEOPOLD, German violinist, composer and conductor, b. Posen, Oct. 22, 1832. Studied under Ries and Bohmer. Appeared as soloist at Magdeburg in 1856 and in 1857 became leading violinist under Liszt of the Court Orchestra at Weimar. In 1860 made numerous successful tours with Von Bulow and Tausig. Came to the United States in 1871 and in 1874 organized the Oratorio Society followed by the Symphony Society in 1878. In 1884 he also placed German opera on a firm basis at the Metropolitan Opera House. As a performer on the violin he was an artist of the highest musical character. Mr. Damrosch had two sons, Frank, now director of the New York Institute of Musical Art (one of the world's finest conservatories) and Walter, conductor of the Symphony Society, founded by his father, endowed by Harry Harkness Flagler, with an annual income of $100,000. D. New York, Feb. 15, 1885.

DANBÉ, JULES, French violinist and composer, b. Caen, Nov. 16, 1840. Studied at the Paris Conservatory and later became director of the conservatory concerts until his resignation in 1892. Compositions include solo pieces of an educational character and transcriptions for the violin. D. Vichy, Nov. 10, 1905.

DANCLA, JEAN BAPTISTE CHARLES, French violinist, composer and teacher, b. Bagneres de Bigorre, 1818. Studied under Baillot at the Paris Conservatory. Appeared as soloist at the "Societé des Concerts," and also held quartet concerts at which he was assisted by his brothers Leopold and Arnaud. In 1857 became professor of violin at the Paris Conservatory. Compositions include more than one hundred and thirty pieces for the violin and several sets of exercises valuable to teachers. His brother, Leopold (1823-1895), was also a violinist of reputation as well as a composer of violin music. D. Paris, 1907.

DANNREUTHER, GUSTAV, American violinist, b. Cincinnati, July 21, 1853. Studied under Joachim and De Ahna. Also visited Paris and London where he resided for four years teaching and playing. Returned to the United States in 1877 to become a member of the Mendelssohn Quintette Club in New York and later of the Boston Symphony Orchestra. In 1884 he founded the Dannreuther String Quartet which was continued until 1917. Since that time he has devoted himself to teaching. Compositions include a work on scales and chord studies for the violin.

DAVID, FERDINAND, German violinist, composer and teacher, b. Hamburg, June 19, 1810. Studied under Spohr and Hauptmann. Appeared as soloist at the Leipzig Gewandhaus in 1825 and later became its concertmaster, remaining at the first desk until his death. Made numerous successful tours through Europe. Became professor of the violin at the Leipzig Conservatory. Compositions include five violin concertos, several concert pieces, a splendid violin method, and a carefully edited collection of works by old masters. As a performer on the violin he combined a solid style with splendid technique and verve. David was a life-long friend of Mendelssohn, who dedicated his concerto to him, after the great artist had aided him for months in perfecting its technical passages. D. Leipzig, July 18, 1873.

DAVID, PETER PAUL, German violinist, b. Leipzig, Aug. 4, 1840. Studied under his father, Ferdinand David. Became a member of the Carlsruhe Orchestra in 1862. Came to England in 1865 and has taught the violin there since that time.

DEANE, THOMAS, English violinist, b. about 1650. He is said to have been the first to perform a sonata of the great Italian master, Corelli, in England in 1709.

DE ANGELIS, GIROLAMO, Italian violinist, b. Civita Vecchia, Jan. 1, 1858. Studied under Bazzini. Became solo violin at La Scala, Milan. Made a successful tour of South America in 1894 and in 1897 became professor of the violin at the Royal Academy of Music, Dublin.

DEBROUX, JOSEPH, Belgian violinist, b. at Liége, May 10, 1866. Studied under Heynberg at the Liége Conservatory. Appeared as soloist with all the great orchestras of Europe and has also specialized in recitals of the works of 18th century masters, often in collaboration with other great artists.

DEVELDEZ, EDWARD-MARIE-ERNEST, French violinist, composer and conductor, b. Paris,

1817. Studied under Habeneck at the Paris Conservatory and was awarded first prize for violin playing. He compiled an anthology of ancient violinists' compositions in which he treated the music so reverently and in such good taste as to make it an everlasting monument to his musicianship. D. Paris, 1897.

DELLA ROCCA, GIACINA, German violinist, b. Dresden, Sept. 8, 1882. Studied under Massart and Sauret. She appeared as soloist at the Salle Pleyel, Paris in 1892. Made numerous tours of Europe and Great Britain. Has toured the United States with great success. Della Rocca has done much on the concert stage toward introducing the violin works of American composers.

DENGREMONT, MAURICE, Brazilian violinist, b. Rio di Janeiro, 1866, of French parents. Studied under Leonard and appeared as soloist in Europe and England with great success in 1877 as a child prodigy, later he toured the United States, but died prematurely in 1893 through ill-health incurred by dissipated habits.

DESSAU, BERNHARD, German violinist and composer, b. Hamburg, Mar. 1, 1861. Studied under Schradieck, Joachim and Wieniawski. Became concertmaster of several famous orchestras and later (1898) of the Berlin Royal Opera. Compositions include a violin concerto and several other splendid works.

DETHIER, EDOUARD, Belgian violinist, b. Liége, Aug. 25, 1884. Studied at Liége and Brussels Conservatories. At the latter was awarded first prize. Appeared in 1902 as the soloist at the Concerts Populaires, Brussels. Came to the United States as soloist with the leading symphony orchestras. Teacher at the Institute of Musical Art since 1906.

DIAZ-ALBERTINI, RAPHAEL, Cuban violinist, b. Aug. 13, 1857. Studied at the Paris Conservatory where he was awarded first prize. Made numerous successful tours throughout Europe. As a performer on the violin his playing recalled Sarasate in its fiery technique and abandon. For a number of years he resided in Brazil. D. Paris, 1917.

DITTERSDORF, KARL (original name Ditters), Austrian violinist and composer, b. Vienna, Nov. 2, 1739. Studied under Konig, Ziegler and Trani. Made a successful tour of Italy in company with C. W. von Gluck, the famous opera composer. Compositions include twelve violin concertos and a great number of operas, oratorios and symphonies. Dittersdorf had not only a wonderful technique but also an expressive tone, which made him a favorite in Vienna over Lolli, the Italian virtuoso. He was also an intimate friend of Haydn, with whom he carefully analyzed each piece of new music performed in Vienna. D. Vienna, Oct. 24, 1799.

DITTLER, HERBERT, American violinist, b. Atlanta, Ga., May 28, 1890. Studied under Sinsheimer, Hartmann, Spiering, and Thibaud. Appeared as soloist at Beckstein Hall, Berlin in 1908. Made numerous successful tours through Germany. Returned to the United States in 1910 and has been concertizing and conducting, as well as teaching at the Columbia University Music School.

DOLMETSCH, ARNOLD, French violinist, teacher and authority on old instruments, b. Les Mans, Feb. 24, 1858. Studied under Vieuxtemps. Taught at Dulwich College and privately in England. Became interested in ancient instruments and devoted years to collecting, repairing and performing on them. Came to the United States in 1902 lecturing at Harvard University, after which he made a lecture tour of the entire country. Mr. Dolmetsch is unquestionably one of the world's greatest authorities on the origin, history, construction and music of ancient musical instruments.

DONT, JACOB, Austrian violinist, composer and teacher, b. Vienna, Mar. 2, 1815. Studied under Bohm and Hellmsberger. Member of the Hofburg Theater Orchestra. Taught the violin at the Academy of Music and was professor of violin at the Vienna Conservatory from 1873. Compositions include a number of études entitled "Gradus ad Parnassum" which are very highly regarded. D. Vienna, Mar. 18, 1888.

DRDLA, FRANZ, Austrian violinist and composer, b. Saar, Sept. 25, 1868. Studied under Hellmsberger at the Vienna Conservatory where he was awarded first prize and a gold medal. Appeared as soloist in Vienna and became a member of the Vienna Opera Orchestra. He is the composer of more than one hundred light violin compositions such as "Souvenir" which have been popularized as encore pieces by Kubelik, Elman and other virtuosos.

DRESSEL, DETTMAR, English violinist, b. London in 1880. Studied under Wilhelmj

PLATE 65

1. FRANZ DRDLA. 2. JOSEPH DEBROUX. 3. HENRI ERNST. 4. GEORGES ENESCO. 5. MISCHA ELMAN. 6. FEDERIGO FIORILLO. 7. CARL FLESCH. 8. STEFI GEYER.

and Ysaye. Appeared as soloist at St. James Hall in 1898. Made successful tour of Great Britain in 1899 and later toured all of Europe. Now teaches the violin in London, devoting his time to pupils of talent. At the time of his debut, Wilhelmj presented Mr. Dressel with his own concert bow.

DREYSHOCK, RAIMUND, Bohemian violinist, b. Zach, Aug. 20, 1824. Studied under Pixis at the Prague Conservatory. Made numerous successful tours of Europe and in 1850 became second concertmaster of the Leipzig Gewandhaus Orchestra and teacher of violin in the Conservatory, in both of which places he was associated with Ferdinand David. D. Leipzig, Feb. 6, 1869.

DUBOURG, MATTHEW, English violinist, b. London in 1703. Studied under Geminiani. Appeared as soloist at the age of twelve. In 1728 was appointed conductor of the Viceroy's Band in Dublin and aided Handel in producing the "Messiah" there in 1742. He afterwards (1752) became leader of the King's Band, retaining this office until his death in 1767. As a performer on the violin he was fond of displaying technical skill. At one time, he introduced a cadenza of such great length into an air that, when he was through, Handel (who was conducting the orchestra) exclaimed "Welcome home, Mr. Dubourg." If this incident is true, it must have been doubly amusing to those who could hear the remark made in Handel's peculiar manner of speaking the English language.

DUESBERG, NORA, Austrian violinist, b. Vienna. Studied under her father and appeared as soloist in Vienna at the age of eleven. She later became a pupil of Sevcik, entering the Meisterschule and gaining the highest honor there which is the state diploma. She visited England with Sevcik in 1911.

DUNN, JOHN, English violinist and composer, b. Hull, Feb. 16, 1866. Studied under Schradieck. Appeared as soloist at Covent Garden in 1882 and has since played with all the leading orchestral organizations in Great Britain as well as Berlin and Leipzig. Mr. Dunn introduced the Tschaikowsky Violin Concerto to British audiences in 1902. Compositions include a number of attractive violin pieces and a set of cadenzas to the Beethoven Concerto.

DUPONT, JOSEPH, Belgian violinist and composer, b. Liége, Aug. 21, 1821. Studied under Wanson and Prume at the Liége Conservatory, to which he was appointed professor of the violin when only 17 years old. Compositions include pieces and études for the violin. D. Liége, Feb. 13, 1861.

DURAND, AUGUSTE FREDERICK (Duranowski), Polish violinist, b. Warsaw about 1770. Studied under Viotti but abandoned his teacher's noble style in favor of his own talent for technical display. As a performer on the violin he was extraordinarily skillful and original, and Nicolo Paganini admitted that his (Paganini's) most striking effects were a result of his study of Durand's playing.

DUSHKIN, SAMUEL, Polish violinist, b. Suwalk in 1895. Pupil of Remy, Auer and Kreisler. Toured England, Germany, Holland, France and made his first appearance in America with the New York Symphony Orchestra on Jan. 6, 1924, playing a newly discovered concerto by Boccherini. Mr. Dushkin has introduced with remarkable success sonatas and other compositions by Blair Fairchild, the American composer residing in Paris.

ECCLES, HENRY, English violinist and composer, b. London. Compositions include twelve violin solos in Corelli's style. Became a member of the King's Orchestra from 1694-1710 and later went to Paris, playing in the Royal Band. D. Paris, 1742.

ECK, FRANZ, German violinist, b. Mannheim, 1774. Studied under his brother, Johann and became court violinist at St. Petersburg. As a performer on the violin he possessed a splendid technique, combined with a beautiful tone. His fame will rest chiefly on the fact that, through the offices of the Duke of Brunswick, he became the teacher of Ludwig Spohr, who thus had inculcated in him the fundamentally sound principles of the famous Mannheim school of violin playing. Eck's unrestrained method of living finally not only disgraced him but affected his health to such an extent that he died insane at Strasbourg in 1804.

ECK, JOHANN FRIEDRICH, German violinist and composer, b. Mannheim, 1766. Studied under Danner. Compositions include four concertos and a concert piece for two violins. As a performer he revealed a broad tone with splendid intonation and soon became one of the greatest players of his time. D. Bamberg, 1810.

EICHBERG, JULIUS, German violinist and composer, b. Dusseldorf, June 13, 1824. Studied under Reitz and was awarded prizes for violin playing and composition. Was appointed professor of the violin at the Geneva Conservatory. Came to the United States in 1857 directing the orchestra at the Boston Museum and in 1867 established the Boston Conservatory of Music, an institution noted for the excellence of its violin teaching. D. Boston, Jan. 18, 1893. Compositions include pieces and studies for the violin.

ELLER, LOUIS, Austrian violinist and composer, b. Graz, June 9, 1820. Studied under Hysel. Made numerous successful tours of the principal European countries, accompanying the pianist, Louis Gottschalk in Spain and Portugal. Compositions include many solos and exercises for the violin. D. Paris, July 12, 1862.

ELMAN, MISCHA, Russian violinist, b. Talnoi, Jan. 20, 1892. Studied under local teachers and with Auer at the Petrograd Conservatory. In 1904 appeared as soloist in Petrograd with great success. Made numerous successful tours of Europe and Great Britain. Came to the United States in 1908 as soloist with the Russian Symphony Orchestra and toured the country many times. Elman has made his home in the United States for many years. He has composed several violin pieces and edited a series of selections from the old masters. As a performer on the violin he ranks among the greatest artists.

ENDE, HERWEGH VON, American violinist, b. Milwaukee, Wisc., Feb. 16, 1877. Studied under Halir and Witek. Member of the Berlin Philharmonic Orchestra. Taught the violin at many well-known conservatories in America and in 1911 founded the Von Ende School of Music. Has been highly successful in chamber music and recital works. His wife is the daughter of Edward Remenyi, celebrated Hungarian violinist.

ENESCO, GEORGES, Roumanian violinist and composer, b. Cordaremi, Aug. 7, 1881. Studied under Hellmsberger and Marsick, winning notable prizes for violin-playing and composition at both the Vienna and Paris Conservatories. Made a successful tour of Europe in 1899 and has toured the United States as soloist with the larger symphonic organizations. Compositions include sonatas and suites for violin as well as much chamber music. As a performer

he ranks among the artists of real musical worth, but he is even better known as a composer.

ENNA, AUGUST, Danish violinist and composer, b. Nakskov, May 13, 1860. Compositions include a violin concerto of great originality. Learned the violin through his own efforts, and later in his life (1888) was enabled (through Niels Gade) to study in Germany, finally becoming a famous operatic and symphonic composer.

ERN, HENRI, German violinist and composer, b. Dresden, Jan. 20, 1863. Studied under Jahn Rappoldi, Joachim and Ysaÿe. Made numerous successful tours through France, Switzerland and Germany. Spent several years in England concertizing and teaching, and now resides in the United States, becoming violin professor at the Cincinnati College of Music. Compositions include a number of pleasing violin pieces.

ERNST, HENRI (HENRICH WILHELM), Austrian violinist and composer, b. Brunn, May 6, 1814. Studied under Bohm and Mayseder. At the age of sixteen made a successful tour of Germany and later toured all of Europe, meeting with the greatest enthusiasm. Compositions include a considerable number of extremely difficult concert numbers, many of which are still used by virtuosos. As a performer on the violin he had an extraordinary technique and a warm colorful tone. He was a great admirer of Paganini, even going so far as to follow him from place to place to observe his style and technique. D. Nice, Oct. 8, 1865.

FARINA, CARL F., Italian violinist and composer, b. Mantua, about 1580. Court Musician at Dresden in 1625. Compositions include a number of violin pieces, one entitled "Capriccio Stravaganti" in which the cries of various animals are imitated on the violin. Farina was one of the first composers to write in virtuoso style for the violin.

FARINELLI, CRISTANO, Italian violinist and composer, b. about 1650. Compositions include a "Follia" which was very popular in England. As a performer on the violin he excelled in performing the airs of Lulli. Lead an orchestra at Hanover with Handel as a colleague.

FARMER, HENRY, English violinist and composer, b. at Nottingham, May 13, 1819. A self-educated player of both the violin and organ; also engaged in the music business. For the youthful player or beginner, his "Airs Variés" on familiar songs are very pleasing. Compositions include violin pieces such as "Airs Variés"; also published several violin instruction works. D. Nottingham, June 25, 1891.

FELLOWS, HORACE, English violinist, b. Wolverhampton, 1876. Studied under Willy Hess at the Cologne Conservatory. Appeared as soloist in Glasgow at the age of twelve. Member of Willy Hess Quartet. Made numerous successful tours of Germany, Holland and Great Britain.

FENNINGS, SARAH, English violinist, b. Essex. Studied under Hollaender, Wilhelmj and Sevcik. Has concertized and taught in England for a number of years. Was appointed professor at Trinity College, London, and is an associated member of the Royal Philharmonic Society.

FERRARI, DOMENICO, Italian violinist and composer, b. Piacenza about 1700. Appeared as soloist at Vienna where he was highly regarded. Visited Paris twice as a virtuoso with great success. Compositions include a number of violin sonatas now forgotten. As a performer on the violin he was particularly skillful at the playing of octaves and harmonics, but it is generally believed that his musicianship was of an inferior degree. D. Paris, 1780, by the hand of an assassin.

FESTING, MICHAEL CHRISTIAN, English violinist and composer, b. London, about 1680. Compositions include several solos for the violin, and orchestral pieces. He was a member of several famous orchestras, but is chiefly remembered as one of the founders of a society for the support and aid of aged or disabled musicians and their families. D. London, July 24, 1872.

FÉTIS, FRANÇOIS JOSEPH, French violinist and musicologist, b. Mons, Mar. 25, 1784. As a violinist, Fétis made no reputation for himself, but his biography of Paganini and his treatise on Stradivarius are among the most important literary works of this character, and will serve to keep him among the elect. D. Brussels, Mar. 26, 1871.

FEUERMANN, SIGMUND, Austrian violinist, b. Kolomea, 1901. Studied under Sevcik. Appeared as soloist at Vienna in 1909, and with the London Philharmonic in 1910. Since then has made numerous successful tours of Europe and the United Kingdom.

FIORILLO, FEDERIGO, German violinist and composer, b. Brunswick, 1753. Studied the mandolin first and later took up the violin. In 1788 he appeared in London as soloist and as viola player in the Salomon Quartet. Compositions include concertos for the violin, concertantes for two violins and his famous "Thirty-Six Caprices" which are a classic among study works for the instrument. Fiorillo was in Paris in 1823, but the date and the place of his death are unknown.

FISCHER, JOHANN, German violinist and composer, b. Suabia, about 1650. Compositions include many solos for both violin and viola. In addition to being a virtuoso with ideas far in advance of his time, Fischer made use of the *scordatura, i.e.* special tunings of the violin strings, later much in vogue with Paganini and other players. D. Schwedt, about 1721.

FITELBURG, GEORG, Polish violinist and composer, b. Dünaberg, Oct. 18, 1879. Studied under Barcewicz. Concertmaster and later conductor of the Warsaw Philharmonic Orchestra. Compositions include violin concerto and sonatas, one of which gained him the Paderewski prize in 1896.

FLESCH, CARL, Hungarian violinist and music editor, b. Moson, Oct. 9, 1873. Studied under Grün and Marsick. Leader of Queen of Roumania's String Quartet. Gave five historical recitals at Berlin in 1909. Taught the violin at Bucharest, Amsterdam and Berlin. As editor has produced admirable editions of Kreutzer, Beethoven, Mendelssohn, Mozart and Paganini. As a performer on the violin he has a magnificent technique and a lofty intellectual style of interpretation.

FODOR, JOSEPH, German violinist and composer, b. Venloo in 1752. Studied under Franz Benda and made numerous successful tours through Europe as a virtuoso. Compositions include many violin concertos and light pieces. As a performer on the violin he was possessed of unusual technical skill, but Ludwig Spohr considered his playing lacking in true musical feeling. D. St. Petersburg, Oct. 3, 1828.

FOLVILLE, JULIETTE, Belgian violinist and composer, b. Liége, Jan. 5, 1870. Studied under Musin and Thomson. Has appeared as soloist successfully in France and Belgium, in addition to conducting her own orchestral works. Became a member of the Liége Conservatory faculty in 1898. Compositions include a concerto, a suite and smaller pieces for violin.

FONTANA, GIOVANNI BATISTA, Italian violinist and composer who published in 1641, eighteen sonatas for violin, accompanied by two or three violins and bass.

FRADKIN, FREDRIC, American violinist, b. Troy, N. Y., 1892. Studied under Schradieck, Remy, Lefort and Ysaÿe, and has been concertmaster of several European orchestras, also of the Boston Symphony Orchestra in 1918-19. Mr. Fradkin has also toured Great Britain with marked success.

FRANCOEUR, FRANÇOIS, French violinist and composer, b. Paris, Sept. 28, 1698. He published two sets of violin sonatas which indicated considerable progress in developing the instrument. One of his peculiarities was employing the thumb of the left hand to play a bass note on the fourth string of the violin. D. Paris, Aug. 6, 1787.

FRANKO, NAHAN, American violinist, b. New Orleans, July 23, 1861. Studied under Rappoldi, de Ahna, Wilhelmj and Joachim. Became concertmaster of the Metropolitan Opera House Orchestra, New York, for many years, and is now conducting his own orchestra for private engagements.

FRANKO, SAM, American violinist, b. New Orleans, Jan. 20, 1857. Studied under Joachim and Vieuxtemps. Appeared as soloist with the Breslau Philharmonic in 1867. Since that time has been in constant demand in the United States as soloist, concertmaster, ensemble player and teacher. Mr. Franko's concerts of ancient music in 1900-1909 were one of New York's distinct musical features. Compositions include a number of charming original pieces and some carefully edited selections from old composers.

FREDERIKSEN, FREDERIK CHRISTIAN, Norwegian violinist, b. Fredrikshold, Nov. 23, 1869. Studied under Sitt, Sauret and Marsick. Appeared as soloist with principal orchestras in Scandinavia, Germany and England. Taught the violin for twenty-five years in London. Is now teaching in Chicago where he plays an important part in the musical life of that city.

GALEAZZI, FRANCISCO, Italian violinist, teacher and composer, b. Turin, 1758. For many years leader of a theater orchestra in Rome and author of one of the earliest known methods for the violin. Compositions include works for the violin and chamber music. D. Rome, 1819.

GARAGUSI, NICHOLAS, American violinist, b. New York, of Italian parents. Studied under Hartmann, Schradieck, Musin and Lichtenberg. Toured the United States at an early age, and has since appeared as soloist and concertmaster of the New York Orchestral Society and the Russian Symphony Orchestra. He is now a member of the Detroit Symphony Orchestra, in addition to important ensemble and solo work.

GARCIN, JULES AUGUSTE, French violinist and composer, b. Bourges, July 11, 1830. Studied under Clavel and Alard at the Paris Conservatory, where he won the first prize in 1853, and later became solo violin and third conductor of the Opera Orchestra. The balance of his life was spent in acting as concertmaster or conductor of various orchestras, the crowning point reached being conductor of the Societé des Concerts. Compositions include a violin concerto and several graceful solos. As a performer on the violin he was a thorough artist, free from mannerisms which detract from real musicianship. D. Paris, Oct. 1896.

GARDNER, SAMUEL, Russian-American violinist and composer, b. Elizabethgrad, Russia. His family migrated at an early age to the United States where he studied under Winternitz in Boston and Kneisel at the New York Institute of Music Art, completing the full artist course. A prize was also awarded him by Columbia University for the composition of a string quartet. Has toured both the United States and Europe. Compositions include a violin concerto, orchestral and chamber music, as well as smaller violin pieces.

GAVINIÉS, PIERRE, French violinist and composer, b. Bordeaux, May 26, 1726. Chiefly self-taught. Appeared as soloist at the Concerts Spirituels in 1741. Became professor of the violin at the Paris Conservatory, being the first incumbent of this post which was founded in 1794. Compositions include his famous "Twenty-four Matinées," six concertos, as well as sonatas for one and two violins. As a performer on the violin, Viotti spoke of him as the French Tartini, and there is no doubt that he aided materially in inculcating the serious Italian principles of violin playing into France. D. Paris, Sept. 9, 1800.

GELOSO, ALBERT, Spanish violinist, b. Madrid, about 1860. Considered a very fine soloist and a remarkable ensemble player. D. Paris.

GEMINIANI, FRANCESCO, Italian violinist

PLATE 66

1. THELMA GIVEN.   2. EDWIN GRASSE.   3. PIERRE GAVINIÉS.   4. SAM-
UEL GARDNER.   5. JACQUES GORDON.   6. FRANCESCO GEMINIANI.
7. HENRY HOLMES.   8. GUSTAVE HOLLAENDER.

and composer, b. Lucca, about 1680. Studied under Lunati and Corelli. Appeared as soloist in Naples, London and Paris and remained a great part of his life in Dublin, with his pupil, Dubourg, who was head of the State Music in Ireland. Compositions include the first known violin method called *Art of Playing the Violin* Op. 9, published in English at London, and many solos, concertos and sonatas. As a performer on the violin he was eccentric, although an exponent of Corelli's masterful style. D. Dublin, Sept. 16, 1762.

GEYER, STEFI, Hungarian violinist, b. Budapest, 1893, studied with Jeno Hubay. Toured Germany, Austria-Hungary, Switzerland and Scandinavia, also appearing in joint recital with Marcel Dupré, the French organist. Her American debut was made in 1924. As a performer, Mme. Geyer is credited with an amazing technique, a broad tone and a noble interpretative style.

GHYS, JOSEPH, Belgian violinist and composer, b. Ghent, 1801. Studied under Lafont. Made numerous successful tours of France, Belgium, Germany, Austria and Scandinavia. Taught the violin at Amiens and Nantes. Compositions include a Violin Concerto, a "Perpetual Motion" for violin with string quartet, and other smaller works. D. St. Petersburg, Aug. 22, 1848, while on a concert tour.

GIARDINI, FELICE DE, Italian violinist and composer, b. Turin, April 12, 1716. Studied under Somis. Member of the Opera Orchestra at Rome and Naples. Appeared as soloist in Italy, Germany, France and England, where he immediately became an immense favorite until Salomon displaced him in public regard. Compositions include twelve violin concertos and much chamber music. As a performer on the violin he had a splendid technique and a powerful but mellow tone. D. Moscow, Dec. 17, 1796.

GIBSON, ALFRED, English violinist, b. Nottingham, Oct. 27, 1849. Studied under Henry Farmer. Appeared as soloist at Nottingham in 1861 and has since become one of England's best-known orchestral and quartet players. Became leader in 1893 of Queen Victoria's private band. Directed the music at both King Edward VII and King George's coronations. Teaches violin and viola at the Royal Academy and the Guildhall School of Music.

GIORGETTI, FERDINANDO, Italian violinist

and composer, b. Florence, June 25, 1796. Compositions include a "Concerto Dramatico" for violin and much chamber music. An admirable virtuoso violinist and teacher at the Florence "Liceo Musicale." D. at Florence, Mar. 23, 1867.

GITTELSON, FRANK, American violinist, b. Philadelphia, June 12, 1896. Studied under Auer and Flesch. Appeared as soloist in Berlin under the baton of Gabrilowitsch. Made a successful tour in Germany, Austria and Holland. Returned to the United States in 1914 as soloist with the Philadelphia Orchestra. In 1919 became professor of violin at the Peabody Conservatory, Baltimore.

GIVEN, THELMA, American violinist, b. Columbus, Ohio, March 9, 1898, pupil of Leopold Auer, with whom she studied for six years. After touring Scandinavia, Miss Given returned to the United States, making her debut at Carnegie Hall Nov. 3, 1918, receiving the highest praise for her interpretative and technical skill.

GLUCK, MARGEL, American violinist, b. Buffalo, N. Y. Studied under Witek, Sevcik and Auer. Appeared as soloist at Aeolian Hall, London, in 1908, under the patronage of the Duchess of Somerset. Has since concertized in Europe and the United States as recitalist and in collaboration with well-known singers.

GOMPERTZ, RICHARD, German violinist and composer, b. Cologne, April 27, 1859. Studied under Joachim. Appeared as soloist at the Gurzenich Concerts, Cologne, and made numerous successful tours of European cities, finally coming to Cambridge, England, and from there to London, in both of which places he was instrumental in raising the standards of quartet playing and of violin teaching at the University and at the Royal Academy of Music. Compositions include a violin concerto, sonatas and smaller pieces.

GORDON, JACQUES, Russian violinist, b. Odessa. Studied under Franz Stupka at the Imperial Conservatory where he was awarded a gold medal. Made a successful tour of Europe and came to the United States where he studied further under Franz Kneisel, in addition to numerous solo and chamber music appearances. At present, Mr. Gordon is concertmaster of the Chicago Symphony Orchestra, leader of the Gordon String Quartet and professor of violin at the American Conservatory of

Music, Chicago. His compositions include a violin concerto (in mss.).

GOW, NEIL, Scotch violinist, b. Strathband, Mar. 22, 1727. Practically self-instructed. Sprang into public notice for his playing of Scotch tunes, and finally became the rage in London. His son, Nathaniel, born in 1763, after the father's death in 1807, succeeded him as performer and composer of the type of dance music popular in Scotland, besides becoming a publisher on a large scale of this class of music. His brothers, William, Andrew and John were also engaged either in the profession or business of music.

GRAAN, JEAN DE, Dutch violinist, b. Amsterdam, Sept. 9, 1852. Studied under Joachim but passed away before he came into the possession of his full powers. D. the Hague, Jan. 8, 1874.

GRASSE, EDWIN, American violinist and composer, b. New York, Aug. 13, 1884. Blind from infancy. Studied under César Thomson. Appeared as soloist at Berlin in 1902, playing the Sinding Concerto. Played the Brahms Concerto at his American debut in 1903. Mr. Grasse is also an organist of the highest rank. Has made numerous successful tours in the United States and his compositions include a concerto, several sonatas and smaller works for the violin and for organ.

GRASSET, JEAN JACQUES, French violinist and composer, b. Paris, about 1769. Studied under Berthaume and became concertmaster of the Italian opera as well as professor of violin at the Paris Conservatory, succeeding Gaviniés. Compositions include three concertos, a sonata, and violin duets. D. Paris, 1839.

GRASSI, ANTONIO DE, Italian violinist, b. near Venice, Feb. 17, 1880. Studied under Joachim, Sevcik and Ysaÿe. First appearance at Petrograd in 1905, followed by concerts in all the principal cities of Europe. Since 1915 has made his home in San Francisco, as the head of an especially fine trio organization, and as a private teacher. Compositions include several interesting violin pieces.

GRAUN, JOHANN GOTTLIEB, German violinist and composer, b. Wahrenbruck, about 1698. Studied under Pisendal and after various engagements, became conductor to Frederick the Great (then Crown Prince) in 1728 and held this position at Berlin the rest of his life. Compositions include violin concertos and much chamber music. D. Berlin, Oct. 27, 1771.

GREGOROVITCH, CHARLES, Russian violinist, b. Petrograd, Oct. 25, 1867. Studied under Besekirsky, Wieniawski, Dont and Joachim. Appeared first in Berlin in 1886 as a virtuoso of the highest rank and has toured Europe and the United States with success.

GRESSER, EMILY, American violinist, b. Newark, N. J., Mar. 11, 1894. Studied under Sam Franko. Has appeared as soloist with famous orchestras in Berlin, Hanover, Munich and Cologne, and has made numerous successful tours throughout Europe. Has toured the United States with success and as a performer on the violin is regarded as one of the best artists of the day.

GRIMSON, JESSIE, English violinist. Studied under Holmes, Gompertz and Wilhelmj. Awarded a scholarship at the Royal College of Music. Appeared as soloist at the Crystal Palace Concerts and founded the Grimson Quartet which has appeared with great success at concerts throughout Great Britain and on the Continent.

GRUENBERG, EUGÈNE, Austrian violinist and composer, b. Lemberg, Oct. 30, 1854. Studied under Heissler and Hellmsberger. Member of Leipzig Gewandhaus and Boston Symphony Orchestras. Since 1899 has taught violin and ensemble playing at the New England Conservatory. Compositions include a suite, a sonata and smaller works for the violin, in addition to two books on teaching subjects.

GRÜN, JACOB, Hungarian violinist and teacher, b. Budapest, Mar. 13, 1837. Studied under Bohm in Vienna. Made numerous successful tours of Europe in addition to becoming concertmaster of the Imperial Opera at Vienna Conservatory where he instructed many famous pupils (among them Franz Kneisel), his labors extending over a period of thirty-two years.

GRÜNBERG, PAUL EMIL MAX, German violinist, teacher and musicologist, b. Berlin, Dec. 5, 1852. Member of several famous European orchestras and instructor at the Stern Conservatory, Berlin. Has written a valuable guide to stringed instrument music.

GUHR, KARL WILLIAM FERDINAND, German violinist, b. Militsch, Oct. 30, 1787. An artist of considerable ability, who wrote down from memory several compositions played by Paganini which without him would never have been known. He is also the author of a book on Paganini's art of playing the violin. D. Frankfort-on-the-Main, July, 1848.

GUICHARDON, ANDRÉ, French violinist, b. Bordeaux in Sept., 1860. Studied under Dancla and Leonard. An artist of high rank now teaching at the Vidon Conservatory.

GUIDI, SCIPIONE, Italian violinist, b. Vincenza, 1884. Studied at the Milan Conservatory, where he later became professor of the violin. Appeared as soloist in Milan in 1895 and in London in 1908. Came to the United States to become a member of the New York Philharmonic Society.

GUIGNON, PIERRE, Italian violinist, b. Turin, Feb. 10, 1702. Studied the violin in Paris, developing a splendid tone and technique and becoming a rival of Leclair. In 1733, he entered the King's service as musical instructor of the Dauphin and was the last "King of the Violins" an office which enabled its holder to collect fees from all musicians, even organists, as "dancing masters."

HAACK, KARL, German violinist and composer, b. Potsdam, Feb. 18, 1751. Studied under Franz Benda and became concertmaster for the King of Prussia. Compositions include concertos and sonatas for the violin. He was an excellent exponent of Benda's school of violin playing, among its pupils being Moser and Maurer. D. Potsdam, Sept. 28, 1819.

HABENECK, FRANÇOIS ANTOINE, French violinist, composer and conductor, b. Mezieres, Jan. 23, 1781. Studied under Baillot at the Paris Conservatory and was awarded first prize in 1804. Appeared as soloist, concertmaster and conductor of prominent Paris orchestras and operatic organizations. From 1825-1848 he taught a special violin class at the Paris Conservatory, among the pupils being Cuvillon, Alard, Clapisson and Leonard. Compositions include violin concertos and solo pieces. Habeneck was the first conductor to introduce Beethoven's Symphonies into fame with French audiences, against opposition of the most determined character. D. Paris, Feb. 8, 1849.

HADDOCK, GEORGE, English violinist, b. near Leeds, July 24, 1824. Studied under Vieuxtemps and Molique and established a large class for violin instruction in Leeds which was eventually merged into the Leeds Conservatory, by his two sons, Edgar and George, founders of same. He was also the author of a violin school in three parts, and made a remarkable collection of old violins and cellos. D. Leeds, 1907.

HAIGH, THOMAS, English violinist and composer, b. London, 1769. Studied composition under Haydn in 1791 and composed a violin concerto and twelve sonatas. He also arranged Haydn's symphonies for violin with piano accompaniment. D. London, 1808.

HALIR, CARL, Bohemian violinist, b. Hohenelbe, Feb. 1, 1859. Studied under Bennewitz and Joachim. Appeared as soloist and concertmaster of various celebrated European orchestras and made numerous successful tours of France, Russia, Germany and England. Visited the United States in 1896. Taught the violin at the Berlin Hochshule under Joachim and was a second violinist of the Joachim Quartet. His interpretation of the Beethoven Concerto was considered incomparable. D. Berlin, Dec. 21, 1909.

HALL, AUTUMN, American violinist, b. New Richmond, Pa., Nov. 16, 1892. Studied under Heerman and Thomson. Made numerous successful tours in Europe. Came to the United States in 1910 as soloist of the Pittsburg Symphony Orchestra under Emil Paur. Since that time has concertized and taught the violin.

HALL, MARIE, English violinist, b. Newcastle-on-Tyne, April 8, 1884. Studied under Wilhelmj, Kruse and Sevcik. Appeared as soloist in Prague in 1902 and at St. James Hall, London, in 1903. Has made successful tours of Europe, Great Britain, the United States, Canada and Australia. As a performer on the violin, Miss Hall possesses a splendid technique, a beautiful tone and a fine sense of musical values.

HALLÉ, LADY. See Neruda, Norman.

HALVORSEN, JOHANN, Norwegian violinist and composer, b. Drammen, Mar. 15, 1864. Studied under Lindberg, Brodsky and Thomson. Has toured Europe and acted as concertmaster of a number of Scandinavian organizations. Compositions include a concerto and two suites for violin with piano accompaniment.

HAMBOURG, JAN, Russian violinist, b. Voronesh, Aug. 27, 1882. Studied under Wilhelmj, Sauret, Heerman, Sevcik and

ˊsaÿe. Appeared as soloist in Berlin in 1905. Made numerous successful tours of Germany, France, Holland, Great Britain and the United States. Has two equally famous brothers, Mark (pianist) and Boris (cellist) with whom he gave about 100 ensemble concerts during a tour of Great Britain in 1909.

HANSEN, CELIA, Russian-Danish violinist, b. at a Russian Cossack Settlement, about 1898. Studied with Leopold Auer, winning first prize at the Petrograd Conservatory in 1914. Toured Finland, Germany, Austria, Czecho-Slovakia and Scandinavia, appearing with all the prominent orchestras. Made her American debut with great success as soloist with the Boston, New York and other symphony orchestras, and is credited with a remarkable technique and tone.

HARMATI, SANDOR, Hungarian violinist and composer, b. Budapest, July 9, 1892. Studied under Jeno Hubay. Appeared as concertmaster with the Budapest Symphony and other famous orchestral organizations and as second violin of the Letz Quartet. Compositions include pieces for violin and piano.

HARRISON, MAY, English violinist, b. Roorkee, India, March, 1891. Studied under Arbor, Rivarde and Auer. Appeared as soloist at St. James Hall at the age of thirteen; with the Madrid Symphony at fifteen; took Kreisler's place at a Mendelssohn Festival in Helsingfors at eighteen; appeared with the Berlin Philharmonic Orchestra at nineteen and has since toured all over the world. Her sister, Beatrice, is a famous cello virtuoso.

HARTMANN, ARTHUR, Hungarian violinist and composer, b. Maté Szalka, July 23, 1881. Studied under Charles Loeffler and at the age of twelve knew practically the whole modern violin repertory. Appeared as soloist with the leading orchestras of the United States and has made numerous successful tours of all Europe, particularly in Paris with Claude Debussy. Taught the violin in New York, among his pupils being numbered Sol Marcosson and Nicholas Garagusi. Compositions include a suite and several solos for violin, also a number of interesting transcriptions, including the discovery and editing of six sonatas by Giardini. As a performer on the violin he is specially noted for a pure tone, splendid technical ability and musicianly interpretation.

HAUSER, MISKA, Hungarian violinist and composer, b. Pressburg, 1822. Studied under Böhm and Mayseder. He made a tour of the world when only twelve years of age, and the balance of an active career, up to about 1860, was spent concertizing all over Europe, America, South America and Australia. Compositions include a Hungarian rhapsody and several "Songs Without Words" which are highly regarded. As a performer on the violin his technique was marvelous and his tone full of passion and animation. D. Vienna, Dec. 9, 1887.

HECKMANN, GEORG JULIUS ROBERT, German violinist, b. Mannheim, Nov. 3, 1848. Studied under David at the Leipzig Conservatory and became concertmaster of orchestras at that city and Cologne. In 1875 formed the Heckmann Quartet, one of the finest organizations in the world, demonstrating conclusively how perfect ensemble can be obtained by the constant association of the same players in rehearsal. D. Glasgow, Nov. 29, 1891.

HEERMAN, HUGO, German violinist, b. Heilbronn, Mar. 3, 1844. Studied under Meerts and Deberiot at the Brussels Conservatory and also for three years in Paris. Appeared as soloist with the Frankfort Orchestra in 1865 and made numerous successful tours of Europe and Great Britain. Came to the United States in 1907 as head of the violin department at the Chicago Conservatory and returned in 1910 to Europe, occupying professorships at various conservatories and editing a new edition of Deberiot's Violin School.

HEGAR, FRIEDRICH, Swiss violinist and composer, b. Basle, Oct. 11, 1841. Appeared as concertmaster and conductor of several notable orchestras in Zurich. Compositions include a concerto for the violin.

HEIFETZ, JASCHA, Russian violinist, b. Vilna, 1899. Studied under Leopold Auer after manifesting musical ability at three years of age. At six years, he appeared as soloist in Kovno playing the Mendelssohn Concerto. Since that time he has made numerous successful tours of Europe, Great Britain, America and the Far East. Came to the United States in 1917 touring as recitalist and as soloist with all the larger symphonic organizations. As a performer on the violin he has an impeccable technique and a broad, fervid style which makes him a virtuoso of the first rank.

HELLMSBERGER, GEORG (SR.), Austrian violinist, teacher and composer, b. Vienna,

April 24, 1800. Studied under Böhm and became professor of violin at the Vienna Conservatory, where he instructed a great number of distinguished pupils including Ernst, Joachim, Hauser, Auer and also his own sons, Georg and Josef. Compositions include two concertos and many other violin pieces. He was one of the world's greatest violin teachers and was held in the highest esteem all his life. D. Neuwaldegg, Aug. 16, 1873.

HELLMSBERGER, GEORG (JR.), Austrian violinist, b. Vienna, Jan. 27, 1830. Studied under his father and made a concert tour in 1847 with him through Germany and England, after which he devoted himself to composing, in addition to becoming concertmaster at the Hanover Opera House. D. Hanover, Nov. 12, 1852.

HELLMSBERGER, JOSEPH (SR.), Austrian violinist, b. Vienna, Nov. 23, 1829. Studied under his father at the Leipzig Conservatory, where he became professor of the violin himself when but twenty-one years old. In 1860 he became leader of the Court Opera Orchestra and three years later succeeded Mayseder as director of the Imperial Band. In 1849 he founded the Hellmsberger Quartet, an organization which not only was one of the finest the world has ever heard, but which awoke the first real general interest in Beethoven's later quartets and in other works by talented composers which had been sadly neglected. D. Vienna, Oct. 24, 1893.

HELLMSBERGER, JOSEF (JR.), Austrian violinist and composer, b. Vienna, April 9, 1855. Studied under his father (Joseph, Sr.), playing second violin in the Hellmsberger Quartet from 1875 and succeeding him as leader in 1887. Also occupies position as professor at the Conservatory and has written several successful operettas.

HENLEY, WILLIAM, English violinist and composer, b. West Bromwich in 1874. Studied with Henry Holmes, Willy Hess, Emile Sauret and August Wilhelmj, acquiring experience in quartet playing under the latter. Has toured England, France and Germany with remarkable success. His compositions are all of the pleasing salon variety; he has also written a book on solo playing and a violin school.

HENRIQUES, FINI VALDEMAR, Danish violinist and composer, b. Copenhagen, Dec. 20, 1867. Studied under Svendsen and Joachim. Member of Court Orchestra at Copenhagen.

Compositions include a violin sonata and suite.

HERBST, GOTTFRIED, German violinist, b. Mulhausen, June 21, 1887. Studied under Joachim. Appeared as concertmaster with orchestras in Gera, Erfurt and Coburg. Came to the United States in 1912 as Professor at the State College, Pullman, Wash. Mr. Herbst gave Mozart's Seventh Concerto, which was discovered in 1907, its first performance at the Coburg Opera House in 1908.

HERING, KARL FRIEDRICH AUGUST, German violinist, b. Berlin, Sept. 2, 1819. Studied under Ries, Rungenhagen, Lipinski and Tomaschek. Made numerous successful tours and became violinist in the Berlin Royal Chapel. Compositions include chamber music and several educational treatises, also a violin method. D. near Magdeburg, Feb. 2, 1889.

HERMANN, FRIEDRICH, German violinist, composer and teacher, b. Frankfort, Feb. 1, 1828. Studied under David at the Leipzig Conservatory. Member of the Gewandhaus Orchestra and in 1848 became violin teacher at the Conservatory. Compositions include chamber music and a trio for three violins. He also edited in a masterly manner many classical violin works for the Peters and the Augener editions.

HERRMAN, EDWARD, German violinist, b. Oberrohweil, Dec. 18, 1850. Studied under Joachim. Appeared as soloist at Stuttgart in 1871. Made numerous successful tours of Germany, Switzerland, Holland and Russia. Came to the United States for a concert at Steinway Hall, New York in 1881. Since then has been identified with the musical life of New York, founding both a quartet and trio, and teaching the violin, among his pupils being the distinguished amateur violinist and musical dilettante, Maurice Sternberger, whose collection of music, musical literature and pictures has been of great assistance in the preparation of this encyclopedia. (Editor)

HERWEGH, MARCEL, French violinist, b. Zurich, of French parents, 1858. Studied under Edward Singer, and has achieved a reputation as a serious artist with a gift for the interpretation of the classics. He has also prepared a splendid edition of Leclair's twelve violin concertos.

HERZFELD, VICTOR VON, Austrian violinist and composer, b. Pressburg, Oct. 8, 1856. Studied at the Vienna Conservatory where

PLATE 67

1. BRONISLAW HUBERMAN.   2. HUGO HEERMANN.   3. JOSEPH HELLMES-
BERGER.   4. CELIA HANSEN.   5. MARIE HALL.   6. MISKA HAUSER.
7. JOHAN HALVORSEN.   8. ARTHUR HARTMANN.

he was awarded first prize for violin playing in 1880. Finally settled in Budapest as professor at the Academy of Music and second violin of the Hubay-Popper Quartet. Compositions include orchestral and chamber music.

HESS, WILLY, German violinist, b. Mannheim, July 14, 1859. Studied under his father and first appeared at eleven years of age in New York, afterwards touring with the Thomas Orchestra. Returned to Europe and in 1876 studied two years with Joachim, after which he held various positions of importance in Germany and England, coming to the United States in 1904. Succeeded Franz Kneisel as concertmaster of the Boston Symphony Orchestra and founded the Hess-Schroeder Quartet. In 1910 he returned to Berlin where he succeeded Halir as professor at the Royal High School and as first violin of the Halir Quartet. His playing combines the intellectual qualities of the German school with a freedom and verve all his own.

HILF, ARNO, German violinist, b. Bad Elster, Mar. 16, 1858. Studied under David, Röntgen and Schradieck. Became professor of violin at the Moscow Conservatory in 1878 under Anton Rubinstein and in 1891 succeeded Brodsky as professor at the Leipzig Conservatory and as leader of the Brodsky quartet. As a performer on the violin he possessed an enormous technique and was rated equally high as a quartet player. D. August 2, 1909.

HILL, HENRY, English viola player, b. London, July 2, 1808. Studied under various teachers but raised himself to the high position as violist which he occupied by ability to study alone and become self-critical. He was one of the founders of the Beethoven Quartet Society and also played the solo viola part in Berlioz's "Harold" Symphony, upon the occasion of its first performance in London in 1848. D. London, June 11, 1856.

HILL, THOMAS HENRY WEIST, English violinist, b. London, Jan. 23, 1828. Studied under Sainton at the Royal Academy of Music. Appeared as soloist at a Royal Academy concert in 1847 and shortly after visited the United States, where he introduced the Mendelssohn Violin Concerto. He afterwards became a distinguished conductor of concerts in London. D. London, Dec. 25, 1891.

HILL, URELI C., American violinist, b.

New York, 1802. Studied under Spohr and was the founder and first president of the New York Philharmonic Society, playing first violin himself in the orchestra. D. New York, 1875.

HILLE, GUSTAV, German violinist, b. Jerichow, May 21, 1851. Studied under Joachim at the Royal High School, Berlin. Came to the United States in 1879 as a member of the Boston Mendelssohn Quartet and the Philadelphia Academy of Music. Compositions include violin sonatas, suites and a concerto for two violins.

HINTON, ARTHUR, English violinist and composer, b. Beckenham, Nov. 20, 1869. Studied violin under Sainton and Sauret and composition under Davenport and Rheinberger. Became assistant violin professor at the Royal Academy but has devoted his time more to conducting and composition. Compositions include a sonata and a suite for violin and piano.

HOCHSTEIN, DAVID, American violinist, b. Rochester, N. Y., Feb. 16, 1892. Studied under Auer and Sevcik and was awarded a scholarship at the Vienna Meisterschule. In 1911 he appeared as soloist at Vienna and made a successful tour of Europe, Great Britain and the United States. He was killed in the World War.

HOEVEL, HEINRICH, German violinist and musicologist, b. Bonn, June 22, 1864. Studied under Konigsloew and Wasielewski. Has taught the violin for twenty-four years in Minneapolis, Minn. Has published a number of important treatises on Bach's violin music, Cremona violins and modern French chamber music.

HOFFMAN, KAREL, Bohemian violinist, b. Prague, Dec. 12, 1872. Studied at the Prague Conservatory under Bennewitz and became leader of the Bohemian Quartet, one of the greatest chamber music organizations in the world.

HOLLAENDER, GUSTAV, German violinist, teacher and composer, b. Leobschütz, Feb. 15, 1855. Studied under David and Joachim. Became professor of violin at Kullak's Academy, and toured Austria with Adelina Patti. In 1881 he became professor at the Cologne Conservatory and leader of its String Quartet, besides making numerous successful tours of Belgium, Holland and Germany. In 1894 he became director of the Stern Conservatory at Berlin. Compositions include concertos, concertinos and smaller violin pieces. As a performer on the violin he combines unusual talent with artistic exactness.

HOLLANDER, BENNO, Dutch violinist and composer, b. Amsterdam, June 5, 1853. Studied under Massart at the Paris Conservatory, taking first prize for violin playing in 1873. After a successful tour of Europe, he came to London in 1876 where he has acted as soloist with and concertmaster of many prominent orchestras (including one founded by him) with great success. Compositions include concertos, sonatas, fantasias and smaller violin pieces.

HEGEDUS, FERENCZ, Hungarian violinist, b. Funfkirchen, Feb. 26, 1881. Studied under Gobbi and Hubay at Budapest Conservatory and at the Royal Academy of Music where he was granted a special diploma at the age of eighteen. Has made numerous successful tours of Europe, Great Britain and the United States. As a performer his playing is marked by fire and racial abandon without overstepping the bounds of artistic restraint.

HOLMES, ALFRED AND HENRY, English violinists and composers, b. at London in 1837 and 1839. Studied under their father from Spohr's Violin School and made their first public appearance as duettists at the Haymarket Theater, July 13, 1847. They then toured Europe with great success, playing at Cassel for Ludwig Spohr, who dedicated his three grand duos to them. In 1864, Alfred Holmes settled in Paris, where he established a quartet and composed a great deal of music, dying there Mar. 4, 1876. Henry Holmes established himself in London, where he became well-known as a concert and quartet performer. He composed a concerto and many solos for the violin. He afterwards came to San Francisco, Cal., where he died, Dec. 9, 1905.

HOLZ, KARL, Austrian violinist, b. Vienna, 1798. Became a member of Schuppanzigh's Quartet in 1824 and was on terms of the closest intimacy with Beethoven. D. Vienna, Nov. 9, 1858.

HRIMALY, JOHANN, Bohemian violinist and teacher, b. Pilsen, April 13, 1844. Studied under Mildner at the Prague Conservatory. Succeeded Ferdinand Laub as professor at the Moscow Conservatory in 1875, also becoming the concertmaster of the Conservatory orchestra and leader of the Mazar Violin School.

HUBAY, JENO, Hungarian violinist and composer, b. Budapest, Sept. 15, 1858. Studied under his father, violin professor at the Budapest Academy of Music and with Joachim at Berlin. Appeared as soloist in Hungary in 1876, followed by concerts in Paris, where he became friendly with Vieuxtemps. Became professor of violin at the Brussels Conservatory and finally succeeded his father as professor at the Budapest National Academy of Music and leader of the Hubay-Popper Quartet, a famous chamber music organization. Compositions include four violin concertos, a "Sonata Romantique" and many violin works of lesser importance.

HUBERMANN, BRONISLAW, Polish violinist, b. Czentstochowa, Dec. 19, 1882. Studied under Michalowisz, Lotto and Joachim. In 1893 he appeared as a child prodigy at Amsterdam, Brussels and Paris, and at Vienna with Adelina Patti. In 1896, he played the Brahms Concerto in Vienna with the composer in the audience, and earned his hearty commendation. Since that time, he has toured all of Europe and America many times. During his Italian tour in 1893, he was requested by the Municipal Authorities of Genoa to play on Paganini's violin, an honor conferred previously on only one other violinist, Camillo Sivori.

HÜLLWECK, FERDINAND, German violinist and teacher, b. Dessau, Oct. 8, 1824. Studied under Franz Schneider. Leader of the Dresden Orchestra and violin professor in the Dresden Conservatory, retiring in 1886. Compositions include a number of valuable educational violin works. D. Blasewitz, July 24, 1887.

HURSTINEN, SULO, Finnish violinist and composer, b. Helsingfors, Dec. 1, 1881. Studied under Sevcik and Halir. Made a successful tour of Germany, Finland and Scandinavia. Taught the violin at the Helsingfors Musical Institute. Compositions include pieces for violin and piano and a violin method.

JACKSON, LEONORA, American violinist, b. Boston, Mass., Feb. 20, 1879. Studied under Joachim at the Royal Hochschule in Berlin, receiving Mendelssohn prize from the government. Appeared as soloist with the Leipzig Gewandhaus Orchestra, and with Paderewski and Adelina Patti. Made numerous successful tours of Europe. Came to the United States to appear with the Boston Symphony Orchestra and at more than 150 concerts in 1901. As a performer on the violin she possessed a splendid technique and a beautiful tone tinged with intense sentiment.

JACOBSEN, SASCHA, Russian-American violinist. Began the study of the violin at the age of eight in Russia, and at eleven came to America with his parents. His artistic education was completed under Franz Kneisel in New York, without the customary finishing touches in Europe, and he is now recognized as among the most promising of the younger artists. Mr. Jacobsen has been soloist with many of the largest symphony orchestras, and has appeared in sonata recitals with Levitzki, Powell, Ornstein and others.

JACOBSEN, SIMON E., German violinist, b. Mitau, Dec. 24, 1839. Studied at the Leipzig Conservatory and resided at Bremen for some years concertizing and teaching. Came to the United States in 1872 as concertmaster of the Theodore Thomas Orchestra, after which he became first violin of the Mendelssohn Quintette Club in Boston, and later teacher of violin at Cincinnati and Chicago Conservatories. D. Chicago, Oct. 3, 1902.

JAFFÉ, MORITZ, German violinist and composer, b. Posen, Jan. 3, 1835. Studied under Ries, Maurin, Massart and Laub. Compositions include much violin music and a string quartet.

JAFFÉ, SOPHIA, Russian violinist, b. Odessa, Feb. 26, 1872. Studied under Auer, Massart and Sauzay. Made numerous successful tours of Germany and upon inheriting a fortune retired from the concert stage.

JANIEWICZ, FELIX, Polish violinist and composer, b. Wilna, 1762. Went to hear Haydn and Mozart conduct their compositions in Vienna, and was preparing to study composition under Haydn when he received an offer to go to Italy under the protection of a Polish gentlewoman which he accepted, thus being enabled to hear Nardini and Pugnani. Later he appeared in London at the Salomon concerts and not only was one of the original members of the Philharmonic Society but also embarked successfully in the music publishing business. Compositions include violin concertos and trios for two violins and bass. D. Edinburgh, 1848.

JANSA, LEOPOLD, Bohemian violinist and composer, b. Wildenschwert, Mar. 23, 1795. Devoted himself to the study of law in accordance with the wish of his father, but

gave it up to devote himself to music. Became conductor of music at the University of Vienna and finally went to London where he developed a teaching practice, one of his pupils being Lady Hallé (Norman Neruda). Compositions include violin concertos, duets and string quartets. D. Vienna, Jan. 24, 1875.

JAPHA, GEORGE JOSEPH, German violinist and conductor, b. Konigsberg, Aug. 28, 1835. Studied under David, Dreyschock, Singer and Alard. Member of Gewandhaus Orchestra at Leipzig. Made numerous successful tours through Germany and Russia. Organized chamber music concerts with Adolf Jensen at Konigsburg and finally became professor of violin at the Cologne Conservatory as well as conductor of the Gurzenich concerts. D. Cologne, Feb. 25, 1892.

JARNOVIC, (GIORNOVICCHI) GIOVANNI, Italian violinist and composer, b. Palermo in 1745. Studied under Lolli. In 1770 he appeared as soloist at the Concerts Spirituels at Paris. Made a successful tour of Europe, reaching London where he met with Viotti, with whom he would have successfully competed if it had not been for his arrogant manners. Compositions include concertos, sonatas and string quartets of light and agreeable character. D. suddenly at St. Petersburg about 1804.

JEHIN (JEHIN-PRUME), FRANÇOIS, Belgian violinist and composer, b. Spa, April 18, 1839. Studied under Deberiot, Leonard, Wieniawski and Vieuxtemps. Appeared as soloist at Dresden and toured Russia with Rubinstein, Jenny Lind and Annette Esipoff. Made a successful tour of Germany, Belgium, Scandinavia and Holland, where he was appointed violinist to the King of Belgium. Came to the United States in 1869 touring with Carlotta Patti, afterwards settling in Montreal, Canada, as teacher and leader of a quartet. He succeeded Vieuxtemps as head of the Belgian school. As a performer on the violin he was endowed with a superb technique and a sweet, pure tone. Compositions include two concertos and many brilliant solo numbers. D. Montreal, Canada, May 29, 1899.

JENKINS, JOHN, English violinist and composer, b. Maidstone, Kent, in 1592. Appeared as a court musician under Charles I but retired into private life during the long period of civil wars. He was the composer of the first sonatas written by an Englishman for the violin.

PLATE 68

1. JASCHA HEIFETZ. 2. JENÖ HUBAY. 3. JOSEPH JOACHIM. 4. CARL HALIR. 5. WILLY HESS. 6. FRANÇOIS HABENECK. 7. SASCHA JACOBSEN. 8. SIMON E. JACOBSOHN.

JENSEN, GUSTAV, German violinist and composer, b. Konigsberg, Dec. 25, 1843. Studied under Joachim and Laub. Member of Konigsberg Orchestra and Professor of counterpoint at the Cologne Conservatory, devoting most of his leisure to composition. Compositions include a violin sonata and chamber music. D. Cologne, Nov. 26, 1895.

JOACHIM, JOSEPH, Hungarian violinist, composer and teacher, b. near Pressburg, June 28, 1831. Studied under Szeraczinski and with Bohm at the Vienna Conservatory, making his debut in 1844 in Maurer's Quadruple Concerto for four violins with Bazzini, Ernst and David. He also appeared with the Leipzig Gewandhaus Orchestra making that city his home until 1849, under the influence of Schumann, Mendelssohn and David who undoubtedly aided in molding his artistic career. For a time he was concertmaster at Weimar under Liszt, and later was appointed head of the Berlin Hochschule, becoming the life and soul of that institution to such a degree that Berlin became the Mecca of all violinists, after the death of David in Leipzig (1873). The quartet which he founded with De Ahna, Wirth and Hausman was without question the greatest chamber music organization the world has ever seen, due to the fidelity with which it performed the works of the great classic composers, and Joachim's solo playing was characterized by breadth and dignity, especially in his performance of the classic violin masterpieces. His quartet appeared frequently in London and on the continent with great success. Joachim's compositions comprise three violin concertos (including the "Hungarian Concerto") and a number of smaller pieces as well as three cadenzas to the Beethoven Concerto. D. Berlin, Aug. 15, 1907.

JULIEN, PAUL, French violinist, b. Brest, Feb. 12, 1841. Studied at the Paris Conservatory where he won first prize in 1850. Appeared in the United States in 1853 and in 1866, when he was drowned in a voyage between New York and Savannah, Oct. 4, 1866.

JUON, PAUL, Russian violinist, b. Moscow, Mar. 9, 1872. Studied under Hrimaly and finished his studies at the Berlin Hochschule, where he became professor of composition in 1906. Has also visited the United States playing and conducting his own compositions. Compositions include a concerto

and a sonata for violin and much chamber music.

KALLIWODA, JOHANNES WENZEL, Bohemian violinist and composer, b. Prague, Feb. 22, 1801. Studied under Pixis at the Prague Conservatory. Became concertmaster to Prince Fürstenberg at Donaueschingen after which he retired to Karlsruhe. Compositions include a concerto, a double concerto and a number of violin solos. D. Karlsruhe, Dec. 3, 1866.

KÄSSMEYER, MORITZ, Austrian violinist and composer, b. Vienna, 1831. Studied under Sechter and Preyer. Became a member of the Vienna Opera Orchestra. Compositions include several humorous but musically well-written string quartets.

KAUFMAN, MAURICE, American violinist, b. New York, June 19, 1876. Studied at several conservatories and with César Thomson. Made numerous successful tours of Europe and the United States; becoming concertmaster of the Russian Symphony, Volpe Symphony and other New York organizations; in addition to quartet playing with Leo Schulz and others. Has taught the violin in New York for over twenty years.

KAYSER, HEINRICH ERNST, German violinist and teacher, b. Altona, April 16, 1815. An excellent violinist and teacher. Compositions include a number of valuable exercises as well as a violin method. D. Hamburg, Jan. 17, 1888.

KES, WILLEM, Dutch violinist, b. Dordrecht, Feb. 16, 1856. Studied under Böhm, David, Wieniawski and Joachim, and while a thorough artist, on the piano as well as the violin, he has turned his attention to and made a splendid reputation as a conductor.

KIALLMARK, GEORGE, English violinist and composer, b. King's Lynn, 1781. Studied under Barthelemon and Spagnoletti and became leader of several well-known orchestras in the United Kingdom. D. Islington, 1835.

KLASS, GEORGE, Polish violinist, b. Warsaw, April 27, 1887. Studied under Barcevicz and Auer. Became concertmaster of the Warsaw Philharmonic Orchestra and assistant concertmaster of the Munich Konzertverein Orchestra under Nikisch, Weingartner and Richard Straus. Now teaching the violin in Minneapolis, Minnesota.

KLEIN, KARL, American violinist, b. New

York, Dec. 13, 1884. Studied under Hilf, Ysaÿe and Wilhelmj. In 1905 appeared as soloist with the Queen's Hall orchestra, and in Leipzig, Berlin and Vienna. Returned to the United States in 1907 as soloist and concertmaster with well-known orchestras in New York where he now resides.

KNEISEL, FRANZ, Roumanian violinist, b. Bucharest, Jan. 26, 1865. Studied under Grün and Hellmsberger at the Vienna Conservatory. In 1882 he appeared as soloist with the Vienna Philharmonic Orchestra, and later became concertmaster of the Bilse Orchestra in Berlin. Came to the United States in 1885 as concertmaster of the Boston Symphony Orchestra and in 1885 founded the string quartet which has made his name famous (see article on "Chamber Music") resigning his position as concertmaster in 1903 in order to devote all his time to the quartet. In addition, Kneisel has acted as assistant conductor of the Boston Symphony and as conductor of the orchestra of the Worcester (Mass.) Festivals. In 1905, he became the head of the stringed instrument department of the New York Institute of Musical Art, disbanding the quartet, in 1917, to devote all his time to pedagogy. The degree of Doctor of Music has been conferred upon him by both Yale and Princeton Universities. As a performer, Kneisel has a splendid technique and an innate musical perception which enables him to play classic or modern compositions with equal delight to his hearers. He has also edited three volumes of violin compositions, and has published a book of advanced exercises.

KOCHANSKI, PAUL, Polish violinist, b. Poland, 1887. Studied under Mlynarski and Thomson at the Brussels Conservatory where he gained the highest prize for violin playing. In 1908 he appeared as soloist at Warsaw, and later in London. Became professor of violin at the Warsaw, Petrograd and Kief Conservatories and has made numerous successful tours of Europe, the Far East and the United States. As a performer, Kochanski is equipped with an adequate technic, but it is his highly musical temperament which proves most satisfying.

KOCIAN, JARASLAV, Bohemian violinist, b. Wildenschwert, Feb. 22, 1884. Studied under Sevcik at the Prague Conservatory from which he was graduated with the highest honors. Made his debut in 1901, and has concertized with extraordinary success in Europe and the United States. Compositions include a Dumka and a serenade for the violin.

KOLAKOVSKI, ALEXIS ANTONOVITCH, Russian violinist, b. Podolia, 1856. Studied at the Petrograd Conservatory where he was awarded a gold medal. Has concertized and taught at famous Russian Conservatories for many years.

KÖMPEL, AUGUST, German violinist, b. Bruckman, Aug. 15, 1831. Studied under Spohr, David and Joachim. Became a member of Cassel, Hanover and Weimar Orchestras and made numerous successful tours of Europe. He was a player with a beautifully refined tone, and an excellent interpreter of Spohr's works. D. Weimar, April 7, 1891.

KONTSKI, APOLLINAIRE DE, Polish violinist, b. Warsaw, Oct. 23, 1825. Studied under his brother and appeared in public at the age of four, later touring Europe and creating a sensation with his technical feats. At one time he became solo violinist to the Czar Nicholas and in 1861 founded a conservatory in Warsaw which proved quite successful. He was at one time said to have been friendly with Paganini, who not only gave him a few lessons, but left him both his violins and compositions in his will. Compositions include a few fantasias of no musical value. D. Warsaw, June 29, 1879.

KORTSCHAK, HUGO, Austrian violinist, b. Graz, Feb. 24, 1884. Studied under Sevcik at the Prague Conservatory where he was graduated with highest honors. Appeared as soloist at the Goldmark Concerts in Prague. Became a member of the Berlin Philharmonic Orchestra, Heerman String Quartet and the Chicago Symphony Orchestra. Founded the Kortschak Quartet in Chicago (later called the Berkshire).

KOTEK, JOSEPH, Russian violinist, b. Kamenez-Poldolsk, Oct. 25, 1855. Studied at the Moscow Conservatory and under Joachim. Taught the violin at the Berlin Hochschule. Compositions include exercises and solos for the violin. D. Davos, Switzerland, Jan. 4, 1885.

KÖTTLITZ, ADOLF, Russian violinist, b. Trier, Sept. 27, 1820. A youthful prodigy who was able to perform Rode concertos at seven years and toured as a soloist at ten years, and, after concertizing through all of Russia, became musical director at Uralsk, Siberia, where he was killed on a hunting trip, Oct. 26, 1860.

KRAHMER, CAROLINE, Austrian violinist, b. about 1790 and regarding whom very little is known except that she performed a Viotti concerto with great effect at Vienna in 1824.

KRAUSS, ARNOLD, Roumanian violinist, b. Bucharest, Aug. 27, 1866. Studied at the Bucharest Conservatory and under Dancla and Thomson. Appeared as soloist under Waldteufel in Paris and under Theodore Thomas and Emil Paur. Has spent more than twenty years of his life in Los Angeles, Cal., concertizing and teaching.

KREINER, EDWARD, Polish violinist, b. Poland, May 1, 1890. Studied under Henri Marteau at the Berlin Hochschule and became violist of the Marteau Quartet as well as assistant teacher at the Hochschule. Came to America to join the New York Symphony Orchestra and became violist of the Letz Quartet.

KREISLER, FRITZ, Austrian violinist and composer, b. Vienna, Feb. 2, 1875. Studied at the Vienna Conservatory and under Massart at the Paris Conservatory, winning the first grand prize. In 1888 he toured the United States with Moritz Rosenthal, and again resumed his studies, making his mature debut in 1899 at Berlin. He has since toured Europe, Great Britain and the United States many times with great success. As a performer on the violin he has a brilliant technique, and a magnetic tone imbued with the highest sincerity of purpose. Compositions include a number of extremely interesting and well-written concert pieces as well as numerous arrangements from the old masters.

KREUTZER, AUGUSTE, French violinist, b. Versailles, Sept. 3, 1781. A brother of the world famous Rodolphe Kreutzer. He was violinist at the Court of Napoleon and succeeded his brother as professor of the violin at the Paris Conservatory upon Rodolphe's enforced retirement, through a broken arm, in 1825. D. Paris, April 18, 1832.

KREUTZER, RODOLPHE, French violinist and composer, b. Paris, Nov. 16, 1766. Studied under Stamitz, but was largely self-trained, through listening to great artists such as Viotti and Mestrino. He became solo violinist to Napoleon and toured Europe with great success. In 1798 he met Beethoven at Vienna, the great composer dedicating to him his famous Sonata Op. 47. While professor of the violin at the Paris Conservatory, a famous violin method was originated by him in collaboration with Baillot. He appeared at concerts in Paris frequently, playing "duos concertante" with Rode. As a performer on the violin he had a splendid technique and a forceful, brilliant style. His compositions include nineteen concertos and two "Symphonies Concertante" for two violins, as well as the "Forty Etudes or Caprices" on which his fame will securely rest as long as the violin is played. D. Geneva, June 6, 1831.

KREUZ, EMIL, German violinist, b. Elberfeld, May 25, 1867. Studied under Japha and Holmes, making a special study of the viola, appearing as soloist on that instrument at London in 1888. Later he became a member of the Gompertz Quartet and of the Covent Garden Opera Orchestra. Compositions include a concerto for viola and a trio for piano, violin and viola.

KRIENS, CHRISTIAN PIETER WILHELM, Dutch violinist, composer and conductor, b. Amsterdam, April 29, 1881. Studied under his father. Made numerous successful tours of Holland, Belgium and France. Came to the United States in 1907 where he founded a successful orchestral school and the Kriens String Quartet. Compositions include a number of pieces for violin.

KRUMPHOLTZ, WENZEL, Bohemian violinist, b. about 1750, who became a warm friend of Beethoven, to whom he is said to have given violin lessons. Krumpholtz was a great admirer of Beethoven and did much to aid in the final recognition of his genius. Among his accomplishments was mandolin playing, and Beethoven wrote a sonata in one movement for this instrument, and also, when Krumpholtz died, a three-part song for men's voices in commemoration. D. Vienna, May 2, 1817.

KRUSE, JOHANN SECUNDUS, Australian violinist, b. Melbourne, Mar. 23, 1859. Appeared at the first desk of the Melbourne Philharmonic Orchestra at nine years of age. In 1875 went to Berlin to study under Joachim and became concertmaster of the Berlin Philharmonic Orchestra and later assistant to Joachim at the Hochschule as well as second violin in the Joachim Quartet, in addition to conducting the Saturday Popular Concerts and several of the Beethoven Festivals. As a performer on the violin he was specially noted for his staccato bowing and trill.

KUBELIK, JAN, Bohemian violinist, b. Prague, July 5, 1880. Studied under Sevcik

PLATE 69

1. PAUL JUON.   2. LEONORA JACKSON.   3. FRANZ KNEISEL.   4. JAN KUBELIK.   5. PAUL KOCHANSKI.   6. FRITZ KREISLER.   7. JARASLOV KOCIAN.   8. RODOLPHE KREUTZER.

at the Prague Conservatory, graduating with highest honors. Appeared as soloist at Prague in 1903 and has since made numerous successful tours of Europe, Great Britain and the United States. As a performer on the violin he has a technique, equal if not superior to that of any contemporary, and accordingly displays great wisdom in playing only that type of music in which such proficiency becomes the chief attraction. Compositions include a concerto and smaller violin pieces.

KUNITS, LUIGI VON, Austrian violinist and composer, b. Vienna, July 30, 1870. Studied under Kral, Grün and Sevcik. Came to the United States in 1893 as concertmaster of the Austrian orchestra at the World's Fair in Chicago, where he taught the violin and founded a quartet. In 1896, he became concertmaster of the Pittsburg Symphony Orchestra, also concertizing and leading a quartet. In 1912, he became professor at the Canadian Academy of Music at Toronto where he plays an active part in the city's musical life. Compositions include violin concertos, études and small pieces.

KÜZDO, VICTOR, Hungarian violinist, b. Budapest, Sept. 18, 1869. Studied under Huber, Lotto and Auer. Appeared as soloist at Budapest in 1882. Made a successful tour of Europe and came to the United States in 1884 as a prodigy and later (1894) settled in New York as a teacher. Compositions include many agreeable pieces for violin.

LABARRE, LOUIS JULIEN CASTELS DE, French violinist, b. Paris, 1711. Studied under Viotti. Became soloist of the Theatre Français and the Grand Opera Orchestra, afterwards fulfilling an appointment in the household of the Emperor Napoleon. Compositions include a number of lighter violin pieces.

LA DIAMANTINA, violinist, b. about 1715, who is described by the English poet Gray, who heard her play about 1740 in Rome, as "a famous virtuoso, playing on the violin divinely."

LAFONT, CHARLES PHILIPPE, French violinist, b. Paris, Dec. 1, 1781. Studied under Berthaume, Kreutzer and Rode. Made numerous successful tours until appointed chamber-virtuoso at St. Petersburg as successor to Rode. As a performer on the violin he imitated Paganini's style, even attempting unsuccessfully to rival him. Lived in Paris from about 1815, appearing as court violinist, meeting his death while on tour, Aug. 14, 1839. Compositions include many light violin pieces and duets.

LAHOUSSAYE, PIERRE, French violinist and composer, b. Paris, Apr. 12, 1735. Studied under Pagin and Tartini. In 1744 appeared as soloist at the Concerts Spirituels and became later concertmaster of several famous Parisian orchestras. Visited London in 1769, and afterwards was appointed professor of the violin at the Paris Conservatory. D. Paris, in 1818.

LALO, EDOUARD (VICTOR ANTOINE), French violinist and composer, b. Lille, Jan. 27, 1823. Studied under Baumann at the Lille Branch of the Paris Conservatory and became a member of the Armingaud-Jacquard Quartet and devoted the rest of his life to composing. Compositions include "Violin Concerto in F" and the "Symphonie Espagnole," both introduced by Sarasate; a Norwegian Rhapsody and a Russian Concerto introduced by Marsick, also a number of smaller works such as the charming "Chanson Villageoise." D. Paris, April 22, 1892.

LAMOTTE, FRANÇOIS, Austrian violinist, b. Vienna, in 1751. At the age of twelve he played a concerto of his own composition before the Austrian Emperor. He made numerous successful tours of Europe, it being said that he played whole pages of music on one string. Compositions include several violin concertos and solos. D. Holland in 1781.

LAMOUREUX, CHARLES, French violinist and conductor, b. Bordeaux, Sept. 28, 1834. Studied under Girard at the Paris Conservatory and became a member of the Gymnase and Grand Opera Orchestra. Founded a string quartet and in 1881 the "Concerts Lamoureux" at which many distinguished violinists have been introduced to Parisian audiences. D. Paris, Dec. 21, 1899.

LANGHANS, FRIEDRICH WILHELM, German violinist and composer, b. Hamburg, Sept. 21, 1832. Studied under David at the Leipzig Conservatory and with Alard at the Paris Conservatory. Became a member of the Gewandhaus Orchestra and after concertizing and teaching in Dusseldorf, Hamburg, Paris and Heidelberg, settled in Berlin where he died June 9, 1892. Compositions include a Concert-Allegro, a Sonata and some violin studies.

LANGLEY, BEATRICE, English violinist, b. Chudleigh, Devonshire. Studied under Joseph Ludwig and Joachim. Appeared as soloist at the Crystal Palace Concerts and made numerous successful tours of Great Britain, the United States, Canada and South Africa. Founder and leader of the Langley-Mukle String Quartet.

LANNER, JOSEPH (FRANZ CARL), Austrian violinist and dance composer, b. Oberdobbing, April 12, 1801. An entirely self-taught violinist, who formed a quartet in which Johann Strauss (later his rival in the dance-orchestra field) played the viola. He is famous as the creator of the modern Viennese waltz and other popular dances. D. Vienna, April 14, 1843.

LAUB, FERDINAND, Bohemian violinist and composer, b. Prague, Jan. 19, 1832. Studied under Mildner and in 1853 succeeded Joachim as concertmaster at Weimar. Made numerous successful tours of Europe and taught the violin from 1855-57 at the Stern Conservatory in Berlin where he founded a string quartet which achieved a brilliant reputation. In 1866 he became professor of the violin at the Moscow Conservatory, retiring after a few years through ill health. Compositions include a Polonaise and several solos for violin. D. Gries in the Tyrol, Mar. 17, 1875.

LAURENTI, BARTOLOMEO GERONIMO, Italian violinist and composer, b. Bologna, 1644. One of the earliest members of the Philharmonic Academy established there in 1666. Compositions include sonatas for violin and cello, also concertos for violin, cello and organ. D. Bologna, Jan. 18, 1726.

LAUTERBACH, JOHANN CHRISTOPH, German violinist, b. Culmbach, July 24, 1832. Studied under Fetis and Deberiot at Brussels where he won a gold medal for violin playing in 1851, and substituted for Léonard at the Conservatory in 1852. Made a successful tour of Holland, Belgium and Germany and came to Munich, where he became soloist and teacher in the Conservatory. In 1873 he became concertmaster of the Dresden Royal Orchestra and professor of the violin at the Conservatory, founding the string quartet which has made his name famous throughout Europe. Compositions include a number of concert solos and smaller pieces for the violin.

LECLAIR, JEAN MARIE, French violinist and composer, b. Lyons, May 10, 1697. Began life as a dancer and ballet-master, and composed some dance music which so attracted Somis that he induced Leclair to study with him for two years, after which he appeared in Paris as a master-violinist. His success was not as great as it should have been, owing apparently to jealousy, and he devoted the rest of his life to teaching and composing. Compositions include sonatas for the violin (see those in the David Violin School) which, through their technical difficulties, vivacity and graceful melodic qualities, place him in the foremost rank of French composers. Leclair was assassinated near his home, Oct. 22, 1764.

LEDUC, SIMON, French violinist and composer, b. Paris, 1748. Studied under Gaviniés and afterwards became one of the conductors of the Concerts Spirituels. Compositions include concertos and solos for the violin as well as a Symphony Concertante for two violins. It is said that shortly after Leduc's death, the adagio in one of his symphonic works so affected the Chevalier de Saint-Georges, who was conducting it, that he burst into tears and let fall the baton. D. Paris, 1777.

LEFORT, NARCISSE-AUGUSTIN, French violinist, b. Paris, June 18, 1852. Studied at the Paris Conservatory, later becoming professor of the violin at the same institution, where he was highly regarded as a pedagogue.

LEHMANN, GEORGE, American violinist, teacher and writer, b. New York, July 31, 1865. Studied under Schradieck and Joachim. In 1883 appeared as soloist with the Leipzig Gewandhaus Orchestra in Joachim's Hungarian Concerto, winning the Helbig prize. Made numerous successful tours abroad and in the United States. Now directs his own violin school in New York, and has published a Violinist's Lexicon.

LÉONARD, HUBERT, Belgian violinist and composer, b. Bellaire, April 7, 1819. Studied under Habeneck at the Paris Conservatory. Made numerous successful tours of Germany, introducing the Mendelssohn Concerto at Berlin in 1844, under the composer's baton. Became successor to Deberiot at the Brussels Conservatory, resigning in 1867 on account of his health, spending the balance of his life in Paris. Léonard was the teacher of many of the most famous modern violinists, among whom may be mentioned Marsick. Compositions include a number of important technical studies, several concertos and concert pieces for the violin. As a performer on the violin he was one of the most brilliant virtuosos of his time. D. Paris, May 6, 1890.

LETZ, HANS, German violinist, b. Ittenheim, Mar. 18, 1887. Studied under Schuster and Joachim. Made his debut at New York in 1908. After concertizing and acting as concertmaster with the Chicago Symphony Orchestra, he became second violin in the Kneisel Quartet, and when it disbanded he organized a very successful quartet under his own name.

LICHTENBERG, LEOPOLD, American violinist, b. San Francisco, Cal., Nov. 22, 1861. Made a tour with Wieniawski through the United States at the age of twelve and afterwards studied with him for three years. Has made numerous successful tours of Europe and the United States, becoming a member of the Boston Symphony Orchestra and professor of violin at the New York National Conservatory of Music, as well as founder of the Margulies Trio which has a splendid reputation in New York. As a performer, Lichtenberg stands in the highest rank of contemporary players, combining technical and emotional qualities. He has also edited many important violin works.

LICHTENSTEIN, VICTOR, American violinist, b. St. Louis, Nov. 15, 1872. Studied under Sitt and Ysaÿe. In 1895 appeared as soloist with the Kranich Concert company at Leipzig and since that time has been connected with every phase of musical life in St. Louis as soloist, teacher, conductor, lecturer and in chamber music work.

LILIENTHAL, ABRAHAM WOLF, American violinist and composer, b. New York, Feb. 13, 1859. Studied under Herman Brandt. Became a member of the Damrosch and Theodore Thomas Orchestras and of the New York String Quartet. Compositions include a sonata for piano and violin, also much highly regarded chamber music.

LINDBERG, THEODORE, American violinist, b. Kansas, Mar. 14, 1874. Studied under Zedeles, Zajic and Listemann. Has taught the violin for more than twenty-five years.

LINLEY, THOMAS, English violinist, b. Bath, 1756. Studied under his father and under Nardini at Florence, where he met Mozart, the result being a friendship and intimacy to which Mozart frequently referred in later years. Upon his return to England, Linley appeared at his father's concerts in Bath and later at the Oratorio concerts in London with great success. His career was cut short by drowning, through the upsetting of a pleasure boat in 1778.

LIPINSKI, KARL JOSEPH, Polish violinist and composer, b. Radzyn, Oct. 30, 1790. Studied the elements of violin playing under his father but otherwise was self-taught. Became concertmaster at the Lemberg Theater, and in 1817 went to Milan where he met Paganini, who took such a liking to him as not only to play in private but at two public concerts as well with him. Later Paganini and Lipinski met at Warsaw, but an artistic rivalry put an end to their friendship. After visiting all the principal cities of Europe and England, he became concertmaster of the Royal Chapel at Dresden. As a performer on the violin, Lipinski had a big broad tone and a magnificent technique. Compositions include several concertos (among them the "Military") and solo pieces of the bravura type. D. Lemberg, Dec. 16, 1861, just after he had been pensioned.

LISTEMANN, BERNHARD, German violinist, b. Schlotheim, Aug. 28, 1841. Studied under Ulbrich, David, Vieuxtemps and Joachim. Made numerous successful tours of Europe and came to the United States with his brother, Fritz, in 1867, becoming concertmaster of the Theodore Thomas Orchestra and the Boston Symphony Orchestra; also founding the Listemann String Quartet and the Listemann Concert Company. From 1893 until his retirement in 1911, he taught the violin in Chicago. Compositions include a violin method and several solo pieces. D. Chicago, Feb. 11, 1917.

LISTEMANN, FRITZ, German violinist, b. Schlotheim, Mar. 25, 1839. Studied under Ulbrich and David and became chamber musician to the Prince of Rudolstadt. Came to the United States with his brother, Bernhard, in 1867, and became a member of the Theodore Thomas and Boston Symphony Orchestras. Played in the Listemann String Quartet and a concert company of the same name, besides teaching the violin for many years. Compositions include two violin concertos and several solos. D. Boston, Dec. 28, 1909.

LISTEMANN, PAUL, American violinist, b. Boston, Oct. 24, 1875, son of Bernhard Listemann (q.v.). Studied under his uncle, Fritz Listemann, and after becoming a member of the Listemann Quartet and Concert Company, continued his studies abroad with Hilf, Brodsky and Joachim. Has been con-

PLATE 70

1. HUBERT LEONARD. 2. CHARLES MARTIN LOEFFLER. 3. JOSEPH LAUTERBACH. 4. LEOPOLD LICHTENBERG. 5. GEOFFREY LUDLOW. 6. JEAN MARIE LECLAIR. 7. BERNHARD LISTEMANN. 8. CARL JOSEPH LIPINSKI.

certmaster of various important American organizations, settling in New York as a teacher and became a member of the Metropolitan Opera House Orchestra.

LOCATELLI, PIETRO, Italian violinist and composer, b. Bergamo, 1693. Studied under Corelli at Rome. Made numerous successful tours and settled at Amsterdam where he gave a regular series of concerts. As a performer on the violin his double stopping was regarded as phenomenal, and his difficult and sometimes technically almost impossible caprices or exercises were evidently written with a view of extending the powers of the violin as a solo instrument. Compositions include *Concerti Grossi* (orchestral concertos), solo concertos and sonatas, all of which contain music of the highest character. D. Amsterdam, Apr. 1, 1746.

LODER, JOHN DAVID, English violinist, teacher and conductor, b. Bath, 1788. Taught the violin at the Royal Academy of Music and in 1845 succeeded Cramer as conductor of the Ancient Concerts. He was the author of a violin method and a work entitled *The Modern Art of Bowing*, published in 1842. D. London, in 1846.

LOEFFLER, CHARLES MARTIN, French violinist, b. Alsace, Jan. 30, 1861. Studied under Léonard, Massart and Joachim. Became a member of the Pasdeloup Orchestra in Paris. Came to the United States in 1881 sharing the first desk of the Boston Symphony Orchestra with Franz Kneisel for many years. Resigned in 1903 to devote himself exclusively to composition. Compositions include a suite and a divertimento for violin and orchestra, also several interesting transcriptions for the violin.

LOLLI, ANTONIO, Italian violinist and composer, b. Bergamo, about 1730. Studied under Nardini for a time but was practically self-taught. In 1773 he went to St. Petersburg, becoming the favorite of the Czarina, Catherine II. Made numerous successful tours of Spain, Austria, Italy, Denmark and Germany but was not well received in England. As a performer on the violin he had a marvelous technique but critics of his time declared him so unmusical that he could not play any slow movement with good taste. His compositions include a number of sonatas and concertos of no musical value. D. Palermo, 1802.

LOTTO, ISIDOR, Polish violinist, b. Warsaw, Dec. 22, 1840. Studied under Massart at the Paris Conservatory. Made extensive concert tours throughout Europe and became solo violinist of the Court Orchestra at Weimar. Also became professor of the violin at the Strassburg and later at the Warsaw Conservatories.

LUDWIG, JOSEPH, German violinist, b. Bonn, April 6, 1844. Studied under Grunwald and Joachim. Came to England in 1870 and has made himself a part of London's musical life, especially as leader of a string quartet of the highest artistic attainments. Compositions include several pieces for the violin.

LULLI, JEAN BAPTISTE, Italian violinist and composer, b. Florence, about 1633. Was the founder of French opera and a violinist, self-taught, as far as our knowledge goes, who became a member of Louis the Fourteenth's private orchestra and creator for him of the band of "Little Violins" (Petits Violons). Charles Perrault's book *Hommes Illustres* speaks of his powers on the violin as attaining a perfection never reached before. Compositions include airs for the violin and chamber music. D. Paris, 1687.

LVOFF, ALEXIS VON, Russian violinist and composer, b. Reval, May, 1799. Studied the violin before entering the army, in which service he rose rapidly to be adjutant to Czar Nicholas I. He succeeded his father as director of the Imperial Court Chapel, and became well-known as a soloist and quartet player. Compositions include a concerto and a duet for violin and cello. Lvoff is also the composer of the music to the Russian National Anthem in use until the recent revolution. D. Kovno, December, 1870.

MACKENZIE, SIR ALEXANDER CAMPBELL, Scotch violinist and distinguished composer, b. Edinburgh, Aug. 22, 1847. Studied under Uhlrich and Sainton. Played the second violin in the Sondershausen Ducal Orchestra where he played the then advanced music of Wagner, Liszt and Berlioz. After he was graduated from the London Royal Academy of Music, he returned to Edinburgh and besides concertizing, formed a string quartet, presenting the Schumann Piano Quintet for the first time in Scotland, later becoming head of the Royal Music Academy, and devoting himself to composition. Compositions include a suite "Pibroch," a Scotch concerto and pieces for violin.

MACKINTOSH, ROBERT, Scotch violinist and composer, b. Scotland, about 1750.

Became a teacher at Edinburgh and leader at the Royal Theatre. He is also reputed to have given lessons to Nathaniel Gow, the most famous of Scotch violin players (q. v.). Compositions include books of Scotch dance music of considerable originality. D. London, 1807.

MACMILLEN, FRANCIS, American violinist, b. Marietta, O., Oct. 14, 1885. Studied under Listemann, Markees, Joachim, Thomson, Flesch and Auer. Won first prize at the Brussels Conservatory, and the Van Hals cash prize of $5,000. In 1903 he appeared as soloist with the Queen's Hall Orchestra, London. Made a successful tour of England, France, Germany and Austria. Returned to the United States in 1907 touring America many times. As a performer on the violin he has a splendid technique and a sympathetic and broad tone. Compositions include a number of engaging violin pieces and transcriptions.

MACPHAIL, WILLIAM, Scotch violinist and teacher, b. at Glasgow, Nov. 18, 1881. Studied under Barmas, Sevcik and Musin. Appeared as soloist with the Minneapolis Symphony Orchestra in 1911, and, after joining the orchestra as first violin, founded the MacPhail School of Music in that city.

MALCHEREK, KARL AUGUST, German violinist, b. Bebra, Apr. 25, 1873. Studied at the Darmstadt Conservatory and under Hugo Heerman at Frankfort, becoming concertmaster of several large German orchestras. Came to the United States in 1899, playing with the Theodore Thomas and Pittsburg Symphony Orchestras, in addition to much concert, chamber music and teaching work which has placed him in the foremost ranks of America's musicians.

MALIBRAN, ALEXANDRE, French violinist, b. Paris, Nov. 10, 1823. Studied under Spohr and founded a musical magazine, Le Monde Musical, in 1864 at Brussels; also published a life of Spohr in 1860. D. Paris, May 13, 1867.

MANÉN, JOAN, Spanish violinist and composer, b. Barcelona, Mar. 14, 1883. Studied piano at first and toured Spain as well as North and South America as a prodigy when seven years old, frequently conducting orchestral works. Later, he was attracted to the violin, studying with Alard and has succeeded to the point of being considered Sarasate's successor. He has appeared recently in the United States with great success as both virtuoso and composer. Compositions include two concertos (one the "Spanish"), caprices, suites, variations and smaller works for the violin.

MANNES, DAVID, American violinist, b. New York, Feb. 16, 1866. Studied under De Ahna, Halir and Ysaÿe. From 1902-11 he acted as concertmaster of the New York Symphony Orchestra; directed the Music School Settlement until 1915 and organized the Music Settlement for Colored People. Gave a series of sonata recitals (with Mrs. Mannes at the piano) in New York, Boston, London and other cities, and in 1916 founded the Mannes Music School and conducts the orchestral concerts at the Metropolitan Museum of Art.

MANNS, SIR AUGUST (FRIEDRICH), German violinist, b. Stettin, Mar. 12, 1825. Studied under a village musician and became first violinist in Gungl's Orchestra at Berlin, and director of the Crystal Palace Music in London in 1854, conducting over 14,000 concerts; introducing hundreds of novelties, and assisting, whenever possible, English composers in getting hearings for their works. D. London, Mar. 2, 1907.

MARCOSSON, SOL, American violinist, b. Louisville, Ky., June 10, 1869. Studied under De Ahna and Joachim. Made successful tours of Germany, Italy, England and America. Became a member of the Boston Mendelssohn Quintet Club, and concertmaster of the Chicago and Cleveland Symphony Orchestras. Now director of the Marcosson Music School, Cleveland, Ohio.

MARINI, BIAGIO, Italian violinist and composer, b. Brescia in 1600. Was court violinist to the Duke of Parma. His compositions include the oldest known sonatas for solo violin, and much chamber music making unusual demands on the performers. D. Padua, 1660.

MARKEES, KARL, Swiss violinist, b. Chur, Feb. 10, 1865. Studied under Wirth and Joachim. Became a member of the Berlin Philharmonic Orchestra, also the Kruse Quartet and the Halir Quartet. Made numerous successful tours as a virtuoso and has written a guide to the technical study of the violin.

MARSICK, MARTIN PIERRE JOSEPH, Belgian violinist and composer, b. Jupille, Mar. 9, 1848. Studied under Léonard, Massart and Joachim and was awarded a stipend by the Belgian government for the completion of his studies under Joachim.

Appeared as soloist at the Paris Concerts Populaires in 1873. Made numerous successful tours of Europe and the United States and succeeded Massart as violin professor at the Paris Conservatory. Compositions include three violin concertos and smaller violin works.

MARTEAU, HENRI, French violinist, b. Rheims, Mar. 31, 1874. Studied under Léonard and Garcin at the Paris Conservatory. In 1888 appeared as soloist with Richter in London. Made numerous successful tours of America, Scandinavia and Russia and succeeded Joachim at the Berlin Hochschule in 1908, being interned during the World War. As a performer on the violin he has an impeccable technique and a warm brilliant tone. Léonard bequeathed him his magnificent Maggini violin. Marteau has also been distinguished by his leadership in chamber music performances. Compositions include two concertos for violin and much chamber music.

MARTENS, FREDERICK H., American critic, musicologist and author, b. New York, 1874. Has engaged in critical work as well as authorship since 1907. His work on *Violin Mastery*, published in 1919, has elicited favorable comment throughout the musical world. He also translated that part of this *Encyclopedia* which was written originally in French. (Ed.)

MASCITTI, MICHELE, Italian violinist and composer, b. Naples, about 1700. Made numerous successful tours of Holland and Germany and settled in Paris where he died about 1750. Compositions include several sonatas which have been republished in standard editions.

MASSART, JOSEPH LAMBERT, Belgian violinist, b. Liége, July 19, 1811. Studied under Rodolphe Kreutzer but never achieved success as a virtuoso because of his excessive shyness. An interesting incident is told of his having the bow uplifted ready to play the Kreutzer Sonata with Franz Liszt, and dutifully lowering it to permit the great piano virtuoso to *first* render a piano fantasia on Meyerbeer's "Robert Le Diable" for which some enthusiast (or idiot) called out from the gallery. Played *after* Liszt's technical "fireworks," the "Kreutzer" naturally fell flat. Became professor of the violin at Paris Conservatory from 1843 to 1890, where he gained great renown, among his pupils being Wieniawski. D. Paris, Feb. 13, 1892.

MATTEIS, NICOLA, Italian violinist and composer, probably born about 1640, although very little is known of his life, except that he became famous after 1672 in London as a violin virtuoso and composer of several suites. His son, Nicola, was also an excellent violinist, accredited with having instructed the famous musical historian Burney in the art of violin playing. D. Shrewsbury, about 1749.

MAURER, LUDWIG WILHELM, German violinist and composer, b. Potsdam, Feb. 8, 1879. Studied under Haack, concertmaster to Frederick the Great, and made numerous successful tours of France, Russia and Germany, settling in Dresden as teacher and soloist. Compositions include several concertos and a highly esteemed concerto for four violins. D. St. Petersburg, Oct. 25, 1878.

MAYSEDER, JOSEPH, Austrian violinist and composer, b. Vienna, Oct. 26, 1789. Studied under Suchs and Wranitzky and became a member of the Schuppanzigh Quartet, later rising to the greatest heights as a concert performer, and also as a teacher and patron of chamber music concerts where Beethoven was often present. He made no tours outside of Vienna but as a· performer on the violin he had a singularly beautiful tone and execution highly praised by Paganini. Compositions include works of all kinds for the violin and much chamber music. D. Vienna, Nov. 21, 1863.

MAZAS, JACQUES FÉRÉROL, French violinist and composer, b. Beziers, Sept. 23, 1782. Studied under Baillot at the Paris Conservatory, and was awarded first prize for violin playing. Appeared as soloist at Paris in a concerto written for him by Auber, composer of "Fra Diavolo." Made numerous successful tours of Europe and became director of the Cambrai Music School. Compositions include many brilliant violin pieces, as well as a method (revised by Hrimaly) and valuable exercises still much used. D. Beziers, 1849.

MAZZUCATO, ALBERTO, Italian violinist and composer, b. Udine, July 28, 1830. Composed a number of operas which had temporary success but were superseded by those of Verdi. Became an eminent violinist, and leader at the La Scala Opera House in Milan for many years and highly successful as a teacher. D. Milan, Dec. 31, 1877.

McCARTHY, MAUD, American violinist. Studied under Fernandez Arbos. Appeared as soloist with the Crystal Palace and Queen's Hall Orchestra in the Beethoven, Tschaikowsky and Brahms Concertos. Has made numerous successful tours of Europe.

MEAD, OLIVE, American violinist, b. Cambridge, Mass., Nov. 22, 1874. At seven years of age she studied under Eichberg and later under Kneisel, appearing as soloist in 1898 with The Boston Symphony Orchestra and since that time has appeared with all the large orchestras and has made numerous successful tours of the United States. In 1904 she organized the Olive Mead Quartet which has proved an organization of real importance in the chamber music field.

MEERTS, LAMBERT JOSEPH, Belgian violinist and composer, b. Brussels, Jan. 6, 1800. Studied under Lafont and Habeneck and became professor of the violin at the Brussels Conservatory in 1835. Compositions include a series of valuable sets of études in all grades, including his "Mécanisme du Violon." D. Brussels, May 12, 1863.

MEGERLEIN, ALFRED, Belgian violinist, b. Belgium in 1880. Came to the United States in 1914 and in 1917 became concert-master of the New York Philharmonic Orchestra.

MEISEL, KARL, German violinist, b. Germany, 1829. Became a member of the Boston Symphony Orchestra, and was the oldest member of the organization at his death in 1908.

MELCHIORI, ANTONIO, Italian violinist and composer, b. Parma, Nov. 25, 1827. A violin virtuoso and teacher who also composed a number of agreeable pieces for the instrument. D. Milan, 1897.

MELL, DAVIS, English violinist, b. Wilton, Nov. 15, 1604. A clockmaker by trade, who lived in London about 1650 and preceded Thomas Baltzar as leader of the King's Band, and is said not only to have played the violin very beautifully, but to have accomplished much in increasing public regard for the instrument before it had been drawn into general notice.

MELSA, DANIEL, Polish violinist, b. Warsaw, Aug. 14, 1892. Studied under Carl Flesch in Berlin and has made numerous successful tours of Europe and Great Britain. He has had the distinction of playing the Brahms Violin Concerto under the baton of Arthur Nikisch.

MENGES, ISOLDE, English violinist, b. Brighton, 1894. Displayed a talent for music at the age of four, and first studied with her father, Director of a Conservatory at Brighton, and in 1909 with Leopold Auer. Since her debut at London in 1913 she has appeared as a virtuoso with unusual success. Miss Menges recently recorded the entire Beethoven Violin Concerto for the phonograph, accompanied by the Royal Albert Hall Orchestra, Sir Landon Ronald conducting.

MESTRINO, NICCOLO, Italian violinist and composer, b. Milan, 1748. Became a member of Prince Esterhazy's orchestra and is said to have perfected his technique while in prison, appearing in 1786 at Paris with great success as virtuoso and teacher and also as concertmaster at the Théâtre Italien under Viotti. Compositions include concertos, duos, sonatas and studies for the violin. D. Paris, 1790.

MEYER, OTTO, American violinist, b. La Porte, Ind., Mar. 22, 1880. Studied under Jacobsen, Suchy, Sevcik and Ysaÿe. Made successful tours of Europe and the United States and has established a conservatory, of which he is director, in Minneapolis, Minn.

MEYER, WALDEMAR, German violinist, b. Berlin, Feb. 4, 1853. Studied under Joachim, who later procured him the position of first violin in the Berlin Court Orchestra. Made numerous successful tours of Europe and became professor of violin at the Stern Conservatory, in addition to forming the Meyer Quartet which has become an organization of high reputation.

MICHALEK, BOHUMIL, American violinist, b. Chicago, Mar. 11, 1885. Studied under Van Oordt and Sevcik and became concert-master at the Prague Opera and assistant to Sevcik. Returned to the United States in 1908 and established a Master School for violinists in Chicago.

MIERSCH, CARL ALEXANDER JOHANNES, German violinist, b. Dresden in 1865. Studied under Rappoldi, Abel and Massart. Became successively concertmaster at Graz, music-teacher at Aberdeen, member of the Boston Symphony Orchestra and Director of the Athens (Greece) Conservatory. Made a successful tour of Europe; returned to the United States in 1902 and in 1910 assumed the professorship of the violin at

PLATE 71

1. HENRI MARTEAU. 2. MARTIN MARSICK. 3. JULES MASSART. 4. JOAN
MANÉN. 5. FRANCIS MACMILLEN. 6. OVIDE MUSIN. 7. MISCHA
MISCHAKOFF. 8. DAVID MANNES.

the Cincinnati Conservatory. Compositions include a concert polonaise for violin and orchestra, and several interesting transcriptions.

MILANOLLO SISTERS, TERESA AND MARIE, Italian violinists, b. Savigliano, Teresa on August 18, 1827, and Marie on June 18, 1832. Teresa studied first under Ferrero, Caldera and Morra and in 1836 went to Paris where she was a pupil of Lafont and Habeneck, and still later of Deberiot in Brussels, thus being trained in the best methods of Italian, French and Belgian schools. She was also teacher for her sister who acquired equal skill, and in 1840 the pair toured France, Holland, Belgium, Germany and England, arousing the greatest interest and enthusiasm. In 1848, Marie died at Paris, and Teresa toured alone with even greater success, marrying a French army officer in 1857, when she retired from the stage. D. Paris, Oct. 25, 1904.

MINCUS, LUDWIG, Austrian violinist and composer, b. Vienna, 1827. Became solo violinist of the Imperial Theatre, Petrograd, and professor at the Moscow Conservatory. He collaborated with Leo Delibes on the ballet "Naila" to which violinists are indebted for the Valse "Pas des Fleurs" so well arranged by Sauret.

MISCHAKOFF, MISCHA, Russian violinist, b. Proskurow, Russia in 1897. He studied under Korgueff, an Auer pupil and was graduated with honors from the Petrograd Conservatory in 1913. He has been concertmaster at Petrograd, Moscow and Warsaw, besides touring all of Europe. His American debut was made in Carnegie Hall in 1923, after which he has appeared many times successfully in recital and as soloist with the New York Philharmonic Orchestra.

MLYNARSKI, EMIL, Polish violinist and composer, b. Poland, July 18, 1870. Studied under Auer and became professor of the violin at Odessa Conservatory, later becoming conductor of the Warsaw Philharmonic Orchestra. Went to England in 1910, assuming the directorship of the Glasgow Choral and Orchestral Unions. Compositions include a violin concerto which gained for him the Paderewski prize in 1898, and several smaller pieces.

MOLIQUE, WILHELM BERNHARD, German violinist and composer, b. Nuremberg, Oct. 7, 1802. Studied under Spohr and Rovelli, whom he succeeded as leader of the Munich Orchestra in 1820. Made numerous successful tours of Germany and England where he spent the rest of his professional life concertizing, quartet playing and teaching, retiring in 1866 to Cannstadt where he died May 10, 1869. Compositions include six concertos, duets and much chamber music.

MOLLENHAUER, EDWARD, German violinist b. Erfurt, April, 1827. Studied under Ernst and Spohr. Came to the United States in 1853 with Jullien's Orchestra and remained in New York, where he founded a violin school for advanced students, besides concertizing and doing orchestral playing. In 1881 he took out a patent (also in England) of a new design for violin construction in which the interior of the instrument was divided into compartments. D. at Owatowa, Minn., 1914. His brother, Friedrich, also a violinist, came to the United States at the same time, and labored together with him; still another brother, Heinrich Mollenhauer, a violoncellist of reputation, followed in 1853 and established a musical school in Brooklyn, still carried on by his son.

MOLLENHAUER, EMIL, American violinist, b. Brooklyn, Aug. 4, 1855. Studied under his father, and after playing at both Niblo's and Booth's Theatres, joined the Thomas Orchestra, the Damrosch Orchestra, and later the Boston Symphony, resigning from the latter to conduct the Boston Festival Orchestra on extensive tours. Mr. Mollenhauer also succeeded B. J. Lang as conductor of the Handel and Haydn Society, and is active in almost every branch of Boston's musical life.

MOLLENHAUER, LOUIS, American violinist, b. Brooklyn in 1863. Studied under his uncle, Friedrich Mollenhauer. Made numerous successful tours in chamber music concerts, returning to Brooklyn in 1889 to succeed his father (Heinrich Mollenhauer) in the management of the well established music school. Has since been active in the musical life of Brooklyn.

MONASTERIO, JESUS DE, Spanish violinist, b. Potes, Apr. 18, 1836. Studied under the best masters in Madrid and at the Brussels Conservatory under Deberiot. He made numerous successful tours of Europe and became professor of the violin at the Madrid Conservatory, in addition to founding the Madrid String Quartet of remarkable excellence, presenting to Spanish audiences classical compositions previously unheard. Compositions include many solos for the violin. D. Santander, Sept. 28, 1903.

MONDONVILLE, JEAN JOSEPH CASSANEA DE, French violinist and composer, b. Narbonne, Dec. 24, 1711. He appeared with great success at the Concerts Spirituels and later became a successful opera and ballet composer at the Royal Court as well as conductor of the Concerts Spirituels. His compositions include six sonatas for solo violin, developing the use of harmonics. D. Paris, Nov. 8, 1772.

MONTANARI, FRANCESCO, Italian violinist, b. Padua, about 1775. Studied under Corelli and became a member of the orchestra at St. Peters in 1700. About 1730 Pasqualino Bini appeared at Rome, and, upon the new arrival being declared by Roman music lovers the finest violinist of the period, Montanari is said by the music historian, Dr. Burney, to have died of a broken heart. Compositions include twelve sonatas for violin.

MONTÉCLAIR, MICHAEL PIGNOLET DE, French violinist, double-bass player and composer, b. Chaumont in 1666. He was one of the first players on the modern type of double-bass; also an excellent teacher of the violin; his *Method of Learning to Play the Violin*, published in 1720, being one of the first works of its kind. D. Paris, 1737.

MOOREHEAD, JOHN, Irish violinist and composer, b. Ireland, about 1750. Came to London at an early age, after playing the violin in country theater orchestras for several years. In 1798, he joined the Covent Garden orchestra, also composing stage music for a number of successful productions. Later he became insane and pronounced cured, joined the navy as an ordinary sailor, soon rising to be bandmaster, but became again insane and committed suicide near Deal in 1804.

MORALT, JOSEPH AND JOHANN, German violinists, b. Mannheim (Joseph in 1775, Johann in 1777). Were members of a quartet in Munich celebrated for their rendition of classical music, especially Haydn's Quartets. The violist of the quartet was another brother, George, and the cellist still another brother, Philipp.

MORGAN, GERALDINE, American violinist, b. New York, Nov. 15, 1868. Studied under Leopold Damrosch, Schradieck and Joachim, being the first American to be awarded the Mendelssohn prize. Made numerous successful tours of Europe and Great Britain, at one time playing the Bach double concerto with Joachim at the Crystal Palace Concerts. She also appeared with the Symphony Society of New York under the baton of Walter Damrosch. D. at New York, May 20, 1918.

MORI, NICOLAS, English violinist, b. London, 1796 or 1797, of Italian parents. He first toured as a child wonder and later studied for six years under Viotti, becoming a famous virtuoso, a member of the Philharmonic Society, and an important factor in London's musical life from about 1810 until his death at London in 1839.

MORIGI, ANGELO, Italian violinist and composer, b. Rimini in 1752. Studied under Tartini and became concertmaster of the Duke of Parma's orchestra, and later Director of the court music for many years. His compositions include six sonatas and six concertos for violin. D. Parma, 1788.

MORINI, ERIKA, Austrian violinist of Italian extraction. Began the study of violin at four years of age, first under her father, and later under Sevcik. Her first important engagement was at Leipzig under the baton of Arthur Nikisch, later under Weingartner and other famous conductors. Her American debut was made at Carnegie Hall, Jan. 26, 1921. Since that time she has toured the United States with remarkable success, combining a marvelous technique, a warm tone and thorough musicianship.

MOSEL, GIOVANNI FELICE, Italian violinist and composer, b. Florence in 1754. Studied under his father (a pupil of Tartini) and under Nardini. He occupied the position of director of music for the Grand Duke Leopold, and had in his possession for a time one of the four violins made by Stradivarius for the Duke of Tuscany about 1700. Compositions include duets and sonatas for the violin. The date of his death is not known.

MOSENTHAL, JOSEPH, German violinist, b. Cassel, Nov. 30, 1834. Studied under Spohr and for several years was leader of the second violins in Spohr's orchestra at Cassel. Came to the United States in 1853 and commenced a busy life of orchestral playing for forty years with the Philharmonic Orchestra, conducting the Mendelssohn Glee Club and playing second violin in the Mason-Thomas Quartet. D. New York, Jan. 6, 1896.

PLATE 72

1. ISOLDE MENGES. 2. ERIKA MORINI. 3. FRANZ ONDRICEK. 4. TIVA-
DAR NACHÉZ. 5. NORMAN NERUDA (LADY HALLÉ). 6. PIETRO NAR-
DINI. 7. MARIE NICHOLS. 8. GUIDO PAPINI.

MOSER, ANDREAS, Hungarian violinist and teacher, b. Semlin, Nov. 29, 1859. Studied under Joachim, but on account of a nervous affection, relinquished the virtuoso career and became Joachim's assistant at the Hochschule. In the editorial field, Moser has also been prominent as co-author with Joachim of an elaborate Violin School, in addition to revisions of Beethoven's string quartets, and Bach's Partitas, violin concertos and sonatas. He has written a biography of Joachim and edited the publication of his letters. Moser's son, Hans Joachim, born at Berlin, May 25, 1889, has also written a biography of Joachim, and a history of string instrument playing.

MOSER, KARL, German violinist, b. Berlin, Jan. 24, 1774. Studied under Bottcher and Haacke. Became a member of the Royal Orchestra after touring for several years and received the title of "Royal Kapellmeister." D. Berlin, Jan. 27, 1851. His son, August, born at Berlin, Dec. 20, 1825, was also a virtuoso of ability; he died while on tour of the United States in 1859.

MOSSEL, MAX, Dutch violinist, b. Rotterdam, July 25, 1871. Studied under Willy Hess and Sarasate. In 1892 appeared as soloist at the Crystal Palace Saturday Concerts and has made numerous successful tours of Great Britain, Europe and America. Settled in Birmingham as a concert director, quartet leader and professor of the violin.

MOZART, LEOPOLD, German violinist, b. Augsburg, Nov. 14, 1719. On the completion of his studies, he became violinist in the Archbishop of Salzburg's Chapel, and in 1756 published a violin method which was long considered the best work of its kind in existence. Later he devoted his time exclusively to the training of his famous son, Wolfgang Amadeus Mozart. D. Salzburg, May 28, 1787.

MOZART, WOLFGANG AMADEUS, German violinist and distinguished composer, b. Salzburg, Jan. 27, 1756. Studied under his father and became an accomplished violinist as well as pianist. He began to write his violin sonatas (42 in all) in 1777, with his pupils in view. They are perhaps, more melodiously charming than profound or stylistically learned. The last, in F (1788), is a sonatina "for beginners." One of the most interesting is that in B Flat Major (1784). The five violin concertos, composed in 1775, show the influence of the French school, and are extraordinarily light, graceful and melodious, with occasional extraordinarily beautiful pages, such as the Adagio from the Concerto in G. D. Salzburg, Dec. 5, 1791.

MÜLLER, GEORG, German violinist, b. Limburg, Dec. 24, 1861. Studied under Joachim and became leader and soloist of the Bilse Orchestra and leader of the London String Quartet, in addition to appearing as virtuoso at all the London concert halls.

MUNCK, CAMILLE DE, Belgian violinist, b. Brussels, in 1839. Studied at the Brussels Conservatory, where he was awarded first prize for violin playing. Made numerous successful tours of Europe and England, settling at Bordeaux (France) in 1866 as soloist and teacher. Compositions include a concerto for violin and a number of salon pieces.

MURPHY, CHARLTON LEWIS, American violinist and teacher, b. Philadelphia, Pa., Apr. 7, 1879. Studied under Winternitz, Grun and Marteau. Appeared as soloist in Vienna and other European cities, finally becoming a member of the Philadelphia Orchestra as well as a prominent figure in the musical life of that city.

MUSIN, OVIDE, Belgian violinist and composer, b. Nandrin, Sept. 22, 1854. Studied under Heynberg and Léonard and was awarded the first prize for violin playing at the age of thirteen. Appeared as soloist with all the principal European orchestras and toured the whole world twice with great success. Came to the United States in 1883 to appear with the New York Symphony Society. Succeeded César Thomson as professor at the Brussels Conservatory in 1897, returning to New York in 1908 to found a Virtuoso school of violin in New York. In 1875, Musin's String Quartet at Paris was the means of first introducing Brahm's chamber music to French audiences. Compositions include many brilliant violin pieces and educational works.

NACHEZ, TIVIDAR, Hungarian violinist and composer, b. Budapest, May 1, 1859. Studied under Sabatiel, Joachim and Léonard. Became soloist under Liszt and at the Pasdeloup Concerts in Paris. Made numerous successful tours of Europe and Great Britain, settling at London in 1889 as soloist and composer. Since 1916 he has lived at Santa Barbara, California. Compositions include two violin concertos, several gipsy dances and revisions of classic concertos.

NADAUD, EDOUARD, French violinist, b. Paris, Apr. 14, 1863. Studied at the Paris Conservatory, where he was awarded the first prize for violin playing, and where, after successful appearances as a soloist, he has become a teacher of the violin.

NARDINI, PIETRO, Italian violinist and composer, b. Fibiana in 1722. Studied under Tartini and in 1753 became soloist at the Ducal Court in Stuttgart, returning to Italy in 1767 to associate again with Tartini, and after the latter's death became director of music for the Duke of Tuscany. As a performer on the violin he had a technique of only moderate caliber, but a beautiful, pure and expressive tone. Compositions include violin concertos, sonatas and solos. D. Florence, May 7, 1793.

NEDBAL, OSCAR, Bohemian violinist and composer, b. Tabor, March 26, 1874. Studied under Bennewitz and became one of the founders of the Bohemian String Quartet; later conductor of the Bohemian Philharmonic Society in Prague. Compositions include a sonata for violin.

NEEDLER, HENRY, English violinist, b. London in 1685. Studied under John Banister, Jr. Became solo violin at the Academy of Ancient Music and was the first to introduce Corelli's compositions to English audiences. D. Aug. 1, 1760.

NERUDA, JOHANN CHRYSOSTOM, Bohemian violinist, b. Rossicz, in 1705. Became celebrated as a performer on the violin, but shortly after became a monk and died in the Praemonstratensian Covent at Prague in 1763.

NERUDA, WILMA MARIA FRANCISCA (LADY HALLÉ), German violinist, b. Brünn, Mar. 29, 1839. Studied under Jansa at Vienna and her debut at seven years of age created a sensation through her remarkable execution and bowing. She then visited the principal cities of Europe, appearing at the London Philharmonic Concerts in a Deberiot Concerto. Made numerous successful tours of Europe and for many years played an important part in London's musical life with Sir Charles Hallé, the pianist, whom she married after the death in 1885 of her first husband, Ludwig Norman, with whom she toured Europe, Australia and South Africa. Lady Hallé also organized a string

quartet which made its mark in chamber music annals, and in 1899 toured the United States, where she was well received, the general feeling being, however, that she should have made the visit while in her prime in order to avoid inevitable comparison with the younger generation of artists. As a player, Lady Hallé, occupied the position among women violinists that Joachim occupied among male performers. D. Berlin, Apr. 15, 1911.

NEUBAUER, FRANZ CHRISTOPH, Bohemian violinist and composer, b. Horzin in 1760. Studied under a village school teacher; traveled to Prague and Vienna where he became acquainted with Mozart and Haydn, and later succeeded J. C. F. Bach as concertmaster at the Royal Court at Bückeburg. Compositions include sonatas and duets for violin. D. through intemperance at Bückeburg, Oct. 11, 1795.

NEUMANN, MLLE. ELEANORA, Russian violinist, b. Russia (date unknown). Studied under Professor Morandi and astounded audiences at Prague and Vienna with her virtuosity, being gifted with a marvelous technique and a tone of soulful beauty.

NICHOLL, ANNE, English violinist, b. about 1728. Appeared before the Duke of Cumberland in 1746 and was credited by contemporary critics with a flexible left hand and an unusual skill in bowing.

NICHOLS, MARIE, American violinist, b. Chicago, Oct. 16, 1879. Studied under Emil Mollenhauer, Halir and Debroux. Appeared as soloist with the Berlin Philharmonic and Queen's Hall Orchestra (London) when she introduced Bruch's Serenade Op. 5. Has toured the United States several times as soloist with the Boston Symphony, Chicago Symphony and other distinguished organizations. Settled in Boston where she is teaching and concertizing extensively.

NIECKS, FREDERICK, German violinist, violist and musicologist, b. Düsseldorf, Mar. 3, 1845. Studied under Langhans, Grünewald and Auer. Appeared in public at the age of twelve and later became violist in Sir Alexander Mackenzie's String Quartet. After two years' study at Leipzig University, he was attracted by musical journalism and authorship in which he has become a leader.

NIKISCH, ARTHUR, Hungarian violinist and famous conductor, b. Szent-Miklos, Oct. 12, 1855. Studied under Hellmsberger at the Vienna Conservatory and was graduated in 1874 with the first prize for violin playing. Did some orchestral playing, but turned his attention to conducting at which he won a distinguished name with the Boston Symphony, the Berlin Philharmonic and the Leipzig Gewandhaus Orchestras. His son, Mitji Nikisch, a distinguished pianist, toured the United States in 1924. D. Leipsig, 1922.

NOAK, SYLVAIN, Dutch violinist, b. Rotterdam, Aug. 21, 1881. Studied under Spohr and Elderling at the Amsterdam Conservatory, and afterwards became a member of the Concertgebouw Orchestra, coming to the United States in 1908 as leader of the second violins in the Boston Symphony Orchestra.

NOREN, HEINRICH GOTTLIEB, Austrian violinist and composer, b. Graz, Jan. 6, 1861. Studied under Massart at the Paris Conservatory and became concertmaster of several orchestras in Belgium, Spain, Russia and Germany, finally devoting himself to composition, in addition to teaching at the Stern and other conservatories. Compositions include a violin concerto, suite, sonata and Divertimento for two violins.

NOVACEK, OTTOKAR, Hungarian violinist and composer, b. Fehertemplon, May 13, 1856. Studied under Dont at Vienna and Schradieck and Brodsky at the Leipzig Conservatory, where he won the Mendelssohn prize in 1885, becoming second violin and later violist in the Brodsky Quartet. Came to the United States about 1889 and became a member of the Boston Symphony and Damrosch Orchestras, devoting himself later entirely to composition. Compositions include concert caprices, Bulgarian dances and a "Perpetuum Mobile" for violin. D. New York, Feb. 3, 1900.

OBERMEYER, JOSEPH, Bohemian violinist and composer, b. Nezabudiez, 1749. Studied under Kammel and Tartini, whose style he followed closely in the playing of slow movements, while possessing a spirit all his own in allegro movements. Entered the service of Count Waldstein, but in 1800 became a gentleman farmer. The exact year of his death is not known, except that it must have been later than 1816. Compositions include several concertos.

OELSNER, BRUNO, German violinist and composer, b. Neudorf, July 29, 1861. Studied under Schradieck and Hermann at the Leipzig Conservatory and became solo viola at the Darmstadt Court Orchestra as well as professor of the violin at the Conservatory.

OGINSKI, PRINCE GABRIEL, Polish violinist, b. Warsaw, 1788. An excellent violinist and music composer, about whom little is known, except that he was driven from Poland, during the revolution of 1831, but later returned and died in Lithuania about 1843.

OLIVEIRA, VALERIO, French violinist, b. Paris, July 7, 1881. Studied under Marsick, and has gained an enviable reputation as a concert player equipped with a splendid technique and a broad sincere tone.

ONDRICEK, FRANZ, Bohemian violinist, b. Prague, Apr. 29, 1859. Studied under Bennewitz and Massart, winning the commendation of Wieniawski at an early age. Has made numerous successful tours of Europe, the Orient and the United States. As a performer on the violin he matured into a player with great ability and depth of conception and later established in Vienna a quartet bearing his name which has a great reputation. Compositions include a violin concerto, cadenzas for the Brahms Concerto and various smaller pieces.

ORTMANN, FREDERICK WILLIAM, American violinist, b. Charleston, S. C., Feb. 6, 1871. Studied under Sitt and Halir. Has settled in New York as orchestral player and teacher, besides writing a loose leaf violin method used in the New York Public Schools.

OTTER, FRANZ JOSEPH, German violinist, b. Nandlstadt about 1760. Studied under Nardini and became violinist at the Salzburg Cathedral for several years and later teacher and soloist at Vienna where he studied composition under Michael Haydn, brother of the illustrious composer. D. Vienna, 1876.

OTTEY, MRS. SARAH, English violinist, b. about 1700, accounted one of the first woman performers on the violin and mentioned by Dr. Burney in his history of music.

OURY, ANTHONY JAMES, English violinist, b. about 1800. Studied under Kiesewetter, Kreutzer, Baillot and Lafont, sometimes practicing fourteen hours a day and made his debut in London (at a concert for the benefit of his former master, Kiesewetter's widow) with great success. Became a prominent member of the musical fraternity in London and married the pianist, Anna Caroline Belleville, with whom he made a nine years' concert tour of Russia, Germany, Austria and France. D. Norwich, July, 1883.

PACIUS, FRIEDRICH, German violinist, b. Hamburg, Mar. 19, 1809. Studied under Spohr and became musical director of the Helsingfors University, holding the position for more than fifty years, and composing as well as producing the first Finnish opera in 1852. D. Helsingfors, Jan. 9, 1891.

PAGANINI, NICOLO, Italian violinist and composer, b. Genoa, October, 1782. Studied under Servetto and Costa, appearing in public successfully at the age of eleven. Studied further with Ghiretti and Rolla at Parma but soon demonstrated his superiority over his masters. Made numerous enormously successful tours of Italy, Austria, France, Germany and England (where he vanquished his rivals Lafont and Lipinski), and after accumulating an immense fortune, retired from the stage and died at Nice, May 27, 1840. Many biographies have been written of this remarkable man, in all of which there is an entertaining mixture of fact and fancy. As a performer on the violin he was unquestionably the greatest technician the violin world has ever known. Compositions include several concertos, airs variés, a perpetuum mobile and the famous "Twenty-four Caprices" for violin solo.

PAGIN, ANDRÉ NOEL, French violinist and composer, b. Paris, 1721. Studied under Tartini and appeared with great success at the Concerts Spirituels, but, as he refused to play any composition in public except those of his master, Tartini, he soon lost public favor. Compositions include six sonatas and several air variés for the violin, one of which is to be found in Leopold Mozart's Violin School, revised by Woldemar. D. about 1770.

PAISIBLE (first name unknown), French violinist, b. Paris, 1745. Studied under Gaviniés and became a member of the orchestra at the Concerts Spirituels. Made a successful tour of Europe as far as St. Petersburg where he hoped to appear before the Empress Catherine, but was prevented through the efforts of Lolli who was then attached to the Royal Court. Discouraged at his failure to obtain a hearing, he died at St. Petersburg by his own hand in 1781. Compositions include two violin concertos.

PANNY, JOSEPH, Austrian violinist and composer, b. Kohlmitzberg, Oct. 23, 1794. Studied under his father and later in Vienna, where he formed a friendship with Paganini, making several joint tours with him. Later they separated and he made a successful tour of German cities and founded a music school at Mainz where he died, Sept. 7, 1838. Compositions include a number of solos for the violin, a scena for violin and orchestra (written for Paganini) and a sonata for the G string.

PANOFKA, HENRI, German violinist and later famous singing teacher, b. Breslau, Oct. 2, 1807. Studied under Mayseder and Hoffman. Appeared as soloist in Munich and Berlin, finally settling in Paris, London and Florence, forsaking the violin for the art of singing. Compositions include sonatas and solos for the violin, and also the translation of Baillot's Violin Method into German. D. Florence, Nov. 18, 1887.

PAPINI, GUIDO, Italian violinist and composer, b. Florence, 1847. Studied under Giorgetti and became court violinist to the Queen of Italy, later appearing at Paris, Lisbon and London, where he achieved artistic success at all the public concerts by performing equally well the sonatas of Corelli or the most modern concertos. Taught the violin at the Royal Academies in Dublin and London. Compositions include two concertos, many charming smaller pieces and a violin school. D. London, Nov. 2, 1912.

PARAVACINI, SIGNORA, Italian violinist, b. Turin, 1769. Studied under Viotti, and attracted, when playing at Milan, the attention of the Empress Josephine, who took her to Paris as instructor for her son, Eugène Beauharnais, but afterwards neglected her. The Italian residents of Paris aided her to get back to Milan, where she made a fresh start. Made numerous successful tours of France, Germany and Austria. As a performer on the violin she had an excellent technique, and a greatly admired refinement in her interpretations. The date of her death is not known.

PARENT, ARMAND, Belgian violinist, b. Liége, Feb. 5, 1863. Studied at the Liége Conservatory and became concertmaster of the Bilse Orchestra at Berlin and the Colonne Orchestra at Paris. Organized the Parent Quartet in 1890, presenting the works of Brahms and the more modern French composers. Compositions include a violin sonata and smaller pieces.

PLATE 73

1. KATHLEEN PARLOW. 2. MAUD POWELL. 3. NICOLO PAGANINI. 4. LOUIS PERSINGER. 5. MAXIMILIAN PILZER. 6. GAETANO PUGNANI. 7. HENRI PETRI. 8. ALEXANDER PETSCHNIKOFF.

PARLOW, KATHLEEN, Canadian violinist, b. Calgary, Sept. 20, 1890. Studied under Henry Holmes in San Francisco and with Leopold Auer at Petrograd. Has made numerous successful tours of Russia, Scandinavia, Germany, Holland, Belgium and the United States, her first appearance on her return from Europe being with the Russian Symphony Orchestra (N. Y.) playing the Tschaikowsky Concerto.

PATTON, ALMA, American violinist, b. Marion, Ind., May 19, 1886, studied under Arthur Hartmann and Michael Press. Has appeared in many concerts in the Middle West and Florida where she has taught in the School of Musical Art at Jacksonville.

PENTE, EMILIO, Italian violinist and composer, b. Padua, Oct. 16, 1860. Studied under Corbellini and Bazzini at the Milan Conservatory. Made his first appearance at Florence in 1895, afterwards teaching and touring Europe, settling at London in 1909 as Professor of violin at the Guildhall School of Music. While in Padua he discovered about forty manuscripts of Tartini which had been lost for more than a century. Compositions include concertos and lighter pieces, in addition to important editions of many classical works.

PEREPELITZIN, POLYCARP DE, Russian violinist and musicologist, b. Odessa, Dec. 14, 1818. Studied under Lipinski and became deeply interested in the history of music, contributing several valuable works, including a history of music in Russia.

PERSINGER, LOUIS, American violinist, b. Rochester, Ill., Feb. 11, 1888. Studied in Leipzig at the Royal Conservatory with Hans Becker, and also with Ysaÿe at Brussels and Thibaud at Paris. In addition to being concertmaster of the Bluthner and Philharmonic Orchestras in Berlin, he has appeared as soloist with concert orchestras throughout Europe and with all the largest organizations in the United States. Is now settled in San Francisco as concertmaster and assistant conductor of the Symphony Orchestra and director of the Chamber Music Society.

PETSCHNIKOFF, ALEXANDER, Russian violinist and composer, b. Yelets, Feb. 8, 1873. Studied under Hrimaly at the Moscow Conservatory where he won a gold medal for violin playing. Made numerous successful tours of Europe and came to the United States in 1906, touring the entire country.

In 1910 he became professor of the violin at the Munich Conservatory of Music.

PETRI, HENRI WILHELM, Dutch violinist, b. Zeyst, April. 5, 1856. Studied under Joachim and appeared as soloist in London with great success, occupying thereafter several positions with European orchestras as concertmaster; finally succeeding Lauterbach at the Royal Chapel in Dresden, acting as violin professor at the conservatory and organizing an excellent string quartet. Compositions include a number of violin pieces, also important revisions of classical instructive works. D. Dresden, Apr. 7, 1914.

PFOUTS, EARL (JOHN), American violinist, b. Bucyrus, Ohio, June 20, 1881. Studied under Musin and Remy, and has toured the United States in company with other noted artists, in addition to acting as soloist with the Metropolitan Opera House Orchestra and other organizations. Has settled in Philadelphia, teaching and concertizing.

PICHL (OR PICHEL), WENZEL, Bohemian violinist and composer, b. Bechin, Sept. 25, 1741. Studied under Dittersdorf and Nardini and became musical director and solo violinist for the Archduke Ferdinand with whom he remained all his life. Pichl was a prolific composer—more than 700 works—among them several violin concertos and solos. D. Vienna, Jan. 23, 1805.

PILZER, MAXIMILIAN, American violinist and composer, b. New York, Feb. 26, 1890. Studied under Schradieck and Joachim. Appeared as soloist in Berlin and made a successful tour of Russia, Austria and Germany. Returned to the United States in 1905, making his debut at Mendelssohn Hall, N. Y. Became concertmaster of the New York Philharmonic Orchestra, but resigned in order to devote his time to concertizing and teaching. Compositions include several graceful solos and transcriptions for the violin.

PINELLI, ETTORE, Italian violinist and composer, b. Rome, Oct. 18, 1843. Studied under Ramaciotti and Joachim. Returned to Rome in 1866 where he, together with Sgambati, founded an association for performing classical chamber music, also a violin school, out of which came the "Liceo Musicale" at which he became professor of the violin. Compositions include a string quartet.

PINTO, GEORGE FREDERICK, English violinist and composer, b. Lambeth, Sept. 25, 1786. Studied under Salomon and Viotti and frequently appeared at Salomon's Concerts and later at Paris with great success. Through dissipation, his health gave away and he died at Little Chelsea, Mar. 23, 1806. Had he lived, Salomon declared he would have been a second Mozart. Compositions include violin sonatas and duets.

PINTO, THOMAS, English violinist, b. England, of Italian parents, 1714. Played Corelli's concertos so beautifully as a boy that he was engaged as leader at great concerts. The adulation of audiences caused him to neglect his playing until the arrival of Giardini as the leader of the King's Orchestra who induced him to practice again, and he shared the honor of leading this organization with the great Italian artist. D. Dublin, about 1780.

PIOT, JULIEN, Belgian violinist and teacher, b. Louvain, Apr. 27, 1850. A celebrated virtuoso and world-famous teacher; author of a highly regarded violin method. D. Paris, June 28, 1923.

PISENDEL, GEORG JOHANN, German violinist and composer, b. Karlsburg, Dec. 26, 1687. Studied under Torelli and Vivaldi and became leader of the Electoral Orchestra at Dresden, besides touring France, Germany, Austria and Italy, finally becoming concertmaster at the Royal Opera. Compositions include several concertos and solos for the violin. D. Dresden, Nov. 25, 1755.

PIXIS, FRIEDRICH WILHELM, German violinist, b. Mannheim, 1786. Virtuoso and teacher of great renown at the Prague Conservatory. D. Prague, Oct. 20, 1842.

PLUNKETT, CATHERINE, Irish violinist, b. Dublin, 1725. Studied under Matthew Dubourg, appearing at Dublin and London with great success about 1744. No facts of her career thereafter are available.

POCHON, ALFRED, Italian violinist, b. Geneva, July 30, 1878. Studied under César Thomson. Made a successful tour of France, Switzerland and Belgium, later becoming assistant to Thomas at the Brussels Conservatory. In 1903, he formed the Flonzaley Quartet in which he voluntarily plays as second violin.

POLAH, ANDRÉ, Dutch violinist. Studied at the Royal Conservatory of the Hague, where he won a gold medal for violin playing and later under Ysaÿe. Made a successful tour with Cyril Scott of England, Belgium, Holland and France. Came to the United States in 1914, as soloist with the New York Philharmonic, Detroit Symphony and other organizations. While in Paris, Polah gave a performance of Eugene Goosen's Violin Sonata with the composer at the piano.

POLK, RUDOLPH, American violinist, b. New York, 1893. Studied under Pasternack, Bendix and Lichtenberg in the United States and under Marteau at the Berlin Hochschule where he won the Joachim prize. Made numerous successful appearances in Europe until 1916 when he enlisted in the American Army, taking up his studies again and making his New York debut at Carnegie Hall in 1919. Since that time he has been studying and concertizing, part of the time on a tour with the Russian bass, Chaliapin.

POLLEDRO, GIOVANNI BATTISTA, Italian violinist and composer, b. Turin, June 10, 1781. Studied under Pugnani and made numerous successful tours, remaining in Russia for five years and in Dresden for ten years, finally accepting an appointment as Director of the Royal Orchestra at Turin where he died, Aug. 15, 1853. Thayer's *Life of Beethoven* states that Polledro met Beethoven in 1812 at Carlsbad and played one of the master's sonatas with him. Compositions include two concertos, several solos and exercises for the violin.

POLLITZER, ADOLF, Hungarian violinist, composer, teacher and editor, b. Budapest, July 23, 1832. Studied under Böhm, playing the Mendelssohn Concerto before its composer, winning his enthusiastic commendation and first prize at the Vienna Conservatory. After touring Germany he studied at Paris under Alard and came to London where he was concertmaster of several organizations and finally professor of violin at the Royal Academy, where he instructed a great many professional and non-professional players. Compositions include caprices and solo pieces for the violin, in addition to editing many of the works of the masters. D. London, Nov. 14, 1900.

POTT, AUGUST, German violinist, b. Nordheim, Nov. 7, 1806. Studied under Spohr and made numerous successful tours of Denmark and Germany, appearing at London in 1838 as soloist with the Philharmonic Orchestra with great success. Compositions include two concertos and various solos for the violin. As a performer on the violin he had an extraordinarily powerful tone. D. Graz, Aug. 27, 1883.

POSZANSKI, BARRETT ISAAC, American violinist and composer, b. Charleston, W. Va., Dec. 11, 1840. Studied under Vieux-temps and, after touring Europe, came to Charleston, but at the outbreak of the Civil War, returned to Paris for several years. In 1866, he came back to New York, touring and finally accepting the directorship of the Illinois Conservatory of Music. In 1879 he settled in London as a teacher, winning a splendid reputation as a teacher, Compositions include an instruction work *The Violin and Bow*, in addition to many charming solos. D. London, June 24, 1896.

POUGIN, ARTHUR, French violinist and author, b. Chateauroux, Aug. 6, 1834. Studied under Alard and became a member of several Parisian orchestras; finally giving up playing and teaching the violin in order to devote himself exclusively to authorship. His published works include a number of biographies of classic violinists. D. Paris, Aug. 8, 1921.

POWELL, MAUD, American violinist, b. Peru, Ill., Aug. 22, 1868. Studied under Schradieck, Dancla and Joachim. Appeared as soloist at Berlin in 1885 and made her debut with the New York Philharmonic the same year. She made numerous successful tours of Europe, Great Britain and South Africa and concertized throughout the United States annually for many years. In 1894, she organized the Maud Powell String Quartet, an excellent chamber music organization. Compositions include many transcriptions for violin of classic and modern pieces and songs. D. Uniontown, Pa., Jan. 8, 1920.

PRESS, MICHAEL, Russian violinist, who made his first concert appearance at the age of ten. Later he toured all of Europe and Great Britain with remarkable success, finally becoming professor of violin at the Moscow Conservatory. After the Revolution, Mr. Press left Russia, and after conducting symphony orchestras in Sweden, took up his residence in the United States.

PRILL, CARL, German violinist, b. Berlin, Oct. 22, 1864. Studied under Hellmich, Wirth and Joachim. Appeared as concert-master with the Bilse Orchestra and the Leipzig Gewandhaus. Later became concertmaster of the Vienna Opera and Philharmonic Concerts, and professor of violin at the Royal Academy. While in Leipzig,

he succeeded Arno Hilf as leader of the string quartet founded by Henri Petri.

PRUME, FRANCIS HUBERT, Belgian violinist and composer, b. Stavelot, June 3, 1816. Studied under Habeneck and became a teacher at the Liége Conservatory; later making a successful tour of Germany, Russia and Scandinavia. He finally became professor of the violin at the Liége Conservatory. Compositions include concertos, concert pieces and a "Melancolie," the latter still popular. D. Stavelot, July 14, 1859.

PUGNANI, GAETANO, Italian violinist and composer, b. Turin, Nov. 27, 1731. Studied under Somis and Tartini and made numerous successful tours, visiting Paris and London, finally establishing a violin school at Turin, among his distinguished pupils being Viotti, Bruni and Polledro. Compositions include violin concertos and sonatas.

PUPPO, GIUSEPPE, Italian violinist and composer, b. Lucca, June 12, 1749. Studied at the Naples Conservatory and spent years in Spain, Portugal, England and Paris, leaving the last named city in 1811 to wander about Italy; finally becoming ill and destitute, dying Apr. 19, 1827, in a hospital at Florence where he was cared for through the good offices of an English friend. Compositions include concertos, studies and duets for the violin.

QUAGLIATI, PAOLO, Italian violinist and composer, b. about 1560, to whom has been traced the first solo written for the violin (called a Toccata) with the accompaniment of a large lute.

RADICATI, FELICE ALLESSANDRO, Italian violinist and composer, b. Turin in 1778. Studied under Pugnani and traveled through Lombardy and visited Vienna in 1818. He died on Apr. 14, 1823, from injuries received through being thrown from a carriage. Compositions include duets and airs variés for violin.

RAIMONDI, IGNAZIO, Italian violinist and composer, b. Naples in 1733. Studied under Barbella and visited Amsterdam, Paris and London where he settled as a performer and composer with considerable success. Compositions include violin sonatas and duets as well as chamber music. D. London, Jan. 14, 1813.

RAPPOLDI, ADRIAN, German violinist, b. Berlin, Sept. 13, 1876. Studied under his father, Joachim and Wilhelmj and became concertmaster of the Bilse Orchestra and other organizations throughout Europe. Now occupies the position of violin teacher at the Dresden Conservatory.

RAPPOLDI, EDOUARD, Austrian violinist and composer, b. Vienna, Feb. 21, 1839. Studied under Jansa, Hellmsberger and Böhm, concertizing and occupying various positions as teacher and concertmaster; finally became Joachim's colleague at the Berlin Hochschule and member of the Joachim Quartet. From 1877 until 1898 he became professor of violin at the Dresden Conservatory and concertmaster with Lauterbach at the Dresden Opera. Compositions include two violin sonatas. D. Dresden, May 16, 1903.

RASOUMOUSKY, COUNT ANDREAS, Russian amateur violinist, b. Lemeschi, Oct. 22, 1752, and was Russian ambassador at Vienna for more than twenty years. He formed a string quartet in 1808, with Schuppanzigh as the first violinist and he himself as second violin. Beethoven's Quartets Op. 59 are dedicated to him.

REBEL, JEAN FERRY, French violinist and composer, b. Paris about 1661. Became a violinist at the Paris Opera and one of the King's "Twenty-four Violins." Compositions include sonatas for violin with double-bass accompaniment. D. Paris in 1747.

REBNER, ADOLF, Austrian violinist, b. Vienna, Nov. 21, 1876. Studied under Grün and Marsick, afterwards succeeding Hugo Heerman as professor of violin at the Frankfort Conservatory, where he founded a quartet with which he toured Germany, France, England and Spain with great success.

REHFELD, FABIAN, German violinist and composer, b. Tuchel, Jan. 23, 1842. Studied under Zimmerman and Grünwald at Berlin. Was appointed royal chamber musician in 1868; was concertmaster of the royal court in 1873 and afterwards devoted himself to private teaching and composing. Compositions include a number of pleasing violin pieces and transcriptions. D. Berlin, Nov. 1920.

REMÉNYI, EDOUARD, Hungarian violinist, b. Heves, 1830. Studied under Böhm at the Vienna Conservatory, and toured the world practically all his life, visiting America first in 1848; England in 1854, where he was appointed solo violinist to Queen Victoria, and returning to Austria in 1860 where he became solo violinist to the Emperor. He soon resumed his touring of the world and continued concertizing in Europe, the Far East and America, dying while on the concert platform at San Francisco, May 15, 1898. As a performer on the violin he had a marvelous technique and a tone at once passionate and full of pathos. During one of his tours of Germany, Reményi had Johannes Brahms as an accompanist. Compositions include a violin concerto and some solos which have little importance.

REUCHSEL, MAURICE, French violinist, b. Lyons, Nov. 22, 1880. Studied under his father and at the Paris Conservatory and toured Europe as violin and viola d'amore virtuoso. Became editor of the Express Musical de Lyon in 1903, also writing a number of interesting essays on matters appertaining to the violin. Compositions include a sonata, concert pieces and suites for violin.

REUTER, FLORIZEL VON, American violinist, child prodigy and composer, b. Davenport, Ia., Jan. 21, 1893. Studied under Bendix, Sauret, Thomson and Marteau and made numerous successful tours of Europe and America and during the World War became director of the Music Academy at Zurich, Switzerland. Compositions include Roumanian Dances and other solos for violin, also an instructive work on the Caprices of Paganini.

REY, LOUIS THEOPHILE, French violinist, b. Strasbourg, Feb. 27, 1852. An excellent violinist, who for thirty years was solo violin of the Geneva Theatre Orchestra, besides playing with the Monte Carlo and Lamoureux Orchestras, and teaching the violin.

REYNOLDS, EDIE, Hungarian violinist, b. Budapest. She was brought to England when a child and began violin study at eight years of age, later entering the Royal Academy of Music under Sauret. Miss Reynolds once had the privilege, at a luncheon given by Sauret, of playing a Bruch and a Tschaikowsky concerto with the composers themselves as her accompanists, both of them being Sauret's guests.

RIES, FRANZ, German violinist and composer, b. Berlin, Apr. 7, 1846. Studied under Massart and Vieuxtemps, taking first prize at the Paris Conservatory and becoming violist in the Vieuxtemps Quartet in London at the Crystal Palace, but in 1872, relinquished the career of virtuoso on account of a nervous affection of the left hand, and entered the music publishing

PLATE 74

1. ERNA RUBINSTEIN. 2. MAX ROSEN. 3. EDOUARD REMENYI. 4. THEO-
DORE SPIERING. 5. ALBERT SPALDING. 6. PIERRE RODE. 7. FRANZ
RIES. 8. JOHANN SVENDSEN.

business, first in Dresden and later in Berlin. Compositions include four famous suites played by most virtuosos.

RIES, HUBERT, German violinist and composer, b. Bonn, Apr. 1, 1802. Studied under Spohr and occupied various posts of distinction as concertmaster, conductor and teacher, including leadership of the Royal Orchestra at Berlin and director of the Berlin Philharmonic Society. Compositions include two violin concertos and a violin method. D. Berlin, Sept. 14, 1886.

RIES, LOUIS, German violinist, b. Berlin, Jan. 30, 1830. Studied under his father, Hubert Ries, and under Vieuxtemps. Settled in London and was a member of the Quartet of the Musical Union for fifteen years and second violin at the Monday Night Popular Concerts for thirty-eight years. D. London, Oct. 3, 1913.

RIETZ, EDOUARD, German violinist, b. Berlin, Oct., 1802. Studied under his father and under Rode. He became a member of the Royal Orchestra, resigning on account of ill health, and founded an orchestral society which he conducted with great success. Rietz was an intimate friend of Mendelssohn, who regarded him highly as a player and a man, dedicating several compositions to him. D. Berlin, Jan. 23, 1832.

RITTER, HERMAN, German violinist and musicologist, b. Wismar, Sept. 26, 1849. Inventor of the "viola alta" an instrument claimed to be an improvement on the ordinary viola, substituting the resonance of the violin for the usual muffled tone of the viola. In 1876, he toured all Europe as a viola virtuoso, becoming professor at the Würzburg Royal School of Music and in 1905 founded the Ritter Quartet, composed of the viola, viola alta, viola tenore and viola bassa. He has written numerous works on the viola and its history.

RITTMEISTER, HEINRICH, German violinist, b. Bremen, Jan. 31, 1881. Studied at Bremen and Munich, playing the Mozart "D Major Concerto" at the age of fourteen with the Bremen Philharmonic Orchestra. Has held various positions as member and concertmaster of orchestras in Munich, Bremen and in the United States with the New York Russian Symphony Orchestra, and the Minneapolis Symphony. He is at present Concertmaster of the Kansas City Symphony Orchestra and leader of the Rittmeister String Quartet.

RIVARDE, SERGEI ACHILLE, American violinist, b. New York in 1865. Studied under Dancla, Simon and Wieniawski, taking first prize at the Paris Conservatory and becoming concertmaster of the Lamoureux Orchestra for several years; later professor of violin at the Royal College of Music, Berlin.

ROBERRECHTS, ANDRÉ, Belgian violinist and composer, b. Brussels, Dec. 16, 1797. Studied under Van der Plancken, Baillot and Viotti, becoming solo violinist to the King of Belgium, later settling in Paris as virtuoso and teacher. Compositions include a romantic fantasy and solo for the violin. D. Paris, May 23, 1860.

RODE, JACQUES PIERRE JOSEPH, French violinist and composer, b. Bordeaux, Feb. 16, 1774. Studied under Fauvel and Viotti. Toured Holland and Germany and became professor of violin at the Paris Conservatory. He also occupied the posts of solo violinist to Napoleon and Czar Alexander of Russia. Boccherini is said to have written a concerto for him and Beethoven the Romance Op. 50. Compositions include the celebrated "Twenty-four Caprices," thirteen concertos, a violin method and smaller works. D. Chateau-Bourbon, Nov. 25, 1830.

ROENTGEN, ENGELBERT, Dutch violinist, b. Deventes, Sept. 30, 1829. Studied under David at the Leipzig Conservatory and became a member of the Opera and Gewandhaus Orchestra; later professor at the Conservatory and successor of David at the first desk of the Gewandhaus Orchestra. He also prepared a scholarly edition of the Beethoven Quartets. His son, Julius, has written sonatas for violin and piano. D. Leipzig, Dec. 12, 1897.

ROENTGEN, JULIUS, Dutch violinist, b. Amsterdam, May 12, 1881. Studied under Cramer, Flesch and Joachim. Became concertmaster at Dusseldorf and came to the United States as second violin of the Kneisel Quartet and teacher at the New York Institute of Musical Art. Now professor of violin at the Rotterdam Conservatory and leader of a chamber music organization.

ROLLA, ALESSANDRO, Italian violinist and composer, b. Pavia, Apr. 22, 1757. Studied under Renzi and Conti and became leader of the Orchestra at Parma where Paganini studied with him. In 1802, he was leader and conductor at the La Scale Opera House, Milan, and professor of violin at the Milan Conservatory. Compositions include several concertos for the violin and the viola, for which he had a great fondness, writing and performing concertos on it in public. D. Milan, Sept. 15, 1841.

ROLLA, ANTOINE, Italian violinist and composer, b. Parma, Apr. 18, 1798. Studied under his father, Alessandro Rolla and became first violin of the Italian Opera Orchestra at Dresden, where he died, May 19, 1837. Compositions include a concerto and several smaller violin pieces.

ROMBERG, ANDREAS JACOB, German violinist and composer, b. Munster, Apr. 27, 1767. A virtuoso of high rank, who toured Holland, France and Austria, settling later at Hamburg and afterwards succeeding Spohr as Court Conductor at Gotha. For several years he toured Europe with his cousin, Bernhard Romberg, an excellent cellist, their duet performances being considered almost perfection itself. Compositions include twenty-three violin concertos. D. 1821.

ROSÉ, ARNOLD JOSEF, Roumanian violinist, b. Jassay, Oct. 24, 1863. Studied under Heissler at the Vienna Conservatory; became concertmaster of the Imperial Court Orchestra in Vienna and later occupied the same position at the Bayreuth Festivals. He then founded the Rosé Quartet at Vienna, one of Europe's most famous organizations and became professor of violin at the Vienna Conservatory.

ROSEN, MAX, Roumanian violinist, b. Roumania, 1900. Came to New York in infancy and studied under Mannes, Sinsheimer, Auer and Hess. Made his debut in Christiania and toured Denmark, Germany, Norway and Sweden; made his New York debut with the Philharmonic Society in 1918; since then has been concertizing in the United States.

ROSS, GILBERT, American violinist, b. Madison, Wisconsin. Studied under Sametini in Chicago and with Leopold Auer, making his debut in 1922 at Berlin and following it with a tour of the principal German cities, closing the tour with a performance of the Brahms and Tschaikowsky Concertos with the Berlin Philharmonic Orchestra. He appeared in New York on Mar. 13, 1923, and has since been concertizing in the United States.

ROSSI, MARCELLO, Austrian violinist, b. Vienna, Oct. 16, 1862. Studied under Lauterbach and Massart. Toured Austria-Hungary, Germany and Roumania with the singer, Padilla-Artot, and was created court violinist to the Emperor Josef of Austria.

In 1889 he made another tour of Austria and Germany, playing on a Stradivarius, formerly the property of Wieniawski and purchased from the great virtuoso's widow.

ROVELLI, PIETRO, Italian violinist and composer, b. Bergamo, Feb. 6, 1793. Studied under Rodolphe Kreutzer, playing at Weimar, at Munich, where Molique was his pupil, and at Vienna; finally returning to Bergamo where he remained until his death, Sept. 8, 1838. Compositions include études and caprices as well as a set of variations for the violin.

ROYER, CLARENCE DE VAUX, American violinist and teacher, b. Lancaster, Pa., May 10, 1874. Studied under Halir, Moser, Ysaÿe and Marsick. Made numerous successful tours of Europe, Canada and the United States and has since taught the violin at well-known colleges and conservatories in the United States and Canada.

RUBINSTEIN, ERNA, Hungarian violinist, b. Hermannstadt, about 1906. Studied under Hubay at the Budapest Conservatory and made her debut with orchestras at Budapest and Vienna. Made a successful tour of Germany, Czecho-Slovakia, Scandinavia and Holland, making her New York debut with the Philharmonic orchestra in 1921. As a performer on the violin she has a splendid technique and a remarkable tone.

RUDERSDORFF, J., Dutch violinist and composer, b. Amsterdam in 1799. Made his first public appearance at the age of eight, later becoming concertmaster at Hamburg and settling in Dublin, where he remained twenty years. In 1851, he went to Berlin, conducting more than one thousand concerts and playing six hundred times himself in six years. Compositions include polonaises and airs variés for violin. D. Konigsberg in 1866.

RUEGGER, CHARLOTTE, Swiss violinist and composer, b. Lucerne, Nov. 17, 1876. Studied under Zajic, Colyns and César Thomson at the Brussels Conservatory, winning the first prize. Made numerous successful tours of Belgium, Germany, Switzerland and France and has since taught the violin at the Oberlin (O.) Conservatory and Meredith College, Raleigh, N. C. Compositions include a concerto, sonatas, solo pieces and études for violin.

RUST, FRIEDRICH WILHELM, German violinist and composer, b. Dessau, July 6, 1739. Studied under his brother, Johann, and with Franz Benda, Tartini and Pugnani. Spent his entire life in Dessau, where he was the leader of musical activities. Compositions include several violin sonatas, one of which has been edited by David and another by Singer. He also wrote a sonata for the E string of the violin.

RUST, JOHANN LUDWIG ANTON, German violinist, b. Dessau, about 1700. An amateur performer whose claims to distinction lay in the fact that he was a member of Johann Sebastian Bach's orchestra in Leipzig and that he was the first instructor of his famous brother, Friedrich Wilhelm Rust.

SACCHI, REGINA, Italian violinist, b. Mantua in 1764. Studied at the Conservatory in Venice. A woman violinist said to have been highly regarded as a performer by Mozart.

SAENGER, GUSTAV, American violinist and editor, b. New York, May 31, 1865. Studied under C. Richter, Leopold Meyer and Leopold Damrosch, entering New York's music life for many years as orchestral player and conductor. In 1909 he resigned all other duties in order to devote himself exclusively to editorial work, consisting chiefly of violin music revision and the editorial management of two important music magazines. Compositions include a concertino, several concert solos and many smaller works for the violin.

SAENGER-SETHE, MADAME IRMA, Belgian violinist, b. Brussels, April 28, 1876. Studied under Jokisch, Wilhelmj and Ysaÿe at the Brussels Conservatory, winning first prize at fifteen years of age. In 1894 appeared as soloist in all the principal cities of Germany, and made her London debut in 1895 where she was favorably compared to Lady Hallé (Norman Neruda). She has since made numerous successful tours of Europe.

SAHLA, RICHARD, Austrian violinist and composer, b. Graz, Sept. 17, 1855. Studied under David at the Leipzig Conservatory. In 1873 appeared as soloist with the Gewandhaus Orchestra. Since then has toured Europe several times and acted as concertmaster of the Vienna Opera, Hanover Royal Orchestra and other famous organizations. Compositions include a Roumanian Rhapsody and other violin solos.

SAINT-GEORGE, GEORGE, English violinist composer and reproducer of old instruments, b. Leipzig in 1841, of English parents. Studied under Mildner at the Prague Conservatory where his interest was greatly excited in the viola d'amore; later becoming a virtuoso on this instrument and appearing with great success as a soloist in England and on the Continent. In addition he has made a number of violins, violas and cellos as well as reproductions of ancient English musical instruments which are declared by experts to be perfect. Compositions include many effective violin pieces.

SAINT-GEORGE, HENRY, English violinist, editor and author, b. London in 1866. Studied under his father, George Saint-George, appearing in London as a soloist in 1881. Since then has concertized throughout the United Kingdom as a violin and viola da gamba virtuoso. Has edited the violin magazine The Strad for years and written a highly instructive work on the violin bow.

SAINT-GEORGE, CHEVALIER DE, West Indian violinist, b. Guadeloupe, Dec. 25, 1745. A mulatto violinist, noted for his eccentricities, who became a pupil of Leclair. His compositions include violin sonatas, concertos and duets. D. Paris, June 12, 1799.

SAINT-LUBIN, LÉON DE, Italian violinist and composer, b. Turin, July 5, 1805. Studied under Polledro and Spohr. Toured Germany and finally became leader at the Konigstadt Theatre, Berlin, for about twenty years. Compositions include five concertos for violin, also an arrangement for solo violin of the "Lucia" Sextette which is still used as a show piece. D. Berlin, Feb. 13, 1850.

SAINTON, PROSPER, French violinist and composer, b. Toulouse, June 5, 1813. Studied under Habeneck at the Paris Conservatory, winning first prize in 1834. Toured Europe with great success and finally became professor of the violin at the Toulouse Conservatory and at the Royal Academy of Music, London, in 1845. He also acted as concertmaster with the Philharmonic and Covent Garden Orchestras. D. London, Oct. 17, 1890. Compositions include concertos and solos for the violin.

SALOMON, JOHANN PETER, German violinist, b. Bonn, 1745. Became a member of the Electoral Orchestra and later went to London, establishing himself as soloist, quartet player and conductor. He was a personal friend of Haydn, for whom he arranged two visits to London and the last quartets the master wrote were composed for him. Salomon was also one of the founders of the London Philharmonic Society, leading the orchestra at the first concert in 1813. D. London, Nov. 28, 1815.

SARASATE, PABLO DE, Spanish violinist and composer, b. Pamplona, Mar. 10, 1844. Studied under Alard at the Paris Conservatory, winning all the highest prizes. Toured Europe, America, South Africa and the Orient; his career as a concert artist ending only with his death. Early in his career, Sarasate played only brilliant pieces such as operatic fantasias, but as his taste matured, he also gave the finest renditions of the classics. Several great compositions, among them Lalo's "Symphonie Espagnole" and Bruch's "Scotch Fantasy," were written for and first played by him. As a performer on the violin he possessed perfect intonation, a marvelous technique and an enchanting tone. Compositions include a number of brilliant solo pieces on the order of his famous "Zigeunerweisen." D. Biarritz, Sept. 21, 1908.

SASLAVSKY, ALEXANDER, Russian violinist, b. Kharkov, Feb. 9, 1876. Studied under Gorski and Grün. In 1893, he toured the Canadian Provinces and later appeared as soloist and concertmaster with the New York Symphony and Russian Symphony Orchestra; also organizing the Mendelssohn Trio Club and the New York Trio. In 1907 he organized the Saslavsky String Quartet, which has toured the United States and has given summer concerts in Denver. D. 1924.

SAURET, ÉMILE, French violinist and composer, b. Dun-le-Roi, May 22, 1852. Studied under Charles Deberiot. Toured Europe and America with great success, besides acting as professor of violin at the Kullak Academy at Berlin; the Royal Academy of Music at London and the Chicago Musical College. In 1908, he became professor at Trinity College, London. As a performer on the violin he had an extremely brilliant style suggestive of Sarasate. Sauret was a great friend of Liszt, who often played with him. Compositions include two violin concertos, two rhapsodies, several smaller pieces and a violin method. D. London in 1919.

SAUZAY, CHARLES EUGÈNE, French violinist and composer, b. Paris, July 14, 1809. Studied under Baillot at the Paris Conservatory, winning the prize for violin playing in 1825 and becoming a member of Baillot's quartet. In 1860 he succeeded Girard as professor of violin at the Conservatory, retiring in 1892. Compositions

include a set of "Etudes Harmoniques" for violin. D. Paris, Jan. 24, 1901.

SCHELLEŘ, JACOB, Bohemian violinist, b. Schettal, May 16, 1759. Studied under the Abbé Vogler at Mannheim and later at Paris, in the Viotti School. Became concertmaster of the Duke of Wurtemberg's Orchestra at Stuttgart; after 1792 he led the life more of an itinerant fiddler, even borrowing a violin to perform on. As a performer on the violin he was famous for his playing of double stops and harmonics. D. about 1803.

SCHIEVER, ERNST, German violinist, b. Hanover, Mar. 23, 1844. Studied under Joachim and joined the Muller quartet; later becoming teacher at the Berlin Hochschule and member of the Joachim Quartet. After organizing a highly successful quartet in Berlin, he came to Liverpool, England, in 1878, conducting the Richter Concerts and forming another quartet which has an enviable reputation in England.

SCHMULLER, ALEXANDER, Russian violinist and musicologist, b. Mozyr, Dec. 5, 1880. Studied under Sevcik, Hrimaly and Auer. Became instructor at the Stern Conservatory, Berlin, and the Amsterdam Conservatory of virtuoso classes. In 1915, he gave a cycle of sixteen violin concertos under the baton of Willem Mengelberg with the Concertgebouw Orchestra at Amsterdam. Came to the United States in 1921, winning admiration for his interpretative originality and vigor. Schmuller is the author of numerous essays of musical interest.

SCHORG, FRANZ, German violinist, b. Munich in 1874. Studied at the Brussels Conservatory under Ysaÿe winning first prize for violin playing. After a long concert tour with the singer, Albani, he specialized for years as a quartet player, forming an organization of his own which has achieved such success as to be considered one of Europe's best chamber music institutions.

SCHRADIECK, HENRY, German violinist and teacher, b. Hamburg, April 29, 1846. Studied under Léonard and David. Became concertmaster of the private concerts in Bremen and teacher at the Moscow Conservatory. Was concertmaster of the Hamburg Philharmonic and Leipzig Gewandhaus Orchestras, succeeding David as professor of violin at the Leipzig Conservatory. Came to the United States in 1883 as violin pro-

PLATE 75

1. OTTOKAR ŠEVČIK.   2. TOSCHA SEIDEL.   3. LOUIS SPOHR.   4. IRMA
SEYDEL.   5. CAMILLO SIVORI.   6. HENRY SCHRADIECK.   7. HANS
SITT.   8. ACHILLE SIMONETTI.

fessor at the Cincinnati College of Music; later at the Broad St. Conservatory, Philadelphia and the Institute of Applied Music in New York. Schradieck had many distinguished pupils, among them Maud Powell. Compositions include many valuable technical studies for the violin. D. New York, Mar. 25, 1918.

SCHROEDER, HERMANN, German violinist and composer, b. Quellinburg, July 28, 1843. Studied under A. Ritter at Magdeburg and founded a music institute in Berlin. Wrote an excellent violin method and an essay on stringed instruments. D. Berlin, Jan. 31, 1909.

SCHUBERT, FRANZ, German violinist and composer, b. Dresden, July 22, 1808. Studied under Rottmeier, Hasse and Lafont. Succeeded Lipinski as concertmaster of the Dresden Orchestra in 1861, retiring in 1873. Compositions include études and pieces for the violin. His dainty composition "L'Abeille" (The Bee) is still much in use. D. Dresden, April 12, 1878.

SCHULTZE, WILHELM HEINRICH, German violinist, b. Hanover in 1827. Came to the United States in 1848 as a member of the Germania Orchestra. Became leader of the Mendelssohn Quintette Club at Boston and professor of music at Syracuse University in 1877. D. Syracuse, Sept. 1888.

SCHUPPANZIGH, IGNAZ, Austrian violinist and composer, b. Vienna in 1776. A member of Prince Rasumovski's private quartet, where were first played Beethoven's great quartets, in addition to those of Mozart and Haydn. He made a successful tour as soloist and with his quartet in Germany, Poland and Russia. Schuppanzigh has the distinction of having taught Beethoven both the viola and the violin. Compositions include a violin solo with quartet accompaniment. D. Vienna, Mar. 2, 1830.

SCIPIONE, GUIDI, Italian violinist, b. Venice in 1884. Appeared in recital at the age of eleven; afterwards entering the Royal Conservatory of Music in Milan, where he was awarded first prize. He also founded the Guidi Trio in London and became concertmaster of the New York Philharmonic Orchestra and member of the New York Trio.

SEBALD, ALEXANDER, Hungarian violinist and composer, b. Budapest, April 29, 1869. Studied under Saphir at the Royal Hungarian Academy of Music and later with César Thomson, becoming a member of the Ge-

wandhaus Orchestra. Resigned in 1903 in order to tour Germany and other European countries. Came to the United States in 1910, touring extensively, and settling in Chicago as a teacher. Compositions include solo pieces and a technical method for the violin.

SEGALL, ARNO, American violinist, b. Savannah, Ga., 1906. Studied under Leopold Auer, at the Brussels Conservatory where he won the highest honors, and is at present concertizing in Germany and continuing his studies under Willy Hess. He will make an American tour in 1925.

SEIDEL, TOSCHA, Russian violinist, b. Odessa, Nov. 4, 1900. Studied under Auer, making his first public appearance in 1915. Has made a successful tour of Norway, Sweden, Denmark, England, France, Australia and the United States, where he first appeared in 1918.

SENAILLÉ, JEAN-BAPTISTE, French violinist and composer, b. Paris, Nov. 23, 1687. Studied under Anet and Vitali. Was a member of Louis XV's "Twenty-four Violins." Composer of fifty sonatas for the violin, which give evidence throughout of their composer's admiration for Corelli. D. Paris, Oct. 8, 1730.

SENKRAH, ARMA, American violinist, b. New York, June 6, 1864. An American girl whose real name was Harkness and who studied under Wieniawski, Massart, Vieuxtemps and Hilf, winning the first prize at the Paris Conservatory. Toured Europe and England successfully for many years. D. New York, Sept. 5, 1900.

SERATO, ARRIGO, Italian violinist, b. Bologna, Feb. 7, 1877. Studied under Sarti, appearing in Berlin as a soloist in 1895. Made a successful tour of Europe and came to the United States in 1914, appearing with distinction all over the country. In 1901 M. Serato first performed Sinigaglia's "A Major Violin Concerto" at Berlin.

ŠEVČIK, OTOKAR, Bohemian violinist and world-famous teacher, b. Horazdiowitz, Mar. 22, 1852. Studied under Bennewitz at the Prague Conservatory. Appeared as concertmaster of the Mozarteum in Salzburg and the Komische Opera at Vienna. Became professor of violin at the Prague Conservatory in 1892 and director of the violin department in 1901. His pupils include Kubelik, Kocian, Marie Hall, Ondricek, Zimbalist, Suchy, Culbertson, Leonora Jackson and many others. In 1909 he became head of the Master School for violin at the Royal and Imperial Academy of Music at Vienna. In 1923 he came to the United States for special teaching work. His compositions include many serious and important technical works, including a method; also Bohemian dances.

SEVERN, EDMUND, English violinist and composer, b. Nottingham, Dec. 10. 1862. Came to the United States and studied under Bernhard Listemann at Boston and Wirth at Berlin. Mr. Severn has taught the violin and concertized in the United States since 1888, becoming in 1907-1914, lecturer for the Board of Education of the City of New York, and since devoting himself to teaching and composing. Compositions include a violin concerto, four suites, many solo pieces and a suite for two violins and piano.

SEYDEL, IRMA, American violinist, b. Boston, Mass., Sept. 27, 1896. Studied under her father, a violinist in the Boston Symphony Orchestra. also under Strube and Loeffler. Appeared with the Gürzenich Orchestra at Cologne in 1909, and has since been soloist several times with the Boston Symphony Orchestra as well as the Berlin Philharmonic, Leipzig Philharmonic and many other famous European orchestras.

SHINNER, EMILY (MRS. A. F. LIDDELL), English violinist, b. Cheltenham, July 7, 1862. Studied under H. Jacobsen, a pupil of Joachim and later of the master-teacher himself. Made her debut in London in June, 1882, at a concert of the London Musical Society, laying the foundation for a successful career as a virtuoso. In 1887 she organized an admirable ladies' string quartet. D. London, July 17, 1901.

SHUTTLEWORTH, OBADIAH, English violinist and composer, b. London, about 1670. An excellent violinist, and one of the earliest English performers of whom there is any account. He became concertmaster of the Swan Tavern Concerts, Cornhill, holding this position until his death about 1735. Compositions include twelve concertos and some sonatas for the violin.

SICARD, MICHAEL DE, Russian violinist, b. Odessa in 1868. Studied under Sevcik, Massart and Joachim. Became concertmaster of the Colonne Orchestra in Paris; toured Europe with great success and was professor of violin at the Kiev Imperial Russian Music School.

SIGHICELLI, a noted family of Italian violinists, composed of Filippo, b. Modena, 1686, d. 1773; Giuseppe, Fillipo's son, b. 1737, d. 1826; Carlo, Giuseppe's son, b. 1772, d. 1806; Antonio, Carlo's son, b. 1802, d. 1835; Vincenzo, Antonio's son, b. 1830, was teaching in Paris in 1855.

SIMONETTI, ACHILLE, Italian violinist and composer, b. Turin, June 12, 1859. Studied under Gamba, Sivori and Dancla and has made successful appearances as a soloist in European cities and in London where he has lived for some years, becoming a member of the "London Trio," established in 1889, and giving a series of subscription concerts annually. Mr. Simonetti is also violin professor at the Royal Academy, Dublin. Compositions include two violin sonatas and a number of attractive salon pieces.

SINGELÉE, JEAN-BAPTISTE, Belgian violinist, composer and arranger, b. Brussels, Sept. 25, 1812. Famous for his skill and industry in arranging fantasias of a light and pleasing character from the melodies of famous operas, these numbering more than one hundred. Compositions include two concertos and many solo pieces. D. at Ostend, Sept. 29, 1875.

SINGER, EDMUND, Hungarian violinist, b. Totis, Oct. 14, 1831. Studied under Ellinger, Kőhne, Böhm and at the Paris Conservatory. Became soloist at the Budapest Theater, concertmaster at Weimar, later and until his death, professor of the violin and leader of a quartet at the Stuttgart Conservatory. Compositions include many solos, a violin method, cadenzas to the Beethoven and Brahms Concertos and revisions of the Etudes of Fiorillo, Gaviniés, Rode, etc. D. Stuttgart, Jan. 23, 1912.

SINSHEIMER, BERNARD, American violinist, b. New York, in 1870. Studied under Joachim and Léonard. In 1886 he appeared as soloist in New York, Paris in 1888, Berlin in 1891. Has been teacher at several institutions and organized his own quartet in 1902, concertizing in New York and other cities. Now teaching privately in New York.

SIRMEN, MADDALENA LOMBARDINI, Italian violinist, b. Venice about 1735. This accomplished lady studied the violin with Tartini, and was the recipient of a letter, dated at Padua, Mar. 5, 1760, containing instructions as to bowing and fingering which constitutes a valuable work of instruction. She toured Europe with enormous success, and was equally well received in London for many years, until she abandoned violin playing and became a singer. Her husband, Ludovico Sirmen, was also a violinist and their performances together were considered of the highest class. Her compositions include several violin concertos and sonatas. The date of her death is not known, but it must have been after May, 1785, when she appeared last at the Concerts Spirituels at Paris.

SITT, HANS, Bohemian violinist and composer, b. Prague, Sept. 21, 1850. Studied under Bennewitz and Mildner at the Prague Conservatory. In 1883 taught the violin at the Leipzig Conservatory and played second violin in the Brodsky Quartet, becoming an important factor in Leipzig's musical affairs until his death. Compositions include six concertos, several concertinos, shorter pieces, exercises and a violin method. D. Leipzig, Mar. 10, 1922.

SIVORI, ERNESTO CAMILLO, Italian violinist and composer, b. Genoa, Oct. 25, 1815. Studied under Restano, Costa and Paganini, the latter taking a great interest in instructing him, and composing a concertino and six sonatas for his use. Toured as a virtuoso all over Europe, Great Britain, the United States, Mexico and South America, imitating Paganini in the technical brilliancy and bravura style of his playing. Compositions include concertos, fantasies and a number of solos for violin. D. Genoa, Feb. 18, 1894.

SKALITZKY, ERNEST, Bohemian violinist and teacher, b. Prague, May 30, 1853. Studied under Mildner and Joachim. Became concertmaster of orchestras in Amsterdam and Bremen; later established himself as teacher and quartet player in Bremen, becoming a member of the Becker and also of the Schumann Quartet.

SLAVÍK, JOSEPH, Bohemian violinist and composer, b. Jince, May 26, 1806. Studied under Pixis at the Prague Conservatory. Concertized in Vienna and Paris with great success. Compositions include two violin concertos and a concerto for two violins. D. Budapest, May 30, 1833.

SMITH, F. LORENZ, American violinist, b. New York, Dec. 25, 1880. Studied under Abel and Walter in Munich; also studied composition with Josef Rheinberger. Awarded a medal for violin playing in 1899. Became a member of the Metropolitan Opera

Orchestra and later of the New York Philharmonic Orchestra.

SNEL, JOSEPH-FRANÇOIS, Belgian violinist and composer, b. Brussels, July 30, 1793. Studied under Baillot at the Paris Conservatory. Became solo violinist at the Grand Theater, Brussels; later founding a music academy and being appointed inspector of music in the army music schools. Compositions include concertos and solos for the violin. D. near Brussels, Mar. 10, 1861.

SOLDAT-ROEGER, MARIE, German violinist, b. Graz, Mar. 25, 1864. Studied under Pleiner in Graz and Joachim at the Berlin Hochschule, winning the Mendelssohn prize. Toured Austria, Germany and England. She is especially noted for her playing of the Brahms Concerto, and her renditions with her own quartet (composed of ladies) of Brahms chamber music, the master being greatly interested in the quartet's work, even directing the rehearsals of some of his chamber music compositions himself.

SOMIS, GIOVANNI BATTISTA, Italian violinist and composer, b. Piedmont in 1676. Studied under Corelli and was himself the teacher of Giardini, Pugnani, Leclair and Chabran. His brother, Lorenzo, was also a violinist and composer of renown. Compositions include a concerto and sonatas for violin. D. Turin, Aug. 14, 1763.

SPAGNOLETTI, P., Italian violinist, b. Cremona in 1768. Studied at the Naples Conservatory and later came to London and was one of the original members of the London Philharmonic Society. He became an important factor in the orchestral concerts in London, and was leader of the orchestra at all of Paganini's appearances in that city. D. London in 1834.

SPALDING, ALBERT, American violinist and composer, b. Chicago, Aug. 15, 1888. Studied under Buitrago, Chiti and Lefort. In 1905 appeared as soloist at Paris with great success. Has made numerous successful tours of France, Germany, England, Scandinavia, Russia, Holland, Italy, Egypt and the United States where he has settled as a concert artist, making frequent tours. Compositions include concertos, a sonata, a suite and many smaller pieces.

SPIERING, THEODORE, American violinist, b. St. Louis, Sept. 5, 1871. Studied under his father in St. Louis, and Schradieck and Joachim. Became a member of the Chicago Symphony Orchestra and in 1893 organized

PLATE 76

1. ADOLPHE SCHMUELLER. 2. PAUL STOEVING. 3. PABLO DE SARA-
SATE. 4. ARRIGO SERATO. 5. PIETRO TIRINDELLI. 6. ÉMILE
SAURET. 7. TERESINA TUA. 8. GUSTAV TINLOT.

a string quartet, giving more than 400 concerts in the United States and Canada. From 1898-1907 he became professor of the violin in many American and German conservatories, and toured England, Germany and Holland from 1907 to 1909. Was concertmaster of the New York Philharmonic in 1909-11. Since that time he has toured extensively and taught violin at the New York College of Music from 1914-1918. Compositions include six "Artist Etudes" for violin solo, also a number of scholarly editions of the classics in collaboration with Rudolf Ganz.

SPOHR, LUDWIG LOUIS, German violinist and composer, b. Brunswick, Apr. 5, 1784. Studied under Kunisch, Hartung and Maucourt at Brunswick; later under Franz Eck, accompanying him to Petrograd. Toured Germany in 1804 with great success; later (1815) toured Italy and Holland, playing his own Concertante for two violins with Paganini. In 1820 he appeared in England with remarkable success, and after further tours, settled in 1821 at Kassel as court conductor and teacher, retiring in 1857. His pupils included David, Kömpel, Böhm, Blagrove and many others. Compositions include fifteen violin concertos, many large and small solos, and a very complete violin method. D. Kassel, Nov. 22, 1859.

STABILINI, GIROLAMO, Italian violinist, b. Rome in 1762. Came to Scotland in 1783 to succeed Puppo as leader at the St. Cecilia Hall Concerts. He was especially famed for his performances of Scotch melodies. D. Edinburgh in 1815.

STAMITZ, JOHANN WENZEL ANTON, Bohemian violinist and composer, b. Deutsch-Brod, June 19, 1717. Studied under his father and became one of the greatest virtuosos of his time, acting as concertmaster of the Mannheim Electoral Orchestra in addition teaching the violin to a number of distinguished pupils, including his sons, Karl and Anton. His greatest service to music was in the creation of the standard classic sonata form, as revealed in his symphonic, solo and chamber music works. Compositions include twelve violin concertos and solo violin sonatas. D. Mannheim, Mar. 30, 1757.

STIEHLE, LUDWIG, German violinist, b. Frankfort, Aug. 19, 1850. Studied under Vieuxtemps, Heermann and Joachim. Especially distinguished as a chamber music player, becoming a member of the Alard

Quartet and also of a quartet at Basle with Hans Huber. D. Mulhausen, July 6, 1896.

STOESSEL, ALBERT FREDERIC, American violinist-composer, b. St. Louis, Oct. 11, 1894. Studied under Hess and Wirth at the Berlin Hochschule. Appeared as soloist with the Bluthner Orchestra in Berlin and became a member of the Willy Hess Quartet. On his return to the United States, Mr. Stoessel appeared with the St. Louis Symphony as soloist in 1915, followed by active service in the U. S. Army during the war, and by the resumption of his concertizing in 1919.

STOEVING, PAUL, German violinist, composer and author, b. Leipzig, May 7, 1861. Studied under Wohlfahrt, Herrman, Schradieck and Léonard. Became a virtuoso of high rank, touring Germany, Sweden, Denmark, Russia and the United States. Became professor of violin at London Guildhall School of Music, Trinity College and at prominent conservatories in New York City, including the New York School of Music and Art. Compositions include a number of solos for violin and several well-regarded historical and instructive books relating to the violin.

STOJANOVITS, PETER LAZAR, Hungarian violinist and composer, b. Budapest, Sept. 6, 1877. Studied under Hubay and Grün and has held several important positions as professor of the violin, in addition to founding a violin school for higher training in Vienna. Compositions include a concerto, a sonata, and technical works.

STOSCH, LEONORA VON (LADY SPEYER), American violinist, b. Washington, D. C., her father being the Count von Stosch and her mother an American. Studied first in America, later at the Brussels Conservatory, and also with Marsick in Paris. Her American debut was made with Anton Seidl's Orchestra, followed by performances with Damrosch and Nikisch. After her marriage, Miss von Stosch left the concert stage, but later returned to it at London with great success. She ranks with artists of the finest musicianship.

STRAUS, LUDWIG, Hungarian violinist, b. Pressburg, Mar. 28, 1835. Studied under Böhm at the Vienna Conservatory. Appeared as soloist at Vienna in 1850 and made a ten-year tour of Europe; came to England in 1864 where he remained as a distinguished virtuoso, orchestral and quartet player in both Manchester and

London, retiring in 1893. D. Cambridge in Oct., 1899.

STRAUSS, JOSEPH, Austrian violinist and composer, b. Brünn, 1793. Studied under Blumenthal and Schuppanzigh. Became a member of the Vienna Court Opera Orchestra, and held many important posts as concertmaster and conductor in Austria and Germany. Compositions include several solos for violin. D. Karlsruhe, Dec. 2, 1866.

STRINASACHI, REGINA, Italian violinist, b. Ostiglia, 1764. A woman virtuoso, of the highest degree of talent, who toured Europe with great success. In the course of her artistic career, she became acquainted with Mozart, who wrote the violin sonata in B flat (Kochel No. 454) for her. D. Dresden, 1839.

STRUBE, GUSTAV, German violinist and composer, b. Ballenstedt, Mar. 3, 1867. Studied under Brodsky and Heermann at the Leipzig Conservatory and taught at the Mannheim Conservatory. Came to the United States in 1891 as a member of the Boston Symphony Orchestra, and conductor of the Promenade Concerts of that organization in the summer. In 1913 he became teacher of theory and composition at the Peabody Conservatory of Music, Baltimore. Compositions include three concertos, a sonata, a suite and several smaller pieces for violin.

STRUNGK, (STRUNCK) NICOLAUS ADAM, German violinist, b. Hanover in 1640. An organist as well as distinguished violin player, greatly praised by Corelli. He held many important positions as both violinist and organist, and was the author of an excellent book of exercises for the violin or viola da gamba. D. Dresden, Sept. 23, 1700.

STRUSS, FRITZ, German violinist and composer, b. Hamburg, Nov. 28, 1847. Studied under Unruh, Auer and Joachim. Became concertmaster of the Berlin Court Orchestra and teacher at the Klindworth-Scharwenka Conservatory. Compositions include two concertos, several pieces and études for the violin.

SUCH, HENRY, English violinist, b. London, Mar. 31, 1872. Studied under Joachim and Wilhelmj. In 1892 appeared as soloist at Berlin and later toured Germany, Austria, Holland and Scandinavia successfully. Settled in London as soloist and professor of the violin at the Guildhall School of Music.

SUK, JOSEPH, Bohemian violinist and composer, b. Krecovic, Jan. 4, 1874. Studied under Bennewitz at the Prague Conservatory, and became second violin in the Bohemian String Quartet in 1892, a post he still occupies. Compositions include a fantasy and several pieces for violin.

SVEČENSKI, LOUIS, Hungarian violinist, b. Osijek, Nov. 6, 1862. Studied under Grün and Hellmsberger and became a member of the Boston Symphony Orchestra and violist of the Kneisel Quartet from 1885 to 1917 when it was disbanded. Compositions include excellent revisions of violin study works and sets of exercises for the violin.

SVENDSEN, JOHANN SEVERIN, Norwegian violinist and composer, b. Christiania, Sept. 30, 1840. Studied under David but was compelled, through paralysis of the hand, to devote himself to conducting and composition. Svendsen was a composer of great ability, a conductor of distinction and a man of the highest character. He was an intimate friend of many great composers and artists, among them being Wagner and Sarasate. Compositions include a violin concerto and several interesting smaller pieces. D. Copenhagen, June 14, 1911.

SZIGETI, JOSKA, Hungarian violinist, b. Budapest, Sept. 5, 1892. Studied under Hubay. Appeared as soloist in 1902 at the Budapest Royal Academy and appeared at London in 1907 where he has been highly successful as a virtuoso, introducing concertos by Harty, Hubay and Busoni, with whom he toured England.

TÄGLICHSBECK, THOMAS, German violinist and composer, b. Ansbach, Dec. 31, 1799. Studied under Rovelli and toured Europe extensively. Finally became concertmaster and conductor to the Prince of Hohenzollern-Hechingen in 1827. Compositions include a military concerto and numerous violin pieces. D. Baden-Baden, Oct. 5, 1867.

TARTINI, GIUSEPPE, Italian violinist, composer and teacher, b. Pirano, Apr. 8, 1692. Was at first a student for the priesthood, but after becoming a law student, he secretly married a niece of the Cardinal Archbishop of Padua, Mgr. Conaro, and while hiding from his displeasure in the Franciscan Monastery at Assisi, he taught himself to play the violin. After a time the Cardinal relented and Tartini, after being greatly inspired by the playing of Veracini, retired to Ancona where he studied hard, becoming so proficient that he was appointed violinist at San Antonio's Church, Padua, he finally established a violin school there which graduated many distinguished pupils including Nardini, Pasqualino, Bini, Alberghi, Manfredi, Ferrari, Pagin, Lahoussaye and Maddelena Sirmen. Tartini also discovered the overtones produced by double stopping and applied this knowledge to perfecting intonation; he also made several changes in the mechanical construction and the method of using the violin bow. His compositions, vitally important in the development of the art of violin playing, include many concertos and sonatas, the best known of the latter being the "Devil's Trill." D. Padua, Feb. 16, 1770.

TAUDOU, ANTOINE, French violinist and composer, b. Perpignan, Aug. 24, 1846. Studied at the Paris Conservatory and won the Grand Prix de Rome in 1869 for musical composition; joined the Paris Opera Orchestra and in 1883 became professor of harmony at the Paris Conservatory. Compositions include a violin concerto.

TESSARINI, CARLO, Italian violinist and composer, b. Rimini in 1690. He is said to have studied under Corelli, and became solo violinist at St. Marks, Venice, in 1729. Little further is known except that he was concertizing in Amsterdam, Holland, as late as 1762. Compositions include solo sonatas and a method for the violin.

THIBAUD, JACQUES, French violinist, b. Bordeaux, Sept. 27, 1880. Studied under Marsick at the Paris Conservatory and was awarded first prize for violin playing. Became a member and later many times soloist of the Colonne Orchestra. Toured Europe with great success, visiting the United States in 1903 for the first time. In 1916, he returned to the United States for another tour, after a year's service in the French army, and showed an improvement in interpretation and general emotional power which at once placed him in the front rank of great artists. Thibaud has also appeared in ensemble recitals abroad with his brothers, one a cellist and the other a pianist. His recitals in the United States with Harold Bauer have been specially noteworthy, especially in the performance of Bach, Beethoven and Brahms works.

THOM, BREAM, English violinist, b. Portsmouth, about 1817. Studied under Robretch, a teacher who shared in the tuition of Deberiot and of Artot. In 1838, he appeared as soloist at the Hanover Square Concert Rooms in London, where he was very favorably received. Later he settled at Brighton where he officiated as theater and concert leader.

THOMAS, EDWARD WILLIAM, Welsh violinist, b. Wales, about 1814. Studied under Oury, Cramer, Mori and Spagnoletti. Appeared in 1832 at Her Majesty's Theater in London, playing the Spohr Dramatic Concerto, later becoming leader of the orchestra and remaining until he left in 1850 to become leader of the Liverpool Philharmonic Orchestra.

THOMAS, THEODORE, German violinist and distinguished conductor, b. Esens, Oct. 11, 1835. Came to America when ten years of age and studied under his father. In 1851, he made a tour of the United States as a violinist, and later toured with Jenny Lind and other noted singers. He was also a splendid quartet player, being one of the founders of the "Mason and Thomas Soirées of Chamber Music" which were a fixture in New York City from 1855 to 1868. Later, Thomas' career is written as the biography of one of the world's greatest conductors, program makers and apostles of good music. D. Chicago, Jan. 4, 1905.

THOMSON, CÉSAR, Belgian violinist and composer, b. Liége, Mar. 17, 1857. Studied at the Liége Conservatory and under Léonard. Made his debut when but ten years old and toured Europe for several years. In 1879 he became concertmaster of the Bilse Orchestra, Berlin; in 1882 teacher at the Liége Conservatory and later professor of the violin. Toured North and South America with success and in 1898 succeeded Ysaÿe as professor of the violin at the Brussels Conservatory, founding a string quartet which has built a splendid reputation. Compositions include a Hungarian fantasy, smaller pieces and a comprehensive violin method.

THRANE, WALDEMAR, Norwegian violinist and composer, b. Christiania, Oct. 8, 1790. Studied under Schall and Baillot and became an important factor in the musical life of Christiania as violinist, conductor and composer of not only the first Scandinavian music with distinct national characteristics and color, but also of the first Norwegian opera. D. Christiania, Dec. 30, 1828.

TINLOT, GUSTAVE, French violinist, b. Clermont-Ferrant in 1887. Studied at the Paris Conservatory where he won first prize; later toured Holland, England, Spain,

France and Germany with Hayot Quartet. He became concertmaster of the New York Philharmonic Orchestra, and was appointed to the jury which awards the prizes at the Paris Conservatory. In 1924 he became concertmaster of the Minneapolis Symphony Orchestra.

TIRINDELLI, PIETRO ADOLFO, Italian violinist and composer, b. Conegliano, May 5, 1858. Studied under Corbellini at Milan, under Grün at Vienna and under Massart at Paris. Appeared with the principal European orchestras and in the United States with the Boston Symphony and Cincinnati Orchestras as soloist. Now professor of violin at the Cincinnati Conservatory. Compositions include a violin concerto as well as smaller works.

TOESCHI, CARLO GIUSEPPE, Italian violinist and composer, b. Romagna in 1724. Studied under Johann Stamitz. Became a member of the Mannheim Orchestra; later concertmaster and finally Director of Music at Munich. Compositions include a number of violin sonatas. D. Munich, Apr. 12, 1788.

TOFTE, LARS VALDEMAR, Danish violinist and teacher, b. Copenhagen, Oct. 21, 1832. Studied under Spohr and Joachim, making his debut at Copenhagen in 1856. He was for many years first violin in the Neruda Quartet and from 1866 to 1904 professor of violin at the Copenhagen Conservatory, Svendsen and Henriques being among his distinguished pupils. D. Copenhagen, May 28, 1907.

TOLLEFSEN, CARL HENRY, English violinist, b. Hull, Aug. 15, 1882. Studied under Lichtenberg, Schradieck and Kneisel. Became a member of the New York Symphony Orchestra and founder in 1909 of the Tollefsen Trio, which has toured extensively in the United States, introducing a number of newer works by American composers. Has held several posts as director of violin instruction.

TOMASINI, LUIGI (ALOYSIUS), Italian violinist, b. Pesaro in 1741. Became a member of Prince Esterhazy's orchestra under the baton of Haydn, with whom he enjoyed an intimate personal relationship. Many of Haydn's quartets and several of his violin concertos were written especially for Tomasini. Compositions include concertos for the violin and much chamber music. D. Esterház, Apr. 25, 1808.

TORELLI, GIUSEPPE, Italian violinist, b. Verona, about 1650. In 1686 he became a music director at Bologna, later in Ansbach, Germany. He is historically and musically important as the first composer to adapt the sonata form to concerted music, his first Concerts Grossi being published at Bologna three years previous to similar works by Corelli. D. Bologna about 1708.

TOTTMANN, ALBERT KARL, German violinist, composer and musicologist, b. Zittau, July 31, 1837. Studied at the Leipzig Conservatory and made his debut at a Gewandhaus Concert. Settled in Leipzig as a teacher and lecturer on musical subjects. His important literary contributions to the violin is a guide through violin music, which contains a running commentary on all the compositions listed. D. Leipzig, Feb. 26, 1917.

TOUCHE, FIRMIN, French violinist, b. Avignon, July 25, 1875. An artist of great distinction who has been solo violinist at the Paris Opera and the Colonne Concerts; also professor of violin at the Paris Conservatory.

TOURRET, ANDRÉ, French violinist, b. Amiens, Feb. 10, 1882. Studied under Hayot, Brun and Lefort. In 1896 became a member of the Colonne Orchestra; later of the Conservatory Orchestra and the Lucien Capet Quartet. In 1913 he came to New York, returning later to Belgium. As an ensemble player his standing is of the highest.

TOURS, BERTHOLD, Dutch violinist and editor, b. Rotterdam, Dec. 17, 1838. Studied at the Brussels and Leipzig Conservatories, and came to London, 1861, first as an orchestral player and later becoming musical adviser to a prominent London publishing house. His "violin method" is one of the most concise and at the same time most complete and thorough works published. D. London, Mar. 11, 1897.

TRNKA, ALOIS, American violinist, b. New York, Feb. 18, 1883. Studied under Sevcik and was graduated from the Prague Conservatory. Toured Austria and has taught the violin in New York since 1907, besides concertizing. His pupils include David Hochstein.

TROOSTWYK, ISIDORE, Dutch violinist, b. Zwolle, July 3, 1862. Studied under Joachim at the Berlin Hochschule and held various positions as leader and teacher in Holland before coming to the United States in 1890. Later became head of the violin department at Yale University, as well as

PLATE 77

1. FRANZ VON VECSEY.   2. JACQUES THIBAUD.   3. CÉSAR THOMSON.   4.
CAMILLA URSO.   5. RAOUL VIDAŞ.   6. GIUSEPPE TARTINI.   7. ANTONIO
VIVALDI.   8. PAUL VIARDOT.

concertmaster of the New Haven Symphony Orchestra.

TUA, TERESINA (MARIA FELICITA), Italian violinist, b. Turin, May 22, 1867. Studied under Massart at the Paris Conservatory, where she was awarded first prize in 1880. Toured Europe with great success, appearing in London in 1883 and the United States in 1887. After her marriage in 1889, she left the concert stage, but resumed playing in 1895, taking up her residence in Rome.

UCCELINI, MARCO, Italian violinist and composer, b. Italy, about 1640. Became concertmaster for the Duke of Modena about 1670 and is historically important as having had much to do with developing the powers of the violin bow.

UHE, ARTHUR EMIL, American violinist, b. Chicago, Dec. 24, 1892. Studied under César Thomson at the Brussels Conservatory, making his debut in 1912. Toured Norway, Switzerland, England and the United States and settled in the middle west as professor of the violin and soloist. Compositions include a violin concerto and smaller pieces.

URHAN, CHRETIAN, French violinist and composer, b. Aix-la-Chapelle, Feb. 16, 1790. Entered the Paris Opera Orchestra in 1816 and succeeded Baillot as concertmaster in 1831. He also was a fine performer on the viola and the viole d'amour and was a member of Baillot's Quartet. Urhan sometimes used a "violin alta" with five strings, four tuned as an ordinary violin and the fifth or lowest, pitched to C, a fifth below the usual lowest string of the violin (G). D. Paris, Nov. 2, 1845.

URSO, CAMILLA, French violinist, b. Nantes, June 13, 1842. Studied under Massart and toured the United States from 1852 to 1855, retiring into private life for seven years to engage in serious study. In 1862 she again made her debut as a serious matured artist, being immediately recognized as one of the world's virtuosi. After extended tours of practically the whole world, she settled in New York in 1895, appearing only occasionally in concert. D. New York, Jan. 20, 1902.

VACARI, FRANCESCO, Italian violinist and composer, b. Modena, about 1772. Studied under Nardini, winning great success when only thirteen years old, by reading a concerto of Pichl's at sight. Later he toured Italy and became concertmaster in the King of Spain's private orchestra. He visited England with success several times. D. Modena about 1823.

VACHER, PIERRE JEAN, French violinist and composer, b. Paris, about 1772. Studied under Monin and Viotti. Became concertmaster at Bordeaux and later at the Théâtre du Vaudeville at Paris, writing several graceful and tuneful romances which became quite popular. Compositions include several solo pieces and duos for violin. D. Paris, 1819.

VACHON, PIERRE, French violinist and composer, b. Arles, 1731. Studied under Chabran at Paris, playing a concerto of his own composition at the Concerts Spirituels in 1758. In 1784 he became concertmaster of the Court Orchestra in Berlin, retiring on a pension in 1798. D. Berlin, 1802.

VALENTINI, GIUSEPPE, Italian violinist and composer, b. Florence, about 1680. Became solo violinist to the Grand Duke of Tuscany. The date of his death is not known. Compositions include concertos and sonatas for the violin with string accompaniment.

VECSEY, FRANZ VON, Hungarian violinist, b. Budapest, Mar. 23, 1893. Studied under his father, Hubay and Joachim, making his debut at ten years of age in Berlin at Beethoven Hall, Oct. 17, 1903. Since that time he has been concertizing in Europe, Great Britain, as well as North and South America. Vecsey is a skilled interpreter of the works of Bach, Beethoven and Brahms.

VENZL, JOSEF, German violinist and composer, b. Munich, Mar. 26, 1842. Studied under Lauterbach at the Royal Music School. In 1858 he joined the Munich Court Orchestra as first violin, and later was appointed Royal Chamber Musician. Compositions include a violin concerto and smaller works. Venzl has also edited works by Campagnoli and Viotti.

VERACINI, FRANCESCO MARIA, Italian violinist and composer, b. Florence in 1685. Appeared in Venice about 1704 with such brilliant success as to cause Tartini to begin the study of the violin with serious purpose. He toured England, Germany, Poland and Italy with great success and at one time was regarded as the greatest violinist in Europe. Later he was succeeded in public favor by Geminiani. Compositions include twenty-four sonatas for violin with bass accompaniment. D. Pisa, 1750.

VERBRUGGHEN, HENRI, Belgian violinist and conductor, b. Brussels, 1874. Studied under Hubay and Ysaÿe at the Brussels Conservatory, winning first prize for violin playing. Became first violin in several orchestras, although later he devoted himself exclusively to conducting, and founded a very successful string quartet in London. In 1915 he went to Sydney, Australia, founding the National Conservatory there and giving Beethoven Quartet Concerts with the same organization as in London. Visited the United States in 1918 as guest conductor, and to study music instruction methods in the United States.

VIARDOT, PAUL, French violinist and musicologist, b. Courtavent, July 20, 1857. A son of the distinguished singer, Mme. Viardot-Garcia. Studied under Léonard and has appeared with great success in Paris and London. Compositions include two sonatas, several concert solos and smaller violin works as well as important contributions to the literature of music.

VIDAS, RAOUL, French violinist, b. Louveciennes, July 17, 1901. Studied first under his father, and later under Henri Berthelier. His first public appearance was made at the age of five, and his American debut in November, 1918.

VIEUXTEMPS, HENRI, Belgian violinist and composer, b. Verviers, Feb. 20, 1820. Studied under De Beriot at the Brussels Conservatory and developed into a virtuoso of the highest rank from both standpoints of technique and interpretation. He toured Europe from 1833 to 1844 when he visited the United States, and in 1846-52 became solo violinist to the Czar and professor of violin at the Petrograd Conservatory. He again visited the United States on two separate tours and finally settled as professor at the Brussels Conservatory, a paralytic stroke in 1873 making solo playing impossible, although he was still able to teach. Compositions include six concertos and a great number of concert violin pieces still in active use by virtuosos and advanced students. D. Mustapha (Algiers), June 6, 1881.

VILIM, JOSEPH ALOIS, American violinist, b. Chicago, Jan. 18, 1861. Studied under Bennewitz at the Prague Conservatory. In 1884 became teacher of violin at the Chicago Musical College; in 1887 Director of the violin department at the American Conservatory (Chicago) and in 1899 to 1918 founder and director of the Vilim American Violin School. Mr. Vilim has also founded several chamber music organizations which have gained reputation and is the author of technical violin works.

VIOTTI, GIOVANNI BATTISTA, Italian violinist and composer, b. Fontaneto da Pò, Vercelli, May 23, 1753. Studied under Pugnani and entered the Turin Court Orchestra; later toured Germany, Poland, Russia, France and England with great success, becoming recognized as one of the greatest virtuosos the world has ever seen. He taught the violin and composed a great deal in Paris (Rode and Baillot being among his pupils) and finally established an Italian Opera House there which was ruined by the French Revolution. After further successes as a soloist in London, followed by financial reverses in concert and opera management which induced him to embark in the wholesale wine business, he finally became settled in Paris as Director of the Opera. He retired on a pension in 1822, and died while on a pleasure trip to London, Mar. 3, 1824. His compositions include twenty-nine concertos, two concert duets, many smaller duos and eighteen sonatas with bass accompaniment for the violin. Viotti developed the sonata form in his concertos more than any of his predecessors, and the orchestration of the accompanying parts has much more of interest for both players and audience.

VITALI, TOMMASO ANTONIO, Italian violinist and composer, b. Bologna, about 1650. A violin player, of excellent reputation, who became a member of the Modena Court Orchestra in 1674, and numbered among his pupils the celebrated player Girolamo Laurenti. Compositions include a "Ciaconna" or "Chaconne" edited by Ferdinand David for his "Hohe Schule."

VIVALDI, ANTONIO, Italian violinist and composer, b. Venice about 1680. A priest before he became a violinist; son of a member of the orchestra at St. Mark's Venice. After occupying several positions of importance in Germany, he settled in Venice as musical director at "Ospedale della Pietà" for girls, remaining there until his death in 1743. Compositions include a number of violin concertos and sonatas which are believed to have had considerable influence on the compositions of Johann Sebastian Bach who not only studied them, but made transcriptions for the piano (or clavier). One of Vivaldi's violin concertos bore the title of the "Cuckoo Concerto."

WALTER, BENNO, German violinist, b. Munich, June 17, 1847. Studied under his father and at the Munich Royal Conservatory, beginning the study of the violin at four years of age, and touring Germany as a prodigy when only eight years old. Three years later he so pleased the King of Bavaria by his virtuosity that he was presented with a Guarnerius. In 1863 he joined the Munich Court Orchestra, and in 1875 succeeded his elder brother, Josef, as concertmaster and professor of violin at the Munich Conservatory. D. October 23, 1901.

WALTHER, JOHANN JACOB, German violinist and composer, b. Witterda, 1650. Became chamber musician to the Elector of Saxony and published a curious collection of Scherzi for solo violin, the last number entitled "Serenade for a chorus of violins, organ tremolo, guitar, bagpipes, two trombones, timpani and harp for a solo violin," showing that Walther was the violin juggler of his period. As music, his compositions are inferior to those of noted contemporaneous composers and his chief claim to distinction lies in the demand of his compositions for the use of the higher positions.

WANHAL, JOHANN BAPTIST, Bohemian violinist and composer, b. Nechanicz, May 12, 1739. Studied under local teachers and later (1767) under Dittersdorf in Vienna, where he spent the rest of his life composing and playing. He was a contemporary of Haydn and a most prolific composer, his works including more than 90 symphonies, 90 string quartets and many sonatas for violin and piano, all of which were popular with amateurs before the works of Mozart and Beethoven became known. D. Vienna, Aug. 26, 1813.

WANSKI, JEAN NEPOMUCENE, Polish violinist and composer, b. Poland, about 1800. Studied under Baillot at the Paris Conservatory and toured France, Spain and Switzerland with great success. Later his health failed him and he became a teacher of the violin. Compositions include a method, technical exercises and solos for the violin. There is no exact record of his demise.

WARE, HELEN, American violinist and composer, b. at Woodbury, N. J., Sept. 9, 1887. Studied under Sevcik and Hubay. Appeared as soloist at Budapest in 1912 and made a successful tour of Bohemia, Hun-

gary, Denmark and the United States, of late turning her attention to literary work and composition. Compositions include many interesting violin pieces, chiefly Hungarian in character, also several literary works on musical subjects.

WASIELEWSKI, JOSEPH WILHELM VON, German violinist and musicologist, b. Gross-Leesen, June 17, 1822. Studied under David and joined the Leipzig Gewandhaus Orchestra. Became concertmaster in 1850 under Schumann at Dusseldorf and in 1855 settled in Dresden as a writer. He wrote an exceedingly interesting biographical work entitled *The Violin and Its Masters* and also another entitled *The Violin in the Seventeenth Century and the Beginning of Instrumental Composition*. D. Sondershausen, Dec. 13, 1896.

WASSERMAN, HEINRICH JOSEF, German violinist and composer, b. Schwartzbach, April 3, 1791. Studied under Spohr and later became a conductor as well as a violinist of note. Compositions include a number of chamber music works, including a set of variations for violin with quartet accompaniment. D. Riehen, Aug. 1838.

WEHRLE, HUGO, German violinist and composer, b. Donaueschingen, July 19, 1847. Studied under his father and played in the Kalliwoda Quartet as a boy. In 1859 studied at the Leipzig Conservatory under David and in 1862 at the Paris Conservatory under Alard. Became a member of the Weimar and Stuttgart orchestras and of the Singer quartet. Retired in 1898 through a nervous affection of the hand. Compositions include several interesting violin pieces, also collections of old violin music.

WEISS, JULIUS, German violinist and arranger, b. Berlin, July 19, 1814. Studied under Henning and Rungenhagen. Taught the violin in Berlin until he succeeded to the management of his father's music publishing business in 1852. He published many instructive and recreative arrangements for the violin. D. Berlin, June 30, 1898.

WÉRY, NICHOLAS LAMBERT, Belgian violinist, b. Huy, near Liége, May 9, 1789. Studied under Baillot at Paris and became solo violinist of the Royal Orchestra and professor of violin at the Brussels Conservatory in 1823. His compositions include three concertos, fifty scale variations and numerous études for the violin. Jean-Baptiste Singelée, the celebrated arranger of operatic fantasias for the violin, was one of his pupils. D. Bande (Luxembourg), Oct. 6, 1867.

WESSELY, HANS, Austrian violinist, b. Vienna, Dec. 23, 1862. Studied under Jacob Grün at the Vienna Conservatory. Appeared as soloist with the principal European orchestras and under Augustus Manns at the Crystal Palace Concerts. Taught the violin at the Royal Academy of Music in London and founded the Wessely String Quartet which has won an enviable reputation. Compositions include a *Violin Method*, a *Scale Manual* and numerous other technical works.

WHITE, JOSEPH, Cuban violinist, b. Mantanzas, Dec. 31, 1839. Studied under Alard at the Paris Conservatory where he was awarded first prize. For a number of years he acted as court virtuoso to the Emperor Don Pedro of Brazil. He was an admirable interpreter of the classics, particularly the Bach Chaconne, and the possessor of one of the finest Stradivarius violins, called the "Swan Song" Strad. D. Paris in 1918.

WHITE, RODERICK, American violinist, b. Grand Rapids, Mich., Feb. 26, 1890. Brother of Stewart Edward White, the distinguished author and Gilbert White, the equally renowned painter. Studied under Max Bendix, César Thomson and Leopold Auer. His debut was made with the Berlin Philharmonic Orchestra in 1913, followed by an extensive European tour. He has also toured the United States with great success.

WIENIAWSKI, HENRI, Polish violinist and composer, b. Lublin, July 10, 1835. Studied under Massart at the Paris Conservatory where he was awarded the first prize. He made numerous successful tours of Russia, Poland, Scandinavia, Germany, Holland, Belgium and England with his brother, Joseph, a famous pianist. He came to the United States in 1872 touring with Anton Rubinstein and succeeded Vieuxtemps at the Brussels Conservatory, later resigning to continue his virtuoso tours, although he finally died in great need through failing health at Moscow, April 12, 1880. He was unquestionably one of the greatest of violinists, endowed with a large and sonorous tone, remarkable temperament and flawless technique. His fame as a composer is no less luminous than as a performer, and most of his compositions, including concertos and virtuoso display pieces, are still used by the greatest artists.

WIER, ALBERT E., American violinist, composer and editor, b. Chelsea, Mass., July 22, 1879. Studied under Emil Mahr at the New England Conservatory of Music, where he was awarded a scholarship, and under John K. Paine at Harvard University. Appeared as soloist with various local organizations and became concertmaster of the Dorchester Symphony Orchestra. Of late years, he has devoted himself exclusively to the editorial side of music. One of his most important contributions to musical literature is *The Ideal Home Music Library*, a ten-volume work designed for home use but his life work has been the editorship of the *Whole World Music Series*, comprising collections of standard music for the recreational use of the serious type of musical amateur. (F. H. M.)

WIETROWITZ, GABRIELE, Austrian violinist, b. Laibach, Jan. 13, 1866. Studied under Joachim at the Berlin Hochschule, where she was regarded as one of his most distinguished pupils. Appeared as soloist with the principal European orchestras and made numerous successful tours of Europe. She taught at the Stern Conservatory and the Hochschule in Berlin and founded in 1905 a ladies' string quartet, in which Joachim himself was intensely interested and which has won a place in European musical life rivaling that of any of the other male organizations.

WILHELMJ, AUGUST, German violinist, b. Usingen (Nassau), Sept. 21, 1845. Studied under Ferdinand David at Leipzig and made numerous successful tours of Europe, afterwards coming to the United States in 1878. Became head of the violin department of the Guildhall School of Music at London in 1894. Compositions include a number of original concert pieces, transcriptions and a *Modern School for the Violin*. As a performer he possessed a magnificent tone united to a wonderful technique and he is justly regarded as one of the greatest performers. D. London, Jan. 22, 1908.

WILLAUME, ALBERT GABRIEL, French violinist, b. Romilly, July 17, 1873. Studied at the Paris Conservatory where he was awarded first prize. He resides in Paris where his reputation as a solo and ensemble artist is of the highest character.

WILLY, JOHN THOMAS, English violinist, b. London, July 24, 1812. Studied under Spagnoletti and became a member of the King's Theater Band, playing under Costa

PLATE 78

1. HENRI WIENIAWSKI. 2. AUGUST WILHELMJ. 3. HENRI VIEUXTEMPS.
4. JOHANNES WOLFF. 5. EFREM ZIMBALIST. 6. JEAN BAPTISTE
VIOTTI. 7. JOSEPE WHITE. 8. RODERICK WHITE.

for many years. In 1849 he gave classical chamber concerts at St. Martin's Hall, at which many famous artists appeared as soloists, including Henri Ernst, Sterndale Bennett, Max Pauer and others. He retired through ill health in 1880. D. London, Aug. 8, 1885.

WIRTH, EMMANUEL, Bohemian violinist, b. Luditz, Oct. 18, 1842. Studied under Kittl and Mildner at the Prague Conservatory and became concertmaster at the Opera and professor at the Conservatory in Rotterdam. Afterwards he succeeded Rappoldi as violinist of the Joachim Quartet and teacher at the Berlin Hochschule, giving trio concerts with Barth and Hausmann. He retired in 1910.

WITEK, ANTON, Bohemian violinist, b. Saaz, Jan. 7, 1872. Studied under Bennewitz at the Prague Conservatory and became concertmaster of the Berlin Philharmonic Orchestra in 1894, remaining with this organization until 1909 when he accepted the same position with the Boston Symphony Orchestra. Witek toured Europe many times with great success, and created a sensation at Berlin in 1895 by playing the Beethoven, Brahms and Paganini Concertos in a single evening. He also was the first to play the newly found A Major Concerto of Mozart in public.

WOLDEMAR, MICHAEL, French violinist, b. Orléans, Sept. 17, 1750. Studied under Lolli and became the head of a wandering troupe of artists who later settled at Clermont Ferrand. Like his master, Lolli, Woldemar added a fifth string (low C in the bass) to his violin, and composed a concerto for this instrument, called the "violin-alto." He also edited Leopold Mozart's Violin Method, adding a scale fugue; also Locatelli's Labyrinth. D. Clermont Ferrand, January, 1816.

WOLFF, JOHANNES, Dutch violinist, b. The Hague, May 12, 1863. Studied under Wirth at Rotterdam and under Massart at the Paris Conservatory, where he won first prize for violin playing. Made numerous successful tours of Great Britain and the Continent, also visiting the United States in company with Josef Hollman, the eminent cellist. He also taught for many years at the Guildhall School of Music in London, and has been decorated with many prize orders and medals.

WOOD, HAYDN, English violinist and composer, b. Slaithwaite, 1882. Studied under his brother and also under Fernandez Arbos and César Thomson at Brussels. Has made numerous successful tours of Great Britain and Canada, being equally successful as a composer for both violin and orchestra, winning prizes both for his playing and his compositions. Wood appears to be one of the coming English musicians.

WRANGELL, LUDWIG HEINRICH, Norwegian violinist and composer, b. Christiania, Oct. 15, 1872. Studied under Gudbrand Bohn at Lindeman's Music School and with Bargheer at Hamburg. Appeared as soloist with orchestras throughout Scandinavia and came to Milwaukee in 1908, founding his own school in 1913. Compositions include many original solo pieces and études.

YOUNG, WILLIAM, English violinist and composer, b. about 1625. Outside of the fact that he became a violinist in the King's Band, information regarding his career is extremely vague. His compositions include twenty-one sonatas for three violins, viola and bass. D. 1672.

YSAŸE, EUGÈNE, Belgian violinist and composer, b. Liége, July 16, 1858. Studied under Wieniawski, Vieuxtemps and Massart. Became concertmaster of Bilse's Orchestra at Berlin in 1880 and professor of violin at the Brussels Conservatory in 1886. Made numerous successful tours of Europe and came to the United States first in 1894, touring the entire country since many times with the greatest success. In 1918, M. Ysaÿe became conductor of the Cincinnati Symphony Orchestra and head of the violin department at the Conservatory, recently resigning in order to return to Europe. As a violinist, Ysaÿe is one of the greatest of all time, possessing a faultless technique, a sympathetic, broad and sonorous tone, coupled to a conception of the noblest character, and a profound appreciation of the composer's intent. He is without question the dean of the contemporary school of great artists.

YUSSUPOFF, PRINCE NICOLAI, Russian violinist, composer and musicologist, b. St. Petersburg in 1827. Studied under Vieuxtemps and maintained a private orchestra in his palace. Compositions include "Concerto Symphonique" and other light pieces. He also wrote a book on violin making entitled Luthomonographie historique et raisonnée which he dedicated to Charles de Beriot. D. Petrograd, Aug. 3, 1891.

ZACHAREVITCH, MICHAEL, Russian violinist, b. Ostrow, Aug. 26, 1878. Studied under Sevcik and Ysaÿe. Appeared as soloist at twelve years of age at Odessa playing the Tschaikowsky Concerto with the composer himself conducting the orchestra. Has made numerous successful tours of Europe and Great Britain. Compositions include many violin solos and a work for violin with string quartet.

ZAJIC, FLORIAN, Bohemian violinist, b. Unhoscht, May 4, 1853. Studied under Bennewitz at the Prague Conservatory and succeeded Sauret as violin professor at the Stern Conservatory at Berlin. Compositions include studies preparatory to Kreutzer and Fiorillo.

ZEDELER, NICOLINE FLORENTINE, Swedish violinist, b. Stockholm, Mar. 8, 1892. Studied under Theodore Spiering and taught the violin in Berlin for several years. Toured both Europe and the United States, in addition to being soloist for Sousa on his world tour in 1910.

ZEUGHEER, JACOB, Swiss violinist, b. Zurich, 1805. Studied under Ferdinand Fränzel and after becoming enthused over chamber music, through a visit to Vienna in 1823, founded the "Gebruder Herrmann Quartet" in 1824, performing successfully in Paris, and afterwards in England, where they introduced quartet music in cities where it had never been heard before. D. Liverpool, June 15, 1865.

ZIMBALIST, EFREM, Russian violinist and composer, b. Rostov-on-Don, Apr. 8, 1889. Studied under Leopold Auer and made his debut at Berlin in 1907, when he made an extraordinary impression through his performance of the Brahms Concerto. He has made numerous successful tours of Europe and Great Britain, coming to the United States in 1912, touring the entire country. He has now permanently settled in America and has become an important factor in its musical life. Compositions include Russian and Hebrew dances, as well as numerous arrangements.

ZIMMERMANN, LOUIS, Dutch violinist, b. Groningen, Holland, July 19, 1873. Studied under Sitt and Ysaÿe. Made numerous successful tours of Germany and Holland, afterwards becoming professor of violin at the Royal Academy of Music at London.

ZOCCA, GAETANO, Italian violinist, b. Ferrara, 1784. Studied under Ballo and Rolla and afterwards became conductor of the Philharmonic Society at Ferrara. He was an artist of high accomplishments, and by his successful efforts to reform the art of bowing in Italy, accomplished much in advancing the art of violin playing in that country. D. Ferrara, Sept. 4, 1834.

CHAPTER XXIII

LITERATURE RELATING TO THE VIOLIN

Literature regarding the violin, dealing with its construction, makers, players and music, is very extensive. Most of these works cover only a single phase and many of the most important books are written in foreign languages and have never been translated into English.

Students or violin lovers who wish to consult such works will find it a difficult task to locate copies of them, except where they have been translated into English and are available through music or book sellers, or where those who seek the books reside in large musical centers where there are important libraries of music or musical literature.

In connection with libraries it will be quite relevant to list the important institutions of this kind in the United States.

Boston, Mass.
> The Public Library contains one of the largest collections of music and musical literature in the world including a number of rare scores and manuscripts.

Chicago, Ill.
> The Newberry Library contains almost 10,000 volumes of music and musical literature including many manuscripts.

Hartford, Conn.
> The Theological Seminary includes about a thousand volumes on music in its library.

New York, N. Y.
> The Public Library contains about 15,000 volumes of music and musical literature including one of the largest collections of ancient publications and original manuscripts.
>
> The library of Columbia University includes about 2,000 volumes on music.

Northampton, Mass.
> The Forbes Library contains about 8,000 volumes relating to music.

Salem, Mass.
> The library of the Essex Institute contains about 5,000 volumes or pamphlets relating to music.

Washington, D. C.
> The Library of Congress contains at least 500,000 books, pamphlets and copies of sheet music.

In addition to the above, the large universities such as Harvard, Yale, Princeton and many others where musical subjects are now taught, have very complete collections of books relating to music, scores and other musical compositions.

There are a number of standard works relating to the violin which are worthy of special mention in the particular field which they cover as they will prove very satisfactory sources of general information where a large assemblage of books is not available.

On the subject of violin making and makers the following books are regarded as authoritative.

ABELE AND NIEDERHEITMANN, *The Violin; Its History and Construction*
APIAN-BENNEWITZ, *Die Geige, der Geigenbau und die Bogenverfertigung*
BACHMANN, A., *Le Violon*
BROADHOUSE, J., *The Violin, Its History and Construction*
CLARKE, A. MASON, *The Violin and Old Violin Makers*
DIEHL, N. L., *The Violin Makers of the Violin School*
DUPUICH, ROBERT, *La Lutherie*
    Les Maitres Luthiers
FETIS, F. J., *Antonius Stradivarius*
FLEMING, J. M., *Old Violins and Their Makers*
FRY, G., *Varnishes of the Italian Violin Makers*
HART, GEORGE, *The Violin, Its Famous Makers and Their Imitators*
HERON-ALLEN, E., *Violin Making as It Was and Is*
LUTGENDORFF, W. L., *Die Geigen und Lautenmacher*
OTTO, JACOB A., *Treatise on the Construction, Preservation, Repairs and Improvement of the Violin*
PEARCE, J., *Violins and Violin Makers*
SAINT-GEORGE, HENRY, *The Bow, Its History, Manufacture and Use*
STAINER, C., *A Dictionary of Violin Makers*
TOLBECQUE, A., *L'Art du Luthier*
VIDAL, ANTOINE, *La Lutherie et les Luthiers*
    Les Instruments a archet

On the subject of great violinists the following books are regarded as authoritative.

BACHMANN, A., *Les Grands Violinistes du Passé*
CLARKE, A. M., *A Biographical Dictionary of Fiddlers*
DUBOURG, G., *The Violin*
EHRLICH, A., *Celebrated Violinists Past and Present*
FERRIS, G. T., *Sketches of Great Violinists*
GROVE, SIR GEORGE, *Dictionary of Music and Musicians*
HART, GEORGE, *The Violin and Its Music*

LAHEE, HENRY C., *Famous Violinists of To-day and Yesterday*
MARTENS, FREDERICK H., *String Mastery*
    Violin Mastery
PHIPSON, DR. T. L., *Biographical Sketches and Anecdotes of Celebrated Violinists*
WASIELEWSKI, J. W. VON, *The Violin and Its Masters*

On the subject of the art of violin playing the following books are considered authoritative.

AUER, LEOPOLD, *Violin Playing as I Teach It*
CARRODUS, J. T., *How to Study the Violin*
COURVOISIER, CARL, *Technics of Violin Playing*
ABERHARDT, SIEGFRIED, *Violin Intonation: Its Absolute and Infallible Mastery*
FLESCH, CARL, *The Art of Violin Playing*
GRUENBERG, EUGENE, *Violin Teaching and Violin Study*
KROSS, EMIL, *The Art of Bowing*
SCHOLZ, RICHARD, *The Technique of the Violin*
STOEVING, PAUL, *The Art of Violin Bowing*
THISTLETON, FRANK, *The Art of Violin Playing*
    Modern Violin Technique

The above selected list of books will be found desirable for general reading on the different subjects which they cover. There is also an interesting series of books on matters relating to the violin published in London and called the *Strad Library*. The volumes are sold separately and at prices within the reach of every music lover.

The following list of books upon matters relating to the violin does not lay claim to being complete in the strict sense of the word. There are many books which it would be useless to list because the matter in them is either obsolete or they are out of print. The list, however, is sufficiently complete so that the violin lover will be able to find in it some book which covers the subject in which he is interested.

ABELE, H., *The Violin and Its Story* (*Strad Library*)
ABELE AND NIEDERHEITMANN, *The Violin: Its History and Construction*
ALLEN, JULIA C., *Famous Violinists*
ALLER, HERMON, *Violin-Making as It Was and Is*
ALTHAUS, BASIL, *Advice to Pupils and Teachers of the Violin* (*Strad Library*)
    Selected Violin Solos and How to Play Them (*Strad Library*)
ANDERS, G. E., *Nicolo Paganini*
ANOMERC, VON, T. S., *The Fundamentals of Violin Playing*
APIAN-BENNEWITZ, *Die Geige, der Geigenbau und die Bogenverfertigung*
ARMSTRONG, ROBERT BRUCE, *English and Irish Instruments*

AUER, LEOPOLD, *My Long Life in Music*
    Violin Playing as I Teach It

BACHMANN, A., *Le Violon*
    Les Grands Violinistes du Passé
BAGATELLA, ANTONIO, *Treatise on the Construction of the Violin*
BAILLOT, PIERRE, *Appreciation of the Great Violinist, J. B. Viotti*
BALFOUR, HENRY, *How to Tell the Nationality of Old Violins*
    The Natural History of the Musical Bow
    What are the Broad, Distinguishing Marks of a Stradivarius Violin?
BARNARD, CHARLES, *Camilla, a Tale of a Violin*
BATES, H. N., *A Treatise on Bow Control*
    A Treatise on Finger Control
BROADHOUSE, J., *The Art of Fiddle Making*
    Facts About Fiddles
    How to Make a Violin
    The Violin, Its History and Construction
    Violins Old and New
BROADLEY, A., *Adjusting and Repairing Violins*
BRODSKY, MRS. ADOLF, *Recollections of a Russian Home*
BULL, SARA C., *Ole Bull: a Memoir*

CARRODUS, J. T., *How to Study the Violin*
CASORTI, *Technique of the Bow*
CHABERT, HENRY, *Le Violon*
CHAPIN, ANNA A., *The Heart of Music: The Story of the Violin*
CLARKE, A. MASON, *A Biographical Dictionary of Fiddlers*
    The Violin and Old Violin Makers
COMMON, A. F., *How to Repair Violins*
COURVOISIER, *Technics of Violin Playing*
COVENTRY, W. B., *Notes on the Construction of the Violin*
CROSBY, M. D., *The Art of Holding the Violin and Bow as Exemplified by Ole Bull*
CUTTER, B., *How to Study Kreutzer*

DANCLA, CHARLES, *Notes et Souvenirs*
DIEHL, N. L., *The Violin-makers of the Italian School*
DISSMORE, G. A., *The Violin Gallery*
DROGEMEYER, HERM. AUG., *Die Geige*
DUBOURG, G., *The Violin*
DUNN, JOHN, *Violin Playing* (*Strad Library*)
DUPUICH, ROBERT, *La Lutherie*
    Les Maitres Luthiers

EBERHARDT, GOBY, *My System of Practising the Violin and Piano*
EBERHARDT, SIEGFRIED, *Violin Intonation; Its Absolute and Infallible Mastery*
    Violin Vibrato; Its Mastery and Artistic Uses
ECKARDT, JULIUS, *Ferdinand David*
EHRLICH, A., *Celebrated Violinists: Past and Present* (*Strad Library*)
    Das Streich Quartett
    Die Geige in Wahrheit und Fabel
EMERY, FREDERIC B., *The Violinist's Dictionary:* Containing nearly 2000
    words, phrases, references, etc., used in the study of the violin
ENGEL, CARL, *Researches into the Early History of the Violin Family*
ERNST, EDUARD, *Die Gymnastik der Hand*

FERRIS, G. T., *Sketches of Great Violinists*
FETIS, F. J., *Antonius Stradivarius,* with comments on the origin and develop-
    ment of bowed instruments, and on François Tourte, inventor of many
    bow improvements
    Biographical Notice of Nicolo Paganini, with an analysis of his composi-
    tions and a sketch of the history of the violin
    Biographie Universelle des Musiciens
FLEMING, J. M., *The Fiddle Fancier's Guide*
    Old Violins and Their Makers
FLESCH, CARL, *The Art of Violin Playing*
FOTHERGILL, JESSIE, *The First Violin*
FOUCHER, G., *History and Construction of the Violin*
    Repairing, Restoring and Adjustment of the Violin
FREDERICK, HENRIETTA, *The Enchanted Violin*
FRY, G., *The Varnishes of the Italian Violin Makers*

GOFFRIE, CHARLES, *The Violin*
GRESSWELL, H. W. and G., *How to Play the Fiddle*
GRILLET, LAURENT, *Les ancêtres du violon et du violoncello*
GROSSMANN, M., *New Cremona: Theory of Harmoniously Attuning the*
    Resonance Boards of the Violin
GROVE, SIR GEORGE, *Dictionary of Music and Musicians*
GRUENBERG, E., *The Violinist's Manual*
    Violin Teaching and Violin Study
GUHR, *Paganini's Art of Playing the Violin*

HAMILTON, J. A., *Catechism for the Violin*
HAND, L. H., *How to Make a Fiddle*
HART, GEORGE, *The Violin, Its Famous Makers and Their Imitators*
    The Violin and Its Music; An account of the progress of the art and its
    professors
HASLUCK, P. N., *Violins and other Stringed Instruments: How to Make Them*

HAWEIS, H. R., *Old Violins*
HAYWARD, JOHN D., *Chamber Music for Amateurs*
HELM, THEODOR, *Beethoven's String Quartets*
HENLEY, WILLIAM, *The Violin: Solo Playing, Soloists and Solos*
HEPWORTH, W., *How to Choose a Violin*
    Information for Players, Owners, Dealers and Makers of Bow Instruments
HERON-ALLEN, EDWARD, *The Ancestry of the Violin*
    De Fidiculus Bibliographa
    Violin Making as It Was and Is
HILL AND SONS, *Antonio Stradivarius: His Life and Work*
    Giovanni Paolo Maggini: His Life and Work
    The Salabue Stradivari
HONEYMAN, WM. C., *Scottish Violin Makers, Past and Present*
    The Secrets of Violin Playing
    The Violin: How to Choose One
    The Violin: How to Make It
    The Violin: How to Master It

JAMES, E., *Camillo Sivori*
JOCKISCH, REINHOLD, *Katechismus der Violine und des Violinspiels*

KELLY AND UPTON, *Edouard Remenyi*
KILBURN, N., *The Story of Chamber Music*
KOECKERT, G., *Les Principes Rationnels de la Technique du Violon*
KOHUT, DR. ADOLPH, *Joseph Joachim*
KRAUSE, EMIL, *Die Entwickelung der Kammermusik*
KROSS, EMIL, *The Art of Bowing*
    How to Hold the Violin and Bow
    The Study of Paganini's Twenty-four Çaprices

LAHEE, HENRY C., *Famous Violinists of To-day and Yesterday*
LA TARCHE, ANDRÉ, *Violin Student's Manual*
LEGGE, *Celebrated Violinists*
LEHMANN, GEORGE, *True Principles of the Art of Violin-Playing*
    The Violinist's Lexicon
LOWE, C. E., *Harmonics for Violinists*
    Hints to Young Violinists
    Lessons in Harmonics
LUTGENDORFF, W. L. F. VON, *Die Geigen und Lautenmacher*

MACDONALD, JOHN, *A Treatise on the Harmonic System*
MACKINTOSH, *Remarks on the Construction of, and Materials employed in, the Manufacture of Violins*
MAILAND, E., *Das Wiederentdeckte Geheimniss des altitalienischen Geigenlackes*
MAITLAND, J. A. FULLER, *Joseph Joachim*

MARTENS, FREDERICK, *String Mastery*
   Violin Mastery
MASSART, L., *The Art of Studying R. Kreutzer's Etudes*
MATTHEWS, J., *The Violin Music of Beethoven (Strad Library)*
MAUGIN, J. C., *Manuel de la Lutherie*
MAYSON, *Violin-Making (Strad Library)*
MITCHELL; C. H., *How to Play a Violin Solo*
MORRIS, *British Violin Makers*
MOSER, ANDREAS, *Joseph Joachim: A Biography*
MURDOCH, A. G., *The Fiddle in Scotland*

NIEDERHEITMANN, F., *Cremona: An Account of the Italian Violin Makers and*
   Their Instruments
NICHOLSON, J., *Designs and Plans for the Construction and Arrangement of*
   the New Model Violin
NOHL, LUDWIG, *Die Geschichtliche Entwickelung der Kammermusik*
   Spohr

OAKES, W. W., *A Review of Ancient and Modern Violin Making*
OSTROVSKY, *New Scientific Method of Violin Teaching*
OTTO, JACOB AUGUSTUS, *Treatise on the Construction, Preservation, Repairs*
   and Improvement of the Violin, etc.

PAINE, JOHN, *A Treatise on the Violin*
PEARCE, J., *Violins and Violin Makers*
PETHERICK, HORACE, *Antonio Stradivarius*
   Joseph Guarnerius, His Work and His Master
   The Repairing and Restoration of Violins
PHIPSON, DR. THOMAS LAMB, *Biographical Sketches and Anecdotes of Cele-*
   brated Violinists
   Confessions of a Violinist
   Famous Violinists and Fine Violins
   Voice and Violin: Sketches, Anecdotes and Reminiscences
PIERRARD, LOUIS, *Le Violon*
POLONASKI, E., *The Value of Old Violins*
PORTER, THOMAS, *How to Choose a Violin*
POUGIN, ARTHUR, *Viotti*
POZNANSKI, I. B., *The Violin and Bow*
PROD'HOMME, J., *Nicolo Paganini—A Biography of His Life and Work*
PURDY, GEORGE, *A Few Words on the Violin*

RACSTER, OLGA, *Chats on Violins*
RADOUX, J. THEODORE, *Vieuxtemps*
READE, CHARLES, *Jack of All Trades*
   A Lost Art Revived

REBS, ALEXANDER, *Anleitung zum Lackiren von Streich-instrumenten*
REGLI, *Storia del Violino in Piemonte*
RIECHERS, AUGUST, *Die Geige und ihr Bau*
 The Violin and the Art of Its Construction
RITCHIE, WALLACE, *Advice to Violin Students*
RUHLMANN, J., *Die Geschichte der Bogeninstrumente*

SAINT-GEORGE, HENRY, *The Bow, Its History, Manufacture and Use* (*Strad Library*)
 Fiddles: Their Selection, Preservation and Betterment (*Strad Library*)
SANDYS AND FORSTER, *The History of the Violin and Other Instruments*
SASS, A. L., *The Secret of Acquiring a Beautiful Tone on the Violin*
SAVART, FELIX, *Mémoir sur la Construction des Instruments à cordes et à archet*
SCHAFER, FERDINAND, *Der naturliche Fingersatz Chromatischer Violinfiguren*
SCHEBEK, DR. EDMUND, *Violin Manufacture in Italy and Its German Origin*
SCHLESINGER, K., *A Bibliography of Musical Instruments and Archæology*
SCHOLZ, RICHARD, *The Technic of the Violin*
SCHROEDER, CARL, *Handbook of Violin Playing*
SCHULZE, CARL, *Stradivaris Geheimniss*
SHELTON, EDGAR, *The Violin and All About It*
SHIRLEY, PAUL, *Right Hand Culture*
SMITH, H. P., *The Construction of the Violin*
SPOHR, LOUIS, *Autobiography*
STAINER, C., *A Dictionary of Violin Makers*
STARCKE, HERMANN, *Die Geige*
STEINHAUSEN, DR. F. A., *Die Physiologie der Bogenfuhrung*
STOEVING, PAUL, *The Art of Violin-Bowing*
 The Mastery of the Bow
 The Story of the Violin
 What Violinists Ought to Know
STORCK, DR. KARL, *Joseph Joachim*
STRATTON, STEPHEN S., *Nicolo Paganini: His Life and Work* (*Strad Library*)

TARTINI, G., *An Important Lesson to Performers on the Violin; a Letter to Signora Lombardini,* translated by Dr. Burney
TAYLOR, T., *Everybody's Guide to Violin Playing*
THISTLETON, FRANK, *Art of Violin Playing*
 Modern Violin Technique
THOMAS, BERTHA, *The Violin Player*
TIETGEN, HANS, *Facts About Violins and Violin-Making*
TOLBECQUE, A., *L'art du Luthier*

VAN DER STRAETEN, E., *The Romance of the Fiddle*
VENZL, JOSEF, *Der Fingersatz auf die Violine*

VIDAL, M., *Les Instruments à archet*
VOLTI, CARL, *Violin Catechism and Text-Book*

WASIELEWSKI, J. W. VON, *The Violin in the Seventeenth Century and the Beginning of Instrumental Composition*
    The Violin and Its Masters
    Instrumentalsatze
WASSMANN, C., *Entdeckungen zur Erleichterung und Erweiterung der Violintechnik*
WESSELY, HANS, *A Practical Guide to Violin Playing*
WETTENGELL, GUSTAVE A., *Complete treatise on the making and repairing of violins*
WINN, EDITH L., *The Child Violinist*
    The Etudes of Life
    Hand Culture, Notation and Rhythm
    How to Prepare for Kreutzer
    How to Study Fiorillo
    How to Study Gaviniés
    How to Study Kreutzer
    How to Study Rode
    Representative Violin Solos and How to Play Them
    Violin Talks
WINRAM, *Violin Playing and Violin Adjustment*
WIT, PAUL DE, *Geigenzettel alter Meister*
WITTING, C., *Geschichte des Violinspiels*
WOLFF, *Fiddle Frauds and How to Detect Them*
WOOD, R., *Tone and Expression in Violin Playing*

YOUSSE, J., *Theory and Practice of the Violin*
YOUSSOPOFF, PRINCE, *Essay on the History of the Violin and Old Violin Makers*

CHAPTER XXIV

THE DEVELOPMENT OF VIOLIN MUSIC

A short historical review of the development of violin music, especially in relation to the master performers on and teachers of the instrument who have so largely contributed to its literature, becomes a fitting preface to the classified list of music which follows.

Bowed instruments of various kinds have existed since the thirteenth century, but the violin in its present form came into general use only about the middle of the sixteenth century. The church played an important part in the development of violin playing, the earliest references to such performances being in connection with masses or psalms.

Gabrieli and Monteverde were pioneers among those who composed for the violin in such a manner as to give it an individuality of its own among other instruments, the latter writing the violin score as high as the fifth position and also indicating tonal effects to be produced by the use of the bow.

The sonata form is the first in which compositions for the violin were written, among the earliest composers being Fontana and Neri, the latter writing both the "Sonata di Chiesa" (Church Sonata) and the "Sonata di Camera" (Chamber Sonata). The church sonata consisted of four movements alternately in slow and fast rhythm; the chamber sonata consisted of dance movements in both stately and lively rhythm. Later the chamber sonata became similar in character to the church sonata, its first great exponents being Giovanni Vitali and his son, Antonio Vitali, whose "Chaconne" is still used on recital programs.

Among the greatest of the earlier violinists who also composed for the violin may be mentioned Heinrich Biber and Thomas Baltzar, the latter credited with having introduced the violin into Great Britain. In Italy, the Vitalis were succeeded by Torelli, who was one of the earliest composers in the concerto form, and also by Corelli, whose concertos and sonatas were so melodious, well harmonized and perfectly balanced that they became the models used by his successors for many generations.

Antonio Vivaldi, who died about 1740, developed both the technique and the tonal possibilities of the violin in his concertos. He also added oboes and horns to his accompaniments, thus enhancing the orchestral color to a degree impossible before with a more limited instrumentation.

Viotti, Veracini and Tartini in turn rendered great service to the art of violin playing, not only in their performances, but also by their development of the concerto and sonata forms. Tartini's contribution of most importance was his development of the technique of the bow, for which he opened up possibilities as yet undreamed of. Somis, Giardini, Pugnani, Geminiani and Locatelli must also be mentioned among those who added to the possibilities of violin technique and bowing, each one paving the way for his successor, who elevated the violin to the point where it became known as "the King of instruments."

In France, Anet, Francoeur, Leclair, Pagin, Lahoussaye, Barthelemon, Gavinies and Boucher were prominent among those who exploited the violin by playing and composing for it, while in Germany, Graun, Carl Stamitz, with his two sons, and the immortal Mozart perpetuated both their own and the violin's fame by their performances and compositions.

Kreutzer, Rode and Baillot, all teachers at the famous Paris Conservatory, constituted a united trio who worked zealously, in the period 1750 to 1840, for the ennobling of the art of violin playing, while Franz Eck was the teacher of Spohr, whose concertos are regarded as among the greatest contributions to violin literature.

Paganini, both through his extraordinary playing and the remarkable nature of his compositions, is another who occupies an exalted position in the history of the violin, chiefly because of his development of the technical resources of the instrument.

The field of salon violin composition was developed by Deberiot, Vieuxtemps, Dancla, Alard and Léonard, while the brilliant compositions of Wieniawski, Ernst and Sarasate are still featured on recital programs, being unique as examples of the virtuoso style.

Ferdinand David's contributions in the form of revision of classical manuscripts are considered by many to be a part of the violin's most important history, while the transcriptions of his pupil, August Wilhelmj, may be found on almost every concert program.

From the year 1800, a long succession of violinists, famous as teachers, performers and composers, all of whom contributed to the pedagogical or virtuoso classes of violin literature, brings us down to the present time, when almost every composer writes in the larger or smaller forms for the instrument. While the modernists' thematic material and its development in many instances are superior in musical value to that of the older composers, lack of technical knowledge on the part of those who compose for the violin often renders performance ungrateful and the actual tonal effect far from pleasing, the orchestral or piano accompaniment frequently overshadowing the violin, and robbing it of its most beautiful characteristics.

What the famous classicists—Bach, Beethoven, Schubert, Haydn and many others—have done for the literature of the violin is almost unnecessary to mention in detail, since they have left a legacy of countless, wondrous works which are constantly heard in concert and recital.

The museums and libraries of the principal European cities contain thousands of unpublished manuscripts written by composers, many of whose names are absolutely unknown at the present time. The musical libraries which contain the greatest treasures in the form of violin manuscripts are:

The British Museum in London.

The Bibliotheque Nationale in Paris.

The Bibliotheque du Conservatoire in Paris.

The (former) Königliche Bibliothek in Berlin.

The Japanesischer Palast (Japanese Palace) in Dresden.

The (former) Königliche und Kaiserliche Bibliothek in Vienna.

In the Japanese Palace at present, for example, there are preserved the manuscripts of one hundred and twenty-seven (127) violin concertos composed by Antonio Vivaldi.

A brief survey of some of the works written for the violin by composers either born in or of long residence in the United States, reveals the fact that most of their published compositions are in the smaller forms, although it is likely that most American composers have conceived works in the larger form which have been performed but not published.

It would occupy more space than is available to review the numerous charmingly original compositions in the smaller forms which have emanated from the pens of American composers. Therefore, the author will concern himself with some of those in concerto, sonata, suite or rhapsodic form.

Cecil Burleigh has composed two concertos, two sonatas and a suite for violin, all of which display originality in theme and development.

John Alden Carpenter, unique in being both a merchant and a composer, has written a sonata for the violin of striking novelty. Equally interesting in that it compares very favorably with works of the romantic period of the same character, is Rossetter G. Cole's violin sonata.

The compositions of Walter Damrosch include a violin sonata of considerable merit and originality in view of the fact that it was a very early work, while Eric DeLamarter, the well-known American organist and conductor, has contributed a sonata of entirely modern characteristics to violin literature.

Arthur Foote's compositions include a sonata, first performed in Boston by Franz Kneisel. Arthur Hartmann, the well-known violinist who, while born in Hungary, was brought up in the United States, has composed a "Suite in the Ancient Style," which reveals musicianship of the highest caliber.

Henry Holden Huss has written several works for the violin, including a concerto and a sonata, and the compositions of Arthur Walter Kramer number among them a symphonic rhapsody for violin with orchestra or piano accompaniment.

The works of Daniel Gregory Mason include a highly interesting and scholastic violin sonata, while John Powell revives memories of the old South in his "Sonata Virginianesque." He has also written another sonata and a concerto for the violin.

Two of the most interesting contributions to American violin literature are offered by Harry Newton Redman in the form of violin sonatas of not too elaborate dimensions, but musicianly to the highest degree in conception. The works of Edmund Severn, English by birth, but American by virtue of long residence, include a concerto, a sonata and three characteristic suites which reveal him as a composer of unusual attainments.

Albert Spalding, the eminent American violinist, has written two concertos, a suite and a sonata for the violin, all of which evidence a talent for composition quite in accord with his abilities as a virtuoso. Passing notice should also be given to the violin works of Samuel Gardner, whose concerto for the violin has been most favorably commented upon by musical authorities.

The foregoing review in no way makes pretense of including all of the important violin works in the larger forms which have been written by American composers, and are in published or manuscript form. Judging by those which the author has seen, it is well worth while for every performer, student or lover of the violin to become acquainted with the works of American composers, not merely because they are American composers, but because the compositions themselves are of an original, a wholesome, and a sincere character.

CHAPTER XXV

A LIST OF MUSIC FOR THE VIOLIN

The following list of music for the violin—either as a solo instrument or in conjunction with other instruments—does not lay claim to being complete in the sense that it includes *all* the compositions for the violin which have been published up to the present time, because it would require several large volumes to catalogue merely the solo compositions and transcriptions which have been written for the instrument.

On the other hand, the author believes that it will be of service to all those who are interested in violin music because it presents in categorical form all of the great violin works and a goodly proportion of the lesser works, thereby enabling the performer, the teacher, the student or the amateur to seek and find successfully the compositions which he may require for any purpose.

The list divides itself into two groups; the first comprises solo music and concerted works, including:

Violin methods	Violin duets
Violin études	Violin duets with piano acc.
Violin solos without acc.	Violin duets with cello
Violin solos with piano acc.	Violin trios
Violin solós with organ acc.	Violin trios with piano acc.
Violin with viola	Violin quartets
Two violins with viola	Violin quartets with piano acc.
Violin with cello	

The second group comprises chamber music works in which the violin plays an important part.

All compositions are listed under the composer's name, the opus number being given wherever possible. Publishers' names have been omitted, due to the fact that in the case of all the classical compositions there are numerous good editions to be procured at varying prices, making it inadvisable to recommend any particular edition. It has also been regarded as advisable to omit compositions which fall into the class of elementary pieces for beginners, as the quantity and variety of this class of music precludes the possibility of inclusion without omitting music of more important character.

There is no reason why any of the compositions mentioned in this list cannot be procured by the local music dealer, who can obtain them for his customers through the large music importing houses, although occasionally the intending purchaser may receive the information that the desired composition is either out of print, or cannot be procured, owing to the many changes in the music publishing business in Europe incidental to the Great War.

VIOLIN METHODS, EXERCISES, SOLOS AND CONCERTED COMPOSITIONS

1. VIOLIN METHODS

Alard, Delphin
Violin Method
Bachmann, Alberto
Violin Method
Baganz, A. F.
Violin School
Baillot, P.
Violin Method (L'Art du Violon)
Bauer, Sigmund
Practical Violin School
Beriot, Charles de
Ecole Transcendante, Op. 123
Violin Method, Op. 102
Bielfeld, A.
Practical School, Op. 139
Blied, Jacob
Elementary School, Op. 24
Brähmig, B.
Practical Violin School
Buttschardt, Karl
Practical School, Op. 10
Campagnoli, B.
Violin Method, Op. 21
Charpentier, A.
Elementary Violin Method
Conte, Jean
Elementary Violin Method
Courvoisier, C.
Violin Method
Crickboom, M.
Le violon théorique et pratique
Czerny, J.
Practical Violin School
Dancla, Charles
Violin Method, Op. 52
David, Ferdinand
Violin School
Depas, Ernest
Complete Violin Method, Op. 28
Dessauer, H.
Universal Violin School
Dont, Jacob
Theoretical and Practical Method
Eichberg, J.
New Violin Method, Op. 21
Flade, O.
Elementary School, Op. 4
Gilis, Ant.
New Violin Method
Gorski, Ladislas
Practical Violin Method
Grolle, John
Rhythmic Melodic Violin Method
Guichard, M.
Complete Grand Method
Hamma, Fr.
Preparatory Violin School, Op. 15

Hauser, Karl
Elementary Violin School
Heinze, L. & Rothe, W.
Theoretical and Practical School
Henning, Ch. & Th.
Violin School
Hering, Karl
Elementary School, Op. 13
Hermann, Fr.
Violin Method
Hertel, Julius
Violin School
Hofmann, Richard
Elementary School, Op. 84
Violin Method, Op. 31
Hohmann, C. H.
Violin School, Op. 31
Houfflack, A.
Easy Method, Op. 32
Joachim, J. & Moser, A.
Violin Method
Jockisch, Reinhold
New Practical Violin Method
Kastner, Georg
Elementary Violin School
Kayser, H. E.
Elementary Violin School
Kewirsch, Th.
Elementary School, Op. 35
Klenck, Robert
Method for the Violin
Kling, H.
Easy Violin School, Op 453
Koch, Gustave
Practical Violin School, Op. 7
Köhler, Pius
Practical School, Op. 24
Kuchler, Ferd.
Practical Violin Method
Lefort, A.
Practical Violin Method
Lehmann, G.
Theoretical and Practical School, Op. 20
Lemaire, A.
Modern Violin School
Léonard, H.
Violin Method, Op. 47
Linnarz, R.
Violin School
Magerstadt, J. F.
Practical Violin School
Mazas, F.
Violin Method, Op. 34
Meerts, L. J.
Elementary School
Meyer, Fritz
Le Petit Ševčik
Mollenhauer, Ed.
Practical Violin School
Mollier, P.
Grand Violin Method

Mozart, Leopold
Method for the Violin
Musin, Ovide
Belgian Violin School
Nejeoly, R.
Practical Violin School
Ondrick & Mittelmann
Violin Method
Panofka, H.
Practical Violin Method, Op. 80
Papini, Guido
Violin School, Op. 57
Pennequin, J. G.
Method for the Violin
Piot, Julien
The Violin and its Mechanism
Rehbaum, Th.
Elementary Violin School
Rieding, O.
Violin School
Ries, Hubert
Violin School
Rosenkranz, Fr.
Practical Violin School
Schatz, Karl
Violin School
Schmidt, Ernst
The Rudiments of Violin Playing
Schöen, M.
Practical Violin School
Scholz, Rich.
New Practical Violin School
Schrader, Hans
Violin School on Modern Principles
Schroeder, Hermann
Violin School
Schubert, Louis
Violin School, Op. 50
Schultz, Aug.
The Art of Violin Playing, Op. 3
Sering, F. W.
Violin School, Op. 31
Singer, Ed. & Seifriz, Max
Theoretical and Practical Violin School
Solle, Fr.
Practical Violin School
Spohr, Louis
Violin School
Trostdorf, L.
Violin School
Vogel, Moritz
School of Violin Playing
Volkmar, W.
Violin School, Op. 2
Wahls, Heinrich
School of Violin Playing, Op. 23

Wassmann, Karl
New Violin Method
Weiss, Julius
Practical Violin School
Wichtl, G.
Violin School, Op. 96

Wilhelmj, Aug. & Brown, James
Violin Method
Witting, C.
Violin School
Wohlfahrt, Fr.
Elementary School, Op. 38

Zimmer, Ferd.
Elementary School, Op. 21
Practical School, Op. 15
Zimmermann, C. F. A.
Practical Violin School

2. EXERCISES AND ETUDES FOR SOLO VIOLIN

Abel, Ludwig
School of Mechanism (2 Vol.)
Six Grand Etudes (On Wagner Motives)
Adelburg, A. d'
Twenty-four Etudes, Op. 2
Alard, D.
Six Etudes, Op. 2
Ten Characteristic Studies, Op. 18
Ten Etudes, Op. 10
Ten Etudes Artistiques, Op. 19
Ten Etudes Brillantes, Op. 16
Twenty Etudes de Genre, Op. 53
Twenty-four Etude-Caprices, Op. 41
Alday, F.
Twenty-four Etudes, Op. 4
Auer, Leopold
12 Characteristic Preludes
Bachmann, Alberto
Nineteen New Caprices and Etudes
Six Caprices du virtuosité
Bagantz, A. F.
Progressive Violin Exercises (2 Vol.)
Baillot, P.
Exercises in All Positions
Twelve Caprices
Baumann, L.
Staccato, Etude, Op. 8
Benoist, André
The Virtuoso's Daily Dozen
Beriot, Ch. de
One Hundred Eighty-seven Exercises (Dessauer)
Six Etudes Brillantes, Op. 17
Three Etudes, Op. 37
Twelve Characteristic Etudes, Op. 114
Bloch, Alexander
Finger Strengthening Exercises
How to Practice
Scales, Studies and Double Stop
Bloch, Jos.
Etudes from Ancient Masters (Ed.)
Twelve Caprices, Op. 8
Blumenthal, Jos.
The Positions, Op. 34
Twenty-four Etudes, Op. 33
Twenty-four Etudes, Op. 68
Boll, H.
Scales and Chord Studies
Bondi, S.
Octave Technique
Bytovetzki, Pavel L.
Double-Stopping for the Violin
Scale Technique
Campagnoli, B.
Art of Improvising, Op. 17
Seven Divertissements, Op. 18
Six Fugues, Op. 10
Thirty-eight Etudes and Studies (Felis)
Capet, Lucien
Daily Exercises

Higher Technique of the Bow, The
Carri, Ferd.
Special Etudes, Op 20
Special Scale Studies, Op. 21 (5 Vol.)
Casorti, Aug.
Etudes, Op. 47
Studies in Double Stops, Op. 61
Technique of the Bow, The, Op. 50
Three Etudes, Op. 41
Catherine, Georges
Scale Study (2 Vol.)
Study of Bowing
Treatise on Harmonics
Centola, Ernesto
Technique of Violin Playing (5 Vol.)
Twenty-four Melodic Etudes
Charpentier, A.
Progressive Exercises
Seven Etudes de difficulté transcendente
Chaumont, E.
Thirty-six Technical Etudes
Chits, John
Thirty Caprices
Coenen, Franz
Twelve Etudes
Consolini, Angelo
Short Daily Exercises
Courvoisier, C.
Finger Exercises
Dancla, Charles
School of Mechanism, Op. 74
Six Etudes, Op. 2
Sixteen Etudes, Op. 128
Ten Etudes, Op. 90
Twelve Etudes, Op. 192
Twenty Etudes, Op. 73
Twenty Etudes, Op. 122
David, Ferd.
Six Caprices, Op. 9
Twenty-six Caprices, Op. 39
Depas, E.
Forty Etudes, Op. 118
Twenty Etudes, Op. 105
Dessauer, Heinrich
Scales, Chords, etc. (2 Vol.)
Technical Groundwork for Modern Violin Playing, The
Domerc, J.
Thirty-five Progressive Double-Stop Etudes
Dont, Jacob
Etudes and Caprices, Op. 35
Scales and Cadenzas, Op. 60
Six Etudes, Op. 54
Theoretical and Practical Technique, Op. 49 (8 Vols.)
Twenty-four Studies Preparatory to Kreutzer and Rode
Dorson, Ch.
Twenty Melodic Double-Stop Etudes
Dupuis, L.
Scales and Exercises
Durand, F. A.
Six Caprices, Op. 15
Eberhardt, Goby
School of Double Stops, Op. 81 (2 Vol.)

School of Violin Technique, Op. 84 (5 Vol.)
Eichberg, Julius
Twenty-four Technical Studies, Op. 80
Eichhorn, Max
Scale and Chord Studies (2 Vol.)
Eichler, F. W.
Etudes Caractéristiques, Op. 3
Eliason, E.
Six Caprices, Op. 12
Eller, Louis
Two Concert Etudes, Op. 11
Ernst, H. W.
Six Grand Etudes
Felis, Paolo
Gradus Ad Parnassum
New Method of Harmonic Study
Fiorillo, F.
Thirty-six Etudes or Caprices
Fischel, Max T.
Double Stop Studies (2 Vol.)
Flesch, Carl
Etude Collections
Book I—51 Etudes
Book II—47 Etudes
Book III—44 Etudes
Art of Violin Playing
Fraatz, Ludwig
Violin Exercises, Op. 11
Gaviniés, P.
Twenty-four Matinées (Etudes)
Gruenberg, Eugene
Elementary Violin Lessons
Foundation Exercises
Scales and Chords
Twenty-five Exercises in the first position
Grunwald, A.
Finger and Bow Exercises, Op. 6
Positions, The, Op. 10
Thirty-six Special Etudes
Haït, M.
Five Caprices de Concert
Thirty Etudes d'Artistes
Halir, Carl
New Scale Studies
Hauser, Miska
Twelve Concert Etudes, Op. 8 and Op. 33
Heim, Ernst (Ed.)
Gradus Ad Parnassum (Selected Etudes)
Hellmesberger, Jos., Jr.
Daily Studies (2 Vol.)
Etudes de Perfection, Op. 220
Exercises in Scale Form, Op. 219 (3 Vol.)
Position Studies
Scale Studies
Hering, Ch.
Twelve Caprices, Op. 18
Hermann, Fr.
Artist Studies, Op. 23
Double-Stop Studies, Op. 27
Orchestra Studies for the 1st Violin (Ed.)
Orchestra Studies for the 2nd Violin (Ed.)

EXERCISES AND ETUDES FOR SOLO VIOLIN

Herrmann, Ed.
Artist Technique, Op. 20
Double-Stop Studies, Op. 27
Individual Position Studies, Op. 9
Position Studies, Op. 10
Six Concert Etudes, Op. 6
Herwegh, M.
Etude de Concert
Hildebrandt, M.
Technique of the Bow The
Hille, Gustav
Twelve Etudes, Op. 47
Twelve Studies, Op. 41
Hillgenberg, Richard
Studies in Thirds, Op. 26
Octave Studies, Op. 12
Hofmann, Richard
Double-Stop Technique (3 Vol.)
Forty Melodic Studies, Op. 108
Forty Studies, Op. 91
Harmonic Technique (1 Vol.)
Orchestral Studies (5 Vol.)
Simple Violin Technique (3 Vol.)
Thirty Melodic Double-Stop Studies
Thirty-two Special Studies, Op. 52
Hoya, Amadeo von der
Foundation of Violin Technique, The
Hrimaly, J.
School of Scales and Arpeggios
Tone and Rhythm Exercises
Hubay, Jenö
Six Etudes, Op. 63
Six Etudes, Op. 64
Ten Etudes Concertantes, Op. 89
Hubl, Otto
School for the Positions
Hüllweck, Ferd.
Elementary Violin Exercises, Op. 10
Orchestral Studies (5 Bks.)
Twenty-five Studies
Hussla, Victor
Technical Studies
Kayser, H. E.
Etudes in the Positions, Op. 28
One Hundred Twenty Daily Studies, Op. 31
Paganini Studies, Op. 53
Thirty-six Etudes, Op. 20
Twenty-four Caprices, Op. 50
Kittel, Bruno
Technical Studies
Kleinecke, Th.
Twenty-four Etudes, Op. 12
Kneisel, Franz
Advanced Exercises (Part I)
Köhler, M.
Thirty Etudes, Op. 51
Köhler, Pius
Double-Stop Studies, Op. 40
Kontski, A. de
L'Echo (Concert Etude), Op. 5
Six Caprice-Etudes, Op. 16
Koopmann, Jules
Progressive Exercises in Double Stops
Kotek, Jos.
Six Studies, Op. 8
Kotlar, I.
Double-Stop Studies
Six Etudes heroïques
Sixteen Etudes on the G String

Kreutzer, R.
Forty-two Etudes
Kreuz, E.
Scales and Arpeggios in Major and Minor Keys (3 Vols.)
Kross, Emil
Art of Bowing, The, Op. 40
Gradus Ad Parnassum (2 Vol.)
Systematic Chord Studies, Op. 98 (2 Vol.)
Systematic Double-Stop Studies, Op. 100 (3 Vol.)
Systematic Scale Studies, Op. 18 (3 Vol.)
Krouszevski, N.
Etude de Concert, Op. 1
Laub, Ferd.
Three Concert Etudes
Lauterbach, J.
Two Etudes de Concert, Op. 5
Lefort, A.
Twelve Etudes
Lemaire, A.
Etudes in the Positions
Lemming, F. C.
Twelve Etudes Fantastiques
Léonard, H.
Twenty-four Etudes Classiques, Op. 21
Twenty-four Etudes Harmoniques, Op. 46
Lévêque, Emile
Six Grand Artist Etudes, Op. 27
Libon, P.
Thirty Caprices, Op. 15
Lichtenberg, Leopold
Scale Studies
Lincke, A. F.
Eight Etudes
Lipinski, Ch.
Three Caprices, Op. 10
Three Caprices, Op. 29
Locatelli, P.
Eight Capriccios (Witting)
Twenty-four Caprices (Bachmann)
Lockwood, Samuel P.
The Scales
Machts, Carl
Ten Etudes & Caprices
Madsen, Thorwald
Daily Studies
Malkin, Jacques
Scale Exercises
Manen, Joan
Studio de Concerto, Op. 10
Manger, Alfred
School of the Fifth Position
Marsick, M. P.
Eureka (Finger Method)
Marteau, Henri
Bow Etudes, Op. 14
Twenty-four Etudes Artistiques
Maurer, L.
Nine Etude-Caprices, Op. 39
Mayseder, J.
Six Etudes, Op. 29
Mazas, F.
Etudes d'Artistes, Op. 36
Etudes Brillantes, Op. 36
Etudes Mélodiques, Op. 36
Etudes Spéciales, Op. 36
Meerts, J. L.
Art of Bowing, The (12 Etudes)
Etudes Rhythmiques
Three Etudes in Fugue Form
Meyer, Clemens
Fifteen Etudes

Minkous, L.
Twelve Etudes
Nadaud, E.
Practical Scale Studies
Neubert, Rich.
Scale and Chord Studies
Novaček, O.
Eight Caprices de Concert, Op. 5
Nowotny, Carl
Chromatic Scale Studies, Op. 7
Chromatic Scale Studies, Op. 9
Twenty-four Studies, Op. 10
Ondricek, Fr.
Fifteen Etudes d'Artistes
Ondricek, Fr. & Mittleman, S.
New Method of Acquiring Master Technique (2 Vol.)
Ortmans, René
Twenty-five Etudes, Op. 8
Paganini, N.
Sixty Variations on the air "Baracuba"
Twenty-four Caprices, Op. 1
Palaschko, Joh.
Six Concert Etudes, Op. 14
Paulli, H. S.
Six Caprices
Pente, Emilio
Six Etudes-Impressions, Op. 8
Petri, Henri
Artist Etudes, Op. 9
Pfriemer, Ernst
Fifty Position Studies, Op. 12
Pichl, W.
Eight Fugues
Six Caprices
Pilet, Ch. E.
Six Caprices
Piot, Julien
Elementary Double-Stop Method
Forty-two Etude-Caprices
Pochon, Alfred
Exercises for the Strengthening of the Fingers
Polledro, J. B.
Six Etudes
Portnoff, L.
Exercises for the Little Finger, Op. 70
Prill, Carl (Ed.)
Orchestra Studies from Richard Strauss' Works
Prume, Fr.
Six Grand Etudes, Op. 2
Six Grand Etudes, Op. 14
Reimert, Gustave
Important Scale Studies for Daily Use
Ries, Hubert
Twelve Etudes in Concert Form, Op. 9
Ritter, E. W.
Scale and Chord Exercises
Rode, Pierre
Twelve Etudes
Twenty-four Caprices, Op. 22
Rolla, A.
Ten Etudes, Op. 10
Rovelli, Pietro
Six Caprices, Op. 5
Twelve Caprices, Op. 3
Sahla, Rich.
Three Studies for Violin
Saint-Lubin, L. de
Six Caprices, Op. 41
Six Grand Caprices, Op. 42
Sass, A. L.
Exercises for Systematic Training of the Left Hand

Sauret, Emile
Artist Etudes, Op. 38
Eighteen Grand Etudes, Op. 24
Gradus Ad Parnassum, Op. 36 (4 Vol.)

Sauzay, E.
Etudes Harmoniques, Op. 14

Schaffner, N. A.
La Folie, Op. 26 (Caprices)

Schatz, Ch.
Etudes, Op. 25

Schill, Otto K.
Scale Studies

Schneider, G.
Double-Stop Studies, Op. 12
Finger and Bow Exercises, Op. 12
Octave and Tenth Studies, Op. 12
Scale Studies, Op. 12
Studies in Thirds and Sixths, Op. 12

Scholz, Richard
The Study of Bowing, Op. 13
The Study of Grace Notes, Op. 15
The Study of the Positions, Op. 22
The Study of Staccato, Op. 11

Schradieck, Henry
School of Violin Technique (3 Vol.)
Twenty-five Studies, Op. 1

Schröder, Hermann
Forty Etudes, Op. 5

Schubert, François
Etudes, Op. 3

Schwendemann, W.
Exercises in the Positions

Sebald, Alexander
Violin Technique (3 Vol.)

Ševčik, O.
Double-Stop Studies, Op. 9
Forty Bow Exercises, Op. 3
Position and Scale Studies, Op. 8
School of Bow Technique, Op. 2 (3 Vol.)
School of Violin Technique,

Op. 1 (7 Vol.)
Trill Studies, Op. 7

Sieber, A. E. (Editor)
Etude Album (3 Vol.)

Singer, Ed.
L'Arpeggio (Etude de Concert), Op. 8

Sitt, Hans
Fifty Daily Exercises, Op. 98
One Hundred Etudes, Op. 32
Scale Studies in Double-Stops, Op. 41
Technical Studies, Op. 92 (2 Vol.)
Twenty Etudes, Op. 69
Twenty-four Etudes, Op. 80
Forty Special Etudes, Op. 134

Sivori, C.
Twelve Etude-Caprices, Op. 25

Slunicko, J.
Five Caprices, Op. 44
Twenty-four Etudes, Op. 54

Sokolowsky, N.
Thirty-five Etudes, Op. 2

Spiering, Th.
Six Etudes d'Artistes, Op. 4

Spohr, Ludwig
Twelve Studies from the Violin School

Stoeving, Paul
Systematic Bow-Arm Development
Right Arm Gymnastics

Svečenski, Louis
Preparatory Exercises for Trill, Vibrato and Staccato
Shifting Exercises

Tartini, G.
Art of Bowing, The (50 Variations)

Temporal, E.
Daily Exercises

Togni, Felice
Training of the Left Hand, The (3 Vol.)

Trienes, Hermann
Scale and Chord Studies

Venzl, Jos.
Thirty-six Etudes, Op. 88

Viardot, Paul
Etudes Mélodiques

Vieuxtemps, H.
Six Concert Etudes, Op. 16
Six Etudes (Posthumous)
Thirty-two Etudes, Op. 18 (Posthumous)

Wahls, Heinrich
Technical Scale and Chord Studies, Op. 11

Walter, V.
Scale Studies
School of Etudes (Selected)

Weisberg, A. H.
Complete School of Shifting
Foundation Exercises
School of Double-Stopping

Weiss, Julius
Etudes, Op. 80
Violin Technique (2 Vol.)

Wery, N.
Fifty Variations on the C Major Scale, Op. 16

Wesseley, H.
Comprehensive Scale Manual

White, Jos.
Etudes, Op. 32

Wichtl, Georg
Twenty-five Studies, Op. 115

Wieniawski, Henri
L'Ecole Moderne (Etudes), Op. 10
Etude Caprices, Op. 10

Wilhelmj, August
Studies in Thirds

Witek, Anton
Fingered Octaves (2 Parts)

Witting, C.
Exercises in the Positions

Wohlfahrt, Franz
Finger, Scale and Chord Studies

Zajic, Florian
Studies for Violin (Simrock)
Thirty Preparatory Exercises to Fiorillo and Kreutzer

Zimbalist, Efrem
One Hour's Daily Exercises

Zinke, Gustave
Scale Studies

3. ETUDES WITH ACCOMPANIMENT OF A 2ND VIOLIN

Abel, Ludwig
Twenty-five Violin Studies

Alard, D.
Etudes Brillantes, Op. 16
Melodic Etudes, Op. 10

Baillot, P.
Etudes in All Positions (Kross)
Twenty-four Etudes (Posthumous)

Beriot, Ch. de
Six Duos, Op. 17
Three Grand Etudes, Op. 43

Bloch, J.
Twenty Etudes, Op. 11

Blumenstengel, A.
Les Positions, Op. 34

David, F.
Etudes, Op. 45 (Violin School)

Dont, Jacob
Sixteen Etudes

Feigerl, Peregrine
Twenty-four Etudes

Fiorillo, F.
Thirty-six Etudes (Acc. by Spohr)

Grunwald, Ad.
Etudes by various masters

Hellmesberger, Jos.
Etudes for two Violins, Op. 184

Hering, K.
Major and Minor Scales

Hom, C. Th.
Fifty Progressive Etudes

Hubel, Otto
Thirty-six Etudes

Hullweck, Ferd.
Six Etudes, Op. 7

Jansa, L.
Sixty Etudes, Op. 55

Kayser, H. E.
Caprices-Etudes, Op. 50
Thirty-six Etudes, Op. 20
Twenty-four Etudes, Op. 28

Kreutzer, Rodolphe
Forty Etudes (Eichheim)

Kross, E.
Etude Album (Alard, Beriot, etc.)

Léonard, H.
Twenty-four Etudes Classiques, Op. 21
Twenty-four Etudes Harmoniques, Op. 46

Mazas, F.
Etudes Brillantes, Op. 39 (Grunwald)

Etudes Speciales, Op. 39 (Grunwald)

Meerts, L. J.
Le Mécanisme du Violon (36 Etudes)
Three Etudes brillantes in Fugue Form
Three Etudes symphoniques in Fugue Form

Panofka, Henri
Twenty-four Etudes, Op. 30

Rode, Pierre
Twenty-four Caprices, Op. 22 (Eichheim)

Rolla, A.
Etudes, Op. 10

Rovelli, P.
Twelve Caprices, Op. 3

Sauzay, E.
Etudes Harmoniques

Schroeder, H.
Special Etudes, Op. 21

Sokolowsky, N.
Thirty-five Etudes, Op. 2

Spohr, L.
Etudes from the Violin School

Viardot, Paul
Etudes melodiques et progressives

Weiss, Julius	White, Joseph	Wieniawski, H.
Etudes, Op. 80	Etudes, Op. 32	Etudes-Caprices, Op. 18

4. ETUDES WITH PIANO ACCOMPANIMENT

Alard, D.
Etudes caracteristiques, Op. 18

Bazzini, A.
Etude de Concert (Les Abeilles)

Benda, Franz
Caprice in B. Major (David)
Caprice in C major (David)

Beriot, Ch. de
Etude de Salon, Op. 85
Six Etudes Brillantes, Op. 17
Ten Etudes, Op. 77
Three Etudes, Op. 37

Carri, Ferd.
Elfentanz, Op. 8

Casorti, Aug.
Two Etudes, Op. 60

Chopin, Fr.
Etude, Op. 25, No. 2 (Burmester)
Six Etudes, Op. 10 and Op. 25 (Klengel)

David, Ferdinand
Six Caprices, Op. 20
Twenty-five Etudes, Op. 39

Dont, Jacob
Three Caprices de concert, Op. 40
Twenty-four Etudes, Op. 37

Gaviniés, P.
Twenty-four Matinées (Tottmann)

Gorski, K.
Petite Etude-Spiccato, Op. 1, No. 2

Hauser, M.
Etude (La Mélancolie), Op. 17
Etude (La Sentimentale), Op. 18

Hubay, Jenö
Five Concert Etudes, Op. 115

Kneisel, Franz
Grande Etude de Concert

Kontski, A. de
Etudes Artistiques, Op. 16

Kreutzer, R.
Forty Etudes (Eichheim)

Lauterbach, Joh.
Two Concert Etudes, Op. 5

Locatelli, Pietro
Le Labyrinthe (Alard)

Loof, Alexis
Twenty-four Caprices

Louis, N.
Caprice-Etudes, Op. 80

Manén, Joan
Aplech, Op. 20
Caprice Catalan, Op. 13
Studio di Concerto, Op. 10

Mestrino, Nicolo
Caprice in C minor (David)

Moscheles, I.
Twenty-four Piano Etudes (Arr. by David)

Nováček, O.
Eight Concert Caprices, Op. 5

Paganini, N.
Twenty-four Caprices (Piano acc. by E. Lassen)

Petersen, J.
Perpetuum Mobile, Op. 10

Rehfeld, F.
Caprice, Op. 49

Ries, Hubert
Concert Etude on the G String

Rode, Pierre
Twenty-four Caprices, Op. 22

Schroeder, H.
Die Biene, Op. 10, No. 1 (Kreutzer No. 9)
Mückentanz, Op. 10, No. 2

Singer, Edmund
Three Caprices, Op. 9
Three Caprices, Op. 23

Sitt, Hans
Two Concert Etudes, Op. 24

Stamitz, J.
Caprice (David)

Stern, J.
Caprice-Etude

Stoeving, P.
Concert Etudes, Op. 6

Tartini, Giuseppe
L'Art de l'archet (David)

Vieuxtemps, H.
Six Concert Etudes, Op. 16

5. VIOLIN SOLO COMPOSITIONS
(without accompaniment)

Bach, J. S.
Chaconne (Fourth Solo Sonata)
Six Sonatas for violin
No. 1 in G minor
No. 2 in B minor
No. 3 in A minor
No. 4 in D minor
No. 5 in C major
No. 6 in E major

Bagge, G.
Sonata in A

Baille, Gabriel
Moto Perpetuo, Op. 90

Barth, Richard
Chaconne, Op. 21
Partita, Op. 10

Campagnoli, B.
Four Preludes (Alard)
Two Fugues (Alard)

Carri, Ferdinand
Fantaisie-caprice, Op. 1

David, Ferdinand
Concert Studies (3 books)
Suite, Op. 43

Eichler, F. W.
Four Songs Without Words, Op. 4

Eller, Louis
Improvisation on a Haydn Theme, Op. 8

Ernst, Henri W.
Fantasy (Last Rose of Summer)
Fantasy (Schubert's Erl-King)
Grand Caprice, Op. 26

Ertel, Paul
Concerto in G minor

Fassbaender, P.
Sonata in D major, Op. 48

Geminiani, Fr.
Sonata in B major

Gorski, L.
Suite, Op. 1

Hait, M.
Légende Orientale
Pastorale

Jarnach, Philippe
Sonata in A minor, Op. 48

Karg-Elert, S.
Partita in D, Op. 89
Sonata, Op. 88

Kreisler, F.
Recitativo and Scherzo-caprice, Op. 4

Léonard, Hubert
Romance, Op. 11

Locatelli, Pietro
Caprices (Catherine)

Meyer, Fritz
Four Songs Without Words

Mikorey, F.
Petite Suite

Mildner, Maurice
Etude de Concert, Op. 10

Mitnitzky, Issay
Fantasy in Ancient Style, Op. 13

Moor, Emmanuel
Four Preludes, Op. 100

Paganini, M.
Duo Merveille
Introduction and Variations (Nel cor più)

Palaschko, Johannes
Suite, Op. 23

Pechan, J.
Two Double-Stop Pieces

Pecoud, F.
Variations Symphoniques, Op. 25

Pizendel, J. G.
Sonata in A major

Purcell, H.
Two Sonatas in Three Voices

Reger, Max
Chaconne, Op. 117
Four Sonatas, Op. 42
Prelude and Fugue in B minor, Op. 117
Prelude and Fugue in E minor, Op. 117
Prelude and Fugue in G minor, Op. 117
Prelude and Fugue on Bach Themes, Op. 117
Preludes and Fugues, Op. 131A
Seven Sonatas, Op. 91

Reichelt, John
Perpetuum Mobile, Op. 7

Rust, F. W.
Sonata in Bb major

Sahla, Richard
Three Studies on Schubert Songs

Saint-Lubin, L. de
Fantasy (on Beethoven's "Adelaide")
Fantasy (on Donizetti's "Lucia"), Op. 56

Sauret, Emile
Suite, Op. 68
Swedish Rhapsody, Op. 59

Sinding, C.
Suite, Op. 123

Stamitz, Carl
First Divertimento (Alard)
Second Divertimento (Alard)

Vieuxtemps, H.
La Chasse, Op. 32, No. 3

6. VIOLIN SOLOS WITH PIANO ACCOMPANIMENT

Babell, William
Sonata in Bb major (Moffat)
Bach, Christian
Berceuse
Bach, J. S.
Air and Gavotte (Ries)
Air on the G string (Wilhelmj)
Bourrée (Papini)
Chaconne (Sonata)
Concerto in A minor
Concerto in E major
Concerto in G minor
Six Solo Sonatas
Bach, P. E.
Complaisante, La (Burmester)
Minuet (Geyer)
Spring's Awakening (Romance)
Sonata in B minor
Sonata in C minor
Bach, W. F.
Grave (Kreisler)
Sonata in B minor
Sonata (Beer-Walbrunn)
Bachelet, A.
Ballade
Bachmann, Alberto
Adagio religioso
Allegro appassionato
Berceuse in A
Capriccio
Chaconne
Chanson Bohémienne
Concertino
Concerto No. 1 in G minor
Concerto No. 2 in A minor
Danse tzigane, No. 1
Danse tzigane, No. 2
Danse tzigane, No. 3
Désir (Longing)
Elégie
Fantaisie sur la vie de Bohème
Fileuse, La
Habanera
"Iberia" Spanish Fantasy
Jota Aragonesa, La
Mazurka brillante No. 1
Mazurka brillante No. 2
Mazurka brillante No. 3
Moto Perpetuo
Papillon, La
Polonaise de concert
Rhapsodie Tzigane
Romance Appassionata
Scènes d'Enfants
Scherzo diabolique
Serenade
Seville
Song of Spring
Tarentelle
Zapateado
Bachmann, G.
Chanson-Ballade
Gigue bretonne
Sylphes, Les (Caprice-Valse)
Bachmeteff, N.
Adagio (Sonata, Op. 27)
Les adieux du guerrier, Op. 19
Baillot, Pierre
Air de Paisiello (Alard)
Concerto, Op. 3
Concerto, Op. 6
Concerto, Op. 7
Concerto, Op. 10
Concerto, Op. 13
Concerto, Op. 18
Concerto, Op. 21
Concerto, Op. 22
Concerto, Op. 30
Rondo sur un air moldavien

Balakirew, A.
Chant du Pêcheur (Hartmann)
Balthazar, Florence
Concerto
Romance
Banck, E.
Mazurka, Op. 8
Barbella, Emanuele
Larghetto from 2nd Sonata
Sonata in E (Alard)
Sonata in G minor (Moffat)
Bargiel, W.
Adagio, Op. 38
Sonata in F minor, Op. 10
Suite, Op. 17
Barmotine, S.
Berceuse (Hartmann)
Sonata, Op. 14
Bains, Ethel
Concertstück
Mazurka
Sonata, Op. 9
Sonata, Op. 24
Swing Song
Barth, R.
Sonata in D minor, Op. 20
Barthelemon, F. H.
Sonata in E minor (Jensen)
Barthelemy, R.
Sérénade coquette
Bartlett, H. N.
Berceuse, Op. 186
Bartók, Bela
Sonata No. 1
Sonata No. 2
Baselt, F.
Berceuse, Op. 23
Bassnine, N.
Sonata, Op. 7
Bastl, Jos.
Sonatine in D, Op. 1
Batiste, E.
Pilgrim of Love (Romance)
Pilgrim's Song of Hope (Andante)
Voix Céleste (Saenger)
Bauer, Marion
Up the Ocklawaha, Op. 6
Bayrhoffer, C.
Mückentanz
Bax, Arnold
Ballade
Bazzini, A.
Allegro de Concert, Op. 15
Ballade, Op. 43, No. 1
Calabrese, Op. 34
Concertino, Op. 14
Concerto in A minor, Op. 38
Concerto in B major, Op. 29
Concerto in E major, Op. 42
Concerto militaire, Op. 42
Dans des Gnomes, Op. 43, No. 2
Elégie, Op. 35, No. 1
Preghiera from Military Concerto, Op. 42
Ronde des Lutins, Op. 25
Scherzo, Op. 41, No. 2
Scherzo Variatio, Op. 13
Six morceaux caractéristiques, Op. 18
Souvenir de Naples, Op. 23
Beach, Mrs. H. H. A.
Berceuse, Op. 40, No. 2
Captive, La, Op. 40, No. 1
Invocation, Op. 55
Mazurka, Op. 40, No. 3
Romance, Op. 23
Sonata, Op. 34 in A minor
Beazley, J. C.
Sonatina in D minor
Becker, Jean
Concerstück, Op. 10

Gavotte
Romance
Becker, Rheinhold
Concerto, Op. 4
Concerto, Op. 100
Beer, J. A.
Concerto in A major
Beethoven, L. van
Adagio (Moonlight Sonata)
Adagio (Sonata Pathétique)
Cavatina (Quartet, Op. 130)
Concerto in D major, Op. 61
Contre-Danses (Seiss)
Dervish Chorus (Auer)
Etude (Auer)
Funeral March (Sonata, Op. 26)
Minuet in Eb, No. 1 (Burmester)
Minuet in G, No. 2 (Burmester)
Minuet, Op. 20
Romance in F, Op. 50
Romance in G, Op. 40
Rondino (Kreisler)
Rondo in G (David)
Scherzo (Auer)
Sonata, Op. 12, No. 1
Sonata, Op. 12, No. 2
Sonata, Op. 12, No. 3
Sonata, Op. 23
Sonata, Op. 24
Sonata, Op. 30, No. 1
Sonata, Op. 30, No. 2
Sonata, Op. 30, No. 3
Sonata, Op. 47 (Kreutzer)
Sonata, Op. 96
Turkish March (Auer)
Behrens, W.
Rêverie Hongroise
Bemberg, H.
Les Larmes (Lament)
Benda, Franz
Sonata in A (Moffat)
Sonata in A minor (Jensen)
Sonata in F (Schering)
Bendall, W.
Chanson d'Amour
Bendel, Franz
Sonata in E minor
Benesch, Joseph
Air varié, Op. 25
Concerto, Op. 20
Bennett, W. S.
The Lake
Benoit, L.
Chanson, Op. 60
Meditation, Op. 59
Nocturne, Op. 55
Berger, W.
Fantasiestück in D, Op. 4
Sonata in A, Op. 7
Sonata in F, Op. 29
Sonata in G minor, Op. 70
Bergh, Arthur
Twilight Musing
Alla Burla
Berghout, J.
Sonatina in G, Op. 34
Beriot, Ch. de
Air Varié No. 1, Op. 1
Air Varié No. 2, Op. 2
Air Varié No. 3, Op. 3
Air Varié No. 4, Op. 5
Air Varié No. 5, Op. 7
Air Varié No. 6, Op. 12
Air Varié No. 7, Op. 15
Air Varié No. 8, Op. 42
Air Varié No. 9, Op. 52
Air Varié No. 10, Op. 62
Air Varié No. 11, Op. 79
Air Varié No. 12, Op. 88
Air Varié No. 13, Op. 122
Air Varié No. 14

Bossi, M. Enrico (Cont'd)
Sonata, Op. 117
Souvenir, Op. 122, No. 2
Suite, Op. 99
Vision, Op. 119, No. 2
Bottesini, G.
Rêverie
Bourges, M.
Sonata No. 2
Bouvard, François
Sonata in F
Bowen, York
Suite in D minor
Boyce, William
Three Pieces, No. 9 (Moffat)
Trio-Sonata, No. 8 (Moffat)
Braga, G.
Angel's Serenade (Pollitzer)
Brahms, J.
Andante (Quartet, Op. 67)
Concerto in D major, Op. 77
Cradle Song (Alder)
Hungarian Dances Nos. 1-13
(Joachim)
Sonata, Op. 78
Sonata, Op. 100
Sonata, Op. 108
Sonata, Op. 115 (Klengel)
Waltzes, Op. 39 (Ritter)
Waltz in A major, Op. 39
(Hochstein)
Branche, Ch. Ant.
Sonata in G minor
Branscombe, Gena
A Memory, Op. 21, No. 3
An Old Love Tale, Op. 21, No. 1
At the Fair, Op. 21, No. 2
Carnival Fantasy
Bresles, Henri
Causette printanière, idylle
Sérénade interrompue
Brink, Jules Ten.
Concerto, Op. 7
Brockway, H.
Sonata, Op. 9
Broustet, E.
Berceuse
Fantaisie on Spanish Airs
Bruch, Max
Adagio Appassionato, Op. 57
Aria, Op. 70, No. 1
Concerto No. 1, Op. 26
Concerto No. 2, Op. 44
Concerto No. 3, Op. 58
Concertstück, Op. 61
Concertstück, Op. 84
Kol Nidrei, Op. 47
Romance in A minor, Op. 42
Scotch Fantasy, Op. 46
Serenade, Op. 75
Swedish Dances, Op. 63
Brull, Ignaz
Concerto in A minor, Op. 41
Sonata, Op. 48
Sonata, Op. 60
Sonata, Op. 97
Suite, Op. 42
Bruneau, Alfred
Romance in F
Brzezinski, Fr.
Sonata in D, Op. 6
Bull, Ole
Adagio (Concerto)
Adagio religioso in G, Op. 1
Mountain Vision, A (Fantasia)
Mountain Visit (Saeterbesog)
Nocturne in D, Op. 2
Polacca guerriera
Saeterjentens Sondag
Solitude sur la montagne
Burleigh, Cecil
Concerto in E minor, Op. 25
Concerto, Op. 43

Cradle Song, A
Eight Characteristic Pieces,
Op. 6
Fantastic Suite "Jack and
the Bean-stalk," Op. 35
Impromptu and Scherzo
Plantation Sketches, Op. 36
Scherzando Fantastique, Op.
12
Six Fancies, Op. 31
Six Nature Studies, Op. 23
Six Pictures, Op. 30
Skeleton Dance, Op. 20
Sonata (Life of St. Paul),
Op. 29
Sonata (The Ascension), Op.
22
Burmester, Willy
Sarba (Roumanian Dance)
Busoni, F. B.
Concerto, Op. 20
Concerto, Op. 35
Sonata, Op. 29
Sonata, Op. 36
Busser, H.
Petite Suite
Romance No. 1
Butzow, W.
Orientale, Op. 3, No. 2
Buziau, Victor
Limpide, La (Etude de
Vélocité)
Byford, Francis G.
Vision d'Amour
Campagnoli, B.
Andante con Variazoni
(Corti)
Concerto in B minor, Op. 15
Romance (Pageli)
Capet, L.
Poème
Sonata in A minor, Op. 7
Carl, M.
Concerto No. 1 in A major
Concerto No. 3 in D major
Carpenter, J. A.
Sonata in G
Carri, Ferdinand
Elfentanz, Op. 8
Carrodus, Bernhard M.
Scotch Rhapsody, Op. 6
Carse, Adam
Norwegian Fantasie
Sonata in C minor
Cartier, Jean B.
"La Chasse" Caprice
(Kreisler)
Casella, C. A. de
Chanson Napolitaine
O Belle Nuit (Sérénade Romantique)
Casorti, August
Concerto, Op. 22
Concerto, Op. 59
Cassado, J.
Flores de Triana (Caprice
Espagnol)
Castillon, A. de
Sonata, Op. 6
Castrucci, P.
Sonata in B (Vatielli)
Sonata in D (Moffat)
Catoire, G.
Poème, Op. 20
Sonata, Op. 15
Cazaneuve, E.
Four Scènes provençales
Centola, E.
Concertino in A minor, Op.
51
Suite Napolitaine, Op. 32
Valse, Op. 10, No. 2
Cervetto, G.
Sonata in C (Salmon)
Sonata in G (Salmon)

Cesek, H.
Barcarolle
Romance, Op. 17
Chabran, Francesco
Largo from Fifth Sonata
(Alard)
Rondo (Nachez)
Chabrier, E.
España Rhapsody (Perier)
Habanera (Alder)
Scherzo-Valse (Loeffler)
Chadwick, Geo. W.
Easter Morn
Chaminade, C.
Capriccio, Op. 19
Guitarre, Op. 32
Lisonjera, La (The Flatterer)
Morena Caprice, La, Op. 67
Romanza, Op. 31, No. 2
Scarf Dance (Callirhoë)
Serenade, Op. 29
Three Morceaux, Op. 31
Chausson, E.
Poème, Op. 25
Cherubini, L.
Anacreon (Overture)
Ave Maria (Ritter)
Chevallier, H.
Concerto in D, Op. 54
Chevillard, C.
Sonata, Op. 8
Chiafitelli, Francesco
Petite Suite
Chiostri, L.
Tarantella, Op. 20
Choisnel, G.
Adagio
Chopin, F.
Berceuse, Op. 57 (Novi)
Etude, Op. 25, No. 2 (Pilzer)
Funeral March, Op. 35 (Herbert)
Introduction and Polonaise,
Op. 3
Larghetto (Concerto, Op. 21)
Mazurka, Op. 7, No. 1
Nocturne, Op. 9, No. 2
(Sarasate)
Nocturne, Op. 15, No. 2
(Bachmann)
Nocturne, Op. 27, No. 1
(Sarasate)
Nocturne, Op. 27, No. 2
(Wilhelmj)
Nocturne, Op. 34, No. 2
(Ritter)
Nocturne, Op. 37, No. 1
(Wilhelmj)
Nocturne, Op. 55, No. 2
(Marx-Goldschmidt)
Polonaise, Op. 26, No. 1
Polonaise Militaire, Op. 40,
No. 1
Prelude, Op. 28, No. 15
(Eberhardt)
Sonata, Op. 65 (David)
Tarantelle, Op. 43 (Lipinski)
Waltz, Op. 18 (Stern)
Waltz, Op. 34, No. 2 (Ritter)
Waltz, Op. 64, No. 1 (De
Ahna)
Chvala, E.
Petite Suite
Cipollone, A.
Capriccietto (Hartmann)
Clark, Scotson
Marche aux Flambeaux
Meditation
Clementi, M.
Six Sonatinas, Op. 36 (Reger)
Cliffe, Frederic
Concerto in D minor

Cliffe, Frederic (Cont'd)
Concerto in G minor (Nachez)

Clutsam, H.
Berceuse Creole (Chanson Nègre)

Coerne, L.
Concerto in D major, Op. 63

Cole, Rossiter G.
Sonata, Op. 8

Coleridge-Taylor, S.
Ballade in D minor
Danse Nègre (African Suite, Op. 35)
Deep River (Transcription)
Four Novellettes, Op. 52
Romance, Op. 39
Suite, Op. 3
Suite Tzigane, Op. 20

Collett, John
Largo cantabile (Moffat)
Sonata in A major, No. 5 (Moffat)

Conus, Jules
Concerto in E minor

Corder, Frederick
Roumanian Dances

Cords, G.
Concerto, Op. 41

Corelli, A.
Adagio and Allegro (Herrmann)
Folia, La (Variations)
Sarabande and Allegro (Kreisler)
Sarabande and Corrente (Moffat)
Sarabande and Giga (Elman)
Three Suites (David)
Twelve Sonatas (Jensen)

Cottenet, R.
Chanson-méditation

Couperin, F.
Aubade Provençale (Kreisler)
Bavolet Flottant (Burmester)
Berceuse en rondeau (Leduc)
Chanson et Pavane de Louis XIII
Cherubins, Les (Salmon)
Fleuri, La (Powell)
Moissonneurs, Les
Précieuse, La
Sarabande (Kross)

Cowen, F. H.
Four English Dances
Minuet d'Amour
Rêverie

Cremont, Pierre
Concerto in A minor, Op. 1

Crist, Bainbridge
Abhisarika (Oriental Poem)

Croft, William
Sonata in G minor (Moffat)

Cui, César
A la mazurka, Op. 50, No. 4
Allegro Scherzoso, Op. 50
Appassionata, Op. 50, No. 14
Berceuse, Op. 20, No. 8
Berceuse, Op. 50, No. 5
Expansion Naïve, Op. 20, No. 1
Kaleidescope (20 Pieces, Op. 50)
Meditation (Donner)
Orientale, Op. 50, No. 9
Perpetuum mobile, Op. 50, No. 12
Petite Suite, Op. 14
Sonata, Op. 84 in D
Suite concertante, Op. 25
Three morceaux, Op. 24
Twelve Miniatures, Op. 20

Cupis, Francesco di Camargo
Moto perpetuo (Nachez)

Czerwonky, Richard
Barcarolle
Gondoliera
Minuet in Ancient Style
Romance
Serenade
Two Album Leaves
Village Festival

Czibulka, A.
Coquette, La, Gavotte, Op. 374
Love's Dream After the Ball, Op. 356
Stephanie Gavotte, Op. 312

Dallier, H.
Contemplation (Organ or piano acc.)

Damare, E.
Gavotte-berceuse (Hayet)

Damrosch, L.
Capricietto
Concerto in D minor
Concertstück
Nachtgesang
Romance

Damrosch, W.
Sonata, Op. 6

Danbé, J.
Amour Maternal (Berceuse)
Andante and Air de Ballet, Op. 21
Andante Appassionato
Angelus, Op. 10
Barcarolle Mignonne, Op. 20
Berceuse, Op. 17
Bolero and Cantabile, Op. 22, No. 6
Canzonetta, Op. 11
Canzonetta, Op. 21, No. 4
Capriccio, Op. 12
Carnival of Venice, Variations, Op. 22
Chant du Bivouac (Kücken)
Dernière Rose, Op. 22
Elégie, Op. 15
Mazurka de Salon, Op. 22
Melancolie
Petite Valse lente, Op. 20
Reverie, Op. 28
Romance, Op. 20, No. 5
Romance and Tyrolienne, Op. 21, No. 1
Serenade, Op. 13
Six divertissements, Op. 24
Six fantaisies brillantes, Op. 22
Six morceaux de salon, Op. 26
Six recreations, Op. 23
Villanelle, Op. 14

Dancla, Chas.
Abeille, L', Valse Brillante, Op. 25
Barcarolle, Op. 187, No. 12
Berceuse, Op. 187, No. 2
Bolero and Romance, Op. 50
Concerto, Op. 78
Eight Petite Pièces, Op. 149
Elégie and Barcarolle, Op. 53
Gavotte Spirituelle
Introduction & Allegro, Op. 152
Minuet, Op. 187, No. 8
Novelette, Op. 187, No. 7
Resignation, Op. 59
Reverie, Op. 66
Romance, Op. 187, No. 10
Romance & Bolero, Op. 50
Romance & Mazurka, Op. 100
Simple Histoire
Six Airs Variés, Op. 89
Six Airs Variés, Op. 118

Sonata in A minor, Op. 138, No. 3
Sonata in D, Op. 138, No. 2
Sonata in D, Op. 138, No. 1
Souvenir, Op. 58
Suite No. 3, Op. 123
Tarantella, Op. 102
Three Solos de Concert, Op. 77
Un Rêve du Soir (Evening Dreams), Op. 187, No. 4
Valse brillante, Op. 4

Dancla, L.
Airs populaires norvégiens, Op. 52
Bluettes, Op. 18
Fantaisie in A, Op. 21
Petite Valse, Op. 48, No. 4

Danglas, J.
Aime-moi (Meditation)
Berceuse (Le sommeil de Jésus)
Love's Awakening
Romance Slave

Danilewsky, M.
Inspiration

Daquin, C.
Cuckoo, The (Rehfeld)

Dauvergne, A.
Sonata in C minor (Alard)

David, F.
Andante & Scherzo Capriccioso, Op. 16
Barcarolle (Gondoliera)
Bunte Riehe, Op. 30 (24 Pieces)
Concerto, Op. 3
Concerto, Op. 10
Concerto, Op. 14
Concerto, Op. 17
Concerto, Op. 23
Concerto, Op. 35
Etude (Perpetuo mobile)
Je Suis le petit Tambour (Variations), Op. 6
Kinderlied, Op. 30, No. 5
Petit Tambour (Variations), Op. 5
Polonaise, Op. 22
Red Sarafan (Variations), Op. 6
Twelve morceaux de salon, Op. 24
Variations de concert, Op. 18

Davidoff, C. H.
At the Fountain, Op. 20
Petite Romance, Op. 37
Romance, Op. 22
Romance sans Paroles, Op. 23

Debussy, Claude
Andante (from 1st String Quartet)
Arabesque, No. 1
Arabesque, No. 2
Ballade (Miersch)
Children's Corner (3 Pieces)
1 Serenade to the Doll
2 The Little Shepherd
3 Golliwogg's Cake-walk
Danse de la Poupée (Roques)
Danse Profane
Danse Sacré
En Bateau
Il Pleure dans mon coeur
L'Enfant Prodigue (Excerpts)
La Plus que Lente
Petit Berger, Le
Petite Suite
1 En Bateau
2 Cortège
3 Minuet
4 Ballet

Elgar, E. (Cont'd)
Pastourelle
Pomp and Circumstance
March (Henley)
Salut d'Amour, Op. 12
Serenade (Wand of Youth)
Sonata, Op. 82
Sursum Corda, Op. 11
Virelai
Elman, Mischa
Romance
Emmanuel, M.
Sonata in D minor
Suite on Popular Greek Airs
Enesco, G.
Sonata, Op. 2
Sonata, Op. 6
Engel, C.
Concerto, Op. 6
Enna, A.
Concerto in D major
Erkel, Fr.
Hungarian Hymn (Hart-
mann)
Erlanger, F. d'
Concerto, Op. 17
Ern, H.
Elégie, Op. 20
Mazurka de concert, Op. 8
Reverie, Op. 22
Ernest, G.
Concerto
Ernesti, T. d'
Introduction & Andante re-
ligioso, Op. 17
Ernst, H. W.
Airs Hongrois, Op. 22
Bolero, Op. 16
Carnival of Venice Varia-
tions, Op. 18
Concerto in D major, Op. 12
Concerto in F♯ minor, Op. 23
Concert Polonaise, Op. 17
Elegy, Op. 10
Fantaisie on "Othello," Op.
11
Morceau de Salon, Op. 9
Nocturne, Op. 8
Rondo Papageno, Op. 20
Two Concert Pieces, Op. 13
Exaudet, G.
Danse des Auvergnats (Na-
chez)
Sonata in D minor (Senart)
Exposito, M.
Sonata in G, Op. 32
Fairchild, B.
Legende, Op. 31
Sonata in C minor
Sonata in G
Famintzin, A.
Russian Rhapsody
Farmer, H.
Airs Variés on Popular Melo-
dies
Farrenc, L.
Sonata, Op. 37
Sonata, Op. 39
Farwell, A.
Song-Flight, Op. 61
Faucheuz, A.
Nocturne
Reverie
Fauconier
Reverie, Op. 114, No. 1
Fauré, G.
Andante, Op. 75
Berceuse in D, Op. 16
Dolly (Berceuse), Op. 56
Elégie, Op. 24
Fileuse (Auer)
Papillon, Op. 77
Romance, Op. 28
Romances sans Paroles, Op.
17

Roses d'Ispahan, Les
Sonata, Op. 13
Sonata, Op. 118
Fauré, J.
Rameaux, Les (The Palms)
(Ritter)
Fernandez-Arbos, E.
Three Spanish Dances, Op. 6
La Zambra
Guajiras
Tango
Fesca, A.
Grande Sonata brillante, Op.
40
Fesch, W. de
Sonata in D minor (Salmon)
Sonata in G (Salmon)
Festing, M. C.
Sonata in B minor (Senart)
Fevrier, H.
Legende
Sonata in A minor
Fibich, Z.
Fancies, impressions & recol-
lections
    1st Series, 10 morceaux
    2nd Series, 10 morceaux
    3rd Series, 10 morceaux
    (Bastl)
Poème (Kubelik)
Sonatina, Op. 27
Field, J.
Nocturne in B♭
Nocturne in D
Nocturne in D minor
Nocturne in E
Fielitz, A. von
Romance in G minor, Op. 25
Finden, A. W.
Four Indian Love Lyrics
(Dyke)
Fiorillo, F.
Sonata
Fischel, A.
Concerto, Op. 40
Flegier, A.
Elégie, romance
Prière d'amour
Stances
Villanelle
Fleuret, D.
Sonata, Op. 28
Foerster, A.
Three Sonatinas, Op. 200
Foerster, A. M.
Concerto in C minor, Op. 88
Fantaisie, Op. 15
Novelette, Op. 26
Romance and Melodies, Op.
17
Sonata in B minor, Op. 10
Spring Song
Suite No. 1, Op. 36
Suite No. 2, Op. 79
Foerster, J. B.
Concerto in C minor, Op. 88
Fontenailles, H. de
Elégie
Foote, A. W.
Canzonetta, Op. 74, No. 1
Legende, Op. 75
Melody, Op. 44
Minuet Serioso, Op. 9
Morgensang, Op. 9
Romanza, Op. 9
Sonata, Op. 20
Song of Sleep, Op. 74, No. 2
Forsyth, C.
Chanson celtique
Concerto in G minor
Foster, S.
Old Folks at Home (Fan-
taisie) (Mollenhauer)
Old Folks at Home (Zim-
balist)

Fourdrain, E.
Serenade impromptu
Fournier, C.
Three Melodies (Souvenir-
Bagatelle-Pastorale)
Franck, C.
Andante Quietoso, Op. 6
Ave Maria
Duo Concertant
Plaintes d'une Poupée, Les
Sonata in A
Sonata in D
Franck, E.
Concerto in E minor, Op. 30
Franck, R.
Sonata, Op. 14
Sonata, Op. 35, No. 2
Francoeur, F.
Aria and Sarabande (Alard)
Arietta (Barison)
Sicilienne and Rigaudon
(Kreisler)
Sonata in B (Moffat)
Sonata in D minor (Moffat)
Franke, Th.
Intermezzo Russe
Franko, S.
Berceuse
Mazurka de concert
Meditation
Franzl, F.
Concerto, Op. 12
Concerto, Op. 13
Concerto, Op. 14
Concerto, Op. 20
Friml, R.
Berceuse, Op. 50
Bygone Days, Op. 65
Canzonetta, Op. 51
Dawn, Op. 82, No. 1
Dumka, Op. 63
Lullaby, Op. 58
Mazurka, Op. 73, No. 2
Melodie, Op. 73, No. 1
Mignonette, Op. 59
O Vermeland, Op. 64
Phantoms, Op. 82, No. 2
Fritz, G.
Sonata No. 1
Fuchs, Rob.
Fantasy Pieces, Op. 104
Serenade in D, Op. 9
Sonata in D, Op. 33
Sonata in E major, Op. 77
Sonata in F♯ minor, Op. 20
Gaal, F.
Rhapsodie Hongroise, Op. 92
Gabriel-Marie
Adagio
Allegresse
Berceuse
Cinquantaine, La
Esquisse
Fantasia
Lamento
Sérénade Badine
Suite (Prelude & Divertisse-
ment)
Tzigane, Mazurka
Gade, N. W.
Berceuse in G
Concerto in D minor, Op. 56
Fantasiestücke
In the Flower Garden, Op. 34
Norwegian Dances, Op. 62
Reminiscences of Scotland,
Op. 1
Romance, Op. 56
Scherzo, Op. 19, No. 2
Sonata in A, Op. 6
Sonata in B♭ minor, Op. 59
Sonata in D minor, Op. 21
Spring Flower, Op. 2, No. 3
Galkine, N.
Serenade

Galliard, J. E.
  Sonata in E minor (Senart)
  Sonata in G (Salmon)
Ganne, L.
  Arlequinade
  Extase, L' (Reverie)
  Gavotte tendre
  Invocation
  Minuet Rose (Alder)
Ganz, R.
  Meditation (Fifth Prelude by
  J. S. Bach)
Garcin, J.
  Canzonetta
  Chanson de Mignon, Op. 11
  Concertino
  Fantaisie concertante (Cop-
  pelia)
Gardner, S.
  Five Preludes, Op. 14
Gaspard, Fr.
  Sonata in D
Gasparini, P.
  Sonata in E minor (Salmon)
Gastaldon, S.
  Forbidden Music (Musica
  Proibita)
Gautier, L.
  Caprice
  Sacret, Le
Gaviniés, P.
  Adagio and Rondo (Nachez)
  Sonata in G minor (Alard)
Gedalge, A.
  Sonata, Op. 12
  Sonata, Op. 19
Geloso, C.
  Berceuse
  Caprice Slave
  Danse Espagnole
  Habanera
  Two Suites in Hungarian
  Style
Geminiani, F.
  Introduction and Allegro
  (Corti)
  Sarabande (Nachez)
  Sonata in C minor (David)
  Sonata in D minor (Jensen)
  Sonata in D minor (Moffat)
Gerke, O.
  Concerto in E minor, Op. 28
German, E.
  Gipsy Suite
  Moto Perpetuo
  Pastorale and Bourrée (Ro-
  meo and Juliet)
  Pavane (Romeo and Juliet)
  Saltarelle
  Three Dances from ''Henry
  VIII''
  Three Dances from ''Nell
  Gwynne''
Gernsheim, Fr.
  Concerto, Op. 42
  Fantasiestück in D, Op. 33
  Introduction and Allegro Ap-
  passionato, Op. 38
  Sonata, Op. 4
  Sonata, Op. 12
  Sonata, Op. 50
  Sonata, Op. 85
Ghys, H.
  Amaryllis (Air Louis XIII)
  Au clair de la lune, Air
  varié
  Berceuse
Ghys, J.
  Concerto, Op. 40
Giardini, F. de
  Chasse, La (Moffat)
  Gigue (Elman)
  Musette (Elman)
  Sonata in E minor (Moffat)

  Sonata in G (Moffat)
  Soupirs, Les (Barison)
Gibbs, J.
  Sonata in D minor (Moffat)
Gillet, E.
  Au Moulin (In the Mill)
  Babillage
  Entr'acte Gavotte
  Lettre de Manon, La (Enoch)
  Loin du Bal
  Passe-Pied
  Précieuse, La
  Serenade Impromptu
Giordani, Th.
  Air ''Caro Mio Ben'' (Rit-
  ter)
Giraud, F.
  Concerto, Op. 12
Glass, L.
  Sonata in Eb, Op. 7
Glazounow, A.
  Concerto in A minor, Op. 82
  Grand Adagio (Raymonda)
  Meditation, Op. 32
  Mélodie Arabe (Ortmans)
Gliere, R.
  Mélodie (Hartmann)
  Romance, Op. 3
Glinka, M.
  Berceuse
  L'Alouette (Balakirew)
  ''Life of the Czar'' Fan-
  taisie (Gavrillof)
  Mazurka (Hartmann)
  Mazurka Russe (Carse)
Gluck, C. W. von
  Air de 'Ballet (Elman)
  Air de Ballet (Manen)
  Andante (Orfeo)
  Andante in G (Burmester)
  Bourrée (Kross)
  Gavotte in A (Singer)
  Mélodie (Kreisler)
  Minuet (Burmester)
  Souvenir d' ''Armide,'' Op.
  97 (Dancla)
  Souvenir d' ''Orphée,'' Op.
  96 (Dancla)
Godard, B.
  Adagio Pathetique
  Au Matin, Op. 83
  Berceuse (Jocelyn)
  Berceuse in G, Op. 78, No. 2
  Canzonetta (Concerto Roman-
  tique)
  Concerto in G minor, Op. 131
  Concerto Romantique, Op. 35
  Danse rustique, Op. 145,
  No. 4
  Five Pieces, Op. 145
  Légende & Scherzo, Op. 3
  Mazurka, Op. 54 (Wier)
  Mazurka sentimentale, Op.
  128, No. 4
  Sérénade andalouse, Op. 128,
  No. 5
  Six morceaux, Op. 128
  Sonata, Op. 1
  Sonata, Op. 2
  Sonata, Op. 9
  Sonata, Op. 12
  Staccato-valse, Op. 128, No.
  6
Godowsky, L.
  Twelve Impressions
    No. 1 Larghetto Lamen-
    toso
    No 2 Profile (Chopin)
    No. 3 Legend
    No. 4 Tyrolean (Schuh-
    plattler)
    No. 5 Poème (Andante
    Cantabile)
    No. 6 Perpetuum Mobile
    No. 7 Elégie

    No. 8 Valse
    No. 9 Valse Macabre
    No. 10 Orientale
    No. 11 Saga
    No. 12 Viennese (Wiener-
    isch)
Goedicke, A.
  Sonata, Op. 10
Goens, D. van
  Cantilene (2nd concerto)
  Chant élégiaque, Op. 45
  Elégie, Op. 10
  Romance sans Paroles, Op.
  12, No. 1
  Scherzo, Op. 12, No. 2
Goldmark, C.
  Air in G (Concerto)
  Ballade in A
  Ballade in G
  Concerto, Op. 28
  Concerto No. 2 (Without
  Opus)
  Queen of Sheba—Ballet Mu-
  sic
  Sonata, Op. 25
  Suite, Op. 11
  Suite, Op. 43
Goldmark, R.
  Call of the Plains, The
  Plaintive Air
  Song of the Troubadour
  Witches' Sabbath
Goltermann, G.
  Andante (Cantilena) from
  Op. 14
Goossens, E.
  Chinese Folk-Song, Op. 4a
  Fantasy, Op. 12
  Sonata, Op. 21
  Two Sketches, Op. 15
Gorski, K.
  Five morceaux, Op. 1 (Rah-
  ter)
Gorski, L.
  Berceuse & Intermezzo ca-
  pricioso, Op. 3
Gossec, F. J.
  Fête en Vallage (Barison)
  Gavotte (Burmester)
  Gavotte in D (Elman)
  Tambourine (Burmester)
Gottschalk, L.
  Last Hope, The
Gound, Rob.
  Suite romantique, Op. 18
Gounod, Ch.
  Ave Maria (Meditation on
  Bach Prelude)
  Berceuse
  Chanson du Printemps
  Dodelinette
  Faust (Fantaisie) (Alard)
  Faust (Fantaisie) (Dancla)
  Faust (Fantaisie) (Kayser)
  Faust (Fantaisie) (Sarasate)
  Faust (Fantaisie) (Singelée)
  Faust (Fantaisie) (Vieux-
  temps)
  Faust (Fantaisie) (Wienaw-
  ski)
  Faust (Waltz) (Wichtl)
  Hymne à Sainte Cecile
  March funèbre d'une Marion-
  ette
  Mireille (Fantasy) (Her-
  mann)
  Mireille (Souvenir) (Hen-
  ley)
  Queen of Sheba (Ballet Mu-
  sic)
  Romeo and Juliet (Fantai-
  sie) (Alard)
  Serenade (Quand tu Chantez)
  Vision de Jeanne d'Arc
  (Meditation)

Lacombe, P. (Cont'd)
Sonata, Op. 98
Suite, Op. 88
Ladoukhine, N.
Mélodie
Petit Suite, Op. 9
Romance
Lafont, C. P.
Concerto No. 1
Concerto No. 2
Concerto No. 3
Lagye, B.
Cradle Song, Op. 33
Le rêve d'un ange, Op. 18
Lahoussaye, P.
Sonata (Alard)
Lalo, E.
Arlequin
Chanson Villageoise, Op. 14,
No. 1
Chants Russes (Concerto, Op.
29)
Concerto, Op. 20
Concerto Russe, Op. 29
Fantaisie norvégienne
Fantaisie originale in A, Op. 1
Guitare, Op. 28
Pastorale and Scherzo, Op. 8
Rhapsody Espagnol
"Roi d'Ys" Fantasy (Her-
mann)
Romance-Serenade
Serenade, Op. 14, No. 2
Sonata, Op. 12
Symphonie Espagnole, Op. 21
Lamarter, Eric de
Sonata in Eb
Lange, G.
Edelweiss (Idyl)
Flower Song, Op. 39
Thine Own (Dein Eigen)
Laparra, R.
Sonata in A minor
Lardelli, G.
Rêve d'Amour
Lassen, E.
Concerto, Op. 87
Concerto, Op. 149
Lates, J.
Sonata in G major
Laub, F.
Four Morceaux, Op. 12
Polonaise de concerto, Op. 8
Rondo Scherzando, Op. 6
Two morceaux, Op. 7
Lauterbach, Joh.
Barcarolle in G minor, Op. 7
Introduction and Polonaise
Légende in G minor, Op. 8
Rondo Scherzando, Op. 6
Tarentelle
Two Concert Etudes, Op. 5
Lazzari, S.
Sonata, Op. 24
Le Borne, F.
Poème légendaire, Op. 67
Sonata, Op. 29
Leclair, J. M.
Andante and Chaconne
Concerto No. 1 in D minor
Concerto No. 2 in D major
Concerto No. 3 in A minor
Concerto No. 4 in F major
Concerto No. 5 in E minor
Concerto No. 6 in G minor
Sarabande and Tambourin
(Ries)
Sonata (le Tombeau) in C
minor (Alard)
Sonata No. 3 (Alard)
Sonata No. 4 (Jensen)
Tambourin (Kreisler)
Lederer, D.
A la Tzigane, Op. 55
Berceuse tendre, Op. 40

Danses Hongroises
Hungarian Poem, Op. 16
Jota Aragonesa, Op. 56
Meditation
Scènes de la Czardas Nos. 1
and 2
Lefebure-Wely, L.
Cloches du Monastère (Noc-
turne)
Clochette du Patrie (Noc-
turne)
Lefèbvre, Ch.
Andante, Op. 103
Romance, Op. 30
Suite, Op. 116
Lefort, A.
Air de Ballet
Barcarolle
Berceuse
Gavotte
Gigue
Mazurka
Minuet
Danse mauresque
Scherzino
Lehmann, Rob.
Elégie, Op. 29a
Le Jeune, A.
Dance des Marionettes
Evening Song
Heiterkeit (Jollification)
Impromptu
Melody
Lekeu, G.
Sonata in G
Lemaitre, L.
Bourrée
Douce ivresse (Melody)
Prelude and Romance
Lemare, E. H.
Andantino
Lenormand, René
Caprice, Op. 11
Légende, Op. 84
Serenade, Op. 11
Léonard, H.
Andante and Allegro de Con-
cert, Op. 31, No. 1
Concerto, Op. 10
Concerto, Op. 14
Concerto, Op. 16
Concerto, Op. 26
Concerto, Op. 28
Fantaisie Militaire, Op. 15
Fantasy on Russian Themes
Grandmother's Tale
Morceau de Concert, Op. 33
Souvenir d'Haydn, Op. 2
Tristezza e Marcia, Op. 31,
No. 2
Valse-Caprice, Op. 43
Variations on a Corelli Ga-
votte, Op. 51
Leoncavallo, R.
Fantasy "Pagliacci" (Wolff)
Prologue (Pagliacci)
Serenade (Pagliacci)
Leroux, X.
Les Perses (Air de ballet)
Une soirée près de lac
(Idylle)
Leutner, A.
Fest Ouverture, Op. 42
Levy, H.
Passacaglia
Lewandowski, L.
Hebraische Melodien, Op. 32
Lewinger, M.
Legende, Op. 9
Leybach, I.
Fifth Nocturne, Op. 52
(Popp)
Liadow, A.
Mazurka

Lindpaintner, P.
Concerto in A major, Op. 42
Lindsay, J.
Aisha (Indian intermezzo)
Tatjana (Intermezzo)
Lipinski, C. J.
Concerto, Op. 32
Concerto Militaire
Liszt, Fr.
Consolation No. 5
Liebesträum (Wier)
Second Hungarian Rhapsody
(Halir)
Second Hungarian Rhapsody
(Joachim)
Second Hungarian Rhapsody
(Sitt)
Litolff, H.
Concerto, Op. 42
Concerto, Op. 45
Serenade, Op. 91
Three Duets (Léonard)
Locatelli, P.
Sarabande and Allegro
Scherzoso
Sonata in B minor (Rieman)
Sonata in Bb minor (Moffat)
Sonata in D (Barison)
Sonata in D minor (Moffat)
Sonata in G (Moffat)
Sonata in G minor (David)
Thème avec variations
(Schering)
Loeillet, J. B.
Air and Allegro Vivamente
(Moffat)
Minuet (Burmester)
Sonata in A minor (Swert)
Sonata in E minor (Moffat)
Loesser, A.
California (Humoresque)
Loewe, C.
Scottish Pictures, Op. 112
Loewe, J. H.
Concerto, Op. 1
Concerto, Op. 3
Lolli, A.
Adagio and Allegro (Elman)
Six Sonatas (Gatti)
Longo, A.
Suite, Op. 33
Lotti, A.
Air "Pur Picesti" (Lang-
hans)
Lotto, I.
Fileuse, Op. 8
Morceau de Concert, Op. 2
Low, J.
Albumblatt (Hermann)
Luigini, A.
Ballet Egyptian
Romance, Op. 22
Romance sans paroles
Voix des cloches, La
Lully, J. B.
Air-Courante and Sarabande
Andantino (Brown)
Gavotte (Burmester)
Gavotte (Kleinmichel)
Gavotte en Rondeau (Elman)
Gavotte and Minuet (Moffat)
Luzzato, F.
Sonata in G, Op. 32
Macbeth, A.
Forget Me Not (Intermezzo)
Love In Idleness (Inter-
mezzo)
MacCunn, H.
Eglantine
Romance in G
Three Romantic Pieces, Op.
27
MacDowell, E.
Idyl, Op. 28, No. 1
Idyl, Op. 62 (Auer)

MacDowell, E. (Cont'd)
Scotch Poem, Op. 31, No. 2
To a Wild Rose, Op. 51, No.
1 (Hartmann)
Macfarren, W.
Sonata No. 1
Sonata No. 2
Mackenzie, A. C.
Concerto, Op. 32
From the North (Nine
Pieces)
Highland Ballad, Op. 47,
No. 1
Invocation, Op. 76
Pibroch Suite, Op. 42
Savannah, La ("Air de Bal-
let"), Op. 72
Six Pieces, Op. 37
Suite, Op. 63
Macklean, Charles
Sonata in E major (Moffat)
Macmillen, F.
Barcarole
Causerie (Prairie Flower)
Gavotte des Ecoliers
Hymn of Love
Nijinsky (Mazurka)
Sérénade Nègre
Magnard, A.
Sonata in G minor, Op. 13
Malaschkine, L.
Romance, Op. 7
Malherbe, Ch.
Romance sans paroles
Malichevsky, W.
Sonata, Op. 1
Malling, O.
Fantaisie de Concert, Op. 20
Sonata, Op. 57
Manen, Joan
Bolero (Morceau de concert),
Op. 27
Caprice, Op. 15a
Carrousel, Op. 3
Chanson, Op. 8, No. 1 (Lied)
Concerto Espagnol, Op. 18
Concerto in E minor
Papillon, Op. 32
Petite Spanish Suite, Op. 26
Rêve, Le, Op. 29
Scherzo Fantastique, Op. 28
Second Caprice Catalan
Spanish Concerto in D major,
Op. 18
Two Tartini Variations, Op. 2
Manfredi, F.
Sonata in G minor (Alard)
Manfredi, P.
Adagio from the Sixth Sonata
(Alard)
Manns, F.
Barcarolle
Eventide
Valse-Serenade
Marais, M.
Five Old French Dances
Marais, R.
Sonata in C (Salmon)
Marcello, B.
Sonata in D (Salmon)
Sonata in E minor (Salmon)
Sonata in G minor (Salmon)
Marchand, L.
Gavotte in D minor (Press)
Marcucci, G.
Concerto in G minor
Marsick, P. M.
Adagio and Scherzando, Op.
6
Berceuse
Capriccioso
Espoir, Op. 22
Fleurs des Cimes, Op. 25
Hesperides, Les, Op. 27
Poème de Mai, Op. 21

Poème d'été, Op. 24
Rêve, Le, Op. 21
Reverie, Op. 4
Romance, Op. 8
Tendre Aveu, Op. 23
Valencia, Op. 26
Marteau, H.
Berceuse, Op. 1
Concerto, Op. 18
Suite, Op. 15
Martin, F.
Sonata in G minor, Op. 1
Martini, G. (Padre)
Andantino (Kreisler)
Arietta (Corti)
Balletto (Barison)
Gavotte (Burmester)
Gavotte (Manen)
Preghiera (Kreisler)
Romance (Lenz)
Suite in G (Bonavia)
Martucci, G.
Sonata, Op. 22
Three Morceaux, Op. 67
Marx, J.
Sonata in A
Mascagni, P.
Fantasia (Bastine)
Intermezzo (Cavalleria Rusti-
cana)
Iris (Fantaisie)
L'Amico Fritz (Fantaisie)
Prelude and Sicilienne (Cav-
alleria Rusticana)
Solo de violon de "L'Amico
Fritz"
Mascitti, M.
Allemanda (Elman)
Preludio and Corrente (Mof-
fat)
Sonata in A major (Moffat)
Sonata in E minor (Moffat)
Mason, D. G.
Intermezzo, Op. 17
Sonata in G minor, Op. 5
Two Pieces, Op. 13
Massart, J.
Words from the Heart (Fan-
tasy)
Massenet, J.
Angelus (Scènes Pitto-
resques)
Aragonaise (Le Cid)
Crépuscule (Twilight)
Elégie, Op. 10
Last Dream of the Virgin
Meditation (Thaïs)
Pensée d'Automne
Scènes Pittoresques (Suite)
Mathias, G.
Sonata, Op. 68
Mathieu, E.
Concerto in D minor
Mattheson, Jos.
Air on the G String (Bur-
mester)
Sarabande and Allemande
(Wehrle)
Maurer, L.
Concerto, Op. 58
Concerto, Op. 59
Concerto, Op. 65
Concerto, Op. 82
Mayseder, J.
Concerto in A minor, Op. 22
Concerto in D major, Op. 28
Concerto in E major, Op. 26
Concerto in E major, Op. 53
Polonaise in A major, Op. 38
Variations Brillantes, Op. 40
Mazas, F.
La Babillarde (Scène-Ca-
price), Op. 37
Melodic Suite

Medtner, N.
Three Nocturnes, Op. 16
Mehul, E. H.
Gavotte (Press-Moffat)
Minuet in A (Burmester)
Melartin, E.
Arietta and Gavotte
Berceuse
Romance
Sonata in E, Op. 10
Mendelssohn, Felix
Concerto in E minor, Op. 64
Confidence
Consolation
Funeral March
Nocturne (Midsummer
Night's Dream)
On Wings of Song. Op. 13
Sonata, Op. 4
Variations, Op. 17
Venetian Gondolier Song
War March (Athalia)
Wedding March
Mendelssohn, Ludwig
Concerto in A, Op. 110
Concerto in D major, Op. 213
Merikanto, O.
Valse lente (Burmester)
Merkel, G.
Romance
Rustic Dance
Six Bagatelles, Op. 149
Messer, N.
Barcarolle
Mestrino, N.
Romance (Kross)
Metzdorff, R.
Concerto, Op. 48
Meyer, G.
Sonata in C minor, Op. 14
Sonata in F, Op. 15
Meyerbeer, G.
Benediction of the Poignards
(Les Huguenots)
Coronation March (The
Prophet)
Fackeltanz No. 3 (Weiss)
Shadow Dance (Dinorah)
Meyer-Helmund, E.
Dialogue, Op. 135, No. 3
Fantaisie in A minor, Op. 44
Mazurka, Op. 40 (Wier)
Melodie, Op. 72 (Wier)
Petite Chanson d'Amour
Petite Sérénade
Petite Valse Mélancolique
Rêve du Volupté
Sérénade Rococo
Wonneträum (Blissful
Dream), Op. 95
Mezzacapo, E.
Le chant du gondolier
Michiels, G.
Magyar-Csardas
Rapsodie russe
Miersch, P. T.
Elégie in F, Op. 27, No. 1
Gavotte, Op. 30, No. 2
Moto perpetuo, Op. 30, No. 3
Migot, G.
Sonata (Mathot)
Milandre, L.
Minuet (Press)
Milanollo, Teresa
Air de Marlborough, Op. 5
Lamento, Op. 7
Rheinweinlied, Op. 6
Milhaud, D.
Sonata No. 1
Sonata No. 2
Mistowski, A.
Concerto in A major
Mitnitzky, I.
Fête orientale, Op. 12

VIOLIN SOLOS WITH PIANO ACCOMPANIMENT 447

Mitnitzky, I. (Cont'd)
Mazurka, Op. 11
Valse con sordino, Op. 9
Mlynarski, E.
Berceuse Slave, Op. 4, No. 2
Humoresque, Op. 4, No. 3
Mazurka, Op. 7
Polonaise, Op. 4, No. 1
Moffat, A.
Danse Paysanne
Espérance
Gavotte in D minor
Mojsisovics, R. de
Sonata in D, Op. 29
Molique, B.
Concerto, Op. 1, No. 1
Concerto, Op. 9, No. 2
Concerto, Op. 10, No. 3
Concerto, Op. 14, No. 4
Concerto, Op. 21, No. 5
Concerto, Op. 30, No. 6
Fandango, Op. 60
Saltarella, Op. 55
Variations and Rondo, Op. 11
Monasterio, J. de
Adieux à l'Alhambra, Op. 12
(Moorish Lament)
Fantasia on Spanish Airs
Sierra Morena (Serenata
Andaluzza)
Mondonville, C. C.
Sonata in F minor
Mondonville, J. de
Chasse, La (Sarasate)
Sarabande (Moffat)
Sonata in F (Alard)
Tambourin (Moffat)
Monti, V.
Csardas No. 1
Csardas No. 2
Serenade (Noël de Pierrot)
Moor, Emmanuel
Aria in D, Op. 83
Concerto, Op. 62
Concerto, Op. 66
Concerto, Op. 72
Rhapsody, Op. 84
Sonata in A minor, Op. 21
Sonata in A minor, Op. 74
Sonata in E minor, Op. 56
Sonata, Op. 54
Suite, Op. 73
Moszkowski, M.
Bolero, Op. 16, No. 2
Cantabile, Op. 56
Concerto in C major, Op. 30
Guitarre, Op. 45, No. 2
Humoreske, Op. 82, No. 4
Hungary (from "In Foreign
Lands")
Mazurka, Op. 10, No. 3
Mélodie, Op. 18, No. 1
Mélodie, Op. 31, No. 2 (Ries)
Mélodie, Op. 82, No. 3
Miniature, Op. 28, No. 1
Minuet, Op. 77
Passepied in A major
Près d'un Berceau, Op. 58
Romance, Op. 42, No. 1
Russia (from "In Foreign
Lands")
Serenata, Op. 15, No. 1
Spanish Dances, Op. 12
Mouret, J. J.
Bourrée (Danbé)
Deux Bourrées (Elman)
Moussorgsky, M.
Boris (Selection)
Gopak (Russian Dance)
Un Larme (A Tear)
Mozart, W. A.
Adagio and Andante (Litolff)
Adagio and Rondo (Jensen)
Andante cantabile (Klein)
Andante and Rondo (David)

Ave Verum Corpus
Concerto No. 1 in B minor
Concerto No. 2 in D major
Concerto No. 3 in G major
Concerto No. 4 in D major
Concerto No. 5 in A major
Concerto No. 6 in Eb major
Concerto No. 7 in D major
Gavotte from "Les petits
riens" (Franko)
German Dance (Burmester)
Gloria (Twelfth Mass)
Minuet (Don Juan)
Minuet in D (Divertimento)
Rondo Concertante in B minor
Rondo in C (Marteau)
Rondo in G (Kreisler)
Serenade (Don Juan)
Sonatas Nos. 1-18
Symphonies (Hermann)
Mraczek, J. G.
Elegy
Nocturno
Muller-Berghaus, C.
Concerto, Op. 60
Murdoch, M.
Recitative and Polonaise
Murkens, H.
Berceuse
Danse Slave
Mazurka
Muscat, H.
Concerto in G minor, Op. 5
Musin, O.
Berceuse, Op. 9
Mazurka de Concert, Op. 7
Mazurka No. 2, Op. 14
Mazurka Romantique No. 3,
Op. 11
Valse de Concert, Op. 7
Nachez, T.
Abendlied (Evening Song)
Concerto, Op. 30
Concerto, Op. 36
Danse Tzigane, Op. 14, No. 1
Danse Tzigane, Op. 14, No. 2
Danse Tzigane, Op. 14, No. 3
Pensée plaintive, Op. 27, No.
1 (Idylle)
Poème de la Puzsta, Op. 33,
No. 1
Polonaise, Op. 26
Rhapsodie Hongroise No. 1,
Op. 16
Rhapsodie Hongroise No. 2,
Op. 25
Napravnik, E.
Fantasy on Russian Themes,
Op. 30
Mélodie russe, Op. 64, No. 3
Nocturne, Op. 64, No. 1
Russian Fantasy, Op. 30
Sonata, Op. 20
Sonata, Op. 60
Suite, Op. 60
Valse-Caprice, Op. 64, No. 2
Nardini, Pietro
Adagio (Concerto in G)
Adagio Cantabile
Adagio in Eb
Adagio and Finale
Concerto in A
Concerto in E minor
Larghetto
Sonata in A
Sonata in B minor (Alard)
Sonata in D (David)
Theme and Variation
(Luizzi)
Nedbal, O.
Romance-Serenade, Op. 6
Sonata in B minor, Op. 9
Nemorowsky, A.
Alla Mazurka (Hartmann)

Meditation, Op. 8
Pensée Musicale, Op. 11
Neruda, Franz
Ballade, Op. 43
Berceuse Slave, Op. 11
Notturno, Op. 45
Nesvera, Jos.
Berceuse Bohemian, Op. 25
Cradle Song, Op. 25
Ricordanza, Op. 97
Suite in G, Op. 53
Neury, J.
Berceuse
Chanson Espagnole
Nevin, Ethelbert
Habanera, Op. 8, No. 2
Melody, Op. 8, No. 1
Narcissus, Op. 13, No. 4
Rosary, The (Transcription)
Newlandsmith, E.
Polonaise-caprice
Nicodé, J. L.
Canzonetta, Op. 13, No. 2
Scène de Bal, Op. 26
Nielsen, C.
Concerto, Op. 33
Niemann, R.
Sonata, Op. 18
Niggli, F.
Sonata in E, Op. 7
Niverd, Lucien
Chacone
Sonata in B
Nolck, A.
Concertino, Op. 178
Noren, H. G.
Capriccio, Op. 43, No. 2
Concerto, Op. 38
Danse Slave, Op. 39, No. 2
Légende, Op. 39, No. 1
Nocturne, Op. 43, No. 1
Sonata, Op. 16
Sonata, Op. 33
Suite, Op. 16
Noskowski, S.
Fantaisie-Mazurka de con-
cert, Op. 21, No. 2
Zingaresca
Novaček, O.
Perpetuum mobile
Oehmler, Leo
Sonata in F, Op. 14
Offenbach, Jacques
Barcarolle (Tales of Hoff-
mann)
Musette, La, Op. 24
Violin Solo (Orpheus in the
Underworld)
Ogarew, M.
Caprice in A minor
Romance in E
Ollone, Max d'
Ménétrier, Le (Poème sym-
phonique)
Olsen, Per
Serenade (Wier)
Ondricěk, François
Barcarolle, Op. 10
Nocturno, Op. 17
Rhapsody Bohme, Op. 21
Romance, Op. 12
Onslow, George
Andante from Fourth Quartet
(Haddock)
Orefice, G.
Sonata in E minor
Orem, Preston Ware
Romance in Eb
Ornstein, Leo
Sonata, Op. 31
Ortemans, René
Concertino in A minor, Op.
12
Concertino in D major, Op.
14

Roussel, Albert
Sonata in D minor
Rozé, Raymond
Extase d'Amour, Op. 28
Rubinstein, Anton
Barcarolle, Op. 30, No. 1
Bayadere Dance (Feramors)
Concerto in G major, Op. 26
Kamennoi Ostrow, Op. 10, No. 22 (Franko)
Melody in F (Auer)
Romance, Op. 44, No. 1
Romance and Caprice, Op. 86
Sonata in A minor, Op. 19
Sonata in B minor, Op. 98
Sonata in G, Op. 13
Toreador and Andalouse, Op. 103, No. 7
Rufer, Phillipe
Concerto, Op. 33
Rust, F. V.
Sonata in D minor (David)
Sonata in G
Sonata Seria in A minor
Sonata Seria in B minor
Rutkowsky, A.
Nocturne, Op. 4
Ryelandt, Jos.
Sonata, Op. 27
Sonata, Op. 53
Saar, L. V.
Boat Song (Gondoliera), Op. 52, IV
Canzonetta, Op. 17 (Schuberth)
Chanson d'Amour, Op. 60, No. 2
En Berceau, Op. 86a (Church)
Romance Mélodique, Op. 78
Sonatas for violin and piano, Op. 44 (Siegel)
Two Pieces, Op. 26 (Schuberth)
Sacchini, Antonio
Air de Dardanus (Franko)
Gavotte de Renaud (Franko)
Sachs, Leo
Sonata, Op. 33
Saenger, Gustave
Caprice, Op. 129, No. 1
Concertino No. 1 in G minor, Op. 83
Improvisation
Rural Sketches
Serenade de Novia, Op. 129, No. 2
Three Concert Miniatures
Saggione, G. F.
Sonata in E
Sahla, Richard
Roumanian Rhapsody
Saint-George, G.
Ancien Régime, L' (1st Suite)
Ancien Régime, L' (2nd Suite)
Confidence
Rondo Brillant, Op. 45
Saint-Lubin, L. de
Adagio religioso, Op. 44
Polonaise, Op. 7
Sainton, Prosper
Concerto, Op. 9
Solo de Concert, Op. 16
Tarantelle, Op. 20
Thème Italien varié, Op. 10
Saint-Saëns, Charles Camille
Barcarolle, Op. 108
Berceuse, Op. 38
Caprice, Op. 52, No. 6
Caprice Andalouse, Op. 122
Concerto in B minor, Op. 61
Concerto in C major, Op. 58

Concertstück in A minor, Op. 20
Cygne, Le (The Swan)
Danse Macabre (Symphonic Poem), Op. 40
Déluge, Le (Prelude), Op. 45
Fantaisie, Op. 124
Havanaise, Op. 83
Introduction and Rondo Capriccioso, Op. 28
Jota Aragonesa, La, Op. 64
Morceau de Concert, Op. 62
Rêverie du Soir (Suite Algérienne)
Romance in C, Op. 48
Romance in C minor, Op. 37
Romance in D, Op. 51
Rouet d'Omphale (Symphonic Poem)
Samson and Delilah (Fantasy)
Samson and Delilah (My Heart at Thy Sweet Voice)
Scherzo-marche, Op. 2 (Lemaître)
Sonata, Op. 75
Sonata, Op. 102
Suite, Op. 16
Suite "Triptique," Op. 136
Une Nuit à Lisbonne, Op. 63
Valse Caprice, Op. 52 (Ysaÿe)
Salmon, J.
Nocturne
Saloman, L.
Concerto, Op. 26
Salomon, H.
Caprice, Op. 61
Samazeuilh, G.
Fantaisie élégiaque
Sonata in B minor
Sammartini, G.
Canto Amoroso (Elman)
Minuet (Barison)
Sonata in A minor (Moffat)
Sonata in G (Salmon)
Sapellnikoff, W.
Lily of the Valley (Wier)
Petite Mazurka (Saenger)
Sarasate, Pablos de
Adieux, Les (Mélodie), Op. 9
Adios, Montañas mías!, Op. 37
Airs Ecossais (Scotch Airs), Op. 34
Barcarolle Vénitienne, Op. 46
Bolero, Op. 30
Caprice Basque, Op. 24
Caprice Espagnol, Op. 35
Carmen (Fantasy), Op. 25
Chansons Russes, Op. 49
Chant du Rossignol, Op. 29
Chasse, La, Op. 44
Danses Espagnoles, Op. 21
Danses Espagnoles, Op. 22
Danses Espagnoles, Op. 23
Danses Espagnoles, Op. 26
Danses Espagnoles, Op. 28
Danses Espagnoles, Op. 29
Danses Espagnoles, Op. 30
Esprit follet, L', Op. 48
Faust (Fantasy)
Habanera, Op. 21, No. 2
Introduction & Caprice Jota, Op. 41
Introduction & Tarantelle, Op. 43
Jota de Pamplona, Op. 50
Jota de San Fermin, Op. 36
Jota Navarra, Op. 22, No. 4
Malaguena & Habanera, Op. 21, No. 1
Mélodie Roumaine, Op. 47
Mignon (Romance & Gavotte)

Nocturne-Serenade, Op. 45
Peteneras (Caprice Espagnol), Op. 35
Playera, Op. 23, No. 5
Rêve, Le, Op. 53
Romanza andaluza, Op. 22, No. 3
Sérénade Andalouse Op. 10
Serenata Andaluzza, Op. 28
Viva Sevilla, Op. 38
Zapateado, Op. 23, No. 6
Zigeunerweisen, Op. 20
Sartorio, Arnold
Chanson sans Paroles
Concerto in C
Sauret, Emile
Andante and Caprice de Concert, Op. 67
Capriccietto, Op. 55
Capriceuse, La (Valse), Op. 41
Chanson sans Paroles, Op. 69
Concerto in G minor
Fantaisie brillante sur des airs Espagnols, Op. 27
Farfalla (The Butterfly), Op. 40, No. 3
Mélodie. Op. 56, No. 2
Rhapsodie suédoise, Op. 59
Rhapsodie Russe, Op. 32
Romance and Tarentelle, Op. 31
Scherzo Fantastique, Op. 9
Serenade in G
Suite Française, Op. 55
Tarantelle, Op. 15
Valse-Caprice, Op. 20
Scalero, R.
Fourteen Variations on a Theme by Mozart, Op. 8
Sonata in D minor, Op. 12
Suite in Olden Style, Op. 15
Three morceaux, Op. 17
Scarlatti, Domenico
Minuet martial (Hermann)
Pastorale (Hauser)
Pavane (Hermann)
Sonata in D (Singer)
Tempo di Ballo
Scassola, A.
Lamento
Meditation
Romance
Scharwenka, Phillip
Alla Polacca in D minor, Op. 104, No. 4
Concerto in G major, Op. 95
Four Pieces, Op. 53
Gondellied (Wier)
Polish Dance, Op. 3, No. 1 (Hollaender)
Romance, Op. 10, No. 1
Scherzo, Op. 10, No. 2
Sonata, Op. 2
Sonata, Op. 110
Sonata, Op. 114
Suite, Op. 99
Suite, Op. 197
Three Concert Pieces, Op. 17
Scharwenka, X.
Five dansen nationales polonaises, Op. 3
Sonata in D minor, Op. 2
Sonata in E minor, Op. 46a
Schatz, Carl
Concerto, Op. 23
Concerto, Op. 26
Schickard, J. C.
Sonata in D minor (Moffat)
Schill, Otto K.
Romance in E, Op. 1
Scherzo in miniature, Op. 7, No. 2
Schillings, Max
Concerto in A minor, Op. 25

Sitt, Hans (Cont'd)
Twelve Pieces, Op. 26
Twenty Short Concert Pieces, Op. 73
Sivori, Camillo
Romances sans paroles, Op. 23
Sjogren, Emil
Morceau de Concert, Op. 45
Poème, Op. 40
Sonata, Op. 19
Sonata, Op. 24
Sonata, Op. 32
Sonata, Op. 47
Two Concert Pieces, Op. 27
Slunicko, J.
Adagio, Op. 2, No. 2
Air, Op. 2, No. 4
Chanson sans paroles, Op. 2, No. 1
Eight Pieces, Op. 98
Tarentelle, Op. 2, No. 3
Smetana, Bedrich
Aus der Heimat, No. 2 (Sitt)
Bartered Bride — Fantasy (Ondricek)
Chant du Soir
Sonatina in D minor, Op. 27
Sodermann, A.
Swedish Wedding March, Op. 12
Sokolow, N.
Berceuse, Op. 35
Elégie, Op. 17
Four Morceaux, Op. 18
Mélodie, Op. 17
Rêverie, Op. 22
Rêverie, Op. 37
Somis, Lorenzo
Adagio and Allegro
Sonata in G (Moffat)
Spalding, Albert
Andantino
Suite
Spendiarow, A.
Berceuse (Wier)
Spiering, Theodore
Concerto in A major
Spies, E.
Capriccio, Op. 45, No. 3
Concerto, Op. 13
Introduction and Polonaise in G, Op. 39
Minuet, Op. 45, No. 5
Romance, Op. 45, No. 2
Serenade, Op. 45, No. 6
Slumber Song, Op. 45, No. 4
Sonatina in D, Op. 44
Spindler, Fritz
Charge of the Hussars
Spohr, Louis
Barcarolle, Op. 135, No. 1
Concertino in A minor, Op. 110
Concertino in E minor, Op. 92
Concerto in A minor, Op. 1
Concerto in A minor, Op. 47
Concerto in A minor, Op. 62
Concerto in A minor, Op. 79
Concerto in B minor, Op. 10
Concerto in C minor, Op. 7
Concerto in D minor, Op. 2
Concerto in D minor, Op. 55
Concerto in E minor, Op. 38
Concerto in E minor, Op. 128
Concerto in Eb major, Op. 17
Concerto in G major, Op. 70
Concerto in G minor, Op. 28
Duo Concertant, Op. 3
Duo Concertant, Op. 9
Duo Concertant, Op. 95
Duo Concertant, Op. 96
Duo Concertant, Op. 112
Fantaisie on themes by Handel

Introduction and Rondo, Op. 46
Irish Fantasy, Op. 59
Morceaux de salon, Op. 127
Morceaux de salon, Op. 135
Morceaux de salon, Op. 145
Polonaise, Op. 40
Rondo, Op. 51
Rondo alla Spagnuolo, Op. 111
Six Salonstück, Op. 135
Squire, W. H.
Adieu, L'
Bourrée, Op. 24
Gavotte Humoristique
Rêve d'Amour
Stamitz, Johann
Andantino and Giave
Concerto in Bb
Concerto in C
Concerto in G
Five Sonatas, Op. 20 (Rieman)
Stanford, Charles Villiers
Concerto, Op. 74
Five Character Pieces
Six Irish Fantasies
Six Irish Sketches
Suite, Op. 32
Stanley, John
Gavotte and Minuet (Moffat)
Sonata in G minor (Moffat)
Steck, Paul
Flirtation (Coquetterie)
Romance, Op. 17
Stern, A.
Andante apassionato, Op. 3
Berceuse, Op. 2
Sternberg, Constantin
Danses Cosaques
Steveniers, J.
Concerto, Op. 9
Stiehl, H.
Andante and Scherzo, Op. 96
Sonata, Op. 37
Sonata, Op. 100
Stoeving, Paul
Am Springquell
Concerto in One Movement
Dervish Dance
Liebeslied
Stöhr, Richard
Concert Fantasy, Op. 50
Sonata in G major, Op. 27
Stoessel, Albert
Amoranza (Spanish Dance)
Five Miniatures
Gymnopedia (Ancient Grecian Dance)
Stojowski, Sigismond
Aubade
Concerto in G minor, Op. 22 (Schmidt)
Mélodie, Op. 1 (Wilhelmj)
Romance, Op. 20 (Peters)
Sonata in G minor, Op. 37 (Heugel)
Sonata in G, Op. 13 (Schott)
Stradella, Alessandro
Air l'Eglise (Danbé)
Sonata in D (Barison)
Sonata in G (Barison)
Strauss, Johann
Artist's Life (Waltzes)
Blue Danube (Waltzes)
Concerto for 'cello (Transcribed)
Pizzicato (Polka)
Roses from the South (Waltzes)
Tales of the Vienna Forest (Waltzes)
Strauss, Richard
An Einsamer Quelle, Op. 9, No. 2

Concerto in D minor, Op. 8
Cradle Song, Op. 41, No. 1
Improvisation (Sonata, Op. 18) (Hayet)
Morning, Op. 27, No. 4
Rêverie, Op. 9, No. 4 (Sitt)
Rosenkavalier Valses (Singer)
Serenade, Op. 7
Sonata, Op. 18
Strelezki, Anton
Fileuse, La
Prière à la Chapelle
Rêverie, Op. 34, No. 1
Romance, Op. 34, No. 2
Scherzo, Op. 34, No. 3
Sérénade Espagnol (Henley)
Serenata
Strube, Gustave
Abendglocken (Sunset Chimes)
Concerto in F# minor
Ein Marchen (A fairy tale)
Mondscheinzauber (Magic Moonlight)
Morgen (Morning)
Sonata
Struss, Fritz
Concerto in A minor, Op. 4
Concerto in D major, Op. 9
Sudessi, P.
Invitation à la tarentelle
Nuit charmante
Suk, Jos.
Appassionato, Op. 17, No. 2
Fantaisie, Op. 24
Sullivan, Sir Arthur
Lost Chord, Paraphrase (Henley)
Lost Chord, Paraphrase (Saenger)
Suppé, F. von
Light Cavalry, Overture (Wichtl)
Poet and Peasant, Overture (Wichtl)
Sutcliff, Wallace
Country Dance
Melody
Svendsen, Johann S.
Concerto in A major, Op. 6
Romance in G, Op. 26
Szymanowsky, K.
Concerto, Op. 35
Romance in D minor, Op. 23
Sonata, Op. 9
Taborowsky, S.
Bohemian Rhapsody
German Rhapsody
Hebrew Rhapsody
Italian Rhapsody
Russian Rhapsody
Taglichsbeck, Thomas
Concerto, Op. 8
Concerto, Op. 14
Taneiew, S.
Rêverie, Op. 23
Suite de Concert, Op. 28
Tartini, Giuseppe
Adagio (Corti)
Adagio Cantabile & Giga (Herrmann)
Adagio Sostenuto (Moffat)
Allegro Animosamente (Elman)
Allegro Festoro (Pente)
Aria in G (Nadaud)
Concerto in A minor
Concerto in D minor
Fifteen Sonatas (Pente)
Fugue in A major (Kreisler)
Pastorale (Pente)
Prelude and Variations in A minor (Pente)
Sarabande (Moffat)

Tartini, Giuseppe (Cont'd)
Sonata in C minor (Schering)
Sonata in E (Nadaud)
Sonata in G minor (Léonard)
Thème Varié (Nachez)
Trille du Diable (Devil's Trill) (Joachim)
Variations on a theme by Corelli (Kreisler)
Taubert, Wilhelm
Concerto, Op. 205
Serenade (Hermann)
Tavan, E.
Gavotte Richelieu
Minuet Mazarin
Ungaria
Telemann, G. Ph.
Rondo (Hermann)
Sicilienne and Rondo
Sonata in E (Moffat)
Tellam, H.
En Sourdine
Petite Sérénade
Tellier, A.
Plainte d'amour
Tenaglia, A. F.
Aria in A minor (Slatter)
Aria in F minor (Ries)
Have Pity, Sweet Eyes (Aria)
Ten Brink
Chanson Mauresque, Op. 2
Concerto Caracteristique
Serenade, Op. 2
Ten Have, W.
Allegro Brillante, Op. 19
Terestschenko, N.
Expansion, Op. 27
Tessarini, Carlo
Sonata in C major (Moffat)
Sonata in D (Moffat)
Sonata in G (Moffat)
Thieriot, Ferdinand
Concerto, Op. 68
Sonata, Op. 58
Thirion, L.
Sonata in C minor, Op. 14
Thomas, Ambrose
Entr'acte-Gavotte (Mignon)
Mignon, Fantasy (Mialko)
Mignon, Fantasy, Op. 114 (Singelée)
Raymond (Overture)
Thomassin, D.
Impromptu, Op. 64
Sonata in E minor, Op. 72
Thomé, Francis
Andante Religioso, Op. 70
Arlequin and Colombine
Clair de Lune
Elevation, Op. 120 (2nd Andante Religioso)
Extase, L' (Pygmalion)
Illusion, Op. 60
Invocation
Pizzicato
Rhapsodie
Romance sans paroles (Mittell)
Simple Aveu, Op. 25
Sonata in C minor
Sous la Feuillée, Op. 29
Thomson, César
Passacaglia (Handel)
Scandinavian Cradle Song
Thuille, L.
Sonata in E minor, Op. 30
Tirindelli, P.
Chanson Plaintive, Op. 7
Concerto in A minor
Concerto in G minor
Histoire, Op. 3
Titl, E.
Serenade

Tobani, Theo. M.
Hearts & Flowers, Op. 245
Tolhurst, Henry
Air de Ballet
Etoile d'Amour, L'
Fern Leaves
Lullaby
Romance
Sunbeams
Tarantella
Valse Caprice
Tombelle, F. de la
Passacaille
Sonata in D minor, Op. 40
Toselli, E.
Serenata
Tosti, F. Paolo
Good-bye (Transcription)
Ninon, Mélodie (Danbé)
Tours, Berthold
Mélodie religieuse
Townsend, L.
Berceuse
Toy, Ernest
Lilma (Lullaby)
Trouselle, Josef
Bumble-Bee, The
Polacca
Saltarella
Tschaikowsky, P.
Album for the Young, Op. 29 (24 Pieces)
Andante Cantabile (Quartet, Op. 11) (Sauret)
Autumn Song, Op. 37
Barcarolle from Op. 37, No. 6 (Sauret)
Canzonetta (Violin Concerto)
Casse Noisette (Suite I)
Casse Noisette (Suite II)
Chanson Russe
Chanson Triste, Op. 40, No. 2
Chant sans Paroles, Op. 2, No. 3
Chant sans Paroles, Op. 40, No. 6
Christmas (Hartmann)
Concerto in D major, Op. 35
Danse russe, Op. 10
Elégie, Op. 48, No. 3 (Hoffmann)
Eugene Onégin (Selection)
Eugene Onégin (Waltz)
Humoreske, Op. 10, No. 2 (Singer)
June Barcarolle, Op. 37a
Melody, Op. 42, No. 3 (Schradieck)
Plainte d'Amour, Op. 71 (Elman)
Romance, Op. 5
Romance, Op. 16, No. 5
Scherzo, Op. 42 (Schradieck)
Seasons, The (12 Pieces), Op. 37
Sérénade Mélancholique, Op. 26
Souvenir, Op. 42 (Schradieck)
Valse, Op. 40, No. 8
Valse (Sleeping Beauty)
Valse-Scherzo, Op. 34
Valses, Op. 39, No. 8 (Kleinecke)
Ye Who Have Yearned Alone (Saenger)
Tscherepnine, N.
Poème Lyrique, Op. 9
Rêverie, Op. 13
Tschetschulin, Agnes
Alla Zingaresca
Berceuse
Gavotte
Uhlig, Theodor
Concerto

Urban, Heinrich
Concerto in D minor, Op. 22
Vachon, P.
Adagio in G (Schering)
Valentine, Robert
Allegro vivace (Moffat)
Sonata in A minor (Moffat)
Valentini, G.
Sonata in B minor (Moffat)
Sonata in B♭ major (Salmon)
Van De Velde, G.
Esperance, L'
Souvenir-Romance
Vecsey, F. von
Caprice No. 1 (Le Vent)
Caprice No. 2 (La Cascade)
Caprice No. 3 (La Lune)
Caprice No. 5 (La Lune glisse)
Nostalgie
Pensée Triste
Rêverie
Venth, Carl
Suite, Op. 65
Venti, Mattia
Sonata (Vatielli)
Venzl, J.
Concerto, Op. 112
Veracini
Cantabile and Giga (Wasielewski)
Giga all'Antico (Elman)
Introduction and Chaconne (Franzoni)
Lento (Montfort)
Minuet (Tirindelli)
Minuet and Gavotte (Wasielewski)
Preludio and Corrente (Wasielewski)
Sonata in A (Wotquenne-Cornelis)
Sonata in A minor (Jensen)
Sonata in B minor (Moffat)
Sonata in D minor (Moffat)
Sonata in E minor (Schering)
Verbrugghe, F. X.
Sommeil d'un ange (Berceuse)
Vercollier, J.
Berceuse aux étoiles
Verdi, Giuseppe
Aida, Fantasy (Alard)
Ballo in Maschera, Fantasy (Alard)
Ernani, Fantasy (Hauser)
Forza del Destino, Fantasy (Sarasate)
Otello, Fantasy (Kadletz)
Requiem (Herrmann)
Rigoletto, Fantasy (Singelée)
Traviata, Fantasy (Alard)
Trovator, Fantasy (Singelée)
Verhey, T. H. H.
Concerto in A minor, Op. 54
Viardot, Paul
Five Concert Solos
Romance, Op. 6
Six Characteristic Pieces
Sonata No. 2 in B minor
Vidal, Paul
Solo de Concert
Vierne, Louis Victor Jules
Sonata in G minor, Op. 23
Vieu, Jane
Au Coin du feu (Berceuse)
Vieuxtemps, Henri
Air varié, Op. 6
Arpèges, Les (Caprice), Op. 15
Allegro de Concert in B minor
Andante and Rondo, Op. 29

454 VIOLIN SOLOS WITH PIANO ACCOMPANIMENT

Vieuxtemps, Henri (Cont'd)
Ballade and Polonaise, Op. 38
Bohémienne, Op. 40, No. 3
Boquet Americaine, Op. 33
Concerto in A major, Op. 25
Concerto in A minor, Op. 37
Concerto in A minor, Op. 49
Concerto in D minor, Op. 31
Concerto in E major, Op. 10
Concerto in F♯ minor, Op. 19
Concerto in G major, Op. 49
Elégie in F minor, Op. 30
Fantaisie-Appassionata, Op. 35
Fantaisie-Caprice, Op. 11
Faust (Fantasy) (Gounod)
Four Romances sans Paroles, Op. 8
Hommage à Paganini, Op. 9
Regrets, Op. 40, No. 2
Rêverie, Op. 22, No. 3
Romance, Op. 24, No 1.
Romance, Op. 40, No. 1
Rondino, Op. 32, No. 2
St. Patrick's Day, Op. 33, No. 2
Sérénité, Op. 45, No. 5
Seven Romances sans Paroles, Op. 7
Six Brilliant Solo Pieces, Op. 22
Sonata in D, Op. 12
Souvenir de Russe, Op. 21
Suite in D, Op. 43
Tarantelle
Yankee Doodle, Op. 17
Villoing, G.
Chant-Fantaisie, Op. 9
Pastorale, Op. 8
Vincent, Thomas
Sonata in A minor (Moffat)
Viotti, Jean-Baptiste
Andante from 28th Concerto (Franko)
Concerto No. 1 in C major
Concerto No. 2 in E major
Concerto No. 3 in A major
Concerto No. 4 in D major
Concerto No. 5 in C major
Concerto No. 6 in E major
Concerto No. 7 in B♭ major
Concerto No. 8 in D major
Concerto No. 9 in A major
Concerto No. 10 in B♭ major
Concerto No. 11 in A major
Concerto No. 12 in B♭ major
Concerto No. 13 in A major
Concerto No. 14 in A minor
Concerto No. 15 in B♭ major
Concerto No. 16 in E minor
Concerto No. 17 in D minor
Concerto No. 18 in E minor
Concerto No. 19 in G minor
Concerto No. 20 in D major
Concerto No. 21 in E major
Concerto No. 22 in A minor
Concerto No. 23 in G minor
Concerto No. 24 in B minor
Concerto No. 25 in A minor
Concerto No. 26 in E♭ major
Concerto No. 27 in C major
Concerto No. 28 in A minor
Concerto No. 29 in E minor
Vitali, G. B.
Ballade and Polonaise, Op. 38
Vitali, Tomaso
Chaconne in G minor (David)
Vivaldi, A.
Adagio (Nachez)
Concerto in A (Guarnieri)
Concerto in A minor (Nachez)
Concerto in C minor (Moffat)

Concerto in G minor (Nachez)
Prelude in C minor (Schering)
Sonata in A (David)
Sonata in D minor (Moffat)
Sonata in G (Moffat)
Sonata in G minor (Moffat)
Vogrich, Max
Andante and Intermezzo
Ballade de Villon
Concerto ''Epur si Muove''
Three Characteristic Pieces after Paganini
Waldstrum
Geisterreigen
Chevalier Mousquetaire
Volkmann, Robert
Allegretto Capriccioso, Op. 15
Chant du Troubadour
Romance, Op. 7
Sonatina in A minor, Op. 60
Sonatina in E minor, Op. 61
Volpe, A. D.
Mazurka in D minor
Tempo di Minuetto
Wachs, Paul
Air de Ballet
Coquetterie
Waghalter, Ignatz
Sonata, Op. 5
Wagner, Richard
Album Leaf (Wilhelmj)
Dreams (Traüme)
Ein Faust Overture
Flying Dutchman
Fantasy (Singelée)
Spinning Song (Press)
Gotterdamerung
Fantasy (Hermann)
Lohengrin
Bridal March
Introduction to Act III
Mastersingers, The
Prize Song (Wilhelmj)
Parsifal
Paraphrase (Hermann)
Paraphrase (Wilhelmj)
Rheingold, The
Fantasy (Hermann)
Rienzi
Prayer
Siegfried
Fantasy (Hermann)
Paraphrase (Wilhelmj)
Death of Siegfried
Tannhäuser
Evening Star (Hullweck)
Elizabeth's Prayer (Lemaître)
Grand March
Pilgrim Chorus (Rehfeld)
Tristan and Isolde
Death of Isolde (Sinding)
Walküre, Die
Fantasy (Hermann)
Siegmund's Love Song (Danbé)
Wailly, P. de
Sonata, Op. 26
Sonata in G minor, Op. 27
Waldteufel, E.
España, Valse (Alder)
Estudiantina, Valse (Alder)
Mon rêve, Valse
Patineurs, Les, Valse
Wallace, Wm.
Maritana (Fantasia)
Scenes That Are Brightest (Saenger)
Sweet Spirit, Hear My Prayer (Saenger)
Walter, Bruno
Sonata in A major

Walther, J. J.
Prelude & Variations in E minor (Schering)
Ware, Helen
Cinka Panna (Hungarian Fantasia), Op. 4
Warlich, H.
Rêverie
Wassilenko, S.
Concerto in D minor, Op. 25
Weber, Carl Maria von
Clarinet Concerto in F minor (Transcribed)
Euryanthe (Overture)
Freischütz, der (Fantasy)
Grand Duo, Op. 48
Jubel Overture, Op. 59
Larghetto (Kreisler)
Nine Variations on a Norwegian Air
Oberon, Fantasy (Bazzini)
Perpetuum Mobile (David)
Polacca, Op. 72
Scherzo Variato (Invitation to the Dance) Themes (Bazzini)
Six Sonatas, Op. 13
Souvenir de Weber (Deberiot, Op. 126)
Weber, Joseph Miroslav
Concerto in G minor
Miniature Suite in G
Weckerlin, J. B.
Five Bergerettes (Romance of the 18th Century)
Weidig, Adolf
Bourrée, Op. 21
Weingartner, Felix
Concerto, Op. 52
Sonata, Op. 42, No. 1
Sonata, Op. 42, No. 2
White, Edward Cameron
Chant
Four Bandanna Sketches, Op. 12
Lament
Negro Dance
Slave Song
White, John Jesse
Concerto in D major
White, Joseph
Romance sans Paroles, Op. 8
Violonesque
Zamacueca
Wichtl, G.
Concerto, Op. 5
Concerto, Op. 24
Widor, Charles M.
Concerto in E minor
Romance, Op. 46
Serenade, Op. 10
Sonata, Op. 50
Sonata, Op. 79
Suite, Op. 21
Suite Florentine
Wieniawski, Henri
Adagio élégiaque, Op. 5
Capriccio-Valse, Op. 7
Caprice in A minor (Kreisler)
Caprice in E♭ major (Kreisler)
Carnaval russe, Le, Op. 11
Chanson Polonaise, Op. 12, No. 2
Concerto, Op. 14
Concerto, Op. 22
Dudziarz (Mazurka), Op. 19, No. 1
Fantaisie Orientale
Faust (Fantaisie), Op. 20
Gigue
Kujawiak (Mazurka)
Legende, Op. 17

Wieniawski, Henri (Cont'd)
Obertass (Mazurka), Op. 9, No. 2
Original Theme with Variations, Op. 15
Polonaise in A, Op. 21
Polonaise in D, Op. 4
Romance (Concerto, Op. 22)
Romance sans Paroles, Op. 9
Rondo Elégante, Op. 9
Scherzo-Tarentelle, Op. 16
Sielinka la Champêtre (Mazurka), Op. 12, No. 1
Souvenir de Moscow (Airs Russes), Op. 6
Souvenir de Posen, Op. 3
Wier, Albert E.
Creole Lullaby
Dream Song
Fairy Tale
Gavotte
Gipsy Dance, Op. 9
Mélancolie, Op. 8
Moment's Play
Petite March
Spanish Minuet
Wiernsberger, J. A.
Sonata, Op. 32
Wihtol, J.
Berceuse, Op. 55
Fantasy on Russian Songs
Mélodie & Mazurka, Op. 2
Rhapsody, Op. 39
Romance, Op. 15
Wilhelmj, August
Album Leaf
Concerto in B minor
Concerto in D major
Concerto in D minor
Deutsche suite (on Bach Themes)
Fantasiestücke, Ballade
Italienische Suite (after Paganini)
Romance, Op. 10
Swedish Melody
Wilkes, R. W.
Adagio, Op. 3
Willaume, Gabriel
Gavotte de Louis XV
Wilm, Nicolai Von
Sonata, Op. 83

Sonata, Op. 92
Suite, Op. 88
Suite, Op. 95
Wilson, Mortimer
Sonata in D
Winkler, A.
Air Finnois Varié, Op. 18
Sonata, Op. 10
Wladigeroff, P.
Concerto, Op. 11
Four Pieces, Op. 12
Wolf, Hugo
Berceuse (Kross)
Wolf-Ferrari, Ermanno
Prayer (Jewels of the Madona)
Sonata, Op. 1
Sonata, Op. 10
Wollenhaupt, Bruno
Scène de Ballet (M Concert)
Wood, Haydn
Lullaby
Vie de Bohème, L
Woollett, H.
Sonata No. 1 in B
Sonata No. 2 in F
Sonata No. 3 in
Wormser, A.
Madrigal (L'En digue)
Meditation (Mart
Rêverie (Suite T
Suite Tzigane
Woycke, Eugen
Concerto, Op. 55
Wuerst, Richard
Concerto in C m
Wullner, F.
Sonata, Op. 30
Wurm, M.
Lullaby, Op. 7
Yost, Gaylord
American Rhap
Youferoff, S.
Elégie, Op. 1 (
Fantaisie de Co
Yradier, Sebastia
Paloma, La
Ysaye, Eugene
Berceuse, Op. 20
Chant d'Hiver, Op. 15

Divertissements, Op. 24
Extase, Op. 21
Mazurka No. 1
Mazurka No. 2
Mazurka No. 3
Poème élégiaque, Op. 12
Rève d'Enfant, Op. 14
Scène au Rouet, Op. 13
Veille Sourdine, Op. 23
Lointain passe, Op. 11
Zarembski, J.
Berceuse, Op. 22
Zarzycki, Alex.
Andante and Polonaise, Op. 23
Chant d'Amour, Op. 19
En valsant, Op. 34, No. 3
Introduction & Cracovienne, Op. 35
...rka in E, Op. 39
... Op. 26

Op. 11

ert Fan-
tyle
is

que

11
f Variations,

rice)

7. VIOLIN SOLOS WITH ORGAN ACCOMPANIMENT

Altes, E.
Adagio religioso (From Sonata, Op. 31)
Bach, J. S.
Adagio in B Minor
Adagio in C minor
Adagio non Troppo (in D minor)
Air for the G String
Andante in D
Andante in G
Aria Cantabile in D
Aria in D
Berceuse-Sarabande-Toccata
Concerto in G minor (Nachez)
Largo (Fifth Sonata)
Largo in D minor
Sarabande
Bach, Philip Emmanuel
Awakening of Spring (Frühlings Erwachen)
Bazzini, A.
Preghiera (Concerto Militaire)
Becker, A.
Adagio, Op. 20
Beethoven, L. van
Adagio (Sonata Pathétique)

Romance in F, Op. 50
Romance in G, Op. 40
Bizet, Georges
Adagietto (l'Arlésienne)
Blemant, L.
Invocation
Boellmann, L.
Prière, Op. 25
Boisdeffre, R. de
Chant d'Eglise
Offertory
Bossi, M. Enrico
Adagio in Ab, Op. 48
Braga, G.
Angel's Serenade
Bull, Ole & Svendsen, J.
Solitude sur la Montagne, Op. 5
Burow, C.
Chant Polonais
Buxtehude, D.
Sarabande & Courante
Campagnoli, B.
Romance in A
Casadesus, F.
Chant d'hymne
Chaine, E.
Elégie, Op. 43
March

Prayer
Romance
Chopin, Fr.
Funeral March
Coleridge-Taylor, S.
Suite, Op. 3
Pastorale
Cavatina
Barcarolle
Contemplation
Corelli, A.
Sonata in D, Op. 5
Sonata in Bb, Op. 5
Sonata in C, Op. 5
Danbé, J.
Elevation
Debussy, Claude
Prelude (La Demoiselle élue)
Donnay, A.
Hymne du soir
Dubois, Theodore
Andante religioso
Mélodie Réligieuse
Ernst, H. W.
Elégie, Op. 10
Fitzenhagen, W.
Consolation, Op. 15
Franck, César
Allegretto de la Sonata "Fragment pour l'Eglise"

456 VIOLIN SOLOS WITH ORGAN ACCOMPANIMENT

Giordani, Th.
Aria (Caro mio ben)
Goldmark, C.
Andante (Violin Concerto, Op. 28)
Gounod, Ch.
Andante religioso
Ave Maria (Meditation)
Hymne à Sainte-Cécile
Nazareth (Chant évangelique)
Offertoire
Grieg, E.
Ave Maris Stella
Guilmant, A.
Andante religioso
Haendel, G.
Air (Judas Maccabeus)
Largo (Xerxes)
Sarabande
Sonata in A
Halvorsen, J.
Andante religioso
Haydn, Jos.
Adagio (Herman)
Largo (Armingand)
Hertel, G. G.
Lento
Hubay, J.
Cortège Nuptial, Op. 95
Stella Maris, Op. 95
Vorbei (Funeral March), Op. 95
Huguenin, Ch.
Meditation
Hure, J.
Air
Kossmaly, C.
Meditation on Bach's 3rd Prelude
Leveque, E.
Andante religioso
Liszt, Fr.
Benedictus (Hungarian Mass)
Offertory (Hungarian Mass)

Locatelli, P.
Aria in A minor
Mailly, A.
Meditation
Manns, Frederick
Eventide
Mascagni, P.
Intermezzo (Cavalleria Rusticana)
Massenet, J.
Le dernier sommeil de la Vierge
Meditation (Thaïs)
Matthison-Hansen, H.
Canzonetta
Mendelssohn, F.
Andante (Concerto, Op. 64)
Merkel, A.
Adagio, Op. 51
Mistowski, A.
Aria
Moor, Em.
Largo, Op. 101
Mozart, W. A.
Ave verum
Nardini, P.
Adagio Cantabile
Concerto in A (Nachez)
Oesten, M.
Moments sacrés, Op. 142
Pergolese, G. P.
Niña (Siciliano)
Raff, J.
Cavatina
Reger, Max
Largo (Suite in D, Op. 93b)
Rehfeld, F.
Adagio religioso, Op. 82
Reuchsel, M.
Andante religioso
Rheinberger, J.
Rhapsody on the Andante from Organ Sonata, Op. 127
Suite, Op. 166
Ropartz, J. Guy
Page d'amour

Saint-Saëns, C.
Prelude (Le Déluge)
Scarlatti, D.
Siciliana (Ritter)
Schumann, Rob.
Evening Song, Op. 85
Träumerei
Simon, Ant.
Berceuse, Op. 28, No. 1
Sitt, Hans
Andante (Violin Concerto)
Svendsen, J.
Romance in G, Op. 26
Thomé, Francis
First Andante Religioso, Op. 70
Second Andante Religioso, Op. 120
Simple Aveu, Op. 25
Tolbecque, A.
Prière
Tschaikowsky, P.
Andante Cantabile (Fifth Symphony)
Canzonetta (Violin Concerto)
Vieuxtemps, H.
Adagio Religioso (Fourth Concerto)
Vitali, Tommaso
Chaconne in G minor (Respighi)
Vivaldi, A.
Concerto in A minor
Concerto in G minor
Wagner, Richard
Amfortas' Prayer (Parsifal)
Elizabeth's Prayer (Tannhäuser)
Melody (Parsifal)
Prize Song (Mastersingers)
Wilbert, F.
Contemplation mystique
Wilm, N. von
Religioso, Op. 127

8. DUETS FOR VIOLIN AND VIOLA

Bach, J. S.
20 Preludes (Hermann)
Beethoven, L. van
Three Duets (originally Clarinet and Bassoon)
Blumenthal, J.
Three Grand Concert Duets, Op. 81
Bruni, A. B.
Three Concert Duets, Op. 24
Fiorillo, F.
Six Sonatas, Op. 9
Fuchs, Robert
Duet, Op. 60
Ghebart, Jos.
Three Duets, Op. 58
Giovanni, N. de
Three Grand Duets
Halvorsen, J.
Sarabande (Handel Theme)
Handel, G. F.
16 Duets (Hüllweck)

Haydn, Jos.
Three Sonatas, Op. 93
Haydn, Michael
Four Sonatas
Jansa, L.
Six Duets, Op. 70
Kalliwoda, J. W.
Two Duets, Op. 208
Kayser, H. E.
Grand Duet, Op. 2
Concert Duet, Op. 27
Klengel, P.
Serenade, Op. 45
Koenig, Ferdinand
Two Duets, Op. 7
Lampugnani, G.
Three Duets
Mayseder, J.
Duet, Op. 30
Duet, Op. 31
Duet, Op. 32

Mozart, W. A.
Duet in Bb major
Duet in G major
Three Duos, Op. 23
Pichl, M.
Six Duets, Op. 18
Pleyel, L.
Three Duets, Op. 30
Three Duets, Op. 44
Three Grand Duets, Op. 69
Rolla, A.
Grand Sonata
Three Concert Duets, Op. 7
Three Concert Duets, Op. 8
Three Grand Duets, Op. 16
Three Duets, Op. 17
Spohr, L.
Duet in G, Op. 13
Three Duets, Op. 3 (Orig. for 2 Violins)

9. TWO VIOLINS AND VIOLA

Akimenko, Th.
Trio, Op. 7
Amani, N.
Trio, Op. 1
Bach, J. S.
15 Inventions (Hofmann)
Boccherini, L.
Six Trios, Op. 14
Six Trios, Op. 38
Beethoven, L. van
Serenade, Op. 3

Grand Trio, Op. 87 (Transc.)
Trio, Op. 3
Variations (La cidarem)
Serenade, Op. 25 (Transc.)
Bruni, A.
Six Trios
Cremont, P.
Three Trios, Op. 13
Dohnanyi, E.
Serenade, Op. 10

Dvořák, A.
Trio, Op. 74
Fuchs, Rob.
Two Trios, Op. 61
Gabrielli, L.
Trio in C major
Trio in D major
Trio in D minor
Trio in E major
Trio in G major

Godard, Benj.
Four Pieces, Op. 5
Haydn, Jos.
Six Divertimenti
Three Trios, Op. 53
Hofmann, Richard
Trio in G, Op. 112
Hollaender, B.
Three Character Pieces, Op. 12
Manus, F.
Serenade

Mazas, F.
Three Trios, Op. 18
Picard, J.
Prelude & Fuge on a Beethoven Theme
Pleyel, I.
Three Trios, Op. 11
Reger, Max
Serenade in D, Op. 77a
Serenade in G, Op. 14a
Schubert, Fr.
Trio in B major

Sinigaglia, L.
Serenade, Op. 33
Taneiew, Serge
Trio in D, Op. 21
Trio in E♭, Op. 31
Thern, C.
Trio, Op. 60
Wranitzky, P.
Six Trios, Op. 17
Three Trios, Op. 20

10. DUETS FOR VIOLIN AND CELLO

Abaco, E. F. dall'
Six Sonatas, Op. 1-4
Albrechtsberger, G.
Six Duets
Battanchon, Felix
Sérénade Espagnole, Op. 43
Beethoven, L. van
Celebrated Rondo (Transcription)
Three Duos (Hermann)
Bessems, A.
Grand Duet, Op. 20
Blasius, F.
Two Sonatinas, Op. 55
Boccherini, L.
Six Sonatas
Bohrer, Antoine & Max
Concert Duet on Swiss Airs
Duets, Op. 41, 42, 43, 44, 47
Breval, J. B.
Three Duets
Dancla, Ch.
Six Duets, Op. 108
Dotzauer, J. F.
Concert Duet (William Tell)
Three Concert Duets, Op. 4
Three Concert Duets, Op. 8
Eichberg, J. & Bockmuhl, R. E.
Grand Duet, Op. 53
Fiorillo, F.
Three Concert Duets, Op. 31
Ganz, Leopold & Maurice
Duet Concertant, Op. 11
Duo Concertant, Op. 7 (Preciosa)
Duo Concert (Freischütz)
Giovanni, N. de
Grand Morceau de Bravoure
Gliere, R.
Eight Pieces, Op. 39

Gottfried, Herrmann
Duet Concertant
Grunberger, L.
Suite, Op. 16a
Halvorsen, J.
Passacaglia (after Handel)
Haydn, Jos.
Duet in D major (Bennat)
Herman, Ad.
Grand duo brillant
Hermann, Fr.
Grand duo brillant, Op. 12
Hoffmann, H. A.
Six Duets, Op. 5
Two Duets, Op. 6
Hofmann, Richard
Five Pieces, Op. 83
Huguenin, Ch.
Fantasy, Op. 20
Gavotte & Musette, Op. 21
Hus-Desforges
Three Duets, Op. 30
Kreutzer, Rodolphe
Three Sonatas, Op. 16
Three Sonatas, Op. 17
Kummer, F. A.
Three duos brillants, Op. 15
Three duos of Concert, Op. 67
Lee, Seb.
Three Duos, Op. 125
Léonard, H. and Servais, F.
First Grand Concert Duet (on English Airs)
Second Grand Concert Duet (on Beethoven Themes)
Third Grand Duet
Fourth Grand Duet (L'Africaine)
Mendes, Fr. L.
Fantasy on "Zampa"

Mollenhauer, E.
Lucrezia (Fantasy), Op. 3
Moor, Emmanuel
Suite in C, Op. 109
Mozart, W. A.
Duet on the Fantasy Sonata, Op. 11
Offenbach, Jacques
Progressive Duets
Perihou, A.
Minuet
Pleyel, I.
Three Duets, Op. 30
Polla, A.
Three Duets
Three Sonatas
Praeger, H. A.
Grand Concert Duet, Op. 41
Nine Duets from Beethoven
Nine Duets from Mozart
Nine Duets from Onslow
Nine Duets from Spohr
Thirty-six Duets
Reicha, J.
Three Duets, Op. 1
Three Duets, Op. 4
Romberg, A. & B.
Three Duets on Mozart Themes
Three Duos concertants, Op. 2
Stamitz, K.
Six Duets, Op. 19
Titz, Anton
Sonata
Vieuxtemps, H. & Servais, F.
Grand Duet on "Les Huguenots"
Viotti, J. B.
Twelve Sonatas

11. VIOLIN DUETS

Alard, D.
Duos brillants, Op. 27
Three Duos brillants, Op. 27a
Aubert, J. (père)
Three Suites
Austri, G.
Divertimento, Op. 7
Bach, J. S.
Concerto in D minor
Five Duets
Baillot, P.
Three Duets, Op. 16
Bender, L.
Three Concert Duets
Bériot, Ch. de
Six Duos, Op. 17
Six Duos caractéristiques
Three Duos concertants, Op. 57
Three Grand Etudes, Op. 43
Spanish Duets, Op. 113
Berou, A.
Three duos concertants, Op. 28

Blied, J.
Musical Recreations, Op. 33
Blumenthal, Jos. von
Six Grand Duos concertants, Op. 80
Three Duos, Op. 86 (Leuckart)
Three Duos, Op. 95 (Leuckart)
Boccherini, L.
Three Duets, Op. 5
Brahms, Johannes
Hungarian Dances
Liebeslieder, Op. 52
Brand, A.
Three Sonatas
Bruni, B.
Six Duos for Concert Use, Op. 19
Bucquet, Pierre
Four Suites for Two Violins
Campagnoli, B.
Six Duos, Op. 14

Clavel, J.
Three Concert Duos, Op. 2
Three Concert Duos, Op. 5
Colyns, J. B.
Three Duets
Dancla, Ch.
Three Duets, Op. 63
Three Duets, Op. 64
Three Grand Concert Duets, Op. 108
Three Sonatas, Op. 138
David, Ferdinand
Sixty Duets
Violin School, Op. 44
Violin School, Op. 45
Depas, A.
Three Duos, Op. 73
Devisien, A. F.
Three Duos, Op. 12
Two Grand Concert Duos, Op. 13
Dont, Jacques
Duet in A minor, Op. 48
Duet in C, Op. 43

Draeseke, F.
Suite, Op. 86
Dubois, C.
Three Duos, Op. 4
Dupierge, F.
Three Themes with Variations, Op. 27
Fiorillo, F.
Six Duos concertants, Op. 10
Six Duos concertants, Op. 14
Fiorillo-Spohr
Thirty-six Studies
Fuchs, Robert
Twenty Duets, Op. 55
Gasse, F.
Three Duos brillants
Three Duos concertants
Geminiani, Fr.
Twelve Instructive Duets
Gliere, R.
Twelve Duets, Op. 49
Gounod, Charles
Meditation (Ave Maria)
Gung'l, Joseph
Sounds from Home (Oberlandler)
Gurlitt, C.
Three Duos, Op. 150
Habeneck, C.
Three Duets
Halven, E.
Three Suites in Canon Form, Op. 11
Hauptmann, M.
Three Duos, Op. 16
Three Grand Duos, Op. 17 (Andre)
Two Duos, Op. 2
Two Duos, Op. 11
Haydn, Joseph
Six Duos, Op. 102
Three Duos, Op. 99
Hellmesberger, G.
Duets, Op. 4
Duets, Op. 14
Henning, C.
Three Duos, Op. 36
Hering, C.
Serenade, Op. 29
Serenade, Op. 31
Sonata, Op. 17
Herman, A.
Three Duos concertants, Op. 130
Hermann, Fr.
Decameron, Op. 16 (10 Pieces)
Three Caprices, Op. 7
Two Grand Duos, Op. 14
Hofmann, Richard
Eight Pieces, Op. 70
Eighteen Duets from Ancient Masters Book 4
Twenty-four Duets from Ancient Masters (Book 3
Jansa, L.
Three Concert Duets, Op. 50
Six Concert Duets, Op. 76
Variations, Op. 19
Jupin, Ch.
Three Duos, Op. 16
Kalliwoda, J. W.
Grand Concert Duet, Op. 244
Grand Duet, Op. 50
Three Duets, Op. 243
Kauer, Ferdinand
Twelve Fugues
Kayser, H. E.
Three Duos, Op. 60
Klengel, P.
Five Duets, Op. 9

Kreutzer, R.
Three Duos, Op. A
Three Duos, Op. B
Krommer, F.
Three Duos Concertants, Op. 2
Three Duos Concertants, Op. 6
Three Duos Concertants, Op. 22
Three Duos Concertants, Op. 33
Three Duos Concertants, Op. 51
Three Duos Concertants, Op. 54
Three Grand Duos, Op. 110
Three Grand Duos Concertants, Op. 94
Kuntze, C.
Duets, Op. 277
Lachner, J.
Sonatina in A, Op. 96
Sonatina in Bb, Op. 98
Sonatina in D, Op. 97
Leclair, J. M.
Six Sonatas
Léonard, H.
Duo de Concert, Op. 25 (La Bataille)
Lequint, A.
Three Duos Concertants, Op. 30
Lolli, A.
Sixth Sonata, Op. 9 (Alard)
Lorenziti, B.
Three Duos, Op. 38
Martinn, J.
Three Duos Concertants, Op. 17
Three Duos Concertants, Op. 18
Three Grand Duos Concertants, Op. 14
Mascagni, P.
Intermezzo (Cavalleria Rusticana)
Maurer, L.
Three Duos Concertants, Op. 61
Mayseder, J.
Air favori russe, Op. 1
Duo Concertant, Op. 30
Duo Concertant, Op. 31
Duo Concertant, Op. 32
Mazas, F.
Nine Duos d'Emulation, Op. 87
Six Concert Duets, Op. 71
Six Duos, Op. 46
Six Duos, Op. 60
Six Duos Brillants, Op. 40
Six Duos Brillants, Op. 72
Six Duos Brillants, Op. 83
Six Duos Brillants, Op. 84
Six Grand Duos de Salon, Op. 88
Three Duos Brillants, Op. 66
Three Duos Brillants, Op. 67
Three Duos Concertants, Op. 34
Mendelssohn, Felix
Songs without Words
Wedding March, Op. 61
Molique, B.
Three Duos, Op. 3
Three Duos Concertants, Op. 2
Moszkowski, M.
Spanish Dances, Op. 12
Mozart, W. A.
Larghetto from Op. 108
Twelve Duets, Op. 70

Nadaud, J. B.
Duo Concertant in C
Pleyel, Ign.
Six Duos Concertants, Op. 17
Six Duos Concertants, Op. 19
Three Duos, Op. 44
Three Duos, Op. 61
Three Duos, Op. 64
Three Grand Duos, Op. 69
Prot, M.
Three Duos Symphoniques, Op. 3
Three Duos Symphoniques, Op. 17
Three Duos Symphoniques, Op. 18
Prume, F.
Duo Concertant, Op. 18
Duo Concertant No. 2, Op. 19
Pugnani, G.
Six Duets (Bachmann)
Reger, Max
Canons and Fugues in Ancient Style, Op. 131b
Ries, Ferdinand
Progressive Duets
Ries, Hubert
Three Duos, Op. 10
Three Duos, Op. 21
Three Duos Concertants, Op. 5
Rode, Pierre
Six Duos, Op. 18
Three Selected Duets, Op. 18
Twenty-four Caprices
Rolla, Alessandro
Three Duets, Op. 3
Three Grand Duos, Op. 9
Three Grand Duos, Op. 28
Romberg, A.
Three Duets, Op. 56
Three Duos, Op. 18
Three Duos Concertants, Op. 4
Sandre, G.
Sonatina in G, Op. 66
Sauret, Emile
Adagio and Rondo, Op. 44
Schloesser, L.
Two Duos Concertants, Op. 18
Schoen, Moritz
Three Fantasy Pieces, Op. 72
Schumann, Robert
Twenty Pieces, Op. 68
Sherwood, P.
Suite in G, Op. 23
Singer, M.
Duo in G
Three Duos Concertants, Op. 2
Sitt, Hans
Ten Duos, Op. 73B
Spohr, L.
Duet in C, Op. 153
Duet in D, Op. 150
Duet in F, Op. 148
Grand Duo, Op. 148
Grand Duo, Op. 150
Grand Duo, Op. 153
Three Duets, Op. 3
Three Duets, Op. 39
Three Duos Concertants, Op. 67
Three Grand Duos, Op. 39
Two Duets, Op. 9
Täglichesbeck, Th.
Three Duos, Op. 11
Viotti, J. B.
Three Duos Concertants, Op. 6

Viotti, J. B. (Cont'd)
Three Duos Concertants, Op. 7
Three Duos Concertants, Op. 9
Three Duos Concertants, Op. 18
Three Duos Concertants, Op. 28

Three Grand Duos Concertants, Op. 22
Weber, C. M. von
Invitation to the Dance, Op. 65
Wéry, N.
Duo Concertant in C, Op. 41
Duo Concertant in G, Op. 30

Duo in G, Op. 35
Three Duos Concertants, Op. 38
Wieniawski, H.
Eight Etudes-Caprices, Op. 18
Zilcher, Herman
Two Pieces, Op. 7

12. VIOLIN DUETS WITH PIANO ACCOMPANIMENT

Alard, D.
Symphonie concertante No. 1 in G, Op. 31
Symphonie concertante No. 2 in D, Op. 33
Symphonie concertante No. 3 in A, Op. 34
Amberg, J.
Five Pièces mignonnes
Ames, J. C.
Canzonetta
André, L.
Alpine Violets, Op. 100
Mountain Echoes, Op. 158
On the High Alps, Op. 140
Andrieu, J. F. d'
Sonata in E minor
Arensky, A.
Serenade
Arne, Thomas
Sonata in E minor, Op. 3, No. 7 (Moffat)
Ascher, J.
Danse Espagnole, Op. 24
Dozia, Op. 23
Fanfare Militaire, Op. 40
Aubert, Jacques
Suite
Avison, Charles
Sonata in E minor
Bach, J. S.
Air for the G String
Concerto for two violins in D minor
Meditation on the first Prelude (Gounod)
Three Sonatas
Bach, Philip Emmanuel
Sonata in B♭ major
Sonata in G
Spring's Awakening
Bachmann, A.
Seville (Suite Espagnole)
Bachmann, G.
Sorrenta (Mazurka)
Badarzewska, Thekla
The Maiden's Prayer
Balfe, M. W.
I Dreamt I Dwelt in Marble Halls
Barbedette, H.
Sonata in A., Op. 183
Barnby, J.
Sweet and Low
Barns, Ethel
Fantaisie
Beaumont, Paul
Mazurka
Serenade
Beethoven, L. van
Minuet in E♭ (Burmester)
Minuet in G (Burmester)
Symphony No. 1
Symphony No. 2
Symphony No. 3
Symphony No. 4
Bendix, Theo.
The Dawn of Love
Beriot, Charles de
Spanish Airs, Op. 113
Twelve Italian Melodies
Biehl, Alb.
Stille Nacht, Op. 151 (Transc.)

Bizet, G.
Adagietto & Minuet (L'Arlésienne)
Entr'acte
Farandole
Intermezzo
Petit Mari
Blon, F. von
Sérénade d'Amour
Vision (Characteristic)
Whispering Flowers
Boccherini, L.
Sonata in C minor
Bohlmann, G. C.
Petite Polka Concertante, Op. 13
Bohm, C.
Gipsy Dance (La Zigana)
Boisdeffre, René de
Adagietto, Op. 15, No. 4
Au Bord d'un Ruisseau, Op. 52
Berceuse, Op. 34
Cantilene, Op. 24, No. 3
Doux Souvenir, Op. 15, No. 2
Boyce, William
Sonata in A (Jensen)
Braga, Gaetano
Angel's Serenade
Brunner, Edward
Sonatina in G, Op. 71
Cahn, L.
Barcarolle, Op. 24
Ein Märchen, Op. 25
Campagnoli, B.
Romance in A
Capua, E. di
Maria, Maria! (Marie, Oh Marie)
O Sole Mio (My Sun)
Chaminade, C.
Callirhoe (Air de Ballet)
Lisonjera, La (The Flatterer)
Chiara, V. di
Spagnola, La (The Spanish Dancer)
Chopin, F.
Nocturne, Op. 9, No. 2
Nocturne, Op. 27, No. 2
Polonaise Militaire, Op. 40, No. 1
Valse Brillante, Op. 18
Corelli, A.
Adagio and Gigue
Six Chamber Sonatas, Op. 4
Couperin, François
Sonata in B♭ minor
Sonata in C minor
Sonata in D minor
Sonata in G minor
Czerwonky, Richard
Serenade
Czibulka, A.
Love's Dream After the Ball (Intermezzo)
Stephanie (Gavotte)
Dancla, Charles
Symphonie concertante No. 2 in A, Op. 10
Symphonie concertante No. 3 in D, Op. 29
Symphonie concertante No. 4 in G, Op. 98

Symphonie concertante No. 5 in E, Op. 180
Symphonie concertante No. 6 in F, Op. 190
Deems, J. M.
The Charm (Air and Variations)
Delbrück, G.
Berceuse (Cradle Song)
Dittersdorf, Karl von
German dance (Burmester)
Donizetti, G.
Sextet from "Lucia di Lammermoor"
Drdla, Fr.
Dialogue, Op. 98
Marche triomphale, Op. 61, No. 1
Tarentelle, Op. 42
Drigo, G.
Serenade (Les Millions d'Arlequin)
Dvořák, Antonin
Humoreske, Op. 101, No. 7
Slavonic Dance No. 1
Eberhardt, Goby
Cradle Song, Op. 101
Ehrich, J.
Dreamy Moments (Landler)
Elgar, Ed.
Salut d'Amour (Love's Greeting)
Engelmann, H.
Four Characteristic Dances
Ernst, Henri W.
Elégie, Op. 10
Ersfeld, Chr.
Slumber Song, Op. 11
Fauconier, B. C.
Evening Recreations, Op. 114
Faure, Jean Baptiste
The Palms (Les Rameaux)
Fesca, A.
Adagio in E
Gabrielli, L.
Duet in C
Duet in D
Duet in G
Gabriel-Marie
La Cinquantaine
Ganne, L.
L'Extase (Rêverie)
Gautier, L.
Le Secret (Intermezzo)
Gillet, E.
Passepied
Glinka, M.
The Lark
Gluck, Chr. W. v.
Ballet Music (Orpheus)
Sonata for two violins
Godard, Benj.
Abandon
Berceuse
Serenade
Six Duets, Op. 18
Souvenir de Campagne
Tristesse
Goens, Daniel van
Romance sans paroles, Op. 12, No. 1
Goossens, Eug.
Suite, Op. 6

Gossec
Gavotte (Burmester)
Goublier, G.
Sous un balcon (Serenade)
Gounod, Ch.
Ave Maria
Serenade (Berceuse)
Grieg, Edvard
Allegretto (Sonata, Op. 13)
An den Frühling
Norwegian Dance, Op. 35, No. 2
Peer Gynt, 1st Suite, Op. 46
Peer Gynt, 2nd Suite, Op. 55
Gung'l Joseph
Oberländler, Op. 31
Gurlitt, C.
Ouverture des Marionnettes, Op. 105
Guzmán, E.
Trio in C, Op. 61
Halevy, J. F. E.
Romance (L'Eclair)
Hammer, R.
Canzonetta, Op. 31
Intermezzo, Op. 32, No. 2
Händel, G. F.
Largo in G
Nine Sonatas, Op. 2
Six Trio-Sonatas
Haydn, Jos.
Andantino
Minuet (C major Symphony)
Minuet in F
Herold, L. J. F.
Zampa (Overture)
Herrmann, Th.
Duo, Op. 29
Hofmann, Karl
Concert-Etude in D, Op. 53
Grand Concerto in D minor, Op. 55
Idylle in G, Op. 54
Romance in A, Op. 52
Huber, Hans
Sonata, Op. 135
Hubl, O.
Concertino in G, Op. 12
Humperdinck, Engelbert
Evening Prayer (Hansel & Gretel)
Jacoby, S.
Concertante in G, Op. 69
Rondo Marziale, Op. 97
Rondo Piacevole, Op. 96
Six Pieces, Op. 100
Jansa, L.
Double Rondeau, Op. 33
Jungmann, A.
Longing for Home, Op. 117
Juon, Paul
Bizarrerie, Op. 9, No. 3
Conte Mysterieux, Op. 9, No. 4
Douleur, Op. 9, No. 2
Idylle, Op. 9, No. 1
Musette Miniature, Op. 9, No. 5
Obstination, Op. 9, No. 6
Silhouettes, Op. 9
Silhouettes, Op. 43
Kalliwoda, J. W.
Concertante in A, Op. 20
Introduction and Grand Polka, Op. 196
Introduction and Rondeau in E, Op. 109
Three Valses Brillantes, Op. 191
Variations concertantes in E, Op. 83
Kayser, H. E.
Three Trios, Op. 72
Keler-Bela
Lustspiel (Overture)

Kontski, A. de
Awakening of the Lion, Op. 115
Korbay, F.
Poème Hongrois, No. 1
Kreutzer, R.
First Symphonie Concertante in F
Labitzky, Aug.
Traum de Sennerin, Op. 45
Lachner, F.
Marche celèbre (Suite, Op. 113)
Lange, G.
Chant du Nord
Flower Song
In the Alpine Hut
Langer, G.
Grandmother, Op. 20
Grandfather, Op. 22
Langey, Otto
Evening Breeze, Op. 60
Laurens, E.
Sieste
Le Beau, Louise A.
Canon, Op. 38
Leclair, Jean Marie
Musette (Slatter)
Liszt, Fr.
Liebesträum
Second Rhapsodie
Locatelli, Pietro
Sonata in D minor
Loeillet, J. B.
Sonata in D, No. 11
Sonata in G, No. 12
Louis, N.
Amitié, L'
Concertino, Op. 12
Lucietto, G.
Fantasia éroica
Petite ouverture
Luigini, A.
Patineuse, La
Rêverie-Caprice
Valse Brillante
Macbeth, Allan
Forget Me Not (Intermezzo)
Love in Idleness (Serenade)
Mahlig, R.
Andante cantabile
Marchioso, G. B.
Priscilla (Serenata)
Mascagni, P.
Intermezzo (Cavalleria Rusticana)
Massenet, J.
The Last Dream of the Virgin
Maurer. L.
Concerto in A, Op. 56
Variations Concertantes, Op. 30
Mendelssohn, Arnold
Trio in A minor, Op. 76
Mendelssohn, Felix
Barcarolle, Op. 19, No. 6
''I Would That My Love,'' Op. 63, No. 1
Midsummer Night's Dream (Overture)
Spring Song
War March (Athalie)
Wedding March
Meyerbeer, G.
Coronation March (Prophète)
Milhaud, D.
Sonata
Mistowski, A.
Aria
Moffat, A.
Petit Duo Symphonique, Op. 31
Suite in Ancient Style (Simrock)

Molique, Bernard
Concertante
Mondonville, J. de
Sonata in G
Moor, Emmanuel
Suite, Op. 144
Moret, V.
Little Symphony in F, Op. 74
Suite Louis XV (on airs by Leclair)
Moszkowski, M.
Hungary (Foreign Lands), Op. 23, No. 6
Serenade, Op. 15, No. 1
Spanish Dances, Op. 12
Suite, Op. 71
Mouchet, Gustave
Pastorale
Mozart, W. A.
Allegro in F (Slatter)
Ave Verum
Concertante in C
Figaro's Wedding
German Dance (Burmester)
Larghetto from Op. 108
Minuet in D
Minuet in Eb
Turkish March
Müller, Otto
Rondino in G, Op. 28
Two Duets, Op. 29
Two Sonatinas, Op. 26
Nesvadba, J.
Loreley (Paraphrase), Op. 17
Nevin, Ethelbert
Au printemps
Au soir (Berceuse)
Gavotte
Pastorale
Vieille chanson
Nicodé, Jean Louis
Barcarolle
Nicolai, O.
The Merry Wives of Windsor (Overture)
Noren, H.
Divertimento, Op. 42
Offenbach, J.
Barcarolle (Tales of Hoffman)
Pache, J.
Characteristic Pieces, Op. 91
Papini, G.
Andante in A
Cinderella March
Home, Sweet Home
Hope March
Pergolesi, G. B.
Three Sonatas (Riemann)
Pleyel, J.
Six Trios, Op. 8
Three Trios, Op. 44
Poldini, Eduard
Poupée Valsante
Pučalka, Ch.
Alpenrosen, Op. 8
Pugnani, Gaetano
Sonata in C
Purcell, H.
Golden Sonata (Jensen)
Sonata in A minor (Jensen)
Sonata in B minor (Jensen)
Sonata in C major (Jensen)
Raff, J.
Cavatina
Ravina, Henri
Petit Bolero, Op. 62
Rehbaum, Th.
Mondnacht, Op. 24
Reissiger, C. G.
The Mill on the Rocks (Overture)

Rheinberger, Joseph
Duet, Op. 156, No. 6
Ricordi, G.
Serenata, Op. 37
Ries, Franz
Perpetuum Mobile (Suite, Op. 34)
Robaudi, V.
Bright Star of Hope
Robberechts, A.
Morceau de concert, Op. 18
Rode, Pierre
Three Violin-Duets, Op. 18
Rossini, G.
Cujus Animam (Stabat Mater)
William Tell (Overture)
Rubinstein, Ant.
Mélodie in F
Toreador and Andalouse
Trot du Cavalerie
Rzhia, F.
Mendelssohnia (Transcr.)
Saar, L. V.
Gondoliera (Boat Song), Op. 52, No. 4
Saint-George, G.
L'ancien régime (1st Suite)
L'ancien régime (2nd Suite)
Saint-Saëns, C.
My Heart at Thy Sweet Voice (Samson)
Sandre, Gust.
Berceuse, Op. 86, No. 1
Petite Suite, Op. 64
Serenade
Sarasate, P. de
Navarra, Op. 33
Scharf, M.
Polonaise in F, Op. 9, No. 1
Two Dances, Op. 21
Waltzes in D, Op. 9, No. 2
Scharwenka, Ph.
Polish Dance, Op. 38b, No. 1
Polish Dance, Op. 38b, No. 4
Scharwenka, X.
Polish National Dance, Op. 3, No. 1
Schneider, F. L.
Arlequin and Colombine
Mazurka
Petit duo symphonique, Op. 59
Schubert, Fr.
Ave Maria
Erl-König (Transcr.)
Grand Marche Héroique, Op. 27, No. 3
Marche Militaire, Op. 51, No. 1

Moment Musical, Op. 94, No. 3
Serenade (Ständchen)
Schuberth, C.
Nocturne in D, Op. 6
Schulhoff, J.
Chant du Berger, Op. 32
Schumann, R.
Evening Song (Abendlied)
Six Pieces, Op. 68
Slumber Song (Schlummerlied)
Träumerei, Op. 15, No. 7
Schytte, Ludwig
Berceuse
Severn, Edmund
Suite
Silvestri, J.
In Days of Knighthood
Simpson, F. J.
Allegro giocoso
Sinding, C.
Serenade No. 1, Op. 56
Serenade No. 2, Op. 92
Sitt, Hans
Moment Musical
Sochting, E.
Concertino No. 1, Op. 95
Concertino No. 2, Op. 95
Spies, E.
Six Character-pieces, Op. 50
Spindler, Fritz
Charge of the Hussars, Op. 140, No. 3
Spohr, Louis
Concertante No. 1, Op. 48
Concertante No. 2, Op. 88
Stiehl, H.
Impressions du soir (Slatter)
Strebelle, L. J.
Andante religioso
Sudds, W. F.
In a Garden of Melody
Swing, The
Suppé, F. von
Light Cavalry (Overture)
Poet and Peasant (Overture)
Tartini, G.
Six Sonatas (Riemann)
Telemann, G. P.
Sonata in E minor
Thomas, Ambroise
Raymond (Overture)
Thomé, Fr.
Andante religioso, Op. 70
Gavotte and Musette, Op. 109, No. 3
Rêve, Le, Op. 55
Simple Confession (Simple Aveu)

Sous La Feuillée (Under the Leaves)
Titl, A. E.
Serenade
Tobani, Theo. M.
Hearts and Flowers, Op. 245
Torelli, J.
Concerto, Op. 8 (Jensen)
Tosti, F. Paolo
Good-Bye (Transc.)
Tours, Berthold
Edelweiss
Petit Duo Symphonique
Tschaikowsky, P.
Barcarolle, Op. 37, No. 6 (Slatter)
Chanson Triste
Chant sans paroles (Slatter)
Eugene Onègin (Fantasy)
Romance, Op. 5
Vecsey, Franz von
Badinage Impertinant
Clair du Lune sur le Bosphore
Veracini, A.
Sonata in C minor
Verdi, G.
Celeste Aïda (Aïda)
Miserere (Il Trovatore)
Quartet (Rigoletto)
Viotti, J. B.
Three Violin-Duets, Op. 19
Vivaldi, Antonio
Sonata in C major
Sonata in E minor
Sonata in G minor
Wagner, Richard
Prize Song (Moffat)
Weber, C. M. von
Freischütz, Der (Overture)
Invitation to the Dance
Wider, Charles
Serenade, Op. 10
Winge, Per.
Berceuse
Marche burlesque
Romance
Scherzo
Yradier, C.
La Paloma (Transc.)
Zarzycki, Alex.
Chant d'Amour, Op. 19
Zedtwitz, K. von
Canon in A, Op. 7
Zilcher, H.
Concerto in D minor, Op. 9
Suite, Op. 15

13. TWO VIOLINS AND CELLO

Abaco, Evaristo Felice dall'
Sonata in A major
Sonata in B minor
Sonata in E minor
Sonata in F major
Bach, Philip Emmanuel
Sonata in Bb major
Beethoven, L. van
Grand trio, Op. 87
Serenade in D, Op. 25
Blumenthal, J.
Trio in C, Op. 36
Trio in F, Op. 34
Trio in G, Op. 35
Boccherini, L.
Six Trios, Op. 9
Bruni, A.
Six Trios

Corelli, A.
Six Chamber Sonatas, Op. 4
Cremont, P.
Three Trios, Op. 13
Gabrielli, L.
Trio in D minor
Trio in E major
Gebauer, J.
Twelve Trios, Op. 10
Gossec, F. G.
Trio, Op. 9, No. 1
Haendel, G. F.
Nine Sonatas, Op. 2
Triple Concerto (David)
Trio Suites (Jensen)
Haydn, Joseph
Twelve Trios, Op. 21
Kreutzer, Rodolphe
Three Trios Brillants, Op. 15

Mazas, F.
Three Trios, Op. 18
Twelve Trios, Op. 38
Mozart, W. A.
Trio in C major
Trio in D major
Trio in F major
Pleyel, J.
Six Trios, Op. 48
Ries, Hubert
Three Trios, Op. 25
Tartini, G.
Six Sonatas (Pente)
Viotti, J. B.
Trio in B minor
Trio in Bb major
Trio in D major

14. THREE VIOLINS

Bachmann, A.
Andante and Bourrée
Battmann, J. L.
Trio in C major
Trio in G major
Trio in G minor
Beethoven, L. van
Religioso (Moffat)
Bella, J. L.
Sonata, Op. 4
Sonata, Op. 13
Blaha, J.
Andante
Elégie
Scherzino
Valse lente
Bloch, Joseph
Trios, Op. 34
Block, O.
Elfentanz (Capriccio), Op. 2
Blumenthal, J.
Trio, Op. 48, No. 2
Trio, Op. 48, No. 3
Bradac, J.
Four Trios
Caemmerer, C.
Gavotte, Op. 15
Chapuis, Auguste
Marche des petits violons
Minuet
Corelli
Corrente (Moffat)

Sarabande and Gavotte (Moffat)
Couperin, François
Minuet in D minor
Dancla, Charles
Six Trios, Op. 99
Dvořák, Antonin
Gavotte
Gluck, C. W. von
Gavotte (Moffat)
Grabner, H.
Concerto in Ancient Style
Handel, G. F.
Largo (Moffat)
Haydn, Jos
Minuet (Moffat)
Three Trios
Hermann, Fr.
Burlesque, Op. 9
Capriccio, Op. 2
Suite, Op. 17
Lachner, I.
Three Sonatas, Op. 90
Three Sonatinas, Op. 92
Liszt, Franz
Au bord d'une source
Mendelssohn, Felix
Songs Without Words (Moffat)
Meyerbeer, Giacomo
Coronation March (Prophète)
Mikuli, C.
Scherzino, Op. 25

Moor, Emmanuel
Suite, Op. 133
Mouchet, Gust.
Pastorale
Mozart, W. A.
Ave verum (Moffat)
Serenade
Rameau, J. Ph.
Minuet in G
Rubinstein, A.
Melody in F
Seitz, F.
Cavatina, Op. 29, No. 2
Gavotte, Op. 29, No. 6
March, Op. 29, No. 1
Minuetto, Op. 29, No. 3
Spies, E.
Etude, Op. 48
Rondo de Concert, Op. 27
Three Morceaux, Op. 75
Spohr, L.
Four Trios
Szeremi, Gust.
Scherzo, Op. 51
Tartini, Giuseppe
Andante con grazia (Moffat)
Tschaikowski, P.
Chant sans paroles
Wichtl, G.
Two Trios, Op. 79
Wiltberger, A.
Suite, Op. 132

15. THREE VIOLINS AND PIANO

Borner, A.
Zur Geburtstagsfeier (March), Op. 36
Bradac, J.
Four Trios
Brahms, J.
Hungarian Dance, No. 6 (Weiss)
Brunner, E.
Abendiche Kahnfahrt, Op. 97
Freud und leid, Op. 94
Cherubini, L.
Anacreon (Overture)
Chopin, Fr.
Nocturne, Op. 9, No. 2
Dancla, Ch.
Petite Gavotte, Op. 155
Six Little Trios, Op. 99
Symphonie concertante, Op. 198
Domerc, J.
Symphony

Eschmann, C.
Petite symphonie, Op. 1
Fowler Ch.
Trio No. 3 in G
Handel, G. F.
Largo (Weiss)
Hellmesberger, J.
Papillon, Les
Serenade
Léonard, H.
Sérénade humoristique à l'espagnole
Liebich, J.
Une soirée en famille
Mistowski, A.
Aria
Rieding, O.
Prelude and Fugue
Saint-George, G.
L'Ancien Régime (Suite)

Schubert, Fr.
Marche militaire, Op. 51, No. 1
Schumann, C.
Schlummerlied
Sommerlust, Op. 17, No. 1
Träumerei (Weiss)
Sochting, E.
Larghetto, Op. 101
Taylor, H. J.
Serenata
Trousselle, J.
Allegretto Scherzando
Andante Cantabile
Barcarolle
Caprice
Gavotte and Musette
Minuet
Vivaldi, A.
Concerto in F (Medefind)
Zielmann, E.
Four morceaux, Op. 102

16. FOUR VIOLINS

Allen, C. N.
Fête champêtre, Op. 24
Scene Pittoresque, Op. 22
Bohm, C.
Quartet
Bohne, R.
Quartet No. 1 in G
Quartet No. 2 in D
Quartet No. 3 in A
Bradac, J.
Twelve Quartets
Burger, M.
Quartet in G, Op. 51
Chapuis, A.
Serenade
Cherblanc, L.
Serenade
Dancla, Ch.
Carnival of Venice (Variations)

Reunion, Le, Op. 203
Variations, Op. 161
Dont, J.
Quartet in E minor, Op. 42
Quartet in F, Op. 45
Dorn, J.
Andante & Allegro, Op. 2
Dvořák, A.
Humoresque, Op. 101, No. 7
Fabian, J.
Albumblatt, Op. 33
Fitzenhagen, W.
Ave Maria, Op. 41
Sarabande, Op. 64
Spinnlied, Op. 59
Gabrielli, L.
Suite
Gaugler, Th.
Quartet in G, Op. 13

Hiller, Ferd.
Capriccio fugate, Op. 203
Hofmann, Richard
Quartet, Op. 98
Koehler, P.
Suite, Op. 37
Kohne, Ridley
Concerto for four violins
Lachner, J.
Quartet in G, Op. 107
Mozart, W. A.
Larghetto
Normand, A.
Les Petits Vieux (17th Century Gavotte)
Potzold, Eug.
Introduction and Polacca, Op. 21
Rihorsky, Ad.
Impressions, Op. 39

Schmidt, E.
All' Albanese
Barcarolle
Schumann, Rob.
Träumerei

Shaw, S.
Rêverie
Sochting, E.
Suite, Op. 58

Spohr, L.
Larghetto, Op. 150
Walder, O.
Sonatina

17. FOUR VIOLINS WITH PIANO ACCOMPANIMENT

Beethoven, L. van
Egmont (Overture)
Larghetto (Symphony No. 2)
Bradac, J.
Twelve Quartets
Cherubini, L.
Anacreon (Overture)
Dancla, Ch.
Quartet, Op. 66
Fowler, C.
Grand Sonata Concertante
Hampeln, C.
Concertante in F, Op. 17
Haydn, Jos.
Symphony No. 1
Symphony No. 2
Symphony No. 4
Symphony No. 9

Hellmesberger, Jos.
Romance, Op. 43, No. 2
Tarantelle, Op. 43, No. 1
Leo, Leonardo
Concerto (Jensen)
Maurer, Louis
Concerto, Op. 55
Mendelssohn, F.
War March of the Priests
Wedding March
Mozart, W. A.
Ave verum
Don Juan (Overture)
Schubert, F.
Ave Maria
Marche Militaire

Schumann, R.
Schlummerlied
Träumerei
Slunicko, J.
Intermezzo, Op. 83
Nocturne, Op. 58, No. 1
Serenade, Op. 58, No. 2
Stang, F.
Fantaisie in D minor
Maienlust (Fantasy)
Tolhurst, A.
Allegretto
Graceful Dance
Intermezzo
Vivaldi, Ant.
Concerto in B minor

18. TRIOS FOR VIOLIN, VIOLA AND CELLO

Abaco, E. F. dall'
Sonata in A minor
Sonata in B minor
Sonata in E minor
Sonata in F major
Akimenko, Th.
Trio in C minor, Op. 7
Amani, N.
Trio in D minor, Op. 1
Andreae, V.
Trio in D minor, Op. 29
Beethoven, L.
Serenade, Op. 8
Serenade, Op. 25 (Arr.)
Trios, Op. 3
Trios, Op. 9
Berens, H.
Two Trios, Op. 85

Berger, W.
Trio in G minor, Op. 69
Boccherini, L.
Six Trios, Op. 38
Dohnanyi, E.
Serenade, Op. 10
Haydn, Jos.
Three Trios, Op. 53
Two Divertimentos
Lendvai, E.
Trio in A minor, Op. 16
Trio in B♭ minor, Op. 11
Trio in F major, Op. 14
Marteau, H.
Trio in F, Op. 12
Mojsisovics, R.
Serenade in A, Op. 21

Mozart, W. A.
Divertimento in E♭ minor
Pleyel, J.
Three Trios Concertants, Op. 11
Reger, Max
Trio in A minor, Op. 77b
Trio in D minor, Op. 141b
Reuchsel, M.
Trio in G minor
Schubert, Fr.
Trio in B♭ minor (Rehfeld)
Sinigaglia, L.
Serenade in D, Op. 33
Sokolow, N.
Trio in D minor, Op. 45

19. TRIOS FOR PIANO, VIOLIN AND VIOLA

Brahms, J.
Trio, Op. 40
Indy, V. d'
Trio in G, Op. 15
Jongen, Joseph
Trio in F♯ minor, Op. 30
Lachner, J.
Trio, Op. 37
Trio, Op. 45
Trio, Op. 58

Trio, Op. 89
Trio, Op. 102
Leclair, J. M.
Sonata in D
Mozart, W. A.
Symphonie concertante, Op. 104
Trio, Op. 14, No. 2
Paqué, Desire
Fourth Suite, Op. 27

Reger, Max
Trio in E minor, Op. 2
Sandberger, Ad.
Sonata, Op. 4
Scharwenka, Ph.
Trio, Op. 105
Trio, Op. 121
Schumann, Rob.
Fairy Tales, Op. 132
Zolotareff, B.
Trio, Op. 28

20. TRIOS FOR VIOLIN, CELLO AND PIANO

Andreae, V.
Trio in E♭ major, Op. 14
Trio in F minor, Op. 1
Anthoime, Eugene
Trio No. 1 in E♭ major
Trio No. 2 in F
Arensky, A.
Trio in D minor, Op. 32
Trio in F minor, Op. 73
Bach, Jean Christian
Trio in D major
Bastard, W.
Trio in G minor, Op. 3
Beethoven, L. van
Grand Trio, Op. 38
Grand Trio in B♭ major, Op. 97
Introduction Variations, Op. 121
Three Trios, Op. 1

Trio in B♭ major, Op. 11
Trio facile in E♭ major
Two Trios, Op. 70
Variations in E♭ major, Op. 44
Bellon, J.
Trio in A, Op. 32
Berens, H.
Three Trios, Op. 95
Boellmann, L.
Trio in G, Op. 19
Bohm, C.
Two Trios faciles, Op. 330
Six Trios faciles, Op. 352
Boisdeffre, R. de
Poème pastorale, Op. 87
Suite in D, Op. 83
Trio in E♭, Op. 10
Trio in G minor, Op. 32

Bossi, M. Enrico
Trio sinfonico in D, Op. 123
Brahms, Johannes
Trio in A minor, Op. 114
Trio in B major, Op. 8 (Revised Ed.)
Trio in B♭ major, Op. 18
Trio in C, Op. 87
Trio in C minor, Op. 101
Trio in E♭ major, Op. 40
Trio in G, Op. 36
Bronsart, H. V.
Trio in G minor, Op. 1
Bruch, Max
Trio in C minor, Op. 5
Buxtehude, D.
Sonata No. 1 in F
Sonata No. 2 in G
Castera, R. de
Trio in D, Op. 5

Castillon, A. de
Trio in B♭ major, Op. 4
Trio in D minor, Op. 17
Catoire, G.
Trio in F minor, Op. 14
Chaminade, Cecile
Trio in A minor, Op. 34
Trio in G minor, Op. 11
Chapuis, A.
Trio in G major
Chausson, Ernest
Trio in G minor, Op. 3
Chevillard, C.
Trio in F, Op. 3
Chopin, Fr.
Trio in G minor, Op. 8
Cimr, E. O.
Trio facile, Op. 9
Corelli, A.
Adagio & Gigue (Stern)
Couperin, François
Concerts royaux
Cras, Jean
Trio in C major
Cutter, Benj.
Trio in A minor, Op. 24
Dancla, Ch.
Three Trios faciles, Op. 117
Destenay, E.
Trio in A minor, Op. 34
Diemer, L.
Trio No. 1, Op. 20
Trio No. 2, Op. 23
Dubois, Theodore
Trio No. 1 in C minor
Trio No. 2 in E major
Dupin, Paul
Trio in C major
Dvořák, A.
Trio, Op. 90 ("Dumky")
Trio in B♭ major, Op. 21
Trio in F minor, Op. 65
Trio in G minor, Op. 26
Fenney, W. J.
Trio in G major, Op. 20
Foote, Arthur
Trio in B♭ major, Op. 65
Trio in C minor, Op. 5
Franck, César
Trio in B major, Op. 2
No. 1 in F♯ minor
No. 2 in B♭ major
No. 3 in B minor
Trio in E major
Gade, Niels W.
Novelettes in A minor, Op. 29
Trio in F major, Op. 42
Glass, Louis
Trio in C minor, Op. 19
Godard, Benj.
Trio in F major, Op. 72
Trio in G minor, Op. 32
Goldmark, C.
Trio in B♭ major
Trio in E minor, Op. 33
Gouvy, Th.
Trio in A minor, Op. 18
Trio in B♭ major, Op. 19
Gretchaninow, A.
Trio in C minor, Op. 38
Haessier, J. W.
Sonata No. 1 in C major
Sonata No. 2 in E minor
Sonata No. 3 in A major
Haydn, Joseph
Trio No. 1 in G
Trio No. 3 in C
Trio No. 7 in A
Trio No. 10 in E
12 Trios (Schott ed.)
Hofmann, Richard
Trio No. 1 in D minor
Trio No. 2 in G major
Trio No. 3 in D

Huber, Hans
Fantaisie pour trio, Op. 83
Trio in E, Op. 65
Trio in E♭, Op. 20
Trio in F, Op. 105
Trio in G♭, Op. 120 (Kist-
ner)
Hummel, J. N.
Trio in E, Op. 83
Trio in E♭, Op. 12
Trio in E♭, Op. 93
Hure, Jean
Suite (on Breton Songs)
Huss, Henry Holden
Trio in D minor, Op. 8
Indy, V. d'
Trio in E♭, Op. 29
Trio in G, Op. 15
Jacques-Dalcroze, E.
Andante cantabile & Rondo
Jongen, Joseph
Trio in B minor
Juon, Paul
Litonial
Trio-Caprice, Op. 39
Trio in A minor, Op. 17
Trio in G, Op. 60
Kirchner, Theodore
Trios faciles, Op. 58
Klassert, M.
Trio facile, Op. 10
Trio in F, Op. 35
Klengel, J.
Two Trios faciles, Op. 35
Two Trios faciles, Op. 39
Two Trios, Op. 42
Korngold, E. W.
Trio in D, Op. 1
Krause, E.
Trio facile in D, Op. 12
Kroeger, E. R.
Trio in E minor
Lacombe, P.
Trio in A, Op. 134
Lalo, Ed.
Trio in A minor, Op. 26
Trio in C minor, Op. 7
Trio in E minor, Op. 55
Lazzari, Sylvio
Trio in G minor, Op. 13
Le Borne, Ferdinand
Trio in D minor, Op. 32
Leclair, J. M.
Chaconne
Gavotte No. 1
Gavotte No. 2
Minuet
Musette
Sonata in D
Lefebvre, Charles
Trio in D minor, Op. 110
Lekeu, Guillaume
Trio in D minor
Loeillet, J. B.
Sonata in B minor (Beon)
Sonata in G major
Lowtzky, H.
Trio in F♯ minor, Op. 2
Luzzato, F.
Trio in C minor, Op. 54
Trio in E minor, Op. 45
Trio in G minor, Op. 37
Magnard, Alberic
Trio in F minor, Op. 18
Marschner, H.
Trio in F, Op. 167
Marx, J.
Trio-fantaisie
Mascitti, Michele
Sonata in G minor
Mendelssohn, F.
Trio in A minor, Op. 66
Trio in D minor, Op. 49
Meyer, L.
Trio facile in G, Op. 1

Trio facile No. 2 in G, Op. 2
Trio facile No. 3 in C, Op. 3
Moor, Emmanuel
Trio in C, Op. 81
Mozart, W. A.
Trio No. 3 in G
Trio No. 6 in E
Trio No. 7 in C
Noren, H.
Trio in D minor, Op. 28
Novak, N.
Trio quasi una ballata, Op.
27
Pfitzner, H.
Trio in F, Op. 8
Quef, Ch.
Trio in C major
Rachmaninoff, S.
Trio élégiaque in D minor,
Op. 9
Raff, J.
Trio in A minor, Op. 155
Trio in C minor, Op. 102
Trio in D, Op. 158
Trio in G, Op. 112
Rameau, J. B.
Five Concertos (Senart)
Five Concert Pieces (Saint-
Saëns)
Ravel, Maurice
Trio in A minor
Reger, Max
Trio in E minor, Op. 102
Reinecke, C.
Trio Facile No. 1 in G
Trio Facile No. 2 in E minor
Trio Facile No. 3 in A
Reissiger, C. G.
Trio in E♭, Op. 85
Trio in G minor, Op. 181
Rheinberger, Joseph
Trio in F, Op. 191
Ropartz, J. Guy
Trio in A minor
Roussel, Albert
Trio in E♭, Op. 2
Rubinstein, A.
Trio in A minor, Op. 85
Trio in B♭ major, Op. 52
Trio in C minor, Op. 108
Trio in F major, Op. 15
Trio in G minor, Op. 15
Sachs, Leo
Trio in G major, Op. 55
Saint-Saëns, C.
Trio d'après le septuor, Op.
65
Trio in E minor, Op. 92
Trio in F, Op. 18
Scharwenka, Philipp
Trio in C♯ minor, Op. 100
Trio in G, Op. 112
Schubert, Fr.
Nocturne in E♭, Op. 148
Trio in B♭, Op. 99
Trio in E♭, Op. 100
Schumann, Rob.
Phantasiestücke, Op. 88
Trio in D minor, Op. 63
Trio in F, Op. 80
Trio in G minor, Op. 110
Schytte, L.
Petites Suites faciles, Op.
132
Sinding, Christian
Trio in A minor, Op. 64
Trio in C, Op. 87
Trio in D, Op. 23
Sitt, H.
Trios faciles, Op. 63
Smetana, F.
Trio in G minor, Op. 15
Sochting, E.
Trio facile in C, Op. 21
Trio facile in C, Op. 51

Sochting, E. (Cont'd)
Trio facile in D, Op. 39
Trio facile in G, Op. 26 (Simon)
Spohr, L.
Five Trios
Strauss, Oscar
Suite in form of dance, Op. 43
Taneiew, Serge Iv.
Trio in D, Op. 22
Thirion, L.
Trio, Op. 11
Thomé, Francis
Trio in A, Op. 121
Tovey, D. F.
Trio in D minor, Op. 1
Tschaikowsky, P.
Trio in A minor, Op. 50

Volkmann, Rob.
Trio in B♭ minor, Op. 5
Trio in F, Op. 3
Vreuils, Victor
Trio in D minor, Op. 1
Weber, C. M. von
Trio in G minor, Op. 63
Weckerlin, J. B.
Trio in A minor
Whitney, S. B.
Trio in C, Op. 30
Widor, Ch. M.
Four Pieces
No. 1 Humoresque
No. 2 Cantabile
No. 3 Nocturne
No. 4 Serenade

Soirs d'Alsace, Op. 52
No. 1 En route
No. 2 Cile d'orage
No. 3 Le calme renait
No. 4 Promenade sentimentale
Trio in B♭ major, Op. 1
Winkler, A.
Trio in F♯ minor, Op. 17
Wolff-Ferrari, E.
Trio in D, Op. 5
Trio in F♯ major, Op. 7
Youferoff, S.
Trio in C minor, Op. 52
Zilcher, P.
Trio facile, Op. 37
Trio facile, Op. 42

21. QUARTETS FOR TWO VIOLINS, VIOLA AND CELLO *

Albert, Eugene D'
Quartet, Op. 8
Quartet, Op. 11
Ambrosio, A. d'
Quartet in C, Op. 42
Andreae, W.
Quartet in B♭, Op. 9
Arensky, A.
Quartet in A minor, Op. 35a
Quartet in G, Op. 11
Bach, Charles Philip Emmanuel
Quartet No. 1 in G
Quartet No. 2 in D
Bach, J. Ch. Fr.
Six Quartets
Bazzini, A.
Quartet in D minor, Op. 75
Beethoven, Ludwig van
Grand Fugue in B♭ major, Op. 133
Quartet in A minor, Op. 132
Quartet in B♭ major, Op. 130
Quartet in C♯ minor, Op. 131
Quartet in E♭ major, Op. 127
Quartet in E♭ major, Op. 130
Quartet in F major, Op. 135
Quartet in F minor, Op. 95
Quartet No. 1 in F major, Op. 59
Quartet No. 2 in E minor, Op. 59
Quartet No. 3 in C major, Op. 59
Boccherini, L.
Nine Quartets
Borodine, A.
Quartet No. 1 in A major
Quartet No. 2 in D major
Borodine, A.-Glazounow, A.-Liadow, A.-Rimsky-Korsakow, N.
Quartet in B♭ on the theme B-la-f
Brahms, Johannes
Quartet in A minor, Op. 51
Quartet in B♭ major, Op. 67
Quartet in C minor, Op. 51
Bretagne, P.
Quartet in B♭ major
Buonamici, G.
Quartet in G major
Capet, L.
Quartet No. 1 in C major
Castillon, A. de
Quartet in A minor, Op. 3, No. 1
Catoire, G.
Quartet in F♯ minor, Op. 23
Cellier, Alexandre
Quartet in D minor

Chausson, Ernest
Quartet in C minor, Op. 35
Cherubini, L.
Quartet No. 1 in E♭ major
Quartet No. 2 in C major
Quartet No. 3 in D minor
Coppet, L. C. de
Quartet in A minor
Dancla, Ch.
Quartet No. 1, Op. 208
Quartet No. 2, Op. 208
Quartet No. 3, Op. 208
Debussy, Claude
Quartet in G minor, Op. 10
Denereaz, A.
Quartet in D major
Dohnanyi, E. von
Quartet in A, Op. 7
Quartet in D♭, Op. 15
Duvernoy, Alph.
Quartet in C minor, Op. 46
Dvořák, A.
Quartet in A minor, Op. 16
Quartet in A♭, Op. 105
Quartet in C, Op. 61
Quartet in D minor, Op. 34
Quartet in E♭, Op. 51
Quartet in F, Op. 96
Quartet in G, Op. 106
Emmanuel, M.
Quartet in B♭ major
Ewald, V.
Quartet in G, Op. 1
Fairchild, Blair
Quartet in G minor, Op. 27
Ferrata, G.
Quartet in G, Op. 28
Fesca, A.
Quartet in D minor, Op. 42
Quartet in F minor, Op. 42
Fibich, Z.
Quartet in G, Op. 8
Theme and Variations in B♭
Foote, Arthur
Theme & Variations, Op. 32
Franck, César
Quartet in D major
Gade, Niels W.
Quartet in D, Op. 63
Gagnebin, H.
Quartet in F minor
Gernsheim, Fr.
Quartet in A, Op. 83
Glazounow, A.-Liadow, A.-Rimsky-Korsakow, N.
Quartet in F (Jour de Fête)
Glazounow, A.
Courante
Five Novellettes, Op. 15
Preludio & Fuga

Quartet No. 1 in D, Op. 1
Quartet No. 2 in F, Op. 10
Quartet No. 3 in G, Op. 36
Quartet No. 4 in A minor, Op. 64
Quartet No. 5 in D minor, Op. 70
Suite in C, Op. 35
Gliere, R.
Quartet in A, Op. 2
Quartet in G minor, Op. 20
Glinka, M.
Quartet in F. major
Godard, Benj.
Quartet in A major, Op. 37
Quartet in G minor, Op. 33
Goldmark, C.
Quartet in B♭, Op. 8
Goossens, Eug.
Fantasy for Quartet, Op. 12
Quartet, Op. 14
Two Sketches, Op. 15
Graener, Paul
Quartet on a Swedish Air, Op. 33
Gretchaninow, A.
Quartet in D minor, Op. 70
Quartet in G major, Op. 2
Grieg, E.
Quartet in G minor, Op. 27
Unfinished Quartet in F
Gromis, Charles
Quartet in A major
Haydn, Joseph
Six Quartets, Op. 1
Six Quartets, Op. 2
Six Quartets, Op. 20
Five Quartets, Op. 50
Thirty Quartets (Eulenberg ed.)
Twelve Quartets (Peters ed.)
Hennessy, Swan.
Suite for Quartet, Op. 46
Hofmann, Richard
Quartet facile, Op. 116
Holbrooke, Jos.
Fantasy in D. Op. 17
Impressions, Op. 59a
Huss, Henry Holden
Quartet in E minor
Indy, V. d'
Quartet in D, Op. 35
Quartet in E, Op. 45
Jaques-Dalcroze, E.
Quartet in E major
Serenade, Op. 61
Jongen, Jos.
Quartet No. 1 in C minor
Quartet No. 2 in A major

---

* Alfred Pochon, of the Flonzaley Quartet, has published an interesting work entitled *A Progressive Method of String Quartet Playing.*—Ed.

Jullien, René
Four Novellettes, Op. 17
Juon, Paul
Quartet in A minor, Op. 29
Quartet in D major, Op. 5
Klose, Fr.
Quartet in E♭
Klughardt, A.
Quartet in D, Op. 61
Quartet in F, Op. 42
Kopylow, A.
Andantino on the theme B-
la-f, Op. 7
Prelude & Fugue, Op. 11
Quartet in A, Op. 32
Quartet in C, Op. 33
Quartet in F, Op. 23
Quartet in G, Op. 15
Kroeger, E. R.
Quartet in D minor
Lacombe, Paul
Quartet in C minor, Op. 101
Ladoukhine, N.
Quartet in F (Tempora Ve-
tusta)
Lalo, Ed.
Quartet in E♭, Op. 45
Lauber, Joseph
Quartet in G minor, Op. 5
Lazzari, Sylvio
Quartet in A minor
Le Borne, Fernand
Quartet in C minor, Op. 23
Lefebvre, Ch.
Quartet in G minor, Op. 80
Lendvai, Ervin
Quartet in E minor, Op. 8
Lewandowsky, M.
Quartet No. 1 in F
Quartet No. 2 in E minor
Luigini, A.
Quartet in D, Op. 5
Luzzato, F.
Suite in G, Op. 51
Magnard, Alberic
Quartet, Op. 16
Mason, Daniel Aregny
Quartet in A, Op. 7
Quartet on Negro Themes,
Op. 19
Mendelssohn, Arnold
Quartet in D, Op. 67
Quartet in F minor, Op. 80
Mendelssohn, F.
Quartet, Op. 12
Quartet, Op. 13
Three Quartets, Op. 44
Quartet, Op. 80
Menu, Pierre
Sonatina for String Quartet
Milhaud, D.
Quartet in A minor
Moor, Emmanuel
Quartet in A, Op. 59
Mozart, W. A.
Quartet in G (Köchel No.
80)
Quartet in G (Köchel No.
156)
Quartet in A (Köchel No.
464)
Adagio & Fugue (Köchel No.
405)
Napravnik, E.
Quartet in A, Op. 28
Quartet in A minor, Op. 16
Quartet in C, Op. 65
Nedbal, O.
Valse triste
Novak, V.
Quartet in D, Op. 35
Quartet in G, Op. 22

Ollone, M. d'
˙ Quartet in D
Pfitzner, H.
Quartet in D, Op. 13
Pogojeff, P.
Quartet in D, Op. 7
Theme & Variations, Op. 3
Powell, John
Quartet, Op. 19
Rabaud, H.
Quartet in G minor, Op. 3
Raff, Joachim
Quartet in A, Op. 90
Quartet in A minor, Op. 137
Quartet in D minor, Op. 77
Quartet in E minor, Op. 136
Quartet in G, Op. 138
Quartet No. 1, Op. 192
Quartet No. 2, Op. 192
Quartet No. 3, Op. 192
Ravel, Maurice
Quartet in F
Reger, Max
Quartet in A minor, Op. 54,
No. 2
Quartet in D minor, Op. 113
Quartet in E♭, Op. 109
Quartet in F♯ minor, Op. 121
Quartet in G minor, Op. 54,
No. 1
Rimsky-Korsakoff, N.
Quartet in F, Op. 12
Rode, Pierre
Quartet in G, Op. 11
Quartet in G, Op. 14
Quartet in G, Op. 18   .
Ropartz, J. Guy
Quartet in D minor
Quartet in G minor
Serenade for String Quartet
Rubinstein, Anton
Quartet in E minor, Op. 47
Quartet in F minor, Op. 106
Quartet in G minor, Op. 90
Quartet No. 1 in G, Op. 17
Quartet No. 2 in D minor,
Op. 17
Quartet No. 3 in F, Op. 17
Saint-Saëns, C.
Quartet No. 1, Op. 112
Quartet No. 2, Op. 153
Samazeuilh, D.
Quartet in D
Scharwenka, Ph.
Quartet in D, Op. 120
Schoeck, O.
Quartet in D, Op. 23
Schubert, Franz
Quartet No. 8, Op. 168
Quartet No. 14 (Death and
the Maiden)
Quartet No. 15, Op. 161
Quartets Nos. 1-7 (Without
Opus)
Schumann, Rob.
Quartet No. 1 in A minor,
Op. 41
Quartet No. 2 in F major,
Op. 41
Quartet No. 3 in A major,
Op. 41
Scontrino, A.
Prelude and Fugue in E mi-
nor
Quartet No. 1 in G minor
Quartet No. 2 in C major
Quartet No. 3 in A minor
Scott, Cyril
Quartet, Op. 28
Quartet, Op. 31
Sgambatti, G.
Quartet in F♯ minor, Op. 17

Sibelius, J.
Quartet, Op. 56 (Voces In-
timae)
Simonetti, A.
Quartet in D minor, Op. 14
Quartet in E♭ major, Op. 16
Sinding, G.
Quartet in A minor, Op. 70
Sinigaglia, L.
Etude de Concert for String
Quartet, Op. 5
Quartet in D, Op. 27
Variations on a Brahms
Theme, Op. 22
Smetana, Fr.
Quartet No. 1 in E minor
Quartet No. 2 in D minor
Sochting, E.
Quartet Facile in A minor,
Op. 70
Quartet Facile in D, Op. 70
Quartet Facile in G, Op. 70
Sokolow, N.
Quartet in A, Op. 14
Quartet in F, Op. 7
Spohr, L.
Quartet in D minor, Op. 11
Quartet No. 1, Op. 4
Quartet No. 2, Op. 4
Quartet No. 2, Op. 45
Stenhammar, W.
Quartet in F, Op. 18
Stojowski, S.
Variations and Fugue, Op. 6
Strauss, Richard
Quartet in A, Op. 2
Suk, Joseph
Quartet No. 1, Op. 11
Quartet No. 2, Op. 31
Svendsen, J.
Quartet in A minor, Op. 1
Taneiew, Serge Ivanovic
Quartet, Op. 1
Quartet, Op. 4
Quartet, Op. 5
Quartet, Op. 19
Tartini, G.
Quartet No. 1 in D
Quartet No. 2 in A
Taubert, E. E.
Quartet in F♯ minor, Op. 56
Tschaikowsky, P.
Quartet in D, Op. 11
Quartet in E♭ minor, Op. 30
Quartet in F, Op. 22
Tscherepnine, N.
Quartet in A minor, Op. 11
Viotti, J. B.
Three Quartets Concertantes
Volkmann, R.
Quartet in A minor, Op. 9
Quartet in G, Op. 34
Wailly, P. de
Poem for String Quartet
Weismann, J.
Quartet in F, Op. 14
Widor, Charles
Quartet, Op. 66
Wihtol, J.
Quartet in G, Op. 27
Winkler, N.
Quartet in C major, Op. 7
Quartet in D minor, Op. 9
Quartet in E♭ major, Op. 14
Wolf, Hugo
Quartet in D minor
Sérénade Italienne in G ma-
jor
Zolotareff, V.
Quartet in A minor, Op. 6
Quartet in D, Op. 5
Quartet in D, Op. 25

22. QUARTETS FOR PIANO, VIOLIN, VIOLA AND CELLO

Beethoven, L. van
Quartet in E♭, Op. 16
Quartet No. 1 in E♭
Quartet No. 2 in D
Quartet No. 3 in C
Bernard, Emile
Quartet in D minor, Op. 50
Boellmann, L.
Quartet in F minor, Op. 10
Boisdeffre, R. de
Quartet in E♭, Op. 91
Quartet in G minor, Op. 13
Braga, G.
Angel's Serenade (Serenata valaque)
Brahms, J.
Quartet in A major, Op. 26
Quartet in D minor, Op. 60
Quartet in G minor, Op. 25
Castillon, A. de
Quartet in G minor, Op. 7
Chausson, Emile
Quartet in A, Op. 30
Destenay, E.
Quartet in G minor, Op. 38
Dubois, Theodore
Quartet in A minor
Dvořák, A.
Quartet in D, Op. 23
Quartet in E♭, Op. 87
Fauré, Gabriel
Quartet in C minor, Op. 15
Quartet in G minor, Op. 45
Fesca, A.
Quartet in C minor, Op. 26
Quartet in D minor, Op. 28
Foote, A.
Quartet in C, Op. 23
Goetz, H.
Quartet in E, Op. 6
Gouvy, Th.
Serenade in E♭, Op. 31
Handel, George Frederich
Nine Sönatas (Orig. 2 Violins, 2 oboes, cello & bass)
Six Sonatas (Orig. 2 oboes & bass)

Herzogenberg, H. V.
Quartet in E minor, Op. 75
Quartet in E♭ major, Op. 95
Hochberg, B. V.
Quartet in E♭ minor, Op. 37
Holbrooke, Jos.
Symphonie Quartet in D minor, Op. 31
Symphonie Quartet in G minor, Op. 21
Huber, Hans
Quartet in E, Op. 117
Quartet in E♭, Op. 110
Indy, V. d'
Quartet in A minor, Op. 7
Jerabek, Jos.
Quartet in D minor, Op. 12
Jongen, Jos.
Quartet in E♭, Op. 23
Juon, Paul
Quartet in G, Op. 50
Rhapsody in F, Op. 37
Kroeger, E. R.
Quartet in D minor
Labey, Marcel
Quartet in G minor
Labor, Jos.
Quartet in C, Op. 6
Lauber, Jos.
Quartet in E♭, Op. 8
Lefebvre, Ch.
Quartet in E♭, Op. 42
Lekeu, Guillaume
Quartet in B minor (Unfinished)
Loeillet, J. B.
Sonata in B minor
Luzzato, Fr.
Quartet in B minor, Op. 58
Malling, O.
Quartet in D minor, Op. 80
Mendelssohn, F.
Quartet in B minor, Op. 3
Quartet in F minor, Op. 2
Quartet in G minor, Op. 1
Mozart, W. A.
Quartet No. 1 (Köchel No. 478)

Quartet No. 2 (Köchel No. 493)
Quartet No. 3 (Köchel No. 452)
Novak, V.
Quartet in C minor, Op. 7
Raff, J.
Quartet in D minor, Op. 202
Quartet in G major, Op. 202
Ratez, E.
Quartet in C minor, Op. 30
Reger, Max
Quartet in A minor, Op. 133
Quartet in D minor, Op. 113
Reinecke, C.
Quartet in D, Op. 272
Roger-Ducasse, E.
Quartet in G minor
Rubinstein, A.
Quartet in C, Op. 66
Saint-Saëns, C.
Barcarolle, Op. 108
Quartet in B♭, Op. 41
Scharwenka, X.
Quartet in F, Op. 37
Schubert, Fr.
Adagio and Rondo Concertant in F (Posthumous)
Octet, Op. 166 (Transc.)
Schumann, Rob.
Quartet in E♭, Op. 47
Strauss, Richard
Quartet in C minor, Op. 2
Taneiew, Serge Iv.
Quartet in E, Op. 20
Weber, Carl Maria von
Quartet in B♭, Op. 8
Widor, Ch. M.
Quartet in A minor, Op. 66
Winkler, A.
Quartet in G, Op. 8
Witte, G. H.
Quartet in A, Op. 5
Zolotareff, B.
Quartet in D, Op. 13

23. QUINTETS FOR TWO VIOLINS, TWO VIOLAS AND CELLO

Alary, G.
Fantasy
Beethoven, L. van
Fugue in D, Op. 137
Quintet in C, Op. 29
Quintet in C minor, Op. 104
Quintet in E♭, Op. 4
Quintet in F, Op. 88
Brahms, J.
Quintet in F, Op. 88
Quintet in B minor, Op. 115
Quintet in G, Op. 111
Bruckner, A.
Quintet in F
Dvořák, A.
Quintet in E♭ major

Ewald, V.
Quintet in A, Op. 4
Gade, Niels W.
Quintet in E minor, Op. 8
Haydn, Jos.
Quintet in C major
Quintet in G major
Mendelssohn, F.
Quintet in A major, Op. 18
Quintet in B♭ major, Op. 87
Mozart, W. A.
Quintet No. 1 (Köchel No. 46)
Divertimento in F (Köchel No. 247)

Divertimento in B (Köchel No. 287)
Divertimento in D (Köchel No. 334)
Reger, M.
Quintet in A, Op. 146
Rubinstein, A.
Quintet in F, Op. 59
Schubert, Franz
Octet, Op. 166 (Transcribed)
Svendsen, J.
Quintet in C, Op. 5
Taneiew, Serge Iv.
Quintet in C, Op. 16
Winkler, A.
Quintet in C, Op. 11

24. QUINTETS FOR TWO VIOLINS, VIOLA AND TWO CELLOS

Ambrosio, A. d'
Suite in E♭ major
Boccherini, L.
Quintet, Op. 16 (L'Uccelliera)
Quintet in A minor, Op. 47
Quintet in D, Op. 37
Quintet in E, Op. 13

Cherubini, L.
Quintet in E minor
Glazounow, A.
Quintet in A, Op. 39
Goldmark, C.
Quintet, Op. 9
Gouvy, Th.
Quintet in G, Op. 55

Klughardt, A.
Quintet in G minor, Op. 62
Schubert, Fr.
Quintet in C, Op. 163
Taneiew, Serge Iv.
Quintet in G, Op. 14
Zolotareff, B.
Quintet in F, Op. 18

25. QUINTETS FOR TWO VIOLINS, VIOLA, CELLO AND BASS

Blanc, Adolphe
Quintet, Op. 15
Quintet, Op. 50
Dvořák, A.
Quintet in G, Op. 77

Mozart, W. A.
Serenade in G (Eine kleine
Nachmusik)
Schaffner, N. A.
Quintet, Op. 32
Quintet, Op. 38

Walckiers, E.
Quintet, Op. 90
Quintet, Op. 108

26. QUINTETS FOR PIANO, TWO VIOLINS, VIOLA AND CELLO

Abaco, E. F. dall'
Concerto da Chiesa in A
minor, Op. 2
Concerto da Chiesa in G
minor, Op. 2
Arensky, A.
Quintet in D, Op. 51
Beach, Mrs. H. H. A.
Quintet, Op. 67
Boisdeffre, R. de
Quintet in A minor, Op. 81
Quintet in Bb major, Op. 43
Quintet in D minor, Op. 11
Brahms, J.
Quintet in F minor, Op. 34
Castillon, A. de
Quintet in Eb, Op. 1
Chadwick, A. W.
Quintet in Eb major
Desjoyeaux, Noel
Quintet in D minor
Destenay, E.
Quintet in Eb, Op. 11
Dubois, Theodore
Quintet in F major
Dupont, Gabriel
Poème in C minor
Dvořák, A.
Quintet in A, Op. 81
Ehrhardt, D.
Quintet in D major
Fairchild, Blair
Rhapsody for Quintet
Fauré, Gabriel
Quintet in D minor, Op. 89
Foote, Art.
Quintet in A minor, Op. 38
Franck, César
Quintet in F minor
Gnessin, M.
Requiem, Op. 11

Goldmark, C.
Quintet, Op. 54
Quintet in Bb, Op. 30
Hadley, Henry K.
Quintet
Holbrooke, J.
Symphonie Quintet, Op. 44
Huber, H.
Divertimento, Op. 125
Quintet in G minor, Op. 111
Hure, Jean
Quintet in D major
Juon, Paul
Quintet in D minor, Op. 33
Quintet in F, Op. 44
Kaun, Hugo
Quintet in F minor, Op. 39
Klemperer, Oscar
Quintet in G minor
Kroeger, E. R.
Quintet in F minor
Lacroix, E.
Quintet
Lauber, Jos.
Quintet on Swiss Themes, Op.
6
Le Flem, Paul
Quintet in E minor
Mandl, Richard
Quintet in G major
Mozart, W. A.
Quintet in Eb major
Mugellini, B.
Quintet in D major
Novak, V.
Quintet in A minor, Op. 12
Pfitzner, H.
Quintet in C, Op. 23
Pierné, G.
Quintet in G, Op. 41

Polignac, A. de
Quintet
Raff, J.
Quintet in A minor, Op. 107
Reger, Max
Quintet in C minor, Op. 64
Rubinstein, A.
Quintet in G minor, Op. 99
Sachs, Leo
Quintet, Op. 77
Saint-Saëns, Camille
Quintet in A minor
Scharwenka, Philip
Quintet in B minor, Op. 118
Schmitt, Florent
Quintet in B minor, Op. 51
Schumann, Robert
Quintet in Eb, Op. 44
Scott, Cyril
Quintet, Op. 57
Sgambati, G.
Quintet in Bb, Op. 5
Quintet in F minor, Op. 4
Sinding, C.
Quintet in E minor, Op. 5
Smith, F. Lorenz
Quintet in C minor
Taneiew, Serge Iv.
Quintet, Op. 30
Telemann, G. P.
Suite
Turina, J. de
Quintet
Wailly, Paul de
Quintet in F minor
Widor, Ch. M.
Quintet in D, Op. 68
Quintet in D minor, Op. 7
Wolf-Ferrari, E.
Quintet, Op. 6

27. QUINTETS FOR PIANO, VIOLIN, VIOLA, CELLO AND BASS

Boisdeffre, R. de
Quintet in D, Op. 25
Hummel, J. N.
Quintet, Op. 87
Labor, Jos.
Quintet in E minor, Op. 3

Macfarren, G. A.
Quintet in G
Nowakowski, Jn.
Quintet, Op. 17
Ries, Ferd.
Quintet, Op. 74

Sachs, Leo
Quintet, Op. 77
Schubert, Fr.
Quintet, Op. 114 (The
Trout)

28. SEXTETS FOR TWO VIOLINS, TWO VIOLAS AND TWO CELLOS

Alary, G.
Thème Varié, Op. 17
Borresen, H.
Sextet in G, Op. 5
Brahms, J.
Sextet in Bb, Op. 18
Sextet in G, Op. 36
Davidoff, A.
Sextet in Eb, Op. 12
Dvořák, A.
Sextet in A, Op. 48
Gade, Niels W.
Sextet in D minor, Op. 44

Gliere, R.
Sextet in B minor, Op. 7
Sextet in C minor, Op. 11
Sextet in D minor, Op. 1
Koehler, B.
Sextet in Ab
Korngold, Eric W.
Sextet in D, Op. 10
Raff, J.
Sextet in Bb, Op. 178
Reger, Max
Sextet in F, Op. 118

Rimsky-Korsakow, A.
Sextet in A
Rubinstein, A.
Sextet in D, Op. 97
Schoenberg, Arnold
Sextet, Op. 4 (Verklarte
Nacht)
Tschaikowski, P.
Sextet in D minor, Op. 70
Wilm, N. V.
Sextet in B minor, O. 27

29. OCTETS FOR FOUR VIOLINS, TWO VIOLAS AND TWO CELLOS

Enesco, George
Octet in C major
Gade, Niels W.
Octet in F, Op. 17
Gliere, R.
Octet in D, Op. 5

Mendelssohn, Felix
Octet in Eb major
Raff, Joachim
Octet in C, Op. 176
Spohr, L.
Double Quartet in D minor,
Op. 65

Double Quartet in Eb, Op. 77
Double Quartet in G minor,
Op. 136
Svendsen, J.
Octet in A, Op. 3
Thieriot, Ferd.
Octet, Op. 78

INDEX

469

(1)